PREFACE

The difficulties of writing recent history are well known. Much of the material is not yet available, the monographs and autobiographies have not yet been written, and many of the actors are still alive, to refute the most ingenious theories. Above all, we are still too close to the events, and too emotionally involved, to see them in their historical perspective.

But the pitfalls of writing recent history are as nothing compared with the pitfalls of teaching it, for it is here that the gap between the generations is at its most unbridgeable. What are everyday events and terms to the teacher are strange mysteries to the student, who finds the nuances, the background, the flavour of events, so familiar to the teacher as to be not worth making explicit, lost on him in a welter of unrecognizable references. The teaching of recent economic history has its own special difficulties, for it enters into the subjects of complex theoretical debate of yesterday, much of which is still unfinished. Yet teaching there must be, if the student is not to carry away with him a blank in his mind regarding the period when 'history' ends and when 'current economic problems' begin —precisely the period in which the minds of his elders were formed, and which some of them, alas, have never succeeded in leaving.

This book arose out of my desire to teach present-day students something about the no-man's land between history and applied economics or current affairs, and my difficulty in finding suitable general introductions, as distinct from specialist treatises and polemical works, of which there are probably too many. The usual tributes paid by the author in his Preface in this case must go to my students who unwittingly, and most likely unwillingly, forced me to write it. It is intended primarily for University students of Economics, Modern History and related subjects, and it assumes a modicum of knowledge of economic terms and institutions, such as any regular reader of the more intelligent weekly press could also command. It is hoped that it may also be of some use to their teachers and, further, to those interested members of the public, graduates, perhaps, in the subjects named here, and now active in business or public affairs, who require some knowledge of recent events to make up their own minds, believing with the author that the infallibility of our professional economic Oracles is by no means assured, even though they conform to their Delphic ancestor's habit of speaking in riddles, and regularly improve on it by speaking with several different voices at once.

A special word needs to be said about the bibliography. Traditionally, books designed mainly as textbooks have their reading lists either at the end of each chapter or at the end of the volume. Both suffer from similar limitations, for while the earnest student will be exasperated by not finding further reading hints on the pages on which his subject-matter occurs, the idle one will be too discouraged by the length of the reading list to make a start at all. Here, therefore (apart from a few general works mentioned at the end), the bibliography occurs in the form of footnotes to the text. These notes, even where they have the ostensible object of referring to the origins of quotations, statistics or unusual views, are all primarily intended as hints to further reading. It follows that the student's reading should extend beyond the page or chapter of the work quoted, according to the demand of his interests.

Each sectional chapter division has been treated as self-contained for the purposes of the bibliography, in the sense that full references are given again, even if the work has been mentioned in earlier sections or chapters. The statistical examples have been chosen deliberately from a wide range of sources, and conflicting series are occasionally given side by side in order to teach a healthy scepticism about economic measurement. The literature has been chosen so that the sum of the footnote references to each section forms the complete bibliography of the section and the sum of the references in each chapter, the bibliography of that chapter. It has, further, been chosen so as to make the student familiar with a wide selection of reading matter available, including books, reprints of documents, articles in learned journals and other periodicals, and official papers and statistics.

S. P.

In this second impression, the bibliography has been brought up to date, and some minor corrections to the text have been made. For some of the latter I am much indebted to Dr. Walter Stern and Mr. C. G. Hanson.

S. P.

7th August 1963

The enlarged edition brings the present volume virtually up to date. The new final chapter runs an even greater danger of showing all the weaknesses of writing on contemporary history, for not only may it stand too close to the events to recognize all the facts, but it may also fall into the trap of taking sides in the controversies. Yet to leave a widening gap between itself and the present would progressively diminish the value of the rest of the book. Amendments and additions to the rest of the book have been kept to a minimum, and mostly concern the literature published since the last revision.

31st May 1968   S. P.

CONTENTS

	PAGE
PREFACE	v
ABBREVIATIONS USED IN FOOTNOTE REFERENCES	ix

CHAPTER I. GREAT BRITAIN AT THE END OF THE LONG PEACE   I

(1) The Idea of Progress   I
(2) British Industry and its Position in the World   3
(3) Industrial Organization and the Growth of Monopoly   10
(4) The Banks and the Money Market   14
(5) Foreign Investment and the Problem of Empire   19
(6) Incomes and the Standard of Living   23
(7) Industrial Relations   28
(8) The Birth of the Welfare State   34

CHAPTER II. THE FIRST WORLD WAR, 1914–1918   42

(1) The Needs of War and Economic Control   42
(2) The Effects of War on British Industry   53
(3) Budgeting and Finance During the War   62
(4) Britain's International Position   72
(5) Labour and the War   76
(6) 'Reconstruction' and Post-War Planning   87

CHAPTER III. BRITISH INDUSTRY AND TRANSPORT BETWEEN THE WARS   92

(1) Progress in Science and Technology   92
(2) New and Growing Industries   99
(3) The Old and Declining Industries   110
(4) The Changing Location of Industry   125
(5) Agriculture   134
(6) Transport and Communications   145
(7) New Forms of Industrial Organization   161

CHAPTER IV. COMMERCIAL AND FINANCIAL DEVELOPMENTS   175

(1) The Changing Pattern of Retail and Wholesale Trading   175
(2) The Course of Overseas Trade   184
(3) Great Britain under Protection   192
(4) The Changing Role of the Budget   200
(5) Economic and Financial Policy in the Nineteen-Twenties   214
(6) The Years of Crisis: 1929–1931   223
(7) Financial Policy and Institutions in the Nineteen-Thirties   229

vii

Contents

PAGE

CHAPTER V. SOCIAL CONDITIONS BETWEEN THE WARS   242

   (1) The Age of Mass Unemployment   242
   (2) Housing, Health and Other Welfare Provisions   254
   (3) The Trade Unions and the Politics of Poverty   267
   (4) Changes in Population and Social Structure   280
   (5) The Rise in the Standard of Living   289

CHAPTER VI. THE BRITISH ECONOMY IN TOTAL WAR, 1939–1945   297

   (1) The War Economy and Economic Planning   297
   (2) Industry in the War Years   308
   (3) Fiscal and Financial Policy During the War   322
   (4) The Problem of the Foreign Balance of Payments   330
   (5) Work and Welfare in the War Years   339
   (6) Plans for Post-War Reconstruction   348

CHAPTER VII. RECONVERSION TO PEACE, 1945–1950   356

   (1) The Dollar Problem and the Sterling Crises   356
   (2) Full Employment Policies in Practice   364
   (3) Industrial Reconstruction   376
   (4) Incomes and Work   391
   (5) The Welfare State   398

CHAPTER VIII. BRITAIN IN THE POST-WAR WORLD, 1950–1967   408

   (1) Industrial Growth and Organization   408
   (2) Foreign Trade and Trading Relations   434
   (3) Finance and the Banking System   460
   (4) Economic Policy: The 'Stop–Go' Cycle   469
   (5) Economic Policy: Government and Society   485
   (6) Wealth and Poverty   499

   FURTHER READING   507

   INDEX   508

ABBREVIATIONS USED IN FOOTNOTE REFERENCES

Amer. Econ. Rev.	*American Economic Review*
Bull. Oxf. Inst. Stat.	*Bulletin of the Oxford University Institute of Statistics*
Ec. Hist. Rev.	*Economic History Review*
Econ. J.	*Economic Journal*
Geog. J.	*Geographical Journal*
J. Econ. and Business History	*Journal of Economic and Business History*
J. Econ. Hist.	*Journal of Economic History*
J. Royal Soc. of Arts	*Journal of the Royal Society of Arts*
J. R. Stat. S.	*Journal of the Royal Statistical Society*
J. Transport History	*Journal of Transport History*
Manchester School	*Manchester School of Economic and Social Studies*
Oxf. Econ. P.	*Oxford Economic Papers*
Q.J.E.	*Quarterly Journal of Economics*
Rev. Econ. Studies	*Review of Economic Studies*
Rev. of Econ. and Statistics	*Review of Economics and Statistics* (formerly *Review of Economic Statistics*)
Scot. J. Pol. Econ.	*Scottish Journal of Political Economy*
Yorkshire Bulletin	*Yorkshire Bulletin of Economic and Social Studies*
H.S.W.W.	(Official) *History of the Second World War*
N.S.	New Series
R.C.	Royal Commission
S.C.	Select Committee
2nd S.	Second Series

Note 1. In references to articles in journals the convention has been followed of separating volume and issue numbers by an oblique stroke: thus 3/12 means Volume 3, Number 12. The date afterwards refers to the date of the number, not necessarily of the whole volume.

Note 2. The British convention has been followed of referring to one thousand million as a 'milliard'; readers preferring American conventions will substitute a 'billion' in each case.

CHAPTER I

Great Britain at the End
of the Long Peace

I. THE IDEA OF PROGRESS

The popular ideas about a country and an age, the ideas which are so all-pervasive that men find it largely unnecessary to express them on paper, take a long time to mature, and they take a long time to eradicate. The ideas which the British citizen imbibed in the last years of the century of peace which came to a close in 1914, as he watched the areas of red spread across the map, and saw fresh technical marvels introduced every year, were based on the experiences of the past two or three generations. These contained a dual promise of progress: the promise that science and industry would continue to improve material conditions of living, and the promise that Britain would continue to be at the head of this march of improvement.

The belief in material progress based on improved technology was still relatively young. It became at all widely held only in the last third of the nineteenth century,[1] when the industrial transformation beginning about 1760 was at last seen to spread visible material benefits among the bulk of the population. Poverty was still so evident all around and in men's recent past that its abolition could not but be considered a worthy aim of society: and thus the foundations of an economy directed towards the multiplication of material goods went unquestioned.

The success of the economy was undoubted, whether measured against the historic past or against other countries at that time. As far as historical comparison was concerned, it had become possible to measure progress no longer merely by the growing number of mills or ironworks, but also, and more pertinently, by the standards of living of the working classes, by methods made respectable by no less an authority than Robert Giffen,[2] whose conclusions were unassailable, even if his statistics were dubious. In international comparisons, equally justifiably, British subjects had come to

[1] S. G. Checkland, 'Growth and Progress: the Nineteenth-Century View in Britain', *Ec. Hist. Rev.*, 2nd S., 12/1, 1959.
[2] 'Progress of the Working Classes in the last Half-Century', *J. R. Stat. S.*, 46/4, 1883, and 'Further Progress', *ibid.*, 49/1, 1886.

assume a superiority over the citizens of other countries, which the latter, in most cases, were not inclined to dispute.

The explanation of British economic success, on the popular level, was still in terms of human institutions and quality of character: the excellence of British institutions had become the theme song of leader writers in the new popular press; the importance of character, as expressed by Samuel Smiles[1] a generation earlier, was firmly embedded in the folk-lore. And indeed, despite the multiplication of costly capital equipment, it was true that the dexterity and ability of the British worker, the connections and knowledge of the market of the British merchant, the integrity of the British banker were relatively much more valuable assets than they have become since, and to that extent personal qualities were of more evident economic importance.

By the early years of the twentieth century the economic optimism sketched here was not unchallenged. The 'Great Depression' of the 1870's and 1880's had given a jolt to British businessmen by showing up for the first time a real threat of foreign competition. Sir William Crookes, conjuring up in his presidential address to the British Association in 1898 a new Malthusian spectre of world famine because of the prospective decline in nitrogenous fertilizers, found listeners and believers. Jevons' forecast, made in 1865, of economic decline for Britain in the foreseeable future because of the exhaustion of the coal supplies, was seriously re-examined by a Royal Commission and by others.[2] Panic was soon proved to have been out of place, but current investigations might have been expected to lead, though they did not, to a questioning of the continued superiority of British industry in the face of nations more richly endowed with land, resources and, as it soon turned out, distance from the European battle-fields. Such publications as stressed the dangers of vigorous foreign competition were too evidently partisan,[3] and the British public proved by the election of 1906 that it still believed in Free Trade and a cheap loaf.

The chief doubt about the prospects of progress arose not so much out of its general direction, but largely out of the glaring inequalities in income and wealth: in 1911–13, it has been estimated, 170,000 persons, or 0·85% of the population, owned 65·5% of the capital in the country, while at the other extreme, over 16⅓ million, or 87·4% of the property-owning population, owned only 8·5% between them.[4] But inequality, of at least the same

---

[1] *Self Help* (1859), *Lives of the Engineers* (1861–2 and 1874) and other works.
[2] W. S. Jevons, *The Coal Question* (3rd ed., 1906); Rt. Hon. L. H. Courtney, 'Jevons' Coal Question: Thirty Years After', *J. R. Stat. S.*, 60/4, 1897; *R. C. on Coal Resources of the U.K.* (1903–5. Cd. 1724, 1990, 2353).
[3] E.g. the Tariff Commission, set up by the Tariff Reformers, issued alarmist reports in 1904–7 on the Iron and Steel, Textile, Agricultural, Engineering, Potteries, Glass, Sugar and Confectionery Trades.
[4] H. Campion, *Public and Private Property* (Oxford, 1938).

extent, had existed before. What gave the dissatisfaction a new edge was the simultaneous appearance of several new factors. Among them were the realization that in the midst of the much-boasted wealth of Britain, poverty was no longer necessary; the fact that after a half-century of growth, the upward movement of real wages had been halted in the last twenty years of peace; and the diversion of much of the new wealth to classes who had not learnt the 'double bluff' of pre-war society noted by Keynes,[1] that capitalists were allowed to appropriate a large part of the nation's wealth, in the face of bitter poverty among the rest of the population, only on condition that they did not enjoy it, but re-invested it in their concerns.

Much of the protest came from the very citadels of privilege and orthodoxy. The first official investigation into 'sweating', the exploitation of helpless labour in domestic industries outside the scope of the Factory Acts, was made by the House of Lords;[2] much of the fundamental thinking on the foundations of the Welfare State was done by the Royal Commission on the Poor Laws (1905–9), presided over by a Tory nobleman; the details of legislation were prepared largely by privileged young men from the Universities; and the Webbs, pursuing their single-minded aim of introducing Socialism into Britain by Fabian methods, found upper-class leaders of the Conservative and Liberal parties at least as helpful as the leaders of the trade unions. 'The landslide in England towards Social Democracy proceeds steadily,' Beatrice Webb noted triumphantly in her diary in 1914, 'but it is the whole nation that is sliding, not the one class of manual workers.'[3]

Change and proposals for change were in the air. It was as if the age of peace and progress had lasted too long. Men who had little to lose, and men who had a great deal, seemed to crave change for its own sake. A spirit of restlessness appeared to pervade the last years of the Long Peace.[4] The concrete causes both for the optimism and for the doubts and misgivings of those years will be examined in the rest of this chapter.

2. BRITISH INDUSTRY AND ITS POSITION IN THE WORLD

From the vantage-point of later years, it is not difficult to point to weaknesses in the British industrial structure before 1914, but they would not have been easy to prove to contemporaries. Total industrial production

---

[1] J. M. Keynes, *Economic Consequences of the Peace* (New York, 1920), pp. 18–22.
[2] *Reports* of the *S.C. of the House of Lords on the Sweating System* (1888. 361 and 448; 1889. 165 and 331).
[3] M. I. Cole (ed.), *Beatrice Webb's Diaries, 1912–1924* (1952), p. 18.
[4] The atmosphere of those years is captured most aptly in Geo. Dangerfield, *The Strange Death of Liberal England* (1936), a book to be recommended more for its intuitive perception than its historical accuracy. Also G. D. H. Cole and R. Postgate, *The Common People, 1746–1938* (1938), chapter 37.

was still growing and 1913 was a peak year on any reckoning. Between 1900 and the averages of the years 1911–13, total industrial output had risen from 43 to 54·6 according to Ridley's index (1948 = 100), and from 77·1 to 93·5, according to Hoffmann's (1913 = 100),[1] while the population had grown by only 11%. This growth of well under 2% per annum compared badly with the growth rates of the mid-nineteenth century, but even without the elaborate statistics which Hoffmann was to assemble later to prove that very point, it could be taken for granted that a mature economy with its advanced industries would grow at a slower percentage rate than an economy in an earlier stage of growth, even though perhaps still at a high absolute rate.

Nor had Britain any general difficulty in selling her manufactures abroad; the export list still showed the strength of the traditional British industries. Thus in 1911–13, textiles still accounted for 51·2% of exports (they had been 67·9% in 1857–9). Other consumer goods accounted for 10·6%, producer goods for 33·7% and other goods for the remaining 4·5%. On a different classification, in 1911–13 raw materials and articles largely unmanufactured represented only 29% of exports (of which coal alone represented 9%), the rest being largely made up of manufactured articles. Among imports, by contrast, manufactures only came to 25% in those years, the rest being chiefly food and raw materials. The proportion, are those of a vigorous industrial nation.

The old 'staple trades' still completely dominated the export figures. Coal, iron and steel, machinery and vehicles, ships and textiles between them accounted for two-thirds of all exports in 1911–13. This reliance on a narrow range of industries was to have severe repercussions in the 1920's and 1930's, but even in the pre-war days the buoyancy of the old staples in export markets was to some extent misleading, as they showed signs of real stagnation. Thus the output of coal per miner had been falling since the early 1880's, and in the Lancashire cotton and Cleveland pig iron industries real costs had not been reduced at all since 1885,[2] while the costs of our chief competitors were still falling.

Coal mining, the most basic of industries, providing the fuel and determining the location of the others, was still expanding. From 223 million tons at the turn of the century, production had increased to 287 million tons in 1913, of which over 94 million tons was for export and bunkering. The United States, however, produced over 500 million tons,

---

[1] T. M. Ridley, 'Industrial Production in the U.K., 1900–1953', *Economica*, N.S., 22/85, 1955; W. G. Hoffmann, *British Industry 1700–1950* (Oxford, 1955), Table 54.
[2] G. T. Jones, *Increasing Return* (1933). The paradox of the export successes of the 'staple' industries in the face of the loss of their relative efficiency is discussed in pp. 20–1 below.

and German output was rapidly approaching the British. The world demand for coal was rising at a rate of 4% per annum and the British demand at 2½% per annum. So far there was no reason for dismay. Though output per manshift was falling, there seemed to be no limit to the population reservoir, both from within old-established mining families and from without, to supply the manpower for the pits: over 1,100,000 were thus employed in 1913. The coalfields were still being extended, notably the difficult, but prolific South Wales field, the rich seams of the Yorkshire-North Midlands area which were followed eastwards as they dipped deeper below the surface, and the newly discovered field in Kent.[1]

Technically, the industry was falling behind other countries. Only 8% of the coal was cut mechanically in 1913, and even less was mechanically conveyed underground; in the use of electricity, concrete, even steel, British pits seemed backward, though the geography of the British fields and the nature of the seams might explain the delay in the introduction of methods which were not yet fully proved. The fields were also broken up into innumerable holdings by companies, many of them small by continental or American standards, while the large numbers of coalfields, each with its own types of coal and its own markets, inhibited organization on a national scale such as was found elsewhere.

Employment in the pig iron and steel works, at little over 100,000, was far smaller than in the mines, but its basic importance for an industrial country was equally evident. Here, also, a considerable growth in British output had been overtaken by the faster growth of Germany and the U.S.A. In 1913 the U.S.A. produced 31 million tons, Germany 16·5 million, and Britain 10·3 million of pig iron. In steel production, the change was equally drastic, and by 1913 the American output was of the order of 13 million tons, the German of 7 million, and the British of 5 million.

Again, home output could not be said to be stagnating: the index of pig iron and steel was rising from 77·3 to 100, and of iron and steel products from 71·3 to 100 between 1900 and 1913, according to Hoffmann, but compared with others the growth was slow. While blast furnaces hardly changed in this country, abroad new building and replacement constantly enlarged their size and raised their efficiency, and the same could be said of the steel furnaces and converters. Britain adopted the cheaper basic processes only very slowly; the final change-over even from puddled iron to steel took place long after it had been completed elsewhere. In the introduction of special alloy steels, which formed one of the most important fields of innovation in the early twentieth century, Britain made her share of the discoveries, but fell behind in their adoption.

In the early years of the twentieth century, the development of coal,

---

[1] H. Stanley Jevons, *The British Coal Trade* (1915).

iron and steel in Britain showed a striking similarity. In each case an early lead over other nations was being lost, yet there was slow progress in output and technique, and the shares and absolute quantities of Britain's output that were exported still greatly exceeded those of her competitors. This might prove that British firms were still competitive, but it also indicated two potential threats for the future. In the first place, foreign markets were much more vulnerable than home markets in an age when so many nations began to build up their own basic industries. In the second place, a larger output and smaller exports by others signified that much larger supplies were diverted to their own home markets. It could be argued that Britain starved herself, neglecting to re-equip her industries and weakening them for the future, while supplying the world with means to outstrip them.

In general engineering and shipbuilding Britain also paid the penalty for being the pioneer. Thus the early excellence of the British marine steam engine and, at the turn of the century, of the steam turbine designed by Charles Parsons, was the direct cause (together with the abundance of steam coal) of the neglect of the oil-fired marine engines and motors in Britain, and it was these which turned out to be the engines of the future. Further, the period of Britain's supremacy was one in which success in industry, whether in coal mining, iron puddling, steel rolling, in textile spinning and weaving, in building or in engineering, depended to a large extent on the skill of craftsmen, their use of tools and machinery, their knowledge of their materials. Britain had a race of craftsmen second to none, and it was precisely the lack of such craftsmen in sufficient numbers in the U.S.A. which forced American employers to pioneer automatic and foolproof machinery as well as 'scientific management'. These, again, turned out to be the methods of the future, but they were resisted here both by masters and men,[1] and adopted only slowly, if at all, before 1914. Pneumatic and electrically driven tools, the milling cutter, cranes and other mechanical aids in engineering works, were slower to appear in Britain than in the U.S.A., and the relative backwardness in the mass-production types of engineering products using interchangeable parts—typewriters, sewing machines, above all, motor cars—were other signs of stagnation. The lag behind Germany in electrical engineering, as well as in chemicals, pointed to another hangover from earlier days: the neglect of university-trained scientists.[2]

Of course, a sensible world division of labour, still the official doctrine

[1] E. H. Phelps-Brown, *Growth of British Industrial Relations* (1959), pp. 94–6.
[2] J. H. Clapham, *An Economic History of Modern Britain*, Vol. 3 (Cambridge, 1938), chapters 1 and 3; A. P. M. Fleming and H. J. Brocklehurst, *A History of Engineering* (1925), chapters 9–11; W. H. G. Armytage, *A Social History of Engineering* (1961), pp. 248–50.

of Free-Trade Britain, required specialization in engineering more than in most industries. In many specialist lines Britain kept, or increased, her lead. In shipbuilding, the United Kingdom still built 60% of the world's mercantile tonnage over the whole period 1900–14.[1] This was the sort of proportion that had been familiar in other industries fifty years earlier.

Textile machinery, bicycles and motor cycles, railway engines and equipment and various types of machines tools were other products which Britain made and sold successfully in many of the world's markets.[2] All told, engineering exports by 1911–13 had increased threefold in value since the early 1880's. In 1907 about half the output of the main sectors of engineering was exported, and (together with shipbuilding) this group employed about 1¼ million workers by 1914.[3] Engineering output is notoriously difficult to measure, but one estimate put the British share of world machinery production in 1913 at 11·8%, compared with the U.S.A., 50%, and Germany, 20·6%.

The textile industries formed the remainder of the old staple trades, which Britain had pioneered and on which her exports still largely depended. Of these, the cotton trade was still by far the most important exporter. In the years 1911–13, it accounted for an average of £123 million, compared with £54 million for all other textile exports combined. Both output and exports (especially of piece goods) were still on the increase, and there were some signs of technical improvement, enlargement of firms, and new processes in some of the finishing sections. But cotton factories are easily set up, and the latest products of the British textile machinery maker were becoming available in Europe and the Far East almost as quickly as in Lancashire.

The woollen and worsted industries were in a less precarious position; their raw material was not entirely foreign, while their markets were also in larger measure based at home. Exports were falling, but the home market was absorbing larger quantities year by year, including imported material, so that the industry was still registering a steady growth. The linen and silk industries had shrunk to relative insignificance, and the output of silk thread and silk goods was actually declining in absolute terms. Jute, concentrated in the Dundee region, was beginning to feel the competition of Indian factories, many of them set up and owned by Scotsmen, and output stagnated.

The numbers employed in all these textile trades were declining at

---

[1] S. Pollard, 'British and World Shipbuilding', *J. Econ. Hist.*, 17/3, 1957.
[2] *Report on Engineering Trades after the War* (1918. Cd. 9073). There were also official reports on Shipping and Shipbuilding, on the Iron and Steel Trades, and on the Textile Industries issued at that time.
[3] Committee on Industry and Trade (Balfour Committee), *Survey of Metal Industries* (1928).

a faster rate than in any other occupation between 1891 and 1911, with the exception of the various groups of 'general labourers' which, it may be suspected, shrank only because of the more accurate classification of successive Censuses.[1] In the hosiery trade, new machinery, mostly of American origin, permitted an increase in output with a falling labour force. The clothing industry, concentrated in factories in London, Leeds and Manchester with their associated dens of sweated outworkers, experienced what could be termed a silent revolution. As the Government forced masters to pay living wages, it encouraged the replacement of cheap labour by better organization and better equipment, including new specialized machines.[2]

There was one other old staple industry, though it had long since ceased to figure in the export statistics: this was agriculture, the chief victim of the Free Trade policy of the nineteenth century. Cheap freights and unrestricted imports reduced the home output of wheat, the Englishman's staple food, from the 1870's onwards, despite a rapidly growing population, until by 1913 less than one-fifth of the wheat consumed was home-grown. By contrast, the quality of home-killed meat left much scope for animal husbandry in Britain, and since 1870, the proportion of cultivated land under permanent pasture had risen from 42% to 53%. Market gardening was another occupation which made economic sense, in a population now largely urban.

The agricultural population as a whole continued to decline, but the numbers of gardeners, nurserymen and seedsmen were actually increasing sharply. With the help of machinery, fertilizer and better methods, output had ceased to fall, and the crisis in agriculture may be said to have been over by 1910.[3] The rising world prices for food in the early years of the century largely contributed to the strength of British, and foreign, agriculture.

By contrast with these old staples, some newer industries promised well for the future by their rapid rate of growth, though they were still relatively insignificant. The statistics of Caradog Jones, quoted above, highlighted some of the fastest growth sectors (the other rapidly growing occupations were professional and some other services and Government employment).[4]

Electrical engineering and supply were based to a considerable extent on British inventions and discoveries, but Britain lagged sadly behind

[1] D. Caradog Jones, 'Some Notes on the Census of Occupations for England and Wales', *J. R. Stat. S.*, 78/1, 1915, 55–78.
[2] Margaret Wray, *The Women's Outwear Industry* (1957), pp. 15–20.
[3] A. D. Hall, *A Pilgrimage of British Farming* (1912); Lord Ernle, *English Farming, Past and Present* (4th ed., 1927), chapters 18 and 19; T. W. Fletcher, 'The Great Depression of English Agriculture, 1873–1896', *Ec. Hist. Rev.*, 13/3, 1961.
[4] See table opposite.

Germany and even America in their development. The gas engine, and the motor car industry, its chief user, were equally the fruits of foreign, rather than British, enterprise.[1]

	Increase in Employment, %	
	1891–1901	1901–11
Tramway service	131	103
Cycle and motor manufacture	128	154
Electrical supply, etc.	259	77
Gas, water, sanitation	46	14
Chemicals, oil, etc.	15	20

More surprising, perhaps, was the relative backwardness of the British chemical industry, for at its base was the making of salt, soap, bleaching powder, and the dyes first discovered by Perkin, all of which were developed while Britain still led the world in industrial technique. In the last years before 1914, however, the British chemical industry appeared increasingly unable to keep pace, being handicapped by the lack of scientists and by being wedded to older processes, e.g. the Leblanc, rather than the Solvay, process of making soda. The war quickly showed up the serious shortcomings in the making of organic chemicals, such as high explosives, the shortage of oleum, one of their basic raw materials, and the neglect of the recent methods of producing fertilizer.[2]

Though perhaps relatively backward, these industries were among the most rapidly expanding ones, together with the allied rubber,[3] oil refining, airplane, artificial silk and scientific instruments industries. There was progress in other industries also, especially in glass, pottery, papermaking and printing, food preparation and boot and shoe making, all of which contributed not a little to the rising standards of comfort in Britain.

Factories (i.e. workplaces under the Factory Acts), however, still employed only a little over one-quarter of the working force in the country, and all the industries enumerated so far, including mining and agriculture, gave employment to only 40% of the occupied population. Millions of others were engaged in the professions, in commerce, transport, retail distribution, building and central and local government. Personal and domestic service still employed more females than any other occupation.

Developments in these occupations are seldom spectacular and they mostly do not compete in foreign markets. Yet they form the essential fabric of society, linking the other industries together, making their rapid technical advances possible and transmitting to the consumer the benefits

[1] Cf. S. B. Saul, *Studies in British Overseas Trade, 1870–1914* (Liverpool, 1960), pp. 37 ff.

[2] T. I. Williams, *The Chemical Industry* (1953), chapter 6; L. F. Haber, *The Chemical Industry during the Nineteenth Century* (Oxford, 1958), chapter 9.

[3] Wm. Woodruff, *The Rise of the British Rubber Industry during the Nineteenth Century* (Liverpool, 1958).

of technical changes which occur far out of his sight. They were growing very rapidly in the last years of peace.

3. INDUSTRIAL ORGANIZATION AND THE GROWTH OF MONOPOLY

By 1914, the early teething troubles of joint-stock companies had been overcome, and they had become the typical form of organization of British firms. Even firms which remained essentially private in ownership and control found great advantages in registering under an Act of 1907 which made special provision for them, freeing them from many of the obligations of other limited companies. By 1914 over three-quarters of all companies, whether registered as 'private' or not, were in fact private companies which did not come before the public for capital.

Such firms, however, were generally small. For large-scale enterprises, a public issue of capital had become the accepted method of financing the enlargement or re-equipment of an existing business. In some fields, as in overseas finance and mining, it was the normal practice to invite the public to subscribe the requisite capital from the beginning, and an increasing number of safeguards had been written into the Acts and developed in City practice to prevent the frauds that seemed inseparable from this form of organization. In other cases, the proceeds of a public issue could be applied to buying up competition or branching out into related enterprises, the process of horizontal and vertical integration becoming increasingly evident from the 1890's onwards.

By the standards of the mid-twentieth century, industrial amalgamation and combination in the last years of peace had not proceeded very far. There were, in effect, two distinct, even if related, movements: a simple growth in size, and an attempt to restrict competition. The two were often confused, but while the former usually took place in order to obtain economies in working, administration, marketing or finance, the latter was, more often than not, directed towards raising prices to consumers.

Improved techniques, not only in production, but also in administration, were exerting a powerful drive towards the enlargement of firms. In the iron and steel trades, for example, large furnace size was an advantage, and at the same time a steady and reliable supply of the raw materials, coal, iron ore and lime-stone, and some control over markets, were invaluable to keep the expensive capital equipment working to full capacity. Thus firms like John Brown and Vickers, of Sheffield, acquired coal mines and ore fields, as well as engineering, shipbuilding and armaments works. In coal mining, large firms like Sir James Joicey & Co. and Henry Briggs, Son & Co. in England, the Fife Coal Co. in Scotland, and the Cambrian Combine and Powell Duffryn in South Wales, arose by amalgamation and purchase. Other sectors in which large-scale operations were found economical included chemicals, glass, grain milling, public utilities, shipping and banking.

Combinations of this kind began to be viewed with apprehension wherever they obtained control over a significant share of their markets; thus in the case of railways, from the 1850's, and the banks in 1918,[1] official policy became expressly opposed to permitting any further reduction in the small number of competing units. Apprehension was increased when associations appeared from the beginning to have as one of their chief objectives the ending of 'destructive' or 'excessive' competition. In a free-trade country like Britain, it was true, monopoly control was more difficult to obtain than in protectionist countries like Germany, France and the U.S.A. Nevertheless, it was attempted in several different fields even here.

In some industries the typical form of organization was an association of independent producers, agreeing on common prices, and often developing common sales organizations and restriction schemes on output in order to protect their prices. These associations were most notable in the iron and steel industry, where they had begun by being regional and transitory, but in the early years of the new century they were becoming national and permanent. Some, like those of the steel rail makers from 1904, the screw makers in the 1890's and again from 1905, and the wire-netting makers, were international. By 1914, some 80 associations were an operation in the industry, each controlling one or a related group of products. Another group of trades in which this type of association was prominent, side by side with single-firm monopolies, was the building materials industry. It was calculated that in 1914 one-quarter of the cost of a cottage was fully price controlled, and a second quarter partially so; some of these monopolistic costs, however, were represented by the wages of skilled workers.[2]

In other industries there were to be found associations, some with international links, which were formed in order to share the benefits of a patent. Among these were the glass-bottle makers, exploiting the American Owens machine of 1906, and the electrical equipment makers. In a different field again were the shipping conferences or 'rings' which had been flourishing since the 1870's. They were normally limited to liner companies which stood to lose heavily if their ships sailed empty at their advertised times, and they brought to perfection a weapon adopted later by other associations: the deferred rebate.[3]

---

[1] Treasury Committee on Bank Amalgamations, *Report* (1918), in T. E. Gregory, *Statutes, Documents and Reports Relating to British Banking*, Vol. 2 (Oxford, 1929).

[2] *Report of the Committee on Trusts* (1919. Cd. 9236). Some of the unpublished material on which this Report was based was used by Clapham, *op. cit.*, chapter 5.

[3] *S.C. on Shipping Rings* (1909. Cd. 4668, 4669, 4670, 4685).

Some associations took the ultimate step of a complete merger to obtain monopolistic powers in this period, especially in the chemical and the textile industries. In chemicals, the early incidence of monopolistic firms was not surprising in view of the economies of scale and the importance of patents and limited access to raw materials. The Salt Union, formed of 64 firms in 1888 with £4 million capital, and estimated to control 90·6% of the British output at its formation, overplayed its hand by rapidly raising prices in an industry which was subject to competition both from abroad and from independent salt companies at home. It suffered severe losses, its capital had to be written down from £4·2 million to £2·6 million in 1902, and its decline was not halted until 1906, when the 'North Western Salt Co. Ltd.' was set up as a combined sales department for the Salt Union, now controlling less than half the British output, and the outside firms, regulating output, prices and distribution.

Another early attempt at monopoly was the United Alkali Company, formed in 1891 out of 48 companies with a capital of over £8 million. It proved equally unprofitable, although it also controlled some 90% of the British soda output at its formation. Much more successful was the firm of Brunner, Mond & Co., which was established in 1881 with a capital of £200,000 and absorbed some other chemical works, reaching a capital of £2·8 million in 1906. Other chemical combines were Borax Consolidated, formed in 1899 out of 12 companies in several countries, the Nobel Dynamite Trust, another international combine established in 1886 out of four constituent concerns, and Curtis & Harvey Ltd., formed in 1898 by a combination of eight of the leading gunpowder makers. The attempt by Lever Bros., then by far the largest soap-makers in the country with a capital of nearly £4 million, to form the 'Great Soap Trust' in 1906 by associating with ten other firms foundered on public opposition; the Soap Manufacturers' Association, however, which was formed in 1914, controlled the selling prices of about 80% of the British output.

In the textile industry, the most successful monopolistic combination was J. & P. Coats, the sewing cotton firm. It was converted into a public company with £5¾ million capital in 1890. By 1896, the four largest and most vigorous competitors had been bought up, and the combine showed excellent results. Fourteen of the remaining, smaller, firms formed a second combine in 1897, called the English Sewing Cotton Co., with the participation of J. &. P. Coats. Its returns were far less satisfactory. Both the British firms joined in 1898 in promoting the American Thread Co., a combine of 13 firms, in the U.S.A., and these three firms, collaborating closely, completely dominated their trade. The other textile combines were mostly formed by amalgamating large numbers of firms with widely scattered premises; the benefits of amalgamation were thus clearly to be higher prices rather than lower costs of production. The most important of them included the Fine Cotton Spinners' and Doublers' Association, formed in 1898 of 31 firms, with 16 more added by 1905; the Calico Printers' Association in 1899, of 59 companies; the Bleachers' Association, formed in 1900 of 53 firms, to which another five were added by 1906; the Bradford Dyers' Association, formed in 1898 of 22 firms, to which were added 13 more by 1903, controlling 90% of the trade; the Woolcombers' Association, formed out of 41 businesses in 1900; and there were several smaller schemes. Of these, only the Fine Cotton Spinners and the Dyers were not complete failures financially. Two chief causes of failure were over-capitalization, i.e. over-payment for businesses bought up, and scattered control, as the former managements generally remained in charge.

There were some notable examples of monopolistic control in other industries also. The Imperial Tobacco Co., a combine of 13 firms, emerged in 1901–2 with the lion's share of the British market and an agreed share of overseas markets after a bitter struggle with the American Tobacco Co. In the wallpaper industry, an amalgamation of 38 firms and three others associated with it, made in 1900, claimed to control 98% of the British output. British Oil and Cake Mills Ltd., a combination of 17 major firms in 1899, controlled over half the output of its industry, while the Distillers' Company, after several mergers, was able in 1907 to raise whisky prices by agreements with the few surviving independents. Lastly, Associated Portland Cement Manufacturers Ltd. was formed in 1900 and quickly controlled 89% of the capacity of the Thames and Medway district, the southern centre of the industry. In 1912, another 33 firms were added to form an Association, and national agreements were to follow after the war.[1]

Towards the end of the nineteenth century, municipalities increasingly undertook the management of public utilities, as the new electricity power stations and electric trams and motor bus companies took their place next to the older railways, water and gas companies. While Manchester Corporation was largely responsible for completing the Ship Canal in 1893, others provided market halls, harbours, cemeteries and baths. By 1913, four-fifths of the consumers of water and of tramway services, two-thirds of the supply of electricity, and two-fifths of the consumers of gas, were provided for by the local authorities. Though Sidney Webb had staked out a claim for municipal Socialism as early as 1894 in an official document, the Minority Report of the Royal Commission on Labour, and 'Gas and Water Socialism' won notable victories especially in the London County Council, the reason for the spread of municipal enterprise was not to be found simply in Socialist doctrine, as yet held by few town

[1] Hermann Levy, *Monopolies, Trusts and Cartels in British Industry* (2nd ed., 1927); F. W. Hirst, *Monopolies, Trusts and Kartells* (1905); Henry W. Macrosty, *The Trust Movement in British Industry* (1907).

councillors, but largely in the need to control natural monopolies, in the hope of relieving the rates, and in a praiseworthy measure of civic pride.[1]

A third method of organization making remarkable progress in the years before 1914 was that of the co-operative society. With a membership of 3 million, the 1,385 societies had total sales of nearly £90 million, and had been transformed from insignificant local associations to a major factor in retail distribution and a few related fields. A significant share of the basic weekly shopping by the working-class housewife in the north was done in the local 'co-op' branch, still working on the 'Rochdale principles' of paying dividends on purchases, not on shares, and keeping to 'one member, one vote'. A few producer societies, and some agricultural societies, notably in Ireland, also worked on co-operative principles. In this period co-operative trading was an important factor in the pioneering of large-scale enterprise in retailing, in promoting the campaign for wholesome and unadulterated food, and in providing convenient facilities for working-class savings.[2]

4. THE BANKS AND THE MONEY MARKET

Among the many changes in the forms of economic organization in the generation before 1914, those in the field of banking were among the most significant. The swallowing up of the private banks by the joint-stock bank engaged in branch banking, 'a trickle in the middle decades of the century, ... had become a headlong rush as the century neared its end. In the new century amalgamations continued to follow one upon the other, and they were now amalgamations between banks already greatly enlarged by earlier absorptions.'[3] This process was all but completed by 1914, when the several hundred private banks had shrunk to fewer than a score, but there now were 20 joint-stock banks with over 100 branches each (the largest, the London City and Midland, having over 700), besides 20 or so with fewer than 100 branches each and local connections only. Between them, they maintained about 7,000 offices in England and Wales. In Scotland, where joint-stock banking had a longer tradition, there were eight banking companies in 1914, with just under 1,200 branches between them.

The core of the banking amalgamations could either be early joint-stock banks, like the London & Westminster or the National Provincial Bank of England, or private bankers, like the Barclays. Amalgamations were carried through to round off a territory, to broaden the basis of a

---

[1] G. P. Jones and A. G. Pool, *A Hundred Years of Economic Development* (1959 ed.), chapter 8; D. H. MacGregor, *The Evolution of Industry* (8th ed., 1928), chapter 8.
[2] C. R. Fay, *Great Britain from Adam Smith to the Present Day* (4th ed., 1937), chapter 20; G. D. H. Cole, *A Century of Co-operation* (1944).
[3] R. S. Sayers, *Lloyd's Bank in the History of English Banking* (Oxford, 1957), p. 241.

bank by entering new territory, to gain entry into the City of London, particularly to share in the coveted rights of the London Clearing House, to acquire an existing goodwill (sometimes after an old private bank had closed its doors) or because 'nowadays . . . prestige was one of the most valuable of a bank's assets'.[1] In the 'race' of amalgamations which began in the 1890's, the objective was increasingly seen to be a national coverage for each firm. In the process, any existing gaps were filled by opening new offices and sub-offices, which increased in number year by year.[2]

The process bespeaks an increasing banking habit of the population: between 1906 and 1914 alone, bank deposits per head of population rose from £18·8 to £23·4, and clearings from £292 to £359. Its consequences were far-reaching. The circulation of private bank notes virtually disappeared, except for Scotland, the cheque system became all but universal, and Bank of England notes were mainly used for wage payments and small retail purchases only,[3] while inland bills were rendered largely obsolete:[4] bills were now used mostly for foreign traffic only. It is noteworthy that Lancashire, the area most familiar with the inland bill, was the most bitterly opposed to the amalgamation of its banks with London-based firms.

A further result of amalgamation was to make banking much safer as resources and reserves were immeasurably increased. Banks became so large and of such wide economic importance that failures could no longer be contemplated, and when in 1910 the Charing Cross Bank failed, dragging the Birkbeck Building Society, now a banking concern, with it, the London & Westminster stepped in and ultimately paid the creditors 16s. 9½d. in the pound. Similarly, in 1911, the Yorkshire Penny Bank was saved by the Midland Bank; a guarantee fund, headed by the Bank of England, had also been raised, but did not have to be used.

National banks worked by internal transfers between branches, and

---

[1] T. E. Gregory, *The Westminster Bank Through a Century*, Vol. 2 (1936), p. 4.
[2] J. F. Ashby, *The Story of the Banks* (1934); P. W. Matthews, *The Banker's Clearing House* (1921), chapter 7; J. Sykes, *The Amalgamation Movement in British Banking, 1825–1924* (1926). Official histories exist of all the large banks, e.g., beside those quoted, H. Withers, *The National Provincial Bank, 1833–1933* (1933); W. F. Crick and J. E. Wadsworth, *A Hundred Years of Joint-Stock Banking* (1936); P. W. Matthews and A. W. Tuke, *A History of Barclays Bank Ltd.* (1926); Ralph M. Robinson, *Coutts'* (1929); *Hoare's Bank, a Record* (1955 ed.); J. Leighton-Boyce, *Smiths the Bankers, 1658–1958* (1958); Sir Eric Gore-Brown, *Glyn Mills & Co.* (1933); C. A. Malcolm, *History of the British Linen Bank* (Edinb., 1950) and *The Bank of Scotland* (Edinb., n.d.); N. Munro, *Royal Bank of Scotland* (Edinb., 1928); Compton Mackenzie, *Realms of Silver* (1954).
[3] Evidence of Governor and Directors of the Bank of England to U.S. National Monetary Commission in 1910, reprinted in T. E. Gregory (ed.), *Selected Statutes, Documents and Reports Relating to British Banking, 1832–1928* (Oxford, 1929), Vol. 2, p. 309; also First Report of Cunliffe Committee, quoted in *ibid.*, pp. 335–6.
[4] W. T. C. King, *History of the London Discount Market* (1936), pp. 271–5.

the old system of 'pyramiding', by which the limited reserve of one London house was regarded as a reserve by several of its provincial correspondents simultaneously, was ended, leading to larger cash reserves, as well as greater caution, after 1890. At the same time the individual banks obtained more power in the money market: just as the decline of the inland bill tended to squeeze the discount houses out of home markets, so the opening of branches or agencies abroad by the joint-stock banks made inroads into the work of other specialist firms. The accumulation of 'private' gold reserves by the banks (the Midland alone held £8 million by 1914, and the others probably £16 million between them) made it more easy for them to defy the central bank, had they so desired,[1] though in fact collaboration with the Bank of England became closer, and a liaison committee was set up in 1911 and justified its existence during the early days of financial panic after the outbreak of war.

The strengthening of the English banking structure by amalgamation also altered the role of the Bank of England as the central bank and banker of last resort. An internal drain having become unlikely since there were very few country banks with their own note issue left, it would appear, to judge from the evidence given to the U.S. Monetary Commission, that the Bank was almost exclusively concerned with the foreign exchanges, and with safeguarding the gold reserve against the dangers of a drain abroad. At the same time it tended to ignore the repercussion of changes in the gold reserve and in general liquidity on the rest of the economy.

The Bank's two main weapons in carrying out its obligations as a central bank were the bank rate and open market operations. The former could sometimes be accompanied by greater selectivity in the kind of paper the Bank would accept for rediscounting; the ideal, however, was to lend freely, but at high rates, in times of need. A rise in the bank rate achieved its primary object if it led to a general rise of interest rates in London. These were then expected to call forth an influx of foreign funds including gold, on the one hand, and to discourage enterprise, lead to a reduction of stocks and to general deflation at home on the other, thus reversing the outflow of gold which was the usual ground upon which the high bank rate policy had been put into operation. 'Open market operations' covered a variety of actions with which the Bank experimented in this period to supplement its bank rate policy by making money scarce or plentiful in the City. They ranged from purchases and sales of securities to influencing market rates (as distinct from bank rate) and the gold market, and included the increasingly effective 'hint from headquarters' to the clearing banks.[2]

---

[1] E. Victor Morgan, *Theory and Practice of Central Banking, 1797–1913* (Cambridge 1943), pp. 210–12.

[2] R. S. Sayers, *Bank of England Operation, 1890–1914* (1936), and 'Open Market

Several circumstances combined to turn the imperfect control of the Bank of England over the market which existed in 1890 into the smooth and perfect instrument of the last years before 1914.[1] In the first place, the gold reserve rose after the mid-1890's, when the vast quantities from the new goldfields of Alaska and South Africa began to arrive in London. From the beginning of 1889 to June 1914, British (net) gold imports amounted to £154 million, of which £17¾ million went to increase the reserve.[2] In the years before 1914, the reserve fluctuated around the comfortable level of £30 million, creeping up to £40 million.

Secondly, the Bank could count on the support of other strong institutions, including foreign central banks, and the joint-stock banks and it could use the growing funds of Colonial Governments and British local authorities to back up its policies. The British Government also strengthened its hand by running budget surpluses to reduce the national debt and by the extension in the use of the Treasury Bill in place of the former Ways and Means Accounts after 1902.

Above all, the powers of the Bank over the City depended on the growth of London as the leading money market in the world. As there were no internal gold hoards to be tapped by a high bank rate, the gold had to come from abroad. Most of the world was on a gold standard by the end of the nineteenth century, but the premier position of London ensured that an attractive rate would bring gold from the four corners of the earth. In fact, at the outbreak of war it was found that despite the position of Britain as the world's chief lender, foreign short-term funds in London exceeded British short-term claims abroad.

The power of a high rate to attract gold was demonstrated in 1907, when, after a serious loss of gold to America, a 7% bank rate brought in speedily £19 million in gold from 24 countries. This proof of the effectiveness of the bank rate impressed itself deeply upon the minds of the directors of the Bank, especially since there were no further serious drains on the Bank's reserve to test the system again before 1914. In 1918, they were to remember the smooth international flow of gold before 1914 and the ease of its control, as far as Britain was concerned, by the Bank of England, without realizing that the conditions which made this possible had been temporary and short-lived.[3]

Operations in English Central Banking' in his *Central Banking after Bagehot* (Oxford, 1957); P. Barrett Whale, 'The Working of the Pre-War Gold Standard', *Economica*, 1937, reprinted in T. S. Ashton and R. S. Sayers (ed.), *Papers in English Monetary History* (Oxford, 1953); A. G. Ford, 'Notes on the Working of the Gold Standard before 1914', *Oxf. Econ. P.*, N.S., 12/1, 1960.

[1] W. E. Beach, *British International Gold Movements and Banking Policy, 1881–1913* (Cambridge, Mass., 1935), chapters 7–9.

[2] R. G. Hawtrey, *A Century of Bank Rate* (1938), pp. 46–8.

[3] Sayers, *Bank of England Operations*, pp. 7, 101, 137, and *Central Banking*, pp. 18,

In the years before 1914, the financial institutions specializing in foreign credits were at the height of their power. They floated foreign loans in unprecedented quantities, they acted as agents for overseas governments and public corporations, accepting foreign bills and engaging in foreign exchange operations. There were only a few large firms engaged in this form of business, and some of the merchant bankers had a standing in the market higher than the Government for which they acted.

While the market for foreign investments was thus extremely well organized, the market for home investment was complex, many-sided, and badly co-ordinated. Local authorities, Railways and public utilities could use the London money market, and their securities were freely quoted on the Stock Exchange. For the rest of the domestic capital needs, however, the Stock Exchange was of little help: in the years before the war, only 10% of real investment in this country was made by issues of industrial firms through the London Stock Exchange, and only 3% by new industrial firms. Neither were the banks, which were quite content to finance the growing volume of Stock Exchange speculation, prepared to finance industry. As a result, capital for industry had to be found largely by personal connections, in provincial centres, and by ploughing back the firms' own profits.[1]

Among the institutional investors, insurance companies were beginning to play a significant part. A process of aggrandizement, not dissimilar from that in banking, had resulted in the creation of a few giant concerns which were beyond the suspicion of failure, though many sound smaller firms survived or came into being in this period. Many of them branched out into new specialist fields, beyond the former main interests of fire, life and marine insurance. Like other institutions in the City of London, they came to rely increasingly on foreign business in the early years of the century. The services performed by all City houses for foreign clients made substantial contributions to the balance of payments: according to a recent calculation, financial, trade and insurance services (excluding shipping) brought in average annual net earnings of £54½ million in 1901–5, £67 million in 1906–10 and £80 million in 1911–13.[2]

61–3; Sir John Clapham, *The Bank of England, a History*, Vol. 2 (Cambridge, 1944), chapter 8; A. I. Bloomfield, *Monetary Policy under the International Gold Standard: 1880–1914* (New York, 1959).

[1] A. K. Cairncross, *Home and Foreign Investment 1870–1913* (Cambridge, 1953), chapter 5; F. Lavington, *The English Capital Market* (1921); and the controversy in A. R. Hall, 'A Note on the English Capital Market as a Source of Funds Before 1914', *Economica*, N.S., 24/93, 1957; A. K. Cairncross, 'The English Capital Market Before 1914', *ibid.*, 25/98, 1958, pp. 142–6; A. R. Hall, 'The English Capital Market Before 1914—a Reply', *ibid.*, 25/100, pp. 339–43.

[2] A. H. Imlah, 'British Balance of Payments and Export of Capital, 1816–1913', *Ec. Hist. Rev.*, 5/2, 1952; reprinted in *Economic Elements in the Pax Britannica* (Cambridge, Mass., 1958).

5. FOREIGN INVESTMENT AND THE PROBLEM OF EMPIRE

Foreign investment in the last years of peace had reached an astonishing level. According to Imlah, capital assets abroad owned by British citizens amounted to about £2·4 milliard at the turn of the century; by the outbreak of war, they had risen to £4 milliard.[1] Further, the pace of foreign investment tended to increase from an average of under £50 million per annum in 1901–5 to about £150 million per annum in 1907–10 and £200 million per annum in 1911–13. From 1907 on, annual investment abroad appears to have exceeded the total of real net investments at home.

How was this vast capital export, amounting in the last years to about one-third of the total export trade, financed? Britain, it must be remembered, showed a substantial unfavourable balance on merchandise trade of the order of £150 million annually. This negative balance, to which must be added (net) bullion imports and tourist expenditure abroad of about £20 million, was almost exactly counterbalanced by large and rising credit items for net invisible exports: banking, insurance and shipping earnings. The surplus was provided by dividends and interest rising from about £100 million to £200 million between 1900 and 1913, and it was these which allowed Britain to increase her foreign investments at an equally rapid rate. This was not merely a statistical coincidence: a large part of the foreign investment was, in fact, direct re-investment of earnings abroad.[2]

Since foreign railways, docks or naval yards, if financed by British investors, would naturally favour British suppliers, a boom in capital exports was bound to be paralleled by a boom in the exports of merchandise, a large proportion of which, as was shown above, consisted of capital goods. There was, at the same time, a high tide of emigration from the United Kingdom, particularly to the countries which received a large share of the British capital. Waves of these exports of capital, of merchandise, and of migrants had gone out during the nineteenth century in cycles, alternating with periods of an exactly opposite character.[3] The years before 1914 formed the second half of the last, and perhaps most powerfully marked, of these cycles, in which the other advanced countries of Europe also registered exceptionally large exports of capital.[4] At the

[1] Other broadly similar estimates are summarized in E. Victor Morgan, *Studies in British Financial Policy, 1914–1925* (1952), p. 328; also see J. H. Lenfant, 'Great Britain's Capital Formation, 1865–1914', *Economica*, N.S., 18/70, 1951.

[2] A dissenting view will be found in A. G. Ford, 'The Transfer of British Foreign Lending, 1870–1913', *Ec. Hist. Rev.*, 11/2, 1958.

[3] Brinley Thomas, *Migration and Economic Growth* (Cambridge, 1954); Cairncross, *op. cit.*, chapter 8.

[4] C. K. Hobson, *The Export of Capital* (1914).

same time British investment, as well as British migration, went increasingly to areas within the Empire. Thus in 1901–10 an annual average of 85,000 migrated from the United Kingdom to Canada, and 23,000 to Australia and New Zealand. In 1911–13, the figures were 189,000 and 85,000 respectively. The proportions of British emigrants making for territories within the Empire were 28% in the 1890's, 63% between 1901 and 1912, and 78% in 1913.

The years before 1914 were also marked by a general rise in world prices, in which food and raw materials, the main British imports, tended to rise faster in price than the manufactured goods which Britain exported. The gross barter terms of trade (aggregate value of exports divided by aggregate value of imports), therefore, turned against Britain, from an index of 82·3 in 1899–1901 to 105·7 in 1911–13 (1880 = 100), while the net barter terms of trade (export prices divided by import prices) declined from 110 to 102 in the same years (1885–1900 = 100).[1] This movement favoured employment in the export industries, which found ready markets as their products were becoming relatively cheaper, but it tended to inhibit improvements in the standards of living here.

This movement, also, may be viewed as part of a longer cycle, extending some fifty years from peak to peak,[2] in which prices, interest rates, terms of trade and general business prosperity moved together. The operative factor in this long-term cycle appeared to be the world price level, which, in turn, depended in part on the world supply of gold, and in part on the main direction of investment: heavy long-term investments, such as railways and docks, as well as costly wars, will push up prices, while peaceful years, and years in which most investments have quick yields while the heavy capital expenditures of the previous period begin to yield their fruits in lowered real costs, will see (cost) price reductions.[3] The period 1896–1914 (and on to 1920) fitted the pattern very well: the world's supply of gold available for monetary use was more than doubled in the twenty years after 1891, there were heavy overseas investments of the slow gestation type, and there were innumerable wars, culminating in the World War itself.

It may now be possible to discern a distinct pattern in the unhealthy reliance of the staple industries on exports, the export boom in capital

[1] H. A. Imlah, *Economic Elements*, pp. 87–8; also 'Terms of Trade of the United Kingdom 1798–1915', *J. Econ. Hist.*, 10/2, Nov. 1950; Cairncross, *op. cit.*, p. 206; W. W. Rostow, 'The Terms of Trade in Theory and Practice', *Ec. Hist. Rev.*, 3/1, 1950, and 'The Historical Analysis of the Terms of Trade', *ibid.*, 4/1, 1951.
[2] N. D. Kondratieff, 'Long Waves of Economic Life', *Rev. of Econ. and Statistics*, 17, 1935; W. W. Rostow, *British Economy of the Nineteenth Century* (Oxford, 1948), chapter 1.
[3] For a critical view, see S. B. Saul, *Studies in British Oversea Trade, 1870–1914* (Liverpool, 1960), chapter 5/1.

goods, the lag behind other countries in technical equipment and progress, the concentration of the City of London on foreign lending, and the downward pressure on real incomes (except for profits), in the last years of peace. Do they all add up to the statement that Britain invested too much abroad, to the detriment of her own industrial future?[1]

The question is to some extent wrongly put, for the direction of the British investment programme was not the outcome of a deliberate decision, but of the choices of innumerable investors. They chose foreign investments, because, even taking risks into account, their yields were substantially higher than those offered at home. Had investors been forced to keep their savings at home, they would have had to accept much lower returns, especially since a large-scale diversion of funds would have still further reduced the marginal productivity of capital in Britain. In relation to the savings available, investment opportunities at home appeared to be distinctly insufficient.

The destination of the funds thus sent abroad was significant.[2] By 1910, when foreign investments totalled some £3¼ million, about £1,550–£1,650 million was invested within the Empire, virtually all of it in four regions, Canada, Australia–New Zealand, Africa, and India–Ceylon, holding just under £400 million each. The United States and the rest of America came next, with over £600 million each, and other areas shared the remainder. By 1913, 47% of British overseas investment was in the Empire. The importance of the Empire stands out, particularly, since, with South America,[3] it formed the area of the fastest increase of investments.

British imperial policy had greatly changed since the last century. Beginning in the mid-1870's, the advanced countries of the West had within one generation carved up the whole continent of Africa, including vast uncharted regions; they had incorporated many areas of Asia into their empires, had partitioned China and other nominally sovereign states into spheres of influence, and were staking out claims for the economic penetration of other regions, including South and Central America. In this scramble for colonies, clashes between the Great Powers could not be avoided. Many were settled without resort to arms, but among the causes of the first World War, imperialist rivalry must take a foremost place.

Modern Imperialism has many roots. It was fed by nationalism and jingoism, perhaps the most potent beliefs in the advanced countries of the

[1] F. W. Taussig, 'Great Britain's Foreign Trade Terms after 1900', *Econ. J.*, 1925; John Saville, 'Some Retarding Factors in the British Economy before 1914', *Yorkshire Bulletin*, 13/1, 1961.

[2] For recent summaries, see Morgan, *Studies*, p. 328; Saul, *op. cit.*, chapters 8 and 9.

[3] J. Fred Rippy, *British Investments in Latin America, 1822–1949* (Minneapolis, 1959), chapter 4.

West before 1914; it owed much to the inspiration of soldiers, poets, missionaries and explorers; and often colonies were sought for their strategic value. But the main root of Imperialism was economic. As far as it had an economic root, it was not so much the search for trade: the proportion of British overseas commerce that went to the colonies had been stationary or declining in the half-century to 1900, despite the growth in their wealth and number. The chief economic significance of the New Colonial Empire, as a brilliant contemporary study pointed out,[1] was its promise of relatively safe, protected and exclusive investment opportunities. The more investment opportunities declined or threatened to yield decreasing returns at home, the stronger the pull of Empire. It has been argued that the decline in home yields coincided with a period when technical improvements and scientific discoveries in transport, the preservation of food and tropical agriculture and hygiene opened out genuine possibilities of development in regions hitherto considered barren and unpromising.[2] Most of British foreign investment, however, continued to flow into fairly well-developed and temperate zones.

Conversion to the new Imperialism had to come slowly. Britain had been brought up to ridicule the fallacies that had built up the Old Colonial Empire and had lost the North American Colonies;[3] though quietly and efficiently rounding off the acquisition of an empire much larger than that of any other power,[4] she wanted free trade and no favours, a cheap loaf and cheap raw materials, and the smallest possible arms budget. The colonies, requiring support, defence and even, perhaps, subsidies, had been a 'millstone round our necks' as late as the mid-century.

It was one thing to make use of the recently established universal education (a potent force in spreading patriotic ideals), and the newly developed popular press which cashed in on the new mass-literacy, to rouse latent jingoistic feelings in Zulu, Kaffir and Boer Wars. To use imperial power to impose tariffs and exclude foreign traders and investors was another. A nascent protectionism was found in a few scattered industries which felt inferior to foreign competitors even in the 1880's.[5] After 1900 economic stagnation at home created more support for a policy

[1] J. A. Hobson, *Imperialism* (1st ed., 1902; 3rd ed., 1938); also V. I. Lenin, *Imperialism, the Highest Stage of Capitalism* (1916, repr. in *Selected Works*, Vol. 5; 1936); Clive Day, *A History of Commerce* (New York, 1907), chapters 37, 38, 53, W. Ashworth, *A Short History of the International Economy, 1850–1950* (1952), chapter 6.

[2] L. C. A. Knowles, *The Economic Development of the British Overseas Empire*, Vol. 1 (1924), Book I, A(3), C(2), Book II, A, B(2)(c).

[3] C. M. MacInnes, *An Introduction to the Economic History of the British Empire* (1935), chapters 20–2.

[4] J. Gallagher and R. Robinson, 'The Imperialism of Free Trade', *Ec. Hist. Rev.*, 6/1, 1953.

[5] B. H. Brown, *The Tariff Reform Movement in Great Britain, 1881–1895* (New York, 1943).

of protection with imperial preference, such as that advocated by Joseph Chamberlain, but his success was limited. He converted large sections of the Conservative Party, but he still failed to convert Britain.

Chamberlain, a former Radical Lord Mayor of Birmingham who became Colonial Secretary in Salisbury's Tory Government and stayed in that office from 1895 to 1903, made this office, formerly a minor one, into one of the key posts in the Cabinet. Though he failed to achieve protection, called 'fair trade', to which he himself had been converted only while in office, the advent of this energetic politician led to a revolution in colonial policy: 'Obstruction ceased. He answered by telegram and usually in the affirmative.' [1] Schools of agriculture and tropical medicine, an Imperial Penny Post in 1898, encouragement of railway building, and the Colonial Loans Act of 1899, which permitted Treasury loans of fifty years' duration to the colonies, were direct or indirect results of Chamberlain's activities.

Other measures taken at the time to further imperial development did, however, prove ultimately to have very little significance. Thus the granting of trustee status to colonial stocks in 1900 had no perceptible effect on the terms on which they borrowed;[2] the attempt to help the West Indies by the sugar convention of 1902 which ended bounties on sugar exports from Central Europe, made no perceptible difference to any British colony; the attempt to further West Indian banana exports by subsidizing the Elder–Dempster shipping line in 1901 failed utterly; and the most controversial measure of all, the cancellation of certain commercial treaties with Germany and Belgium in order to take up the offer of a preference in the Canadian market made in 1897, had again no noticeable effect on trade, either with Canada or with the other Dominions which followed her example. The only effective protectionist measure was the prohibitive export duty on Malayan tin ore in 1903, which kept the smelting capacity within the Empire.[3] Yet in his term of office, which ended in 1903, Chamberlain, together with his energetic followers, had made sufficient converts to lay the basis for a swing to protection less than thirty years later.

6. INCOMES AND THE STANDARD OF LIVING

In the second half of the nineteenth century it became one of the unspoken tenets of all classes that total national output per head would

---

[1] C. R. Fay, *Great Britain from Adam Smith to the Present Day* (4th ed., 1937), p. 82.

[2] A. S. J. Baster, 'The Colonial Stocks Act and Dominion Borrowing', *Economic History*, 2/8, 1933.

[3] S. B. Saul, 'The Economic Significance of "Constructive Imperialism" ', *J. Econ. Hist.*, 17/2, 1957.

rise in the long run and that those performing some useful economic function would normally share in the increased wealth. Long-term upward movements do not, however, exclude movements in the opposite direction for substantial periods of time, and in the first fourteen years of this century, while the total national product increased as before, the real wages of labour remained stationary or declined.

According to Hoffmann, the index of industrial production rose from 77·1 to 100·0 between 1900 and 1913, both of these being peak years; the index of ocean shipping stood at 59·6 in 1900, railway goods traffic at 74·8, gas output at 67·7, 1913 in each case being valued at 100. According to Kuczynski, output in mining and manufacturing rose by 30% between 1900 and 1913. Productivity in other sectors, notably the services, did not increase as fast, but 'unearned' income in the form of interest and dividends from abroad rose even faster. Total national income at constant prices, according to Prest, grew by 20·3% between 1900 and 1913.[1] In view of a population increase from 41·2 million in 1900 to 45·7 million in 1913, or of 11%, real national income per head rose by about 8½%,[2] and productivity per worker employed rose by 7% in those years.

This increased national output was not necessarily reflected in increased personal consumption, for the price rises occurred largely in food and textile raw materials, the bases of consumers' expenditure, while the relative prices of capital goods fell. Thus the volume index of total consumers' expenditure stood at 111·4 in 1911 and 111·7 in 1912, 1900 being 100, so that it was only just keeping pace with the growth in population.[3] Food consumption, in fact, was falling behind the population figure. Wage-earners stood to lose most by the relative movement of prices, since about seven-tenths of their incomes were spent on food and clothing.

To make matters worse, wages were falling relatively to other incomes, declining as a proportion of total incomes, from 41·3% in 1900 to a bare 36·2% in 1913.[4] Thus real wages experienced an absolute fall, according to Kuczynski, by 5% between 1900 and 1913, according to Cairncross by 3%, and according to Layton and Crowther[5] by 5%. These two years were, however, peak years in the pattern of the trade cycle, 1913, in

---

[1] Hoffmann, *op. cit.*; J. Kuczynski, *A Short History of Labour Conditions in Britain, 1750 to the Present Day* (1946 ed.), p. 121; A. R. Prest, 'National Income of the United Kingdom, 1870–1946', *Econ. J.*, 58/229, 1948.

[2] Prest's figures as corrected by C. H. Feinstein yield an increase of 4% only: 'Income and Investment in the United Kingdom, 1856–1914', *Econ. J.*, 71/282, 1961.

[3] A. R. Prest and A. A. Adams, *Consumer Expenditure in the United Kingdom, 1900–1919* (Cambridge, 1954).

[4] Feinstein's figures are: 41·5% and 37·8% respectively. Cf. also A. L. Bowley, *The Change in the Distribution of the National Income, 1880–1913* (Oxford, 1920).

[5] W. T. Layton and G. Crowther, *An Introduction to the Study of Prices* (3rd ed., 1938).

particular, being a year well above the ordinary. More important was the fact that for the whole of the period 1902–12, real wages were well below the levels reached in 1899–1901, and in some years, especially 1909–11, they were less than 90% of the earlier figures. The failure of wages to rise with the country's prosperity, against all expectation, was bound to cause unrest and bitterness in the ranks of labour, without an understanding of their causes. Only towards the end of the period did statistics prepared by the Labour Department of the Board of Trade, and by A. L. Bowley and G. H. Wood, show the fall in real wages.[1]

Statistics of this kind should not be credited with too great an accuracy, but the general trend of real wage indices is established beyond doubt. Within these general figures of wage changes, however, three developments stand out: differences in the payments for different jobs, differences as between families of varying sizes, and the incidence of unemployment and cyclical variation of employment.

The difference between the nominal weekly wage rates of skilled and unskilled men was, perhaps, at its widest in this period. It had been materially reduced in the 1890's with the organization of trade unions for general labourers, but since then the main pressure on real wages had been exerted by rises in the cost of living, slowly to 1907, faster from then on, so that there was need for positive trade union action to raise money wages, and for such action most unskilled men were badly prepared. Many of the general unions of the 1890's found it difficult to hold their mass membership in the face of low wages and irregular employment. Thus, the gap between the skilled and unskilled widened again. The unweighted average of unskilled wages in five industries (coal, cotton, engineering, building and railways) was 60% of the skilled wage in 1886 and 58½% in 1913. It was to rise to 77·7% in 1920, and then settle around the 67% mark in the inter-war years.[2] Artisans' wages were in the region of 40s. to 50s. per week in all but the smallest towns, and labourers' still round the 25s. mark.[3] Other wages ranged between these limits, and women's industrial wages were around one-third to one-half of a man's wage. In addition to the textile industry and domestic service, two new occupations had recently been opened to women; shop work from the 1860's on, and office work from the 1890's, while teaching and nursing were other growing female occupations.

[1] Another contemporary calculation produced these index figures for real wages: 1895—163; 1900—179; 1910—161. J. A. Hobson, *Gold, Prices and Wages* (1913), chapter 7.

[2] K. G. J. C. Knowles and D. J. Robertson, 'Differences Between the Wages of Skilled and Unskilled Workers, 1880–1950', *Bull. Oxf. Inst. Stat.*, 13/4, 1951, p. 111.

[3] J. F. W. Rowe, *Wages in Practice and Theory* (1928), chapters 1, 2 and 3 and Appx. 1: Board of Trade, *Report on Earnings and Hours of Labour* (1911. Cd. 5814).

The differences in the wage rates between the skilled and the unskilled were widened by the fact that it was often the labourers' jobs that were the most irregular, employers preferring to keep their skilled crews together. Further, there were employments which were by their nature irregular and in which men could seldom, if ever, hope to work six days in the week, such as navvying, building work generally, and dock labour, and the inquiries made by Charles Booth and his assistants in 1887–92 showed how far this type of employment was responsible for primary poverty, at least in London.

A wage of £1 per week or under might provide all the necessities of life for a single man or a couple, but would cause hardship and want for a family with several children. Families were getting smaller: from a normal family of 5–6 children, the average for marriages contracted in 1900–7 had fallen to just over 3, and in 1910–14 to under 3. But there were growing class differences, the lower the social status of the family, the larger being the number of its children. At a time when the distribution of incomes was turning decisively against the wage-earner, this was a potent factor aggravating the adverse relative movement—just as, in more recent years, the reduction in the size of the average family has been an important factor in the rising standards of comfort in this country.

If the 'average' working-class family, consisting of two adults and three children, enjoyed an income of an equivalent of 1½ adult wages, or 45s., in 1914, 20s. of such income was spent on food and 7s. 6d. on rent, fuel and light, leaving 17s. 6d. for everything else, including clothing, travel, entertainment, contributions, doctors' fees, etc. Perhaps as much as 6s. per household went on drink.[1] If this was a tolerable standard, the life of householders who belonged to that half of the labour force which brought home an average of 20s. or less per week, or who had a ratio of dependants to earners less favourable than 5 to 1½, was bound to be a life of economic hardship or distress.

Charles Booth found in London that about one-third of the population lived below a standard which kept them physically efficient, later called the 'poverty line'. This discovery, in the richest city of the world, was soon confirmed by the recruiting sergeants and by other inquiries, made in York in 1899 by B. S. Rowntree, and in the four towns of Northampton, Warrington, Stanley and Reading, undertaken in 1912–13 by A. L. Bowley and A. R. Burnett-Hurst.[2] The numbers of those whom the economic system had condemned to an existence of dire want in the

---

[1] E. H. Phelps-Brown, *Growth of British Industrial Relations* (1959), pp. 19–20.
[2] Ch. Booth, *Life and Labour in London* (1904 ed.); B. S. Rowntree, *Poverty, a Study of Town Life* (1902); A. L. Bowley and A. R. Burnett-Hurst, *Livelihood and Poverty* (1915); *Report of Inter-Departmental Committee on Physical Deterioration* (1904. Cd. 2175).

midst of a rich society was too large to be accounted for merely by personal defects, nor, even if it were, could the even larger proportion of children in primary poverty be defended on such grounds. Among the men who in 1911 received less than 25*s.* if in regular work, there could not have been fewer than 2 million who were married and who would have dependent families, numbering 8 million souls all told. All of them were 'underfed, under-housed and insufficiently clothed. The children among them suffer more than the adults. Their growth is stunted, their mental powers are cramped, their health is undermined.' [1]

The growing understanding of social problems of this kind was accompanied by a growing understanding of the problem of cyclical unemployment. [2] Skilled men, when out of work, could normally draw trade union benefit, and it was the unskilled labourers who bore the brunt of the fluctuations in employment, but this was a scourge which threatened more than the submerged third of the population. Unemployment fluctuated round an average of 4% among trade union members, but in the very worst years it rose up to 11%; in 1908 and 1909, for example, it was over 8½%. In such years, standards of consumption would deteriorate still further and debts would have to be incurred. [3] Mass unemployment, like poverty, was not, of course, a new phenomenon in the early twentieth century, but it was the new interest in social conditions, the rising flood of Socialist propaganda, and, not least, the remarkable growth of cities receiving a great impetus by the development of the tram and the motor bus, which brought this long-standing evil to inescapable public notice.

Unemployment relief was a local responsibility, but the basic Poor Law provision, administered by the elected Guardians of local 'Unions' of parishes, had been found increasingly ineffective in dealing with the bulk of cyclical unemployment. As a result, local authorities, subject to increasing pressure from their working-class voters, had begun to supplement the work of the Guardians by supporting Public Relief Committees and providing public works in slack periods. The Unemployed Workmen Act passed in 1905 by the Conservative administration attempted to regularize such aid by establishing Distress Committees in all the large

---

[1] (Mrs.) Pember Reeves, *Round About a Pound a Week* (1913), p. 214.
[2] It is to this period that we owe the first descriptions and analyses in English of the phenomenon of the trade cycle. D. H. Robertson, *A Study of Industrial Fluctuation* (1915, repr. 1948); H. M. Hyndman, *Commercial Crises in the Nineteenth Century* (1892, 2nd ed., 1902); A. C. Pigou, *Unemployment* (1913); R. G. Hawtrey, *Good and Bad Trade* (1913); W. C. Mitchell, *Business Cycles* (1913); F. Lavington, *The Trade Cycle* (1922); W. T. Hutchison, *A Review of Economic Doctrines, 1870–1929* (Oxford, 1953), chapters 22–4; J. A. Hobson, *The Economics of Unemployment* (1922).
[3] W. H. Beveridge, *Unemployment, a Problem of Industry* (1909, repr. 1930 as Part I of a new edition).

towns of over 50,000 inhabitants and by encouraging local labour exchanges and the provision of work, but it merely added to the confusion of principles, authorities and funds by which poor relief and unemployment relief were granted or refused. The appointment of the Royal Commission on the Poor Laws and the Relief of Distress at the end of 1905 symbolized the widespread conviction that a new approach to this, as to several other social problems, was now required.

7. INDUSTRIAL RELATIONS

Before describing the actions taken by the State to deal with poverty and some of its results, it will be best to consider the actions taken by working men themselves. Their main defence organization, the trade union, was rapidly, if erratically, achieving official recognition. In the few employments in which trade unions were not 'recognized', the railways and the Shipping Federation being the outstanding examples of such conservative management, industrial disputes before the war largely took the form of attempts to enforce such recognition. Trade union membership, reaching over 4·1 million in 1913–14, covered perhaps 30% of the eligible working force, but, as always, this average hid a very high percentage of membership in a few sectors, such as the skilled grades in engineering, building, printing, textiles, transport and the mines, and an almost complete absence of organization elsewhere, as in agriculture and among shop-assistants.

The adverse legal decision of the House of Lords in the Taff Vale Case of 1901, which cost the Railway Servants' union £23,000 in damages and a similar sum in other costs, appeared to trade unionists to shatter at one blow their power of striking, and thereby their bargaining power, built up over a long period.[1] Most of the leaders of the large unions were, in politics, Liberals and some were Conservatives, but the need to reverse the Taff Vale judgment by legislative action and to strengthen the Labour pressure group in Parliament generally, induced them to flock to the recently formed 'Labour Representation Committee', an organization made up of trade unions and various small Socialist societies with the object of securing the election of 'labour' representatives to Parliament and local government bodies.

The L.R.C. had been formed mainly by Socialists who had hoped to make this body the vehicle of introducing Socialist policies and convictions among the trade unionists who adhered to it. Before they could develop their programme, however, they were now swamped by a trade

[1] S. and B. Webb, *The History of Trade Unionism, 1666–1920* (1920 ed.), chapters 9–11; G. D. H. Cole and R. Postgate, *The Common People 1746–1938* (1938), chapters 38, 39; Pauline Gregg, *A Social and Economic History of Britain, 1760–1950* (1950), chapter 19.

union membership which provided the numbers and the funds for leaders who were often bitterly anti-Socialist, and who saw themselves merely as Liberals entrusted with the special duty of representing the working-men's point of view. It needed the genius of J. R. MacDonald, the secretary of the party, to hold together Socialist crusaders and Liberal–Labour die-hards, and to put forward independent programmes while yet concluding widespread electoral alliances with the Liberals.[1] He held the party together, but its devious actions in Parliament contributed materially to the contempt with which large groups of workmen turned away from political action in those years and turned to direct industrial action instead.

In terms of immediate results, however, the L.R.C. campaign was crowned with success. In the General Election of 1906, which registered a Liberal landslide, the L.R.C., soon re-named the 'Labour Party', secured 29 seats, and there were a dozen or more working men returned as Liberals, many of whom adhered to the Labour group later. Labour, finding itself in alliance with the Government Party, could exert some influence on legislation, and this position was maintained, to a lesser extent, after the two General Elections of 1910, from which the Liberal Party emerged still as the governing party, but only by virtue of the votes of its allies, the Irish and the Labour groups. Moreover, when Parliament met in 1906, members of all parties were found to have pledged themselves to undo the damage done by the Taff Vale decision, and the resultant Trade Disputes Act of 1906, passed without serious opposition, freed the trade unions from liability for civil actions in respect of any wrongful act committed by or on behalf of the union.

It is possible that the attack on cherished trade union privileges by the House of Lords contributed to the worsening of industrial relations in this period, especially since it was preceded by other hostile judgments in the courts[2] and was followed by a second unfavourable decision in the House of Lords, the Osborne judgment, in 1909, which prevented the trade unions from spending money on political objects, until it, in turn, was reversed by the Trade Union (Amendment) Act of 1913. It may also be that universal education since 1870, which had created the first generation of fully literate wage-earners, had contributed to the feeling of discontent and to the industrial tension before 1914.[3] There may, further, have been special factors in certain industries to cause unrest, and it was noticeable

---

[1] Henry Pelling, *The Origins of the Labour Party, 1880–1900* (1954); Henry Pelling and F. Bealey, *Labour and Politics 1900–1906* (1958).

[2] John Saville, 'Trade Unions and Free Labour: The Background to the Taff Vale Decision', in Asa Briggs and John Saville (ed.), *Essays in Labour History* (1960).

[3] This is the argument strongly put forward by Prof. Phelps-Brown, *Growth of British Industrial Relations* (1959).

that the main disputes took place within only a handful of industries. Finally, the disregard for established authority, manifesting itself in the years before 1914 among upper-class suffragettes, and Conservative leaders plotting mutiny and insurrection over Irish Home Rule, may also have transmitted itself to industrial disputes. The tendency of the Government to settle major disputes by enforcing unpalatable decisions on employers, on the apparent grounds that large firms could be coerced while numerous workmen could not, was also a source of bitterness among some powerful employers' associations.[1]

Basically, however, there can be little doubt that the series of extensive and often violent industrial disputes which occurred in Britain between 1908 and 1914 was called forth by the failure of real wages to rise and by the actual decline of some of them, at a time when the wealthy classes were evidently becoming richer. Several of the disputes arose behind the backs of the official trade union leadership, others brought out many non-unionists, and in a few cases there were strikes without any discoverable trade union at all. Strikes of this nature are normally the symptom of a background of dissatisfaction, rather than the result of a disagreement over any specific issue. By 1911–13 some 20 million working days were lost every year in disputes.

One of the most disturbed industries was railway transport, the industry in which both the Taff Vale and the Osborne cases were fought out. There were here two special causes for unrest. One was the inability of the railway companies to raise rates in a period of rising prices because of the Act of 1894, and the consequent attack on costs, including wages. The other was the refusal of the railway managements, with the exception of the North-Eastern Railway Co., to recognize the unions, and their demand for military discipline. Yet union membership grew rapidly, especially that of the Amalgamated Society of Railway Servants, the largest union, which absorbed in 1913 virtually all other groupings except for the Railway Clerks and the Locomotive Engineers and Firemen.

Early in 1907 the A.S.R.S. launched an 'all grades movement', i.e. a request for improvements for all grades and on all lines simultaneously. The refusal of the companies even to recognize the union and the men's decision to call a national strike led to intervention by Mr. Lloyd George, the President of the Board of Trade, who persuaded both parties to accept the compromise formula of Conciliation Boards, on which employers met trade union officers without actually recognizing the union as such. Wages, however, remained extremely low in the face of rising prices, about two-fifths of the adult men being paid 20s. a week or under, and in the summer

---

[1] R. V. Sires, 'Labor Unrest in England, 1910–1914', *J. Econ. Hist.*, 15/3, 1955.

of 1911, after a series of local 'unofficial' railway strikes, a national strike was actually called, despite the intervention of Mr. Winston Churchill, the Home Secretary, and the troops he dispatched to strategic centres. The effects of the strike on British industry were such that the Prime Minister himself decided to intervene and oblige the employers to meet the unions. After a Special Committee of Inquiry, the companies were forced to recognize the unions by a Commons resolution and by an implied threat of specific legislation. As a result, the powers of the Conciliation Boards were greatly extended.

The docks were another centre of unrest. In 1910 Tom Mann and Ben Tillett formed the National Transport Workers' Federation, embracing three dozen unions among seamen, dockers and carters. There was much dissatisfaction in all these employments, but the first to attack was the National Sailors' and Firemen's Union, which called strikes in port after port in 1911, emerging victorious everywhere after short struggles. Their action set off a strong movement of dockers, carters and others about the Port of London, which culminated in a strike affecting the whole riverside in August. Again it needed Government intervention to force the Port of London Authority to parley with the strikers, and ultimately grant most of their claims.

Dock strikes were often fought with much violence, since it was relatively easy to procure blacklegs from other areas. In the 1911 strikes, violence was particularly noticeable in Hull, where the dispute was settled with the help of the Labour Department of the Board of Trade. In Liverpool and in Manchester, Government intervention was also needed to arrive at a settlement. After the London strike had been settled, trouble flared up again in Liverpool, largely arising out of the railwaymen's claims, but also involving tramwaymen, carters and dockers, who had come out again, and the city was in a virtual state of siege for several days, soldiers and police being used against the strikers before peace was restored.

Unrest in the docks continued in 1912. There were bitter and long-drawn-out disputes in Glasgow, Manchester, Liverpool and Birkenhead, before a major dispute flared up in London over the refusal of Lord Devonport of the P.L.A. to meet the Transport Workers' Federation, or to accept Government mediation. The Federation called a nation-wide strike but was defeated. This set-back of the men led to a period of relative peace until 1914, except for a local dispute in Hull and the famous Dublin strike of 1914 which had James Larkin's Irish transport workers at its core but involved many other groups.

Yet another disturbed industry was coal mining, where again there were special problems. While the increased cost of working deeper and more difficult seams, coupled with the export tax and safety legislation, tended to raise expenses, the men had finally united in a national Miners' Federation with the adhesion of the last remaining outsiders, Northumberland and Durham, in 1908, and were trying to use it to establish national minimum wages in the face of the varying traditions and methods of work in the different districts. Normal tonnage rates differed widely according to the ease of working, but in difficult places it had been customary to fix a minimum 'fall-back wage'. It was this wage that was the first to be attacked when colliery managers were told to economize, and it was over this that many of the disputes were fought, especially in South Wales. The Cambrian Colliery strike of 1910, fought over 'abnormal places', introduced dangerous methods of terror and violence, and saw the use of troops and police against strikers. The application of the miners' eight-hours' Act of 1908 also led to many disputes in 1910 and 1911.

The largest of the pre-war disputes in terms of man-hours lost was the national miners' strike of 1912, fought over the establishment of a national minimum wage, when nearly a million miners stopped work for over a month. Again the dispute was settled only by the intervention of the Government, this time by an Act of Parliament rushed through while the men were out, granting the principle of a minimum wage, but leaving the actual figure to be settled by the areas. The fixing of minimum wages for well-organized adult men introduced a novel principle into British legislation. The Government could not be sure whether the Act would, in fact, end the dispute, but after some hesitation both sides of industry decided to accept it.

There were major strikes and lock-outs also in other industries, as for example in the Lancashire cotton industry in 1910 and 1911, among the London builders in 1914, among woollen and worsted workers in 1911, and among the boilermakers in 1908 and 1910. But the unions in the railways, transport and mining did, in a sense, act as pacemakers for the others, and in 1914 they combined in a 'Triple Alliance'. Originally intended to ensure that all their contracts were terminated, and all their claims made, at the same time, it was quickly looked upon as an undertaking to call sympathetic strikes by the other two if any one of them was under attack. The powerful threat to the economy, and thus in the last resort to the Government, implied in an alliance of the workers in these three basic industries, could hardly be ignored. At the same time it was a symbol of a different development.

Since about 1910, there had spread among large sections of the trade union world a new outlook, called 'Syndicalism'. Its intellectual origins lay in France and America, but its concrete base was the depression of wages, together with the apparent apathy and ineffectiveness of the official Labour Party and trade union leaders and the mounting violence of both sides in conducting industrial disputes. Beside Syndicalism, there were also the closely related programmes of Industrial Unionism, and Guild Socialism.

The Syndicalists opposed both the bourgeois State and the State-Socialist parties within it. They believed in 'direct action', the political strike, using the trade unions to capture political power and administer the new society, especially its industries, and they distrusted any class collaboration as a stratagem designed to keep labour in subjection. In practice, there were two immediate tasks before them. One was to inaugurate a militant trade union policy, and their success in this field, whether in fact brought about by their own action or by the conditions of the day, has already been described. The other was to reorganize innumerable splintered craft societies and others into a few large, powerful industrial unions, each covering one industry, and each standing ready to take over the control of its own industry.

In their support for industrial unions, they were swimming with the tide. Under Tom Mann, the most influential Syndicalist leader, the Transport Workers' Federation had been formed in 1910. The Miners' Federation of 1908 and the railwaymen's union in 1913 were perhaps the nearest British approaches to industrial unionism so far. In South Wales, an unofficial committee had issued *The Miners' Next Step* in 1912, in which the new policy was preached, and in 1913, Larkin, the Irish leader, raised large audiences for other 'forward policies'. There was the Triple Alliance and in 1914 there began an unofficial movement among the building workers, perhaps the most scattered among all the craft unions, to combine in one industrial union. Even the conservative Trades Union Congress declared in favour of amalgamation in 1911 and 1912. There was also a further lesson of those years which was not lost on trade unionists. The more extensive and the more potentially destructive their strikes, the more likely were they to succeed at least in part, since they would bring in the Government which would suggest a compromise in which at least a part of the men's claims would be granted.[1]

Syndicalism did not survive in any strength after 1914, while Guild Socialism, always more a movement of intellectuals than of trade union members, experienced a brief efflorescence after the war, and then also

---

[1] For information on the trade union developments in this period, see the works quoted above by E. H. Phelps-Brown, S. and B. Webb, Pauline Gregg (chapter 19) and Cole and Postgate. Also Elie Halévy, *A Short History of the English People in the Nineteenth Century*, Vol. 6, *The Rule of Democracy*, Book 1 (1952 ed.); G. D. H. Cole, *A Short History of the British Working-Class Movement, 1900–1927*, Vol. 3 (1927), chapters 4 and 5, and *The World of Labour* (1913); Branko Pribićević, *The Shop Stewards' Movement and Workers' Control, 1910–1922* (Oxford, 1959), chapters 1, 4, 7; B. C. Roberts, *The Trades Union Congress, 1868–1921* (1958), chapter 7; George Dangerfield, *The Strange Death of Liberal England* (1936), Part II, chapter 4.

sank into insignificance. There was, however, one other relic of the disturbed industrial scene of 1910–14 which was destined to grow into major importance. This was the 'machinery' for settling disputes and for conciliation and arbitration, strongly supported by the Labour Department of the Board of Trade and its Chief Industrial Commissioner, Sir George R. (later Lord) Askwith. Until 1906, the machinery of the Conciliation Act had been used only about 20 times per annum; in 1907–9 it was used on over 50 occasions, and in 1911–13 on over 300 occasions a year. It has since become a major part of the British structure of industrial relations; at the time it was of particular importance in enabling employers and men to meet round the table on a basis of equality.[1]

8. THE BIRTH OF THE WELFARE STATE

While the working classes reacted to their persistent poverty in the midst of a wealthy society with much impatience and violence, their protests did not remain without effect on the Government. Public provisions for various human needs were not new. The Poor Law had existed for centuries, and in the past fifty years public health provisions and general elementary education, among others, had greatly increased the range of activities of the public authorities devoted to social welfare. Nevertheless, there was a noticeable change in emphasis and direction, amounting to a change in basic principles, in the years to 1914: 'measures which only ten years ago would have been dismissed as impracticable were now (1906) debated seriously'.[2]

Most of the causes of this change have been mentioned already: the discovery of widespread poverty by the new social science, the stagnation of real wages, the realization that unemployment was beyond the power of the individual to avert. There was also the cumulative effect of the power of civil servants, health and factory inspectors, and local government officers, who had a professional interest in further reform. Their influence must not be underrated, as 'England was becoming bureaucratic': employment in local and central government rose from 104,000 in 1891 to 226,000 in 1911.[3] Overriding all these was the workmen's suffrage, granted by the Reform Acts of 1867 and 1884, which the working classes had learnt to manipulate after about a generation.

The vote was not used by working men to ensure that their majority in the country was reflected by a majority in Parliament, since the main

---

[1] G. R. Askwith, *Industrial Problems and Disputes* (1920).

[2] E. H. Phelps-Brown, *Growth of British Industrial Relations* (1959), p. 253.

[3] E. Halévy, *A Short History of the English People in the Nineteenth Century*, Vol. 6, *The Rule of Democracy*, Book 1 (1952 ed.), p. 262. On a different calculation, excluding 'industrial' employment, such as in dockyards, post office, gas and water works, but including teachers, the central and local authorities employed 632,000 persons in July 1914.

political divisions were conceived to run on different lines. The Labour Party, which was indeed founded in those years, was established only as a minority pressure group, with no agreed policies of its own other than those relating to the interests of labour. It did, for example, include Imperialists and Little Englanders, Socialists and believers in *laissez-faire*. If it had really been intent on capturing a voting majority, it would have devoted more energy to enfranchising the 40% of the male adult population still without a vote, and would not have allowed a bill to give the vote to some 2½ million people (about a third of the electorate), most of whom were clearly of the working classes, to be dropped for lack of interest.

More important, at least in the short run, than the arrival of the Labour Party was the fact that politicians of all parties began more consciously to address themselves to the new electorate, knowing the balance of forces and the ingrained allegiance of the old. Thus protection, the Boer War, even the Licensing Act were debated increasingly with the working-class voter in mind. Above all, labour was to be propitiated by welfare provisions. This preoccupation subtly and imperceptibly changed the attitude of Governments: the initial drive may have been the concern to secure votes, but the effect was none the less that for the first time in British history 'the poor' were considered to be full citizens, deserving as much consideration as the more fortunate classes. What had been a matter of charity to one's inferiors was becoming a matter of rights to one's equals.[1]

In 1897 the Workmen's (Compensation for Accidents) Act was passed, as one of the fruits of Joseph Chamberlain's attempts to win the Conservative Party for social reforms, which were also to include pensions and arbitration in labour disputes. Though limited in scope, the Act introduced a new principle. Hitherto, compensation for accidents at work was still based on the degree of liability by the employer, while the trade unions were concerned to close the loophole of 'contracting out' and to prevent the 'German system of compulsory insurance to strike at the root of trade unionism'.[2] The novel principle of 1897 was, according to Chamberlain, 'that the right to compensation of any person injured in the ordinary course of his employment is a public right and a national obligation'.[3] Thus what had been a private contractual relation was transformed into one of public concern. In 1899 agriculture was brought

---

[1] See, in general, Gertrude Williams, *The State and the Standard of Living* (1936), esp. chapters 1 and 4.

[2] The phrase was used by Henry Broadhurst, a working-man M.P., in the House in 1888. W. C. Mallalieu, 'Joseph Chamberlain and Workmen's Compensation', *J. Econ. Hist.*, 10/1, 1950.

[3] Quoted in Gertrude Williams, *op. cit.*, p. 145.

in, and by a further Act in 1906 virtually all employments, including now also many very small firms, while compensation for certain industrial diseases was also enacted. The Act of 1906, which added 6 million workers to the 7¼ million encompassed by the existing legislation, was one of the earliest of that complex of social welfare Acts passed by the Liberals in the last nine years of peace.

Another one of their early subjects for legislation was the relief of the old. As a rule old age held the terror of destitution for all those who earned their bread by manual work. The existing Poor Law and its institutions were so feared and detested among respectable workmen, that the greatest hardship was suffered before resort was had to them. A Royal Commission on the Aged Poor, reporting in 1895, found that only one-third of those who reached the age of 65 depended in part on public assistance. The rest eked out a living from payments by Friendly Societies—often insecure and badly run actuarially—by private charities, or they were supported by their families. As a result, from 1878 on, when Canon Blackley began his agitation for compulsory national insurance against old age, schemes for the provision of some kind of old age pension attracted increasing public support. By the 1890's, many Guardians relaxed the conditions of relief for the aged, and by 1905, when the Royal Commission on the Poor Laws met, national relief for the destitution of old age had secured general approval.

The Old Age Pensions Act, passed in 1908, provided for non-contributory payments, since under any sound contributory scheme at least twenty years would have had to elapse before the first pension was actually paid. All respectable persons over 70 years of age whose income did not exceed £21 a year were to receive 5s. a week (7s. 6d. for a married couple), and those with incomes of £21 to £31, proportionally smaller pensions. The 'tests' of respectability were inevitably relaxed, and by 1913 three-fifths of the population over 70 was in receipt of pensions. The cost, first put at £6 million per annum, had risen to double that figure by 1913, but to compensate for this, there was a large drop in the number of old persons depending on the Poor Law.

In contrast with old age pensions, the two main welfare provisions embodied in the two parts of the National Insurance Act of 1911 caused considerable controversy. Much of the debate was carried on within the meetings of the Royal Commission on the Poor Laws and the Relief of Distress, which sat from 1905 to 1909 and included a wide range of opinion amongst its members. The disagreement was in part about principles. At one extreme was the view of Sidney and Beatrice Webb, expressed in the Minority Report of the Commission (of which Beatrice was a member), favouring the 'break-up of the poor law', i.e. the provision of separate and functionally different institutions for the able-bodied unemployed, the sick, the old, the orphans, and the lunatics. It also favoured a 'national minimum of civilized life', open to all, provided by the State, a kind of safety net to offer security in the face of every conceivable calamity. At the other extreme were members of the Charity Organization Society and others who feared that payments as of right would destroy the character and self-reliance of the poor, and therefore opposed them, while they also objected to being drawn into a discussion of the causes of destitution, preferring to take it for granted and merely discuss relief measures.[1]

Beside the opponents on principle, there were also the vested interests. Trade unions and Friendly Societies wanted to keep their benefit functions; doctors were afraid of losing their poor law practices and the 'industrial' insurance companies threatened to kill by a whispering campaign of their ubiquitous agents any scheme that would harm their interests. The debate, necessarily, was about means as well as about principles, and the two could not be separated. The resulting Act was a compromise, and the main principles and practical methods of application of the two parts of the National Insurance Act differed from each other as much as they differed from the Old Age Pensions Act.

Both parts of the Act had in common tripartite contributions, by employee, employer and the State, but otherwise there were great differences between them. Part II, dealing with unemployment insurance, disturbed no existing interests, except those of the trade unions, which had insured about 700,000 members against unemployment, and on whose practices it was largely based. Its main object was to protect workmen from the worst effects of cyclical unemployment by compulsory insurance. Seven industries only, mainly those considered most liable to cyclical fluctuation, were included in the scheme, with about $2\frac{1}{4}$ million workers in 1911, or one-sixth of the total industrial labour force. It was administered by the Labour Exchanges, and by those trade unions which adapted their existing out-of-work benefits to it. All other trade unions received a subsidy of one-sixth of the unemployment benefits paid out of their own funds. The benefit was 7s. a week, payable for up to fifteen weeks in a year only, with the additional limitation that no more than one week's benefit would be paid out for every five contributions paid in.[2]

Part I, dealing with health insurance, by contrast, was well-nigh universal, affecting about 13 million workers. It was based on the German model, but was modified by the claims of the existing entrenched institutions, which became 'approved societies'[3] under the Act; only a small

---

[1] Beatrice Webb, *Our Partnership* (1948), pp. 341–2, 383, 418, 482.

[2] W. H. Beveridge, *Power and Influence* (1953); Sir Frank Tillyard and F. N. Ball, *Unemployment Insurance 1911–48* (Leigh-on-Sea, 1949), chapters 1 and 2.

[3] The 'approved societies' were made up as follows in 1912: industrial life offices, 41·5%, friendly societies without branches, 22·8%, friendly societies

minority of members became 'deposit contributors' receiving their benefits direct from the local insurance committees. In addition to paying monetary benefits, the scheme had to be integrated with medical and other services, arousing an opposition thereby which more than once threatened to wreck the Bill. In the end, medical benefit, panel doctors and sanatoria were paid directly by the insurance committees set up in local government areas, while the contributions from the workers were collected and the sickness allowances were paid out by the 'approved societies'. The societies were required to pay for certain basic medical benefits, but they could add various additional benefits for their members if their funds permitted. Both schemes were thus run nominally on insurance principles, with accrued benefits. as of right, and both paid out their first benefits in January 1913.[1]

The two Acts of 1908 and 1911 were central to the welfare legislation of those years, but they were flanked by many other measures conceived in the same spirit. Thus the belief that much of the existing unemployment was 'frictional' led to an Act authorizing the establishment of Labour Exchanges in 1909, on the model of the (London) Central Unemployment Body, set up under the Act of 1905. The first Exchanges were opened in February 1910, and by the end of 1912 there were over 400 of them. At the outset, their success in bringing jobs to workers was, perhaps, smaller than had been hoped.

The Fair Wages Clause, based on a resolution by the House of Commons, according to which all Government contracts had to be worked by labour paid at current local trade union rates, dated from 1891, and since the Lords' Committee on Sweating there had been a growing public revulsion against the exploitation of helpless workers in 'sweatshops'. Sir Charles Dilke, after his fall, led a campaign for the enforcement of minimum wages, securing the appointment of a Select Committee of the House of Commons in 1908, and, on its favourable report, the passing of the Trade Boards Act of 1909. Under the Act, four Trade Boards were to be set up in the sweated trades of ready-made tailoring, paper-box making, lace making and chain making, and there were powers to make orders establishing Boards for other industries. Each Board consisted of an equal number of employers' and workers' representatives together with some official 'appointed' members, and had powers to lay down minimum time and piece wages, which were then enforceable at law. In 1913, when

---

with branches, 23·7%, trade unions, 11·5%, and employers' provident funds, 0·5%, of the membership of 12,390,000. Sir William Beveridge, *Social Insurance and Allied Services* (Beveridge Report) (1942. Cmd. 6404), para 53.

[1] H. N. Bunbury (ed.), *Lloyd George's Ambulance Wagon* (1957); R. W. Harris, *National Health Insurance in Great Britain, 1911–1946* (1946), chapters 2–4; M. Bruce, *The Coming of the Welfare State* (1961), pp. 156–89.

four more trades were added, altogether half a million workers were covered by this minimum wages legislation.[1] It represented a remarkable break with the past, and was followed quickly by the minimum wage legislation for coal miners in 1912, as noted above.[2]

Balfour's Education Act of 1902, which transferred power over schooling from the School Boards to the local authorities and made a beginning with the provision of secondary education, was not only an important measure of social reform[3] in itself, but was also used as a basis for public health and other reforms. Thus school medical inspection, made permissive in 1902, became obligatory on local authorities in 1907; in 1906 school meals for needy children were permitted, and in 1907 higher grants were provided for secondary schools which gave at least a quarter of the places to 'board' scholars. At about the same time, in 1908, a Children's Act made various acts of cruelty to children illegal, and in 1914 the Government undertook to subsidize milk depots, local welfare centres and other similar institutions of progressive local authorities.[4] Thus the public care for children led to many general social reforms, while, in turn, the growing body of teachers was added to that of doctors and administrators to provide professional support for further progress.[5] An energetic attack on infantile mortality, one of the most serious problems of the early twentieth century, began effectively with an Act of 1902 providing for the training of midwives and the exclusion of the unqualified.

Medical interests secured two further sets of measures of far-reaching social significance. The first was a provision of the Factory and Workshops Act of 1891 under which the Home Secretary was empowered to enforce safety regulations for occupations he considered dangerous: by 1910, elaborate precautions had been enforced in 22 industries, and certain dangerous occupations prohibited altogether.[6] The other was the Housing and Town Planning Act of 1909, representing for the first time a positive, rather than a restrictive, approach to the building of towns and cities.[7]

Hours of work were regulated by Shop Acts in 1904 and 1911, and in the mines by the Miners' Eight Hours Act of 1908.[8] Lastly, the previously

[1] *Report of Committee on Trade Board Acts* (1922. Cmd. 1645); Stephen Gwynn and G. M. Tuckwell, *Life of Dilke*, Vol. 2 (1917), chapter 52.

[2] p. 32.

[3] G. A. N. Lowndes, *The Silent Social Revolution* (1937).

[4] W. M. Frazer, *History of English Public Health, 1834–1939* (1950), Part III and Part IV, sections 1 and 2.

[5] J. M. Mackintosh, *Trends of Opinion about the Public Health, 1901–1951* (1953), sections 1 and 2.

[6] H. A. Mess, *Factory Legislation and its Administration, 1891–1924* (1926), chapters 2–9.

[7] W. Ashworth, *The Genesis of Modern British Town Planning* (1954), chapter 7.

[8] B. McCormick and J. E. Williams, 'The Miners and the Eight-Hour Day, 1863–1910', *Ec. Hist. Rev.*, N.S., 12/2, 1959.

ineffective legislation to provide for small holdings for agricultural workers and others was replaced by the Small Holdings and Allotments Act of 1907, which enabled the Board of Agriculture to induce County Councils to use their compulsory powers to acquire land for small holdings. By 1914, 14,000 small holdings had come into existence under the Act.[1]

The Small Holdings Act of 1907 was one of the few welfare measures arousing violent *party* feelings, for while it was the Conservatives' declared intention to create a landowning peasantry, the Liberals wished to protect tenants against existing landlords, while at the same time attacking the landlords' position in other ways also. Otherwise views on the new social legislation did not as a rule differ along party lines: the political battle was fought out over the raising of the necessary finance.

From 1908 onward, the Liberals attempted to use the growing tax burden itself as a weapon to re-distribute income in favour of the poorer classes. The budget of 1907/8 made the first important changes by creating earned income relief on the income tax while increasing the death duties. There was little change in the budget of 1908/9, apart from the ominous warning by Asquith, who presented it, 'that the democratic neo-liberalism of the twentieth century had little in common with Gladstonian Liberalism, that the Cabinet did not intend to govern on the cheap and that a large increase in the amount and the sources of expenditure was inevitable'.[2] It was the budget for 1909/10, the first to be presented by Lloyd George, that was the basis of the most bitter party strife, and of a major constitutional crisis, two General Elections and the Parliament Act of 1911.

In view of the heavy new commitments for the navy and the welfare legislation, the Chancellor of the Exchequer had been faced by a prospective deficit of £15¾ million at existing rates of taxation. To find this sum, the income tax was promoted to become the 'sheet anchor' of taxation and was increased to 1s. 2d. in the pound, the grading was made steeper, and a supertax, to yield £2·3 million in a full year, was put on incomes over £5,000 a year. At the same time, death duties were made heavier, stamp duties were raised, and an additional £3·5 million was to be raised by increasing tobacco and spirit duties. The most controversial issue, however, in this 'People's Budget' was the imposition of the 'land taxes', designed to tax part of the 'unearned increment' in land values—a stock proposal of Radical reformers for decades. Threatening the privileges of landed property, which the Conservative Party was pledged to defend, it led to the last attempt by the House of Lords to throw out a money bill. Considerable confusion resulted in the actual

---

[1] Hermann Levy, *Large and Small Holdings* (Cambridge, 1911), chapter 8; W. Hasbach, *History of the English Agricultural Labourer* (1908), chapters 5 and 6.
[2] Halévy, *op. cit.*, p. 287.

administration by the delay in its passage, and it was not until 1911 that normal budgeting was resumed. For the remaining years of peace, the main changes occurred in the amounts, rather than the forms, of taxation.[1] The revenue (excluding the relatively small land value duties) increased from £131·7 million in 1909/10 to £197·5 million in 1913/14.

Without any single major change, the budgetary reforms yet represented a not insignificant transfer of purchasing power from the rich to the poor. Direct taxation, as a proportion of revenue, was raised steadily from about 50% in the last years of the Conservative Government to 57·5% in 1912/13, at a time when the working classes were virtually excluded from its incidence. The stormy last years of peace saw not only the foundations laid for the present Welfare State, but also the faint beginnings of the use of the budget, not merely to provide the means of the Government's expenditure, but also as an instrument of social policy.

[1] J. F. Rees, *A Short Fiscal and Financial History of England, 1815–1918* (1921), chapter 7.

CHAPTER II

The First World War, 1914–1918

I. THE NEEDS OF WAR AND ECONOMIC CONTROL

When Britain declared war on Germany and her allies in August 1914, it was almost a century since a major war had been fought by this country and its lessons had long since been forgotten. The more recent experiences, particularly of the Crimean War, waged against a European power, and the Boer War, had not involved more than the furnishing of expeditionary forces and the temporary expansion of the Royal Navy, without fundamental readjustments to the rest of the economy. There was thus no experience of the economic stresses and the industrial efforts involved in waging modern full-scale war. Views as to the economic effects of the war were further distorted by the belief, common at the outbreak of all wars, that it would be short.

In so far as the economic problems were considered, they were thought of as specific, not general. It was recognized, for example, that recruitment for the army would have to be greatly expanded, and, indeed, so effectively was this done that before long the volunteers outran the supplies to clothe and arm them. Further, wars had never in the past been financed out of current revenue, and the Government prepared to borrow heavily. Foreign trade and the foreign exchanges were likely to be affected, and special provision had to be made for them. But these and a few minor actions of a specific nature were thought to exhaust the list of economic actions of the Government, and as for the rest, there would be 'business as usual'.[1]

In practice, until Lloyd George's Ministry of December 1916, which formed a watershed in the conduct of the war, the apparatus of Government control was limited almost entirely to such specific examples of intervention, though they were more extensive than had at first been assumed. Thus the strategic importance of railways had been a commonplace since the Franco-German War of 1870–1, and the British companies were placed at once under Government control, though the actual management was left in the existing hands, shareholders receiving fixed returns. The supply of sugar, some two-thirds of which had come from the Central

[1] Samuel J. Hurwitz, *State Intervention in Great Britain, A Study of Economic Control and Social Response, 1914–1919* (New York, 1949), chapter 2.

Powers in peace-time, gave rise to anxiety, and within a few days of the declaration of war, on 7th August 1914, the Government began to buy up supplies in the West Indies, and some days later it established an (executive) Royal Commission on Sugar Supplies. The Government also began to build up a secret reserve of wheat and assumed control over the food crops of India, but took no other measures to secure the grain supplies.

The War Office, seeking to procure its necessary supplies, began as early as October 1914 to purchase meat abroad itself, instead of relying on contractors, and before long, turning to other commodities, it found itself forced to assume responsibility for competing civilian supplies also, by the need to prevent speculative price rises and the interruption of established markets. Thus the sandbag shortage, felt in 1915, led it ultimately in August 1916 to undertake the buying and control of the whole jute crop just as it was obliged to buy, as sole agent, the Russian flax crop in March 1916, Indian kips (for army boots) in May 1916, and the home wool clip, for blankets, in November 1916. Some strategic stocks were wholly requisitioned, the beginning being made with toluol in November 1914.

Another group of early Government controls was concerned with preventing the specific dangers of financial panic, and this will be treated in greater detail in section 3 below. The shortage of labour, which appeared first in the munitions industry, will also be considered in greater detail in a later section. Lastly, the control over shipping appeared in the early stages of the war as a specific problem, namely the requisitioning of a certain number of ships for use by the Admiralty.

The Government policy of intervening only at a few selected points of the economy, and even there only at the dictate of strategy rather than economics, followed the experience of the relatively minor wars of the more recent past; it was also congenial to the orthodox economic thinking of the time.

> The idea that industry would have to be deliberately organized for war production encountered subconscious resistance in a Government committed to the doctrines of free trade and individualism. It is not surprising that the necessity for State intervention was only gradually admitted by Ministers who had spent the greater part of their political careers in exploding the fallacies of Protectionism on the one hand and Socialism on the other.

In order to obtain the necessary supplies of war materials in the early months of the war, 'it was thought preferable to rely on private enterprise and the laws of supply and demand'; 'a prosperous state of trade, regular employment at good wages and high profits for the Revenue to tax and the Treasury to borrow, were regarded with good reason as essential conditions for the successful prosecution of the war'.[1]

[1] E. M. H. Lloyd, *Experiments in State Control* (Oxford, 1924), pp. 22, 23, 261.

43

This attitude failed to reckon with the sheer magnitude of the military demand in an all-out war against a European power under modern conditions, and with the distortions that this would impart to the civilian part of the economy. What appeared at first as a specific need or shortage often quickly became a symptom of a much wider alteration in supply and demand relationships. Some relatively minor control, to deal with an immediate issue, often had repercussions which required Government intervention further and further back, until the State found itself directing a major part of the country's industries, and controlling or licensing most of the remainder. Thus a sudden demand for blankets would set up an immediate rise in the price and lead to the hoarding of wool tops, which would affect other sectors of the woollen and worsted industries; and this, in turn, might affect British agriculture or imports from Australia, and so on in unending progression. This lesson was learnt slowly, because it was learnt reluctantly. It was driven home, first of all, in the 'munitions' industry, the industry most immediately affected.

'Munitions' included arms and ammunition, transport of all kinds, including aircraft, and optical instruments used by the Forces. Deficiencies in their supply appeared with the very first recruiting drive of the war. The pre-war system of army contracts, which allowed only a limited number of firms to tender, made the shortage even more acute than it need have been, for it disregarded the productive capacity of the firms not on the official lists of suppliers, while elaborate safeguards evolved in peacetime, including inspection and audit, further slowed down the process of ordering and testing. A proposal to nationalize the munition firms was rejected by the Cabinet early in the war, and suggestions to overhaul the system of contracts were rejected by the War Office. Instead, the Service Departments were given virtually unlimited spending power, and it was hoped that by offering sufficiently high prices, the supplies would be forthcoming.

The normal price mechanism was, however, quite unable to cope with orders which quickly increased from quantities to supply 100,000 men (the original recruitment figure) to 500,000, one million, and ultimately three million men. Neither the equipment nor the factories nor the workers were available, and relative price movements were too slow a method, even if they had not been weakened by contrary movements of private demand, for bringing about the required switch in resources. The need for physical controls was all the more easily accepted in this field, since the main shortage, that of shells, was causing serious losses at the front and was turned into a major political issue as the 'Great Shell Scandal'.[1]

[1] D. Lloyd George, *War Memoirs*, Vol. I (1933); *History of the Ministry of Munitions*, Vol. 1 (1922).

A Cabinet Committee on Munitions, appointed in October 1914, had been ineffective. A new committee was set up in April 1915, the Board of Trade made efforts to attract labour to the booming munitions works, and greater powers were given to the Government under the Defence of the Realm Act (D.O.R.A.) in March 1915, to take over any existing factory or workshop making munitions; but they all failed to speed the supply of shells. More comprehensive and far-reaching powers were needed, and were provided in May 1915, with the creation of a new Ministry of Munitions under Lloyd George, increasingly the strong man in the Government.

From the very beginning, the new Minister found that he had to cast his net of control and direction very wide indeed. One of the first necessities was an expansion of the labour force in the industry. By June 1915, 19·5% of the male workers in the engineering trades had enlisted. Few of them could be got back, but the further recruitment of skilled engineering and metal workers was blocked by a system of exemption 'badges', later converted into a list of 'starred occupations'. Having stopped the outflow of labour, the Minister had next to organize a large-scale recruiting drive of workers from outside the industry to provide for expansion, and for this, the consent of the trade unions concerned had first to be obtained.

Within a few days of his appointment the Minister had arranged for a meeting with their leaders and had agreed to put the important concessions which they had granted in the Treasury Agreement of March 1915, into his Munitions of War Bill, which became law early in July. The unions were to permit 'dilution', i.e. the substitution of skilled labour by unskilled or semi-skilled men and women; they agreed to abolish other cherished trade union practices which had the effect of restricting output and to renounce the right of the individual worker to leave his employment without the permission of his firm; and lastly, they were prepared to forgo the right to strike, and accept arbitration instead, for the duration of the war. In return, the trade unions obtained a guarantee that their practices would be restored at the end of the war, that the concessions would apply to munitions firms only, and that profits in these 'controlled' firms would be limited to the pre-war level plus an excess of one-fifth. By September 1915, 715 of the main engineering establishments were thus 'controlled'.

This Munitions Act was to lead to much labour unrest later in the war; its immediate result, however, was a considerable extension of the Government's powers of economic control. It formed the beginning of a system of Government-directed production of the weapons of war, which quickly included Government-owned shell factories, the purchase and control of the supply and distribution of certain metals and chemicals, and a whole network of regulations stretching back to the raw material supply and the provision of machine tools and precision gauges, both of which were in short supply, and forward *via* the control of labour, the direct allocation of orders, the auditing and price control, and the provision of capital for expansion, to the transport of the finished articles to the fighting units.

The final step was to assume responsibility for all visible supplies, to control all private importation and distribute material to non-munitions as well as munitions trades, thereby virtually bringing the industries connected with the munitions supply, and all the industries using munitions materials, including private as well as munitions trading, under the control of the Department.[1]

From a beginning of 20 clerks in the Army Contracts Department in August 1914, the Ministry of Munitions had grown to employ a staff of 65,000 by November 1918; it controlled the employment of 2 million workers directly, and 3·4 million all told; it managed 250 Government factories, quarries and mines and supervised operations in 20,000 'controlled' establishments; and between June 1915 and March 1919 it disbursed £2,000 million.

Though partial or specific controls led irresistibly to general controls, the Government was reluctant to take up the additional powers called for, always hoping that prices and the profit motive would operate to make State action unnecessary. Hence its actions were generally taken as late as possible, its powers were as restricted as was consistent with the purpose in hand, and the success of the war effort was constantly jeopardized by the tardy application of the central guiding hand. Not until 1917 did controls begin to be comprehensive, and it was only in the last year of war that the British economy could be said to be on a full war footing.

By the end of 1916 there were also developing certain general stresses in the economy, quite apart from material shortages, which could be met only by an active general economic policy. The basic cause was undoubtedly the growth of the munitions industry which had absorbed so much of the country's raw material and capital resources and, together with the recruitment of a full-scale expeditionary force, was now creating a pressing labour shortage. Superimposed on this was the growing shortage of imports, largely caused by the diversion of resources from exports and the consequent shortage of foreign exchange. And lastly, as the most generalized symptom of the maladjustment of resources, the Government was spending vast sums on the war without withdrawing equivalent amounts from the purchasing power of the population, and a marked inflation had set in.

By the end of 1916 it had become abundantly clear that the free price mechanism had failed to serve the country at war. The symptoms were

[1] J. Hurstfield, 'The Control of British Raw Material Supplies, 1919–1939', *Ec. Hist. Rev.*, 14/1–2, 1944, p. 2.

many. The Government could not get the deliveries it ordered, while resources were diverted to private luxury consumption. Price rises led to profiteering, but did not bring forth increased supplies. Distribution of commodities as well as of incomes was erratic and unjust, and caused unrest among workers whose standard of living was being eroded by inflation. All through 1915 the optimistic assumption was made that 'while Germany is using all her means only the fringe of our resources in men, money, foodstuffs, and raw materials have been touched'.[1] In 1916, however, it began to be dimly understood that the diversion of millions of men and of commensurate resources to the unproductive activities of war had created real shortages for which unco-ordinated measures of price control, or allocation, or rationing, or profit limitation alone would not work. What was required was a comprehensive system of control, using all available means together.[2]

The apparatus of control, as perfected in 1917 and 1918, used many different methods. There was direct control of productive capacity, either by taking over the management of firms, as in the case of the railways, the National Shell Factories, the collieries, the flour mills and the Irish distilleries, or control by requisitioning of output or by licensing; there was State purchase of raw materials, especially abroad; there were restrictions of dealings, especially of imports and exports, by licensing and other means, and similar restrictions of capital expenditure. There was also price fixing, usually on a cost-plus basis, after a thorough check of accounts; control of distribution, both of consumer goods and of raw materials; and control of labour, including military conscription, first undertaken with selected groups in March 1916. By the end of the war, the Government had direct charge of shipping, railway and canal transport; it purchased about 90% of all the imports and marketed over 80% of the food consumed at home, besides controlling most of the prices. Direct or indirect control over industry and agriculture was virtually all-pervasive. Reasons of space forbid a detailed description of its development after December 1916, but it will be illustrated by three examples: shipping, war production other than munitions, and food consumption.

At the outbreak of hostilities, Britain possessed about 42% of the world's ocean-going steamer tonnage (45% if the rest of the Empire is included) and about 60% of the world's shipbuilding capacity. There appeared to be little cause to fear a shortage of shipping, therefore, particularly since there was much unemployed tonnage in 1914, and up to the end of 1916 the carrying capacity of the mercantile fleet was probably up to the demand.

[1] E. Crammond, 'The Cost of the War', *J. R. Stat. S.*, 78/3, 1915, p. 399.
[2] The best concise discussion will be found in E. V. Morgan, *Studies in British Financial Policy, 1914–25* (1952), chapter 2.

Some 4 million tons were at once requisitioned out of the total sea-going tonnage of 19 million gross tons in 1914, and by 1916 the requisitioned vessels, for British and Allied Governments, rose to 37% of the total. Further, some 4 million tons were immobilized in enemy ports and elsewhere. Certain ports were closed to mercantile vessels, and ships were re-routed for reasons of safety, thus making journeys longer, while the remaining ports became congested and turn-round was slowed down. Ships as well as docks and railways lost men by enlistment, and crews were further depleted by the departure of foreign sailors. Enemy submarines, at first of minor significance, increased their effectiveness, and by August 1916 had sunk a total of 1·7 million gross tons under the British flag, while British shipyards were obliged to work almost exclusively for the Admiralty, and mercantile launchings, averaging over 1·8 million gross tons in the years 1911–13, had fallen to a third of that figure in 1915 and 1916. Against this, as compensating factors, a large tonnage of enemy shipping was impounded at the outbreak of war, and more was captured; from November 1915 a Port and Transit Executive Committee speeded turn-round, and in 1916 shipping began to be co-ordinated to much greater effect; and ships were withdrawn from overseas routes and used on the home trade routes, while export restrictions, from 1915 on, reduced the demand for tonnage still further. Altogether, until about August 1916 these two tendencies roughly cancelled out, and the supply and demand for tonnage were not seriously out of step.

Nevertheless, freights had risen enormously, in some cases to four or five times their peace-time level. The cause lay in the piecemeal or specific form which Government control had taken. A large part of the shipping fleet had been requisitioned for purposes of war and was paid at so-called 'blue book' rates, roughly commensurate with costs and therefore not subject to much inflation. Early in 1915 requisitioning was extended to non-military uses such as the Government overseas purchases of sugar and meat, and later also of nitrate, pyrites, flax and timber. Meanwhile, in November 1915 a committee of shipowners withdrew yet a further proportion of tonnage from the free market, amounting to about 19%, by 'directing' it into the North Atlantic grain trade, keeping rates down on this special route by directing rather more tonnage into it than was strictly required. By these means the Government had so depleted the 'free' shipping available that in a market of notoriously inelastic demand, freights rocketed, profits soared, and large capital gains were registered in mergers and purchases.

The outcry caused by this profiteering, rather than any seriously felt shortage, caused the Government to extend its control over virtually all the shipping at the end of 1916; but the newly appointed Controller of Shipping and his Ministry, created in the Cabinet reorganization of

December 1916, was overwhelmed almost at once with a shipping crisis of major proportions. Sinkings had risen to 160,000 tons monthly in September–December, and with unrestricted U-boat warfare from 1st February, they reached 545,000 tons in April, the total annual sinkings being 3,730,000 gross tons of British shipping alone. Neutral shipping was driven away from British ports; convoy sailings and other precautions reduced the efficiency of the remaining fleet; and the failure of the North American harvest in 1916 forced Britain to divert ships to the longer Australian run for the home wheat supply.

The control exercised by the new Ministry never embraced all shipping. The largest single step towards full control was taken in the spring of 1917, when all available liners were put on the North Atlantic track, to collect grain, and in order to ensure equal treatment, the whole of the liner tonnage was requisitioned, the companies working on a hire basis, handing all their surplus earnings to the Government. Again, in March 1917 imports were restricted by licence, in January 1918 coastal vessels came under much closer direct control, including the control over bunkering, ballast and repairs, and the decision to give the Government direct ownership over new ships being built greatly enlarged the fully nationalized part of the merchant fleet, which had hitherto been mainly limited to vessels taken as prizes. It led to the design and construction of 'standard' ships to a handful of basic designs, to much indirect control over the shipyards, and to a greatly enlarged mercantile building programme.

These vigorous measures kept the supply lines to Britain open, even though the tonnage 'deficit' had risen to 3 million tons by February 1918, while a further 20% was tied up in direct military service. The total losses were $7\frac{3}{4}$ million tons (38% of the tonnage under the British flag in 1914), and the tonnage available at the armistice was 18% less than at the declaration of war. World tonnage as a whole was little, if anything, below the 1914 figure and a high rate of launching in 1919–20 created a surplus of tonnage. As a result market freight rates were driven below controlled rates in the summer of 1920, the licensing system was quickly dismantled, and the Government-owned ships sold off.[1]

The Army Contracts Department, organizing the supply of all army supplies other than those which were the responsibility of the Ministry of Munitions, necessarily competed directly with civilian demands. Some of its early exercises in general control before December 1916, including bulk purchase of raw materials abroad, have been noted above; in 1917 and

[1] C. E. Fayle, *The War and the Shipping Industry* (1927), and *History of the Great War: Seaborne Trade*, 3 vols. (1920, 1923, 1924); Sir Arthur Salter, *Allied Shipping Control* (1921).

1918, however, its powers were very much extended. One of its earliest problems was the settlement of prices for requisitioned commodities. Initially done by using the Crown prerogative of making *ex gratia* payments against which there could be no appeal, the later definitions of 'fair price' when, in 1915, Defence of the Realm Regulation (D.O.R.R.) 7 gave power to order manufacturers to produce, led to difficulties.

It was only in 1916 that an amendment to D.O.R.R. 7 made it clear that the 'fair prices' to be paid by the War Office referred to costs, not market prices, which had soared owing to profiteering, when sudden large demands, backed by a limitless purse, met restricted supplies. This, in turn, led to the development of a large apparatus of auditing and accounting control to establish actual costs. The cost-plus method of payment was first used by the Ministry of Munitions in September 1915, for certain metals, and by the War Office itself in June 1916, in buying up the whole of the domestic wool clip. Powers to examine the books of firms were obtained in February 1916, and became not only the basis of a widespread network of output and price control but also introduced accounting into many firms which had previously got by without it.

The power of Government trading was at first obtained indirectly, by the power to grant licences given under D.O.R.R. 30. A monopoly, e.g., of imports, was then obtained by the War Office by the expedient of granting only one licence—to itself. Later this was strengthened by the more direct powers under D.O.R.R. 2E, and the control of imported raw materials, in turn, gave the Department the power of allocation and thus of determining the output of individual firms. Thus the leather allocation was the basis of the control over the production of boots, including, from early 1918 onwards, a scheme for producing standard boots for the civilian population, on a cost-plus basis.

One of the most complex schemes of control was that evolved for meat, since it had to cover both imports and home-grown meat for both military and civilian use. As long as supplies were sufficient to meet effective demand, the only direct Government action was the bulk purchase of imported meat for the use of the Forces; by early 1917, however, the sinkings by submarines, the growing demands by the Allies, and the fact that army rations were much higher than the quantities consumed by many of the men as civilians, caused a shortage which led to immediate price rises, without any evident parallel rises in costs. The first measure taken was a price control on retail butchers, who, it was hoped, would be forced to lower their own bids for meat and thus reduce prices all down the line to the farmer or stockbreeder. This policy worked for a time, but towards the end of 1917, the Government had to step in, in the face of a real shortage, by ordering heavy slaughtering and purchasing all meat from the farms from December–January 1917-18 onwards. All the firms engaged in slaughtering and wholesaling were turned into agents of the Government by April 1918 and finally meat was rationed to consumers.[1]

Consumer food rationing was the task of the Ministry of Food. The appointment of a Food Controller, authorized by the outgoing Ministry in November, was one of the many changes introduced by Mr. Lloyd George as Prime Minister in December 1916. In the case of food the conjunction of shortage of supply, unwarranted price increases ('profiteering') and maldistribution touched on a peculiarly sensitive spot in the war economy, the morale of the working population. 50–60% of the typical working-class household budget was still being spent on food and drink, and it was the workers whose consumption was reduced first when shortages pushed up prices.

Food control was largely seen in terms of its effects on industrial unrest. As long as it was believed, with the Departmental Committee of the Board of Trade set up in the summer of 1916, that the benefits of full employment outweighed the fact that food prices had risen much faster than wages, no action was taken. But when in 1917, the Commission of Enquiry into Industrial Unrest found that its 'eight panels [were] unanimous in regarding the opinion of the working classes, that they have been exploited by the rise of food prices, as the universal and most important cause of unrest',[2] positive action over food followed at once. A prominent labour leader, J. R. Clynes, was appointed to the post of Food Controller, and his advisory 'Consumers' Council' was made up almost entirely of representatives of labour organizations. In July 1917, the prices of wheat, sugar and meat were fixed. Within the next six months, a food crisis of major proportions had enlarged the scope of the Ministry beyond all expectation.

Britain was at no time in actual danger of starvation or even malnutrition. Total consumption in terms of calories per adult male fell only very slightly, and even in the worst year of 1917 amounted to 3,320 per day, compared with 3,442 in 1909–1913 and 3,300 as the minimum laid down by the Allied Scientific Commission. Within these totals, distribution was probably much more equitable in war than in peace. Men in the forces were well fed, while unemployment, the chief cause of poverty, was virtually abolished, and overtime and women's work brought additional earnings into working-class homes. Of some foods there was never a shortage: the supply of flour, of potatoes, of bacon and ham and of margarine and lard increased throughout the war years, and some of these acted as substitutes for meat, butter, milk and sugar, the consumption of which declined. The food crisis of November 1917 to February 1918 was, in fact, largely psychological: fear of shortages set up a tendency to hoard and

[1] E. M. H. Lloyd, *Experiments in State Control* (Oxford, 1924).
[2] E. Cannan, 'Industrial Unrest', *Econ. J.*, 27/108, 1917, p. 456.

created the conditions of highly inelastic demand in which a slight shortfall was translated into a substantial price rise.

By November 1917 all the main categories of food were price-controlled, control reaching back in some cases through several earlier stages of production, and the bread subsidy began on 1st September. The first commodity to be rationed was sugar, the supply of which began to decline seriously. Some 2,000 local Food Control Committees were appointed to deal with sugar rationing, and were soon to provide much of the initiative for the rationing of other goods. They supervised the allocation of sugar to wholesalers and retailers according to the number of ration cards left with them by the consumers. This system of 'registering' or indirect allocation was to be supplanted by a personal, 'non-tied' coupon system, to begin with the New Year, 1918, but plans were overtaken by events, and the system adopted for other foods was essentially also one of 'registration' with certain shops.

By December 1917 shortages apeared in meat, butter, margarine, tea, bacon and cheese, caused partly by losses at sea, but in part by the panic buying itself. Queues collected in all large towns with surprising speed: in London, 1½ million people stood in queues weekly, and in Sheffield and Coventry munitions workers threatened to queue in working hours. An answer had to be found quickly, but both extra supplies from abroad and a general individual rationing scheme would have taken too long to organize. Instead, some local Food Control Committees rationed other food in short supply and tied it to the sugar registration cards. Gravesend introduced this system, followed by Pontypool, and Birmingham was the first large city to ration tea, butter and margarine, from New Year's Day. By February, the London and Home Counties' scheme was completed, and by April a meat scheme had been applied to the rest of the country. There was, however, no uniform national rationing scheme: thus by mid-March there were 31 million persons rationed for butter and margarine, 16 million for tea and meat, 2 million for cheese and 1·2 million for lard, and there was the 'national' sugar scheme on a parallel basis.

Food rationing proved difficult to abolish after the war: the milk control scheme only *began* in the winter of 1918–19. The Government was hostile to the continuation of control, but the world shortage of wheat and sugar was felt more severely in 1919 than in earlier years, and control had to stay. The Ministry of Food earned the gratitude of the Cabinet by maintaining the flow of food during the railway strike of September–October 1919, and in August–September of that year, meat, butter and sugar were re-controlled (the latter two commodities until 1920); but control was exercised increasingly in the interests of and under pressure from the producers rather than the consumers, except in so far as it was used to reduce working-class unrest by keeping prices down. The attempt to placate both producers and consumers could be met only by subsidies, and these were paid, in growing amounts, on wheat (at a rate of £50 million per annum), and on sugar, meat, bacon and cheese. Despite these, however, the Ministry of Food made, from first to last, a profit of over £6 million on a turnover of £1,200 million. With the collapse of world prices in the second half of 1920 food control and subsidies were no longer necessary and the Ministry of Food itself was wound up in March 1921.[1]

There were few other war-time controls which survived long into the early disturbed post-war years. Socialists, in favour of planning generally, civil servants who had come to appreciate their powers, and industrialists who preferred a settled share of the market and cost-plus to the strenuous conditions of competition, might wish to continue them, but economists looked with horror on 'the vast expansion of Government control which has taken place during the war (and was) without parallel in the history of the world',[2] and businessmen, misled by illusions about the opportunities for British industry, hoped for a quick release from the shackles of control. In any case, much of the apparatus depended on D.O.R. Regulations, which were valid only 'during the continuance of the present war', suitably defined, so that decontrol would be the automatic result of inaction. ' "Back to 1914" became a common cry',[3] and by the middle of 1922 virtually the whole machinery of Government control was dismantled.

2. THE EFFECTS OF WAR ON BRITISH INDUSTRY

The major distortions of normal economic life described in the last section caused far-reaching shifts in British industry. There were further upheavals in the immediate post-war period, superimposing yet another distortion on the artificial pattern left by war conditions. The need for adjustment was often hidden beneath the temporary dislocations of those years, and it was only later in the 1920's that the irreversible alterations in the structure of British industry caused by the war came to be better understood.

In spite of the mobilization of 5,700,000 men in the fighting services, of shortages of materials and losses at sea, the total output of British industry had hardly declined at all in the years of war. According to Hoffmann, the index of industrial production (excluding building) declined from 100 in 1913 to the lowest point of 80·8 in 1918, but 1913 had been an exceptional

---

[1] W. H. Beveridge, *British Food Control* (1928).
[2] A. C. Pigou, 'Government Control in War and Peace', *Econ. J.*, 28/112, 1918, p. 363; also *Aspects of British Economic History, 1918–1925* (1948 ed.), Part IV.
[3] R. H. Tawney, 'The Abolition of Economic Controls, 1918–21', *Ec. Hist. Rev.*, 13/1–2, 1943, p. 14.

year and the decline was hardly steeper than that in any ordinary trade cycle; according to Ridley's more recent statistics, industrial production fell only from 57·3 in 1913 to 53·7 in 1918.[1] These results were achieved largely by longer hours of labour and more intensive work, by better organization, better equipment and better management. Even those who had been most critical of Britain's competitive position before 1914 had to admit that the stimulus of war had infused a fresh spirit of enterprise into British industry.[2] Pressure of war needs, urgent appeals and direct aid by Government departments, and acute shortages of materials, fuel, machinery and labour created a new outlook and a more active approach which were not entirely lost even after the emergency had ended.

Scientific research, for example, unduly neglected by British industrialists, was stimulated by the Government which set up in July 1915 a department to promote scientific research in industry. In 1916 it became the Department of Scientific and Industrial Research, sponsoring research not only directly in Universities and elsewhere, but also encouraging industry to set up its own research associations.[3] The discovery of applied science by British industry may be said to have dated from those years, though it was still in an embryonic stage.

Some industries had hardly existed at all in this country before the war and had to be established in war-time to maintain supplies formerly drawn from Germany. They included the making of scientific instruments, of ball bearings, of chemical and laboratory glassware, of tungsten and of chemical products including benzol, toluol and ammonia liquor.[4] Others, again, had been in infancy in 1914 and grew to manhood only because of military demands, the most important being the aircraft industry.

In general, improved processes, the saving of labour and material, the use of scrap metal, the standardizing of components, the re-planning of factory layouts were encouraged by war conditions in the best firms, and often imposed by the Government in others. The 'practical application (of control) to munitions and non-munitions industries, aided by the control of materials and the operation of the priority principle, resulted in an enormous increase in output, more efficient industries, and great economies in production'.[5] Again, the need to provide figures for cost-plus con-

[1] W. G. Hoffmann, *British Industry, 1700–1950* (Oxford, 1955), Table 54; T. M. Ridley, 'Industrial Production in the U.K., 1900–1953', *Economica*, 22/85, 1955.
[2] E.g. the articles in the *Economic Journal*, reprinted in J. W. Lea, *Britain's Decline* (Birmingham, 1922).
[3] R. S. Sayers, 'The Springs of Technical Progress in Britain, 1919–1939', *Econ. J.*, 60/238, 1950, pp. 279–80; R. S. Edwards, *Co-operative Industrial Research* (1950), chapter 4; Sir Harry Melville, *The Department of Scientific and Industrial Research* (1962), chapter 2.
[4] E.g. C. M. Whittaker, 'The British Coal-Tar Colour Industry and its Difficulties in Times of War', *J. Royal Soc. of Arts*, 65/8th Dec. 1916.
[5] *History of the Ministry of Munitions* (1922), Vol. 7, Part 1, p. 87.

tracts, as well as for Excess Profits Duty, introduced up-to-date accounting practices into many firms. Problems of large-scale management were often tackled systematically for the first time. In its turn, the Government was obliged to collect new sets of statistics which could be of assistance to industrial management.[1]

Further, the controls and allocation and rationing schemes 'established a strong presumption in favour of organization'[2] and the formation of trade associations. The war 'stimulated organization and combination among manufacturers; advertised rationalization; strengthened the demand for tariffs; and encouraged, in another sphere, the settlement of wages and working conditions by national rather than local agreements'. At the same time, 'by breaking down trade jealousies and secrecies and accustoming firms engaged in the same industry to joint action through a representative organization, the Ministry (of Munitions) encouraged the formation of trade combinations, involving great aggregations of capital and unions of producers formidable to consumers'.[3] Many of these associations did not survive the war, but they often left skeleton structures which could quickly take on flesh and blood when depression encouraged restrictive practices.[4] On the other hand, the amalgamations encouraged by the war, such as those in the steel industry, in shipping, in banking and, in effect, among the railways, survived to become permanent.

Among major industries, engineering was changed most. Before the war, British engineering firms had tended to undertake too many different jobs, and had failed to get long enough 'runs' of repetition work. They were able to do this by using highly skilled labour, and relatively little specialized machinery: 'It would probably be true to say that no country in the world could show such a high level of workmanship, or so much out-of-date machinery.'[5] This did not survive the war, for under the stress of the voracious demands for arms, ammunition, motor vehicles and machinery for other war-important industries, the Government was soon forced to impose rationalization.

Some changes, as for example, the transformation of shell making into a mass-production industry staffed largely by unskilled female labour in new premises specially erected, had few permanent effects, for at the end of the war the women left the industry and the buildings were converted to other uses.[6] Other innovations were bound to leave more permanent

---

[1] E. M. H. Lloyd, *Experiments in State Control* (Oxford, 1924), pp. 389–92.

[2] J. F. Rees, *A Social and Industrial History of England, 1815–1918* (1920), Suppl. chapter.

[3] R. H. Tawney, 'Abolition of Economic Controls, 1918–21,' *Ec. Hist. Rev.*, 13/1–2, 1943, p. 8; *Ministry of Munitions*, Vol. 7, Part 1, p. 102.

[4] Hermann Levy, *Monopolies, Cartels and Trusts in British Industry* (1927 ed.), pp. 177–81.   [5] *Ministry of Munitions*, Vol. 7, Part 1, p. 94.

[6] G. D. H. Cole, *Trade Unions and Munitions* (Oxford, 1923), chapter 14.

marks. Thus the machine tool industry was encouraged to expand with Government assistance and obliged to produce more efficiently a large quantity of standardized units. Limit gauges, used by non-skilled labour on mass-production processes, were introduced into British engineering firms in large numbers.[1] Automatic welding became more common in the shipyards. New types of output bonus were introduced, and other more enlightened practices of labour management, including an official series of studies of industrial fatigue, became more widely accepted. Towards the end of the war, when the erection of so many new works seriously strained the supply of experienced engineering managers, there was some 'dilution' in management also, the Ministry of Munitions transmitting the accumulated experience of the industry to new factories by means of strict instructions.

Much of the war-time capacity in engineering could, as noted above, be scrapped after the war with little hardship on capital or labour. Much of the rest, particularly the building of motor vehicles and aircraft and of machine tools, faced a promising future in a world eager for improved capital equipment and hoping to progress by mechanization, and there were potential markets both in the backward areas of the globe and among the chief industrial rivals. Apart from the products for industries which themselves suffered contraction, such as textile machinery, railway locomotives or marine engines, in the engineering industry no permanent reduction was necessary from the inflated war-time capacity.

Shipbuilding was less fortunate. In the early years of the war, the Admiralty had monopolized most of the building capacity of the country, but the heavy sinkings beginning at the end of 1916 had forced an enlargement of the mercantile building programme, while the provision of new tonnage became one of the chief contributions of the United States to the Allied cause. Japan, Holland and Scandinavia, deprived of British ships, also enlarged their building capacity. Thus by 1918, world output had regained the pre-war level at just under 3 million gross tons, but as the transport difficulties and dislocations of 1919 simulated a world shipping shortage much greater than actually existed[2] while shipyards rapidly converted from building warships to building merchant vessels, world output reached almost $5\frac{1}{2}$ million tons in 1919, 7 million in 1920 and nearly 6 million in 1921. While the fall in British output from 2,056,000 gross tons in 1920 to 646,000 gross tons in 1923 was not as large as the American drop, from 3,580,000 gross tons in 1919 to 79,000 gross tons in 1922, the main legacy of the war was a greatly inflated building capacity, which had to compete against an even more greatly inflated capacity elsewhere.

[1] *Ministry of Munitions*, Vol. 8, Part 3.
[2] Fayle, *The War and the Shipping Industry*, chapters 21, 25; p. 49 above.

The war-time demand for armaments and ships quickly outran the capacity of the existing steelworks, denuded as they were of labour by heavy recruiting. Ultimately the steelmaking capacity of the country was enlarged by 50%, though much of this was completed only in the years 1919–20, when the war demand was past and costs of construction were at their highest. Employment in the iron and steel industry increased from 311,000 in July 1914 to 403,000 in January 1920. This expansion was fostered by the Government, which sometimes bore part of the actual cost of new plant, and in most cases granted loans on easy terms as well as very generous tax concessions. Capacity in the rest of the world was also greatly and permanently enlarged in war-time, particularly, again, in the United States, where capacity rose by 15 million tons, or 50%, to produce over two-thirds of the world output of steel in 1918. The subsequent decline in world demand and in output, both in the U.S.A. and in the European countries, was less steep than in shipbuilding, but it was still sufficient to make over-capacity a permanent feature of the inter-war years.[1]

In this period of Government-stimulated growth, some major technical changes were taken in hand. By far the most important was the long-overdue expansion of basic open-hearth capacity to make use of the extensive ore fields of the East Midlands in place of the high-grade ore from overseas, at a time of shortage of shipping tonnage and of foreign currency. This change to open-hearth furnaces also allowed steelmakers to use more scrap and waste, and during the war years the steel scrap ratio was raised from 15% to 50%. The new works were more efficient than much of the existing capacity in other respects also. At the same time the large contracts for the production of shell steel, which had to be accurately controlled in the melting, taught many firms to make steel to closer specifications.

War conditions gave the industry 'a taste of collective research'.[2] New alloys for aircraft and tanks were developed; heat treatment was introduced into the making of tank components which improved the tensile strength in a revolutionary way and methods were perfected in Sheffield of making tool steel from home ores as well as from the high-grade Swedish ores. Basic slag began to be converted into fertilizer on a large scale. Metallurgists were improving manufacturing methods of cupronickel, were learning to build up worn mechanical parts by electro-deposit methods, and were introducing extrusion processes for brass rod and copper tubing.[3]

[1] T. H. Burnham and G. O. Hoskins, *Iron and Steel in Britain, 1870–1930* (1943); M. S. Birkett, 'The Iron and Steel Trades during the War', *J. R. Stat. S.*, 83/3, 1920.
[2] D. L. Burn, *The Economic History of Steelmaking, 1867–1939* (Cambridge, 1940), pp. 350, 369.
[3] *Ministry of Munitions*, Vol. 7, Part 1, chapter 6, and Vol. 7, Part 2.

The expansion of capacity during the war was carried out under the control of the industry itself. It therefore largely took the form of extensions to existing works to balance their capacity, e.g. of the annual output of blast furnaces, steel furnaces and rolling mills, and this had the immediate result of reducing the burden on the transport system, and of reducing some cost, but it prevented a major shift in favour of the areas with the lowest costs. In 1918 the National Federation of Iron and Steel Manufacturers was formed under the stress of war, but it remained weak and unimportant; on the other hand, regional and specialist associations came closer together and the industry thereby acquired a habit of collaboration.

Beside the munitions industry and the metallurgical and chemical industries associated with them, the sectors of the economy most affected by the war were agriculture, coal mining and rail transport. At the outbreak of war, Britain imported from abroad four-fifths of the cereals consumed, two-fifths of the meat, three-quarters of the fruit, besides all the sugar and colonial products and substantial proportions of other foodstuffs. Yet no special attention was paid to the food supply of the country in the first two years of the war, apart from the establishment of War Agricultural Committees in the counties to organize the supply of labour, fertilizer, machinery and feeding stuffs; and these were to form the main instruments of the emergency policies of 1917 and 1918.

Shipping losses and a poor harvest in North America drew attention to the need to increase home food supply towards the end of 1916. By that time the farmers had been denuded of labour and of horses, and fertilizer and feeding stuffs, being largely imported, were controlled and in short supply. It was possible to increase the proportion of the population living on the produce of British acres by only one method, and that was to plough up pasture land for potatoes and, above all, grain, and thus reverse the slow process which had continued since the 1870's: it was calculated that 100 acres would maintain only 9 persons if used as meat-producing pasture, and 41 if used as milk-producing pasture; but they would maintain 172 persons if planted with oats, 208 if planted with wheat, and 418 with potatoes.[1]

It was too late to do more for the harvest year of 1917 than add about one million acres to tillage. For 1918, however, some 3 million acres more than in 1916 were ploughed up, and compared with the average harvests of 1904–13, the wheat production increased from 1·56 million to 2·58 million tons, oats from 3·04 to 4·46 million, barley from 1·52 to 1·56 and potatoes from 6·59 to 9·22 million tons in 1918.[2] This was achieved at the

[1] G. P. Jones and A. G. Pool, *A Hundred Years of Economic Development* (1959 ed.), chapter 16.

[2] T. H. Middleton, *Food Production in War* (Oxford, 1923), pp. 112, 154, 192, 241.

cost of reducing the grassland by 3½ million acres and decreasing the home output of milk and meat. This large-scale switch could be justified for the sake of raising food production quickly for a short time, since newly ploughed grassland will, for a season or two, yield high returns with little effort, though it was opposed in some quarters on the grounds that farming as it was distributed just before the outbreak of war yielded the highest possible food return.[1]

To help the British farmer in these efforts, the Food Production Department of the Board of Agriculture distributed and allocated scarce fertilizer and equipment; it supplied 22,000 men, including prisoners of war, 300,000 part-time women workers and a women's land army which at its maximum numbered 16,000, this special labour being responsible for 2·2 million out of the 3 million extra arable acres; and it spread knowledge of improved methods. Above all, several thousand tractors were sent out, to open up a new era in British farming: 'in the spring of 1917 the tractor was a new, untried, and rather distrusted implement, and although by the end of 1918 it was familiar and was eagerly sought after by farmers in every county, its rapid introduction and progress in favour had been secured as a result of an immense amount of effort, and at a high cost'.[2]

The tractor remained a permanent feature of British agriculture, but the distribution of land between pasture and the different crops reverted quickly to the pre-war proportions and the crops of 1924–8 (excluding the Irish Free State) bore a striking resemblance to the crops grown in 1909–13.[3] The ploughing policy of 1917 and 1918 had been achieved only by compulsory powers given to the Board of Agriculture on the one hand, and by a minimum price guarantee for wheat, oats and potatoes, on the other. Both were to be valid for six years, under the Corn Production Act of 1917, but were repealed before their time, allowing agriculture to revert to its pre-war state. The protective and directive policy of the 1930's was, however, to a large extent, to be anchored on the experience of State control of farming in war-time.

In coal mining, after a decline of 11% of output, and a loss of a quarter of a million men in the first year of war, there was built up a most complex system of control, beginning with price control and export licensing in 1915 and ending, in 1918, with a state of virtual nationalization of the mines. Though the former managers were still in charge of individual pits, the Government had taken over control of the mines of South Wales in December 1916 and all the other mines in February 1917. Under an Act of February 1918, the Coal Controller received 15% of the

---

[1] E.g., Sir R. Henry Rew, 'The Progress of British Agriculture', Pres. Address, *J. R. Stat. S.*, 85/1, 1922.   [2] Middleton, p. 226.

[3] A. W. Flux, 'Our Food Supply Before and After the War', Pres. Address, *J. R. Stat. S.*, 93/4, 1930.

excess profits of the industry as a fund to pay the guaranteed dividends to high cost companies, and only 5% was to be kept by the owners; the remaining 80% was to be paid in tax. During the period of control, the State determined capital investment, it 'zoned' all coal supplies to save transport, and it allocated scarce resources, in particular pit props, by central direction.

The reason for the close official control of the coal mines was only in part the need to maintain the supply of a basic fuel and raw material; in large measure it sprang from the desire to keep down the price of coal to consumers while permitting wages to rise in line with other wages and the cost of living. Despite the powers under D.O.R. Regulations, the miners, and those of South Wales in the first instance, were not disposed to forgo their right to strike, and by successive wage demands which were granted by Government intervention over the opposition of the mine owners, they forced the Government to take over the industry and subsidize all wages out of the very high prices secured by that part of the coal output that was exported.

Despite all efforts to improve productivity and fill the places of the miners who had enlisted, coal output seriously declined towards the end of the war. The tonnage produced in 1918, 228 million, was almost 50 million short of the peak of 1913, and the burden of the reduction had to be carried by exports. With most of the western European coalfields damaged or out of action, there was an insatiable demand for coal after the armistice, which allowed the Government to hold down home prices while recouping itself by soaring export prices, benefiting the budget to the extent of £170 million in one financial year. In these conditions the Government kept control over the industry, while a Royal Commission, headed by Mr. Justice Sankey, failed to agree on its future.[1] The mines were handed over to the former owners in March 1921, when prices had collapsed and the bitter task of bringing wages down likewise lay ahead. The legacies of the war were, therefore, a capacity larger than normal peace-time exports could warrant, and a bitter hostility between employers and workers on principle as well as on day-to-day wage rates and working conditions.[2]

The British railway companies were taken over by the Government on the outbreak of war, and administered as a single unit by a Railway Executive Committee, consisting of the General Managers of ten of the main lines. Returns to shareholders were guaranteed at the very generous level of 1913 out of a pool, shared among the 130 companies taken over.

[1] pp. 111–12 below.
[2] R. A. S. Redmayne, *The British Coal Mining Industry During the War* (Oxford, 1923); W. H. B. Court, 'Problems of the British Coal Industry Between the Wars', *Ec. Hist. Rev.*, 15/1–2, 1945.

Detailed administration, as in the case of the coal mines, was left in the hands of the former managers, but the ending of competition permitted many economies to be introduced, such as the closing of duplicated services over rival lines and the concentration of parcels in certain stations only. The pooling of rolling stock, avoiding wasteful shunting, sorting and empty return, began with standard open wagons between the Great Central, Great Eastern and Great Northern Companies in December 1915, and by January 1917 it had extended to all companies, involving 307,000 wagons. By June 1919 over 500,000 wagons were embraced in the scheme, though it proved impossible to incorporate more than a fraction of the 600,000-odd privately owned wagons into it.

Rates and fares, like coal prices, were held down in order to stabilize the cost of living, but the bitter rail strike forced the Government to allow wages and rates to rise at the end of 1919. A Select Committee of 1918 reported in favour of ultimate unification with nationalization as one of the possible forms it might take, and the arguments for preserving the economies secured in war-time were too strong to be ignored. To avoid nationalization, the Railway Act of 1921 forced all existing lines, apart from some suburban and some light railways, into four companies, to be privately owned and run for profit.[1]

In contrast with the industries enumerated so far, cotton may be taken as an example of an industry which was not considered of importance to the war, and in which recruitment for the Forces proceeded apace, unhindered by badges or starred lists, though much of the labour force was female and remained. Throughout the war, 'Egyptian' cotton was at no time in short supply, but from 1916 onward supplies of raw cotton from the United States were restricted, and the association established by the industry to deal with this shortage was destined to be much more symbolic of the associations of the next twenty years than the organizations of other industries in war-time designed to expand capacity to meet insatiable buyers.

As the supply of American cotton dried up, free dealings in Liverpool were suspended, and a Cotton Control Board was set up by the Board of Trade in June 1917. It consisted of manufacturers in the different branches of the industry, together with a few trade union leaders, and its objective was to ration out the limited supplies of American cotton. Restriction of output was achieved by limiting the proportions of spindles and looms that could be worked, and collecting a levy on those worked in excess. Those at work, mainly the spinners and weavers of 'Egyptian' cotton, could recoup themselves by charging higher prices, while the price of raw cotton was kept down simply by limiting its demand. The workers, most of whom

---

[1] E. A. Pratt, *British Railways and the Great War*, 2 vols. (1921), esp. chapters 8, 9, 11, 47, 48, 49, 74; C. E. R. Sherrington, *The Economics of Rail Transport in Britain*, Vol. 1 (1928), chapter 12.

agreed to be stood off a week at a time on a 'rota' system, received unemployment benefit out of the levies so collected.[1]

Until wage disputes broke out in the summer of 1918, the scheme satisfied the employers, the workers and the unions, though it could be held against the industry that it was wantonly hoarding labour desperately needed elsewhere. Its temporary success was largely due to the fact that the reduction was in the supply of the raw material, not in the demand, so that its costs could be borne by the public who were charged higher prices, a solution not open to the restrictive schemes of the inter-war years, when the main problem was the collapse of effective demand.

Thus the permanent effects of war on British industry were not confined to the fostering of new techniques or the creation of up-to-date productive capacity. At least as important were the lessons it taught in collaboration and organization: trade associations for raw material allocation, common research projects, price control or other purposes were formed in many industries for the first time. The process of amalgamation of firms was also speeded up by the war. The Committee on Trusts of 1919 was 'satisfied that Trade Associations and Combines are rapidly increasing in this country, and may, within no distant period, exercise a paramount control over all important branches of British trade'.[2] In a contemporary view, 'the Trust Report shows that the power of these associations of all kinds was considerably increased as a result of war experience'.[3]

The war also taught the country to look at its national equipment in a new light, not as private property alone, but as the capital helping to provide the national income. This was particularly so in industry administered nationally, like shipping, the railways or the coal mines, and it was no accident that it was under the influence of war that compulsory amalgamation of collieries and nationalization of coal royalties, unification of all internal transport, including roads and canals, and a reorganization of the building industry, as well as a national electricity grid were first seriously considered,[4] or that protection of 'key' industries found general favour. Lastly, the war, by causing fluctuations in demand and supply of hitherto undreamt-of range and speed, accustomed industry to the more prolonged and pervasive fluctuations of the years to follow.[5]

3. BUDGETING AND FINANCE DURING THE WAR

At the outbreak of war it was assumed that the task of the Chancellor of the Exchequer would be the collection of sufficient funds, both by

[1] H. D. Henderson, *The Cotton Control Board* (Oxford, 1922).
[2] *Report on Trusts* (1919. Cd. 9236), p. 11.
[3] J. M. Rees, *Trusts in British Industry, 1914–21* (1922), p. 27.
[4] R. H. Tawney, 'Abolition', p. 11; Redmayne, *op. cit.*, pp. 81–2; *Ministry of Munitions*, Vol. 8, Part 3, chapter 4.
[5] W. Ashworth, *An Economic History of England 1870–1939* (1960), chapter 12.

taxation and by borrowing, to allow the Government to bid in the open market, in competition with others, for such commodities and services as it required. It was understood that this would imply some transfer of resources from peaceful uses to uses of war, and that prices would be raised thereby; but the extent to which the economy would have to be driven and cajoled to provide for modern mass armies and withstand a blockade was not even dimly appreciated at first.

When the economic controls began to be applied, from early 1917 onwards, many lessons were learnt in the fiscal sphere also. It had become clear by then that there was a dual objective of taxation in war-time: the provision of funds for Government departments, and the removal of funds from private hands in which they would have helped to raise prices and divert resources to inessential uses. The fiscal theory of the second World War was not fully developed in the first—the relation between savings and the contributions to Government loans, in particular, was by no means wholly understood—but from early 1917 onwards enlightened opinion had an adequate grasp of the main principles of fiscal policy in war-time.[1] 'In the face of extravagance and inflation', wrote the *Economist*,[2] 'the only cure was surely taxation or compulsory borrowing which alone could have taken out of the hands of thoughtless and ignorant people the power to warp the economic energy of the country from the war work on which it should be concentrated.'

Under the stresses of war, there were several new developments in the techniques of taxation. Owing to the state of unpreparedness, the early weeks of hostilities had to be covered, not by a supplementary budget, but by votes of credit, and these were found so convenient that they formed the major part of the Parliamentary vote, rising from £362 million in the fiscal year 1914–15 to £2,500 million in 1918–19, and amounting to a total of £8,742 million between August 1914 and March 1919. The ordinary budget was left to carry on annually with only token votes for the fighting services, and with civil votes on a peace-time basis.

Faced with the need to enlarge revenue at once, the first reaction of the Chancellor of the Exchequer was to increase the burden evenly over all the different groups of taxpayers. Thus in November 1914, the income tax and supertax rates were doubled, at the same time as the rates of duty on beer and tea were raised: in this way, both the chief direct and indirect taxes were affected simultaneously.[3] In the long run, however, such simple apportionment could not bear the strain of tax levels at several times their peace-time values. In particular, the taxes on consumption, falling mainly

---

[1] E.g. Hartley Withers, *Our Money and the State* (1917); A. W. Kirkaldy (ed.), *Industry and Finance* (1917), Preface; cf. also A. C. Pigou, *The Economy and Finance of the War* (1916).   [2] *The Economist*, 5th May 1917.
[3] D. Lloyd George, *War Memoirs*, Vol. 1 (1933), pp. 116–19.

on the poor, would find little margin for 'luxury' spending, and would merely lead to demands for higher wages. Customs and excise revenue likewise arose from commodities the consumption of which had to be limited for various reasons in the later stages of the war.

Thus the main additional burden of taxation had to fall on the direct taxes. The 'normal' rate of income tax was raised, by steps, from 1s. 2d. in the pound in 1913–14 to 6s. in the two years 1918–19 and 1919–20, while the exemption limit was lowered from £160 to £130 in 1915. Since, at the same time, prices and wages were rising to about double the pre-war level by 1918, and treble by 1920, the total numbers liable to income tax rose from 1·2 million in 1913–14 to 4·5 million in 1917–18 and 7·8 million in 1919–20, and the number of incomes actually paying the tax rose from 1·13 million in 1913–14 to 3 million in 1917–18 and 3·9 million in 1919–20.[1] Supertax rates were similarly raised.

To these direct taxes was added the Excess Profits Duty, beginning with the second budget of 1915. It had been preceded by the so-called Munitions Levy, which was applied to 'controlled' establishments in the munitions industry to end profiteering, as part of the bargain under which the trade unions had agreed to give up certain cherished rights and practices for the duration of the war. The Munitions Levy was assessed at 100% on all profits above a pre-war 'standard' plus 20%, and as such was mostly evaded by capital expenditure, wear and tear allowances and other methods which made the concept of the 'standard' meaningless. Its yield was negligible.

E.P.D., like the Munitions Levy, was designed in part to meet the popular complaints of profiteering, and was levied on firms, not on individuals—an innovation of considerable importance in British taxation practice. Its rate was originally 50% of the excess profits over the pre-war standard, but it was raised to 80% in 1917 for political reasons, cut to 40% at the end of the war in the expectation of a slump, and raised again to 60% in 1920, too late to have much influence in stopping the boom. Its average rate over the period was 63% of the excess profits made, but the actual amount collected has been estimated to have been but 34%; it was subject to much evasion, delay and fraudulent practices. Yet it yielded, until its repeal in 1921, £1,154 million, or one-quarter of the total tax revenue in this period.[2]

By these means, as well as the simple effect of the inflation, the yield

---

[1] Sir Bernard Mallet and C. Oswald George, *British Budgets (Second Series), 1913–14 to 1920–21* (1929), pp. 324–5; T. J. Kiernan, *British War Finance and the Consequences* (1920).

[2] J. R. Hicks, U. K. Hicks and L. Rostas, *The Taxation of War Wealth* (Oxford, 1941); A. W. Kirkaldy (ed.), *British Finance, During and After the War, 1914–21* (1921), chapter 7.

from direct taxes was raised from £94 million in 1913–14 to £508 million in 1917–18 and £721 million in 1919–20, or as a proportion of total tax revenue, from 57·5% in 1913–14 to about 80% in the last two years of war, to fall again to 68·2% in 1920–1. Indirect taxes, therefore, increased relatively much less and barely kept pace with the rise in prices to the end of the war, showing a real rise only in the boom years of 1919 and 1920. Of pre-war duties, tobacco proved to be the most buoyant, bearing increases in the rate from 3s. 8d. to 8s. 2d. per lb. without reduction in consumption. Consumption of alcoholic drinks, by contrast, was deliberately restricted during the war, in order to conserve grain and to reduce absenteeism among war workers. The sugar duties bore the largest percentage increases, from 1s. 10d. per cwt. to 25s. 8d., and the tea duties were also raised. Among the more important new imposts were the entertainments duty, easy to collect and acceptable as taxing a 'luxury', and the so-called 'McKenna Duties' introduced in 1915. These were a tax of 33⅓% *ad valorem* on such luxuries as motor cars and cycles, watches and clocks and musical instruments, and a specific duty on film. They were principally designed to discourage unnecessary imports and thereby save foreign exchange and shipping space; in 1919–20, however, they became revenue collectors of some moment, and they were later turned into openly protective duties. None of these innovations, however, became a major source of revenue: in 1920–1, four-fifths of the indirect taxation came from alcohol and tobacco and one-seventh from the 'breakfast table' duties; the new war duties raised less than 7%.

The strong concentration of the additional taxation on direct taxes tended to increase somewhat the redistributive effect of the tax system, at least in the higher ranges. The percentages of incomes paid in taxes compared as follows:[1]

	1913–14	1918–19
Earned: £100	6·0%	13·8%
£500	5·8%	13·1%
£10,000	8·1%	42·6%
Unearned: £10,000	15·1%	50·3%

This shift towards greater equality may in part have reflected the general preoccupation with the need to maintain the morale of the working classes, but it was mainly based on the belief that there was little additional taxable capacity left among the poor, so that all the additions had to come from the pockets of the rich.

By these means, revenue was increased four-fold to 1918–19 and

[1] Rt. Hon. Herbert Samuel, 'The Taxation of the Various Classes of the People', Pres. Address, *J. R. Stat. S.*, 82/2, 1919; Mallet and George, *op. cit.*, Table XXI.

six-fold to 1920–1, the peak year; in real terms, it was more than doubled. Expenditure, however, grew at a vastly greater rate (£mn.):

United Kingdom

Financial Year	Revenue	Expenditure	Surplus or Deficit	
1913–14	198·2	197·5	+0·7	—
1914–15	226·7	560·5	—	−333·8
1915–16	336·8	1,559·2	—	−1,222·4
1916–17	573·4	2,198·1	—	−1,624·7
1917–18	707·2	2,696·2	—	−1,989·0
1918–19	889·0	2,579·3	—	−1,690·3
1919–20	1,339·6	1,665·8	—	−326·2
1920–21	1,426·0	1,195·4	+230·6	—

It will be noted that revenue did not fully meet expenditure until almost two years after the armistice. Further, it is evident that had taxation been as vigorous in the early years as it became later in the war, and as sensibly concentrated on profits during the war-time profit inflation, borrowing could have been kept down to more manageable proportions, especially before 1917.[1]

It was a mixture of motives which induced successive Chancellors to be gentle with taxpayers in the first three years of the war. At first, the duration, the cost, and the price rises of the war were greatly underestimated. Moreover, the Government was not, apparently, averse in principle to raising most of its war expenditure by borrowing, and it appeared in 1916 that the Chancellor was satisfied as long as the sums raised in taxation were sufficient to meet the interest and the sinking fund for repayments on the debts outstanding, besides the normal peace-time expenditure. Lastly, the country would certainly not have been ready, in the earlier years of war, for the level of taxation which it was willing to accept in 1917 and 1918. Over the whole period from 1914–15 to 1919–20, revenue only covered some 36% of expenditure: in the worst year of 1915–16, the proportion was only 21·6% and in the next two years just above one-quarter. The total deficit on the war budgets amounted to £7,186 million, and the national debt was increased by about the same sum. This increase completely dwarfed the pre-war national debt of £650 million.

Contemporaries were much preoccupied with the 'burden' of this vast national debt created during the war. A heavy load of interest and repayments would have to be borne by later generations, and this would represent an undesirable tax liability on the active part of the population, including manufacturers who would have to compete with foreign industry, while the payments would accrue to inactive rentiers. Matters were made worse

[1] J. M. Keynes, *A Treatise on Money* (1930), Vol. 2, pp. 170–6; W. Ashworth, *An Economic History of England, 1870–1939* (1960), pp. 270–3.

by the fact that war-time borrowing was made, in 1917–19 at least, in depreciated pounds and at high rates. Long-term loans were mostly raised at 5%, often in addition to other concessions, while short-term borrowing on Treasury Bills of 3, 6, 9 or 12 months was made at rates which occasionally even exceeded that figure. The average interest on the war debt was 4·65%, but several loans had been issued at less than par. Only in September 1917 did the Government begin its continuous issue of War Bonds, which had the advantage of withdrawing savings regularly as they were made, in place of the earlier fixed subscription period loans involving extensive temporary bank loans.[1] Had the Government taken firmer measures to discourage other forms of investment, it could have secured far more favourable rates. This large deadweight debt, together with a floating debt which rose from £16 million at the outbreak of war to a maximum of £1,570 million in June 1919, created most serious problems for the Treasury in the post-war years.

More important, perhaps, was the question how far the fiscal policy of successive Chancellors succeeded in diverting the necessary resources to the Government's war effort with the greatest possible efficiency and the least possible disturbance.[2] Deducting loans to Dominions and Allies, and certain capital transactions, Government expenditure on internal current account rose from one-twelfth of the national income to four-ninths by 1916–17 and over half in 1918–19: this was much more than could have been financed out of normal savings. With private capital issues still running at an average of £52 million per annum in the years 1915–18, Government borrowings in 1914–17 were at about three times the pre-war level of savings,[3] and the deficit alone amounted to one-third of the national income in 1915–16 and to 40% of the national income in 1917–18. Budget policy was clearly the major factor in the war-time rise of prices.

The monetary mechanism, by which the Government's attempt to divert to its own uses a larger proportion of the nation's current income than the nation was willing to forgo was translated into inflation, has been described in a classic passage of the Interim Report of the Cunliffe Committee of 1918:[4]

> Suppose, for example, that in a given week the Government require £10,000,000 over and above the receipts from taxation and loans from the public. They apply for an advance from the Bank of

---

[1] Frank L. McVey, *The Financial History of Great Britain, 1914–1918* (New York, 1918).

[2] The best account will be found in E. V. Morgan, *Studies*, pp. 99 ff.

[3] Morgan, *op. cit.*, pp. 41–2, 264.

[4] Committee on Currency and Foreign Exchanges after the War, *First Interim Report* (1918), para. 10, reprinted in T. E. Gregory, *Banking Statutes and Reports*, Vol. 2.

England, which by a book entry places the amount required to the credit of Public Deposits in the same way as any other banker credits the account of a customer when he grants him temporary accommodation. The amount is then paid out to contractors and other Government creditors, and passes, when the cheques are cleared, to the credit of their bankers in the books of the Bank of England—in other words is transferred from Public to 'Other' Deposits, the effect of the whole transaction thus being to increase by £10,000,000 the purchasing power in the hands of the public in the form of deposits in the Joint Stock Banks and the bankers' cash at the Bank of England by the same amount. The bankers' liabilities to depositors having thus increased by £10,000,000 and their cash reserves by an equal amount, their proportion of cash to liabilities (which was normally before the war something under 20 per cent) is improved, with the result that they are in a position to make advances to their customers to an amount equal to four or five times the sum added to their cash reserves, or, in the absence of demand for such accommodation, to increase their investments by the difference between the cash received and the proportion they require to hold against the increase of their deposit liabilities. Since the outbreak of war it is the second procedure which has in the main been followed, the surplus cash having been used to subscribe for Treasury Bills and other Government securities. The money so subscribed has again been spent by the Government and returned in the manner above described to the bankers' cash balances, the process being repeated again and again until each £10,000,000 originally advanced by the Bank of England has created new deposits representing new purchasing power to several times that amount. Before the war these processes, if continued, compelled the Bank of England . . . to raise its rate of discount, but . . . the unlimited issue of Currency Notes has now removed this check upon the continued expansion of credit.

In place of the pre-war bank notes backed by a highly sensitive gold reserve, there were now 'currency notes' in circulation, created by the Treasury early in August 1914, in denominations of £1 and 10s. They were to have been issued to the banks, as a loan at current bank rate, to aid them in staving off the expected run on their deposits, but since no run developed, and the banks were unwilling to pay interest on loans they did not require, the Treasury issued these notes freely to the public *via* the Bank of England and the joint-stock banks. The Bank was obliged to open a 'Currency Note Redemption Account', which became, in effect, a lender to the Government and a direct means of creating credit.

The direct inflationary effect of these notes was, however, small. The value of the notes in circulation, taking the average of the last quarter of the year, rose from £34 million in 1914 to £299 million in 1918 and to a peak of £354 million in 1920, after which it declined, but to some extent the notes were merely replacing the gold in circulation before the war and now withdrawn or hoarded. According to the Cunliffe Committee, legal tender money (excluding token coins) in circulation and held by the banks had risen only from £200 million in June 1914 to £383 million in July 1918.

Compared with the increase in the 'immediately available purchasing power' which doubled between 31st December 1913 and 1st August 1919 from £1,588 million to £3,151 million (at a time when the quantity of goods and services available had clearly shrunk), this increase in the note issue was small. Of the rise of over £1,560 million in the quantity of money, £1,130 million was accounted for by the rise in commercial bank deposits,[1] and there were increases also in savings banks and Bank of England deposits, and in notes issued by Scottish and Irish banks; the only decline was registered in the quantity of gold in the hands of the public.[2] Most of the gold was absorbed by the Bank of England, the holdings of which rose from about £30 million before the war to £87 million at the end of 1914, £107 million in 1918 and a peak of £155 million in 1920. The share of the financial system in the price rise during the war was thus largely the creation of sufficient liquidity to allow the inflationary budgeting to proceed unchecked.

The causes of the inflation were not, however, purely monetary. In the early days, there was some panic among consumers and shopkeepers, causing isolated price rises, but prices usually fell again quickly. Bottlenecks in the supplies of certain materials needed in the war caused some slight rises in wholesale prices in the winter of 1914–15, but the real cost inflation raged from the middle of 1915 to the middle of 1917, aided by such outside factors as shortage of materials and labour, losses at sea and consequent rises in freight and insurance costs, and rising costs of imports. From June 1917 until the middle of 1919, price control kept rises in the cost of living again to a minimum.[3]

If the consumer was considered only very belatedly, the financial institutions of this country were protected by a large number of comprehensive measures from the very beginning of the war. At the outbreak of war, London was a short-time debtor to the rest of the world, but was a long-term creditor, besides being the main foreign exchange market of the world. The actual declaration of war by Britain had been preceded, at the end of July 1914, by financial panic in many continental cities, a collapse of the price of securities and a stampede to sell. When London houses attempted to call in their loans, the frantic search on the Continent

---

[1] Cf. also Mallet and George, *op. cit.*, p. 374.

[2] A. W. Kirkaldy (ed.), *Industry and Finance* (Supplementary Volume) (1920), p. 144.

[3] Morgan, *op. cit.*, pp. 291 ff.; S. E. Harris, *Monetary Problems of the British Empire* (New York, 1941), Part II, Book 4.

for sterling to meet obligations turned all foreign exchanges (except that of Paris, which was in a short-term creditor position) in favour of London. There was thus no question of a foreign exchange crisis, or a gold drain, in London itself: on the contrary, in the critical days of late July and early August 1914, the world was engaged in attempting to make payments to London.

What strain there was, was internal and had several causes, but perhaps the most important was the fear that foreign debtors would be unable to meet their obligations on the bills of exchange. There were about £350 million outstanding, of which some two-thirds were payable by foreign firms in London, but while the payments by the foreign houses remained uncertain, the accepting houses were committed to find payment for those bills which were falling due at a rate of £3 million per day. The joint-stock banks, in anticipation of demands for accommodation by the acceptance houses, called in their loans, and tried to strengthen their own position with the Bank of England. Between 22nd July and 1st August, the Bank of England's 'other securities' rose from £33·6 million to £65·4 million, and 'other deposits' from £42·2 million to £56·8 million, while £6·4 million in notes and £14·3 million in gold were passed into circulation, and the reserve fell from £29·3 million to £10 million.[1]

On 1st August, the Bank raised its discount rate to the panic level of 10%, but in the then state of the City, this was not considered sufficient. A Bank Holiday was declared to Thursday, 6th August inclusive, in order to give five clear days for emergency measures. On 1st August, the Government authorized an increase in the fiduciary issue if necessary; in the next few days the decision to issue £1 and 10s. Treasury notes, mentioned earlier, was taken, and Scottish and Irish bank notes and postal orders were made temporary legal tender, while a moratorium was imposed on bills. When the banks reopened on 7th August, the bank rate could safely be lowered to 6%, and from 8th August onward it reverted to 5%.

The exchange market, still paralysed, was assisted by the Government decision, on 13th August, to ask the Bank of England to re-discount all outstanding pre-moratorium bills, the Government guaranteeing any losses, and to help acceptors in September by loans at 2% on easy terms. Other early measures to steady the money market included a general debt moratorium on 6th August, a scheme to allow joint-stock banks to advance money on new bills with a Government guarantee in November, and a scheme, announced on 31st October, to help those who held shares on margins and might be hit by the expected price falls. Altogether, the Government guaranteed about £500 million of securities, many of them

[1] This account, as much else in this section, is based on Morgan, *op. cit.*

enemy securities, and all but a very small proportion were ultimately recovered.[1]

These elaborate and costly defences against financial disaster turned out to have been largely unnecessary. There was no sign of a run on banks, no drain of gold abroad; most of the internal drain seems to have been to the coffers of the joint-stock banks. The extraordinary care taken to shelter the money market at a time when the greatest sacrifices were demanded from the rest of the nation had several causes. First, the City, and the joint-stock banks in particular, showed a greater disposition to panic than other comparable groups of the population, and therefore needed special treatment; secondly, even in a Government of Liberal–Radical orientation like that of Asquith in 1914, the influence of finance over the Cabinet was very great, and it could advance its special claims in a way which no other interest could; and thirdly, it was genuinely and widely held that economic life would break down without a trouble-free financial system of traditional pattern, and that it was therefore the duty of the Government to cushion it from shocks at almost any cost.

Protected in this way, the financial institutions survived the war with few outward changes. The most important was the virtual completion of the process of amalgamation among the large banks. In 1914, there were still 38 independent joint-stock banks in England and Wales, with just under 5,900 branches. By 1920, there were only 20 independent banks left, having 7,257 branches between them, but of these, the five largest companies controlled 83% of the deposits. Out of the amalgamations of the war and the years immediately following had emerged the 'Big Five'.

> The economic and financial changes associated with the war indirectly influenced the banking structure and are the ultimate explanation of the rapidity of the amalgamation movement which characterized the war period, particularly the last twelve months, and which in a relatively short space of time altered British banking, it may almost be said, from top to bottom.[2]

The major mergers of 1917–18 were of firms already possessing an extensive and wide coverage over much of the country[3] and it was feared that these and further amalgamations were designed not so much for the

---

[1] E.g. A. W. Kirkaldy (ed.), *British Finance, 1914–21*, chapters 1 and 2, and *Credit, Industry and the War* (1915), p. 197; R. G. Hawtrey, *A Century of Bank Rate* (1938), p. 125; R. S. Sayers, *Central Banking After Bagehot* (1957), p. 67; D. Lloyd George, *War Memoirs*, Vol. 1 (1933), pp. 101 ff.; *A Century of Bank Rate* (1938), p. 125; R. S. Sayers, *Central Banking After Bagehot* (1957), p. 67; D. Lloyd George, *War Memoirs*, Vol. 1 (1933), pp. 101 ff.

[2] T. E. Gregory, *The Westminster Bank Through a Century*, Vol. 2 (1936), p. 10.

[3] J. F. Ashby, *The Story of the Banks* (1934); A. W. Kirkaldy (ed.), *Industry and Finance*, Supplementary Volume (1920), p. 121.

convenience of the public, nor yet to open new territories to existing companies, but to eliminate competition. Public disquiet led to the appointment of a Treasury Committee which reported in 1918.[1] It found that while larger banks possessed the advantages of serving wider areas and had the capacity of making larger single loans, they might prejudice the public interest by reducing competition, perhaps leading ultimately to a single combine or a close association of a few firms, and they tended to accelerate the fall in the ratio of bank capital to deposits, which at the time was still considered to be a factor of some importance. On balance, the Committee held that the dangers of further amalgamation outweighed the possible benefits, and recommended legislation to require Government sanction for any future amalgamation, such sanction to be withheld where it would tend to eliminate local competition, or where it would make a single bank overwhelmingly strong. A Bill was prepared by the Chancellor of the Exchequer to that effect, but was withdrawn on the undertaking given by the banks to follow the recommendations of the Committee. Thus banking in this country has remained an oligopoly, yet strongly competitive in some respects.

In war-time, as the Government flooded the country with notes, the deposits held by the joint-stock banks rose, particularly after 1916, and since investment by traders was limited by controls and shortages, the proportion of bank advances fell. Instead, there was a rise in 'investments', mainly in Government stocks. There was also a large increase in discounts, largely in the form of Treasury Bills, and in cash and money at call and at short notice. The banking system was becoming exceedingly liquid in the later years of the war, ready to support a vast expansion of credit the moment the controls were taken off. At the same time, the volume of short-term debt (Treasury Bills) outstanding ensured that the Government would be quite incapable of checking this expansion, even had it had the desire to do so.

4. BRITAIN'S INTERNATIONAL POSITION

In the last years of peace, British overseas investments were increasing at a rapid rate, and by the outbreak of war her total capital holdings abroad had risen to about £4,000 million. This British creditor position was as strong in the dollar countries as in any other part of the world. Investments in the U.S.A. held by British citizens amounted to some $4,000 to $4,500 million (£800–900 million), and in Canada to an additional $2,500 million, and the annual claims of interest, dividends and service charges from the U.S.A. brought in a sum approaching $400 million in dollar exchange.

As noted in the last section, British houses also had large short-term

[1] The Report is reprinted in Gregory, *Statutes and Reports*, Vol. 2.

loans outstanding, mostly in the form of discounted bills of exchange. When in the disturbed period that preceded and followed the declaration of war country after country closed its Exchange and declared a moratorium, British firms called in their loans and refused to discount new foreign bills, and the world was left searching for sterling to meet its short-term obligations. Only New York had remained open, and the debtors of several continents turned to it to use their dollar securities and holdings as means of payment to London. American houses, obliged to make these remittances to London, could not offset them because of the moratoria, 'so that New York, as the centre of American finance, was called to pay one side of a running account for the whole world'.[1] For a time, the rate on London rose from its normal $4·90 to $6·50, and New York had to be saved by the raising of a gold fund of $100 million to support the dollar exchange.

The early weeks of the war thus served to confirm the long-established assumptions that the pound sterling was the world's most coveted currency, and that Britain was in comfortable long-run balance with the rest of the world, allowing her to maintain a steady stream of investments abroad. The deterioration of the position of sterling on the American exchanges and in other neutral centres within a few months of the war was thus little regarded, and viewed as a purely temporary phenomenon. In fact, however, it marked a fundamental shift in the patterns of the international balance of payments, and in the world position of the pound sterling.

By early 1915, the dollar exchange had not only recovered its pre-war gold parity; it was beginning to push up beyond it. As British productive capacity was switched from exports to war production, and as exports of merchandise, as well as of shipping and financial services, consequently began to fall off, while imports increased to supply the booming war factories, the balance of payments and the exchanges began to turn heavily against Britain. The U.S.A., in particular, became a source of imports of all kinds for which no equivalent goods or services could be exported, directly or *via* another country, and inevitably, the pound began to fall in New York. Gold was transferred to America by the Bank of England and from Ottawa, and some dollar securities were sold, but the exchanges kept falling from $4·86 in January to $4·76¼ in July, $4·55½ in September and $4·49 in October. It became clear that the British deficits on current account with the U.S.A. were of an order of magnitude which was beyond the power of the gold reserve to sustain. Instead of deflating after her initial loss of gold on the pre-war model, Britain was launched on a headlong career of inflation.

[1] F. L. McVey, *The Financial History of Great Britain, 1914–1918* (New York, 1918), p. 62.

To finance purchases from America on the required scale, the monetary reserves, which in 1914 amounted to $165 million in central gold reserves and $600 million other monetary gold for all purposes, could be supplemented by dollar securities worth $2,600 million.[1] At first, at the time of the visit of the Anglo–French Commission to the U.S.A. to raise a $500 million loan in September–October 1915, it had been intended to use British-held dollar securities as collateral for loans only. By the end of 1915, however, it had become clear that some might have to be sold in order to maintain payments to America and to stabilize the exchange rate. To operate effectively it was necessary to unify the control over the British-held dollar securities, and the scheme eventually evolved by the Treasury foreshadowed significantly the methods of monetary control resumed twenty years later.

The 'Mobilization of Securities Scheme', in operation from the end of 1915 onwards, was voluntary at first, tempting private owners to sell or lend American securities to the Treasury by offering very attractive terms. A proportion approaching one-half of the securities was, in fact, handed over. In January 1917, with the balance of trade deteriorating further, it was felt necessary to give the Treasury powers to conscript the remainder, but the entry of the U.S.A. into the war in April, and the large loans made available at once for the Allies, made an addition to the Treasury-held securities unnecessary; from September 1917 on, in fact, the list of these securities was reduced.[2]

The actual sales of dollar securities were minimal, amounting to only £207 million in 1915–19, plus perhaps another £54 million of sterling and other securities:[3] but by a judicious use of loans, gold payments, high interest rates, and direct operation on the sensitive exchange markets, the Government successfully held the dollar exchange at between $4·76 and $4·77 from January 1916 to February 1919, while at the same time financing large and growing purchases from the U.S.A. and acting as an exceedingly generous lender to her Allies. From the outbreak of war until the end of the financial year 1918/19, Britain had lent some £1,741 million, including £171 million to countries within the Empire, £434½ million to France, £568 million to Russia and £412½ million to Italy. As against this, she had, in turn, received loans to the amount of £1,365 million, of which £1,027 million came from the U.S.A., £135 million from Canada and the remainder mostly from neutral countries. British loans, therefore, exceeded British borrowings by some £350 million, and American loans had, in a sense, been transmitted to other Allies, the British Government acting, as London finance houses had often done

---

[1] U.S. Federal Reserve *Bulletin*.
[2] Kirkaldy, *British Finance, 1914–21*, pp. 183 ff.
[3] Morgan, *Studies*, pp. 327 ff.

before, as intermediaries who interposed their credit between lender and borrower. The position may be made clear by the following table.[1]

Estimated Balance of Payments of the U.K., 1914–19 (£ mn.)

Year	Deficit on Merchandise Account A.	Government Payments Abroad B.	Credit on Invisible Items C.	Miscellaneous[2] D.	Balance Before Government Loans, etc. (A + B + C + D) E.	Sale of Foreign Investments F.	Government Borrowing Abroad G.	Government Lending Abroad H.
1914	−170	−20	+315	−125	0	0	0	0
1915	−368	−50	+395	+225	+202	+43	+53	−298
1916	−345	−50	+520	−24	+101	+110	+319	−530
1917	−467	−80	+575	−57	−29	+60	+532	−563
1918	−784	—	+580	+97	−107	+23	+381	−297
1919	−663	—	+605	+109	+51	+29	+57	−139

Britain will be seen to have fought the war out of her own resources, the sale of foreign securities (Column F) roughly balancing the net loans to the Allies (Columns G + H).

This conclusion emphasizes the comfortable balance of payments position of Britain, in spite of the buoyant demand for imports in the war years at a time of severe cuts in exports. In values, exports (including re-exports) remained fairly stable, the average for 1914–18 being £547 million, compared with £578 million in 1911–12. Retained imports, however, rose roughly in proportion with prices, from £601 million in 1914 to £1,285 million in 1918.

To some extent, the British position was aided by an improvement in the terms of trade. The diversion of the manufactures of the chief industrial nations to an exhausting war was itself a major cause of improvement, as it raised the relative prices of such manufactured goods as did continue to enter foreign trade. In addition, the Government's direct intervention, such as the bulk purchase of raw materials by the Ministry of Munitions or the War Office, must have materially lowered the prices paid to foreign sellers. There were similar gains also in the growth of the 'invisible exports' in the table above (column C), referring to shipping, banking, insurance and similar services, which showed a substantial increase in monetary terms in the war period, while they must have shrunk in volume. Finally, the balance of payments was strengthened by contracting overseas long-term investment to a mere trickle, an average of some £20 million annually in 1915–18.

As far as the United States was concerned, she changed within the

---

[1] Based on Morgan, *op. cit.*, p. 341.
[2] Short-term loans, gold movements, etc.

short span of the war from a major debtor to a major creditor nation, and there was a sharp increase in the American share of world production of many key commodities, while the European nations were locked in combat. The same could be said, on a smaller scale, of Canada. The flow of international trade was also diverted from the Central Powers mainly to the countries of North America. At the return of peace, British exports to that region had fallen below the pre-war level, but imports were higher, and the adverse trade balance with the dollar countries remained. It expressed one of the most profound permanent economic changes wrought by the war.

5. LABOUR AND THE WAR

The unemployment of the first few weeks of the war, mainly caused by uncertainty and the collapse of certain specific markets,[1] quickly gave way to a labour shortage which continued to worsen as the war progressed. It had been one of the first tasks of the newly established Ministry of Munitions to ensure a sufficient supply of labour to the armament works, but the voracious demands both of the army and of the munitions industries for manpower soon denuded the rest of industry and created an overriding shortage which dominated the history of labour in the war.

Initially, the cry was for volunteers, and several million were quickly recruited by powerful appeals to their patriotism. But it soon became evident that there were more men in uniform than there were arms available to equip them, and there was a still greater shortfall in the stocks of ammunition to keep them supplied at the front. The Ministry of Munitions was established essentially to rectify this serious error of over-recruitment, and quickly realized that the manpower budget of a country at war had to extend further back than the recruiting sergeant.

Some of the early mistakes were beyond repair. Key personnel of engineering works, coal mines and elsewhere, once they had been accepted into the fighting forces, were virtually impossible to retrieve, though many of them naturally drifted to the repair depots set up overseas, or did other work in which their skills were used. Within twelve months, the workers in all war-important skilled crafts were exempt from recruitment, and some order was introduced into the labour market, but even then the drain of manpower to the army posed a most complex problem for staffing the home industries. For while young men as potential recruits were found in all industries, some industries could well afford to contract their employment, others had to make good any losses of manpower by recruitment, and others still had actually to increase their labour force, while furnishing some men for the forces. After the initial pool of unemployment

[1] G. D. H. Cole, *Labour in War Time* (1915).

men had been used up in the early weeks of 1915, the only substantial reserve of labour was to be found among the women who could be induced to enter industry for the first time.

There was thus carried out, as a by-product of recruitment and change-over to war production, a transformation of the labour market of fundamental and, to some extent, lasting importance. Everywhere there was some substitution of female labour for male, and in the munitions industry there was, in addition, substitution of unskilled labour for skilled, known as 'dilution', because of the impossibility of training skilled men requiring several years' apprenticeship fast enough to fill the rapidly expanding munitions works.

This policy was not always carried out smoothly. Even though there was some central direction after the establishment of the Man-Power Distribution Board under Austen Chamberlain in August 1916, there were often divided counsels, and at the worst time, after the beginning of compulsory military service in 1916, some men found themselves shuttled backwards and forwards between industry and the front. Again, the German spring offensive of 1918 led to a temporary panic in which military commanders forced the destruction of carefully laid plans to harness key workers to such vital industries as coal mining, agriculture and even engineering, for the sake of filling the depleted battalions with the last reserves of able-bodied men.

Yet the extent of the transfer carried through was remarkable. Several occupations in which women had begun to replace men to a slight extent before 1914, were turned permanently into female preserves. These included work in shops and offices, in hotels, theatres and cinemas, and to some extent on public transport. On the other hand, in many factories attracting large numbers of female workers, the male labour was easily re-absorbed in the course of 1919, and much of the female labour which had replaced it left industry again.

One by-product of this shift in employment was a revolutionary advance in the economic position of women, whose new-found economic independence was rewarded with the vote after the war with virtually no opposition. Another important by-product was a greater concern for workers' welfare in industrial work, as distinct from the abolition of abuses and the reduction of danger with which previous factory legislation had been mostly concerned. Encouraged by tax concessions, and partly also by a desire to reduce drunkenness among war workers, 867 works canteens were built between November 1915 and November 1918. In September 1915 a Health of Munitions Workers Committee was appointed, and one of its first tasks was the sponsoring of inquiries into industrial fatigue[1] and

---

[1] E.g. *Memorandum* No. 12 (1916. Cd. 8344), and *Industrial Efficiency and Fatigue* (1917. Cd. 8511); also, Henry Carter, *The Control of the Drink Trade* (1918).

hours and conditions of factory work. By November 1918, about 1,000 women supervisors had been appointed to observe and regulate the conditions of work of women, at a time when some 1,600,000 were employed, directly or indirectly, by the Government.[1] It was in the first World War that some of the earliest experiments were made which proved the connection between welfare and efficiency.

400,000 temporary women war workers were drawn from domestic service, but most others had taken up paid employment for the first time and total female employment in industry, transport, commerce and the professions increased from 3,280,000 in July 1914 to 4,950,000 in November 1918, or by over 1½ million. This compared with a loss of 2½ million men in the same occupations in this period. Total employment was thus reduced, but in some trade groups it had declined much more than in proportion.

Among the manufacturing industries, textiles and clothing, paper and printing and wood were the heaviest losers, and there were reductions in employment also in building, transport and in hotels and the entertainments industry. These groups lost, between them, nearly 1·4 million male workers, and gained only some 90,000 female workers, thus sustaining a net loss of 1·3 million. In most other occupations, the loss of men was made good to a greater or lesser degree by an increase of employment of women; Thus food, drink and tobacco lost 113,000 men, but gained 34,000 women; commerce and finance lost 555,000, but gained 449,000; and the Civil Service and Local Government Service lost 173,000 men, and gained 201,000 women. The only civilian sector which increased its employment not only of women but even of men between July 1914 and November 1918 was the munitions industry, including the metals and chemical industries and the Government industrial establishments. Despite initial volunteering, and later recruitment and comb-outs, the number of men employed rose from 1,869,000 to 2,309,000, and of women from 212,000 to 945,000, a total net increase of nearly 1,200,000 workers.[2] It was there that the chief labour problems of the war were bound to occur.

The general scarcity of labour might have been expected to push up wages; instead, workers seemed content to allow the value of their real wages to be whittled away by the creeping inflation of 1915–17. Most money wages were raised slightly in the course of these years, but not nearly as much as prices, until by July 1917 real wages had dropped by one-fifth compared with their immediate pre-war level: Bowley's wage index of those in full time employment stood then at 135–140, with the cost of

[1] D. Lloyd George, *War Memoirs* (1933), Vol. 1, pp. 292, 341 ff.; Asa Briggs, *Social Thought and Social Action* (1961), chapter 5.
[2] A. W. Kirkaldy (ed.), *Industry and Finance* (1920), p. 96.

living at 160–180 (July 1914 = 100); according to Kuczynski, real wages had dropped from 97 to 74 (1900 = 100), and according to Layton and Crowther, from 174 to 142 (1850 = 100).[1]

There were several causes of this parodoxical behaviour of wage-earners. First, trade unions never fight as hard against a drop in real wages caused by rising prices as against a cut in money wage rates. Secondly, in the early months the war was generally expected to be of short duration, and the loss in real wages was felt to be an appropriate sacrifice on the part of those who stayed behind, to match that of the volunteers. Thirdly, the replacement of men by women (paid at 50–60% of men's rates even when doing a man's job) greatly reduced the pressure on the labour market. Fourthly, with trade unions voluntarily disarmed by their Treasury Agreement of March 1915, later incorporated in the first Munitions of War Act, which forswore the strike weapon, and prominent labour leaders joining the Civil Service and even the War Cabinet, the main instrument of working-class pressure had been voluntarily laid aside, and nothing else was yet in sight. And lastly, the decline was in real wage *rates* only; earnings, with secure full employment, overtime, night work, and bonus or piece payments, taken in conjunction with long hours of repetition work in various industries, secured for the workers rising earnings which, on the whole, roughly kept in step with the rises in the cost of living.

There were some signs of dissatisfaction from an early date. The miners, for example, refused to accept any curb on their right to strike, and the South Wales miners actually went on strike, defying the Act within a few days of its passing, and emerged victorious. The agreement to suspend restrictive trade union practices was, in many areas, more honoured in the breach than in the observance:

> Trade unions were anxious that when the war was over and when the men came back, they should not return to find their positions taken up by underpaid labour; that they should not have been worsened in their circumstances for having given their services voluntarily and freely for the benefit of their country.[2]

A pacifist section of the I.L.P. opposed the war from the beginning, while on the Clyde, much influenced by the Socialist Labour Party and the I.L.P., trouble was brewing in the engineering trades from early 1915 onwards. There was a strike in the armaments works there in February, when a claim for 2*d.* an hour, justifiable even on pre-war grounds, was

[1] J. Kuczynski, *A Short History of Labour Conditions in Great Britain, 1750 to the Present Day* (1946 ed.), p. 120; A. L. Bowley, *Prices and Wages in the United Kingdom, 1914–1920* (Oxford, 1921), p. 106.

[2] Alfred Evans, a moderate, quoted in A. W. Kirkaldy (ed.), *Credit, Industry and the War* (1915), p. 58.

turned down in spite of price rises since, and the Committee on Production, in its first arbitration award, awarded 1*d*. only in March 1915. By and large, however, despite falling wage rates, more intensive work, and many inconveniences, the working classes showed no serious signs of dissatisfaction in the first two and a half years of the war.

It was in the course of 1917 that all the factors which had kept wage claims within narrow limits seemed to break down at once. The impotence of the official trade union leadership was neutralized by the shop stewards on the one hand, and a more complete system of arbitration on the other. New members flocked into the trade unions, whose membership was doubled in the course of the war, from 3,959,000 in 1913 to 8,023,000 in 1919. Feelings of patriotism and self-sacrifice were giving way to disillusionment at the sight of the uninhibited profiteering and luxury spending of the rich, when it contrasted with the food shortages and queues, and occasional complete breakdowns in supplies of tea, sugar, meat, fats or potatoes in the working-class quarters. The intensity of work, and thus the bonus earnings, could be increased no farther, while prices went on rising, and there was growing dissatisfaction with the capriciously high earnings of unskilled men on piecework by the side of the fixed datal rates of skilled men. Other grievances noted by the commissions on industrial unrest and the Select Committee on National Expenditure were the inability of workers in some industries to make up earnings by piecework and overtime, the restrictions on liberty, especially the licensing laws affecting the sale of alcohol, the powers of employers over the mobility of their workers by the withholding of the leaving certificates, and compulsory arbitration.[1]

Taking July 1914 as 100, controlled food prices stood at 118 in January 1915, 160 in August 1916 and 202 in August 1917, when they were stabilized for about a year, before being allowed to rise to 233 in November 1918 and a maximum of 291 in November 1920. Uncontrolled foods stood at 213 in July 1917 and 384 in November 1918, textiles at 234 and 307, and soap at 133 and 233.[2] In the face of these rising prices the Committee on Production, which had statutory powers of arbitration for all Government work, jettisoned its previous policy of holding down wages.[3] Other wage rates followed, and by the middle of 1919 the pre-war level of real wage rates was almost reached again. While in 1915 and in 1916 the weekly wages bill (of some £9 million) was estimated to have

[1] *Select Committee of H.o.C. on National Expenditure*, 167 (1917); E. Cannan, 'Industrial Unrest', *Econ. J.*, 27/108, 1917; Cole and Postgate, *The Common People* (1938), chapter 41; M. B. Hammond, *British Labor Conditions and Legislation during the War* (New York, 1919), chapter 9.
[2] W. H. Beveridge, *British Food Control* (1928), pp. 322–3.
[3] W. H. Beveridge, *Power and Influence* (1953), pp. 133–4.

increased by £600,000–700,000 over the previous year, in the three years 1917, 1918 and 1919 the increase in the weekly wages bill amounted to £2–3 million every year.[1]

Meanwhile, however, there had set in a serious decline in morale, particularly in the centres of the munitions industry, the Clyde, Sheffield, Barrow and Coventry. The March Revolution in Russia, and signs of revolt among the peoples of Germany, France, Austria and other belligerents, had alerted the British Government. From early 1917 onward, the morale of the working population became one of its principal preoccupations. A separate Ministry of Labour was created, and 1¼ million additional munitions workers were brought within the scope of the unemployment insurance provisions. Special commissions reported on 'industrial unrest'. Much of the control apparatus, including food rationing and subsidies, excess profits duties, exemption schemes from conscription, and wage arbitration awards as well as the plans of the newly established Ministry of Reconstruction were drawn up very much under the shadow of the threat from the war-weary and rebellious working classes.

The problem was most acute in the munitions industries, which may be taken to epitomize the difficulties of adaptation to the war conditions, and the critical importance of morale. Here the key section was the engineering industry, and by far the most powerful trade union concerned was the Amalgamated Society of Engineers. Other craft unions of importance were the Boilermakers' Society (in the shipyards), the Ironfounders, the Patternmakers, the Machine Workers, and the Steam Engine Makers. All these and some others organized the skilled men, while several of the recently founded general workers' unions had a scattered but growing membership among the labourers and helpers in the engineering works and the shipyards. Altogether, there were some 200 skilled engineering unions with 450,000 members, some 12 unskilled unions had 75,000 members in engineering workshops, and the National Union of Railwaymen had 30,000 in railway workshops. Thus 550,000 men were organized, about one-third of the industry, and of these 161,000 were in the A.S.E.[2]

The engineering industry had been in the throes of some painful changes and readjustments at the time of the outbreak of war. There was, on the one hand, the new, semi-automatic, specialized machinery which made it possible to subdivide the work and replace skilled men by 'semi-skilled' workers who would be proficient in one part of the trade only, and get appropriately lower wages. There was also, in combination with the

[1] A. L. Bowley, *Prices and Wages*, p. 95.
[2] Branko Pribićević, *The Shop Stewards' Movement and Workers' Control 1910–1922* (Oxford, 1959), p. 27.

first change, the growing movement to introduce 'scientific management' as established in the U.S.A., involving time and motion study, re-allocation of work and complex premium bonus systems designed to get the maximum of work out of each worker. The A.S.E. as the chief spokes-man of the skilled crafts was opposed to both trends and had fought the costly 1897–8 strike over the issue of piecework. The strike had been settled on the employers' terms, but the A.S.E. was gradually trying to win back some of the ground given up then. Superimposed on this potentially explosive situation was a series of wage claims and disputes, based on the rising prices since 1908, and a movement for an 8-hour day in which the rank-and-file membership appeared to be far more militant than their leadership.[1]

The Treasury Agreement of March 1915, and the Munitions Act which incorporated it, had obliged the unions to give up precisely the main points of contention of peace-time. Division of jobs so as to allow 'dilution' by semi-skilled workers, unskilled men and even women, and piecework with incentive schemes were all to be admitted into the workshops, while the unions voluntarily laid down any powers they might have had of controlling the detailed methods of introducing all these concessions, by their acquiescence in compulsory arbitration and the outlawing of strikes. It is true that there was a Government promise that all the pre-war conditions would be restored at the end of the war, but few men believed that the march of history could be reversed in this way.

Dilution itself proceeded by several stages. In March 1915, the Shells and Fuses Agreement permitted women and young persons to work special single-purpose machines, involving virtually no skill, while the Treasury Agreement, of greater potential significance, permitted the employment of semi-skilled workers on tasks and on machines hitherto solely the pre-serve of fully-skilled men. By the dilution scheme of October 1915, formerly skilled work could be further sub-divided and rearranged so as to allow unskilled men and women to take the place of the 'semi-skilleds', who, in turn, could be up-graded. About a year later, in September 1916, followed a general substitution scheme, as the inflow of semi-skilled men ceased and many of them were called up to the forces, and more and more machines were manned by unfit men, cripples and women, who could be up-graded at will. The last stage began in the summer of 1917, when even skilled men began to be called up. There was now no limit to substitution and up-grad-ing, and there were many signs that the quality of the work was beginning to suffer as a result. In January 1916 the Ministry of Munitions had ap-pointed special Dilution Commissioners for the Tyne and the Clyde respec-tively, composed of employers, workers and officials, to design dilution

[1] J. B. Jefferys, *The Story of the Engineers, 1800–1945* (1945), chapters 7 and 8.

schemes to fit the special condition of each separate works, but they were later disbanded and the Ministry undertook to apply the policy directly, causing much friction in the process.[1]

These changes occurred while new sets of payments by results and bonus rates had to be negotiated shop by shop, including minimum wages for women, until special arbitration tribunals for dilutees were set up under the Munitions of War (Amendment) Act of 1916, and while extension of premises, or moves to newly established works, brought fresh problems. Before the war, employers had negotiated separately with representatives of the various craft and other unions represented in their shops, whose district or national executive took the major decisions on wages and conditions. Now, the unions had largely abdicated their role, and many leaders were engaged in speeding war work and in enforcing national agreements; at the same time the problems which multiplied in the works were not those of just one craft, but those affecting the workmen as a whole, whatever their divided union allegiance.

These conditions favoured the rise of the shop stewards as the representatives and leaders of the men in the engineering shops, shipyards and arsenals irrespective of which union they belonged to or, indeed, of whether they belonged to a union at all. Before the war the shop stewards' main tasks had been the collection of union dues, the checking of membership cards and the negotiations over the settlement of piece rates, but now they became the obvious authority to settle many immediate questions. The shop stewards forming their factory works committees, with chief shop stewards or conveners at their head, came to be taken, by employers and Government alike, as the accredited spokesmen of the munition workers.[2]

The shop stewards and the works committees developed spontaneously, without any central direction or initial planning, and they did not conform to a single pattern. In large munitions centres representatives from all works formed a district Workers' Council. Some, as in Coventry or Sheffield, collaborated closely with their official District Committee of unions such as the A.S.E., others were looked upon as usurping the functions of the established societies and their officers. Many of the leading shop stewards had a background of Syndicalism and the Amalgamation Committee Movement in the immediate pre-war years, and before long the workers' councils began to grope for a philosophy and national organization of their own. Under the leadership of J. T. Murphy of Sheffield, an attempt was made to link up the workers' councils in the different centres, to form local and National Industrial Committees for the different industries, and local and National Works Councils. These

---

[1] G. D. H. Cole, *Trade Unions and Munitions* (Oxford, 1923).
[2] G. D. H. Cole, *Workshop Organization* (Oxford, 1923).

were held to be the direct and true representatives of the working classes and they were to be used for distinctly revolutionary purposes. There were, in fact, four important national conferences held, and the shop stewards wielded much power for a time, but the movement was largely limited to engineering, with some embryonic organization in the boot and shoe, cotton and woollen industries, in mining and on the railways. The power of the shop stewards' movement waned as soon as the war was over; the National Workers' Committee Movement, established with a new constitution in 1921, represented their last flicker of independent life.[1]

Meanwhile, however, the shop stewards' organizations bore the brunt of the war-time disputes. The Clyde Workers' Committee was the first, being formed out of the delegates to the Clyde 'Central Withdrawal of Labour Committee' of the strike of February 1915. In November of that year it led the 'rent strike', which persuaded the Government to take the momentous decision of keeping rents down to near their pre-war level by the Rent Restriction Act. In the winter of 1915–16 the Clyde committee began to attack the worst abuses of dilution and the Munitions Act in general, and its delegates roused the shop stewards in other armaments centres. A renewed strike flared up on the Clyde in March 1916, in the teeth of opposition by the official union leadership, after the arrest of some of the leaders and repeated suppression of the local workers' paper, on the right of a convener to visit all the sections of his firm, and several of the leaders were deported from the Clyde without charge or trial. At the same time, the Government began to treat the Clyde with particular care and circumspection, and there were no further major interruptions of work there for the rest of the war.

Elsewhere there was mounting indignation towards the end of 1916 at the growing number of skilled men called up in breach of the Government's specific pledges of exemption. As a result of a strike of munition workers in Sheffield on this issue, organized by the local shop stewards' committee, the 'trade card' scheme of exemption for skilled men was instituted by the Government. The scheme, in effect, handed over completely to the trade unions the task of certifying who were the skilled men who should be exempt from military service. Such an administrative device might be taken as a proof of the incompetence of the Manpower Board and the Director-General of National Service, Neville Chamberlain; but it could also indicate the delicate manner in which trade unions and shop stewards had by that time come to be handled.

The trade card scheme, which exempted many workers in non-war trades, and did not protect others in key jobs, as it was organized by

[1] Pribićević, *passim.*

84

unions and not by occupations, had, indeed, little to recommend it. But the announcement by the Government in April 1917 that the mounting labour shortage required its scrapping, together with an extension of dilution to private, non-war work, and a scheme of wholesale volunteer industrial enlistment, sent up a wave of protest. It was the proposal to extend dilution to private work which caused the most bitter opposition, superimposed as it was on the breach of trust implied by the unilateral abandonment of the trade card scheme, as also on the war-weariness and hardships, the suspicion of the Government's war aims and other causes of political dissatisfaction. When a small firm near Rochdale tried to apply dilution to private work without even waiting for the promised Government sanction, there broke out the most widespread engineering strike of the war in May 1917. 60,000 workers were on strike in Lancashire, 15,000 in Sheffield and Rotherham, 30,000 in Coventry, and the men came out from the munition centres in the whole of southern England. The only major centres to remain at work were the Clyde and the Tyne. These strikes were exclusively organized by the shop stewards.

The first reaction of the Government was to arrest the strike leaders, but the men ultimately won their point. Winston Churchill replaced Dr. Addison as Minister of Munitions, the dilution clause was withdrawn, the 'leaving certificate', the most resented aspect of earlier Munitions Acts, was also abolished, and by the new Munitions Act of 1917 national wage advances were to apply to non-federated as well as federated firms. The trade card scheme, however, was replaced by a 'schedule of protected occupations', under which wholesale recruitment of skilled men in April–December 1917 was carried through, and a revised, even stricter schedule limited the exemption still further in 1918, under the threat of the German spring offensive. These measures were applied in spite of bitter opposition on the part of the engineering workers. An attempt in 1918, under D.O.R.R. 8A, to prevent certain firms from employing men with certain scarce skills by 'labour embargoes' was defeated by a strike in Coventry.

Perhaps the most important result of the labour unrest in 1917–18 was the belated upward revision of wage scales. In the munitions industry, where the Committee on Production, as arbitration tribunal, had powers to make legally binding awards, wage awards were to be national by an agreement in February 1917 between employers and some 50 engineering trade unions, and the wage scales were to be revised every four months. The new system proved much more flexible than the old. At the time of its inauguration in February 1917, after $2\frac{1}{2}$ years of war, the total increases amounted to only 7s. per week for the main group of skilled engineering craftsmen; in the course of six awards to December 1918, this was raised to 28s. 6d. Further, the awards of the munitions industry were applied with little or no change in the chemical, shipbuilding, heavy engineering, tool and cutlery making, and other industries. In May 1917 the Committee on Production was re-grouped in several panels to get through its work more quickly. It became the Court of Arbitration under the Wages (Temporary Regulation) Act of 1918, and in 1919 it became the Industrial Court under the Industrial Courts Act of that year. The system of changing wages uniformly over the whole country and the whole industry by arbitration continued into 1920.

One of the most striking changes wrought by the war of 1914–18 was the relative rise in the wage of the unskilled, as compared with that of the skilled man. Thus in the engineering and shipbuilding trades, representative wage rates moved as follows (July 1914 = 100):[1]

	Skilled Fitter and Turner	Skilled Plater	Unskilled Labourer
July 1917	134	130	154
July 1918	173	169	213
July 1920	231	223	309

This difference may, to some extent, be ascribed to the simple effect of granting flat-rate increases: thus the 7s. awarded to engineers by early 1917, if added to a pre-war wage of 40s. for skilled men, added $17\frac{1}{2}\%$ to the index; if added to the labourer's pre-war 20s., it added 35%. In turn, these flat-rate increases and the reduced differentials resulting from them could be justified on the grounds that during emergencies the skilled men might suffer a drop in real wages while those of the unskilled men at the margin of subsistence should not be lowered. This kind of consideration could also apply at other times, e.g. in depressions, and the shift in relative incomes of skilled and unskilled men was never fully reversed after the war and represented a powerful secular trend in the direction of reducing the differentials between the skilled craftsmen and the unskilled labourers, in earnings as well as in status. But an important trend of this kind was bound to have a deeper cause than the accident of awarding flat-rate, instead of percentage, increases. It represented the underlying reality in most industries of the declining importance of manual skill of the old type, and the growing predominance of semi-skilled or virtually unskilled machine-minders.

The tensions created by this process even before the war were aggravated in the munitions industry in war-time by the fact that skilled engineers were often on time rates, while the dilutees worked on piece rates and bonus work which might give them earnings in excess of those of the skilled men, who often set up or maintained the machines they worked on. Where skilled men were on piece rates also, it had been the rule, before the war, that the delicate jobs on which piece rates produced

[1] Bowley, *Prices and Wages*, p. 131.

low earnings, were fairly mixed with straightforward work yielding fat wage packets. Dilution meant that the lucrative, repetitive jobs went to the unskilled dilutees, while the skilled men were permanently on the intricate and difficult jobs, yielding lean earnings only.

There was thus a set of special grievances among skilled munitions workers which came to a head late in 1917. A strike of skilled iron moulders who were earning less than their labourers induced the Committee on Production to grant a $12\frac{1}{2}\%$ increase in October to all skilled datal workers in the munitions industry. The lines between skills and earnings in practice were not very clearly drawn, however, and the $12\frac{1}{2}\%$ award set off a series of strikes in different centres, at a time when the Government had its hands full with quite a separate complete stoppage at Coventry over the recognition of shop stewards. In December 1917, therefore, the $12\frac{1}{2}\%$ was extended to all time workers, skilled and unskilled alike, and in January 1918 a $7\frac{1}{2}\%$ bonus was granted, in compensation, to all piece workers.

These developments in the engineering and allied industries were mirrored, more or less faithfully, in most others. In many, the status and wages of the unskilled labourer and semi-skilled machine-minder improved and led to the demand of these workers to enter the formerly exclusive craft unions. The practice of industry-wide, in the place of local, collective bargaining, which first emerged in 1914–18,[1] was destined to spread in the inter-war years, while the Trade Board Act of 1918, extending the original Boards in the sweated trades to wherever 'no adequate machinery exists for the effective regulation of wages throughout the trade', further emphasized the trend towards national wage bargaining. Lastly, the war-time shop stewards' movement furnished much of the drive behind the giant amalgamations of the early 1920's, of which the Amalgamated Engineering Union, created out of the A.S.E. and nine other societies, was the earliest.[2]

6. 'RECONSTRUCTION' AND POST-WAR PLANNING

As early as December 1914 the Board of Trade considered that there was an 'urgent need' to discuss the problem of unemployment after the war.[3] By the end of 1916 the labour unrest was lending new poignancy to this view, while the sustained sacrifices demanded of all classes of the population during the war were giving birth to the widespread feeling that victory should bring more than a mere return to pre-war conditions. The later phrase of 'homes fit for heroes' expressed a general hope that out of the horrors and deprivations of the war there should emerge a

[1] S. and B. Webb, *History of Trade Unionism* (1920 ed.), chapter 9; B. C. Roberts, *The Trades Union Congress, 1868–1921* (1958), chapter 8.
[2] Jefferys, *op. cit.*, pp. 189 ff.
[3] W. H. Beveridge, *Power and Influence* (1953), p. 136.

society more worthy of the sacrifices it had demanded in its defence. 'Government emphasis on reconstruction grew out of the sufferings and the low spirit of the citizens during the three bitter years beginning in 1914.'[1]

The Government did not remain unaware of this mood, and it was also conscious of the post-war problems that were likely to arise out of the violently changed trading and financial conditions.[2] It set up a Reconstruction Committee in 1916 which was turned, in July 1917, into the Ministry of Reconstruction under Dr. Addison.[3] The Ministry did its work through committees, some of which had been sub-committees of the earlier organization, the two most important being those discussing demobilization and machinery for dealing with labour questions.

Demobilization plans were drawn up with some care, and included transitional unemployment pay, housing, and provisions for both munition workers and soldiers and sailors. In the event, the carefully worked-out scheme broke down after November 1918 as soldiers refused to wait their turn and made their own way home, but their re-absorption into civilian posts caused much less trouble than expected. Trade union statistics of unemployment never rose above the 2·9% level of March 1919, the able-bodied men found employment very quickly, while within a year, three-quarters of a million women workers left paid employment with hardly a trace, and others returned to domestic service.

Labour questions were discussed by a committee under J. H. Whitley, later Speaker of the House of Commons. Its first report in 1917, the 'Whitley Report', proposed standing joint industrial councils, made up of representatives of employers and workers, on national, district and works level, as a peaceful means of resolving differences on labour questions and others. These proposals, although by no means new,[4] excited much attention in view of the existing labour unrest, and the Minister was urged to appoint Interim Industrial Reconstruction Committees until either these Joint Industrial Councils or Trade Boards, proposed in the Whitley Committee's second report, could take their place. In the event, Joint Industrial Councils were set up in a large number of minor industries by 1921, though few had any district sub-committees, and few survived for long or were of much importance; their only really successful application came to be in the Government service, including the Civil Service, the dockyards and the Post Office, when the Cabinet could at last be persuaded to permit them.

[1] S. J. Hurwitz, *State Intervention in Britain. A Study of Economic Control and Social Response, 1914–1919* (New York, 1949), pp. 286–7.

[2] W. H. Dawson (ed.), *After-War Problems* (1917).

[3] Ch. Addison, *Politics From Within, 1911–1918*, 2 Vols. (1924), Vol. 2, chapters 14, 15, 18.

[4] E.g. A. W. Kirkaldy (ed.), *Labour, Finance and the War* (1916), pp. 42 ff., and *Industry and Finance* (1917), pp. 160 ff.; M. B. Hammond, *British Labor Conditions and Legislation during the War* (New York, 1919), pp. 272–9.

'Reconstruction' and Post-War Planning

The Ministry of Reconstruction also considered the post-war supply of raw materials for Britain, the Empire and the Allies, as well as industrial capacity and demand, and organized special inquiries into several industries. By March 1918, there were also in existence committees on education, on scientific and industrial research, on Empire settlement and on civil air transport, among others. These activities of the Ministry of Reconstruction show a disposition to carry out a fair modicum of economic planning, though no formal machinery for it was ready when peace came. There was a rash of new departments, but this was a victory for bureaucracy as much as for reconstruction planning: besides the Ministry of Transport (1919), the D.S.I.R. (1916) and the Ministry of Labour (1916), mentioned already, and the purely war-time departments like the Ministries of Munition and of Shipping, and the Coal Control, there were also the Ministry of Health (1919), the Ministry of Pensions (1917), the Forestry Commission (1919), the Medical Research Council (1920) and the Electricity Commissioners (1919).

However radical its proposals, the Government was in continual danger of being outflanked on the left. The successes of a largely planned economy, introduced by adherents of private enterprise doctrines as the only means to save the country from economic chaos, made many converts to Socialism, while the trade union membership went up by leaps and bounds and came increasingly under the influence of its militant wing. The official leadership of the Labour Party had been loyal supporters of the Liberal Government and Liberal–Conservative coalition, and had been rewarded with several ministerial posts; but the resignation of Arthur Henderson, Labour's representative in the War Cabinet, because of the Government's refusal to consider a negotiated peace, though he was replaced by another Labour adherent, absolved a section of the party from further loyalty to the coalition, and combined the .pacifist instincts of some with the revolutionary ardour of others in drawing up a new independent programme.[1] The new constitution of 1918 allowed individual membership of the Labour Party, tempering the conservatism of the large trade unions, and in place of the pre-war Liberal attitude, there was a new Socialist programme, drawn up largely by Sidney Webb and supported by Henderson, embracing in its four main points the 'universal enforcement of a National Minimum', the old demand of the Webbs, 'democratic control of industry', including nationalization, as well as proposals for a capital levy and further redistributive taxation.

Labour (together with the independent, non-Coalition Liberals) was badly defeated in the General Election immediately following the war, but that 'khaki election' had been won by the Coalition Government largely by appealing to the passions of hatred of Germany, rather than

[1] S. and B. Webb, *History of Trade Unionism* (1920 ed.), chapter 11.

by a reconstruction programme at home: the question of reconstruction was still open in 1919–21. Labour's policy of nationalization had much widespread support because of the sheer technical and economic efficiency of the nationally managed undertakings,[1] and while the Socialist demands for a widely planned economy[2] were soon pushed aside by the overwhelming desire of businessmen for freedom to profit from the incipient boom, a few Government-controlled industries and services, notably coal mining, shipping and the railways, could not be so easily disposed of. The main battle was fought over coal, especially since the miners themselves were insistent that it be nationalized.

The immediate post-war years, with their frequent strikes, both for political and economic aims, their unsettled markets, the confident demands of Labour and the apparent weakness with which employers and the Government were prepared to give in to them, have sometimes been considered years of potential revolution. The example of Russia was feared to be infectious, and indeed it was on the issue of arming the enemies of the young Soviet State that the Labour Movement most directly defied and defeated the Government. According to this view, it was Lloyd George's skilful delaying tactics, especially by calling the Industrial Conference and by appointing the Sankey Coal Commission, until the appetite for nationalization had evaporated, which preserved the free enterprise system in this country.[3]

This view exaggerates the revolutionary mood of the Labour Party. If the Socialists of Germany, Austria and her successor states failed to overturn the established order in countries in which the social fabric and traditional loyalties had been disrupted so fundamentally, it seems unlikely that British capitalism was ever in any serious danger. All that can be said is that the period of 1918–21 was the high point of Socialist endeavour—organization, membership and propaganda being at a higher level than ever before, while the comforts of office and the frittering away of energies in piecemeal reforms had not yet set in.

Though the danger was small, the delaying tactics were undoubtedly effective. The Sankey Commission of 1919 produced a report which kept the parties talking and thus prevented a change in ownership of the coal mines. The National Industrial Conference of employers' and trade union representatives failed to establish a permanent peaceful meeting ground of capital and labour, and, having met its objective of delay, was allowed to expire quietly in 1921. At the same time, the inflationary price rises of

---

[1] p. 53 above.

[2] E.g. Sir Leo Chiozza Money, *The Triumph of Nationalization* (1920).

[3] Charles Loch Mowat, *Britain Between the Wars, 1918–1940* (1956 ed.), chapter 1, sect. 9; G. D. H. Cole and R. Postgate, *The Common People 1746–1938* (1938), pp. 535 ff.

1918–20, which forced the unions to spend most of their energies on raising wages, did as much as any deliberate action to divert interest from grand schemes of nationalization.

Something remained of the high hopes and militant actions of the years 1917–21. The Industrial Courts Act of 1919, one of the results of the Whitley Report, extended the Ministry of Labour's power of conciliation and Inquiry, without power of compulsory arbitration. There was progressive legislation in many fields, such as the Housing and Town Planning Act of 1919, and the extension of insurance by the Unemployment Insurance Act of 1920. Less widely noted was the general reduction in working hours in 1919, a result of post-war trade union power as well as of studies in industrial fatigue. In virtually every industry, the working day was reduced from 9 hours[1] to about 8, and 46½–48 hours became the standard working week, at no loss of wages; even in the steel works, where two shifts of 12 hours average had been worked, the change was to three 8-hour shifts.[2] The miners reduced their shift to 7 hours, but this could not be held for long. In the other occupations, this reduction in hours of work became firmly established, and remained perhaps the most valuable permanent gain from all the high hopes of post-war 'reconstruction'.

[1] In contemporary terminology, a 9-hour day meant a 54-hour week, usually 9½ hours on weekdays, 6½ on Saturdays.
[2] A. L. Bowley, *Prices and Wages*, Appx. III.

CHAPTER III

British Industry and Transport between the Wars

I. PROGRESS IN SCIENCE AND TECHNOLOGY

During the long peace to 1914 the certainty of material progress had become an idea widely and firmly rooted, but between the wars the prevailing belief was mostly one of stagnation, if not decline, in the economic sphere. This change in the economic climate did not become evident immediately. There was, for a time, a wild boom in which fortunes could be made quickly and industrialists and bankers talked glibly of returning to pre-war positions, improved by the defeat of Germany, the chief foreign competitor before 1914. Even the slump of 1921 was believed to be the result of a mere temporary adjustment. It was only when Britain proved unable to steer herself out of the doldrums of the 1920's, in Pigou's phrase, when she failed to take part in the world boom of 1925-9, and then sank, with the rest of the world, into the depression of the 1930's, that pessimism began to gain the upper hand. While Socialists proclaimed that the last great crisis of capitalism was at hand, the defenders of the existing order, with few (if significant) exceptions, could only counsel control, restriction, retrenchment and decline.

The ordinary citizen may remember the inter-war years chiefly for the queues of the unemployed, the idle factories, yards and mines, the hunger marchers and the spiritual impoverishment and economic insecurity which sent some other countries, not very differently placed from this, down into the abyss of a willing acceptance of Fascist dictatorship. In Britain political democracy was preserved but no Government, whether Conservative, Labour or National, knew how to cure the blight on the body economic. The waste of human and material resources of those years has become all the clearer when compared with the world economic progress since 1945.

But beside the waste, there was also the most vigorous industrial and technological development, a general rise in standards of living, and a greater diffusion of wealth and welfare. If progress was not always smooth, it must be remembered that British industry had to undergo a radical change in a short period, undertaken in the midst of a world depression and without very clear notions of the task to be accomplished. From undue and over-long reliance on the old staple export industries, Britain had to engineer a major switch to new industries, requiring different skills and raw materials, different locations, and aimed increasingly at a rising home market. As it was done without planning and with scarcely an understanding of its direction, it was done hesitantly, clumsily, and expensively. This, in a nut-shell, is the story of British industry since 1919.

The change was accompanied, and was partly caused by, rapid technological progress which changed the structure of many existing industries and created others by introducing new products and services, materials or processes. While the rate of technical progress is difficult to measure, it seems safe to say that in the inter-war years the consumer was offered more new products, and the industrialist more new machinery and materials, than at any comparable period in history.

There was still a considerable time lag between invention and application. The major new industries which emerged into full maturity in 1919–39[1] were all based on inventions or discoveries made in the generation before 1914, if not earlier, just as the major discoveries of the inter-war years (e.g. television, penicillin, the jet engine and nylon) were turned to practical use only after 1939. Yet it would be true to say that it was in this period that at least some part of British industry became interested for the first time in technological discovery itself. It was significant that in a country which had so long maintained an industrial superiority by the skill of its artisans, and in which industrialists (not to mention dons) were content to rest in ignorance of the natural sciences,[2] this consciousness for the need of scientific training and research arose first because of military needs.[3]

With the aid of the Department of Scientific and Industrial Research, set up in 1916 to provide Government support, financial and otherwise, for scientific research with possible industrial applications, much research work was carried out by independent institutions, such as Universities, and 13 successful grant-aided co-operative research associations for whole industries were established in the period 1918–21, 8 in 1923–38, and 4 in 1941–4. In 1918–23, 24 research associations altogether were licensed by the Board of Trade.[4] The Medical Research Council (1920), the Agricultural Research Council (1931) and several research stations, of which the National Physical Laboratory (1900) was the earliest, also received Government funds.

[1] Including electrical engineering, chemicals, rayon, radio, motion pictures, aircraft and motor engineering.
[2] E.g. R. F. Harrod, *The Prof.* (1959), pp. 17–27, 53.
[3] p. 54 above.
[4] Sir H. Frank Heath and A. L. Hetherington, *Industrial Research and Development in the United Kingdom* (1946), chapter 32 and Appx. II.

Apart from Government sponsorship, which declined in importance after the early 1920's, private industry was itself turning increasingly to research and systematic control techniques to improve its methods and products and discover new ones. The effects were most uneven, and perhaps half the industrial research expenditure was incurred in three industries only, electrical engineering, chemicals and aircraft, each with strong military associations. Even there, however, the Balfour Committee found in the mid-1920's that research expenditure by British firms was quite inadequate when set against that of comparable firms in the U.S.A. and Germany.[1]

Yet, compared with the pre-war years, progress had been rapid. Partly with official sanction,[2] a quiet revolution in the relative status of scientific and technical education was beginning,[3] no less powerful for being unrecognized, and technical colleges and research laboratories in firms increased steadily and unobtrusively in number and standing.[4] 'Our youth should be taught the facts of science,' pleaded Lord Moulton in 1917,[5] 'they must also be trained in its methods. In every industry there is scope for research and on it must depend the maintenance of our position in the industrial struggle for existence.' Interest in the technical marvels of the new age, such as radio, aircraft, photography and film, more powerful telescopes and faster means of land transport, helped to popularize science from the 1920's onwards among wide sections of the population.[6]

Even in the industries most tenaciously clinging to 'practical experience', as distinct from scientific training, in coal, iron and steel, engineering and shipbuilding, it could be said at the end of the 1920's that

> the scientific spirit in these days is a vital factor in manufacturing success. Its importance cannot be exaggerated. It is not too much to say that in the research laboratory lies the source of prosperity in the future to labour and capital alike. Research secures the means of reducing costs and increasing output, but it goes far beyond this . . . In this country we have long hung in the rear of the application of science to industry. The relations between the two have often been marked by a degree of mutual depreciation, if not actual contempt,

---

[1] Committee on Industry and Trade (Balfour Committee), *Survey of Industries*, Vol. 1 (1927), pp. 318–20.

[2] *Natural Science in Education* (1918. Cd. 9011).

[3] I.A.A.M. and S.M.A., *The Teaching of Science in Secondary Schools* (1958 ed.) pp. 8–9.

[4] Balfour Committee, *Report*, Vol. 1, pp. 178 ff.

[5] In his introduction to the notable volume, *Science and the Nation* (1917, Cambridge), ed. by A. C. Seward, pp. xix–xx.

[6] C. L. Mowat, *Britain between the Wars* (1956 ed.), pp. 219–22.

which has isolated each from the other and kept them apart. We have seen this disposition changed, and scientific research is now regarded with respect by even the most conservative of our industrial leaders.[1]

In many fields, notably in the various branches of the chemical industry, in electrical and mechanical engineering, including motor engineering, in aircraft and ship design, and also to some extent in metallurgy, in food processing and agriculture, research came to be undertaken on a large scale, involving the collaboration of scientists of various disciplines, a measure of planning and co-ordination, and the much more costly work of 'development'. In the twentieth-century invention, 'the origin of the idea may have been far back, perhaps in the genius of some inventive individual: but it has no significance for investment until it has passed, in some firm or institution, through the difficult and costly stage of development or design'.[2] This, in turn, helped to intensify two existing tendencies: the growing participation of the Government in industrial research, and the concentration of production in the hands of very large firms in all the industries which relied heavily on scientific or technological innovation. The fact that new ideas always arise in individual brains, not in teams, and that large organizations become administratively top-heavy and may oppose change even when they are research organizations charged specifically with initiating it,[3] did not invalidate these general trends.

Technical progress is not normally, and was not in this period, a matter merely of spectacular brainwaves: it was the gradual adaptation and improvement, often of only humble parts of machines or materials; the linked development of one new process waiting for improvements in others before it can be applied; and the constant pressure on the average firm to reach the level of the best by installing machines and methods already known. Beside the new industries or new materials, such new techniques as the extension of welding to many aspects of shipbuilding, new alloy metallurgy, precision control,[4] cellulose spray painting, the dozens of improvements which tell the expert almost to within a year when a particular car or a particular aircraft was built, contributed equally to the rising output and the rising standards of living of this period.

Last, but by no means least, science and research invaded the very citadel of entrepreneurship itself. The management of men, the layout of plant, the grouping, selecting, training of staff, work study and study of

---

[1] Lord Aberconway, *The Basic Industries of Great Britain* (1927), pp. 353–4.
[2] C. F. Carter and B. R. Williams, *Investment in Innovation* (1958), p. 138.
[3] John Jewkes, David Sawers, Richard Stillerman, *The Sources of Invention* (1958).
[4] R. S. Sayers, 'The Springs of Technical Progress in Britain, 1919–1939', *Econ. J.*, 60/238, 1950.

fatigue, besides many others, became aspects of 'scientific management' which were being introduced from across the Atlantic in at least a few large and progressive firms, and developed to fit the native soil.[1]

In view of the large-scale waste by unemployment of productive resources in the inter-war period, the substantial rise in home output was achieved largely by technical progress. While in the twenty years before 1914 capital accumulation consisted largely of adding similar, or very little improved types, in 1924–38 'a very low rate of accumulation went with the coming into being of new techniques, which only now obtained a general application and exploitation on the large scale'.[2]

Definitions of 'industrial' output vary, but all available statistics agree that total industrial output reached the pre-war level by about 1924, rose substantially to 1929 and after falling back in the depression, rose quite spectacularly in the late 1930's, with 1937 as the pre-war peak. This increase is all the more remarkable since 1913 was a record year, far above the average run of pre-war years:

Index of Industrial Production in the United Kingdom (1924 = 100)

	Including Building		Excluding Building		
	Ridley[3]	Lomax[4]	Hoffmann[5]	O.E.E.C.[6]	Lomax[4]
1913	94·2	90·5	110·3	97·1	92·6
1920	102·3	90·3	100·2	97·1	92·4
1924	100	100	100	100	100
1929	117·3	115·8	116·5	112·9	113·3
1931	99·0	103·7	99·9	97·1	101·9
1935	130·8	130·3	125·8	128·6	127·9
1937	153·1	150·5	144·4	152·9	147·7

This increase was achieved in spite of shorter hours of work. For manufacturing only, the figures are shown opposite.

[1] L. Urwick and E. F. L. Brech, *The Making of Scientific Management* (1957 ed.), esp. Vol. 2; E. F. L. Brech (ed.), *The Principles and Practice of Management* (1958 ed.), pp. 56–64.

[2] E. H. Phelps-Brown and B. Weber, 'Accumulation, Productivity and Distribution in the British Economy, 1870–1938', *Econ. J.*, 63/256, 1953.

[3] T. M. Ridley, 'Industrial Production in the United Kingdom 1900–1953', *Economica*, 22/85, 1955. Recalculated from 1948 = 100.

[4] K. S. Lomax, 'Production and Productivity Movements in the United Kingdom since 1900', *J. R. Stat. S.*, 122/2, 1959, p. 196.

[5] W. G. Hoffmann, *British Industry, 1700–1950* (Oxford, 1955), Table 54. This index has been generally criticized as showing too slow a rise after the 1914–18 war, e.g. W. A. Cole, 'The Measurement of Industrial Growth', *Ec. Hist. Rev.*, 2nd S., 11/2, 1958.   [6] O.E.E.C., *Industrial Statistics* (Paris, 1955).

Output in Manufacturing in 1935 (1907 = 100)[1]

	Total Manufacturing Output	Manufacturing Output per Employee Year	Manufacturing Output per Employee Hour
Iron and steel	147·9	139·6	154
Engineering, shipbuilding, vehicles	271·5	177·6	196
Non-ferrous metals	135·2	121·0	131
Chemicals	222·6	157·7	174
Textiles	109·1	134·6	155
Clothing	125·3	125·3	146
Leather	131·8	120·9	136
Food, drink, tobacco	129·6	96·8	108
Timber	176·0	132·0	147
Paper, printing, publishing	262·6	192·7	208
Clay and building materials	213·3	160·3	180
Miscellaneous	362·0	207·8	228
Total Manufacturing	176·6	151·9	171

On the 'favourable' weighting of this tabulation the compound annual rate of growth between 1907 and 1924 was 1·7% (1·2% on the least favourable basis), and between 1924 and 1935, 2·7% on either weighting.[2] Total industrial output *per head* in the United Kingdom rose from an index of 218 in 1913 (1850 = 100) to 224 in 1925 and 332 in 1937:[3] total real product *per man-hour* from 0·366 'International Units' in 1913 to 0·576 in 1939, or by 57%.[4]

While even the 'stagnating' industries showed some rise over pre-war productivity (though not necessarily over total pre-war output), the main growth sectors of the economy were the new industries. Thus the *annual* increase in output was 15·7% for artificial silk, 10·2% for electrical goods, 10·1% for motor cars, 5·3% for dyestuffs, but only 1·9% for British industry as a whole.[5] Indices of output of the major new industries compared as shown overleaf.[6]

[1] A. Maddison, 'Output, Employment and Productivity in British Manufacturing in the Last Half-Century', *Bull. Oxf. Inst. Stat.*, 17/4, 1955.

[2] Other estimates put the increase in output per man-hour at 50% between 1c.14 and 1931 and in output per worker at 37% between 1924 and 1937. Sayers, *o6l cit.*, p. 276.

[3] M.S.A. Mission to U.K., *Economic Development in the United Kingdom, 1850–1950*. No source given for this series.

[4] Colin Clark, *The Conditions of Economic Progress* (1957 ed.), p. 63.

[5] W. G. Hoffmann, 'The Growth of Industrial Production in Great Britain', *Ec. Hist. Rev.*, 2nd S., 2/2, pp. 171–2. Lomax puts the annual increase of manufacturing output in Britain at 2·9% over the period 1920–37. *Op. cit.*, p. 201.

[6] A. E. Kahn, *Great Britain in the World Economy* (1946), p. 106. Based on the Census of Production.

	1924	1930	1935
Electrical goods	55	67	100
Electricity supply	45	71	100
Automobiles and cycles	42	61	100
Aircraft	23	65	100
Silk and rayon	20	47	100
Hosiery	70	69	100
Chemical and allied goods	67	69	100
Share of above, plus scientific instruments[1]	12·5%	16·3%	19·0%

The changing weight of different industries was an inevitable concomitant of economic progress:

The shift of emphasis from one area within the productive system to another in addition to knowledge, new technology, and innovation means changes in the identity of the new and rapidly growing industries. By the same token there is a tendency towards retardation in the rate of growth of older industries, as the economic effects of technical progress and innovation within them slacken and as they feel increasingly the competition of the newer industries for limited resources. To put it differently, a sustained high rate of growth depends upon a continuous emergence of new inventions and innovations, providing the bases for new industries whose high rates of growth compensate for the inevitable slowing down in the rate of invention and innovation, and upon the economic effects of both, which retard the rates of growth of the older industries. A high rate of over-all growth in an economy is thus necessarily accompanied by considerable shifting in relative importance among industries, as the old decline and the new increase in relative weight in the nation's output.[2]

'Britain had reached a point at which the maintenance of a high level of prosperity depended on exceptionally drastic shifts in the use of productive resources and greater ingenuity in the development of new types of finished products.'[3] It was the tragedy of British industry in the inter-war period that the shift had to be made too quickly, that few were aware, until the 1930's, of its necessity, and that it had to be carried out not only in the midst of a world depression, but in the midst of a particularly difficult time for Britain's old staple export industries, owing to a change in the terms of trade, a restrictive monetary policy until 1931 and an open home market, until 1932, in a world of rampant protectionism.

The shift that did occur was not insignificant. Numbers in the main groups of occupations changed as shown opposite.

[1] In 1907, it had been 6·5%.
[2] Simon Kuznets, *Six Lectures on Economic Growth* (Illinois, 1959), p. 33.
[3] W. Ashworth, *An Economic History of England, 1870–1939* (1960), p. 321, also pp. 331–5, 414–16.

New and Growing Industries

Numbers employed in the United Kingdom (000)[1]

	Average 1920-1	Average 1937-8	Change
Agriculture, forestry, fishing	1,112	762	−350
Mining and quarrying	1,204	791	−413
Manufacture	6,668	6,539	−129
Building and contracting	840	1,159	+319
Gas, water, electricity	185	291	+106
Transport and communication	1,482	1,513	+31
Distribution, insurance, banking	2,120	2,897	+777
National, local government	1,381	1,222	−159
Professional services	721	950	+229
Miscellaneous services	2,025	2,755	+730
Grand total	17,738	18,879	+1,141
Salaried workers	3,758	4,810	+1,052

Numbers employed in certain industries as % of the numbers employed in Manufacturing[2]

	Average 1921-2	Average 1937-8
Ceramics, glass, etc.	3·4	4·5
Metal manufacture	6·1	6·5
Engineering, shipbuilding, electrical engineering	17·2	17·6
Vehicles	5·75	8·85
Other metal goods	3·6	4·95
Textiles	21·4	16·15
Clothing	11·0	9·8

2. NEW AND GROWING INDUSTRIES

One of the most critically important of the new industries was electrical engineering, together with the supply of electricity. It could be taken as the symbol of the new industrial Britain, freeing other industries from dependence on the coalfields of the north and west and setting in motion a vast migration to the Midlands and the south-east. Backward technically until 1918, and behind other countries in consumption per head in the 1920's, by the late 1930's the industry was close, if not equal, to its foreign rivals, while the British 'Grid' constituted a method of distributing electric power which had no equal anywhere in the world.[3]

---

[1] Agatha L. Chapman and Rose Knight, *Wages and Salaries in the United Kingdom, 1920–1938* (Cambridge, 1953), p. 18; cf. also Mark Abrams, *The Condition of the British People, 1911–1945* (1945), p. 63; Sir William Beveridge, *Full Employment in a Free Society* (1945 ed.), pp. 316–20; Phyllis Deane and W. A. Cole, *British Economic Growth 1688–1959* (Cambridge, 1962), chapters 4, 5 and 9, sec. 3.

[2] Chapman and Knight, p. 20.

[3] *Committee on the Position of the Electrical Trades after the War, Report* (1918. Cd. 9072); M. E. Dimock, *British Public Utilities* (1933), p. 197.

The early haphazard and scattered development had led to much technical inefficiency in an industry such as electricity generation. In 1925 there was still a bewildering variety of voltages and, in the case of A.C., of cycles in use. Although larger stations were much more economical than smaller ones, in 1925 28 stations generated 50% of the power between them, and another 88 generated 39%, but the remaining 11% was shared between 322 suppliers.[1] Each carried its own surplus capacity for meeting the heavy peak demands, and at less than peak demand, the efficient stations ran at less than full capacity, while the inefficient stations were kept going also.

The Electricity (Supply) Act of 1919 which attempted to encourage amalgamations remained a dead letter, but following the Weir Committee Report of the Ministry of Transport in 1925, the Electricity (Supply) Act of 1926 introduced more effective changes. A Central Electricity Board was set up and given the right to monopolize all the wholesaling of electricity. With funds derived from powers to borrow money at fixed interest, it successfully pursued a policy of concentrating all output in a small number of base load stations and new super-stations (144 by 1935), while closing down large numbers of the smaller, inefficient ones. The whole system was connected by means of a national 'grid' of high-tension transmission cables which incidentally employed about 100,000 people at the bottom of the slump, and total output rose from 6,600 million units in 1925 to 26,400 million units in 1939.[2]

Improved technical and thermal efficiency, the falling price of coal, and the 'grid', allowing the closing of high-cost stations and a reduction in the proportion of idle capacity, all helped to lower costs, and as electricity became cheaper, it came within reach of new classes of the community. There were 730,000 electricity consumers in 1920, 2,844,000 in 1929 and 8,920,000 in 1938; in the late 1930's, consumers were being added at a rate of 700,000–800,000 a year.[3] With the spread of new electrical consumer durables, cookers, radios, refrigerators, washing machines, vacuum cleaners and electric irons, each of these households increased its consumption of electricity, while the new industries established away from the coalfields, electric street lighting, and the conversion of some railway

---

[1] H. H. Ballin, *The Organization of Electricity Supply in Great Britain* (1946), chapter 8.

[2] Heath and Hetherington, *op. cit.*, chapter 7; J. G. Crowther, *Discoveries and Inventions of the 20th Century* (1955 ed.), pp. 95–8; Sir Henry Self and Miss Elizabeth Watson, *Electricity Supply in Great Britain* (1952), chapter 4; Lincoln Gordon, *The Public Corporation in Britain* (1938), chapter 3.

[3] British Association, *Britain in Recovery* (1938), p. 265; Richard Stone, *Measurement of Consumers' Expenditure in the United Kingdom, 1920–1938* (Cambridge, 1954), p. 418; Alfred Plummer, *New British Industries in the Twentieth Century* (1937), chapter 2/1.

traction added further important sources of demand. Thus, with falling marginal costs and an elastic demand, the growth in the output of electricity was not reversed even in the slump, and in the 1930's its rate of growth in Britain exceeded that in the rest of the world.

These conditions offered great opportunities for electrical engineering. Employment rose particularly fast in the 1930's, and the number of insured workers grew from 173,600 in 1924 to 367,000 in 1937. The export record of the industry was good, and although there were large imports of various electrical goods from Germany and of lamps and valves from Holland, the British industry kept control of its home market, aided as it was by protective measures in 1921 and 1926.[1] There were several innovations that originated in Great Britain. These included the discharge lamp; the development of thermionic valves, invented by Sir Ambrose Fleming in 1904; and, fostered by the distinctive organization of wireless broadcasting in this country, complex multi-channel radio sets and television, even earlier than in the U.S.A. Another series of important discoveries in Britain made Radar possible in 1936.[2]

A high degree of specialization allowed innumerable small firms to survive, but, as in other countries, the industry came to be dominated by a few large firms. Further, in an industry so dependent on constant inventions and patents[3] it was perhaps not surprising that restrictive associations of producers were particularly rampant, especially those providing for the exchange of patents and the exclusion of newcomers from them. Most of these, including, for example, the Electric Lamp Manufacturers' Association, which was perhaps the best known,[4] had international links, and so had some of the leading firms, such as E.M.I. (Electrical and Musical Industries), a combine formed in 1931.

Comparable in importance with electricity in the inter-war years was the motor industry. The motor car changed people's habits of living, shopping, travelling and holidaying; it affected the layout of towns and of suburbs; it created the first true conveyor-belt factories and stimulated innumerable ancillary industries, some of them of major importance in

---

[1] Balfour Committee, *Survey of Industries*, Vol. 4, chapter 3; Plummer, *op. cit.*, chapter 2/II; Lord Aberconway, *The Basic Industries* (1927), pp. 317 ff.; A. E. Kahn, *Great Britain in the World Economy* (1946), pp. 43–120.

[2] Crowther, *op. cit.*, p. 372; S. G. Sturmey, *The Economic Development of Radio* (1948), p. 179.

[3] Thomas Wilson, 'The Electronics Industry', in Duncan Burn, *The Structure of British Industry*, Vol. 2 (Cambridge, 1958), pp. 132–49.

[4] Monopolies Commission, *Report on the Supply of Electric Lamps* (1951. 287), esp. chapter 2; cf. also *Report on the Supply of Insulated Electric Wires and Cables* (1952. 209), chapter 4; *Report on the Supply of Electric Valves and Cathode Ray Tubes* (1956. 16), chapters 2–4; *Report on the Supply and Export of Electrical and Allied Machinery and Plant* (1957. 42), chapter 1.

their own right, including oil refining, rubber, electrical goods, glass, metallurgy, both ferrous and non-ferrous, and mechanical engineering.

Before the war, motor vehicles had been made singly or at best in batches; 34,000 motor vehicles of all kinds were built in 1913, but among the cars alone there had been 198 different models,[1] and apart from vans, cabs and omnibuses, the motor vehicle was available only to the very rich or eccentric. During the war, motor engineers benefited greatly by the experience of building military trucks and engines, though the output of luxury cars had to be suspended. The war also left the McKenna duty of $33\frac{1}{3}\%$ *ad valorem* on imported cars, first intended to preserve scarce foreign exchange and shipping space, but remaining, under different pretexts, an effective protectionist measure in practice, with a single break in 1924–5.

After 1918 the industry grew quickly out of its pre-war methods. By 1921 Austin had started on the production of his first 'mass car', the Austin 7, and by 1925 Morris, who had also introduced a production line, made 41% of the total output of British cars in his class.[2] Some of the leading makers, like Ford's, a branch of the American firm, built a planned complete production unit at Dagenham, while others, like Morris, of Cowley, evolved by buying up innumerable specialist firms, suppliers and rivals; but all the large motor firms were by the end of the 1920's reaping the advantage of mass production, mass markets and of new manufacturing techniques. Omitting motor cycles, the annual output of motor vehicles rose from 95,000 in 1923 to a peak of 511,000 in 1937; employment rose more slowly, from 220,000 insured workers in 1924 to 380,000 in 1939 (including aircraft); and the average factory value of private cars made in Great Britain fell from £308 per car in 1912 to £259 in 1924 and £130 in 1935–6.[3] Falling costs and an elastic market thus went together as in the case of electricity.

In this period, the number of makers fell from 96 in 1922 to 20 in 1939. By 1929, 75% of the output (by numbers) was accounted for by three firms, 60% being accounted for by the two largest alone. There was also a geographical concentration in Birmingham, Coventry and the London region, and a concentration of models in the 1930's, while many components were used interchangeably in different models. On the other hand, the two leading firms of cheap car makers, Morris and Austin, lost their predominance and by 1939 the market was shared more evenly among the 'Big Six'.[4] In the production of commercial vehicles, concentration went

[1] P.E.P., *Engineering Reports II: Motor Vehicles* (1950), p. 5.
[2] P. W. S. Andrews and Elizabeth Brunner, *The Life of Lord Nuffield* (Oxford, 1955), p. 112.
[3] G. C. Allen, *British Industries and their Organization* (1959 ed.), p. 204; Plummer, *op. cit.*, p. 87.
[4] G. Maxcy, 'The Motor Industry', in P. L. Cook (ed.), *Effects of Merger* (1958).

less far, though most of the large private car producers also made commercial vehicles. Several motor firms survived by catering for narrowly specialized markets in the luxury car and sports car range.

The slump affected the industry here less than elsewhere, as real incomes of the middle classes kept up better, and the industry was just beginning to tap an extremely elastic section of its market in the early 1930's.[1] Exports were never of outstanding importance, amounting usually to $\frac{1}{7}$ or $\frac{1}{8}$ of output,[2] largely because the system of taxation here led to the production of engines which were unsuitable for overseas markets; the motor cycle industry, however, which had exported over 40% of its output in the 1920's, suffered a serious contraction when foreign demand declined in the 1930's.

Closely linked with the development of the motor car engine was the development of aircraft production. Until 1930 the instability of the air transport companies made aircraft building excessively risky, but from 1930 onwards the needs of the R.A.F. provided a backbone of orders as well as research, and in the early 1930's some 30,000 people were employed in aircraft manufacturing. Rearmament, and the erection of 'shadow' factories from 1936 onward, drew several of the larger motor firms into the production of aircraft.

Some new industries were based on advances in the science of chemistry and in chemical engineering. One of the most significant of them was the man-made fibre industry, limited, before 1939, almost entirely to rayon and rayon staple, based on cellulose derived from wood-pulp or cotton linters. In 1913, over 6 million lb. of rayon filament had been produced in Britain, about 27% of the world output, but development was retarded during the war and the pre-war level was exceeded only in 1921. In 1927 Britain produced 53 mn. lb. of filament and 2 mn. lb. of staple, the figures rising to 115 mn. lb. and 58 mn. lb. respectively by 1939, representing 7·7% of the world output. The rate of growth of this new industry was thus very rapid, but even in 1939 all man-made fibres together only accounted for 8–9% of the fibres used in the world's textile industries.

In the early stages, the thin continuous filament with its smooth, lustrous surface suggested its use as a substitute for silk, and rayon became widely known as 'artificial silk'. In the 1920's, improvements both in methods of production and in handling made possible the production of mixed fabrics, and even the substitution for cotton and finally for wool and linen: in 1934 spinning of rayon staple began in a Rochdale mill and weaving in another demonstration plant, and a similar plant was opened in Bradford also to show the possibilities of 'fibro' in the worsted trade; high-tenacity types of viscose rayon could be used in the industrial field, e.g. for

---

[1] G. Maxcy and A. Silberston, *The Motor Industry* (1959), chapter 1.
[2] L. F. Duval, 'The Motor Industry', in *Britain in Recovery*, Part II, chapter 7.

tyre cords.[1] Nevertheless, the chief successes were scored in replacing silk and in opening wider markets for goods formerly made of silk, helped by the marked decline in its costs and prices.[2] By 1936, the total number employed in the rayon industry was about 100,000.[3]

The industry was from the beginning dominated by a small number of large firms. Before 1914, Courtauld's, an old-established silk-throwing firm which acquired the various British patents and factories in 1904, had not only a virtual monopoly in Britain, but also a large share of the total world output. Several other firms were established in the 1920's, but even in 1939, while the issued capital of Courtauld's was £32 million, and that of British Celanese £13·5 million, that of the other nine firms combined only came to £5·2 million.[4] The hegemony of the two leading firms was assisted by price agreements in the 1930's, by disguised protection since 1925, by international links with the main producers abroad, and by maintaining a high rate of technical improvement.[5]

The 'chemical industry' proper came to mean in this period particularly the production of explosives and dyestuffs, heavy chemicals, industrial gases, fertilizers, fine chemicals (including medicinal) and plastics.[6] At its centre stood Imperial Chemical Industries Ltd., formed in 1926 by a merger of four companies. One of these, British Dyestuffs Corporation Ltd., had been set up in 1918 largely with Government financial support and protection by licensing (for synthetic dyestuffs) and by a $33\frac{1}{3}\%$ duty (for other organic chemicals). The Government shares were bought out in 1925. The other constituent firms were Brunner-Mond Ltd., a combine that had rapidly extended in 1918–26 beyond its original alkali interests and had put up the first large-scale British plant for fixing nitrogen from the air at Billingham, Stockton-on-Tees, in 1923; United Alkali, the other large producer; and Nobel Industries, dominating the explosives industry. The company had an initial capital of £65 million. Several other chemical firms were absorbed soon after,[7] and the company joined international cartel agreements with the chemical combines of Germany, France and Switzerland in 1932. While it might have exploited its monopolistic position at times to keep up prices, there is no doubt that

---

[1] R. Robson, *The Man-made Fibres Industry* (1958), pp. 19–29.
[2] D. C. Hague, *The Economics of Man-made Fibres* (1957), p. 86.
[3] Plummer, *New Industries*, chapter 4/II, 'Rayon'.
[4] Hague, *op. cit.*, p. 78. Courtauld's and British Celanese, the main producers of acetate yarn, merged in 1957. G. C. Allen, *British Industries*, p. 288.
[5] Balfour Committee, *Survey of Industries*, Vol. 3, chapter 3, 'The Artificial Silk Industry'; H. A. Silverman, 'The Artificial Textile Industry', in *Studies in Industrial Organization* (1946), ed. H. A. Silverman, pp. 307 ff., 334.
[6] W. B. Reddaway, 'The Chemical Industry', in Duncan Burn (ed.), *The Structure of British Industry*, Vol. 1 (Cambridge 1958), pp. 223 ff.
[7] Stephen Miall, *History of the British Chemical Industry* (1931), pp. 61–2; A. F. Lucas, *Industrial Reconstruction* (1937), pp. 178–90.

the scale of the enterprise helped to raise the technical efficiency of the British industry to the level of its chief foreign rivals.[1]

Few sectors of the chemical industry remained outside the control of I.C.I., exercised by agreements, by control of patents or ingredients, by control of subsidiaries and by other methods. The soap industry, however, was dominated by the vast Lever combine, which joined with its chief Dutch rivals, Jurgens' and Van den Bergh (the Margarine Union of 1927), in 1929 and had interests in other industries also.[2] Oil refining was another related industry, dominated from the beginning in this country by large firms. Thermal cracking began in 1913, and catalytic cracking plants were developed just before the second World War. In the 1930's, however, an increasing proportion of motor spirit was imported, while the output of British refineries actually fell from 604 mn. gallons in 1929 to 455 mn. gallons in 1938.[3]

Another industry which showed remarkable technical progress and came to be dominated by a single large firm was glass making. Just before the first World War, American patents for glass bottle making (Owen's patent) in 1907 and for sheet glass (Lubbers' process) in 1909 had introduced novel techniques into Britain. Sheet glass making was revolutionized by Pilkington's adaptation of the Slingluff process of the Pittsburgh Plate Glass Co. in 1930. Plate glass making, in turn, was changed into a continuous flow process between rollers; continuous polishing and grinding, a development in Britain in 1922–3 of a process pioneered by Ford's in Detroit for the making of windscreen glass, was also perfected at Pilkington's.

During the first World War, the formerly neglected production of optical glass and chemical and heat-resisting glassware had been established, and in the inter-war years laminated and armour plate or toughened glass was developed from a pre-war British discovery.[4] These developments occurred at a time when demand was rising by leaps and bounds by the needs of motor vehicles, by the building boom and by the rapidly growing sales of light bulbs, glass containers used in food preservation, milk bottles, etc.

Domestic and ornamental glassware continued to be produced by large numbers of small firms, severely hit by competition from abroad, in spite of protection, but flat glass making, including plate and window glass, became dominated by a single firm, Pilkington's. Chance's, the

[1] Plummer, chapter 6/1, 'Synthetic Dyestuffs'.

[2] Charles Wilson, *The History of Unilever*, 2 vols. (1954); Ruth Cohen, 'The Soap Industry', in P. L. Cook (ed.), *Effects of Mergers* (1958).

[3] Duncan Burn, 'The Oil Industry', in *Structure of British Industry*, Vol. 1; P.E.P., *The British Fuel and Power Industries* (1947), pp. 199–209.

[4] Heath and Hetherington, chapter 10; L. M. Angus-Butterworth, *The Manufacture of Glass* (1948), chapters 16–19.

leading competitor in the nineteenth century, were bought out between 1936 and 1955; James A. Jobling, the makers of Pyrex, about the same time; and the Triplex Co., makers of safety glass, were linked by a joint subsidiary.[1]

If glass making was typical of the old industries which were being revolutionized by new techniques, the working of aluminium, rubber and plastic typified the new industries based on new materials. Though aluminium is one of the most common metals found on earth, the electrolytic process of isolating it was discovered only in 1886, in the U.S.A., and the British Aluminium Co. was established only in 1894. In the inter-war years, the peculiar qualities of the metal encouraged its widespread use in many fields: its ductility when cold made it ideal for cooking utensils; its light weight encouraged its use in aircraft; its great strength as an alloy led to its use in engines and machinery; and its low resistance to electric current made it sought after as an electrical conductor. World output of aluminium rose by 330% between 1913 and 1929, and by 165% between 1929 and 1939, British production of virgin aluminium increasing from 10,000 to 25,000 metric tons between 1913 and 1939, and consumption from 16,000 metric tons in 1925 to 90,000 metric tons in 1939. Economies of scale led to an early concentration in large firms: in 1923 an international cartel agreement protected the European market, and after 1929 it was extended also to America and Canada.[2]

Rubber was used for rainwear and other purposes in the nineteenth century, but the rubber industry became of importance only with the motor vehicle of the twentieth. By 1937, two-thirds of the world's rubber supplies were used for motor tyres and tubes.[3] Rubber tyre making in Britain was dominated by the largest firm, Dunlop's,[4] and there were price agreements and far-reaching international links among the leading firms, particularly after a 33⅓% tariff in 1927. Rubber footwear was similarly organized.[5]

The plastics industry may be said to have dated from 1908 with the discovery of 'bakelite'. In Britain, however, little progress was made until the 1930's. The discoveries of this period, including alkathene in Britain

---

[1] Working Party Reports, *Hand-blown Domestic Glassware* (1947); T. C. Barker, *Pilkington Brothers and the Glass Industry* (1960); P. L. Cook, 'The Flat-Glass Industry', in P. L. Cook (ed.), *Effects of Mergers* (1958).

[2] Plummer, *New Industries*, chapter 4/1; J. D. Edwards, F. C. Frary and Z. Jeffries, *The Aluminium Industry* (New York, 1930), Vol. 1, pp. 43–7.

[3] G. Rae, 'The Statistics of the Rubber Industry', *J. R. Stat. S.*, 101/2, 1938, p. 340; Audrey G. Donnithorne, *British Rubber Manufacturing* (1958), chapter 3.

[4] In 1951–2, the company accounted for 47% of British sales. Pre-war figures are not available, but were similar. Monopolies Commission, *Supply and Export of Pneumatic Tyres* (1955. 133), p. 82.

[5] Monopolies Commission, *Rubber Footwear* (1956. 328).

and nylon in the U.S.A., had to wait in turn for the period after 1939 before they were exploited on a large scale.[1]

Lastly, there was a whole range of consumer goods and services which expanded with the rising standards of living. The 'services', including communications and the retail trades, will be considered elsewhere; here we must limit ourselves to considering a few representative consumption goods industries as they were affected by changing techniques and by changes in demand.

The boot and shoe industry, for example, showed no fundamental technical innovations in this period, yet adopted a steady stream of minor improvements which allowed it to produce a rising output with a shrinking labour force. Between 1924 and 1935 output was estimated to have increased from under 10 million to over 11 million dozen pairs, while rubber footwear increased much more rapidly to 3 million dozen pairs. At the same time the labour force fell by 5% from 1924 to 1939, and within that total a large proportion of male labour was replaced by female. There was a serious decline in exports in the 1930's, but home consumption was rising more than proportionately.[2]

In the hosiery industry, similarly, without any major change apart from the introduction of rayon, employment increased by about one-third between 1924 and 1935–9, yet output of stockings and socks rose by 41%, of underwear by 97%, and of outerwear by 20% between 1924 and 1937. A serious fall in exports was more than compensated for by the drastic fall in imports after the imposition of a tariff in 1932.[3] In hosiery, more clearly than in footwear, an elastic demand ensured that falling costs and prices led to a marked expansion of sales.

Flour-milling, an industry once to be found in every village, had moved to the ports in large and efficient units before 1914 in order to deal with imported grain. During the war, many inland mills were revived to cope with the increased home wheat production so that by the early 1920's there was much surplus capacity. This was aggravated by technical improvement at a time when the consumption of flour hardly rose at all between 1907 and 1939. The enormous technical advantages of size led to domination by a handful of firms, and at the end of 1938, Rank's, Spiller's and the Co-operative Wholesale Societies between them controlled 65–70% of the industry's capacity. The latter did not join any rationalization

---

[1] Heath and Hetherington, chapter 18; A. J. Brown, *Applied Economics* (1947) chapter V/4.

[2] Working Party Reports, *Boots and Shoes* (1946), section 5; H. A. Silverman, 'The Boot and Shoe Industry', in *Studies in Industrial Organization* (1946), ed. Silverman.

[3] H. A. Silverman, 'The Hosiery Industry', in *ibid.*; F. A. Wells, 'The Hosiery Trade', in *Britain in Depression* (1935); Working Party Reports, *Hosiery* (1946), esp. chapters 2, 7, 8.

schemes or price agreements, but under the leadership of the other two giants the industry was 'rationalized' in 1929, by the purchase and removal of much redundant capacity by the 'Purchase Finance Co. Ltd.', owned by the seven largest firms. Prices were effectively maintained by a quota system, organized by the 'Millers' Mutual Aid Association', an offshoot of the old-established National Association of Millers. The results of the cartel on the profit rates of its members were most satisfactory.[1]

The canning of food, on the other hand, faced a rapidly expanding market in the inter-war years. The consumption of canned vegetables is estimated to have risen from an average of 24,000 tons p.a. in 1920–2 to 193,000 tons in 1937–8, and the home production of canned and bottled fruit from 30,000 cwt. to 180,000 cwt. in the same years.

An infant industry, established during the war with the aid of the Ministry of Agriculture, canning was killed by American imports in the post-war years. In 1924 special commissioners reported in favour of reviving it, and with the help of the Ministry, the tin-plate makers and existing canners, the National Food Canning Council was set up. From 6 factories in 1926, the industry grew to 80 factories in 1934, helped by great improvements in canning, in temperature control, and in mass-growing, e.g. of peas in Lincolnshire and the Vale of Evesham, for the canneries; the Metal Box Co., a firm with international links established in 1921, controlled 90% of the British output of cans. Imports, especially of canned fruit and vegetables, still however accounted for the bulk of consumption.[2]

One of the industries most disorganized during the first World War was building, since nearly all private work had been stopped and the labour force dispersed: from 920,000 in July 1914 it fell to 438,000 at the time of the armistice and by July 1920 had recovered only to 796,000.[3] From then on a series of public programmes and favourable conditions for private building kept the industry booming throughout the inter-war years, except for a brief interval in 1928–30. The housing boom of the early 1930's saw the most rapid rate of house building in British history and was widely believed to have helped to pull the country out of the slump,[4] yet at the time house building accounted for only about one-third of the output of building and contracting, including repair. There was little rise in productivity, so that most of the increased output was achieved by increased employment, but labour flocked in faster than it could be employed, and unemployment in the industry remained high throughout

[1] H. V. Edwards, 'Flour Milling', in *Further Studies in Industrial Organization* (1948), ed. M. P. Fogarty.
[2] Richard Stone, *The Measurement of Consumers' Expenditure* (Cambridge, 1954), Tables 36, 40; Plummer, *New Industries*, chapter 5, 'Canning of Foodstuffs'; W. E. Minchinton, *The British Tinplate Industry* (Oxford, 1957), pp. 178–80.
[3] Quoted in G. C. Allen, *British Industries*, p. 304.
[4] pp. 239–41 below.

the boom, one of its worst features being the irregularity of employment.[1]

Despite the size of the building industry as a whole, employing up to ¾ million workers, plus 300,000–400,000 in directly dependent industries, there were few large firms, and these mostly in civil engineering. Competition was severe among the 72,690 firms enumerated by the Census of Production in 1935.[2] By contrast, the suppliers of many building materials, following in the footsteps of the Portland Cement industry before the war, became strongly cartellized in this period.[3]

The new or growing industries were thus of several types. Some were directly replacing an old industry, enjoying a temporary scope for substitution': they included artificial silk, motor cars, aluminium and canned food. Others represented genuinely new products or services which came to absorb much of the additional wealth available: among them were radio, aircraft and electrical goods. Others still were long-established industries for which the home market was growing: these included building, boots and shoes, and hosiery. Quite a number fell into more than one category.

Some of the new industries, such as electrical and motor engineering, had substantial export sales, but fundamentally, unlike the old staples, they were based on a buoyant home market. Similarly, most of the prosperous industries were 'sheltered' from the competition of foreign makers, by costs of transport, tariffs or by the nature of their supply. Many of the new industries depended on State support, encouragement or sponsorship; many required a high degree of scientific knowledge, and a surprisingly large number of them were dominated by a single large firm, or a few firms strongly cartellized, often with international links.[4] Such small firms as there were, existed in an environment dominated by the giants.

Again, few of the new and growing industries were tied to the coalfields or even to the ports. Electric power and cheap internal transport, or raw material of little bulk, gave greater freedom of location, and with the exception of those in heavy chemicals, industrialists preferred to settle in the Midlands, to benefit from the old-established skills in working metals, or farther south, particularly round the largest single market of the metropolis. Thus the industries in the new industrial suburbs to the north and west of London which formed an important part of the national output were the motor industry, the electrical industry, engineering, chemical

---

[1] Monopolies Commission Reports, *The Supply of Buildings in the Greater London Area* (1954. 264), p. 67.

[2] Alfred C. Bossom, 'The Building Industry since the War', in *Britain in Depression*; Sir Harold Bellman, 'The Building Trades', in *Britain in Recovery*.

[3] E.g. Monopolies Commission Reports, *Cast Iron Rain Water Goods* (1951. 136); P. L. Cook, 'The Cement Industry', in P. L. Cook (ed.), *Effects of Mergers* (1958).

[4] Plummer, *op. cit.*, chapters 1, 6 and 7; H. Clay, *The Post-War Unemployment Problem* (1929), p. 108

engineering, and the manufacture of foodstuffs, furniture, musical instruments and office equipment and stationery.[1] The geographical shift was distinctly away from the centres of the old staple industries in certain regions in the north and west.

3. THE OLD AND DECLINING INDUSTRIES

Coal had been the symbol of the old industrial Britain. It had driven her industries and it determined their location since the days of the Industrial Revolution. The decline in the output of coal after the peak of 1913 was equally symbolic. The coal industry was buffeted by all the storms which drove the other old staple trades before them in this period, and was dragged down by them into depression and secular decline.

Prior to 1914, the traditions and organization of this industry had been geared to a steadily expanding market; few industries showed such consistent rise of output and employment over the years. In the war, while output fell heavily because of the high rate of recruitment of miners, demand was far in excess of supply, and in the years 1917–19 in particular, the coalfields were driven as hard as possible to raise the maximum tonnage of coal with their depleted manpower. Even after the collapse of the boom of 1920, a series of fortuitous events helped to prolong the illusion of a continuing sellers' market in coal, including the strike of April–July 1921, the American coal strike of 1922, and the French invasion of the Ruhr in 1923. Up to the end of 1924, in fact, unemployment in coal was below the national average.[2] It was not until 1925 that the industry was brought up against a sharp fall in demand, and it took some years longer before it recognized that the reduction in the aggregate demand for coal was permanent.

That part of the demand for coal which came from the home market ceased to grow for the first time in centuries: home consumption, including coastwise bunkers, was estimated at 183·8 million tons in 1913 and at 185 million tons in 1937–8.[3] The rising demand from power stations, gas works and domestic users was counterbalanced by the decline in the demand from iron and steel works and from general industry, as well as by substitution by oil and by greater fuel efficiency.[4]

While domestic demand stagnated, exports, including foreign bunkers

[1] D. H. Smith, *The Industries of Greater London* (1933), pp. 131, 154.
[2] Cf. J. M. Keynes, *The Economic Consequences of the Peace* (New York, 1920), p. 93; W. H. B. Court, 'Problems of the British Coal Industry between the Wars', *Ec. Hist. Rev.*, 15/1–2, 1945, p. 8; Henry Clay, *The Post-War Unemployment Problem* (1929), p. 41.
[3] R. Stone, *Measurement of Consumers' Expenditure* (Cambridge, 1954), p. 235; A. M. Neumann, *Economic Organization of the British Coal Industry* (1934), p. 98.
[4] G. P. Jones and A. G. Pool, *A Hundred Years of Economic Development* (1959 ed.), pp. 284–5.

which were at a level of about 100 m.t. in 1913 and again in 1923 because of freak market conditions, reached only about 50 m.t. even in the relatively good years of 1937–8, and the shortfall of demand as against capacity was thus of the order of 40–50 m.t. yearly. In part, this reflected the drastic slowing down in the increase of the world's demand for coal, from 4% p.a. before 1913 to 0·3% p.a. in 1913–37,[1] largely because of substitution by oil and water power, and the depressed state of industry in the 1930's. In part, it reflected the improved performance of the coal industry abroad, especially in Germany, Poland and the Netherlands.

Technically, the British industry fell behind its foreign competitors after 1918. Output per man-shift rose, between 1913 and 1936, by 117% in Holland, 81% in the Ruhr, 73% in Poland, 50–51% in Belgium, 22–25% in France and 10% in Britain. In 1927, output per man-shift measured in tons was much the same in Britain, Holland, Poland and the Ruhr; 10 years later, the other three areas had improved by 50–70%, and Britain alone was still near the old figure.[2] There was some progress: in 1913 8% of the coal was cut by machine, in 1929 28%, in 1934 47% and in 1939 61%, while mechanical conveyance was used on 12% of the coal in 1928, 37% in 1934 and 54% in 1938.[3] The large modern pits sunk in the eastward extensions of the coalfield in Yorkshire, Nottinghamshire and Scotland, in particular, showed very favourable cost figures and high output per man-shift.[4] By and large, however, the British industry became technically inferior to its main foreign competitors, while its older coalfields forced it to work less accessible seams.

The organization of the industry made it hard for it to put its house in order. The typical British colliery was too small to be efficient and there were too many independent and competing firms to form voluntary associations which could stand up to the German coal cartel or similar foreign organizations. Reorganization was bedevilled by the strongly felt demand, among miners and others, for the nationalization of the coal mines, on political as well as on technical and economic grounds.

The Sankey Commission of 1919 was the first of a series of official bodies which attempted to deal with the problem of organization in the coal industry in this period. Composed of owners' and miners' representatives in equal numbers with a judge as chairman, an agreed set of

[1] W. H. B. Court, *op. cit.*, p. 11.
[2] A. Beacham, 'Efficiency and Organization of the British Coal Industry', *Econ. J.*, 55/218–19, 1945, p. 207.
[3] P.E.P., *Report on the British Coal Industry* (1936), p. 2; G. C. Allen, *British Industries* (1959 ed.), p. 70; E. C. Rhodes, 'Labour and Output in the Coal Mining Industry in Great Britain', *J. R. Stat. S.*, 94/4, 1931. Cf. also Balfour Commission, *Survey of Industries*, Vol. 4, chapter 5.
[4] E. C. Rhodes, 'Output, Labour and Machines in the Coal Mining Industry of Great Britain', *Economica*, N.S., 12/46, 1945.

recommendations was most unlikely to emerge. In the event, the chairman appeared to use his casting vote in favour of nationalization, mainly on technical grounds, and virtually all members agreed on a recommendation to nationalize the coal royalties. Both suggestions were ignored by the Government, and the only permanent result, apart from the miners' Welfare Fund financed by a levy of 1*d.* per ton of coal, was the lasting suspicion of the miners that they had been tricked by the Government by means of the Commission into delaying their demands until their post-war economic and political strength had been dissipated. There were, however, some temporary results. These included a reduction of working hours to 7 per shift in 1919 and the setting up of a Mining Department within the Board of Trade under the Coal Mines (Emergency) Act of 1920. In March 1921, when prices and wages were tumbling down from their inflated heights, the industry was decontrolled, and the newly found 'freedom' was ushered in by one of the most costly and bitter strikes in the history of coal mining.[1]

The dispute was settled by a complex agreement on the division of the surplus profits and wages, on a regional basis, but this broke down as soon as over-production and heavy unemployment began to affect the industry in 1925-6. A temporary Government subsidy of £23 million enabled the owners to cut prices while keeping up wages in 1925-6, but in the end they insisted on cutting wages, increasing hours from 7 to 8 and making regional in place of national wage agreements. The miners resisted in a seven-months strike, ushered in by a General Strike called in sympathy by the T.U.C., but ultimately had to give in.

Meanwhile, the Samuel Commission had been set up in 1925 to report on the changed competitive position of the industry. Its main suggestion was to encourage amalgamations of neighbouring collieries, and the Mining Industry Act of 1926 attempted to implement this by remitting stamp duties and by authorizing the Railway and Canal Commission to coerce unwilling minorities into colliery amalgamation schemes. But the initiative had still to come from the industry, and the Act had negligible results.

Such amalgamations as took place were the results of purely private initiative. In 1920-9, there were 20 amalgamations, involving over 200 pits, and there were further significant combinations in South Wales and in Lancashire in 1929-30.[2] In 1927-8 some of the districts evolved more ambitious cartel schemes. Scotland tried to limit output by closing down inefficient mines, compensated by a levy on all coal sold at home, and South Wales attempted to keep to a system of minimum prices by a levy

---

[1] A. R. Redmayne, *Coalmining During the War* (Oxford, 1923), chapters 14–16.
[2] Neumann, *op. cit.*, pp. 152 ff.; Lord Aberconway, *The Basic Industries of Great Britain* (1927), p. 22.

and compensation scheme. More effective was the Midland scheme which embraced Lancashire, Yorkshire, Nottinghamshire and Derbyshire and had a large and secure home market as base: for two years from 1928 it was fairly successful in restricting output, subsidizing exports and controlling the Humber Coal Exporters' Association. Its success seemed to point to a way to prevent further price falls, losses and industrial disputes.[1]

The Coal Mines Act of 1930, the most important measure affecting the industry in the inter-war years, attempted to apply the lessons of the 1920's. By Part III of the Act, the Labour Government carried out its long-standing pledge to reduce the hours per shift by one-half to $7\frac{1}{2}$, symbolizing the end of the period in which the problems of the industry were to be solved at the expense of the miners. This provision was linked with Part IV, which provided for the Coal Mines National Industrial Board to regulate wages nationally, but that part of the Act foundered on the owners' refusal to give up their cherished right to negotiate district by district.

Part I of the Act set up a compulsory cartel scheme. A Central Council, representing the coal owners, was to determine the allocation of sales quotas between the seventeen districts into which the country was divided, and the districts, in turn, allocated quotas to individual collieries. But this quota system was not backed by an effective national price maintenance scheme, and price competition, particularly between districts, continued with undiminished bitterness. Similarly, only a few districts set up common selling agencies before selling schemes were made general by official pressure in 1936.[2] Nevertheless the cartel scheme established by Part I of the Act of 1930 helped to reduce output and keep up prices and profits, and since quotas were transferable, it led to some concentration of production.

These cartel powers were designed to raise the price of coal temporarily. Part II of the Act was to effect a permanent cure. It set up the Coal Mines Reorganization Commission, charged with the task of reorganizing the industry mainly by amalgamations and concentration of production. In the face of the determined opposition of the industry, however, the Commission was unable to carry out its task.[3] Its powers were transferred to the Coal Commission by the Coal Act of 1938, which also authorized the nationalization of coal royalties, ultimately completed in 1942 at a cost of £66½ million.

The history of the coal industry has been described at some length since

---

[1] J. H. Jones, G. Cartwright and P. H. Guénault, *The Coal-mining Industry* (1939), chapter 6.
[2] J. H. Jones *et al.*, *Coal-mining Industry*, pp. 127–33.
[3] Ivor Thomas, 'The Coal Mines Reorganization Commission', in W. A. Robson (ed.), *Public Enterprise* (1937).

it illustrates better than any other the fundamental problems of the declining staple industries in the inter-war years. Largely because of the fall in exports, there was a drop in output from an annual average of 268 millions tons in 1907–14 to 232 million tons in 1927–33 and 228 million tons in 1934–8. Even these figures were only achieved by drastic price cuts. In 1929, perhaps the best inter-war year, it was estimated that one-quarter of the German industry, one-quarter to one-third of the British, and one-half of the Polish were surplus to requirements. Since productivity was on the increase, employment fell drastically from 1,100,000 in 1913 and a peak of 1,226,000 in 1920, to 970,000 in 1929 and 702,000 in 1938. After 1925, unemployment was seldom under 20% and generally well above this figure, while at least 200,000 miners drifted out of the industry.[1]

The iron and steel industry was another of the basic staple trades which suffered a decline in its vital exports. Moreover, the war had created a large surplus capacity and the post-war boom of 1919–20, in which the nine largest firms increased their nominal capital from £20 million to £67 million, burdened it with much watered capital, and this hung like a millstone round its neck until the re-armament of the late 1930's.

Until 1937, British pig-iron production declined steadily from its absolute peak of $10\frac{1}{4}$ million tons in 1913. In part, this was due to its replacement by scrap, the proportion of the latter rising from 40% in 1918 to 60% in 1933,[2] for steel output itself rose from just under 8 million tons in 1913 to well over $9\frac{1}{2}$ m.t. in 1917–18, and after a period of decline, began to soar in 1935 to a peak of 13 m.t. in 1937. These figures may be compared with a capacity of 12 m.t. for both pig iron and steel after the war.[3] There was thus, throughout, much redundant capacity and a high level of unemployment, generally fluctuating around the 20% level.

The British industry fared relatively worst in the 1920's, when tariffs abroad and foreign cartels reduced exports, while the home market was flooded with cheap foreign steel. In 1911–13 the average annual excess of exports of iron and steel over imports had been $2\frac{3}{4}$ million tons; by 1921–2, it had shrunk to about $1\frac{1}{4}$ m.t. and in 1927–9 to a mere $\frac{3}{4}$ m.t. At the same time, while the world output of steel had risen from 75 m.t. in 1913 to 118 m.t. in 1929, the British output had increased by only 2 m.t.[4]

---

[1] G. C. Allen, *British Industries*, chapter 3; J. H. Jones, G. Cartwright, and W. Prest, 'The Coal Industry', in *Britain in Depression*; J. H. Jones, 'The Coalmining Industry', in *Britain in Recovery*; P.E.P., *Report on the British Coal Industry* (1936), pp. 23–5.

[2] H. G. Roepke, *Movements of the British Iron and Steel Industry, 1720–1951* (Urbana, Ill., 1956), p. 111.

[3] E. D. McCallum, 'The Iron and Steel Industry', in *Britain in Depression*.

[4] T. H. Burnham and G. O. Hoskins, *Iron and Steel in Britain, 1870–1930* (1943), Tables 91, 93; M. S. Birkett, 'The Iron and Steel Industry since the War', *J. R. Stat. S.*, 93/3, 1930, p. 373.

Significantly, domestic consumption, which was just over 5 m.t. of steel a year in 1910–14, rose to 7·6 m.t. in 1927–31 and 10·6 m.t. in 1935–8.

In the post-war period Britain's capacity was still geared too much towards puddled bar iron and acid steel instead of basic steel, and, besides, her steelworks were antiquated, the furnaces too small, mechanical aids insufficient, and the layout of works dictated by history rather than technical needs.[1] Blast furnaces were particularly backward and inefficient. The British industry, it was said, was inferior by the 'nature of labour supply, character of home market, lack of sufficient scientific training, oldness of plant, changing conditions of ore supply, dearness of transport, unsuitable sites of older works, inflexibility in face of new circumstances'.[2] Improvements did take place: there were several major and innumerable minor extensions and modernization schemes, output per man employed grew by 50% in the inter-war years, the basic open-hearth capacity was greatly extended (Britain refused to follow the Continent into extending the basic Bessemer capacity), and in 1924 a Fuel Economy Committee was set up, which became the Iron and Steel Research Council in 1929.[3]

The main geographical shift was towards the Lincolnshire and East Midland ore fields, which produced 18·7% of the pig iron in 1920 and 37·4% in 1932. The increase in the steel capacity was more widely diffused. In North Lincolnshire large integrated works were set up on the ore field, about 20 miles from the coal, but there was much expansion also in Sheffield, badly sited from almost every point of view, but containing 80% of the British electric furnace capacity, as well as in Consett and the Lancashire Steel Corporation, both away from the coast and the ore. If there was no clear move to better sites, there was little progress made towards regional self-sufficiency either, and millions of tons of ore, coke and coal had regularly to be transported over long distances.[4]

There were several amalgamations in the industry in the 1920's, including South Durham and Cargo Fleet, Dorman Long and Bolckow-Vaughan, Cammell-Laird and Vickers, Guest, Keen & Nettlefold and Baldwin, Colville and Beardmore, the Lancashire Steel Corporation and the United Steel Companies. In 1929 the British Steel Exports Association was formed, but it was unable to stand up to the powers of foreign cartels.

The world depression hit the iron and steel industry with particular

[1] E.g. Burnham and Hoskins, pp. 190–3; D. L. Burn, *The Economic History of Steelmaking, 1867–1939* (Cambridge, 1940), pp. 362–70, 408–13, 427; J. C. Carr and Walter Taplin, *History of the British Steel Industry* (Oxford, 1962), parts 4 and 5; Balfour Committee, *Survey of Industries*, IV, pp. 21–32.

[2] Roepke, p. 118, summarizing Burn.

[3] Heath and Hetherington, *op. cit.*, chapter 13.

[4] Roepke, pp. 115–16; I.D.A.C. (May Committee): *Report on the . . . Iron and Steel Industry* (1936. Cmd. 5507), p. 61.

force because of its dependence on capital goods. The production of pig iron dropped by 53% between 1929 and 1932, and of steel by 45%. A large part of the industry's capital had to be written off, £42 million being thus wiped off among 37 firms in 1927–36.[1] The subsequent recovery was equally remarkable, assisted by a 33⅓% tariff in 1932. By 1934 output returned to the level of 1929, and continued to expand. If iron and steel did worse in Britain than in the rest of the world in the 1920's, it did better in the 1930's: the country's share of the world's steel output rose from 7·6% in 1931 to 9·7% in 1937.

Like Part I of the Coal Mines Act of 1930, the tariff on iron and steel in 1932 was granted on the understanding that reorganization was to follow, 'to maintain co-ordination of the various sections of the industry and co-operation between constituent concerns, and facilitate such adjustments in productive capacity and prices as would place the industry on a reasonable profit-earning basis and make possible that technical development and re-equipment which was becoming so urgently necessary'.[2] The Government looked for the benefits of monopoly, tempered by planning in the national interest. Accordingly, the British Iron and Steel Federation was formed in April 1934, and was given fairly strong powers. In 1935–6 it took over the price-fixing functions of earlier sectional associations, and it negotiated with foreign cartels to impose quantitative restrictions on imports, after establishing a position of strength by getting the tariff on steel raised temporarily from 33⅓% to 50%; it bought foreign scrap and pig iron for the industry as a whole and sold them cheaply to home producers, financing the transaction with a levy.

With a controlling organ owing its existence largely to Government action and its funds derived mainly from a consortium headed by the Bank of England, the steel industry found that its major construction schemes became political issues. Thus Richard Thomas's plans for a works at Redbourne, Lincolnshire, were thwarted and the firm was forced to build its modern plant at Ebbw Vale, on a restricted site away from the coast, as a measure to relieve local unemployment. The B.I.S.F. itself, representing as it did interests of steelmakers only, was widely accused of restricting the building of modern plant for the sake of keeping up steel prices, particularly after the abortive attempt to lay down a new plant at Jarrow.[3]

Under pressure from the banks, there were further mergers and schemes of 'rationalization' and integration after 1928. In 1932, ten vertical combines had 47% of the pig-iron capacity and 60% of the steel capacity between them.[4] These mergers and the officially supported cartel

---

[1] P. W. S. Andrews and E. Brunner, *Capital Development in Steel* (Oxford, 1951), p. 85.   [2] May Committee, *Report*, p. 12.
[3] Roepke, chapter 6; Burn, pp. 461–4.
[4] G. C. Allen, *British Industries*, p. 115.

policy certainly kept up prices and profits but it is not certain that they contributed greatly to economic efficiency: the history of the steel industry in the 1930's was still described as one of 'retarded development'.[1] It was the moderate boom beginning in 1935, and the re-armament orders which followed, which led to a phenomenal increase in the output of steel in the late 1930's[2] from 5·2 million tons in 1931, to 9·85 m.t. in 1935, 13·0 m.t. in 1937 and, after a relapse in 1938, to 13·2 m.t. in 1939.

Shipbuilding suffered even more than steelmaking in the depression from the decline in the demand for capital goods. In the war years, particularly in 1917–18, a depleted working force had had to labour to the utmost to replace the tonnage sunk by U-boats, and was quite unable to meet foreign orders at the same time. As a result other centres, formerly dependent on British-built tonnage, were forced to supply their own, and the U.S.A. in particular forged ahead in this industry as in many others. Orders for replacements of war losses kept the world's shipyards busy in 1919–20 and the combined result of the war and the post-war boom was that the world shipbuilding capacity was more than doubled, while the world's shipping tonnage, and thus the potential demand for ships, hardly increased at all.[3]

From 1920 onwards the tonnage under construction fell, though the years 1927–30 were relatively good years, British launchings then running at about 75% of the level of 1911–13. In the slump, with millions of tons of shipping laid up, the building of new tonnage virtually came to a standstill: in 1933 the launchings from British yards fell to 7% of the pre-war figure. Throughout the early 1930's a large part of the industry was idle, and its unemployment rate was among the highest in the country.

The expansion of building capacity abroad in 1915–19 had lowered the British share of world output from 58·7% in 1909–13 to 35·1% in 1920, but thenceforth it remained at about the 40% level, reaching 64% in 1924 and being well over 50% in 1927–30, launchings for foreign owners continuing to form a substantial proportion of the output.[4] Britain was slow in adopting some newer types of ship: thus in 1927–30 British yards built 65% of the world's tonnage of steamships, but only 41% of motor vessels. Yards were older, sites often restricted, steel prices and labour costs higher here than elsewhere, but the problem of the industry was not so much its relatively high costs—it held its own quite well with other countries—as the low level of the world's needs compared

[1] D. L. Burn, p. 483; McCallum, *loc. cit.*, pp. 274–5.

[2] E. D. McCallum, 'The Iron and Steel Industry', in *Britain in Recovery*.

[3] Cf. pp. 49, 56–7 above. Warship building in private yards in Britain averaged 133,000 displacement tons in 1911–13, 242,000 d.t. in 1919, 18,000 d.t. in 1920, and none in 1921–2.

[4] Leslie Jones, *Shipbuilding in Britain* (Cardiff, 1957), p. 64.

with the available capacity. The world's building capacity, much larger in the 1920's than before the war, yet faced a demand of only 2½% of world tonnage a year, as against 6% in 1900–14. Surplus ships, laid up after 1920, but capable of being brought into use again, and estimated at 11 million tons in 1922 and 6 million in 1925–6, kept down freight rates and orders for new tonnage, despite the new types of ships needed, such as motor vessels and oil tankers. In Britain, a capacity estimated at between 3 m.t. and 4 m.t. p.a. in the 1920's,[1] compared with an output which fluctuated between 640,000 and 1,540,000 tons.

There was a heavy decline of the labour attached to the industry, and large financial losses were incurred, four of the leading firms alone reducing their capital by £15 million in 1925–9. Few firms actually went out of business, but many saved themselves only by mergers, like Harland & Wolff of Belfast and the Clyde, Palmer's and the Northumberland Shipbuilding Co. on the Tyne, Hawthorne–Leslie and Vickers–Armstrong.[2] The disastrous collapse of markets in 1929–33 threatened to obliterate much of the industry altogether, and it was forced to turn to an organized scheme of restriction, 'National Shipbuilders' Security Ltd.', formed in 1930 with the support of nearly the whole of the industry. Supported by the 'Bankers' Industrial Development Co.', an organization set up by the Bank of England and the clearing banks to reorganize and reduce the capacity of the various staple industries, it could raise funds, to be repaid by a 1% levy on the sales of participating firms, in order 'to assist the Shipbuilding Industry by the purchase of redundant and/or obsolete shipyards, the dismantling and disposal of their contents and the resale of sites under restriction against further use for shipbuilding'. In the slump years the berths and yards bought up for dismantling were acquired at very low prices. By 1937, 28 firms with a capacity of over 1 million tons out of a total of perhaps 3½ m.t. had been bought up and destroyed, while a number of others, less fortunate, had been forced into liquidation. 'National Shipbuilders' Security' was then converted into a private company and virtually ceased operation.

There was also the so-called 'scrap and build' scheme of Part II of the British Shipping (Assistance) Act of 1935, made valid for two years. Its object was to help the builders of cargo tramp vessels in particular, since cargo freight rates, and hence orders for new vessels, were the last to recover after the slump. In return for an undertaking to scrap 2 tons of existing tonnage for every ton newly built, the Treasury offered loans on favourable terms to owners. Tramp ship owners availed themselves of

<hr>

[1] Balfour Committee, *Survey of Industries*, Vol. 4, chapter 4; Jones, *op. cit.* p. 124.
 [2] H. M. Hallsworth, 'The Shipbuilding Industry', in *Britain in Depression*, pp. 255–6, and 'The Shipbuilding Industry', in *Britain in Recovery*, p. 358.

this offer only to a limited extent, however, not least because of Part I of the same Act which gave them direct subsidies on sailings and thus discouraged the scrapping of tonnage.

Reorganization with a view to reducing costs, particularly by specialization and concentration of production, was intended to follow the work of National Shipbuilders' Security Ltd., but little was achieved. Instead, from 1934 onwards attempts were made to raise prices. Even in the years 1936–8 annual launchings still averaged less than 1 million tons, or half the level of 1920, launchings for export orders, in particular, failing to pick up again in the face of foreign subsidies and protection. On the contrary, in the mid-1930's even some British owners began to place their orders abroad,[1] deriving some indirect benefits from foreign subsidy payments.

In the engineering industry, some sections, such as motor engineering and electrical engineering, were expanding rapidly and absorbing much capital and labour from the declining sectors. Among the latter, those that suffered most were those which had been particularly successful before 1914, notably steam engine making, including locomotive and marine engineering, and the building of textile machinery. As in her industrial structure as a whole, it was the misfortune of Britain to have concentrated before 1914 precisely on the engineering sectors which were destined to decline.[2]

Engineering in the widest sense had expanded faster than any other occupation during the war: the Census figures showed an increase in employment from 1,779,000 in 1911 to 2,491,000 in 1921, and the insurance figures, calculated on a different basis, registered an increase from 1,028,000 in 1913–14 to 1,647,000 in 1919–20.[3] The necessary reductions were less painful than they might have been because of the large numbers of women workers involved, but in some sectors male workers were affected also. According to the Census of Production, engineering output in 1924 was only slightly higher than in 1907. It then rose to 121 in 1929 (1924 = 100), dropped heavily in the depression, then rose quickly after 1933. By 1937, it was perhaps 60% above the 1924 level, employing 30% more workers, the increases being largely due to motor and electrical engineering, while general engineering and other sections showed substantial reductions in employment.[4]

Though there were some large specialist firms in the industry, e.g. Babcock & Wilcox, boilermakers, or Platt Bros. Ltd., textile machinery makers, most firms in general engineering were of small or medium size.[5]

---

[1] G. C. Allen, *British Industries*, p. 155.   [2] *Ibid.*, pp. 137–8.
[3] Balfour Committee, *Survey of Industries*, Vol. 4, pp. 132–3; H. Clay, *Unemployment*, pp. 84–6.
[4] E. Allen, 'Engineering', in *Britain in Depression*.
[5] P.E.P., *Agricultural Machinery* (1949), p. 10.

It was not at all certain that large size necessarily promoted efficiency, which depended largely on technical innovation; good progress was being made particularly in mass-production and in accepting standard specifications for components, in association with the British Standards Institution which had arisen out of the British Engineering Standards Association. Among new processes widely adopted, an example was flash-butt welding, introduced in 1922: the weight of coated electrodes made and sold in the United Kingdom increased from 7·8 million lb. in 1932 to 46 million lb. in 1940 and 97 million lb. in 1943.[1]

In the inter-war years, technical progress still depended largely on improved mechanical aids and on efficient prime movers, that is, on engineering. Direct comparisons of efficiency with other countries can only be made separately for each subsection of the engineering industry, if at all. Until 1929, world trade in engineering products was growing so fast that even British exports were increasing in absolute terms, though they declined as a proportion of world exports. This picture changed radically in the 1930's, when export markets collapsed. The industry then came to rely increasingly on the home market, largely protected by the tariff of 1932 and increasingly prosperous after 1933.[2] In this it was typical of much of industry in Britain.

The cotton industry had grown up as an export trade, and despite the rapid growth of competing industries in other countries in the generation before 1914, Britain's share in the international trade of cotton yarns and piece goods was still 65% in 1909–13.[3] The importance of cotton exports for the British economy may be judged by the fact that about 75% of the British output was exported in 1913, and 70% in 1920–6, the proportion of piece goods being 85% in both periods, and that cotton goods accounted for 25% of total British exports by value in 1910–13.

During the war, the output of cotton textiles had been curtailed both because of the loss of manpower and because of the reduction in raw cotton imports to save shipping space. As a result of the pent-up demand created thereby, prices rose excessively in the boom years 1919–20, and many cotton firms were lured into over-capitalization by bonus issues of shares at inflated values.[4] When the bubble was pricked, the highly competitive spinning and weaving sections suffered a disproportionate fall in prices, since the monopolistic finishing sections succeeded in maintaining their margins fairly well.

---

[1] Heath and Hetherington, chapter 13.
[2] E. Allen, 'The Engineering Trades', in *Britain in Recovery*.
[3] G. C. Allen, *British Industries*, p. 217.
[4] Balfour Committee, *Survey of Industries*, Vol. 3, pp. 36–8, 123–7; G. W. Daniels and J. Jewkes, 'The Post-War Depression in the Lancashire Cotton Industry', *J. R. Stat. S.*, 91/2, 1928, pp. 170–80.

The decline in the cotton industry which followed, especially in the case of piece goods, was wholly due to the fall in exports; home sales, in fact, were rising. The fall in yarn production was a reflection of the fall in the output of woven goods, though declining exports also contributed to it. Thus the problem of the industry was its decline in exports, too great to be made up by home sales:[1]

	Yarn (million lb.)		Piece Goods (million sq. yds.)		Machinery		Labour in Spinning, Doubling, Weaving (000)
	Production	Exports	Production	Exports	Spindles (mn. mule equivalent)	Looms (000)	
1912	1,982	244	8,050	6,913	61·4	786	621·5
1930	1,047	137	3,500	2,472	63·2	700	564·1
1938	1,070	123	3,126	1,494	42·1	495	393·0

The fall in exports could not be ascribed to a fall in the world's cotton goods consumption, but was due to the rise of newly established competitors abroad. The erection of textile mills, often equipped by Lancashire engineering firms with the latest machinery, had particularly drastic effects on the markets of India and the Far East. For India, the largest pre-war market, the change was as follows:[2]

	Cotton Piece Goods (million linear yards)		
	Average 1909–13	1938	Change
Indian home production	1,141	4,250	+3,109
Total imports into India	2,741	724	−2,017
of which from the U.K.	2,669	258	−2,411
from Japan	4	441	+ 437

[1] Working Party Reports, *Cotton* (1946), p. 6; R. Robson, *The Cotton Industry in Britain* (1957), Appendix. The piece goods figures for 1912 are in millions of linear yards, but the difference is negligible: in millions of linear yards, the export figure for 1930 would have been 2,490 instead of 2,472. The figures for 1930 and 1938 include small quantities of spun rayon and mixtures. Imports were negligible, except in 1930, when they reached 10% of home consumption. Cf. also A. C. Pigou, *Aspects of British Economic History 1918–1925* (1948 ed.), Part III, chapter 4.

[2] R. Robson, *op. cit.*, p. 10; cf. also A. R. Burnett-Hurst, 'Lancashire and the Indian Market', *J. R. Stat. S.*, 95/3, 1932; F. W. Daniels and H. Campion, 'The Cotton Industry and Trade', in *Britain in Depression*.

Lancashire was inclined to blame this loss entirely on the cheap labour of the East, but other Western countries showed that it was possible, by operating with high wages and first-class equipment, to stand up to low wages competition. The British industry was unable to reorganize at a time when markets, prices and profits were falling away, and output per man-hour rose very slowly compared with such countries as Japan or the U.S.A.[1] Its proportion of the world's mill consumption of cotton fell from 20% in 1910–13 to 9% in 1936–8, and its share of the world's cotton goods exports, from 58% to 28%. Cotton goods as a proportion of British exports fell from 25% in 1910–13 to 20% in 1927–9 and 12% in 1937–9. The producers of finer counts suffered less than the makers of coarser yarns and fabrics, but competition became effective in increasingly higher levels of quality.

Up to 1930, some attempts were made to improve efficiency in the industry, but after that the world depression turned the emphasis away from technical improvements to a panic reduction in capacity. Both methods, according to the official Clynes Report of 1930,[2] required reorganization in the industry. There had been some amalgamations in the post-war boom, including the Amalgamated Cotton Mill Trust Ltd. of 1919, Crosses and Heatons (1920) and the absorption of other concerns by Joshua Hoyle & Sons Ltd. in 1917–20, but most firms remained small and agreement was difficult to reach among the hundreds of independent producers in the spinning, doubling and weaving sections; even in the finishing sections the pre-war amalgamations claimed by 1939 to control only one-third of total capacity.

In 1925, the Joint Committee of Cotton Trade Organizations had been formed, representing the associations of spinners, manufacturers, converters and merchants, and, from 1928 on, the trade unions in the industry, but its powers did not include the sanctioning of restriction schemes. The first of these on the other hand, the Cotton Yarn Association, was established in 1927 to keep up prices, but failed within a few months, as was inevitable in an industry consisting of so many small units, and working with costs higher than those of foreign makers. A new approach was required, and with the help of the Bankers' Industrial Development Corporation, the Lancashire Cotton Corporation was set up in 1929 for the American section of the industry. It quickly acquired 9 million spindles, which it reduced to $4\frac{1}{4}$ million by 1939, at the same time modernizing the property it retained. In the smaller Egyptian section, the banks set up the Combined Egyptian Mills Ltd. in 1929, which bought up 3 million

---

[1] Working Party Reports, *Cotton*, pp. 8–9, 50, chapter 6; L. Rostas, 'Productivity of Labour in the Cotton Industry', *Econ. J.*, 55/218–19, 1945, p. 199; A. J. Brown, *Applied Economics* (1947), chapter V/3.

[2] *Report of the Committee on the Cotton Industry* (1930. Cmd. 3615).

spindles capacity. The Quilt Manufacturers' Association was formed in the same year. These 'voluntary' actions were reinforced by the Act of 1936, which set up the Spindles Board, with powers to raise a compulsory levy, used to acquire and scrap, by 1939, 6 million spindles out of the 13½ million still thought to be redundant. The figures on p. 121 show that looms were also being scrapped in large numbers, but that action was unorganized and still left far too many looms in operation.

As early as 1923 the Government had intervened in the industry by levying 6*d.* per bale to continue the finance of the Empire Cotton Growing Corporation, established to reduce dependence on outside raw cotton. It intervened to more purpose in the 1930's. In 1934, the Cotton Manufacturing Industry (Temporary Provisions) Act gave statutory sanction to wages and working conditions to which the two sides of the industry had agreed. The Cotton Industry (Reorganization) Act, passed in 1936, authorized the setting up of a Spindles Board, as noted above, and the Cotton Industry (Reorganization) Act of 1939 created machinery for fixing compulsory minimum prices by setting up a Statutory Cotton Industry Board.[1] The State, having ensured the reduction of capacity, thus created a compulsory cartel to raise prices. The outbreak of war prevented the functioning of the Cotton Board as originally intended, and its powers were modified by an Act of 1940.

Structurally, the woollen and worsted industry was not dissimilar from the cotton industry. It consisted of large numbers of small firms, though in the woollen section vertical integration was common and most firms engaged in both spinning and weaving. In 1935, the average employment per firm was 160, and half the working force worked in establishments employing fewer than 300 workers. There were a few amalgamations in this industry also, including Illingworth, Morris & Co. Ltd., and Paton & Baldwin Ltd., the knitting wool combine, both formed in 1920, but apart from the combing and finishing sections, where near-monopolies had been formed before 1914, the industry remained highly competitive.[2]

Since it had always relied less on exports and more on the home market than cotton, it suffered less by the general decline in the former and benefited more by the buoyancy of the latter in the 1930's. Moreover, the British woollen and worsted industry did not lose its share of world exports, but suffered only from the decline in total world trade, caused by crippling tariffs in some countries and growing self-sufficiency in others. This was largely due to the continued importance of the quality trade, in which the traditional skill of British labour continued to be an advantage. As far as the mechanical equipment was concerned, however, too much of

---

[1] H. G. Hughes and C. T. Saunders, 'The Cotton Industry', in *Britain in Recovery*, pp. 448–9.

[2] Balfour Committee, *Survey of Industries*, Vol. 3, pp. 177 ff.

it was antiquated, and output per man-hour or per spindle was only a fraction of the American figure.[1]

After 1929, the more serious drop in exports was not fully made up by the growing home market of the 1930's, though the tariff of 1932 had reduced imports at once from 50 million to 7 million square yards of cloth. Employment declined steadily in the inter-war period, and unemployment was above the average, reaching 36·4% in 1931, the worst year. Schemes of control were being considered more seriously in the 1930's,[2] mainly with a view to ending price cutting in the home market, but pleas for an enabling act to permit re-organization to take place on the model of the cotton industry were not widely supported and were dropped when sales increased in 1935-7 in the home market.

The pottery industry was smaller than those considered so far, yet it has occupied an important place in British industrial production and exports since the Industrial Revolution, and like the other old staples, it is highly localized so as to form the main livelihood of a substantial region of the country, the 'Potteries'. In some sectors of the industry, notably electrical porcelain accessories, there was growth rather than decline, but the industry as a whole, especially domestic pottery, suffered from the over-expansion of the post-war replacement boom. A certain decline at home became inevitable, while tariffs abroad reduced export sales by half between 1924 and 1935. The British industry received protection under the Safeguarding Act from 1927 on. With exports of domestic pottery worth £2 million, imports £290,000 and sales to the home market £5·5 million in 1935, and similar figures for other sectors of the industry,[3] the readjustment to declining markets was not as drastic as in coal or cotton, but was nevertheless substantial.

Technical progress was not negligible, even though many of the innumerable small firms were chronically short of capital and the installation of automatic or semi-automatic machinery for table-ware was far behind. Tunnel kilns, perfected in 1910, gradually spread in the inter-war years, replacing the beehive kilns, and firing by gas or electricity became more common. The production of tiles and electric fittings was mechanized in the 1920's.[4] These improvements led to further declines in employment, and the industry had a high level of unemployment in the inter-war period, reaching 38·8% in 1931 and about 45% in 1932.

The staple industries which were in a state of depression or in absolute decline in the 1920's and 1930's were thus, to a large extent, victims of the same set of circumstances. There was, first, the contraction of vital

[1] Working Party Reports, *Wool* (1947), pp. 66-7, chapter 8.
[2] A. N. Shimmin, 'The Wool Textile Industry', in *Britain in Recovery*, p. 467.
[3] Working Party Reports, *Pottery* (1946), pp. 1, 36-7.
[4] John Thomas, 'The Pottery Industry', in *Britain in Depression*, p. 413.

foreign markets, largely because of self-sufficiency or tariffs abroad. Secondly, the British share of world trade was shrinking, as the British industries appeared antiquated, badly sited for expansion or in relation to raw materials, operating often under increasing costs, and in a period of low profits unable to modernize their equipment, preferring, instead, restrictive and monopolistic schemes. Thirdly, the staple export industries on which Britain had concentrated in the past were no longer the growth sectors in world demand. With greater purchasing power in western countries, 'instead of demanding fine, durable British cottons and woollens, china, or cutlery, consumers in protected markets, subjected to high-pressure salesmanship, turned to new mass-produced cheap luxuries—silks and rayons, radios, automobiles, household gadgets, movies, phonographs—and to the home market goods and services—electric light, newspapers and books, sports, housing and leisure'.[1] Fourthly, after 1925 the relative loss of markets was aggravated by the over-valuation of the pound, and it is monetary causes which largely account for the fact that unemployment was worse in Britain than elsewhere in the 1920's, but lighter here than in the other major industrial nations in the 1930's. The growth in output was fairly fast by historical standards in both decades. There were marked sectoral differences: manufacturing and distribution grew faster in the 1930's, and most other sectors in the 1920's.[2]

In addition, there were often specific causes for the depression in particular industries. Thus steel and shipbuilding suffered from the unhealthy over-expansion during the war; coal from being replaced, in part, by oil and hydro-electric power; and cotton from the ease with which backward low-wage countries could install up-to-date machinery.[3] Finally, the more the world's governments turned for remedies to autarchy, restrictions or bilateral agreements, the more they were bound to injure the industries which depended for their health on free access to the world's markets.

4. THE CHANGING LOCATION OF INDUSTRY

The interaction between the declining staple industries and the new and expanding trades was one of the most decisive influences on the British economy in the inter-war years. It underlay the changes in the volume and terms of Britain's foreign trade, and the marked rise in the standard of living as resources formerly devoted to the staple exports to acquire food and raw materials were devoted to home-produced consumer goods. It was also responsible for a decisive shift in the geographical location of British industry and population between 1920 and 1939.

[1] A. E. Kahn, *Great Britain in the World Economy* (1946), p. 74.
[2] J. A. Dowie, 'Growth in the Inter-War Period: Some More Arithmetic', *Ec. Hist. Rev.*, 21/1 (1968), and literature quoted there.
[3] W. A. Lewis, *Economic Survey 1919–1939* (1949), pp. 42, 87.

British Industry and Transport Between the Wars

Some of the declining industries including railways, shipping and agriculture were widely scattered geographically, but mostly they were highly concentrated in small and clearly defined areas. Some of these held concentrations of two or three of these old basic industries and were utterly dependent on their prosperity. They were all to be found in that part of England and Wales lying north and west of a line drawn from the Severn Estuary to the Humber, and in the Lowland Belt of Scotland. The south and east, apart from London, had been largely by-passed in the industrialization of the nineteenth century.

The original location of these centres of the nineteenth-century staple industries had been determined largely by the location of easily accessible coal and iron deposits, by water power available from mountain streams, and by other materials, such as salt in Cheshire, fireclay near Stourbridge, and grindstones near Sheffield. Once established, an industry would call into being others of an ancillary or complementary nature, as well as a large labour force, a canal and railway network, and these would in turn attract yet other industries by a snowball effect, the whole depending ultimately on steam power based on coal. Thus, by 1914, much of Britain's basic staple industry was to be found in a few areas in South Wales, Lancashire and the West Riding, the industrial West Midlands, the north-east coast and Clydeside.

The effects of the decline and depression of the old staple industries on employment and prosperity generally were naturally felt with particular force in these narrowly limited areas, and they were not relieved by a parallel establishment of the new industries in the same districts. Wherever the expanding industries settled in old industrial areas, as in Birmingham, Coventry, Nottingham, Leicester and Derby, or in parts of London, they found much of the existing equipment, the public utilities, the skill and adaptability of the work force, of great advantage. But, in general, the new industries settled in new areas, mainly in the Midlands and the south. This is illustrated in the following tables:

Percentage of Net Output of Industry in Regions, 1924–35[1]

	1924	1930	1935
Old Industrial Regions[2]	49·6	42·4	37·6
New Industrial Regions[3]	28·7	33·4	37·1
Rest of Great Britain	21·7	24·2	25·3
Total Great Britain	100	100	100

[1] P.E.P., *Report on the Location of Industry in Great Britain* (1939), p. 44.
[2] Lancashire and Cheshire, West Riding, Northumberland and Durham, South Wales and Monmouthshire and West Central Scotland Regions of the Census of Production.
[3] Greater London, Warwickshire etc. Regions of the Census of Production.

The Changing Location of Industry

Percentage of Total Population and Insured Population in Regions, 1921–37[1]

	Total Population		Insured Population	
	1921	1937	1923	1937
1. Lancashire	11·6	10·9	15·7	13·8
2. West Riding, Notts and Derby	10·9	10·8	13·0	12·2
3. Northumberland and Durham	5·2	4·8	5·7	4·9
4. Mid-Scotland	6·2	6·0	7·3	6·6
5. Glamorgan and Monmouth	4·0	3·4	4·2	3·3
6. London and Home Counties	23·5	25·7	22·4	26·0
7. Midland Counties[2]	9·5	9·7	11·2	11·7
Old Industrial Areas (1–5)	37·9	35·9	45·9	40·8
New Industrial Areas (6–7)	33·0	35·4	33·6	37·7
8. Rest of Great Britain	29·1	28·7	20·5	21·5
Total Great Britain	100	100	100	100

In June 1923, the four southern Divisions of the Ministry of Labour (London, South-East, South-West and the Midlands) contained 46·6% of the insured population, and the rest of the United Kingdom (including Northern Ireland) the remaining 53·4%: in June 1938 these figures had been almost exactly reversed, the south now having 53·9% and the north 46·1% of the insured population. There was thus a remarkable shift in the distribution of the total population; it was considerably larger in the insured population; and it was larger still when measured by net industrial output.

This shift was not so much the result of a southward 'migration' of industry, as the result of its original distribution, for it was the south and east which contained mainly industries which were destined to expand, while the typical industries of the north and west were declining. The extent of that factor is illustrated in the table overleaf, which should be compared with the second of the two tables above.[3]

To some extent, however, every industry showed rather better results in the expanding areas than in the declining ones,[4] the multiplier effect

[1] *Report of the Royal Commission on the Distribution of the Industrial Population* (Barlow Commission) (1940. Cmd. 6153). Based on the Ministry of Labour Regions. Cf. also Mark Abrams, *The Condition of the British People, 1911–1945* (1945), p. 22.

[2] Industrial Midland Counties, except Notts and Derbyshire.

[3] M. P. Fogarty, *Prospects of the Industrial Areas of Great Britain* (1945), p. 16.

[4] R. C. Tress, 'Unemployment and the Diversification of Industry', *Manchester*

	Percent of Insured Workers in each Region Employed in:				Total Change in Employment, %	Hypothetical Change if Employment in 21 Industries had changed alike in All Regions
	16 expanding industries		5 declining industries			
	1923	1937	1923	1937		
1. Lancashire	9	16	36	24	+8	+11
2. West Riding, Notts, Derby	9	14	43	32	+15	+9
3. Northumberland, Durham	6	9	49	33	+5	+4
4. Mid-Scotland	10	13	24	15	+10	+18
5. Glamorgan and Monmouth	4	6	59	41	−4	+1
6. London and Home Counties	21	25	1	1	+43	+40
7. Midland Counties	26	30	12	7	+28	+29
Great Britain	14	19	23	14	+22	+22

of local prosperity being particularly evident in 'local', as distinct from 'basic', industries, such as local transport, distribution, hotels and entertainments services.[1] Building, above all, as might be expected, showed quite disproportionate increases in the growing areas and was correspondingly slack in the depressed areas.

The substantial migration of labour involved in the geographical shift was entirely voluntary, induced by the classic economic forces of supply and demand. The pull of higher wages was relatively unimportant here: it was the comparative levels of unemployment—as well as the distance—which were the most powerful factors affecting the decision to migrate.[2] Yet the resistance to migration was high also, for to the end of our period the northern and Welsh 'unemployment figures remained obstinately at double the southern rates, migration having been quite insufficient to level them out. The July averages of the proportion of the insured population unemployed in the eight years 1929–36 compared as follows:

%
South-west 7·8 ⎤
London 8·8 ⎥ South Britain 11·0%
South-east 11·1 ⎥
Midlands 15·2 ⎦

School, 9/2, 1938; D. G. Champernowne, 'The Uneven Distribution of Unemployment in the United Kingdom, 1929–36', *Rev. Econ. Studies*, 6/2, 1938; A. M. Carr-Saunders and D. Caradog Jones, *A Survey of the Social Structure of England and Wales* (Oxford, 2nd ed., 1937), p. 43.

[1] S. R. Dennison, *The Location of Industry and the Depressed Areas* (1939), pp. 40–1, 158; J. H. Jones, in Appx. II to Barlow Commission, *Report*, pp. 274–6.

[2] H. Makower, J. Marschak and H. W. Robinson, 'Studies in Mobility of Labour', *Oxf. Econ. P.*, 1/1, 1938.

North-west 21·6⎫
Scotland 21·8⎪ North Britain and Wales 22·8%
North-east 22·7⎪
Wales 30·1⎭

The difference was even more marked in the case of protracted unemployment, of 12 months or over: in June 1936, for example, this ranged from 9% in London and the south-east to 37% in Wales.[1]

Even these figures do not measure the true extent of the difference in employment opportunities between the prosperous and the declining parts of the country. There was more underemployment in the latter, seen in the lower figures of net output per head, and, apart from the textile industries in which women habitually went out to work, there was a markedly smaller percentage of the population seeking employment: while the *proportion* of the population insured went up by 20·8% in London in 1922–31, it went up by only 2·6% in Wales.[2] Where most of the men were out of work, women, youths and old men did not even trouble to sign on at the Labour Exchange. By contrast, in the Greater London Region and the Midlands, there was a much tighter labour market, including local and temporary severe labour shortages.[3] Lastly, for a man on the unemployment register, the chances of re-absorption into industry were much higher in the prosperous than in the depressed areas.[4] None of these differences was ironed out by migration; they remained as strongly marked at the end of our period as at the beginning.

The new industries of the southern half of Britain differed from the old staples not only by the fact that they were growing instead of declining. They were also industries of a different character. The main pre-condition of the southern industrial renaissance was the fact that the new industries were no longer tied to any particular area by bulky fuel or raw material needs. In place of localized coal for steam power and heat, electricity was available everywhere, especially after the completion of the grid. Likewise, few of the new industries were troubled by high transport costs of bulky raw materials. In some cases, the raw material formed only a very small item in total costs, as for example the steel used in motor or electrical engineering. In others, the raw materials were imported, and any port could become a good location: thus timber and wood pulp, landed in

[1] H. W. Robinson, 'Employment and Unemployment', in *Britain in Recovery* (1938), p. 97.
[2] J. H. Jones, in Appx. II to Barlow Commission, *Report*, pp. 264–5. The differences also emerge from a comparison with the table on p. 127 above.
[3] S. R. Dennison, 'The Effects of Recovery on the Various Regions', in *Britain in Recovery*, p. 109; Board of Trade and Scottish Office, *Distribution of Industry* (1948. Cmd. 7540), p. 7.
[4] H. W. Singer, 'Regional Labour Markets and the Process of Unemployment', *Rev. Econ. Studies*, 7, 1939–40.

London, were the raw materials of the flourishing furniture, paper and printing industries of the metropolis. At the same time, the development of road transport made industry altogether less dependent on the old rail and canal networks and forced down railway rates to 'exceptional', i.e. lower rates, while 'tapering' charges on the railways made long distances less disadvantageous. Industry was thus more footloose and had greater freedom of choice of location than in the nineteenth century. In 1924, 55% (or including cotton and wool, 70%) of the declining industries were tied to their location by heavy transport costs, and in 1934 the proportion was still 50% (65%). By contrast, among the growing industries the proportion was only 10% in both years.

Moreover, in place of skilled or brawny male labour, most of the new industries required adaptable but essentially unskilled labour, much of it female. In place of the capital goods and foreign markets of the old staples, the new industries were largely mass-producing consumer goods for the home market. Proximity to the market, whether this consisted of the ultimate consumer or a consumer-good industry, often became the decisive consideration, and the relaxation of the old localizing restrictions permitted industry to follow it.[1] As a result, London, forming the largest concentration of home consumers, became the main location for new industries: in 1932-7, it accounted for five-sixths of the net increase in the number of factories, two-fifths of employment in new factories and one-third of all factory extensions undertaken, even though it had only one-fifth of the population. Birmingham and its conurbation formed another large market attracting the new industries. Even in the depressed parts of the country, the large cities were exempt from the worst effects of industrial decline: thus the Manchester and Liverpool areas were omitted from the original list of depressed (or 'special') areas, and even in the areas so designated, the boundaries were drawn so as to exclude the main population centres of Cardiff, Newcastle and Glasgow. In following the market as the main factor in location, industry was concerned not so much with transport costs as with speed and regularity of supplies, and immediate knowledge of changes in markets, tastes and fashions. This was considered so important that some firms set up what were, in effect, duplicate factories for each main centre of population.

In many cases, however, the rationality of the geographical shift can easily be exaggerated.[2] In preferring the south to the north, industrialists moved into areas of higher rents and higher wages; they left areas with well-developed public utilities and plentiful labour for districts in which good roads and other services had still to be laid out, and where labour was scarce, untrained and had to travel long distances to work. Nor was

[1] P. G. Hall, *The Industries of London since 1861* (1962).
[2] G. D. H. Cole,, *Building and Planning* (1945), p. 23.

it true that trade unions were more restrictive in the north;[1] in fact, the only clear-cut case in this period of an industry driven out by high wages and trade union power was the printing industry, which migrated out of Central London to such places as St. Albans, Cheltenham and Ipswich, largely because of the accident that the London and provincial trade unions of typographers had not amalgamated. Constricted space, high rents and traffic jams forced other industries also to move out of London into the suburbs, to make the outer ring of London the fastest growing area in the country: between 1901 and 1938, the population of the County of London declined by 150,000, but that of Greater London grew by 1,600,000.[2] There may have been a few industrialists who consciously preferred the climate or the amenities of the south, and there may have been a few others who worked out comparative costs in some detail. But largely, industry moved south because the south was expanding and prosperous,[3] and London and the Midlands thus benefited by the same kind of snowball effect which had created the industrial centres of the north and Wales in the past.

There was, however, one major difference. While, broadly speaking, the general rate of expansion of the economy before 1914 was such as to allow the re-absorption of displaced labour by the growth areas, the expansion of the inter-war period had been slowed up, and the locational and other changes accelerated, to such an extent as to render such easy readjustment by the direct pull of market forces impossible. As the staple industries contracted, the populations of whole districts were thrown out of work, without hope of alternative employment. Ancillary trades and finally local service trades suffered, and as the most energetic workers left, the areas affected became caught up in a vicious circle of depression and decline. In the depression of the early 1930's the problem had grown to such dimensions that Governments could no longer ignore it. In some areas, up to 80% of the insured population was out of work: even after recovery had begun, in May 1934, 74·1% of the insured males were unemployed in Brynmawr, 73·4% in Dowlais, 69·1% in Merthyr and 65·7% in Ferndale,[4] while high unemployment rates even in 'prosperous' areas robbed migration of its purpose.

[1] *First Report of Commissioner for the Special Areas (England and Wales)* (1935. Cmd. 4957), pp. 14–16.

[2] P.E.P., *Location of Industry*, p. 47, map on p. 171; D. H. Smith, *The Industries of Greater London* (1933); Fogarty, *Prospects*, chapters 14, 15; Mowat, *Britain between the Wars*, p. 225; Brinley Thomas, 'The Influx of Labour into London and the South-East, 1920–36', *Economica*, N.S., 4/15, 1937.

[3] P.E.P., *Location of Industry*, chapter 3; Dennison, *Location of Industry*, pp. 30–2; R. C. on the Geographical Distribution of the Industrial Population (Barlow Commission), *Minutes of Evidence* (1937), *passim*.

[4] Ministry of Labour, *Reports of Investigations into the Industrial Conditions in Certain Depressed Areas* (1934. Cmd. 4728), p. 136.

Surveys were sponsored by the Board of Trade and carried out by the provincial Universities in five of the most hard-hit areas,[1] to which a private investigation added a sixth.[2] Their main conclusion was that with the collapse of export markets, and in some areas, the exhaustion of the coal or other mineral deposits, there was little hope of rehabilitating the local staple industries which had formed the mainstay of employment in those districts. This was confirmed two years later by official investigators, who went over the ground again in large parts of four of the original six areas. Their reports, published in November 1934,[3] led to the official designation of these four areas as 'depressed', quickly renamed 'special areas' in 1934, by the Special Areas (Development and Improvement) Act, 1934.

Under the Act, two Commissioners were appointed, one for the Scottish Special Area, and one for England and Wales, responsible for the other three Special Areas of South Wales and Monmouth, West Cumberland and Tyneside with part of Durham. At first their powers were very seriously limited as they were not simply to give relief, nor were they to supplement the grants of other departments, e.g. for roadmaking, or to give direct grants to concerns working for profit. As a result, though nearly £17 million had been spent on grants by September 1938, the benefits were negligible.

Indeed, it was becoming clearer that the problem of the Special Areas, which was the problem of the whole of the old industrial regions in an accentuated form, was that the local industries would never expand again to employ their former numbers, while it was yet inconceivable that the social capital represented by houses and public utilities, and the deeply rooted local communities, should be sacrificed by evacuating their populations. The only feasible solution was the introduction of new industries into the Special Areas, and this became the official policy. It came to be administered mainly on the basis of two further Acts, the Special Areas Reconstruction (Agreements) Act of 1936, and the Special Areas (Amendment) Act of 1937. Further help was given by the Finance Act of 1937, which permitted the Treasury to remit the defence contribution of firms in the Special Areas.

Under the Act of 1936, Special Area Reconstruction Associations were set up, with a Treasury guarantee, to finance firms settling in those areas. This financial aid was supplemented in 1936 by the Nuffield Trust, and

---

[1] *Industrial Surveys* of: *South Wales* (University College of South Wales and Monmouth, 1932); *Lancashire Area, excluding Merseyside* (University of Manchester, 1932); *Merseyside* (University of Liverpool, 1932); *North East Coast Area* (Armstrong College, 1932); *South West of Scotland* (University of Glasgow, 1932).
[2] J. Jewkes and A. Winterbottom, *An Industrial Survey of West Cumberland* (1933). [3] Cmd. 4728, quoted above.

by the outbreak of war £¾ million had been spent by S.A.R.A.'s and £2·2 million by the Trust. The Act of 1937 gave the Treasury authority to provide direct assistance to firms settling in the Special Areas or in certain designated distressed districts, and £1·1 million had been loaned under this part of the Act by 1939. The Commissioners, at the same time, were permitted to make contributions towards the rent, rate and tax payments of firms settling there, and to provide factories for letting.

This last was perhaps the most valuable of the powers granted, and led to the establishment of industrial estates which could attract more effectively than small direct financial grants the new diversified light industry which was expected to save the Special Areas. Industrial estates had proved themselves in other parts of the country since the creation of the Trafford Park estate in 1894, which by 1939 had become the largest in the country with 1,200 acres and 200 works, employing 50,000 people. Other large and successful estates were at Slough and in Welwyn and Letchworth garden cities, all three in the outer ring of London suburbs, and Manchester and Liverpool Corporations were on the point of launching their own at Wythenshawe and Speke, respectively. On these and other estates the owners provided the land, the buildings and all services, such as power, light and roads, and manufacturers often had the further convenience of specialist service firms, such as packers, printers or laundries, on the estate. Industrialists renting a factory on an estate thus saved much of their capital costs, and had the further advantage that is their business expanded or declined, there were other factories of different sizes available. The Commissioners laid out large trading estates of this type in the Special Areas at Hillington, Treforest and Team Valley, providing by the outbreak of war employment for 1,600, 2,500 and 3,300 respectively, though they were still largely in the building stage. There were also minor schemes at Pallion (Sunderland), St. Helens Auckland, Larkhall and Cyfarthfa, and employment for a total of 12,000 had been found by 1939.

These results, while gratifying, could scarcely be said to have made much impression on a surplus population in the Special Areas, variously estimated at between 200,000 and 400,000 insured workers with their families. In 1938, the gap in the unemployment percentages between them and the rest of the country was, if anything, wider than in 1934, when the programme began, despite the new industries, and despite heavy emigration. Similarly, the transfer (assisted migration) scheme of the Ministry of Labour, undertaken on the recommendation of the Industrial Transfer Board in 1928, scarcely touched the surface of the problem: the numbers transferred were small, and about half of them were known to have returned to their original homes in the period 1928–37. Nor did the preference in placing Government orders, or the compulsory diversion of firms established by foreigners, make any appreciable difference. The Barlow Report in 1940 was in favour of authority to prohibit the establishment of new industries in certain areas, while its Minority Report, as well as P.E.P., demanded more drastic powers still to curb development in any expanding area, on the grounds of the evils of overcrowding, as well as of the evils of starving the old industrial areas. These plans were set aside by the war, but meanwhile the re-armament boom of 1938–9, and the war-time and post-war revival of many of the staple industries, brought new employment opportunities for most of the older centres of industry.

5. AGRICULTURE

In the war years, agriculturists had found themselves in a sellers' market, and when unrestricted U-boat warfare began to threaten the food supply of these islands, the depleted labour force on the land was stretched to the utmost to produce the largest quantity of foodstuffs that the soil would yield. The Corn Production Act of 1917 gave farmers and farm workers the necessary security of prices and wages beyond the war years,[1] and the policy of deliberate encouragement of a high level of corn production was continued, largely for strategic reasons, by the Agriculture Act of 1920. This aided the farmers by guaranteeing minimum prices for wheat and oats, and the tenants by greater security of tenure, and spread some benefits to farm workers also by continuing the machinery of fixing agricultural wages.

An Act of this nature, passed in peace-time, represented a sharp break with the past by ending a tradition of neglect, and introducing a positive policy towards the land. Moreover, home supplies, even with the campaigns of 1917–19, still only formed a small proportion of food grains available to the British housewife, so that substantial aid could be given to British farmers at a relatively low cost to the consumer. Farmers might have been forgiven for believing that the policy of *laissez-faire*, which had all but ruined British agriculture in the nineteenth century, had been truly reversed as a result of the war experience.

No sooner was the Agriculture Act on the statute book, however, than world grain prices began to crash down from their inflated post-war height. The emergency which the Act was designed to meet had arrived much sooner than expected. The wheat harvest sold at an average of 86s. 4d. a quarter in 1920, 49s. in 1921 and 40s. 9d. in 1922,[2] and it was estimated that the State would have to meet a bill of some £20 million

---

[1] R. J. Hammond, 'British Food Supplies 1914–1939', *Econ. Hist. Rev.*, 16/1, 1946, p. 2.

[2] Jones and Pool, *A Hundred Years of Economic Development* (1959 ed.,) pp. 327–8.

under the guarantee laid down by the Act.[1] At this the Government took fright and went back on its word, and within a few months of their enactment, the price guarantees were repealed by the Corn Production (Repeal) Act of 1921. Wage fixing by the Agricultural Wages Board was also abolished and wage levels were reduced at once.

As world prices of foodstuffs continued to fall rapidly to 1923, and after an interval, again from 1926 onwards, British agriculture reverted to its pre-war trends. More and more farmers gave up their arable farming and concentrated on the products in which their proximity to the home markets outweighed the disadvantages of high rents and small fields: fruit, dairy produce and meat. With a rising standard of living, the consumption in the United Kingdom of all types of meat rose from an average of 48·6 mn. cwt. a year in 1920–2 to an average of 58·3 mn. cwt. in 1937–8, of eggs from 3,915 million to 9,385 million, of milk from 849 to 1,000 mn. gallons and of butter from 4·1 to 10·0 mn. cwt.[2] These increases represented a considerable growth potential for British farming, but falling costs abroad and more efficient methods of packing, grading and preserving ensured that home farmers were not to be allowed to enjoy these growing markets unchallenged. In the period 1924–8, for example, while consumption of meat, dairy produce and vegetables was at roughly the level of 1909–13, the proportions imported had grown,[3] even if the supplies from the Irish Free State are deducted from the 'imports' of the post-war years. The quantity of home-produced meat fell from an average of 29·6 mn. cwt. in 1911–13 to 24·8 mn. cwt. in 1920–2 and 22·4 mn. cwt. in 1924–9.[4] With its former strongholds now also under attack, agriculture again turned into a declining, and generally depressed, industry.

There was some scattered Government aid in the 1920's. After the heavy war fellings, the Forestry Commission was set up as early as 1919 to speed afforestation by buying or leasing land for planting and by assisting private and local authority owners in the preservation and extension of their timber reserves. It was provided with a grant of £3½ million over the next ten years and £5½ million for the ten years following, and by 1939 about 1 million acres had been acquired, including 120,000 acres of Crown land.[5]

---

[1] C. S. Orwin, *A History of English Farming* (1949), p. 84. Cf. p. 59 above.

[2] Richard Stone, *Measurement of Consumers' Expenditure* (Cambridge, 1954); Viscount Astor and B. Seebohm Rowntree, *British Agriculture* (1938), p. 3.

[3] A. W. Flux, 'Our Food Supply Before and After the War', *J. R. Stat. S.*, 93/4, 1930, p. 541.

[4] E. M. Ojala, *Agriculture and Economic Progress* (1952), pp. 203, 209.

[5] E. P. Stebbing, 'The Forestry Commission in Great Britain', *Quarterly Review*, 256/508, 1931; Sir R. G. Stapledon, *The Land Today and Tomorrow* (1944 ed.), chapter 7; John Parker, 'The Forestry Commission', in W. A. Robson (ed.), *Public Enterprise* (1937).

The pre-war encouragement of small holdings was continued, first by the Land Settlement (Facilities) Act of 1919, under which 17,000 ex-servicemen were settled on small farms, and then by the Small Holdings and Allotment Act of 1926 and the Agricultural Land (Utilization) Act of 1931. These provided Central Government subsidies to County Councils which let small holdings under the earlier enabling Acts, but the policy proved very costly and availed little to stem the decline of small holdings.

In 1928 agricultural land and buildings were relieved of local rate burdens, and more generous credits were made available under the Agricultural Credit Act of 1928. The Agricultural Mortgage Corporation was established, financed by the banks, including the Bank of England, and by the Treasury, with powers to borrow up to £5 million, to be used for long-period loans on mortgage; for Scotland, a similar Act was passed in 1929. Part II of the Act of 1928 provided for the creation of an 'agricultural charge', based on any of the farmer's assets, including chattels, as security against bank loans. All these schemes, however, came up against the farmers' objection against mortgaging his property, and as they did not come into operation until 1930, when an agricultural slump of calamitous proportions had set in, while their money was raised at high rates just before the introduction of cheap money, they were not very effective. Lastly, the Agricultural Holdings Act of 1923 gave the tenant freedom of cropping and greater security of tenure, though it permitted his eviction for bad husbandry.[1]

The most significant Government gesture of the 1920's in aid of agriculture was the creation of a beet sugar industry. Aided by heavy subsidies, sugar beet had been grown on the Continent for many years, and experimental plantings in Britain proved that the country was well suited by soil and climate for the plant, and that the land would benefit from the deep cultivation and heavy manuring of the crop and the by-products, including pulp for livestock fodder.[2] In view of the large surplus capacity of the cane sugar plantations in the colonies and of the subsidized and experienced beet sugar industry in Europe, the British Sugar Subsidy Act of 1925 was passed, granting a subsidy for ten years, but of declining value, in the hope that at the end of the period the industry would be able to stand on its own legs.

The experiment was not unsuccessful. The acreage under sugar beet rose from virtually nothing to well over 350,000 over most of the 1930's, even after protection and subsidies had helped to increase the cultivation of other crops,[3] while the crop provided employment for an additional 32,000 men in agriculture, beside others in the factories, and became a

[1] Aston and Rowntree, *op. cit.*, pp. 378 ff.
[2] Orwin, *op. cit.*, p. 85.
[3] Noel Deerr, *The History of Sugar*, Vol. 2 (1950), pp. 481, 497.

valuable source of cash to many farmers in the depression. The costs, however, were substantial. The subsidies in the original ten years' period of 1925–34 amounted to £30 million, to which has to be added the sum of £10 million in abatement of excise duty; on renewal, the annual cost of the subsidy was about £3¼ million. The Sugar Industry Inquiry Committee reported in 1935 that such heavy expenditure could be justified only if the producers were forced to reorganize. Accordingly, under the Sugar Industry (Reorganization) Act of 1936, the Government amalgamated the existing 18 factories into the British Sugar Corporation Ltd., with a nominal capital of £5 million. Its chairman and two members of the Board were Government nominees, and while the subsidy continued, the profits of the Corporation were limited to 4% plus a declining proportion of any surplus beyond that level, the remainder to benefit the Treasury. The total subsidy was limited to 560,000 tons of white sugar, estimated to represent 375,000 acres. There was also a Sugar Commission appointed, to supervise research, education and other matters.[1]

Compared with this Government-sponsored development, the voluntary schemes organized by the farmers remained singularly ineffective Thus the hop growers, after the war-time control over the growing and marketing of hops had been wound up in 1925, organized themselves as 'English Hop Growers Ltd.' to consider a joint sales policy. Although about 90% of the producers joined, within little more than three years overproduction and bitter competition led to widespread secessions[2] and the collapse of the scheme. The failure of this scheme (as of others) strengthened the growing belief that in agriculture, where innumerable producers competed freely with each other and usually with importers as well, organized marketing could survive only with the help of statutory compulsion.

Agricultural co-operation also made very little headway in Great Britain. The Agricultural Organization Society, founded in England in 1900 (a separate A.O.S. was set up in 1905 in Scotland), promoted the Agricultural Wholesale Society during the war, and when the latter was overwhelmed by the collapse in prices in 1923, the A.O.S. was dragged down with it and was wound up in 1924 when it lost its Government subsidy. It was left to the National Farmers' Union to take English agricultural co-operation under its wing, a task which it performed without much enthusiasm.[3] The Welsh section of the A.O.S., which had separated from the mother society, survived, and even in England the demise of the A.O.S. did not destroy the co-operative societies. By 1935

---

[1] Heath and Hetherington, chapter 8; Plummer, *New Industries*, chapter 6/II.
[2] C. S. Orwin, 'Agriculture: Grain and other Crops', in *Britain in Depression*, pp. 100–1.
[3] C. R. Fay, *Co-operation at Home and Abroad*, Vol. 2 (2nd ed., 1948), chapter 13.

there were, apart from the small holding and allotment societies, about 230 co-operative societies in England, 81 in Wales and 88 in Scotland, with total sales of £12·6 million. Most of them were purchasing societies, buying in feeding stuffs, seed and other requirements of their members. Many of the remainder were organized to pack and sell co-operatively their members' produce, mainly eggs, dairy produce and meat.[1] Agricultural credit societies had never taken root here and altogether the contribution of co-operation to British farming remained of minor significance only.

As the world depression spread in the early 1930's, most of the world's food, produced by farmers and peasants in conditions of inelastic supply, fell drastically in price and huge stocks accumulated in the food exporting countries, threatening further price falls and hampering any possibility of relief by curtailing production. The cutting off, by the war, of Russian and Danubian supplies had encouraged expansion of overseas producers for the British and other European markets. Canadian acreage under wheat rose from 10 to 15 million, Australian from 6 to 12 million and Argentinian from 14 to 16 million,[2] and these fertile areas were flooding the world with unwanted grain. The world stocks of wheat, which had averaged 635 million bushels in 1922–8, rose to a record of 900 million in 1931 and finally to 1,140 million in 1934. The index of wheat prices in Britain, taking 1911–13 as 100, fell from 130 in 1929 to 76 in 1931, that of barley from 125 in 1929 to 96 in 1932, and of oats from 125 in 1929 to 80 in 1933.[3]

In 1931 the Government abandoned free trade in manufactured goods, and there were now no grounds of principle left to oppose the protection of agriculture also. In the course of the next two years British agriculture was turned into a highly protected, organized and subsidized sector of the economy, mainly by the Wheat Act of 1932, the Import Duties Act of 1932 and the Agricultural Marketing Acts of 1931 and 1933.

The Wheat Act provided the most direct subsidy. Producers were assured of the 'standard guaranteed price' of 10s. a cwt., equivalent to 45s. a quarter, and the difference between the prices actually realized at that time, about one-half of the guaranteed figure, and the guaranteed price was paid over by the Government to the growers in the form of a subsidy, up to a maximum of 27 mn. cwt. By an ingenious provision, each grower was to be paid the average shortfall in price per cwt. sold,

[1] M. Digby, *Producers and Consumers* (1938), chapters 6–8; Horace Plunckett Foundation, *Agricultural Co-operation in England* (1930).

[2] C. S. Orwin, 'Agriculture: Grain and Other Crops', in *Britain in Recovery*, p. 166.

[3] Royal Institute of International Affairs, *World Agriculture* (1932).

so that those who sold at a higher than average price would keep their differential advantage. At the same time it was hoped that the limitation on the total crop to be subsidized would prevent a large expansion of wheat production in an overstocked world.

After 1933 wheat prices gradually began to rise from their slump levels, not least because of the joint action of producer and consumer countries in the International Wheat Agreement of 1934, and British prices rose from an average of 4*s*. 7½*d*. in 1933 to 8*s*. 10*d*. a cwt. in 1936, so that the deficit payments to British farmers declined sharply. The hope of limiting the acreage under wheat was not, however, fulfilled; it rose from 1·2 million acres to over 1·7 million in 1934 and the limit of 27 mn. cwt. was exceeded nearly every year; the Agriculture Act of 1937, in fact, raised the limit of the subsidized crop to 36 mn. cwt.

Import duties under the Act of 1932 and under a special Act were at first applied to horticultural produce only, but were soon extended to oats and barley also. In 1937 this protection was considered insufficient and was supplemented by subsidies to the growers of these crops, and in 1939 these were extended still further. When given a choice, the British farmer in this period preferred protection to any other measure of Government support, since it allowed him to make the most of the large prosperous home market at his doorstep, and in the end, under pressure from the farmers, protection was added to almost every other Government aid programme for agriculture, including the Marketing Acts.

The Agricultural Marketing Act of 1931 enabled two-thirds of the producers of any agricultural commodity to prepare a scheme for organized marketing, and with Parliamentary approval, this became compulsory on all. It was hoped that farmers would be able to exploit the monopoly powers given them under this Act to raise prices, but in the event the only price control scheme set up under this Act was that of the Hop Marketing Board, which had the benefit of the earlier organization of the growers and a later quota restriction on imported hops, and even then had difficulty in enforcing its acreage quota restriction.

For other commodities, the farmers argued convincingly that the powers of collective marketing given under the Act of 1931 were insufficient. They obtained the Agricultural Marketing Act of 1933 which added two new sets of powers. The organized producers were now authorized to control output as well as prices of their commodities, while the Government could add protection to any scheme that required it. On the basis of this formidable battery of powers, several schemes were organized with some differences of detail, but on the same basic principles. The Potato Marketing Board, set up early in 1934, dealt with a crop which had little to fear from imports, except for 'earlies', but had suffered in the past from a highly variable yield as against a most inelastic demand.

Of all the marketing schemes it was the most successful. It succeeded in stabilizing the acreage grown by a penal levy on excess acreage, it administered a quantitative control of imports from 1934 onwards, and it regulated the seasonal variations in supply by a simple method of control, the 'riddle': by varying the gauge of the riddle through which all potatoes had to pass before sale, it could vary the share of the crop sold for human consumption.

The Milk Marketing Boards, for England and Wales and for Scotland respectively, formed at the end of 1933, could build on earlier unofficial but effective collective agreements. Since 1922, the Permanent Joint Milk Committee, representing producers, distributors and manufacturers, had controlled a dual price system, consisting of the basic price, for the minimum of milk supplied throughout the year for sale in liquid form, and a much lower price for additional seasonal output, used for manufacturing into butter and cheese. Such a scheme of stable prices attracted much capital and labour from other types of farming into dairying, but prices kept up until 1930, since imports were small and home demand rising. Then the fall in world prices for dairy products led farmers who had hitherto sold to manufacturers to invade the liquid milk market and threaten the scheme as a whole. In 1932 high tariffs were put on dairy products, but as imports from Empire countries were exempt, the British farmer was not much benefited thereby, and compulsory organization by the Milk Marketing Boards was thought necessary. The Boards controlled the sales of all registered producers and maintained the dual price, or discriminatory monopoly, system. In 1933-4, for example, the average price for liquid milk in England and Wales was $13\cdot6d.$ per gallon, and for milk to manufacturers, $5d.$ per gallon. The farmers, however, received uniform prices according to the total sale of the regional 'pool'. The Boards were also active in stimulating consumption and improving the quality of milk, and in grading and attesting 'accredited' and 'attested' herds.[1]

The Bacon and Pig Marketing Boards, established in 1933, were the least successful. Attempting to stimulate home production at the expense of imports, they controlled the contracts between producers and curers, providing temporary Government loans where the resulting prices were unsatisfactory. Home supplies did increase as a result, but the rising demand of the later 1930's exceeded the ability of British growers to supply it and at the same time fill the gap left by the drastic reduction in imports. The main result was a marked rise in prices to consumers. By

[1] A. W. Ashby, 'The Milk Industry', in *Britain in Depression*, and 'The Milk Industry', in *Britain in Recovery*; C. R. Fay, *Co-operation at Home and Abroad*, Vol. 2 (2nd ed., 1948), chapter 14. See, in general, H. T. Williams, *Principles for British Agricultural Policy* (1960), chapter 2.

1936 the original scheme had virtually broken down and the Bacon Development Board, set up in 1935, was reorganized in 1938 under the Bacon Industry Act, to include independent members in addition to representatives of the growers.

Marketing schemes for other livestock proved to be even more difficult to execute and had to be abandoned. Instead, severe and diminishing quota restrictions were imposed on imports of meat from non-Empire countries, mainly from South America, and by the Cattle Industry (Emergency Provisions) Act of 1934 large subsidy payments were made to home producers. In the three years 1934–7 £11·4 million was paid out under this head. The Livestock Industry Act of 1937 altered the method of payment of this subsidy; protective duties were levied on imports under the Agricultural Marketing Act of 1933 and the revenue from the import duties was used to pay for part of the subsidies.[1]

The massive State intervention in agriculture in the 1930's sketched here reversed a policy of *laissez-faire* which was nearly a century old. Initially, strategic considerations played no part in it, and it was not until 1937 that the military importance of an enlarged food production began to be considered. It was judged, therefore, on economic grounds alone, and as such was subjected to criticism on various counts. Viewed in the broadest possible perspective, the world was suffering from a surfeit of food, and Britain, the world's chief food market, reacted to this glut by closing her frontiers to imports and encouraging her farmers to add to the world output by expanding their high-cost production. There was, further, the standard objection to making the home consumer pay higher prices than was necessary: the annual costs of agricultural subsidies and protection in the 1930's were variously estimated at between £32 and £41 million;[2] including the additional costs of raising food at home which could more cheaply have been bought abroad, it might well have been £100 million. Even then, prices barely rose to levels at which British farmers could make a profit: the index of agricultural prices, taking 1927–9 as 100, fell as low as 77 in 1933, but even by 1937–9 had only crept back to 90–90½.[3]

Apart from the potato scheme, the Marketing Boards were criticized as mere elaborate excuses for protection and import restriction. The bacon scheme, in particular, inflicted serious damage to Denmark, the chief foreign supplier, without stimulating home production in return: as a

---

[1] A. W. Ashby, 'The Livestock and Meat Industry', in *Britain in Depression*, and 'The Livestock and Meat Trade', in *Britain in Recovery*.

[2] R. J. Thompson, 'State Expenditure on Agriculture in Great Britain in 1938–9', *J. R. Stat. S.*, 101/4, 1938, p. 737; Sir A. Daniel Hall, *Reconstruction and the Land* (1942), pp. 41–2.

[3] R. J. Thompson, 'The Future of Agriculture', *J. R. Stat. S.*, 106/1, 1943.

result of the work of the Marketing Board, total supplies fell from 13·7 mn. cwt. in 1932 to 10·0 mn. cwt. in 1938.[1] Lastly, it was evident that Britain could not simultaneously hope to benefit her home farmers and the Empire growers whom she was pledged to support under the Ottawa Agreement of 1932, and clashes of policy resulted.[2]

The policy of agricultural protection, however, could not be judged in isolation. In a world of rising tariffs, international commodity schemes, bilateral trade agreements and managed currencies, such as the world of the 1930's had become, British agriculture alone could not be left un-protected. It might, nevertheless, be pertinent to ask what results were achieved by the drastic revision of British agricultural policy in the narrow field of agriculture itself and in particular how far the unfavour-able trends of the 1920's, and indeed, of the whole period since the 1870's, were reversed by it. It did not change the general downward trend in British farming. The flight from the land continued: employ-ment in agriculture and forestry in the United Kingdom fell from an average of 1,004,000 in 1920–2 to an average of 735,000 in 1937–8, or from 6·3% to 3·9% of total employment, parallel with the decline of the contribution of agriculture to the national income from 5·9% in 1920–2 to 3·2% in 1935–9.[3] Workers left the industry at the rate of 10,000 a year, and the exodus of the young men was particularly marked: the number of young male workers under 21 declined by 44% between 1921–4 and 1938.[4] By contrast, the number of farmers and members of their families working on their own farms declined but little, though accurate figures are not available.

The drift from the land had various causes. Low wages formed one of them. The Agricultural Wages (Regulation) Act introduced by the Labour Government in 1924 had set up a system very much akin to the Trade Boards, but based on the counties, and this had succeeded in raising the relative level of agricultural wages, but in absolute terms they were still far below the industrial: thus in 1924 agricuitural workers were paid an average of 28*s*. a week, builders' labourers 55*s*. 6*d*. and bricklayers 73*s*. 5*d*., while in 1936 the figures were still 32*s*. 4*d*., 52*s*. 2*d*. and 69*s*. 4*d*. In Scotland, statutory minimum wages had to wait until the Agricultural Wages (Regulation) (Scotland) Act of 1937.[5]

In addition to low wages, agricultural workers complained of long and irregular hours of work, poor opportunities for advancement, poor

[1] Charles Smith, *Britain's Food Supplies* (1940), chapter 6.
[2] Cf. esp. Astor and Rowntree, *passim*; R. J. Hammond, *op. cit.*, pp. 4–10.
[3] Agatha L. Chapman and Rose Knight, *Wages and Salaries in the United Kingdom, 1920–1938* (Cambridge, 1953), pp. 18, 20; Ojala, *op. cit.*, p. 67.
[4] *Report of the Committee on Land Utilization in Rural Areas* (*Scott Report*) (1942. Cmd. 6378), p. 16; Edgar Thomas, *Introduction to Agricultural Economics* (1949), p. 65.   [5] Astor and Rowntree, p. 313; Thomas, pp. 91–4.

housing, the system of tied cottages, poor schools and few provisions for leisure activities. Other amenities were also lacking. In 1939 it was estimated that only 25,000–30,000 of the 366,000 agricultural homesteads were served with electricity. Under an Act of 1934, the Government made available £1 million for improving the rural water supply, but even by 1939 it was still deficient in many areas. Finally, as late as 1939 there were at least 5,186 parishes without a sewage system.[1]

Most statistics agree that gross agricultural output in the 1920's was around the pre-war level and rose in the mid-1930's beyond it, stimulated by subsidies, protection and the buoyant home market,[2] though at least one recent index puts the volume of gross agricultural production even in the 1930's well below the pre-war peak.[3] The output was maintained in the face of a shrinking labour force by rising labour productivity: on a sample of East Anglian farms, output per worker was found to increase by nearly 4% per annum; the output per person engaged in agriculture over the country as a whole was estimated to have risen by 20% between 1921 and 1941, or 1% per annum.[4] Partly these results were achieved by mechanization, such as the employment of combine harvesters, milking machines and tractors: there were 55,000 of the latter on British farms by 1939.[5] Agricultural research, starting with the Development Fund of £2 million in 1910, was greatly expanded, the Government spending £646,000 on this account in 1938–9.[6] Yields, pest control and farm management generally were greatly improved, though crop yield per acre (as distinct from output per worker) in England and Wales rose but little between the ten-year periods 1886–95 and 1926–35: the yield of wheat went up from 15·8 to 17·7 cwt.; of oats from 13·8 to 15·8 cwt.; and that of potatoes from 6·0 to 6·4 tons. The yield of turnips per acre actually declined. Yet much marginal land had gone out of production in the interim. In Scotland, progress was more marked.[7]

Modern techniques did not lead to any substantial growth in the average size of holdings, or in the number of large holdings. Among all holdings in Great Britain over 5 acres, holdings over 300 acres in 1924–5 accounted for 3·9% and for 3·3% in 1939; those of 50–300 acres, for 38·6%

[1] *Scott Report*, pp. 16–19.
[2] Astor and Rowntree, p. 53; L. C. Mowat, *Britain between the Wars* (1956 ed.), pp. 253–6; Leo Drescher, 'The Development of Agricultural Production in Great Britain and Ireland from the Early Nineteenth Century', and T. W. Fletcher, 'Drescher's Index, a Comment', in *Manchester School*, 23/2, 1955.
[3] E. M. Ojala, *Agriculture and Economic Progress* (1952), pp. 208–9.
[4] R. M. Carslaw and P. E. Graves, 'The Changing Organization of Arable Farms', in *Econ. J.*, 47/187, 1937; Thomas, *op. cit.*, pp. 86–7.
[5] P.E.P., *Agricultural Machinery* (1949), p. 6.
[6] P.E.P., *Report on Agricultural Research in Great Britain* (1938).
[7] Hall, *op. cit.*, p. 93.

and 34·4% respectively, and small holdings of 5–50 acres, for 57–5% and 62·3% respectively. It was not, in fact, certain whether at the stage which British farming technique had reached in the inter-war period, large holdings were necessarily more efficient than small. Expert opinion was divided, and it could not be denied that the yield per acre was much higher on the smaller holdings.[1]

The main trend of the pre-war years, the decline of arable, continued after the interruption of the war years. For Great Britain as a whole, it fell from 14·44 million acres in 1921–5 to 11·86 million in 1938, while permanent grass increased from 16·2 to 17·4 million acres and rough grazing, etc., from 14·5 to 16·1 million acres.[2] Livestock and livestock products remained by far the most important products of farming in Britain, accounting in 1937–8 for 70·5% of the value of output, with farm crops valued at 16·1% and horticultural products at 13·4%.[3] There was a considerable increase in market garden produce in the inter-war period to supply the growing and still sheltered markets of the cities, the acreage under brussels sprouts for example rising from 14,950 in 1922 to 41,280 in 1938, that under peas from 43,500 in 1925 to 86,440 in 1938, and that under flowers growing in the open, from 5,500 to 13,100.[4] However, even at the end of the period there were scarcely more than ¼ million acres under green vegetables.

There was one important respect in which a pre-war trend was reversed. The number of owner-occupied holdings rose substantially, from 10% in 1914 to over 20% in 1921 and 37% in 1927 in England and Wales, and there was a corresponding change in Scotland. The reasons included tax changes in war-time which favoured owner-occupancy compared with tenancy, a buying spree in 1919–20, and, after a lull in sales, renewed transfers to tenants in 1924–5, when a slight improvement in agricultural prices persuaded tenants that now was the time to buy, and landlords that now was the time to sell.[5] Moreover, many landlords were unwilling to risk the large capital which had now become necessary for modern farming and they preferred to break up their estates.

After 1925 the buying of land by tenants ceased. This was one of the most significant symptoms of decline, and of the deep depression which even the Government apparatus of protection and support of the 1930's could not fully stem.

---

[1] R. L. Cohen, *The Economics of Agriculture* (1940), chapter 4; A. W. M. Kitchin, 'Small Holdings and the Agricultural Structure', *Econ. J.*, 44/176, 1934.
[2] L. Dudley Stamp and S. H. Beaver, *The British Isles* (1937 ed.), p. 153.
[3] Thomas, *op. cit.*, p. 11.
[4] Stamp and Beaver, p. 180; Hall, p. 97.
[5] S. G. Sturmey, 'Owner-Farming in England and Wales, 1900–1950' *Manchester School*, 23/3, 1955.

· These changes in agricultural conditions were reflected in many parts of the countryside. Less arable land was to be seen in the landscape; the number of derelict fields, rank with coarse matted grass, thistle, weeds, and brambles, multiplied; ditches became choked and no longer served as effective drains; hedges became overgrown and straggled over the edges of other fields; gates and fences fell into disrepair; farm roads were left unmade. Signs of decay were to be seen also in many of the buildings . . . the landscape of 1938 had, in many districts, assumed a neglected and unkept appearance.[1]

Agriculture was the oldest and still one of the most important of the declining staple industries.

6. TRANSPORT AND COMMUNICATIONS

The Railway Act of 1921 bore many marks of the political compromise which had brought it about, and of its various objectives, not all were fully compatible with each other. In the first place, it was designed to preserve the unified rates and charges over the whole country, achieved during the war, and the four main lines which emerged as a result of the Act were grouped partly with the aim of ensuring that each had its due share of revenue-earning and losing lines. The existing capital, including the compensation payable for neglected repairs and replacement, fixed at £60 million, was all converted into the new railway stock.

The four systems, the London and North Eastern Railway, the London Midland and Scottish Railway, the Great Western Railway and the Southern Railway, each covered a large region within which all competition ceased. To prevent the exploitation of this monopoly by the main lines, the Act laid it down, in the second place, that the railways were to provide reasonable service and that rates were to be fixed so as to secure to the companies a net revenue equivalent to the earnings of their constituent lines in 1913, plus an allowance for the capital invested since: the total sum thus arrived at was about £51 million per annum, allocated in fixed proportions among the companies. In place of the Railway and Canal Commission, which had merely laid down maximum rates before the war without any direct consideration of the resulting total revenue, a Railway Rates Tribunal was set up to control actual, not only maximum, rates on the new principle of securing this agreed total net revenue,[2] as well as keeping to the former principles of equity as between traders. At the same time Part III of the Act gave greater

---

[1] *Scott Report*, p. 15, para. 50.
[2] Sir Hubert Llewellyn Smith, *The Board of Trade* (1928), p. 142; C. I. Savage, *An Economic History of Transport* (1959), pp. 98–114; E. A. Pratt, *British Railways and the Great War* (1921), chapters 47, 48; C. E. R. Sherrington, *The Economics of Rail Transport in Great Britain*, Vol. 1 (1928), pp. 251 ff.

flexibility of charging by creating 21 classes of goods in place of the former eight.

In the third place, the Act established a permanent system of negotiation and conciliation with all grades of staff, in notable contrast with the pre-war refusal of the companies even to recognize the unions. Starting from sectional and departmental councils, the pyramid of organization was topped by a Central Wages Board for the whole industry, from which, in turn, appeals were possible to the National Wages Board which included outside neutral nominees: 'Parliament', it was said, 'has definitely asserted the right to intervene to secure in the public interest harmony and co-operation in railway management.' [1] The system broke down in 1933, however, over a demand by the companies for a 10% reduction in pay, and new machinery was set up in 1935. It had a Railway Staff National Council at its centre, and as its final, though non-compulsory, arbitration body, the Railway Staff National Tribunal.

Lastly, the amalgamation of lines was expected to lead to great economies in running, and the Minister of Transport was authorized by Part II of the Act to require the companies to standardize their equipment and collaborate by common working, common use of rolling stock and similar means in the interest of economy. Estimates of possible economies varied from £4 million a year to £45 million, a sum almost as large as the total permitted net revenue of the four main lines.[2]

In sum, the Act of 1921, which dominated the history of railways in Britain until the outbreak of the second World War, marked the end of an epoch. After almost a century of retreat from its original anti-monopoly position, the State had at last granted the railways the right to a monopoly of transport in the interest of efficient working, but with the most stringent measures of control to protect the public at the same time. It was ironic that at the very moment when the long campaign for railway amalgamation and monopoly had at last been won, it should turn into a hollow victory by the rise of the motor vehicle, which represented more dangerous competition than ever one railway line had offered another.

As a result, much of the Act became pointless if not directly harmful. Instead of the earlier system which had fixed maxima only, leaving railway rates at least flexible and free to move downwards, the new system of fixing actual rates proved far more rigid in a period of falling costs and prices. Before long, 'exceptional' rates became the rule: by 1935, 84% of the tonnage carried, and 68·4% of gross receipts, came from exceptional rates; and in 1936 only 7% of passengers paid standard fares, the remainder

---

[1] Sir W. M. Acworth, 'Grouping under the Railways Act, 1921', *Econ. J.*, 33/129, 1923, p. 19.
[2] Acworth, *loc. cit.*, p. 35; M. E. Dimock, *British Public Utilities and National Development* (1933), p. 80.

travelling at reduced rates.[1] The 'standard net revenue' of £51 million, beyond which the public was to share the benefits, was in fact never reached between the wars. Receipts fell markedly from 1923, the date of the compulsory amalgamation. In 1928, when the new rate system came into operation, the net earnings stood at £41 million; they then fell to about £25 million in the depression of 1932–3, rose again to a peak of £38 million in 1937, only to decline once more as the boom broke.[2] Net revenue might have been even lower if costs had not been reduced sharply also. Though there was no labour unemployment, the railways became a seriously depressed industry. In 1932, £260 million of their capital went without any dividend. There was a permanent decline in passenger traffic from about 1,100 million (excluding season ticket holders) before the war and a peak of 1,200 million in 1920, to 800–950 million in the inter-war period. Similarly, goods traffic fell from over 300 million tons in 1919–20 to 250–280 m.t. in most years in the 1930's.

Apart from the vast nominal capital of the constituent companies, amounting to £1,085 million, which bore no relation to present or future earning power, and the special statutory restrictions to prevent the exploitation of their crumbling monopoly, the railways had three other sources of weakness in the inter-war years: their own inability to lose the monopoly mentality and to modernize and improve their working; the falling off of heavy mineral traffic, including coal and iron ore, owing to the depression; and the competition of the motor vehicle. These will be examined in turn.

The Royal Commission on Transport made one of the most severe criticisms on the first head. While making allowances for the grave post-war problems facing railway staffs, it believed

> that in the days of their monopoly the railways had in some way, insufficiently studied the needs of the public, and their policy had become utterly conservative. Although between the most important centres of population there were excellent services of trains . . . the passenger services generally were unnecessarily slow and often inconveniently timed . . . The truth of the doctrine that facilities create traffic appears to have been forgotten . . . It is in the short and moderate distance journeys that the railways have lost passenger traffic by failing to make full use of their capacity for speed . . . It is certainly remarkable that there has been practically no improvement in locomotive speed in this country during the last eighty years.[3]

---

[1] H. M. Hallsworth, 'Rail Transport', in *Britain in Recovery*, p. 292.

[2] H. M. Hallsworth, 'Rail Transport', in *Britain in Depression*, p. 193, and *Britain in Recovery*, p. 286; Savage, *op. cit.*, p. 114.

[3] Royal Commission on Transport, *Final Report: The Co-ordination and Development of Transport* (1931. Cmd. 3751), pp. 37–8.

Such a sweeping indictment was hardly fair. For one thing, there was some competition even between railways: in 1932, for example, the L.M.S.R. and L.N.E.R. felt obliged to pool about half their traffic receipts over competing northern routes. Secondly, the competition of the roads was unlikely to allow a monopoly mentality to survive for long. But thirdly, the railways' record of innovations was by no means negligible. Containers were introduced, easing the transport of fragile goods; railhead facilities were greatly improved; door-to-door services inaugurated. Electrification speeded up suburban services in the Manchester, Newcastle, Liverpool and London areas. The Southern Railway electrified its main line to Brighton and Worthing in 1933 and to Portsmouth, Reading, Maidstone and Chatham later in the 1930's. Diesel engines were put on shunting services and some passenger railcars were used by the G.W.R. From 1935 onward the main line companies began to introduce faster non-stop long-distance services, often with specially named trains: by 1938 there were 107 daily trains with average speeds of over 60 m.p.h., compared with 25 in 1934 and 4 in 1914.[1] The provision of fresh capital was difficult in view of the poor returns on existing railway capital, since outside investors were discouraged and there was little surplus arising out of the companies' own earnings. Some help came, however, from a loan of £26·5 million for railway modernization made under the Railways (Agreement) Act of 1935. In the depression years of 1930–3 some 900 miles, mostly of branch lines, were closed to traffic.

The falling off in mineral traffic, caused by the decline in the production of coal, iron and steel, was bound to hit the railways more than any other means of traffic. In 1936, for example, coal accounted for $177\frac{1}{2}$ million tons of the total railway goods traffic of 281 million tons; in 1913 the railways had still carried $225\frac{1}{2}$ m.t. of coal and coke, and as late as 1929 it had still been 207 m.t.[2] Road transport did not compete in this field, and did not suffer by this decline.

Basically, however, the railways were in decline because of the rise of road motor transport, growing particularly fast from about 1926 onward: indeed, much of the traffic lost in the strike of that year was lost permanently. The extent of the loss of traffic to the road cannot be estimated with certainty, but compared with pre-war traffic, and bearing in mind changing needs in the interim, the main lines had lost, by 1933–5, about half their traffic to the roads.[3]

Against road competition, the railways contended, they were unfairly handicapped by statutes and orders, legacies of the days of potential rail-

[1] Hallsworth, in *Britain in Recovery*, pp. 294–5; Jones and Pool, *A Hundred Years of Economic Development*, p. 354.
[2] Gilbert Walker, *Road and Rail* (1947 ed.), p. 20.
[3] *Ibid.*, p. 128.

way monopoly, from which road operators were exempt. Thus their rate structure was rigid and publicized: their competitors' rates were neither, and when in competition, could always be reduced just below the railway rates. The railways were obliged to charge so much a mile to passengers; bus and coach fares tapered with distance, and thus became the more attractive, the longer the journey. In the case of goods, the railway charges depended in part on the value of the cargo, while road haulage charges depended only on size and ease of handling; thus the more valuable cargoes tended to travel by road, and for both passengers and goods the roads skimmed off the cream and the railways were left with the less desirable traffic. Further, they had to run services between the less populous centres, and they had to accept all traffic, while the road haulier need only accept what suited him, and, knowing the railway rate, could overcharge for any load he did not want to carry. There was also the long-standing grievance of privately owned mineral trucks on the lines, causing much empty running.

As their difficulties increased, the railways were relieved of some of their handicaps. In 1928, they were given powers to run road passenger vehicles, and within two years had invested £9½ million, mostly in joint omnibus undertakings with road companies. In 1934 they absorbed Carter Paterson and Pickford's, the leading road cartage contractors. The de-rating of railway property to the extent of 75% provided the companies with a freight rebates fund out of which to grant rebates. In 1930 and 1933, the competing road vehicles were also restricted by legislation; and finally, in 1939, after a campaign of the railways for a 'square deal', they were promised the repeal of many of their rate restrictions.[1] In spite of the triumphant advance of road transport, the railways were still by far the most important conveyers of goods and merchandise: in 1939, they carried 265 million tons of freight, compared with 100 m.t. by road and under 50 m.t. by canal and coastal shipping; and though the 4,526 million passengers carried by road greatly outnumbered the 1,237 million carried by rail, the figures looked different in terms of passenger miles: the average fare of the former was 2½d., of the latter, 1s. 6d.[2]

The motor vehicle, however, had captured a firm place in modern society. As a heavy goods vehicle, it could make deliveries from door to door without reloading and, if need be, loading and unloading could be done by or under the supervision of the traders. As the minimum economic load was smaller than that of a train, it was a much more flexible carrier. For relatively small deliveries, such as supplies to retail shops or deliveries to the home, it not only replaced the horse-drawn vehicle, but also opened

[1] Gilbert Walker, *op. cit.*, p. 233; M. R. Bonavia, *The Economics of Transport* (1954 ed.), pp. 200–1.
[2] Savage, *op. cit.*, p. 175.

out entirely new forms of distributive trade. In the case of public passenger service, motor vehicles rapidly replaced all other forms of the town omnibus, the 'stage carriage' of official terminology, and were also turned into 'express carriages', i.e. long-distance coaches, and 'contract carriages', or coaches hired as a whole. Meanwhile, the private motor car and motor cycle gave a new freedom of movement to its owners and diverted traffic from both trams and buses, as well as creating much new traffic. All these had been in their infancy in 1914; they appeared to sweep all before them in the inter-war years.

In 1914, the total number of motor vehicles licensed was 389,000. Of these, 132,000 were private cars and 82,000 were goods vehicles, and in 1919 these figures had all fallen by 10–20%. By 1929, there were nearly 2,200,000 motor vehicles registered, including 981,000 private cars, and in the 1930's the motor cycle lost in popularity, while the output and possession of the small car of 8–10 h.p. expanded further. By 1939 there were over 3 million motor vehicles on the road, of which 2 million were private cars.[1] The motor car had become the normal means of transport for the middle classes, just as the motor goods vehicle had become indispensable to many businesses. Both vehicles and their fuel became large-scale sources of taxation: direct taxation yielded £1½ million in 1920 and £34½ million in 1937, while net fuel tax and import duty receipts rose from £5 million to £46½ million in the same period. Earmarked for road improvement by the Road Act of 1920, the Road Fund receipts were first 'raided' by Winston Churchill in 1926, and the Fund was finally wound up in 1936–7, the revenues going directly to the Exchequer. Expenditure on the roads was nevertheless considerable, rising from £26½ million in 1920 to £65½ million in 1930. The mileage of class 1 and 2 roads rose from 38,000 in 1924 to 44,000 in 1937, but the mileage of unclassified roads fell in the same period by some 4,600, so that the net addition was only 1,600 miles. It was only in 1930 that County Councils became responsible for the classified roads in their areas, and it was not until the Trunk Roads Act of 1936 that the trunk roads outside London and the County Boroughs and large Burghs were wholly transferred to the Ministry of Transport. The number of motor vehicles per mile of road rose from 0·8 in 1909 to 7·5 in 1924 and to 16·4 in 1937.[2]

The speed with which road transport developed in the 1920's created new problems faster than legislation could cope with. Three, in particular, stood out: safety on the roads; the regulation of public service vehicles used for passenger transport; and the regulation of goods vehicles. The

[1] Savage, *op. cit.*, pp. 96, 142; L. F. Duval, 'The Motor Industry', in *Britain in Recovery*, p. 317.
[2] Duval, *loc. cit.*, pp. 312–15; K. G. Fenelon, 'The Road Transport Industry', in *Britain in Depression*, p. 213.

Royal Commission on Transport urged road safety measures in its first
Report:

> Legislation is greatly overdue. The present statute law (i.e. the
> Motor Car Acts of 1896 and 1903) on the subject, passed many years
> ago when traffic was in its infancy, is obsolete, and many of its pro-
> visions are generally disregarded. Probably not one motorist in a
> thousand observes the general speed limit of 20 miles per hour, and
> in many parts of the country no attempt is made to enforce it . . . The
> sooner an obsolete law, which is clearly no longer applicable to present
> circumstances and which public opinion refuses to support, is repealed
> or amended, the better.[1]

Following this report, the first of the three main statutes affecting road
traffic in the inter-war years, the Road Traffic Act of 1930, included the
abolition of general speed limits for private cars and compulsory insurance
against third party risks. The Road Traffic Act of 1934 introduced provisions for a 30 m.p.h. limit in built-up areas, a driving test, and powers to
establish pedestrian crossings, amending also the Act of 1933.

The remainder of the Act of 1930 dealt with the regulation of road
passenger transport, largely on the lines laid down by the second report
of the Royal Commission.[2] Up to that time, the bus and coach services
outside London had grown up virtually without control. In rural areas,
some 5,000 operators of one or two vehicles each continued to function,
having in 1931 20% of the existing buses between them. At the other end
of the scale, the Tillings Group controlled, by interlocking directorates,
holding companies and other means, together with the two other large
'associated' groups, British Electric Traction and Scottish Motor Traction,
some 40% of the buses in the country. Tillings' came to an agreement in
1929 with the railway companies to share any bus company in which both
were interested, in equal holdings. Many municipalities had also acquired
powers to run their own bus services, either jointly with private companies or alone, and in 1929 there were 100 such, operating 4,700 buses.[3]

The Act of 1930 introduced a strict system of control of public service
vehicles with the dual objective of providing full and co-ordinated public
regular services, and of protecting existing operators against wasteful competition by newcomers. 13 traffic areas were created, each under the control of one full-time Traffic Commissioner and (except in London) two
part-time Commissioners, and they took over the licensing of public service
vehicles from the 1,300 previously existing authorities. They had powers to

[1] R.C. on Transport, *First Report, The Control of Traffic on Roads* (1929. Cmd.
3365), p. 3.
[2] R.C. on Transport, *Second Report, The Licensing and Regulation of Public Service
Vehicles* (1929. Cmd. 3416).
[3] Savage, *op. cit.*, chapter 6.

grant licences to bus operators, bearing in mind the suitability of the route, and the alternative services available, and to regulate conditions of service, including the fares to be charged. In addition, vehicles had to meet various safety and other requirements before receiving a licence. In the event, the Commissioners interpreted their duties very rigidly, giving preference to the 'prior' service and strongly discouraging new services. Some 4,000–5,000 vehicles were withdrawn voluntarily, either as being surplus or as not roadworthy under the new regulations, but, broadly speaking, the general structure and even the fare system of road passenger transport was frozen in the position it had reached in 1930, except that amalgamations still remained possible.[1]

The Act also laid down conditions of service for drivers and conductors, including a system of licensing of drivers, maximum hours of work, and a 'fair wages clause'. While the regulation of hours was fairly well enforced, the attempt to control wages was not successful. Machinery of voluntary conciliation was established in 1934, but the decisions of the Conciliation Board were not recognized as necessarily providing the standard of 'fair wages'.

The other important measure relating to road transport was the Road and Rail Traffic Act of 1933, which regulated the carrying of goods on the road, and attempted to co-ordinate road and rail traffic, following the Final Report of the Royal Commission on Transport and the Salter Report.[2] Part I established a licensing system for goods vehicles, operated by the existing Traffic Commissioners. Three classes of licences were created: class 'A', for public carriers carrying exclusively for hire or reward; 'B' for firms carrying partly for others and partly on their own behalf; and 'C' for firms carrying exclusively their own goods. 'C' licences were issued freely, but the granting of 'A' and 'B' licences by the Commissioners was handled perhaps even more restrictively than the licensing of passenger vehicles, so that existing operators were even more secure from competition. The numbers of vehicles on 'A' and 'B' licences actually fell in the years following the Act, though 'C' licences continued to increase very rapidly.

There were also, as in the earlier Act for passenger vehicles, regulations as to speed limits and the condition of the vehicles before any of the three types of licences could be granted, and there were clauses relating to the hours of work of drivers and to their wages. Ultimately, joint boards were established and the Minister of Labour was given power to determine

---

[1] D. N. Chester, *Public Control of Road Passenger Transport* (Manchester, 1936), pp. 50, 87.

[2] R.C. on Transport, *Final Report: The Co-ordination and Development of Transport* (1931. Cmd. 3751); *Report of the Conference on Rail and Road Transport* (Salter Committee) (1932).

wages by order under the Road Haulage Wages Act of 1938. Part II of the Act referred to railway rates, permitting 'agreed charges' to traders who would agree to send all their traffic by rail, at a flat rate per ton; by 1948, agreed charges amounted to 7% of railway freight receipts.[1] Part III established a Transport Advisory Council to advise the Minister of Transport on measures for co-ordination, but little was achieved in this direction outside London. Unlike the public service companies, firms in the road haulage industry remained small: even in 1938, the average number of vehicles among 'A' licence holders was three, and 85% of operators had fewer than five.[2]

The only thoroughgoing scheme of co-ordination was that applied to the passenger transport of the Metropolis. London was served by main line and suburban railways, by Metropolitan and underground railways, by trams, buses and, later, trolley buses, belonging to many different companies. From 1922 onward more intense competition and the practices of 'chasing', racing and boxing in buses of rival companies had become an inconvenience, as well as a danger, to the public. The Underground Railway combine was especially hard hit, as it had used the profits on its buses to subsidize the tubes. As there was no power to refuse bus licences, there were by 1924 nearly 500 independent vehicles running in London, besides those of the London General,[3] while outlying districts were left without any service at all.

The London Traffic Act of 1924, following a strike of tramwaymen and omnibus workers, created a powerful apparatus of control by the Minister and the licensing authority over London buses. Routes could be limited, schedules could be laid down or amended, and stricter safety regulations enforced. As a result, most of the independent bus proprietors combined and in 1927 formed the London Public Omnibus Company, which quickly came to an agreement with the dominant firm, the London General.

Other means of transport were also crying out for unification. Lord Ashfield, the forceful chairman of the Underground Group, itself an amalgamation which included the London General Omnibus Co., pointed to the need for the extension of the electric and underground systems to the suburbs, but before these were built, demanded an assurance that no duplicate lines would be permitted. In 1928 the Underground, the Metropolitan and the main line railways decided to pool their London revenues, and finally, the London Passenger Transport Bill of 1931, the work of Lord Ashfield and Herbert Morrison, Minister of Transport in the second

---

[1] J. R. Sargent, *British Transport Policy* (Oxford, 1958), p. 43.

[2] Savage, *op. cit.*, p. 136; Alfred Plummer, *New British Industries in the Twentieth Century* (1937), chapter 3/I.

[3] London Transport (publ.), *London General—The Story of the London Bus, 1856–1956* (1956).

Labour Government, proposed complete unification. It was enacted by the National Government in 1933.

The Act set up a public body, the London Passenger Transport Board, which took over the property of 5 railway companies (excluding the main lines), 17 tramway undertakings (including 14 municipally owned) and 66 bus companies, plus parts of 69 other companies, to run them as a unified service. The members of the Board were appointed by a panel of trustees of public standing, and were thus made as far as possible independent of outside influence, except that the stockholders (many of whom were private persons) had the power to put in an official Receiver if certain minimum rates on the capital were not paid. Surpluses could be used to redeem capital or improve services. The L.P.T.B. had a monopoly of passenger transport in London and a region about 30 miles from Charing Cross, except for the four main line railway companies, with which all the Metropolitan revenues were pooled. In the last years before the war Green Line bus services were multiplied, rolling stock standardized and in part modernized, and about half the tram lines converted into trolley-bus services. The L.P.T.B. stock amounted to £109 million on inception, and in 1936 the Board employed some 72,000 persons.[1]

While road transport gained from the rising standard of living at home, of which a large part was consumed in the form of suburban housing and motoring, British shipping suffered sharply from the world depression and the decline in overseas trade. The shipping slump started as early as 1921. Freights tumbled from an index of 374 in 1920 to 166 in 1921, falling further to 115 in 1929. Tramp freights fell even faster, from 602 in March 1920 to 141 in 1921 and 106 in 1929.[2]

While the British tonnage remained fairly stationary, the world tonnage, stimulated in part by subsidies, actually continued to increase, from 59 million g.t. in 1921 to a maximum of over 70 m.g.t. in 1931. The carrying capacity increased even faster, with increased efficiency of the new tonnage. The British share of the world's trade thus fell, and competition was felt particularly from the ships of nations which paid lower wages or kept costs down by less stringent safety provisions, like Japan or Greece. Until 1929, however, the industry could still secure employment on an economic basis, and some 20% of British shipping, bringing in 10% of its earnings, still plied entirely between foreign ports. Between 1929 and 1932 the index of world trade fell from 130 to 97 (1913 = 100), while the shipping tonnage increased, and as a result British tonnage laid up rose from 630,000 g.t. in 1929 to 3,610,000 g.t. in 1932, while large fleets were sold to foreign flags, presumably to compete with the remaining British tonnage

---

[1] Plummer, *op. cit.*, pp. 146 ff.

[2] C. E. Fayle, *The War and the Shipping Industry* (1927), chapter 25 and Table 2, p. 415; L. Isserlis, 'Shipping', in *Britain in Depression*, p. 239; p. 56 above.

either with the aid of subsidies, or lower wages costs, or both. Tramp freight rates suffered particularly heavily, falling in 1933–5 to somewhere below three-quarters of the already low level of 1929,[1] and though other rates did not fall quite as far, most shipping capital became unprofitable and many companies could not even provide sums for normal depreciation.[2]

By June 1935 world tonnage had been reduced by 5¼ million g.t. compared with June 1931,[3] but freights were still low. Tramps, being without the resources of the large lines, without backing or subsidy, were the hardest hit, being driven out of their international routes by the discriminating legislation of other countries. As a counter-measure, the British Government introduced subsidies to tramp vessels in Part I of the British Shipping (Assistance) Act of 1935. They were to amount to not more than £2 million a year, and were to be reduced as the freight levels approached those of 1929. A Tramp Shipping Subsidy Committee was to administer this part of the Act; at the same time, the Tramp Shipping Administrative Committee was to encourage the industry to reorganize and eliminate competition. It was successful to the extent of aiding the setting up of minimum freight schemes, including foreign tonnage, for the grain trade from Australia, Canada and the Argentine to Europe. The 'scrap and build' subsidy under Part II of the Act was noted above.[4]

Liner companies with their large resources, and the regular incoming payments of mail and other contracts, as well as their well-organized 'rings' to keep up freights, found it easier than tramps to withstand the slump; nevertheless, several groups only survived by amalgamation. About one-quarter of the British tonnage, i.e. one-half of the liner tonnage, came under the control of the 'Big Five'—the P. & O., Royal Mail, Cunard, Ellerman and Furness-Withy groups.[5] Of these, the Royal Mail group, an £80 million concern controlling the largest merchant fleet in the world, collapsed early in 1931, the whole of the ordinary capital of the company being lost.[6] Only the Cunard Company received a subsidy, on condition that it amalgamated with the White Star line (which in 1927 had been acquired by the Royal Mail group). It took the form of a loan on very easy terms to finance the construction of two new giant liners for regular transatlantic service, the *Queen Mary*, on which work had begun and had been suspended, and the *Queen Elizabeth*.

From 1936 onward freight rates began to rise. British and world tonnage had been allowed to run down, and prosperity at home raised the weight

[1] L. Isserlis, 'Tramp Shipping Cargoes and Freights', *J. R. Stat. S.*, 101/1, 1938, pp. 78–9, 94.
[2] M. R. Bonavia, *The Economics of Transport* (1954 ed.), p. 19.
[3] L. Isserlis, 'British Shipping since 1934', in *Britain in Recovery*.
[4] p. 118 above.
[5] C. E. Fayle, *A Short History of the World's Shipping Industry* (1933), p. 298.
[6] *Economist*, 7.2.1931, pp. 299–300.

of imports, which had fallen from 60½ million tons in 1929 to 52 m.t. in 1932, again to over 75 m.t. by 1937. Exports, however, did not recover, largely because of the lagging sales of coal, and this, in turn, forced British shipping to make outward journeys in ballast and deprived it of one of its main competitive advantages.[1] Passenger traffic to Europe exceeded the peak level of 1929 by a wide margin in 1937, but on routes to areas other than Europe the figures of the 1920's were not reached again. Passenger shipping had to face the competition of a new form of transport, the commerical aircraft.

The heavier-than-air craft had proved itself in military missions during the war, and in August 1919 two air services to Paris began in tiny ramshackle planes. Several other companies followed, but apart from providing the main airports and navigational aids under the Air Navigation Act of 1920, the British Government refused to subsidize these services. Unable to withstand the competition of the heavily subsidized foreign aircraft, the British companies folded up one by one, and for a time, in 1921, there was not a single commercial airline left in this country. The strategic importance of civil aviation could not, however, be ignored for long, and Winston Churchill, up to 1921 Secretary of State for War and Air, secured a subsidy for the three, and later four, existing companies. In return, in 1922 the Government ordered the companies to end their costly competition on the most popular route to Paris and open up certain new routes instead.

The system of subsidies was reviewed in 1923 by the Hamblin Committee, and on its recommendation the four subsidized lines were amalgamated into a single company, 'Imperial Airways', in 1924.[2] It had two Government-appointed directors in a Board of eight, headed by Sir Eric Geddes, and a declining 10-year subsidy. Imperial Airways, starting with 13 small aircraft with a total seating capacity of 112, and a staff of 260, quickly proved technically successful, and opened up new routes to India, the Far East, South Africa and Australia, experimenting, in 1937–9, with transatlantic flights also. By 1939, it had a fleet of 77 aircraft of 191,000 h.p. and a staff of 3,500, but financially it was still dependent on the Government. The direct subsidy and Government payments for carrying the air mail totalled 68·6% of revenue.[3]

Services to Europe were neglected by Imperial Airways and an experimental service in 1930 to Birmingham, Liverpool and Manchester was soon abandoned. Other companies were more successful, and by 1935,

---

[1] Peter Duff, *British Ships and Shipping* (1949), p. 21.

[2] A. J. Quin-Harkin, 'Imperial Airways, 1924–40', *J. Transport History*, 1/4, Nov. 1954; E. Birkhead, 'The Financial Failure of British Air Transport Companies 1919–24', *ibid.*, 4/3, May 1960.

[3] Sir Osborne Mance and J. E. Wheeler, *International Air Transport* (1944), pp. 45–6.

19 companies operated 76 services within the British Isles, though that number was later reduced.[1] In that year, British Airways, a merger of three companies, was also given a subsidy, together with a monopoly of services to Berlin and Scandinavia and a share in the lucrative London–Paris route. With rising subsidies both companies soon showed high profits, but were severely criticized in the official Cadman Report. As a result, the two companies were to be merged, to share the European and Empire services between them. The British Overseas Airways Act was passed in August 1939, buying out the former shareholders and nationalizing the property, and B.O.A.C. came into operation after the outbreak of war, in November.

Modern communications, like modern transport, posed problems as to the methods of ownership and control, and the choice between private monopoly or State control. The pre-war history of the telephone had set unfortunate precedents. Numerous private and municipal telephone companies had been licensed by the Postmaster-General and the resulting inefficiency, muddle and poor service forced the Post Office to nationalize the telephone system (except for the Hull Corporation network) in 1912 at a cost of £12½ million. This action had been expected for some years, so that the equipment taken over was badly out of repair, and little could be done to improve it before the first World War. With only 700,000 subscribers in 1912, the proportion of the population linked up was far smaller than in most other civilized countries. The number of subscribers reached 1 million at the beginning of 1922, 2 million in 1932 and 3¼ million in 1939. The only special efforts made to extend the service were those offering subsidized terms to rural subscribers, and these greatly encouraged the spread of the telephone into the countryside.[2]

Unlike the telephone services, the British Post Office letter service remained second to none and was enormously expanded in 1919–39. Among its technical innovations in this period were the special electric underground railway, authorized in 1913 but completed only in 1927, linking six sorting offices and two main line stations by 6½ miles of line below some of London's busiest streets, and the air mail service. The first regular air mail contract began in 1926 on the Egypt–Karachi section of the Indian route, the direct London–India service starting three years later. In 1931 regular flights from Cairo to Cape Town began, and in 1934 the first air mail service in the British Isles was inaugurated, from Inverness to the Orkneys. By 1935, 19 million letters were sent by air mail.[3] The

[1] Plummer, *New Industries*, chapter 3/II.
[2] Sir Evelyn Murray, *The Post Office* (1927), chapter 8; Arthur Hazlewood, 'The Origin of the State Telephone System in Britain', *Oxf. Econ. P.*, N.S., 5/1, 1953.
[3] Howard Robinson, *The British Post Office, a History* (Princeton, New Jersey, 1948), chapter 30.

telegraph service, however, declined to about half its volume between 1920 and 1940, driven out by the telephone on the one hand, and wireless communication on the other.

The original commercial application of wireless telegraphy, following Marconi's first English radio patent of 1896, was to link ships with the shore and with each other. The Marconi International Marine Communication Co. Ltd., formed in 1900, dominated the field here by controlling most of the necessary patents, though there were some rival companies.[1]

The next step was to establish radio communication between fixed points, and the Marconi Wireless Telegraphy Company sent the first signal across the Atlantic in 1901, establishing a regular service in 1902. This posed an immediate threat to the established transatlantic cable companies, British and foreign, which had up to then succeeded in keeping up rates by a tight agreement to make large profits on a limited traffic. The other services from Britain were owned by a single combine, the Eastern Telegraph Co. Radio, though not at first as reliable as the cable service, expanded by undercutting the cable rates by a large margin, and the strategic importance of wireless links was also becoming obvious. In 1911, the Imperial Defence Committee urged the Post Office to establish wireless links with various parts of the Empire at once, and the contract was awarded to the Marconi Co., as the only one capable at that time of fulfilling it. Nevertheless, there were widespread allegations of corruption, the so-called 'Marconi scandal', in 1912, and though a new contract was signed with Marconi's in 1913, no stations had been built by the outbreak of war owing to the delay.

The need of war called forth important technical improvements, and innumerable signallers were trained who were, in the 1920's, to play a major part as 'hams' or amateur radio enthusiasts. After the war, imperial radio links were demanded more urgently than ever by the Imperial Communications Committee and the Empire Press Union. The British Post Office, mindful of the 'scandal' of 1912 and years of bad relations since, refused to give the contract to Marconi's, yet was unable either to build the stations itself or find other organizations able to do so, but the Dominions had become less obedient to the mother country during the war, and in 1922 the Australian and South African Governments made their own contracts with Marconi's.

Britain herself remained without intercontinental radio links as late as 1924. In that year, Marconi's announced a revolutionary discovery, the 'beam', or directed short wave transmission, which used far less power than the previously undirected transmissions, yet could send a minimum of 250 words a minute simultaneously in both directions. The invention

[1] S. G. Sturmey, *The Economic Development of Radio* (1958), chapter 3; H. E. Hancock, *Wireless at Sea* (1951).

forced the hands of the Post Office. Marconi's received the Imperial contract and, by 1928, 'beam' links had been established with Canada, South Africa, India and Australia. At the same time, the Post Office opened its own valve transmitter at Rugby, then the most powerful in the world, for radio telephony.

The two separate services, the cable systems and the wireless stations, were compulsorily amalgamated after the Imperial Wireless and Cable Conference of 1928, and the Post Office was forced to lease to the resulting organization its own beam station, which it finally made over in 1938. Financially, the new organization, controlled by a holding company, Cables and Wireless Ltd., was not a success: it had had to take over the obsolescent cable system at inflated prices, £12 million of the total capital of £53 million being paid for goodwill. In 1937–8, the company was reconstituted, and £22 million of its capital written off. The company also suffered from a decline in the volume of traffic after 1929. Cables and Wireless had some of the attributes of a Public Corporation: its rates and services were scrutinized by an official Advisory Committee, its distribution of profits was limited in the public interest, and two of the directors, including the chairman, had to be approved by the Government. But compared with other Public Corporations formed at that time, the shareholders' interests were more powerfully represented, and the deals shaping its financial structure more doubtful.[1]

Wireless broadcasting, as distinct from point-to-point communication, was entirely a post-war development. Marconi's Chelmsford station sent out broadcasts early in 1920, but this was done merely for the sake of technical experiments; the idea of public information and entertainment arose in the U.S.A. as a by-product of an advertisement campaign by the Westinghouse Company in Pittsburgh. By the time broadcasting was considered in Britain in 1922, the American listening public had been thoroughly antagonized by the interference on the air caused by unregulated competing independent stations, as well as by the advertising which spoilt their programmes. The Post Office, the licensing authority in Britain, also traditionally preferred monopolies, so that there was general approval for the decision that broadcasting, when established in this country, would be a monopoly controlled in the public interest.[2]

It was handed over to a consortium of the six principal wireless equipment makers, united as the 'British Broadcasting Company'. The 'Big Six' subscribed £60,000 of the authorized capital of £100,000, and other manufacturers ultimately another £11,500. The B.B. Co. was given all

[1] Sturmey, *op. cit.*, chapters 4–6; Dimock, *op. cit.*, chapter 4; H. F. Heath and A. L. Hetherington, *Industrial Research and Development in the United Kingdom* (1946), pp. 209 ff.

[2] Lincoln Gordon, *The Public Corporation in Great Britain* (1938), chapter 4.

the manufacturing patent rights and its income was derived from the heavy royalties charged on each receiving set sold and from a share of the receiving licences, issued by the Post Office. The large manufacturers were induced to finance the broadcasting company in this way in order to create a demand for their sets, and they were rewarded with the restriction of receiving licences to British-made sets only, at a time when foreign-made sets were generally both cheaper and better. The small makers and assemblers joined in order to share in the patent rights. The B.B. Co., using some of the existing stations of the Marconi Co., which had begun regular broadcasting in 1922, started its regular services in 1923. At the end of 1922 there had been 36,000 licences issued; at the end of 1924, there were 1,130,000; at the end of 1926, when the B.B. Co.'s existence ended, the number had risen to 2,178,000.

From the first, the broadcasting company and its programmes were dominated by the General Manager, J. C. W. (later Lord) Reith, who imposed on it a distinct shape which not only survived his own tenure of office in the company, but also influenced the structure and objectives of other Public Utility Corporations in this country. In Reith's view, the company was to be a monopoly established under the auspices of the State, but not subject to day-to-day public control: the B.B. Co. had had to accept powers of direction and censorship by the Postmaster-General, but these were never exercised. Further, the company was not to be run to make profits, but to provide a public service, with a conscious social purpose. It held a stewardship to contribute 'constantly and cumulatively to the intellectual and moral well-being of the community', with idealism playing a part, 'perhaps a determining part'.[1]

Reith succeeded in imposing his conceptions not only on his subordinate staff, but also on the two official committees of inquiry into broadcasting, the Sykes Committee of 1923 and the Crawford Committee of 1925, and on the public in general. When the extended licence of the B.B. Co. expired at the end of 1926, the British Broadcasting Corporation, formed according to the new conception of a Public Corporation, took it over. Its Governors, though appointed by the Government, were not responsible to it; and operating within a secure income of licence fees, it was not in need of revenue from advertisers or others. 'Those directing the policy of the Corporation were not influenced by the profit motive. They were not interested in the material welfare of the Corporation; their interest was in the intellectual and ethical welfare of the listeners.'[2]

Broadcasting did indeed become a major influence on the information,

[1] M. E. Dimock, *Public Utilities*, p. 268; R. H. Coase, *British Broadcasting, a Study in Monopoly* (1950), chapter 3.
[2] Coase, *op. cit.*, p. 118; Asa Briggs, *The History of Broadcasting in the United Kingdom*, Vol. 1 (1961); J. C. W. Reith, *Into the Wind* (1949), Part 2.

on the political and other views, the culture and entertainment of modern nations. By the end of 1929, there were almost 3 million licence holders in Britain; after 1930 sets became available on hire purchase terms and at the end of 1938 nearly 9 million, or the large majority of homes in this country, possessed them. A growing number, reaching over ¼ million by 1938, received their programmes by wire relays. The B.B. Co. had handed over 9 main stations, 11 relay stations and the high-power station at Daventry. This network was built out by the Corporation, which ultimately broadcast two complete sets of programmes, one national and one for the seven regions.[1]

Television was based on scientific discoveries made before 1900, especially the reactions of the selenium cell and the cathode ray tube, but it was not until the 1920's that television broadcasting was seriously considered as a commercial proposition. In Britain the main initiative came from J. L. Baird and his sponsoring companies. They exercised great influence for a time and from 1929 persuaded the B.B.C. to allow broadcasts from its stations, even though the Baird mechanical scanning system was palpably inferior to several other systems then being developed abroad. The system ultimately adopted was based on the experiments made with a cathode ray tube by V. K. Zworykin in America in 1931 and developed here by the Marconi–E.M.I. combine. The B.B.C. turned to it exclusively in 1937, providing the only regular television broadcasts anywhere before the war, received by an estimated 20,000 sets by 1939.[2]

7. NEW FORMS OF INDUSTRIAL ORGANIZATION

The earlier sections of this chapter contain numerous references to new forms of business organization and to a greatly extended range of functions of the Government and other public authorities in industry, agriculture and transport. These developments were evidence of a new attitude towards economic policy and represent a distinct phase in the economic development of this country.[3]

The paid-up capital of registered joint-stock companies with limited liability, the typical form of industrial enterprise, rose from £2½ milliard in April 1914 to £4·1 milliard at the end of 1921 and to over £6 milliard in 1938.[4] The large increase between 1914 and 1921 was partly the result of war-time extensions, but in part it reflected the share boom of 1919–20 in which capital was increased by watering, by the ploughing back of the results of war-time profiteering and by speculative promotion at greatly

---

[1] Sturmey, *op. cit.*, chapters 8, 9.
[2] Sturmey, *op. cit.*, chapter 10.
[3] W. Ashworth, *An Economic History of England, 1870–1939* (1960), chapter 15.
[4] Balfour Committee, *Survey of Industries*, Vol. 1 (1927), p. 125; A. Beacham, *Economics of Industrial Organization* (3rd ed., 1955), p. 6.

inflated prices.[1] Much of this fictitious capital was lost again in the slump of the early 1920's, but throughout the inter-war period the expansion of genuine joint-stock enterprise continued and many of the remaining individually owned firms and partnerships were converted to the joint-stock form of organization. By 1938 the partnership or the individual trading on his own had become very exceptional in industry, though they still persisted in retail distribution, in agriculture, in the professions and in a few other sectors. The share of joint-stock enterprise in the economy is difficult to estimate: according to the tax returns, it obtained about 85% of the profits of manufacturing industry in the late 1930's.[2]

The number of public joint-stock companies on the register actually declined in this period, but at the same time there was a large increase in the number of private companies, as partnerships and even one-man firms registered to obtain the various benefits of the company acts; to some extent, they were also recruited from among the public companies which found the more restricted, but also more privileged position of the private company more appropriate to their needs. The private company, as the typical form of organization of the family firm, was, on the average, much smaller than the public company. In 1938, while the private companies outnumbered the public companies by ten to one, they had an aggregate capital of only £1,900 million, compared with the £4,100 million of the latter.[3]

A large share of industry and transport was, even in the 1920's, not controlled by private enterprise at all, but by various types of public or non-profit-making organizations and their growth is one of the most significant aspects of the period. Among the most important of them were the co-operative societies, registered under the Industrial and Provident Societies Acts, and the building societies, registered under the Building Society Acts; enterprises administered by charitable, educational and similar bodies; local authorities, administering over one-third of the gas works, two-thirds of electricity supplies, four-fifths of water supplies and of tramway mileage, virtually all the trolley-bus systems as well as a large proportion of omnibus and other services. There were, further, *ad hoc* authorities such as dock and harbour boards, including those of London, Liverpool and Glasgow, and the Metropolitan Water Board, established in 1902; companies established by Act of Parliament, mainly in the public utility field, including the railways; enterprises administered directly by the State, including the Post Office, the dockyards, and the Crown Lands; and the Public Corporations. In 1928 the Liberal Industrial Inquiry found

[1] H. W. Macrosty, 'Inflation and Deflation in the United States and the United Kingdom, 1919–1923', *J. R. Stat. S.*, 90/1, 1927, pp. 70–2.
[2] P. Sargant Florence, *The Logic of British and American Industry* (1953), p. 170.
[3] A. B. Levy, *Private Corporations and their Control*, Vol. 1 (1950), sections 18 and 20.

that the capital administered by these authorities came to about £4 milliard (including £1¼ milliard for roads and £1·15 milliard for railways) and was thus of the same order of magnitude as the aggregate capital of all joint-stock companies. Public property as a proportion of total property was estimated to have risen from 6–8% in 1911–13 to 8–12% in 1932–4.[1]

The extension of the joint-stock type of organization was, from the beginning, associated with the need for large sums of capital, and it proceeded fastest in industries composed of large firms and using much capital per worker. Technical needs and market conditions favoured the large unit in this period, and the typical form of organization changed with the increase in the typical size of the firm. In one industry after another the family firm gave way to the registered company with its numerous and anonymous shareholders and its elected Board of Directors.

By the end of the 1930's, one of the consequences of this development, the divorce of ownership from control, had become very marked. In most of the larger companies the proportion of the shares held by any single holder (or indeed by the Board) had become insignificant and there were thousands, and even tens of thousands of shareholders; large holders were often found to be not individuals but other companies. Thus a relatively small holding might dominate a company in view of the scattered nature of the rest of the holdings, and this might mean 'government by bloc-holder', but more commonly left control in the hands of a self-perpetuating Board of Directors who were administering an institution rather than their own property.[2]

Keynes noted the tendency as early as 1924

> of Joint-Stock Institutions, when they have reached a certain age and size, to approximate to the status of public corporations rather than that of individualistic private enterprise . . . A point arrives in the growth of a big institution—particularly a big railway or big public utility enterprise, but also a big bank or a big insurance company—at which the owners of the capital, i.e. the shareholders, are almost entirely dissociated from the management, with the result that the direct personal interest of the latter in the making of great profit becomes quite secondary. When this stage is reached, the general stability and reputation of the institution are more considered by the management than the maximum of profit for the shareholders . . . This is particularly the case if their great size or semi-monopolistic position renders them conspicuous in the public eye.[3]

---

[1] Liberal Industrial Inquiry, *Britain's Industrial Future* (1928), chapter 6; Balfour Committee, *Survey of Industries*, Vol. 2 (1928), chapter 8; H. Campion, *Public and Private Property in Great Britain* (1939), chapter 5.

[2] E.g. P. Sargant Florence, 'The Statistical Analysis of Joint-Stock Company Control', *J. R. Stat. S.*, 110/1, 1947; also his *Logic*, pp. 176 ff., and *Ownership, Control and Success of Large Companies* (1961).

[3] J. M. Keynes, 'The End of Laissez-Faire' (1924), in *Essays in Persuasion* (1931), pp. 314–15.

In 1939 it was more generally accepted that

> with the increasing use of joint-stock principle and the limited liability company . . . the owners of industry are the ordinary shareholders. Their ownership does not amount to a control over concrete objects, but to a right to share in the profits of the concern . . . The increasing dominance of industry by combines and cartels has given a further twist to the meaning of ownership. It is becoming less a right to draw a share in the profits, and more a right to draw dividends in perpetuity —the factor of risk, the short-term risk at least, is declining. Absentee ownership, as Veblen has called it, is no longer at the mercy of competition.[1]

A further consequence of the growing size of firms was that an increasing proportion of workers was to be found in large firms. By 1935 there were three industries in which more than half the workers employed worked in *plants* employing 1,000 workers or more (electrical machinery, motor and cycle manufacturing and iron and steel rolling and smelting) and in a further four industries (silk and art silk, newspaper production, shipbuilding and sugar and sugar confectionery) over 40% did so. The proportions of workers in plants employing 500 and over varied from 58·4% to 83·5% in these seven industries. All told, of about 5·2 million workers in the industries enumerated by the Census of Production, 21·5% worked in *plants* employing 1,000 and over, and another 13·9% in plants employing 500–999 workers. But concentration was also evident in the absorption of several plants by one firm. The proportion working in *firms* employing 1,000 and over was 31·2% in 1935; and those in firms employing 500–999, 13·3%, i.e. nearly half the labour force was to be found in firms employing 500 workers and over.[2]

Even this does not show fully the extent of industrial concentration, for many firms, while nominally independent, were being combined in groups, not only in the traditional 'horizontal' or 'vertical' forms of integration, but also in other complex ways inadequately described as 'lateral' or 'diagonal' integration. Thus a steel firm might expand not only into coal mining, iron mining and engineering, but also into electrical engineering, chemicals or telecommunications. Textiles and clothing, boxes, paper and printing, public utilities and building, shipping and banking were other industries with 'groups' which straddled several of them. The links between the firms forming a group were sometimes economic or technical, but often they were little more than financial. Holding companies or subsidiaries were the most common means of control, but there were also interlocking capital holdings, frequently unknown to the public, and interlocking directorates. In 1936 it was found that among a sample

---

[1] M. Compton and E. H. Bott, *British Industry* (1940), p. 128.
[2] Florence, *Logic*, pp. 24, 34.

of 623 directors of large firms with capitals of over £500,000 each, only 25% held single directorships. No fewer than 81 (13%) held ten or more.[1]

In their pioneer study[2] Leak and Maizels, using the Census of Production of 1935, found that 55% of all workers enumerated, or just under 4 million, worked in 'units' (i.e. industrial groups) employing 500 men or over. Among the most highly concentrated trade groups were mining and quarrying (89%), public utilities (78%), engineering, shipbuilding and vehicles (67%), iron and steel, chemicals (both 59%), food, drink and tobacco (50%) and textiles (49%). Sub-groups with specially high proportions of employees in units of 500 and over included blast furnaces (92%), aircraft (91%), coal mines (94%), tramways (94%), tobacco (88%), biscuits (82%), iron and steel rolling and melting (87%) and railways (100%). Nearly 1·7 million workers worked in the 135 largest units employing 5,000 each or over and producing 44·5% of the gross output. Equally telling was the share held by the three largest units in any one industry, as a measure of concentration. Among the main industrial groups, there were five in which the three largest units employed 39% of the labour force or more; when industries were further sub-divided, there were no fewer than 33 trades in which the largest three units accounted for 70% of the total employment or more. Concentration had made remarkable and measurable progress since the turn of the century, particularly among 'surviving' firms: new firms and new industries, starting from a small scale, could not counter-balance this general tendency.[3]

Concentration of industry has often been equated with monopolistic control. The mere growth in the size of firms need not, however, by itself restrict competition, nor was the motive of the organizers necessarily the monopolistic control of markets. In part, it derived from the technical and economic advantages of size, aided also by the contemporary revolution in office equipment and administrative techniques. In part it was the new mass consumers' markets and efficient means of transport and distribution to supply them, which called forth mass production by single large firms. New industries especially, including electrical engineering, rayon, aluminium, motors, films and chemicals, were dominated by a few giant concerns, but new techniques or marketing opportunities also led to concentration in older industries, such as brewing.[4] In part, concentration was the

---

[1] Florence, 'Joint-Stock Company Control', p. 14, and *Ownership*, chapter 4. J. M. Rees, *Trusts in British Industry, 1914–1921* (1922), pp. 28, 31, 71 ff.; H. Levy, *The New Industrial System* (1936), § 20.

[2] H. Leak and A. Maizels, 'The Structure of British Industry', *J. R. Stat. S.*, 108/1–2, 1945.

[3] P. E. Hart and S. J. Prais, 'The Analysis of Business Concentration: A Statistical Approach', *J. R. Stat. S.*, 119/2, 1956.

[4] Hermann Levy, *New Industrial System, passim*; A. Plummer, *New Industries of the Twentieth Century* (1937), chapter 7; J. E. Vaizey, 'The Brewing Industry', in

result of the growing control of companies by financial interests which looked for extensions, either to invest surplus capital or to make promotional gains.[1]

In the main, however, growing concentration was associated with restriction of competition and the creation of monopolistic markets, either as a deliberate aim, or because a handful of large and powerful firms found it easier to make and enforce agreements than innumerable competing small firms.[2] The logical conclusion of this development was the creation of a single large monopolistic firm dominating an industry by controlling, say, 70% or more of its capacity. Several of these survived from the period before 1914,[3] including those in textile finishing, sewing cotton, wallpaper, Portland cement, tobacco, flat glass, and salt and other chemicals. Among the new combines established to dominate their markets as monopolists or quasi-monopolists were those in chemicals (1926), whisky distilling (1925), soap and margarine (1929), matches (1927), glass bottles, yeast and seed crushing.[4] In almost every case, increased prices and profits were easier to find as a result of mergers, than increased efficiency.[5]

Apart from the single firm, the most widespread form of monopoly organization to arise in the inter-war years was the trade association. There had been a few in existence even before 1914, but many more were formed in war-time, when the planning and controlling ministries were glad to avail themselves of any existing organization of firms to represent their industries, and this gave greater standing to them and provided a strong incentive for firms to join them. At the end of the war, the Committee on Trusts enumerated 93 associations in many different industries which had had dealings with the Ministry of Munitions, 35 associations being enumerated in the iron and steel industry alone, mostly with price-fixing functions, in a list which was stated not to be exhaustive.[6] John Hilton, the Secretary of the Committee, estimated that over 500 associations were then in existence. The Federation of British Industries had been formed in 1916 with 50 affiliated organizations and by 1918 it had 129, mostly of the trade association type, claiming a membership of 16,000

P. L. Cook (ed.), *Effects of Mergers* (1958), pp. 413–19; and *The Brewing Industry 1886–1951* (1960), pp. 25–45, 149–155.

[1] H. A. Marquand, *The Dynamics of Industrial Combination* (1931), chapters 7–11.
[2] Compton and Bott, *British Industry*, chapter 3.
[3] Cf. chapter 1, section 3 above.
[4] P. L. Cook (ed.), *Effects of Mergers*; H. Levy, *Monopolies, Trusts and Cartels in Britain To-day* (1927 ed.), chapter 9.
[5] E.g. A. F. Lucas, *Industrial Reconstruction and the Control of Competition* (1937), chapter 8; G. C. Allen, 'An Aspect of "Industrial Reorganization" ', *Econ. J.*, 55/218–19, 1945; Ernest Davies, *National Capitalism, The Government's Record as a Protector of Private Monopoly* (1939).
[6] Min. of Reconstruction, *Report of the Committee on Trusts* (1919. Cd. 9236).

firms with an aggregate capital of £4 milliard; the National Union of Manufacturers also evolved at the same time, in 1917, out of the British Manufacturers' Association of 1915.

Many of these trade associations collapsed in the slump of 1921–2, but in the 'rationalization' movement of 1924–9, much of it Government-supported, others were formed. By the late 1930's there were probably 1,000–1,200 in existence in manufacturing alone, with a similar number to be found in distribution and other spheres.[1]

Some associations were little more than gentlemen's agreements on terms, prices or trading areas, and others were formed for purposes of information, common research or advertising rather than restricting competition. Most, however, were driven sooner or later by shrinking markets and falling prices, or by the actions of other trade associations, to concern themselves with price fixing and control. Where the power of these associations was bolstered either by the power of a quasi-monopolistic firm acting as price leader, as in soap making, rayon, tyres or matches, or by patents, as in electric lamps, pharmaceutical products or shoe making machinery, the fixed price was virtually unchallengeable.[2]

Some trade associations went further and approached those of the German-type cartel by controlling not only prices, but also output quotas or capacity. Thus the Sulphate of Ammonia Federation, the National Benzol Co., and the Nitrate Producers' Association acted as selling agencies allocating orders to their members. The Cable Makers' Association manipulated the tenders of its members so that orders were allocated according to a prearranged quota plan, and similar methods were in use among large building and civil engineering contractors. Government-sponsored Marketing Boards and the coal industry after the Act of 1930 operated in a similar way in the 1930's. The Shipping Conferences continued to exclude competition by their well-tried methods of deferred rebates. Finally, some associations sponsored subsidiary companies which systematically bought up and destroyed excess capacity. This occurred in shipbuilding, grain milling, wool combing, and among licensed houses, as well as (with Government assistance) in cotton spinning.

Some cartels shared out international markets according to prearranged quotas, including the international rail cartel, revived in 1926, and the associations among makers of electric lamps, chemicals, minerals, tobacco and glass bottles, among others. The oil industry was dominated by a few competing giant international concerns with price agreements and understandings in any individual market, such as the United Kingdom.[3] On the other hand, the international cartels of such raw materials

---

[1] P.E.P., *Industrial Trade Associations* (1957).
[2] Lucas, *op. cit.*, chapter 9.
[3] Patrick Fitzgerald, *Industrial Combination in England* (1927), chapter 19.

as tin, rubber, coffee and sugar had only temporary effects at best.[1] Finally, some large monopolistic firms spread networks of agreements across many frontiers: among them were Courtauld's, Unilever, the Swedish Match Co., Dunlop, J. & P. Coats, Nestlé, the International Nickel Co., the Amalgamated Metals Corporation Ltd., E.M.I., I.C.I., Ford's, General Motors, the Singer Sewing Machine Co., and the (American) General Electric Co.[2]

Some of these associations to curb competition were the result of adverse market conditions; in other words, they were defensive rather than aggressive. Some were the result of the natural growth of firms in search of economies of size for mass-produced articles, until there were only a few concerns left, which found it easy to combine; others were formed to exploit their markets by monopoly powers; and others still were the result of State initiative. Whatever the origins, monopolistic combination was immeasurably extended during the inter-war years. It is true that even in 1919, the Report of the Committee on Trusts began by asserting: 'We find there is at the present time in every important branch of industry in the United Kingdom an increasing tendency to the formation of trade associations and combinations, having for their purpose the restriction of competition and the control of prices.' But they were describing an economy still closely organized by war-time controls which were dismantled in the following twelve months or so. By the end of the inter-war period restrictive practices had become the normal framework of economic life, buttressed as they were by associations, agreements and Acts of Parliament. Trade 'was the subject of the most extensive, though not always co-ordinated, control instituted by the producers, distributors, and consumers'. 'As a feature of industrial and commercial organization,' wrote an observer in 1937, 'free competition has nearly disappeared from the British scene.'[3]

At least as striking as the extension of monopolistic market conditions was the reversal of the public attitude towards it. The Committee on Trusts, at the end of the war, took it for granted that monopoly was undesirable. It proposed Tribunals of Investigation, and under the Profiteering Act of 1919, some thirty reports on restrictive practices and price increases were completed, before the Act was allowed to lapse. In 1919, also, the Treasury enforced a gentlemen's agreement on the banks to abstain from further amalgamation. The slump of 1921–2 with its bank-

---

[1] P.E.P., *Report on International Trade* (1937), pp. 102 ff., gives some details of 28 international cartels and mentions 28 others.

[2] Alfred Plummer, *International Combines in Modern Industry* (3rd ed., 1951); E. Hexner, *International Cartels* (1946).

[3] *Committee on Trusts*, pp. 2, 13; J. Hurstfield, 'The Control of British Raw Material Supplies, 1919–1939', *Ec. Hist. Rev.*, 14/1–2, 1944, p. 1; A. F. Lucas, *op. cit.*, p. 64.

ruptcies and price falls diverted attention from the potential powers of monopolies to raise prices, but even in 1923 and 1925, for example, there were abortive private members' bills against restraint of competition, and the report of the Royal Commission on Food Prices of 1925 was equally hostile.[1]

These, however, were the last symptoms of a dying era. The drive towards the 'rationalization' of industry, introduced in this country from Germany about 1924, was perhaps the first sign of change. It began as a movement to improve techniques, but it was soon mainly looking for savings by structural and economic, rather than technical, reorganization, 'the right arrangement of the relations of producers to each other'.[2] This often required the collaboration of firms to provide common services, or the amalgamation of firms in order to use each other's facilities or, more commonly, to provide a full load for the more up-to-date plant while scrapping the less efficient. Such measures could produce only limited results if confined to small groups of firms and were more logically applied to the whole of an industry, and thus rationalization led directly to schemes of control and monopoly. The height of the 'rationalization' movement was passed in 1929, for the slump created the fear that 'over-rationalization' would lead to higher output and more unemployment,[3] and the problem became less that of reducing real costs than that of reducing total capacity Thenceforward 'planning' became the favoured term. Meanwhile, however, the former attitude to competition and monopoly had been largely reversed.

The first straw in the wind was the official blessing, by a Departmental Committee, of the co-operative selling of coal in 1926.[4] More significant was the cautious support given to industrial control schemes by the influential Balfour Committee on Industry and Trade in its Final Report in 1929, as one of the ways of overcoming the weakness in exports with which it was mainly concerned.[5] By 1931 the Macmillan Committee added its powerful voice to the clamour of industry for organization and association. 'It has been represented to us strongly in evidence', it reported,

that a great deal remains to be done in more than one important

---

[1] P.E.P., *Industrial Trade Associations* (1957), chapter 1; G. C. Allen, 'Monopoly and Competition in the United Kingdom', in E. H. Chamberlin (ed.), *Monopoly and Competition and their Regulation* (1954).

[2] D. H. MacGregor *et al.*, 'Problems of Rationalisation', *Econ. J.*, 40/159, 1930, p. 352; cf. also L. Urwick, *The Meaning of Rationalisation* (1929), and Walter Meakin, *The New Industrial Revolution* (1928).

[3] T. E. Gregory, 'Rationalisation and Technological Unemployment', *Econ. J.*, 40/160, 1930.

[4] *Report of the D.C. on Co-operative Selling in the Coal Industry* (1926. Cmd. 2770).

[5] Balfour Committee, *Final Report* (1929), pp. 297, 304, 308.

industry in overcoming sectional and individual opposition to desirable amalgamations and reconstructions designed to eliminate waste and cheapen costs. It was stated to us that very important economies and much greater efficiency are possible if there are concerted movements to that end. We believe this to be the case,

and, after suggesting that financial houses might assist in these movements, the Committee expressed its 'strong opinion that sectional interests should not be allowed to stand in the way of re-organizations which are in the national interest'.[1] In the same year, the Greene Committee on Restraint of Trade (in retailing) was equally emphatic that monopolistic practices should be tolerated in the name of 'freedom of contract'.

The new attitude was to be found among all shades of opinion. The Labour members of the Committee on Trusts had as early as 1919 emphasized their belief that evolution towards combination and monopoly was 'both inevitable and desirable',[2] as long as it was controlled in the public interest. Conservative opinion by the early 1930's was equally strongly in favour of regulation and control. Some Conservatives were even prepared to go further, and plan industry as a whole.

Such a policy [wrote Mr. Harold Macmillan in 1932][3] is impossible without the co-operation of industry. Production cannot be planned in relation to established demand while industries are organized on competitive lines. *In present circumstances there are no channels through which any economic policy at all can be effectively administered throughout the field of productive effort* [H. M. italics]. It is for this reason that I regard it as a matter of primary importance to produce an orderly structure in each of our national industries amenable to the authority of a representative directorate conducting the industries as self-governing units in accordance with the circumstances of the modern world.

He was also co-author of an earlier work in which the divorce of ownership from control was noted, and in which the tendency of many large firms to change their basic motivation to that of public utilities, in accordance with the 'Socialist theory, namely, the production of essential commodities for use rather than profit',[4] was applauded.

Even the Liberal Industrial Inquiry of 1928, signed by some of the leading Liberal politicians as well as economists, was prepared to see free competition in industry displaced. In many industries, it reported, public enterprise had proved itself superior and there 'the *ad-hoc* Public Board

---

[1] *Report of the Committee on Finance and Industry* (Macmillan Report) (1931. Cmd. 3897), para. 385.
[2] *Report of the Committee on Trusts* (1919. Cd. 9236), p. 13.
[3] Harold Macmillan, *Reconstruction, A Plea for a National Policy* (1933), pp. 9–10.
[4] R. Boothby *et al.*, *Industry and the State* (1927), pp. 157–8.

points to the right line of evolution'. Elsewhere, they were averse to restoring

the old conditions of competition, which often involve waste and [? of] effort, the uneconomic duplication of plant or equipment, and the impossibility of adopting the full advantages of large-scale production. In modern conditions a tendency towards some degree of monopoly in an increasing number of industries is, in our opinion, inevitable and even, quite often, desirable in the interest of efficiency. It is, therefore, no longer useful to treat trusts, cartels, combinations, holding companies and trade associations as inexpedient abnormalities in the economic system to be prevented, checked, and harried ... We believe that there is still room ... for large-scale enterprises of semi-monopolistic character which are run for private profit and controlled by individuals.

As for trade associations,

we think that cases may arise in which it is in the legitimate interests of a trade or industry that a small minority shall be required to conform to the rules which the majority have decided to impose upon themselves ... we suggest, therefore, that, where an Incorporated Association can show that 75 per cent. of those affected are in favour of a trade rule or instruction ... the Association shall have the right to apply for powers to issue an order enforcing the rule in question on all members of the trade or industry or of the appropriate section of it, whether within the Association or not.[1]

The *Economist* was equally prepared to shed its traditional views. 'The time is surely coming', it stated, 'when public opinion will cease to tolerate the impotence of mismanagement in the sacred name of individualism.' 'A very wide measure of public control will be necessary if the badly needed work of rationalization is ever to make any real progress.'[2]

With such backing, it was not surprising to find a Committee of the F.B.I. in 1935 strongly urging legislation to strengthen trade associations, or Political and Economic Planning, as well as Lord Melchett on behalf of the Industrial Reorganization League, in the House of Lords in 1934, sponsoring bills giving compulsory powers to the majority of producers in any one industry to enforce schemes of reorganization on the rest, 'with the general object of promoting greater efficiency, eliminating wasteful competition, and facilitating production, manufacture and supply of the products of that industry'.

These bills were stillborn, but there were, in fact, innumerable Government measures to encourage industrial combinations since 1930,

[1] Liberal Industrial Inquiry, *Britain's Industrial Future* (1928), pp. 77, 93–4, 99.
[2] *Economist*, 21st July 1934, 25th Aug. 1934. Cf. also Arthur Salter, *Recovery* (1932); and *The Next Five Years, an Essay in Political Agreement* (1935), written by 152 professional people of all parties.

at least. The compulsory railway amalgamation of 1921 was the first specific step. In 1930 came the Coal Mines Act with its compulsory cartel scheme and Reorganization Commission, and in 1931–3 the Marketing Boards of producers which had as 'their most directly common interest restricted production as a means of monopoly exploitation',[1] though they had other subsidiary functions as well. In 1930 and 1933 competition in road transport was restricted by Traffic Commissioners, in 1934 a Herring Industry Board was set up, and in 1936 the Spindles Board was established to restrict competition in cotton spinning. Subsidies were made the occasion by the State to restrict or end competition in beet sugar production, civil aviation and transatlantic passenger shipping, and tariffs were used to restrict competition in iron and steel making, among others. In the Finance Act of 1935 the Government provided that 'if a scheme of reorganization covering the majority of an industry had been certified by the Board of Trade as being of assistance in reducing excess capacity, contributions to it might be deducted from income for tax purposes'.[2]

In the course of the 1930's, the State thus played an active part in the cartellization of industry. It created favourable conditions for industries, in which combination was easy, and it intervened directly to provide a monopolistic framework where firms were too weak or too scattered, as in the old staples of coal, cotton, iron and steel, shipbuilding and agriculture. For a third type of industry, the public utility, the country groped its way through to a new and significant form of organization, the Public Corporation.

Public Corporations had been pioneered by Dock and Harbour Boards before 1914. Between the wars the most important new authorities were the Forestry Commission (1919), the Central Electricity Board (1926), the British Broadcasting Corporation (1926), the London Passenger Transport Board (1933) and the British Overseas Airways Corporation (1939). In addition, Treasury control over the Post Office was relaxed and more financial independence given to it, following strong criticism, especially by Lord Wolmer and the Bridgeman Committee,[3] and the organization of that ancient Department was thus modelled more closely on that of the Public Corporation.

The Public Corporation was an attempt to cope with the problem of the administration of large or nationally important industries, mostly requiring large capital sums, secure control of their market and a strong interest in general or social, as distinct from sectional, welfare. It was a compromise, to avoid both the exploitation of the public by a private

---

[1] Lincoln Gordon, *The Public Corporation in Great Britain* (1938), p. 325.
[2] P.E.P., *Industrial Trade Associations* (1957), p. 29.
[3] Lord Wolmer, *Post Office Reform* (1932); *Report of the Committee of Enquiry on the Post Office* (Bridgeman Committee) (1932. Cmd. 4149).

monopoly, and the day-to-day political interference to which ordinary
Departments of State are normally subjected. The Corporations, while
differing in detail, were built up on similar principles. They were controlled by Boards which had to meet fixed interest charges on their capital,
but beyond that had to provide the best possible public service out of the
revenues arising from direct charges or, as in the case of the B.B.C., from
licence fees. Though in other respects the Corporations were much like
joint-stock companies, the profit motive, as normally understood, was
removed, and the public interest substituted. The British Public Corporation has been described as the outcome of an attempt to create consumers',
in place of producers', economics, and in some cases, notably the Port
of London Authority, consumers were very strongly represented on the
governing bodies. The capital might be held by the State or by former
owners, including private shareholders, but there was the most complete
separation possible between ownership and control. Despite its decisive
rejection by the Haldane Committee in 1918,[1] the Public Corporation
enjoyed general support and roused widespread interest as a new administrative device.[2]

The manifold new developments of industrial organization described
here implied a fundamental change in thought as much as in actual
practice. The nineteenth-century belief in an unlimited extension of
markets parallel with the extension of productive capacity was shattered
by the experience of declining export markets in the 1920's and world-
wide deficiency of purchasing power in the 1930's. Technical and organizational problems were thus transformed, and the main task was, not how
to supply ever-extending markets at the lowest cost, but how to cater for a
stagnant demand without an excess of unemployment.[3]

For the manufacturer, the limits and capacity of his own industry thus
acquired a new significance as it had to be measured against a known
static demand. They 'forced the individual producer to forego his traditional isolation. The whole re-organization movement is premised upon a
common purpose, a unified policy, and concerted action.'[4] It seemed as
though the country was moving inexorably into a corporate economic
structure, the solution tried in several fascist countries.

In the event, the extremes were avoided. Large sectors of the economy

[1] *Reports of the Committee on the Machinery of Government* (1918. Cd. 9230).
[2] See esp. W. A. Robson (ed.), *Public Enterprise* (1937); T. H. O'Brien, *British
Experiments in Public Ownership and Control* (1937); Lincoln Gordon, *The Public
Corporation in Great Britain* (1938); J. F. Sleeman, *British Public Utilities* (1953);
M. E. Dimock, *British Public Utilities and National Development* (1933); Balfour
Committee, *Survey of Industries*, Vol. 2, chapter 8 (2); Ernest Davies, *National
Enterprise: The Development of the Public Corporation* (1946), chapters 2, 3, 9.
[3] Levy, *New Industrial System*, p. 28.
[4] Lucas, *Industrial Reconstruction*, p. 43.

still remained unorganized, dominated by small units, or at least subject to bitter oligopolistic competition. Associations and agreements, as long as they were not State-supported, were not always permanent. The economy proved more flexible than had been allowed, changes from old to new industries were carried through with greater speed in the 1930's and aggregate demand began to expand again during and after the 1939–45 war. In retrospect, it seems that much of the organizational, anti-competitive phase of history in 1919–39 was directly derived from the world economic depression. Its character was all the more easily forced into a restrictive mould, because of the existence of a long-term trend, making necessary ever larger agglomerations of capital for maximum productive efficiency, and providing at the same time the administrative, transport and distributive means to manage them. This trend was evident before 1914, as it has continued after 1939.

CHAPTER IV

Commercial and Financial Developments

I. THE CHANGING PATTERN OF RETAIL AND WHOLESALE TRADING

The main theme of the last chapter was industrial change; above all the decline of industries producing for export and the growth of production and services for domestic use. This trend was bound to reduce the relative volume of international trade of the United Kingdom and to have other effects on her international commercial and financial relationships with the rest of the world. The causal connection was, however, by no means all one way. It was often developments abroad which forced the changing industrial pattern on Britain, and, at the same time, the striking differences between the industrial history of the 1920's and the 1930's were at least in part due to the differences in financial policy. The history of these commercial and financial developments, and their interaction with the changing pattern of industry, will be the theme of this chapter.

The industrial revolution of the eighteenth century had mainly transformed the production of capital goods and semi-manufactures. As far as the consumer was concerned, there were still local bakers and blacksmiths, carpenters and upholsterers, tailors and cobblers to supply him with the goods he needed, on a small scale and often bespoke. It was only from the 1850's onwards that shoemaking and sewing machines, and similar inventions in other trades, made mass-production possible and craftsmen suppliers of consumption goods began to be displaced. In the inter-war years this change was greatly speeded up and virtually completed, while at the same time a whole host of new factory-made consumer goods appeared on the market, from electrical goods to patent polishes and cleaning powders, and from plastic containers to artificial silk stockings and photographic apparatus. The rise of the new industries, both a cause and a consequence of a prosperous home market, particularly in the late 1930's, was an aspect of the opening of the era of mass-consumption.

One of the sectors most immediately affected was retail distribution. It had begun to change slowly even before 1914, but after 1919 its changes were greatly accelerated. The old-established boundaries between retailers were being broken down. New goods called forth new retailing specialists, and some of these, like electrical goods suppliers, had to undertake the new function of after-sales services. In other cases the change was in the opposite direction, as manufacturers increasingly performed many of the traditional functions of the retailer, such as weighing, packing and pricing, in the factory, where they could be undertaken more economically, and then substituted their own reputation for that of the retailer in the eyes of the consumer.

Information and salesmanship by the shopkeeper was increasingly replaced by advertising by the manufacturer. In this period, the mass-production of consumer goods for a national market and the rise of new media such as mass-circulation newspapers, radio and film afforded new opportunities for the advertiser. By 1938, it was estimated that about £106 million a year was being spent on advertising, of which the manu-facturers' share was about 53%, the retailers', 11%. Press advertising alone, according to another calculation, had risen from £22 million in 1907 to £60 million in 1930. The formation of the Advertising Association in 1926 and of other associations of advertisers at about the same time set the seal on the creation of the profession of advertising agents.[1]

What was significant was not only the increase in the volume of advertising, both absolutely and as a proportion of national income, but also its change of direction. Before 1914, the bulk of advertising was either informative, or it took the form of local advertising by shopkeepers. The only consumer goods advertised nationally on any scale were branded medicines, cigarettes and toilet requisites, about which consumers have always been most gullible. Between the wars this picture changed considerably as manufacturers succeeded in turning all kinds of consumption goods into 'household words' by advertising, free gift schemes and similar methods. Cosmetics, cigarettes and medicaments were still among the most heavily advertised, 20–50% of the retail price being accounted for by advertising costs; but other commodities, including alcoholic drinks, manufactured foods and fountain pens, had now joined this group of highly advertised commodities.[2]

Motor transport also exerted great influence on retail distribution. From the early 1920's onward, motor vans and lorries gave greater free-dom of location to shops, they permitted direct delivery from manufacturer or importer, or from depots to multiple branches, and they also replaced

---

[1] N. Kaldor and R. Silverman, *A Statistical Analysis of Advertising Expenditure and of the Revenue of the Press* (Cambridge, 1948), pp. 7 ff.; F. P. Bishop, *The Economics of Advertising* (1944), pp. 54–5; Ralph Harris and Arthur Seldon, *Advertising in a Free Society* (1959), pp. 5–11, 25, Appx. C.

[2] Kaldor and Silverman, *op. cit.*, Table 75, pp. 144–7.

the errand-boy. At the same time the rural motor bus brought villagers regularly into the market towns and transformed their shopping centres. In the 1930's, the acquisition of private motor cars by large sections of the middle classes allowed many of them to live in the country, thus helping to transform the traditional village shop, while keeping the city department store within easy reach. In the last years before the war, however, increasing traffic congestion in city centres began to favour the well-equipped suburban shopping area at the expense of the central one for many types of shopping.

The third important influence on retailing in the inter-war period was the growth of the residential suburb, middle-class or council-built, in loose rings around the tightly packed nineteenth-century inner towns. The typical shop on an estate was often designed with some forethought, had a larger turnover, and was generally more efficient, than the shops in the old residential areas. Since the opening of a new shop on the estate seldom led to the closing down of an equivalent shop elsewhere, however, the creation of new housing estates was one of the most potent causes of the increasing number of shops in this period.

Lastly, there was the effect of the general rise in living standards, bringing an enlarged spending power to a middle class rapidly growing in numbers, and even allowing greater freedom to spend to the working classes in the prosperous industries and districts in the 1930's. Broad groups of the population began to demand better shops, greater choice, style, and fashion, and other improvements, and a different collection of goods. The weighting of the official cost-of-living index bears eloquent witness to the changes in the consuming habits of the working classes, though the earlier figures are not too reliable:

Working-class Expenditure

Proportions spent on:	Budget of 1904 (1914 Cost-of-Living Index)	Budget of 1937–8 (1947 Cost-of-Living Index)
Food	60%	35%
Rent and rates	16	9
Clothing	12	9
Fuel and light	8	7
Other items in 1904 Budget	4	16
	100	76
Items not in 1904 Budget	—	24
	100	100

For the whole population of the United Kingdom, proportions of retail sales have been estimated as follows:[1]

	1910	1920	1939
Food	57·7%	50·7%	46·6%
Clothing	18·8	24·6	19·4
Reading, writing materials, confectionery, tobacco	8·8	9·3	14·4
Other goods	14·7	15·4	19·6
Totals, in £ million	892	2,863	2,302

The effects of all these influences on retail trading were complex. One major trend, however, stands out: the growth of capital and employment in the retail trades, absolutely and in relation to other trades. Few reliable statistics exist, but what was not in dispute, was that the number of shops was increasing. One estimate put the annual increase in the years 1924–32 at about 6%, at a time when the population increased by 0·55% per annum, though other estimates put the rate of increase rather lower.[2] Wherever official figures existed for licensing or other purposes, they confirmed this rapid rise. Thus the number of tobacco licences grew from 352,000 in 1911 to 530,000 in 1939; vendors paying medicine stamp duties increased from 46,000 in 1920 to 164,000 in 1938; the number of butchers' shops in the 72 largest towns in Britain rose from 13,021 in 1913 to 16,176 in 1928; the number of milk producer-retailer licences rose from 46,000 in 1934 to 63,000 in 1938; and the number of confectionery outlets grew from 100,000 in 1913 to 250,000 in 1938.[3] Furniture, hardware, electrical goods and other 'non-essential' types of shops were growing even faster in numbers than these.

The number of workers engaged in distribution (including wholesaling) grew from an average of 1,661,000 in 1920–2 to 2,436,000 in 1937–8, or from 10·4% to 12·9% of total employment. There was an actual increase even in such areas as the four depressed counties of South

[1] J. B. Jefferys, *Retail Trading in Britain, 1850–1950* (Cambridge, 1954), pp. 44–5.

[2] Henry Smith, *Retail Distribution* (2nd ed., 1948), pp. 35–7, 90–106; P. Ford, 'Competition and the Number of Retail Shops, 1901–31', *Econ. J.*, 45/179, 1935, and 'Decentralisation and Changes in the Number of Shops, 1901–1931', *ibid.*, 46/182, 1936; also P. Ford and G. V. White, 'Trends in Retail Distribution in Yorkshire (West Riding), 1901–1927', *Manchester School*, 7/2, 1936.

[3] Hermann Levy, *The Shops of Britain* (1948), pp. 31–43, 50, 56, 71; Jefferys, *op. cit.*, p. 53.

Wales[1] which lost population in this period, though there were indications that the prosperous areas had more shops per head than depressed areas which were similar in other respects.[2] Including owner-managers and working proprietors, distribution employed about 3 million people in 1939, mostly in the retail field.

The increase in resources devoted to distribution was natural, in view of the fact that the economies of mass-production automatically threw greater burdens of costs on the distributive network (though the saving on the one greatly outweighed the additions to cost of the other);[3] that further, there were few improvements in the technical equipment of shops; and lastly, that distribution required personal services at a time when a rising standard of living implied that the cost of labour rose as compared with that of goods. Nevertheless, the increase was quite out of proportion to any increases likely on those grounds, and it was widely held that there were 'too many shops', and too many people engaged in distribution. According to one estimate, the volume of sales per assistant fell from 100 in 1924 to 90 in 1931 and 79 in 1938–9,[4] though another calculation showed a slight fall in the man-hour costs of distributing a general aggregate of foodstuffs from 1·20 in 1932 to 1·02 in 1939.[5]

The main cause of the growth of the resources devoted to the distributive trades was the decline of price competition in ever wider fields of retailing, and its replacement by competition in ever more lavish services. 'It appears as safe as any general assumption can be to conclude that the dominant factors in the growth of retail costs between the wars have been the imperfections in the retail market, and the opportunities which a period of falling wholesale prices and unemployment have provided for that imperfection to be deliberately increased.' [6] As in industry,[7] these 'imperfections' were fostered by monopolistic associations, and these, in turn, were related to the increase in the size of firms.

Alfred Marshall had noted as early as 1896 that 'the retail trade is being transformed, and the small shopkeeper is losing ground daily',[8] but large-scale enterprise became really significant only in the inter-war years. The proportions of trade held by different types of retailer changed as shown on the next page.[9]

---

[1] Henry Smith, *op. cit.*, p. 106; A. L. Chapman and Rose Knight, *Wages and Salaries in the United Kingdom, 1920–38* (Cambridge, 1953), p. 18.

[2] British National Committee, International Chamber of Commerce, *Trial Census of Distribution in Six Towns* (1937).

[3] Sir Arnold Plant, 'The Distribution of Proprietary Articles', in *Some Modern Business Problems* (1937), p. 313.

[4] Henry Smith, pp. 85–7.

[5] Colin Clark, *Conditions of Economic Progress* (1951 ed.), p. 342.

[6] Henry Smith, p. 145.   [7] Cf. chapter 3, section 7 above.

[8] Quoted in Levy, *Shops of Britain*, p. 1.

[9] Jefferys, *op cit.*, pp. 29, 73.

	1915	1939	Change
Co-operative societies	$7\frac{1}{2}$–9%	10–$11\frac{1}{2}$%	+$2\frac{1}{2}$%
Department stores	2–3	$4\frac{1}{2}$–$5\frac{1}{2}$	+$2\frac{1}{2}$
Multiple shops	7–$8\frac{1}{2}$	18–$19\frac{1}{2}$	+11
'Independents', owning 1–9 shops each, by difference	$79\frac{1}{2}$–$83\frac{1}{2}$	$63\frac{1}{2}$–$67\frac{1}{2}$	−16

The growth of the 'multiple' shops retailer, owning ten or more shops, was the most outstanding of these developments. Between the wars, this type of organization spread to virtually every trade, and to all price and quality ranges.[1] Only the chains of variety stores or bazaars continued to rely mainly on their price appeal.

Among the multiple firms, in turn, the growth occurred largely among the larger chains. Between 1920 and 1939, the number of branches of firms owning 10–24 shops grew only from 4,111 to 5,474, while the branches owned by those with 25 shops or more increased from 20,602 to 39,013; among these, the number of shops in firms with 200 branches or more grew from 10,942 to 21,283. Variety chain stores grew from 300 to 1,200 in the same period. Some of the growth was accounted for by mergers among the larger chains, but other firms grew rapidly without amalgamations: thus Boots' had 200 branches in 1900 and 1,180 in 1938, while Marks & Spencer had 140 in 1927 and 230 in 1938.

Even before 1914, many chains were linked with manufacturing or importing organizations, either by the forward integration of manufacturers, or the backward integration of the stores. Such integration was especially common among chemists', grocers' and footwear chains.[2] In the inter-war years, the large chains, additionally, began to exert considerable influence on their suppliers, without actually owning them.

By comparison with the expansion of the multiples, the growth of department store trading was modest. Unlike the chains, pre-war department stores had generally started as exclusive ventures for the middle classes, but they also were concerned to tap a wider market after 1920, though there were some notable exceptions. Stores began to be built in suburban shopping centres and in smaller towns, and these were from the beginning more popular in appeal. Many sought lower costs by combining in groups, and by 1939 there were four large groups, controlling 200 stores between them.

Co-operative retail societies remained in this period the only significant

[1] J. B. Jefferys, *The Distribution of Consumer Goods* (Cambridge, 1950), pp. 120–2.
[2] Hermann Levy, *Retail Trade Associations* (1942), pp. 29–34; H. Compton and E. H. Bott, *British Industry* (1940), chapter 6.

and successful examples of co-operation in Britain. Their working-class origins were strongly marked by their concentration in the industrial quarters in Britain, their main strength being in Lancashire and the West Riding, north-eastern England and Scotland. In the inter-war years, however, they spread rapidly into the co-operative 'deserts' of the south, and the southern and Midlands areas showed much more rapid increases in co-operative trade than the older areas, though they were still far below them in co-operative penetration even in 1939.[1] The trading pattern of co-operative retail societies remained that of the basic needs of working-class households. About two-thirds of the societies' sales was still in groceries and other food. The share of the co-operative societies in the total retail trade in 1939 was estimated to have been 14·1% in food and 13·8% in coal, but only 9·1% in footwear, 6·6% in textiles and clothing, and 3·5% in furniture and hardware.[2] In many non-essential articles and services it was negligible.

The growth in the total share of co-operative retailing is shown on p. 180 above. Membership, however, increased much more rapidly, from 3 million in 1914 to 4½ million in 1920 and 8½ million in 1939. The growth in the war years was accompanied by a fall in the average sales per member from £28·7 in 1914 to £22·0 (in 1914 prices) in 1919–20, but afterwards this level was held, the sales (in 1914 prices) in 1939 being valued at £22·3 per member.[3] This might be thought disappointing in view of the growing purchasing power of the working classes, but was merely a reflection of the increase in the number, and fall in the size, of families. In 1919, with 4·1 million members, co-operative societies held 10·7 million sugar registrations, while in 1940, with 8·5 million members, they only held 13·5 million registrations.

Among co-operative retail societies the large organization also made headway against the small. In part, this was brought about by the geographical shift to the south, where societies were larger, but in part it was the result of mergers. In London, in particular, there were 33 societies with 134,000 members in 1913; by 1935, there were only 14, with an aggregate of 844,000 members.[4] The average membership of all societies rose from 3,054 in 1914 to 8,643 in 1939: by 1935, 56½% of the members were in large societies of 20,000 members and over.

In retail distribution, the decline of price competition, mainly by the spread of 'resale price maintenance', depended basically on the existence

[1] J. A. Hough, *Co-operative Retailing, 1914–1945* (1949); S. M. Bushell, 'The Relative Importance of Co-operative, Multiple and Other Retail Traders', *Economica*, 1/1, Jan. 1921, Table I.
[2] Levy, *Retail Trade Associations*, p. 28.
[3] G. D. H. Cole, *A Century of Co-operation* (Manchester, 1944), pp. 371–2.
[4] A. M. Carr-Saunders, P. Sargant Florence, Robert Peers *et al.*, *Consumers' Co-operation in Great Britain* (1938), pp. 45–6.

of branded, identical goods with a very wide, and preferably a national, market.[1] Thus it was that price maintenance was first found in bookselling as early as the eighteenth century, and by the 1890's had begun to spread to groceries and proprietary medicines.[2] The latter were protected by the 'Proprietary Articles Trade Association' (P.A.T.A.), established in 1896, which became a model for other associations and exerted great power. In 1938 it had 3,000 different articles on its protected list, and in its efforts to beat the price cutter, it made 10,000 purchases and discovered the source of supply of 2,035 of these by means of code-marking.

In the inter-war years, associations to fix and maintain retail prices sprang up in most mass-production goods trades. Their methods of control, including stop lists, boycotts and deferred rebates, needed the collaboration of manufacturers. Other associations attempted to reduce competition by distance limits, the most successful being newspaper vendors and sellers of photographic goods, and by licensing, usually tied to some necessary qualification, as in the case of pharmacists and motor and cycle dealers. Price maintenance itself covered about 3% of the domestic consumer's expenditure on goods in 1900; by 1938, this had grown to 30%.[3] The official Committee on Restraint of Trade, reporting in 1931,[4] deplored the propping up of prices and the restrictions of entry practised by many associations, but it felt that there was no 'compelling reason' for intervention by the State.

In the atmosphere of expanding sales, protected prices and widening margins, even the small shop managed to survive. There were other reasons, also, for the survival of the small unit in distribution: the absence of important technical advantages of size, the personal qualities of the shopkeeper, advantages of site, inertia on the part of the housewife, and the relatively small capital required. At the same time, advertising, packing, weighing and branding by manufacturers or wholesalers reduced the necessary skill of keeping many types of shop. Thus retail distribution became one of the last refuges of the small entrepreneur. By 1938, of an estimated 747,000 shops, all but 90,000 were still in the hands of small firms with 1–9 branches, the overwhelming majority being single shops managed by working proprietors.

The changing conditions in which retailers operated were not without effect on the wholesale trade also. The decades before 1914, which had seen the widespread replacement of producer-retailers by large-scale manufacturers or bulk importers, had greatly favoured the development

---

[1] Levy, *Retail Trade Associations, passim.*
[2] B. S. Yamey, *The Economics of Resale Price Maintenance* (1954), chapters 7 and 8.
[3] *Report of the Committee on Resale Price Maintenance* (Lloyd Jacob Committee) (1949. Cmd. 7696), p. 1; Jefferys, *Retail Trading*, pp. 53, 96–7.
[4] *Report of the Committee appointed . . . to Consider Certain Trade Practices* (1931).

of wholesaling, and to some extent this tendency continued into the post-war period, especially in the fruit and vegetable[1] and various made-up wear trades. The tendency of the retailers to carry lower stocks also increased the importance of the wholesaler, and in co-operative trading the Scottish and English Wholesale Societies extended their scope greatly as producers, importers and bankers.

The main changes of the period, however, worked in the opposite direction. Packing, blending and breaking bulk, even selection and pricing, were increasingly carried out by the manufacturer. Manufacturers of branded and advertised goods began to send their travellers and delivery vans direct to retailers, cutting out the wholesaler completely, and this was particularly so in commodities in which condition at the time of sale, or after-sale service and guarantee, were important, including biscuits, flour, meat, soap, books, electrical goods, photographic and sports goods and furniture. The larger chains, at the same time, did their own wholesaling, and their growth thus further reduced the scope of the specialist firm. In 1930, it was estimated that while retailers bought 29% of their turnover from wholesalers, multiple shops bought only 5% and bazaar stores, 7%.[2] By 1938, there were some 25,000–30,000 wholesaling firms left, and a further 20,000 wholesaler-retailers, handling about 40% of the consumer goods sold.[3]

The scope of the merchant firms trading overseas was reduced by similar factors as well as by the decline in Britain's international trade, and the artificial barriers put up by many countries against foreign imports.

> The merchants were . . . losing a great deal of their influence in Britain's foreign trade. The general reduction in world trade necessarily reduced their scope and numbers, while the growth of bilateral trading, which required that at least the preliminary negotiations should be undertaken by government departments, made some of their work unnecessary . . . The expansion of integrated industrial organizations also tended to supersede the activities of the merchant class internationally as in the domestic sphere.[4]

Britain's entrepôt trade fell from £110 million in 1913 to £62 million in 1938, when prices were higher, and of this diminished total, the proportion of raw materials had declined from 58% to 48%.

---

[1] Ministry of Agriculture and Fisheries, *Report of the Departmental Committee on the Distribution and Prices of Agricultural Produce* (Linlithgow Committee) (1924).

[2] E. H. Phelps-Brown and G. L. S. Shackle, *Statistics of Monetary Circulation in England and Wales, 1919–37* (Royal Economic Society Memorandum No. 74. 1938), p. 21.

[3] Jefferys, *Retail Trading*, pp. 47–9, and *Distribution of Consumer Goods*, pp. 21–9, 46–8, 117–18; D. C. Braithwaite and S. P. Dobbs, *Distribution of Consumable Goods* (1932).

[4] J. Hurstfield, 'The Control of Raw Material Supplies, 1919–1939', *Ec. Hist. Rev.* 14/1–2, 1944, pp. 19–20.

British merchants also suffered from the direct competition of foreign firms, often enjoying stronger financial and other support by their home Governments and banks than the British house, as well as a more adaptable joint-agency system and more go-ahead staff.

> British overseas trade [it was being said] has been conducted in the past too much, as it were, in the English Club, in the seaports and with a 'take it or leave it' attitude to the 'dagoes' who are the inhabitants of the country and the customers of British trade. Individual instances of failures on the part of British manufacturers to meet local requirements occur almost daily. Most of these are relatively trivial, but they typify an ignorance of, and lack of contact with, foreign markets which are symptomatic of fundamental shortcomings.

In this, British manufacturers were not without blame, for in their packaging, style and language of instructions accompanying their goods they took less account of local wishes than competing manufacturers from other countries.[1]

In the changing nature of trade with formerly backward, but now rapidly developing parts of the globe, the better technical training of foreign representatives became more important than the knowledge of the international market for raw materials which was the *forte* of the British merchant. In the case of complex manufactured products or large installations which took a growing share of the export trade, he was squeezed not only by foreign houses, but also by the large British manufacturers. For if he succeeded in opening a region to large sales, the manufacturer was tempted to send out his own representative and keep the merchanting profits for himself; tariff regulations might also force him to open branch factories. If, on the other hand, the merchant failed to sell the product, the manufacturer was equally tempted to by-pass him and try other channels. The shift from merchant to manufacturers' agent was detrimental to British trade as a whole, since the latter, unlike the former, had no interest in return cargoes. At the same time the British merchant, who had often acted as local banker and shipper, was pushed out by developing native or Government-sponsored firms, reducing further the demand for British financial and shipping services, already weakened by the decline in British overseas investment.[2] A long phase of the history of British overseas commerce was coming to a close in the inter-war years.

2. THE COURSE OF OVERSEAS TRADE

The decline in the position of the British overseas merchant, and the fall of the share of British trade, are best seen in their proper perspective

---

[1] P.E.P., *Report on International Trade* (1937), pp. 140–1; cf. also A. E. Kahn, *Great Britain in the World Economy* (1946), p. 79.
[2] P.E.P., *ibid.*, pp. 12–14, 131 ff.

by glancing at world trade as a whole in the inter-war period. The war and the revolutions which followed it had disrupted many of the established trade connections, notably those between the two sides to the conflict; between Russia and the rest of the world after the Bolshevik revolution; and between the industrial European countries as a whole, and the less developed overseas areas which found themselves deprived of manufactured imports and had to attempt to create their own industries instead. The war also created some new trade links. The United States, in particular, emerged as a large exporter and shipowner and, above all, as a large-scale international lender.

The boom of 1919–20 and the runaway inflations of several countries, including Germany, in the early 1920's[1] further dislocated established trade connections, but world trade as a whole recovered remarkably quickly and soon began to grow beyond its pre-war level. In this growth the industrial progress and rising national incomes of the advanced countries, including the United States, Germany and Japan, played a major part, but the exports of primary producers were lagging. This was probably due to the decline in the rate of population increase in Europe and to an inadequate rate of transfer of population from the land to industry, leading to tariffs to protect an over-large peasantry in European countries, and to substitute home-produced commodities for imports.[2] At the same time, the continued high rate of population increase in overseas areas made it easier to keep much of the primary production in the country of origin.

These factors, together with the over-stimulation of the production of primary products during the war, caused a certain weakness in the world demand for them even in the 1920's. In the depression of the early 1930's it suffered a disastrous collapse. As a result, the primary producing countries, which were generally also international debtor countries, found it impossible to service their debts or pay for imports from the advanced countries. Here was one of the main causes of a vicious circle of shrinking world trade in the 1930's.[3]

Before 1914, it was Great Britain which had, by a flexible monetary policy, a free market for gold as well as for imported commodities, and by large overseas investment operations, held the balance between the world's raw material and manufactured exports. After the war, this role should have fallen to the United States by virtue of her economic strength

---

[1] League of Nations, *The Course and Control of Inflation* (Geneva, 1945).

[2] W. A. Lewis, *Economic Survey, 1919–1939* (1949), pp. 149 ff., 196, and 'World Production, Prices and Trade, 1870–1960', *Manchester School,* 20/2, May 1952. F. Benham, 'The Muddle of the Thirties', *Economica*, N.S., 12/45, 1945.

[3] A. E. Kahn, *Great Britain in the World Economy* (1946), pp. 42–3, 63; A. J. Brown, *Industrialization and Trade* (1943), pp. 11, 56–7.

and her emergence as the world's main lender. Long-term foreign investments had changed as follows (in £ million):[1]

	1914	1929
Great Britain	4,004	3,737
France	1,766	719
Germany	1,376	226
U.S.A.	513	3,018

The U.S.A., however, was unable to play her role in world trade quite as Britain had played it.

There were several reasons for this. For one thing, the U.S.A. retained her high tariff and, in any case, had far less need of imports than had the British economy in its days of economic leadership. Britain, in fact, remained the world's chief free market for most raw materials and food products, the 'dumping ground of foreign exporters',[2] before 1931 and the largest market even after that date, while becoming too weak to stand the financial strain which such a position involved.

Secondly, the U.S.A. had become the world's chief lender at a time when international capital movements and indebtedness were being bedevilled by war loan repayments and reparations of vast dimensions. Germany, above all, was quite unable to pay the annual reparations instalments, even after they were scaled down by the Dawes Plan of 1924 and the Young Plan of 1929. They had largely to be advanced by the U.S.A., and since these loans, in turn, were written off after 1932, very little was actually paid over by the losers of the war as such.[3] As far as the war loans among the Allies were concerned, moratoria and standstill agreements lightened the burdens of the weaker nations, but the U.S.A. insisted on *some* repayments, based on ability to pay, so that Britain actually repaid more to the U.S.A. than she could collect from the financially weaker allies whom she had helped during the war. These payments also gained little for the creditors and, in the depression of the 1930's, would have become a positive embarrassment to the receiving countries suffering from heavy unemployment.[4] Meanwhile, however, they caused much harm to the debtors and to the vanquished nations, they disrupted the flows of international payments, and they created a new phenomenon, the highly industrialized debtor nation, of which

---

[1] Colin Clark, *Conditions of Economic Progress* (1951 ed.), p. 514.
[2] P.E.P., *Report on International Trade* (1937), p. 63.
[3] A. J. Youngson, *The British Economy, 1920–1957* (1960), pp. 51–3, but note that there was no such currency as the Austrian 'mark': it was the Krone (crown) which collapsed in 1922; cf. C. Bresciani-Turroni, *The Economics of Inflation* (1953 ed.), p. 334.
[4] H. W. Arndt, *The Economic Lessons of the Nineteen-Thirties* (1944), p. 28.

Germany, Japan and Italy were the leading examples. These countries were forced by their position into ever tighter control and artificial restriction over foreign trade and payments, including the creation of several artificial exchange rates by which they hoped to extract forced loans from abroad.[1]

Thirdly, American lending differed greatly in character from the overseas investments of Britain before 1914. It arose out of the war rather than out of normal trade relations, and in the absence of firms in New York with long experience of overseas connections, too much of it was speculative or merely to pay off former loans. Much of it, also, was politically directed, but without effective political control over the territory in which the investment was made, such as was normally insisted on by the investor of the nineteenth century. Above all, for the American investment market foreign investment was marginal, and was easily jettisoned, as in 1928, when the boom in American home securities diverted all funds to Wall Street. Yet for the rest of the world, the reversal of the outflow of American investments appeared to be of staggering proportions. In the course of 1919–1930, $11·6 milliard long-term capital and $1 milliard short-term capital was sent abroad, as against only $3·3 milliard repaid or invested by foreigners in the U.S.A.[2] This outflow was replaced, in the 1930's, by a *net* investment by the rest of the world in the U.S.A. of the order of $320 million a year. Similarly, there was a flight of short-term funds into the U.S.A. from 1934 onwards, converting a net export of short-term capital into a net import which averaged $650 million a year in 1934–9.

Nor was this all, for with the onset of the American slump in 1929, imports into the U.S.A. fell off drastically and were further reduced by the tariff of 1930:[3] payments on merchandise import account fell from $4,399 million in 1929 to $1,323 million in 1932. The amount of dollars thus made available to the rest of the world by American lending and purchases fell from $7,400 a year to $2,400 in the course of three years, 1929–32, or by 68%, and if the fixed debt payments which had to be met out of these totals are deducted, the dollars available to foreigners for other purposes were cut by an even greater percentage margin.

A cut of such magnitude, caused by sudden reversals of the trade and lendings flows, created an overpowering dollar shortage, related to, though not quite of the same nature as, the more prolonged dollar shortage of the post-war years.[4] It forced other countries to deflate and ultimately

[1] P.E.P., *International Trade*, pp. 19–20; Sir Arthur Salter, *Recovery* (1932), pp. 51 ff., also 100–7 and chapter 3.
[2] Hal B. Lary *et al.* (U.S. Dept. of Commerce), *The United States in the World Economy* (Washington, 1943, London, 1944), pp. 89 ff., Appx., Tables I–III.
[3] J. K. Galbraith, *The Great Crash* (1955), pp. 162–3.
[4] A. J. Brown, 'Dollars and Crises', *Ec. Hist. Rev.*, 2nd S., 12/2, Dec. 1959; Donald MacDougall, *The World Dollar Problem* (1957), pp. 35–42, Appx. IA.

to go off the gold standard, while as part of the large-scale capital inflows, $10 milliard of gold was sent to America in 1934-9 and duly re-interred there without being allowed to affect the value of the dollar. Meanwhile, gold was mined at a hitherto unheard-of rate in view of its high price after most of the world had come off the gold standard and had depreciated its currencies.[1] Thus, the United States, instead of acting as a buffer, and using its vast gold reserves to stabilize world trade when threatened by the dislocations of the slump, tended by its policy to make matters worse.

The reduction of American overseas trade to less than a third in value in the depression (though the reduction was much less in terms of volume) was accompanied by reductions in world trade between other countries in the 1930's. Currency and trade restrictions, Government-sponsored autarchy, bilateral and regional agreements, all tended to reduce still further the flow of goods across frontiers, already affected by the depression. In the recovery which followed, world trade expanded again, but it failed to reach the levels of 1929; the volume of trade in manufactured goods was 14% lower, and in foodstuffs 7% lower, in 1937, values being subject to much greater reductions still. In 1938 the cyclical downward turn in world trade began again, but was interrupted by the outbreak of war.

In the 1920's, Britain's volume of imports was steadily increasing, and her exports steadily declining.[2] As world trade as a whole was expanding, the British share of world imports remained about the same, being 16% in 1913 and 15·4% in 1929, but the share of the world's exports fell from 13–14% to 10·86% in the same years.[3] In the slump, Britain suffered rather less than many other countries, and her share of world exports rose slightly, from 9·36% in 1931 to 10·37% in 1933, but it was back at 9·8% in 1937. Britain's share of the world export trade in manufactured goods fell from 27·5% in 1911–13 to 23·8% in 1921–5 and 18·5% in 1931–8, and as a proportion of national income, overseas trade declined as follows:[4]

Ratio of Exports to National Product		Ratio of Imports to National Income	
1907	33%	1913	31%
1924	27%	1929	25%
1938	15%	1938	16%

---

[1] R. G. Hawtrey, *The Gold Standard in Theory and Practice* (5th ed., 1947), p. 180.
[2] H. S. Booker, *The Problem of Britain's Overseas Trade* (1948), chapter 3.
[3] H. W. Macrosty, 'The Overseas Trade of the United Kingdom, 1924-31', *J. R. Stat. S.*, 95/4, 1932; G. D. H. Cole, *British Trade and Industry* (1932), chapter 9.
[4] W. A. Lewis, *op. cit.*, pp. 82, 85. For slightly different figures, see G. D. A. MacDougall, 'General Survey, 1929-37' in *Britain in Recovery* (1938), p. 13.

With a strongly rising volume of imports, and an equally marked fall in the volume of exports, Britain would have been faced with a rapidly widening unfavourable trade gap, if it had not been for a remarkably favourable trend of relative prices.[1] The improvement in Britain's terms of trade was one of the outstanding characteristics of the whole period:

	Quantum of Trade		Terms of Trade	
	Quantum of Imports	Quantum of Exports	Export Prices/ Import Prices, 1913 = 100 [2]	Net Terms of Trade 1938 = 100 [3]
1908–13	92	91	97	143
1921–9	104	79	127	115
1930–7	115	64	138	103

It was this change in the terms of trade which permitted, and in part caused, the rising standard of living in Britain while condemning the export industries to unemployment and decline. If labour and other resources could have been transferred quickly enough from export goods to new and expanding industries, these remarkably favourable terms could have given Britain a splendid opportunity to raise living standards at a quite exceptional rate. As it was, part of it was wasted by unemployment in the export sectors. In 1929 it was estimated that the unemployment in the six leading staple export trades caused by the fall in exports since 1913 alone amounted to 700,000–800,000 workers, or virtually the whole of the intractable core of the unemployment of the 1920's.[4] Meanwhile the low prices of primary products on the world markets were ruining many of the primary producers who had been the chief customers of Britain.

In the 1930's Britain was much more successful in transferring resources from the old export industries and benefiting by the favourable trade terms, and in increasing the exports of the growth industries.[5] Rising incomes and standards of comfort led to an expansion of employment in the service trades, building and other sheltered industries, and the nature

[1] Elliott Zupnick, *Britain's Postwar Dollar Problem* (New York, 1957), pp. 24–7.
[2] Lewis, Appx., Table XV, p. 202.
[3] B. R. Mitchell and Phyllis Deane, *Abstract of British Historical Statistics* (Cambridge, 1962), p. 332.
[4] E. V. Francis, *Britain's Economic Strategy* (1939), pp. 55–6.
[5] W. A. Lewis, p. 78; for a different tabulation for 1927–8 see F. H. Awad, 'The Structure of the World Export Trade, 1926–1953', *Yorkshire Bulletin*, 11/1, 1959, p. 35.

of import demand also changed. After 1929, virtually the whole of the increase in imports was in the form of consumption goods, mainly food, drink and tobacco.[1]

Compared with pre-war trade the 1920's saw a growth in the trade with Commonwealth countries, and a corresponding decrease in the trade with Western European nations and with Russia.[2] As far as trade with North America was concerned, exports showed a substantial decline, while imports were rising. The resultant strain on sterling was aggravated by the fact that other European countries also had an unfavourable trade balance with the U.S.A., covering it by American loans and investments, and by running a surplus with Britain which was its surplus with her colonies. A large quadrilateral world trade thus had to be kept in balance by the dollar earnings of the British overseas territories which were members of the sterling bloc.[3]

In the 1930's this complex system of trade was subjected to intolerable pressure and virtually broke down. One limb, the dollar earnings of the colonies, shrank disastrously with the price fall of primary commodities and the decline in the American demand for industrial raw materials in the slump. A second limb, the European (and American) surplus with Britain, was reduced in size by Britain's effective, if belated, entry into the international game of beggar-my-neighbour in 1931, with policies of protection, currency manipulation and more direct aids. In the same period, she allowed her balance of trade with the Commonwealth and South America to deteriorate by about the same amount, but these two movements were in no sense 'compensating': they were both the consequences of decline, a decline in British purchases from Europe and the U.S.A., and in sales to the tropics and other primary products suppliers,[4] and the deflationary effects of these tendencies further aggravated the two main problems, the unemployment in the British export industries and the low income of the overseas trading partners.

The favourable price trend was approximately of the right order of magnitude to counteract the unfavourable volume movements and keep the visible trade gap in the inter-war years on a fairly even keel. It averaged £225 million in 1921–4, rose to an average of £396 million in 1925–31, fell to £276 million in 1932–5 and then showed a strongly rising tendency again, increasing to well over £400 million by 1937.[5]

[1] G. N. Butterworth and H. Campion, 'Changes in British Import Trade' *Manchester School*, 8/1, 1937.
[2] Figures will be found in the *Annual Statistical Abstracts of the United Kingdom*.
[3] A. E. Kahn, *op. cit.*, chapters 12 and 13; Zupnick, pp. 37–8.
[4] Lewis, *op. cit.*, pp. 169–70.
[5] Annual figures will be found in E. V. Morgan, *Studies in British Financial Policy, 1914–25* (1952), p. 341; A. E. Kahn, *Great Britain in the World Economy* (1946), p. 126, also chapters 9 and 10; G. D. A. MacDougall, 'General Survey,

To meet this adverse merchandise trade gap of £200–400 million a year, Great Britain relied largely on her income from overseas investments, and on the 'invisible' earnings from shipping, banking, insurance and similar services.

These invisible earnings, apart from the income from gilt-edged securities expressed in sterling, were all dependent on prosperity abroad and a high level of international trade. As long as world prosperity held up reasonably well, they were more than sufficient to cover the visible trade gap. With shipping income estimated at £120–140 million a year, investment income around £250 million and commissions, etc., about £80 million, there was an annual surplus on current account of £50–100 million in the 1920's, except for the strike year of 1926, and this surplus was regularly invested abroad. It was smaller than the overseas investment of 1910–13, but it was a balance on the right side, and the cumulative effects of these overseas investments were by no means negligible.

With the onset of the depression, both exports and imports fell away, and except for the single year of 1930, the visible trade gap was reduced, from 1931 on, in proportion to overseas trade. Meanwhile, however, there was a far more drastic fall in net invisible earnings which had accounted for about a third of the balance of payments in the 1920's. Shipping incomes dropped to a nadir of £65 million in 1933, investment income to £150 million in 1932, and commissions and miscellaneous incomes to a bare £40 million: a fall for these three items together by £200 million. The small regular surplus available for foreign investment disappeared in 1930, and in 1931 became a deficit, leading to a repatriation of capital on balance to the extent of £104 million. The drastic steps taken in that year, including protection and depreciation of the currency, reduced the unfavourable balance (including 'invisibles') to £51 million in 1932 and to much smaller amounts later, but throughout the 1930's repayments of capital slightly exceeded foreign lending[1] for the first time since the Industrial Revolution.

What little lending occurred in the 1930's was made almost entirely within the Empire. New capital issues indicate the trend (in £ million)[2] (see table on next page).

1929–1937' in *Britain in Recovery*, p. 22; and C. L. Mowat, pp. 264, 435. They are all based on Board of Trade Returns.

[1] Sir Robert Kindersley, 'British Overseas Investments, 1938', *Econ. J.* 49/196, 1939, p. 694. His main figures are summarized in A. E. Kahn, *op. cit.*, p. 187; Royal Institute of International Affairs, *The Problem of International Investment* (1937); Tse Chun Chang, 'The British Balance of Payments, 1924–1938', *Econ. J.*, 57/228, 1947

[2] A. J. Youngson, *op. cit.*, p. 124; J. H. Richardson, *British Economic Foreign Policy* (1936), p. 73 and chapter 3.

	1911–12	1925–9	1932–6
Home investment	38	165	124
Overseas investment: Empire	67	67	28
„ „ Elsewhere	95	48	3
Totals	200	280	255

This switch was partly due to Treasury control from 1931 on. In 1932, the Chancellor asked for the suspension of all new issues over part of the year in order to make his conversion operations a success, and when the conversion was over in September, the embargo on foreign lending continued, and was extended in 1933 to the purchase of blocks of existing foreign securities. Control over these issues was transferred in 1936 to the Foreign Transactions Advisory Committee, which later became the Capital Issues Committee.

With these capital repayments and large-scale defaults, the nominal value of British overseas investments fell from £4,100 million in 1927 to £3,490 million in 1939;[1] the fall in the real value, in terms of earning power, was certainly greater, since over £1,900 million of this investment was in the form of equity and loan capital of companies. Holdings within the Empire accounted for 47% in 1913, 59% in 1929 and 61% in 1936. In that year, £505 million was held in Australia, £443 million in Canada and Newfoundland, and £438 million in India and Ceylon. The peak of investments in areas outside the Empire, of which South America held the largest share, was reached in 1927–9.[2]

3. GREAT BRITAIN UNDER PROTECTION

It was noted above that one of the emergency measures taken in 1931, to rectify the unfavourable trade balance was the imposition of protective tariffs. This decision represents such a complete reversal of traditional British economic policy that it deserves separate treatment.

Perhaps what was remarkable was not so much the adoption of protection, but its delay until 1931 in the face of the protectionism of all the other leading industrial states. The continued free-trade policy in Britain was imposed, in part, by the choice of the electorate, which had decisively defeated the Conservative Party on the two occasions when it made protection an important electoral issue, in 1906 and in 1923, and even

[1] Bank of England figures; Kindersley's are slightly higher throughout.
[2] J. Fred Rippy, *British Investments in Latin America, 1822–1949* (Minneapolis, 1959), chapter 5; series of articles by Sir Robert Kindersley in the *Economic Journal* in the 1930's.

in 1931 could scarcely be said to have given the 'National' Government a mandate for ending free trade. Economists and economic advisers were also all but united on opposing protection, and their views were summarized in the brilliantly argued *Tariffs: the Case Examined*,[1] which appeared in the year in which protection was finally to triumph.

There had been many digressions from the narrow path of free trade even before 1931, but they could all be deemed to have been measures dealing with particular issues which still left the main principle intact. During the war, in 1915, the so-called 'McKenna duties' were imposed, consisting of a duty of 33⅓% *ad valorem* on some imported luxury goods. Their original object was the saving of foreign exchange,[2] but they were not repealed after the war, except briefly by the Labour Government of 1924, and when re-imposed, they were extended in 1926 to commercial vehicles and parts. They allowed such industries as motor manufacturing to grow to maturity behind a substantial tariff wall which was high enough to keep out most imports in what was nominally a free-trade country.[3]

In the later years of the war, shortage of shipping space, as well as shortages of foreign currency led to further restrictive measures. Prohibition of imports, except under licence, was extended to a wide range of commodities until September 1919, and was kept on afterwards for the products of certain 'key industries', such as dyestuffs and other chemicals, scientific instruments, laboratory glassware and magnetos, for all of which the country had depended mainly on imports before the war. When the High Court declared this continued prohibition to be illegal, it was reimposed in two new Acts.

The Dyestuffs (Import Regulation) Act, 1920, dealt with dyestuffs only. It prohibited their imports for ten years, except under licence, and this period was sufficient to permit the vigorous growth of the industry in Britain. The second measure, the Safeguarding of Industries Act of 1921, was more complex. It protected the other 'key industries' by a tariff of 33⅓% *ad valorem*, but by Part II it also permitted the extension of such protection to other industries (which could make no claim on grounds of military importance), provided they could show that foreign products undersold them either by selling below costs of production or by the depreciation of a foreign currency. No use was made of the anti-dumping provision, and it was repealed in 1930, but under the other clause, relating to currency depreciations, a few minor manufactures, including fabric gloves, glassware, hollow-ware and gas mantles, were protected by tariffs. In 1924 this section of the Act lapsed, though the

---

[1] W. H. Beveridge *et al.*, *Tariffs: The Case Examined* (1931).
[2] p. 65 above.
[3] P.E.P., *Engineering Reports, II: Motor Vehicles* (1950), p. 75.

duties themselves ran on for their allotted span of years, some until 1929. Meanwhile, the German Reparation (Recovery) Act of 1921 permitted the Treasury to impose duties of up to 50% *ad valorem* on German imports in part payment of reparations, and despite a complex and ingenious machinery devised to prevent this, the duties were in fact protective, to the extent of 26% *ad valorem* on the average.[1]

In 1925 the conditions making imports dutiable under the Safeguarding Act were somewhat extended. Industries might be granted protection if they satisfied a committee of inquiry that the imports competing with their products enjoyed unfair advantages by virtue not only of currency depreciation, but also of subsidies or bounties, or by inferior conditions of employment abroad. Under these clauses, protection was extended to cutlery, pottery, lace, buttons, wrapping paper and some very minor industries, but it was withheld from the steel industry, among others. There were also silk duties and hop duties imposed in 1925, which in spite of their complex provisions had a clear, if limited, protective effect, as had the petrol and sugar duties. The McKenna duties were re-imposed in the same year.[2]

A special type of protection was extended to the film industry. This was in danger of complete extinction in 1926–7 owing to the mass influx of American films which had covered their overhead costs in the U.S.A. and could be shown here at little more than their (negligible) prime costs. The Cinematograph Films Act of 1927 established a compulsory minimum quota of British pictures, rising from $7\frac{1}{2}$% for renters and 5% for exhibitors, by steps of $2\frac{1}{2}$% to reach 20% for both in 1936–8. The quota system was an undoubted success, and by 1936 the British film industry had by its own efforts exceeded the minimum quota at home, and had established a growing export market for its products.[3]

All these measures together did not constitute a protectionist policy. In 1930 only 17% of imports by value were dutiable, mostly by revenue duties only: protective duties did not affect more than 2–3% of imports. Nor did protection seem likely, for the total balance of payments of Britain was still active, and the pressure on the exchanges originated from financial policies and transactions rather than from merchandise trade. Above all, it came to be generally recognized and confirmed by the influential Balfour Committee on Industry and Trade, that Britain's main problem lay not in keeping out imports, but in solving the difficulties of the export

---

[1] E. B. McGuire, *The British Tariff System* (1939), chapter 17.

[2] G. P. Jones and A. G. Pool, *A Hundred Years of Economic Development in Great Britain* (1959), pp. 317–23; J. H. Richardson, 'Tariffs, Preferences and other Forms of Protection', in *Britain in Recovery* (1938), p. 126; Sir Hubert Llewellyn Smith, *The Board of Trade* (1928), pp. 185–8.

[3] Alfred Plummer, *New British Industries in the Twentieth Century* (1937), chapter 6/IV.

industries, which could not be helped, and might be harmed, by tariffs. J. M. Keynes, however, argued ingeniously for a tariff to be worked in such a manner as to neutralize, in effect, the British handicap of the over-valuation of the pound sterling under the gold standard.[1]

All this was changed in the economic blizzard of 1931, which drove Britain off the gold standard, created a large unfavourable balance of payments[2] and brought in, by the snap election of October, a vast Conservative majority under the guise of supporters for the 'National' Government,[3] eager to impose protection. While protection was being debated, a temporary Abnormal Importations (Customs Duties) Act was passed at once, to stop the rushing in of imports in anticipation of later duties. The Act permitted *ad valorem* duties of up to 100%, though only 50% was generally imposed in practice on a wide range of manufactured goods. Another early protective measure was the Horticultural Products (Emergency Duties) Act, also passed before the end of the year.

The breathing space thus created was used to institute an inquiry by the 'Balance of Trade Committee' under Neville Chamberlain. Its labours were perfunctory, and in February 1932, the Import Duties Act inaugurated the protectionist era in Britain. The Act was not to apply to Empire goods for the time being, nor to the commodities covered by earlier protectionist legislation. There was also a specific free list, including wheat, meat and other foodstuffs, as well as all important industrial raw materials. On other commodities, a general tariff of 10% *ad valorem* was imposed and an Import Duties Advisory Committee (I.D.A.C.) under Sir George May was appointed, to suggest alterations in that general tariff.

I.D.A.C. reported in April 1932.[4] It recommended that duties on manufactured goods in general should be increased by 10% to a total of 20% *ad valorem*, on luxury goods to 25% or 30%, on bicycles and some chemicals to 33⅓% and on certain industrial raw materials and semi-manufactures to 15%. These rates were adopted at once. After the alterations agreed to at Ottawa later in the year, the total effect was to leave about one-quarter of imports duty free (many of them, however, restricted by other methods), one-half paying 10–20%, 8% paying new duties of over 20% and the remainder of imports paying the old McKenna and Safeguarding Duties.[5] In the following years innumerable alterations of specific duty rates were suggested by I.D.A.C. and put into force; of these,

[1] Beveridge *et al.*, *Tariffs: The Case Examined*, pp. 76–88; P. J. Grigg, *Prejudice and Judgment* (1948), p. 184.

[2] See p. 191 above.

[3] C. L. Mowat, *Britain Between the Wars* (1956 ed.), pp. 409–12.

[4] (Cmd. 4066). Also see *Recommendations of the I.D.A.C.*, 45 pts., Parliamentary Papers, 1932–3, XVI.

[5] J. H. Richardson, in *Britain in Recovery*, p. 129. Also F. Benham, *Great Britain Under Protection* (New York, 1941), chapter 2.

the most important was the duty of $33\frac{1}{3}$% imposed on steel imports on condition that the industry was reorganized, and the temporary raising of the steel tariff to 50% in 1935 in order to force the European steel cartel to grant better terms to the British industry.[1] Of the other protectionist measures introduced in the 1930's, the most important ones were those relating to agricultural products, noted in chapter 3, section 5 above.

As long as Britain kept to a free-trade policy, there was little opportunity of granting preferential tariffs to Dominions and Colonies. Empire preference, to the extent of one-sixth of the duty rate, as instituted in 1919, could work effectively only on commodities on which there was a revenue duty, e.g. tea, sugar and cocoa, and this excluded the white Dominions from any major benefit. Even the trade from India and the Crown Colonies benefited to the extent of 5–6% only in 1920. The reduction of one-third in the McKenna duties, granted to Empire countries in 1919, and the complete exemption from the 'key industry' safeguarding duties of 1921 and the one-third reduction on others were also of little practical importance to members of the Commonwealth.[2]

Much more important than tariff preference was the encouragement given to investment within the Empire by a provision in the Finance Act of 1919, exempting it from double taxation. Investment was thereby to some extent channelled to the Empire, and often, as in the case of India and South Africa, led to an expansion in trade. From 1922 on, the Colonial Office also instructed colonies to discriminate in favour of British imports.[3]

As noted above, imports from Empire countries were exempted from the original tariff of 1932. Britain's new system of protection made it possible for her to build up a system of imperial preferences and to this end an Imperial Economic Conference assembled in Ottawa in July–August 1932, hoping to expand trade among the members of the British Commonwealth in a world of shrinking commerce and rising trade barriers. These hopes were to be largely disappointed, for in fact neither Britain nor the Dominions had much room to manœuvre.

In the first place, there was no hope of making the Empire economically self-sufficient. In 1924–9, about 60% of the exports of Britain, India and Canada, about 50% of the exports of Australia, and 36% of the exports of South Africa had gone to countries outside the Empire,[4] and the Empire countries could not replace these markets. If they depended on sales to outsiders, they must needs allow foreigners to import goods in return, and

[1] D. Abel, *A History of British Tariffs, 1923–1942* (1945).

[2] C. L. Mowat, *Britain Between the Wars*, pp. 109, 367; E. V. Francis, *Britain's Economic Strategy* (1939), pp. 104–14.

[3] J. Hurstfield, 'The Control of British Raw Material Supplies, 1919–1939', *Ec. Hist. Rev.*, 14/1–2, 1944, p. 5.

[4] P.E.P., *Report on International Trade* (1937), p. 66.

their exports could not be sold in preferential Empire markets at prices higher than the ruling world level.[1]

In the second place, the mercantilist conception of an industrialized mother country linked with primary producer colonies, which underlay much Empire preference propaganda, had become grossly anachronistic by 1932. The Dominions had infant industries, which they were determined to protect even against the United Kingdom, while Great Britain had at last decided to protect her farmers. As a result, all that could be achieved, after weeks of bitter wrangling, was a series of bilateral treaties, seven of them between Britain and the Dominions[2] (except the Irish Free State), according to which Britain would use a system of quotas and licences to ensure that Empire imports would increase at the expense of foreign importers and not British farmers, while the Dominions granted their preference in return, not by lowering tariffs to British exporters but by raising them still higher against other countries. British tariffs on imports from the rest of the world were also raised in the aggregate by the Ottawa agreements:[3]

		1930	1932	
			Before Ottawa	After Ottawa
% of imports free of duty		83·0	30·2	25·2
% of foreign imports subject to new duties at:	10%	—	32·9	28·3
	11–20%	—	15·3	21·8
	over 20%	—	4·6	7·7
		83·0	83·0	83·0

The network was completed by the imposition, in the months which followed, of imperial preference on the Colonies also. Only the Irish Free State stood out, being engaged in a tariff war with Great Britain, largely of political origin.

The result of the imperial preference system was not an increase in trade, but a diversion of part of the trade formerly conducted with outside regions towards Empire regions.[4] Even then, it is not certain how far Ottawa was responsible for this diversion, for it was in line with a long-

---

[1] Benham, *op. cit.*, pp. 80–1.
[2] *Imperial Economic Conference at Ottawa, Summary of Proceedings and Copies of Trade Agreements* (1932. Cmd. 4174).
[3] Francis, *op. cit.*, p. 203; J. H. Richardson, *British Economic Foreign Policy* (1936), p. 128.   [4] P.E.P., *International Trade*, pp. 66–74.

term trend, and with the trend of investments,[1] as well as being furthered by the exchange stability within the sterling bloc in contrast with the exchange uncertainties in the rest of the world. As the following tabulation shows, the rest of the Empire benefited more from Ottawa than the United Kingdom, but Britain had started in a more favourable position:[2]

U.K. Trade with Empire Countries (excluding Irish Free State)

	% of U.K. Imports from Empire	% of U.K. Exports to Empire
1913	25·0	32·9
1924–9 (average)	26·8	35·2
1931	24·5	32·6
1933	34·3	36·0
1937	37·3	39·7

The new tariffs and quotas also permitted Britain to offer concessions, or threaten retaliation, to other countries. Normally Britain insisted on the most-favoured-nation clause, which tended to have a general downward effect on tariff rates. The 1930's were not propitious for such liberalizing tendencies, and great ingenuity was shown in so defining commodities that mutual concessions were limited to the contracting parties only, where most-favoured-nation clauses were in operation. In any case the latter tended to go out of favour. Commercial agreements became strictly bilateral, the proportion of world trade conducted bilaterally or by barter rising to 12%, and Britain made 20 such agreements in 1933–8.[3] With countries with which Great Britain had large unfavourable balances, like the Baltic countries and the Argentine, she could insist on forcing an increase in the sale of her own goods, such as coal. Other industrial nations, notably Germany, did likewise, and as a result there was a strong trend towards bilaterally balanced trade relations,[4] an obvious retrogression from the earlier system of multilateralism. Specially high retaliatory duties, apart from the Irish case, were used by Britain only twice, in 1934, against France and against Japan.

Thus the world was increasingly divided into economic, as well as political blocs, with currency restrictions, barter agreements, and quota and tariff barriers between them replacing the former trade flow. There were few downward revisions. The most important was the trade agreement between Britain and the U.S.A. made in November 1938 after three years of delicate negotiations, but there was no opportunity of

---

[1] Cf. p. 191 above.
[2] Richardson, in *Britain in Recovery*, p. 138; F. C. Benham, *Great Britain Under Protection* (1941), pp. 256–7. [3] McGuire, chapter 19.
[4] H. S. Ellis, *Exchange Control in Central Europe* (Cambridge, Mass., 1941).

developing it before the outbreak of war; a treaty with Germany in 1939 was similarly thwarted by political events.

It is not easy to summarize the total effects of protection in the 1930's on Britain's trade and prosperity. The theoretical argument for maintaining a free-trade policy, even when the rest of the world is protectionist, cannot be gainsaid on its own assumptions, but few of these assumptions were operative in Britain in 1931. The claim that free trade will ensure the most efficient use of resources was irrelevant when 20% of the national resources or more were idle; the doctrine of comparative costs had to be greatly modified when applied in a context of exchange manipulation, tariffs, quotas and subsidies abroad and international or foreign cartels which could and did freely engage in dumping or in discriminatory pricing. The structural alterations required of British industry were too great to be carried out satisfactorily without State aid, including protection. Lastly, it was felt that at a time when all countries were attempting to export their unemployment, the multiplier effect of deflation and increasing unemployment could be cut off by cutting off imports, though the problem was not put in such terms at the time.

The arguments actually used in 1931 were far less sophisticated. Statesmen appeared to be looking for the more direct effects of protection —the salvaging of individual industries, the prevention of undercutting by ill-paid labour—of the kind which in normal times economic theory had little difficulty in showing up as illusory or mistaken. Some hoped for rising prices as a possible cause of a cyclical upswing, others wanted simply to stop the unfavourable trade balance by the crudest method available, or to raise revenue. The British 'National' Government had a 'doctor's mandate' to try any remedy in 1931 and prescribed protection as a nostrum for a variety of ills and with a variety of motives.

It may be doubted whether protection helped greatly to pull Britain out of her exchange difficulties, still more out of the slump. When she used her economic power to force her coal on Scandinavia, Polish and German coal, squeezed out of that market, turned south and drove British coal out of Italy and France, so that little was gained by that manœuvre. If British manufacturers enjoyed a preference over Americans in Canada, the Americans retaliated by opening branch factories in Canada which then enjoyed preference over imports from Britain. On the other hand, the ill-effects of protection feared by orthodox economists were equally hard to find. Apart from the special case of agriculture, it would be hard to point to a single industry fostered in Britain by the tariff which was obviously uneconomic or inappropriate for this country. Again, the British consumer would have benefited little if foreign imports in the 1930's had been allowed to ruin British steelmaking, agriculture or shipbuilding. Continued free trade, while it would have driven prices down still further for the consumer, might well have robbed him of the purchasing power to make use of his opportunity.

Even the immediate effects of protection are difficult to isolate. There was, certainly, a sharp reduction in imports, and in the sequel home production rose much faster than imports, pointing to a possible replacement of one by the other. At the same time, however, there was also an even larger fall in exports, and the fall in total foreign trade as a proportion of home production was part of a secular trend, and may well not have been caused by the tariff as such. Similarly, protection did not seem to have led to any noticeable rise in prices: these continued to fall to 1932–3, and then rose slowly as the cyclical upswing began, as might have been expected:[1]

	Wholesale Prices (1929 = 100)			Cost of Living (1929 = 100)
	(Board of Trade)	(Economist)	(Statist-Sauerbeck)	(Min. of Labour)
1931	76·8	70·2	72·8	89·9
1932	74·6	67·7	70·7	87·8
1933	75·0	68·2	69·8	85·4
1937	95·2	89·3	90·0	93·9

In the last resort, protection in Britain was only one in a long chain of measures, and by itself it could neither reverse nor speed up the world's march to economic disruption and stagnation evident in the Great Depression of the 1930's. Its imposition in 1932 was motivated at least as much by politics as by economics. It arose out of the desire of the Government to be seen to make a gesture and take some novel action to stave off economic disaster, and at the same time to please some of its friends, rather than out of a careful balancing of economic advantages. In this, it resembled other economic policies of Governments more closely than is commonly allowed.

4. THE CHANGING ROLE OF THE BUDGET

The dislocation of the public finances caused by the war, as described in chapter 2, section 3 above, could not be ended immediately by the armistice. The budget continued to be unbalanced for a further two years the deficit being about £1,690 million in 1918–19 and £326 million in 1919–20, or a total of £2,000 million.[2] The budget of 1920–1 was the first

[1] G. D. H. Cole, *Money, Trade and Investment* (1954), p. 95.
[2] p. 66 above; E. V. Morgan, *Studies in British Financial Policy, 1914–25* (1952).

to achieve a surplus, and it may thus be considered to have been the first 'normal' peace-time budget.

There were, however, several legacies left of the war even after 1920 which made a simple return to the pre-war type of budget quite impossible. On the expenditure side, the changes, in Morgan's 'adjusted' terms, were as follows (in £ million):[1]

	1913–14	1920–1	1924–5
Consolidated Fund Services	37	378	394
Fighting Services	86	354	138
Munitions	—	33	—
Revenue Departments	30	76	64
Other Civil Departments	55	466	257
	208	1,306	853
Less Appropriations in Aid[2]	12	150	54
	196	1,156	799

When the much higher prices of the middle year in this tabulation are borne in mind, it will be noted that the main changes occurred in the course of the war: the budget of 1920–1 was, broadly, representative of the inter-war budgets which were to follow.

Among the changes since 1913–14, the striking increase in the 'Consolidated Fund Services' stands out, representing mainly the national debt. In money terms, its burden increased tenfold, and unlike the other items of expenditure, it could not be reduced when prices and costs fell. Compared with the pre-war position, the national debt increased from $\frac{1}{40}$ to $\frac{1}{4}$ of the total private property in the country; the annual interest payments, negligible before the war, rose to over 40% of the budget, and as prices fell in the early 1920's, the real burden of this debt, both on the budget and in more general terms, as a payment from mainly the active part of the population to mainly the inactive, became distinctly heavier.

The total national debt was at its maximum in March 1920, when it stood at £7,830 million. Of this, only £315 million was funded, £1,230 being external, and the rest consisting of a 'floating' debt of some £1,250

---

p. 98. On Professor Morgan's 'adjusted' figures, showing the sums actually collected and spent in the economic, rather than the administrative sense of the official figures, there was, in fact, a surplus of £110 million in 1919/20, p. 104.

[1] *Ibid.*, p. 101.

[2] Sales by Departments to other Departments or to the private sector.

million and of other unfunded debt of nearly £5,000 million with varying repayment dates and contracted at different terms and with differing privileges. The floating debt was tackled first, and within three years the Treasury Bills outstanding were reduced from over £1,100 million to little more than half this sum, while Ways and Means advances, standing at over £200 million in March 1920, were almost wiped out at the end of the decade.[1] The funding of this part of the floating debt, in the then existing market conditions, could only be done at great cost. With the annual interest obligations remaining the same, total obligations had to be increased in nominal amount: the reduction of £440 million in short-term debt in the four financial years 1921–5 was achieved only by raising the nominal value of long-term issues by £1,000 million. Moreover, the forcing of these additional sums on an already gorged market was bound to raise long-term interest rates.

As it was, most critics were agreed that the war debts had been contracted at too generous a rate, and that several opportunities had been missed, in 1915, 1917 and again in 1919, to raise more revenue by taxation and thereby reduce the need for borrowing.[2] Moreover, with £2,100 million of the unfunded debt in 1920 falling due for repayment in 1–7 years, and £2,900 million in 8–10 years from the date of issue, repayments and renewals followed each other so closely in the 1920's that the whole tended to coagulate into one single mass of war debt, to be dealt with together. Actual repayments out of budget surpluses, often needlessly disguised as 'sinking funds', reached £583 million in 1925–6, but the nominal national debt fell by less than this, partly because of unfavourable conversions, and partly because some of the debt was held by the National Debt Commissioners. The nominal total was brought down by £300 million, to £7,530 million, in 1931. In the 1930's the position was further improved, and by 1935, of the £5,590 million of public debt held outside the Departments, only £371 million was in bills, etc., of 3 months, £736 million was in debt of 1 to 15 years, and £4,483 million over 15 years or undated.[3]

The burden on the economy, however, was still high. The debt service fluctuated round 7% of the national income and rose to 8¼% in 1932 with the fall of incomes in the depression. Relief came only with the great War Loan Conversion of 1932, and the associated fall in short-term rates, which reduced the annual payments by £55 million on the funded debt

[1] A. T. K. Grant, *A Study of the Capital Market in Post-War Britain* (1937), pp 86 ff.

[2] Ursula K. Hicks, *The Finance of British Government, 1920–1936* (1938), p. 317; E. V. Morgan, *op. cit.*, p. 139, also 94–7, 115–51; A. W. Kirkaldy (ed.), *British Finance During and After the War, 1914–21* (1921), pp. 161–2.

[3] *Report of the Committee on the Working of the Monetary System* (Radcliffe Committee) (1959. Cmnd. 827), Table 26.

and £31 million on Savings Certificates and Treasury Bills. The debt service burden then fell to 5·45% of national income in 1933, 5·00% in 1934 and 4·65% in 1935.

Next to the increase in the Consolidated Fund Services, the most striking increases occurred in the expenditure on the social services, though part of these were derived from special contributions under the insurance schemes (in £ million):[1]

Payments Made:	Area Covered	1913–14	1921–2	1933–4
Poor Relief	G.B.	16½	46	47
Health Insurance	G.B.	14½	24½	32
Old-Age Pensions	G.B.	10	22	58½
Widows', etc., Pensions	G.B.	—	—	22½
War Pensions	U.K.	—	88½	44
Unemployment Insurance	U.K.	½	53	88½
Totals		41½	234	292½
Contributions Levied				
Health Insurance	G.B.	17	25	26
Pensions	G.B.	—	—	23
Unemployment Insurance	U.K.	2	30½	39½
Totals		19	55½	88½

War pensions were declining, but the expenditure on old-age pensions was growing inexorably with the rising proportion of older people, and unemployment and poor relief constituted a large and highly fluctuating item. Housing and education were other costly services, both of which also derived some share of their incomes from local authorities. As a result, the budgets of the local authorities were rising as rapidly as those of the Central Government. The changes between 1913–14 and 1938–9 may be tabulated as shown on the next page.[2]

Most of this expansion occurred during the war or in the immediate post-war years, as a response to the claims or threats of Labour, but substantial increases were also voted in 1924 and 1925, especially towards housing, education, contributory old age, widows' and orphans' pensions,

[1] G. D. H. and M. Cole, *The Condition of Britain* (1937), pp. 328–9; C. L. Mowat *Britain Between the Wars*, p. 497.
[2] A. R. Prest, *Public Finance in Theory and Practice* (1960), pp. 181–2.

Commercial and Financial Developments

Local Authorities Expenditure and Revenue (£mn.)

Current Expenditure (excl. Trading)	1913-14	1938-9	Revenue	1913-14	1938-9
Education	36	118	Rates	82	215
Health	9	86	Current Grants	27	164
Roads	23	68	Trading and		
Other	54	114	Other	12	19
Totals	122	386	**Totals**	121	398
Capital Expenditure (incl. Trading)					
Housing	0	67			
Roads	4	16			
Trading	5	37			
Other	16	52			
Totals	25	172			

and supplementary unemployment payment. Measured as a proportion of national income, social expenditure by the public authorities, national and local, increased from 5·5% in 1913 to 10·3% in 1924 and 13·0% in 1938; in the depression, when national income declined while relief payments kept up, it had risen even further, to 15·8% in 1932. At the same time, expenditure on roads, the Post Office and other public enterprises rose from 4·7% in 1913 to 5·8% in 1924 and to 7·7% of the national income in 1938, and the cost of Government and of Defence from 4·5% to 4·5% and 9·3% in the same years.[1]

A permanent increase in expenditure of such magnitude was bound to call forth major changes also in the methods of raising revenue. In broad outline, the total changes are summarized in the tabulation (in £ million) shown opposite.[2]

Again, the main alterations occurred in the war years, the only important change after 1920 being the imposition of the tariff in 1932. Income tax, standing at 6s. in 1920–1, was far too convenient a tax to be lightly discarded, and never fell below 4s. in the pound in the inter-war years. Such high levels over wide ranges of income had no previous parallel in peace-time. To mitigate some of its effects, more generous

[1] Ursula K. Hicks, *Public Finance* (1947), p. 32. Also Alan T. Peacock and Jack Wiseman, *The Growth of Public Expenditure in the United Kingdom* (1961).
[2] Prest, *op. cit.*, pp. 157–8; *Statistical Abstract of the U.K.*, Annual.

The Changing Role of the Budget

National Expenditure	1913–14	1924–5	1932–3	1938–9
National Debt	25	357	308	231
Defence	77	115	103	272
Civil, Collection, etc. (excl. self-balancing)	69	257	365	424
Totals	171	729	776	927
National Revenue				
Inland Revenue	88	419	411	520
(of which Income Tax)	(44)	(274)	(251)	(336)
Customs and Excise	75	234	288	341
Miscellaneous	10	64	45	66
Totals	173	717	744	927

allowances for dependent relatives, and a differential in favour of earned incomes, suggested by the Royal Commission on the Income Tax in 1920,[1] were adopted, and were largely responsible for the form which the British tax structure assumed in the inter-war years. Other direct taxes imposed at the time of war and post-war boom proved less successful: Excess Profits Duty was abolished in 1921 (arrears continuing to be collected for a decade after) and Corporation Profits Duty was repealed in 1924.

Among indirect taxation, the duties on tobacco and alcoholic drinks were retained at a high level after the war, and to these the hydrocarbon oil taxes and motor duties were added, surprising successive Chancellors by their inexorable tendency to expand. Higher taxes on low incomes and on necessities were thus largely avoided, though there were temporary increases in the 'breakfast table' duties on tea and sugar. The search for new sources of taxation which began again in 1925, largely in order to finance the growing social programme, did, however, lead to some additional tax burdens on the very poor. Apart from entertainments duty and the abortive betting tax of 1926, the most important of these were by-products of protection and agricultural price support. The tariff, even in the depression, yielded £40 million a year, and artificially raised food prices constituted a further large burden.

Before the war, 57·5% of the revenue had been in the form of direct taxes. This rose to a peak of 82·7% in 1917–18 and 68·2% still in 1920–1 and remained at about this level until 1931–2, when it stood at 65·88%

[1] Royal Commission on Income Tax, Report (1920. Cmd. 615), paras. 126–140.

It then fell somewhat with the imposition of protective duties in 1932. The lowering of real wages by taxing the consumption of the working classes was, in fact, one of the aims of the protectionists.

Larger social welfare expenditure and a heavier burden of steeply progressive direct taxation were bound to lead to a marked redistribution of incomes. The vastly increased war-time revenue could, by definition, not be collected from those living near the subsistence level, but had to fall almost exclusively on the higher incomes, so that the war was the great leveller. Rates were pushed back afterwards in favour of the rich, but not all the redistributive effects were lost, particularly since Snowden's budgets of 1924 and 1930 were designed to benefit the lower income groups.

The following examples show the changing burden of total taxation, including the estimated shares of indirect taxes, etc., expressed as a percentage of income, on a family of two adults and three dependent children, living on earned income only at different levels of income:[1]

Income of	£100	£200	£500	£1,000	£10,000
1913–14	5·4	4·0	4·4	5·2	8·0
1918–19	9·9	7·9	10·2	16·9	42·5
1923–4	14·1	11·8	8·0	14·1	37·1
1925–6	11·9	10·2	6·2	11·0	31·2
1930–1	11·0	9·6	4·5	9·7	35·8
1937–8	10·4	8·4	5·6	11·8	39·1

British taxation, it will be observed, was not as 'progressive' as is often supposed. Taxes on smaller families, and local rates, were even more regressive over a wide range. On the other hand, death duties and profits taxes, which fell more heavily on the rich, are omitted from this table.

Thus the British tax structure, as it evolved in the inter-war years, when taxation for the first time absorbed an appreciable part of national income, was steeply progressive at the upper end, largely because of income tax and surtax, and equally steeply regressive at the lower end (which included the large bulk of the population), with medium incomes between £250 and £1,000 a year enjoying the lowest percentage burden of taxation. The heaviest burdens on the poorer families were duties on tea, sugar, tobacco, alcohol and, latterly, taxes on production, such as wheat and coal.[2]

As far as the allocation of expenditure was concerned, it also worked in the direction of redistribution in this period. According to one estimate,

[1] G. Findlay Shirras and L. Rostas, *The Burden of British Taxation* (Cambridge, 1942), p. 58; cf. also Sir Bernard Mallet and C. Oswald George, *British Budgets (Second Series), 1913–14 to 1920–21* (1929), Appx. Table XXI.

[2] Shirras and Rostas, p. 37; Hicks, *Finance of British Government*, chapter 16.

while in 1913 the working classes received less in social services than they paid in taxes, by 1925 they contributed only 85% of the cost (receiving the excess of £45 million from other classes) and in 1935 they contributed but 79%, receiving an excess of £91 million.[1] For 1937 it was found that, on various assumptions, the sums redistributed to the poorer income groups (receiving under £125 a year) were in the range of £193–274 million. For those with incomes of £125 to £250 a year, the additions were in the range of £3–74 million. The total redistributed amounted to 5–6% of the national income.[2] Other calculations put the amount of redistribution lower than this.

After the efforts made over several generations, and the onerous burden of taxation borne by the British people in the inter-war years in order to achieve a greater measure of social justice, this result may seem, at first sight, to be disappointingly small. There were several causes for it. In the first place, a large proportion of the welfare schemes was financed by the working classes themselves: the employees' weekly insurance payments alone rose from 1·9% of average earnings in industry in 1912 to 2·3% of the higher earnings in 1938. This steeply regressive poll tax was matched by the regressive nature of indirect taxation, including protective tariffs, which by 1938 added an average of 7·2% to the prices of all goods. The percentage was particularly high for tobacco (49·4%) and alcoholic drinks (37·8%), widely consumed by the poorer classes.[3]

Secondly, not all the benefits of social welfare provisions went to the poorer families. Some, including pensions and assistance and unemployment benefits, mainly benefited the very poor. The housing subsidies, on the other hand, benefited chiefly the better-off manual workers and the white-collar workers and lower middle classes. The benefits of public provision for education were greatest for families still higher on the income scale. One estimate puts the incidence of divisible benefits in 1937 at the following annual rates *per capita* (£):[4]

Income Class	Education	Public Health	Health Insurance	Assistance and Unemployment Insurance	Pensions	Housing
Under £125	2·1	1·2	0·7	4·2	5·1	0·4
£125 and under £250	3·1	1·2	0·4	0·8	1·1	0·7
£250 „ „ £500	3·7	1·3	—	—	0·3	—

[1] Mowat, *Britain Between the Wars*, p. 492; Colin Clark, *National Income and Outlay* (1937), pp. 145–8.
[2] T. Barna, *The Redistribution of Incomes through Public Finance in 1937* (Oxford, 1945), pp. 229–30.
[3] Prest, *Public Finance*, p. 360.   [4] U. K. Hicks, *Public Finance*, p. 298.

Lastly, the large annual national debt payments added a further strong regressive element to the tax system.

The budget, originally designed merely to meet the necessary expenditure of the Crown and the Government, had even before 1914 acquired the secondary duty of assisting in carrying out other desirable social and economic aims, by the nature of the taxes collected and the expenditure disbursed. These functions were greatly expanded in the inter-war years, as the public authorities came to spend about one-quarter of the national income, about half of this in ways which tended to alter the distribution of incomes. At the same time, such expenditure, heavily concentrated as it was on investment, was bound to become an autonomous influence on the economy as a whole, and the capital market in particular. Public gross fixed capital formation, running at £312 million in 1938 (compared with £49 million in 1913), represented over 30% of the total of some £1,000 million. Local authority borrowing alone, directly or through the Public Works Loans Board, came almost to equal all non-Government capital issues in the 1930's, and in one year, 1932, to exceed it.[1]

Thus it was that the support of official monetary policy, and above all the maintenance of the value of the currency, became a third task to be placed upon the budget between the wars. This task, though much debated at one time, had receded into the background and had become pointless in the century of peace before 1914, when the value of the pound sterling was maintained in terms of gold by the free convertibility at the Central Bank. However, since the abrogation of the gold standard, in practice in 1914 and legally in 1919, there had occurred a considerable measure of inflation, which could plausibly be blamed on the over-expansion of the currency by the Government. As the restoration of the pound to its pre-war parity with gold became an aim of policy from 1919 onward, the Government was bound to accept the responsibility of playing itself a major part in the necessary deflation. The runaway inflations which occurred in the early 1920's in several countries, including such advanced economies as that of Germany,[2] and which were everywhere accompanied, even if not always caused, by the activities of the Government printing presses, also seemed to point to the conclusion that sound currency could only be achieved by 'orthodox' finance, which consisted in balancing the budget.

In spite of the seeming simplicity of the canons of financial orthodoxy, the issues raised by the policies adopted in the 1920's were complex, and

---

[1] U. K. Hicks, *British Public Finances, Their Structure and Development, 1880–1952* (1954), p. 65, and *Finance of British Government*, pp. 25, 130; also A. R. Ilersic, *Government Finance and Fiscal Policy in Post-War Britain* (1955), p. 12; Mallet and George, *British Budgets*, Third Series (1933), pp. 459–60.

[2] C. Bresciani-Turroni, *The Economics of Inflation* (1953 ed.).

were made more difficult still by the parallel attempts to prevent, or cure, industrial fluctuations leading to mass unemployment. These turned, after years of debate, into yet a fourth task of the budget.

This new aspect of economic policy had several roots. It derived from the proposals of the Swedish economists in the late 1920's, from the budding 'national income' approach of economists, and the doctrines on money, interest, investment and saving propagated by J. M. Keynes.[1] It received its most complete exposition in Keynes' *General Theory*,[2] and it is with his name that it is generally associated.

In the narrow sense, the new doctrine asserted that in depressions it was the duty of the Government to expand its activities and to create additional incomes by programmes of public works and other inflationary actions,[3] as well as to encourage investment by low interest rates. This was in direct contrast to the current 'Treasury view', described by the then Chancellor, Winston Churchill, in the House of Commons in April 1929 as 'the orthodox Treasury doctrine which has steadfastly held that, whatever might be the political or social advantages, very little additional employment and no permanent additional employment can, in fact, and as a general rule, be created by State borrowing and State expenditure'.[4] The official view did not change throughout the depression years.[5]

In the wider sense, the new doctrine held that it was the duty of the Government, by budgetary as well as other means, to control the economy so as to keep it at a steady and high level of activity. This doctrine, com mon property and widely adopted now, made little impression on the Government in the 1930's. Sweden, Australia, New Zealand and, above all, the U.S.A. carried out policies which, however unconsciously, were in line with the new economics; but in Britain the pragmatic efforts of the Labour Government of 1929–31 to foster public works by the Development (Loan Guarantee and Grants) Act and the Colonial Development Act of 1929, and to admit more progressive economic thought by the Economic Advisory Council set up in January 1930 to advise the Prime Minister, were a failure. Although Keynes made many converts among academic economists, it was not until the early years of the war that the

[1] J. M. Keynes, *A Treatise on Money*, 2 vols. (1930), and *The Means to Prosperity* (1933); also R. F. Kahn's fundamental contribution, 'The Relation of Home Investment to Employment', *Econ. J.*, 41/162, 1931.

[2] J. M. Keynes, *General Theory of Employment, Interest and Money* (1936).

[3] R. F. Bretherton, F. A. Burchardt, R. S. G. Rutherford, *Public Investment and the Trade Cycle* (1941), chapter 1.

[4] Quoted in S. H. Beer, *Treasury Control* (1956), pp. 1–2.

[5] U. K. Hicks, *Finance of British Government*, chapter 13; A. D. Gayer, *Monetary Policy and Economic Stabilisation* (1935), chapter 10; Richard W. Lyman, *The First Labour Government, 1924* (London, 1957), chapter 9; K. J. Hancock, 'The Reduction of Unemployment as a Problem of Public Policy, 1920–29', *Ec. Hist. Rev.*, 2nd S., 15/2, 1962, pp. 335–8.

new economics received official sanction in budgetary policy and else-where.[1] It followed from the new, and now generally accepted doctrine, that British budgetary policy in the inter-war years was of a nature to aggravate the ill-effects of the trade cycle.

In the financial year 1919–20, when all the Government's efforts should have been directed to restraining inflation, it added to it by a budget deficit. The consequent increase in the national debt, much of which was held in the form of short-term paper, especially Treasury Bills, as noted on p. 202 above, was doubly unfortunate since it weakened the Bank of England's control over the market. In 1920–1, by contrast, the Government determined to achieve a surplus and reduce the floating debt in order to regain control over the market and prepare the way for the ultimate return to gold at the old parity. Technically the reduction of the floating debt, partly by repayment and largely by funding, was highly successful,[2] but the fact that the immense deflationary pressure was applied by the Government from April 1920 onwards, when the boom began to sag, greatly aggravated the effects and extent of the slump. Budgetary policy was similarly ill-timed in the recurring crises and difficulties of the remainder of the inter-war years.[3]

Deflationary policies were maintained in all the budgets of the early 1920's, and throughout the decade it proved possible to devote regularly, year by year, a sum averaging £50 million for debt redemption. With expenditure falling by £470 million in 1919–20 and another £116 million in 1920–1, it was also possible to abolish the Excess Profits Duty and make other concessions while still balancing the budget. Meanwhile, however, the severe depression continued, and the accepted doctrine for a rigidly orthodox Chancellor in such a case was to reduce taxation, but only if he could impose equivalent cuts in expenditure. Some tax remissions were made in 1922–3, while the fall in incomes would clearly reduce the yield from all existing taxes: the problem was to find the reductions in expenditure. The original plan was to suspend debt redemption and to make other savings totalling £175 million, but departments proposed cuts of £75 million only. A committee of businessmen, headed by Sir Eric Geddes, was therefore set up to suggest economies leading to a reduction of the remaining £100 million, and in three reports[4] recommended cuts totalling £87 million, quickly dubbed the 'Geddes axe'. The remaining £13¼ million were to be found by curtailing the naval programme.

---

[1] U. K. Hicks, *Public Finance*, chapter 17; H. W. Arndt, *The Economic Lessons of the Nineteen-Thirties* (1944), chapters 2 and 8. Also chapter 6, section 3, below.

[2] F. W. Paish, 'The Floating Debt, 1914–1939', in T. Balogh, *Studies in Financial Organization* (Cambridge, 1947), p. 192.

[3] Cf. also sections 5, 6 and 7 of this chapter.

[4] *Committee on National Expenditure, Reports* (1922. Cmd. 1581, 1582, 1589).

Few departments escaped the axe. Some large savings were to be achieved on the military service votes, but the most severe cuts were reserved for the social services, including education and tuberculosis, maternity and child welfare services. Among others, the Ministry of Transport, the Mines Department, the Electricity Commissioners, the Department of Overseas Trade, the Ministry of Labour and the Employment Exchanges were to be abolished. These disastrous proposals were not accepted in their entirety by the Chancellor; nevertheless, some of the social services, above all education, took over a decade to recover from the cuts imposed in 1922. As it turned out, there was a large surplus of over £100 million achieved in 1922–3, used for debt redemption. In the next year, revenue was down by £77 million, largely owing to cuts in income tax, profits tax and beer duties, but as expenditure was also down by £24 million, there was still a sizeable surplus.

Snowden's budget of 1924 represented a partial reversal of the trend of successive Chancellors since 1920 to wipe out the egalitarian legacies of the war, by cutting social services and the direct taxes to finance them. He made substantial reductions in indirect taxation, notably among the (revenue) customs duties, and the McKenna duties were also repealed, with the thorough approval of the Liberals on whom the Government depended in the House. The result was virtually to wipe out the surplus of earlier years and to end the era of surpluses of the early 1920's: henceforth budgets were more closely balanced, and over the rest of the inter-war years, surpluses and deficits roughly cancelled out.

Winston Churchill's budget of 1925 was the second important budget of the decade. Apart from the re-introduction of the gold standard, the budget speech was notable for reversing the previous deflationary emphasis. The new Widows', Orphans' and Old Age Contributory Pensions Act laid extra burden on the Exchequer, particularly in years to come. Churchill's budget of 1928 added further expenditure and so did Neville Chamberlain's Local Government Act of 1929, which, among other reforms, included a major measure of derating. Agricultural land and property, subject already to substantial measures of derating enacted in 1896, 1923 and 1925, were freed completely from rates, and industry and the railways were derated to the extent of three-quarters. The Treasury was to make up the losses of rates to local authorities, estimated at £30 million, by 'block' grants, which, unlike earlier grants, favoured the authorities with the poorer incomes and higher costs by taking into account their population, the number of children under five, rateable value, the unemployment percentage and the population per mile of roads. Existing Treasury grants paid on a percentage basis were, however, not affected.[1]

[1] C. L. Mowat, *Britain Between the Wars*, pp. 199–200, 339–42; P. J. Grigg *Prejudice and Judgment* (1948), pp. 194–209.

While expenditure was thus increased in 1925, income tax rates were cut. Inevitably, the year 1925–6 ended with a deficit and so did the next year, and Churchill balanced his budgets only by such windfalls as an abortive betting tax, two raids on the road fund, using capital (such as loan repayments by the Allies) to balance revenue, and making changes in the timing of the income tax and beer duty which gave, for once only, a yield of parts of two years in the course of one financial year. These inflationary budgets were introduced just at a time when the re-establishment of the gold standard forced deflationary policies on the monetary authorities.

Snowden's budget of 1930 was introduced in an atmosphere of worsening trade and mounting unemployment. Forced to find additional revenue to meet the shortfall expected because of declining incomes and mounting pension and relief payments, the Chancellor added heavily to direct taxes, including 6*d.* on the income tax, but raised only one indirect tax, that on beer, by 1*d.* a gallon, while allowing a whole series of safeguarding duties to lapse. No important changes were made in the budget of 1931, except for an increase in the petrol tax. The threatening deficits were to be met by raids, anticipations and transfers on Churchillian models. Further, two long-term changes were in the offing: a nation-wide valuation of land for the purpose of a tax on land values, and proposals for reducing expenditure expected from a Committee presided over by Sir George May. The former proved still-born; the latter, however, had a large share in bringing down the second Labour Government and setting thereby the political course for the 1930's.

Technically, the May Report was concerned with the narrow problem of making an estimate of the budget deficit to be expected, and suggesting means of meeting it. Within this relatively narrow framework, however, it is difficult to avoid the conclusion that the Report was intended to be, and certainly turned out to be, a political document designed to do the maximum damage to the Labour Government and its social welfare programme, especially the increased unemployment payments which it had authorized. The Committee's estimates rested on the most pessimistic assumptions: the costs of the increasing numbers of old-age pensions were stressed without the mention of the parallel relief by the decline in the number of school children under working age;[1] the annual payment of £50 million to the Sinking Fund was assumed to be immutable; and the Exchequer was charged equally with the £30 million transitional benefit and the £40–50 million deficit on the Unemployment Insurance Fund.[2] The expenditures singled out for special comment were those with a welfare content. The Unemployment Insurance Fund, which had kept solvent

[1] *Committee on National Expenditure, Report* (1931. Cmd. 3920), p. 12.
[2] P. J. Grigg, *op. cit.*, p. 255.

throughout the heavy unemployment of the 1920's, but was now running a deficit, received particular attention, and defaults on its existing rates of payments were among the Committee's strongest recommendations, while reductions in the national debt payments, running close on £300 million a year, were not even considered, though they were recommended by the Macmillan Committee reporting at about the same time,[1] and in the event were carried out without a hitch in the following year. By such means, it was possible for the May Committee to forecast a total budget deficit of £120 million a year. This the Committee proposed to meet by raising another £24 million in taxes and cutting expenditure by £96 million, of which two-thirds was to be accounted for by slashing unemployment pay.

The proposals for economies were as drastic as those of the Geddes Committee earlier. Several members of the Cabinet were not prepared to see relief cut to the extent demanded, but after the Labour Government had split on this issue, and a 'National' Government formed in August 1931, many of the May Committee suggestions were adopted by Snowden in his autumn budget.[2] Direct and indirect taxes were heavily increased, and unemployment contributions raised. On the expenditure side, there were reductions in the appropriations to the sinking fund, in salaries of civil servants, police, teachers and others, and a 10% cut in unemployment benefit rates and other reductions in benefits.

> Not only was the entire tax structure raised, more or less proportionately, from end to end, but social insurance contributions were increased and benefits down. The resulting tax structure was considerably higher than any of its predecessors. Salary cuts and rigid economy at the centre were backed up by the enforcement of the most severe retrenchment in local government. Economy circulars of an almost mandatory tone were sent round. Public works grants were abruptly discontinued. An (unofficial) embargo was placed on local borrowing on the stock exchange. The fall in rate-receipts due to the depression and the activities of local economy committees, their nerves completely shattered by the magnitude of the disaster, caused an even greater collapse of local than of central spending.[3]

In the event, the budget balanced almost exactly, at £851 million.

From 1932 onwards, Chancellors operated in a less restrictive environment. For one thing, the successful conversion of some £1,970 million of War Loan from 5% to 3½% in the course of 1932 ultimately relieved the budget to the extent of £80 million, while the newly imposed tariff brought in additional revenue. Secondly, the experience of other countries from

---

[1] *Committee on Finance and Industry, Report* (1931. Cmd. 3897), Addendum, I, paras. 28–30.　　　[2] C. L. Mowat, *op. cit.*, pp. 379–412.
[3] U. K. Hicks, *Finance of British Government*, pp. 361–2.

1933 on showed that an unbalanced budget did not necessarily lead to financial or economic disaster. Thirdly, with Britain off gold, the pound sterling was less vulnerable, and the balance of payments position was never again as weak as it had been in 1931.

Neville Chamberlain's budget of 1932, providing for a slight surplus, actually resulted in a deficit of £32 million. Hence revenue was further increased, adding further deflation to an economy still severely depressed, and in 1933-4 the budget showed a nominal surplus of about the same amount, achieved, however, only by suspending the repayment of debt. In 1934, expecting a surplus, Chamberlain greatly eased conditions: the cuts of 1931 in unemployment rates were restored, and half the cuts in Government salaries, the rest being made good in 1935-6; at the same time, the standard rate of income tax was reduced by 6*d.*, from 5*s.* to 4*s.* 6*d.* in the pound.

The 1936 budget was the first in which defence expenditure rose significantly, by £50 million to £187 million. It was met by a rise in the income tax rate to 4*s.* 9*d.*, and a large increase in the tea duty, besides absorbing the whole of the road fund and the increase in the revenue due to rising prosperity. In 1937, the defence votes were increased further, largely paid for by raising the income tax to 5*s.* and levying a 5% profits tax (in place of the abortive 'National Defence Contribution'). For 1938-9 they were estimated at £253 million (plus £90 million to be provided by borrowing) and for 1939-40 at £250 million (plus £380 million by borrowing). The last budget was not destined to survive the financial year. A September budget, after the outbreak of war, increased income tax from 5*s.* 6*d.* to 7*s.* 6*d.* in the pound and introduced an excess profits tax of 60%, besides making other changes.

5. ECONOMIC AND FINANCIAL POLICY IN THE NINETEEN-TWENTIES

The war ended with wholesale prices 140%, and the cost of living 120-125%, above the level of July 1914, and the apparatus for manufacturing further purchasing power by Government borrowing generally in full swing. Technically, deflation might have been possible in 1919, but politically it was unthinkable.[1] As demobilized soldiers returned to civilian employment by the million, the fear among members of the Government and their advisers was of widespread unemployment, not of runaway inflation. Instead of restricting credit, Britain went formally off gold in March 1919 (having been *de facto* off gold since the outbreak of war) and allowed the credit expansion of the war years to go on into 1920.

On this swelling stream of easy credit, employment picked up rapidly in the summer of 1919, the demand coming from the backlog of necessary consumer goods restricted during the war years, translated into demands

[1] J. M. Keynes, *A Treatise on Money* (1930), Vol. 2, pp. 176-7.

for stocks and capital goods, also run down during the war. With demand outrunning supply, prices rose sharply, and in the prevailing climate of optimism the rapid price rise added a speculative element to the boom, feeding on itself to drive prices up still faster. Thus the boom of 1919–20 was largely one of prices, not output: at no stage did industrial output approach, let alone exceed, that of 1913.[1] Wages and other costs, while rising, rose less than prices, and there was a shift in the distribution of incomes in favour of profits, used in part to carry through a substantial programme of capital investment and re-equipment of British industry. This may have been, in the circumstances, the only way of carrying through some of the necessary capital developments interrupted by the war,[2] but it was done at the cost of a rate of over-capitalization which was to burden several major British industries with top-heavy capital structures or the next two decades.

With costs lagging behind prices, the impetus behind the inflation of 1919–20 was largely a demand-pull, furthered by the Government-induced credit inflation. In April 1920, the Government took fright: a deflationary budget and determined action to reduce the floating debt was accompanied by a rise in bank rate, and there followed one of the most precipitous declines in British industrial history, unemployment rising from 2% to 18%, and the index of industrial activity falling from 117·9 to 90·0 in the space of one year.[3]

Some months before this reversal of policy, the influential Cunliffe Committee on Currency and Foreign Exchanges after the War had reported to recommend the restoration of the gold standard at the earliest possible opportunity. 'Nothing can contribute more to the speedy recovery from the effects of the war, and the rehabilitation of the foreign exchanges, than the re-establishment of the currency upon a sound basis,' it stated in its first interim report in August 1918,[4] before the end of the war. By 'sound currency' it meant, inevitably, the pound freely convertible into gold in a framework like that of the last decade or so before 1914, 'the golden age of gold standards',[5] when the Bank of England had been in easy control not only of the credit market in London, but virtually of the world.

Oblivious of the changed post-war conditions, and in spite of much opposition from some quarters, the Cunliffe Committee strongly re-affirmed its original recommendations in its final Report which appeared on 3rd December 1919,[6] in the midst of the post-war inflation. It was

---

[1] A. C. Pigou, *Aspects of British Economic History, 1918–1925* (1947), p. 62.
[2] Colin Clark, *National Income and Outlay* (1937), p. 266.
[3] W. H. Beveridge, *Full Employment in a Free Society* (1944), p. 313.
[4] Cd. 9182, reprinted in T. E. Gregory, *Select Statutes, Documents and Reports Relating to British Banking, 1832–1928* (Oxford, 1929), p. 335.
[5] Chandler, quoted in E. Nevin, *The Mechanism of Cheap Money, 1931–1939* (Cardiff, 1955), p. 8. [6] Reprinted in T. E. Gregory, *loc. cit.*, pp. 366 ff.

content to retain notes for small payments in place of the gold sovereigns of pre-war years, and therefore was prepared to enlarge the fiduciary issue by amalgamating the Treasury notes, in circulation since 1914, with the Bank of England note issue of which up to then only some £17 had been fiduciary. For large transactions, however, the cheque and the bank deposit system was to be brought back to gold by restoring the power of the Central Bank to force the joint-stock banks to vary the aggregate of their deposits in accordance with the state of its gold reserve. But in 1919 Britain was still far from such equilibrium. In order to regain a 'currency upon a sound basis', a stringent financial policy was necessary. The budget would have to be balanced, foreign lending suspended (except to borrowers who were capable of repaying their loans), foreign trade brought into balance, and the large surplus of bank notes reduced. On the latter point, the Committee suggested that the minimum note issue of one year should become the maximum issue of the next.

This programme was accepted by the Government in principle and in detail.[1] The severe deflation induced from April 1920 onward became the first step in a consistent policy which had one over-riding aim: the restoration of the gold standard at the old parity at the earliest possible moment.[2] Unemployment, never below 10% until December 1924 and standing at 11·1% in April 1925 when the gold standard was re-imposed, was at a frighteningly high level. There were exceptional capital losses in industry, and there was an obstinate inability of British exports and shipping services, or even industrial production, to return to pre-war figures. But these and other troubles were ignored or even aggravated (except in the brief Labour administration of 1923–4) in the single-minded attempt to restore the gold standard. The efficacy of the gold standard which, once established, would restore British trade, prosperity and prestige, became a Sorelian myth in the City.

At the time, the most that Government economic policy was expected to do was the prevention of fluctuations in exchange rates and prices, and the avoidance of the credit cycle.[3] As late as 1927, the World Economic Conference in Brussels pronounced in favour of 'balanced Budgets, stable prices, lower tariffs, abolition of subsidies, credit control, a common currency standard, stable exchanges and the elimination of artificial price restrictions in external trade'.[4] In this list of *desiderata* there is no mention of

[1] Treasury Minute of 15th December 1919 (Cmd. 485), reprinted in Gregory, *loc. cit.*, p. 371.

[2] A. C. Pigou, *Aspects of British Economic History, 1918–1925* (1947 ed.), Part V, chapter 1; S. E. Harris, *Monetary Problems of the British Empire* (New York, 1931), Part II, Book 5; Lawrence Smith, 'England's Return to the Gold Standard in 1925', *J. Econ. and Business History*, 4, 1931–2, p. 230.

[3] *Report of the Committee on the Working of the Monetary System* (1959. Cmnd. 827), para. 53.   [4] E. V. Francis, *Britain's Economic Strategy* (1939), p. 93.

a high level of economic activity, economic growth, or prevention of un-employment. Meanwhile, in 1920-5 (as in 1914 and in 1931) the City was benefiting from the convenient doctrine that its own prosperity, security and comfort, at no matter what cost to other sectors of the economy, was the only way to benefit the British economy as a whole.

Imbued with these ideas, the Government pursued its deflationary policy with consistent ruthlessness. A bank rate of near panic level, at 7%, was kept on for a year, until April 1921, at a time of disastrous un-employment, and even afterwards the rate was reduced but slowly, to reach 3% only in July 1922. The 'Geddes axe' became a by-word for callous meanness. Agricultural price support, in spite of a statutory guarantee for four years, was overthrown with indecent haste as soon as it became operative.[1] But, within its limits, the policy began to work.

The budget was balanced, and a favourable foreign balance of pay-ments restored. The short-term debt, which had destroyed the power of the Bank over the market, was greatly reduced, even though this was only achieved by raising the rate of interest on long-term capital still further above that of pre-war days. The note issue was also reduced, and bank deposits fell from over £2,000 million in December 1920 to £1,800 million in June 1925.[2] Above all, prices came down almost as fast as they had climbed: wholesale prices, which had risen from about 210 in March 1919 (1913 = 100) to a peak of 310–340 in mid-1920, were down to 190–210 in March 1921 and 160–170 in February 1922, then remaining fairly steady around 160–180 until 1925. Wage rates, which did not reach their peak until early in 1921, proved very flexible also (quite a number had been tied to the cost-of-living index) and fell from 275 in the winter of 1920–1 (July 1914 = 100) to 173 in the winter of 1923–4, rising slowly to 181 in March 1925.[3] From 1922 onwards it was even possible to pursue more normal policies appropriate to a slump, such as a lower bank rate, and a slight recovery was nursed up in 1922–4, though the preparations of the authorities for the return to gold helped to hold it back well below the recovery of other countries.

Substantial as this deflation in prices and costs was, however, it had just not gone far enough to match American prices and permit an easy return to gold at pre-war parities. The dollar rate of exchange, which had fallen to below $3.50 in the autumn of 1920, rose to about $4.70, or near parity, in the winter of 1922–3.[4] Later in the year the rate fell again, coming down to $4.30 in the early months of the Labour Government. Taking the period as whole, the inevitable short-term fluctuations

[1] W. Philip Jeffcock, *Agricultural Politics* (Ipswich, 1937), p. 6.
[2] E. V. Morgan, *Studies in British Financial Policy, 1914–25* (1952), pp. 73, 155–6, 220–31. Also p. 202 above.   [3] *Ibid.*, pp. 73, 271–86.
[4] A. J. Youngson, *The British Economy, 1920–1957* (1960), p. 29.

occurred, not about a mean of the pre-war gold equivalent rate of $4.86, but about a rate around $4.40 or $4.50, i.e. 10% less. Home prices, costs and wages, were stuck at a level about 10% too high, and in spite of the 'capitalist offensive' fought from 1921 on to bring them down,[1] wages could not be reduced any further without risking more industrial violence. The attempts to force down wages were all the more doomed to failure since wages in export industries had been sharply lowered already, while wages in the 'sheltered' home industries remained immune to pressure,[2] and the campaign to reduce the former thus merely served to increase the gap between the industries and the bitterness of the less fortunate workers. Combinations of capital and cartel agreements made other prices increasingly sticky, especially downwards, and high taxes added further rigidities.[3]

If the stickiness of home costs was one reason for making the return to gold difficult, the level of the gold reserve was another. It had stood at about £150 million when the Cunliffe Committee reported, and this became accepted, for no very sound reason, as the safe minimum, but it was no easy task to keep the reserve at that level. With a weakened balance of trade, and an established machinery for overseas investment, erected on a scale appropriate to the pre-war surpluses, grinding on arranging for foreign loans much larger than the current trade balance could warrant, in spite of the unofficial embargo on foreign loans by the Bank of England,[4] there was a tendency for gold to flow out, avoided only by attracting short-term funds to London, sources of trouble later.

From the middle of 1924 on the authorities began to push up the exchange rate of the pound to a level which would make free convertibility possible. London rates of interest were raised substantially above those ruling in New York, and funds began to flow in. The belief that an attempt would be made to restore the pound to its old parity in the course of 1925, before inconvertibility would lapse automatically at the end of the year, attracted further funds, and the Government helped the favourable movement along by raising credits in New York and by other means. By April 1925 the pound had virtually reached its pre-war parity with the dollar, and Mr. Churchill, the Chancellor of the Exchequer, announced the return to gold.

This carefully planned resumption of the gold standard was a considerable achievement for the monetary authorities, in view of the post-war weakness of the British economy. When the Treasury note issue was amalgamated in 1928 with the Bank of England note issue which raised

---

[1] W. A. Lewis, *Economic Survey, 1919–1939* (1949), pp. 43–4.

[2] Henry Clay, *The Post-War Unemployment Problem* (1929), p. 93.

[3] E. Nevin, *The Mechanism of Cheap Money, a Study of British Monetary Policy, 1931–1939* (Cardiff, 1955), pp. 23, 32; A. D. Gayer, *Monetary Policy and Economic Stabilisation* (1935), chapter 3; J. M. Keynes, *A Treatise on Money* (1930), Vol. 2, pp. 180 ff.

[4] Sir Henry Clay, *Lord Norman* (1957), pp. 144–5.

the total fiduciary issue to £260 million, the programme of the Cunliffe Committee had been fully achieved. Britain could claim to have made a major contribution to the stabilization of the foreign exchanges after the stress of wars and revolutions, and a large number of other countries returned to gold in the next year or two, though not all at pre-war parities.

Nevertheless, the decision to return to gold at the old parity was one of the most controversial of the period. It called forth a large volume of criticism, among the most intelligent and far-sighted of which was that associated with the name of J. M. Keynes.[1] Although Keynes had most of the orthodox economic opinion against him at the time, there would be few today who would deny that Keynes' misgivings were warranted, though not necessarily for the right reasons.[2]

Keynes' criticism ran along two lines. The first was concerned to show that at the old parity the pound would be over-valued to the extent of about 10%. This was borne out not only by the exchange rates of 1923–4, but also by the internal price levels: with pre-war at 100, British internal prices even in the favourable month of April 1925 stood at 176 compared with 165 in the U.S.A. Some of those who were responsible for the decision to return to gold in 1925 later defended it on the grounds that they hoped that world prices were about to rise up to the British price level and thus remove the handicap they had put on British industry. Their hopes, and the hopes of those who had assumed a period of price stability, were misplaced; world prices fell after 1925 and several other countries, including France, Belgium and Germany, returned to gold at lower parities, thus making the competitive disability of British prices greater still. It was unlikely that a Government less responsive to the demands of the City would have taken such appalling risks with British industry. The decision to return, in fact, was a City decision, which might have become a political necessity[3] and had, perhaps, as its ultimate aim the salvaging of industry also, but it was emphatically not a decision of the industrialists: 'had their views been given as much weight as those of the City, it is unlikely that the change would ever have been made'.[4]

The forecasts of the critics as to the consequences of returning to gold

[1] J. M. Keynes, *Tract on Monetary Reform* (1923) and *The Economic Consequence, of Mr. Churchill* (1925). Cf. also André Siegfried, *England's Crisis* (1931), chapter 2, § 1; K. J. Hancock, 'Unemployment and the Economists in the 1920's', *Economicas* N.S., 27/108, 1960, pp. 308–11.

[2] For a rare recent contrary view, see Youngson, *op. cit.*, chapter 7; also R. S. Sayers, 'The Return to Gold', in L. S. Pressnell (ed.), *Studies in the Industrial Revolution* (1960), and T. E. Gregory, *The First Year of the Gold Standard* (1926), and *The Gold Standard and its Future* (3rd ed., 1934), chapters 3 and 4.

[3] C. L. Mowat, *Britain Between the Wars* (1956 ed.), p. 200.

[4] Alan Bullock, the *Life and Times of Ernest Bevin*, Vol. 1 (1960), p. 267, cf. also pp. 428–9, and F. E. Gannett and B. F. Catherwood, *Industrial and Labour Relations in Great Britain* (1939), p. 283.

at too high a level soon began to come true with fateful precision. A price differential of 10%, or somewhat less (the exact figure has been disputed),[1] while encouraging imports, formed a most severe handicap to the export industries in their most difficult period, when Britain was falling most calamitously behind other industrial countries.

The ill-effects of the high interest rates which the Bank of England was forced to maintain to prevent the loss of gold as a result of the weaker trade balance were more pervasive still. They kept up the burdens of the national debt charge, and thus of taxation. They burdened enterprise with many fixed payments at an unnecessarily high rate. They attracted foreign and British speculative funds of dangerous instability into London. Above all, dear money was designed to depress enterprise directly, and to preserve the foreign exchanges by creating deflation and unemployment at home. This high structure of interest rates in a period of depression was to be described later as 'putting on the brake when going uphill'; in a period when investment was slack, and the 'natural rate of interest' low, the market rate was pitched above it and choked off what little investment there was.[2]

These issues were debated at length in the evidence and in the Report of the Macmillan Committee which sat in 1929–31;[3] most dramatically, they came up in the exchanges between Montagu Norman, Governor of the Bank of England throughout this period, and a key figure in the working of the gold standard, and his questioners, above all Keynes and Ernest Bevin. The Governor at first denied that the high bank rate he was forced to impose to maintain the gold standard was responsible for creating unemployment (Questions 3328, 3334–8, 3343–51); he was then driven to concede that it had some such effect (Qs. 3390–2, 3398–9); and finally to admitting that his high bank rate was designed directly to create unemployment (Qs. 3492–3). The burden of his evidence to the Macmillan Committee was that he was under such constant pressure to keep up rates to prevent a drain abroad that he could not, even had he wished, consider the effects on industry, but that until 1930, at least, he had not greatly troubled about them.[4] His deputy, Sir Ernest Harvey, showed a much

[1] W. Ashworth, *An Economic History of England 1870–1939* (1960), p. 387; Keith Hancock. 'Unemployment and the Economists in the 1920's', *Economica*, N.S., 27/108, 1960, p. 317.

[2] R. G. Hawtrey, *The Gold Standard in Theory and Practice* (5th ed., 1947), pp. 108, 119; J. M. Keynes, *A Treatise on Money*, Vol. 2, pp. 377 ff.

[3] *Report of the Committee on Finance and Industry* (1931. Cmd. 3897); *Minutes of Evidence*, 2 vols. (1931); cf. also A. T. K. Grant, *A Study of the Capital Market in Post-War Britain* (1937), pp. 8 ff.

[4] *Minutes of Evidence*, 18th Day. Even then, Norman's evidence as published was doctored: his own words showed even less concern with industry. A. Boyle, *Montagu Norman* (1967), p. 258; T. Gregory; 'Lord Norman: A New Interpretation', *Lloyds Bank Review*, 88 (1968), p. 38.

greater understanding of the needs of trade, in the course of his evidence to the Committee.

In retrospect, it seems impossible to deny that the preparations and the return to gold at too high a rate contributed to the depressed conditions of British industry in 1925-9, at a time when the rest of the world enjoyed a prolific boom, just as the removal of the handicap in 1931 was responsible for the sudden spurt of British exports relatively to other countries.

Keynes' second line of criticism was that in post-war conditions the international gold standard would not be allowed and would not be able to work as freely as the idealized pre-war standard was said to have done. At best, it might stabilize either price levels or exchange rates, but it could not do both; and Britain would do better to concentrate on stabilizing prices. Moreover, the large gold hoarders, the Bank of France and the Federal Reserve Board of the U.S.A., would not play the game according to the rules, but would 'manage' their currency in spite of compensating gold flows, thus rendering impossible the task of a country like Great Britain with a gold reserve of barely £150 million to maintain stability in the sterling area as well as among several minor currencies.

This forecast, also, was abundantly justified by later events.[1] Indeed, the rigidities of the system, and the tendency of the authorities of all the main financial centres to neutralize, rather than obey, the gold movements from time to time, turned out to be even greater than Keynes had suggested. In Britain, changes in the banking structure and in the money market further interfered very seriously with the automatic regulative function of the gold reserve of the Bank of England, described with such great confidence by the Cunliffe Committee.[2] For one thing, by 1925 a high bank rate did not bring in any provincial funds, as in former periods, for there were none.[3] Instead, it merely attracted short-term foreign funds, which left again the moment the London rate was reduced; in other words a bank rate change caused short-term funds to move long before it could have any effect on the general price level. If, on the other hand, a high bank rate did succeed in compressing incomes and creating deflation in Britain, with the consequence of a rise in exports and an influx of gold or funds, this would, under existing conditions, merely spread deflation abroad and thus counteract the British deflation.[4] It was an essential part of the mechanism of the pre-war gold standard that there was a single credit centre, London, which could enforce its monetary policies

---

[1] A. D. Gayer, *Monetary Policy and Economic Stabilisation* (1935), chapter 2; W. A. Morton, *British Finance 1930-1940* (Madison, 1943), pp. 87, 97-101.

[2] *First Interim Report*, paras, 4-7.   [3] p. 17 above.

[4] R. G. Hawtrey, *A Century of Bank Rate* (1938), p. 137, and *The Gold Standard in Theory and Practice* (5th ed., 1947), pp. 124-5; A. E. Kahn, *op. cit.*, pp. 20-1; Keynes, *Treatise on Money*, pp. 309-15; Gayer, p. 23.

on the rest of the world. After the war, there were two major centres, London and New York, and several minor ones, and the mechanism was, therefore, likely to show very different responses.[1]

Secondly, the large quantities of Treasury Bills still outstanding even after the conversion and funding of 1921–5 greatly altered the effectiveness of the apparatus of monetary control. At its very centre was the assumption by the authorities that the credit structure of the country depended on the joint-stock banks, that these, in turn, regulated their credit by their 'reserve' (of cash and balances at the Bank of England), rigidly held to about 8% of liabilities, and that this cash reserve could be operated on by the Central Bank, which could thus enlarge or diminish the whole of the credit outstanding. But with a weekly issue of £40 million of Treasury Bills to be absorbed, neither open-market operations, nor a high bank rate to stem losses of gold, as imposed in November 1925 or September 1929, for instance, induced a stringency in the money market: 'the banks and the money market had the power of maintaining their cash in spite of losses of gold by abstaining from buying Treasury bills',[2] and the Bank of England was forced to take up these bills and render its own restrictive policy nugatory. The Macmillan Committee failed to note this development, though it found that one-half of the short-term assets of the clearing banks consisted of Treasury Bills even in the 1920's,[3] but it was discussed by Lord Bradbury, in a dissenting Memorandum.[4] The official recognition of this mechanism had to wait for the Radcliffe Report of 1959,[5] which at last killed the concept, 'given an extra thirty years' lease of life by the Macmillan Report, that the effective basis of credit resides in the cash reserves of the banks'.[6]

Lastly, a true international gold standard assumes that changes in the foreign exchange position, as communicated to the economy *via* the gold reserve and the action taken by the monetary authorities, would be rectified by changes in home prices. But industry in Britain (and elsewhere) in the 1920's was too rigid to stand this flexible price system, even had it been on other grounds desirable to impose it. The City, ill-informed as it was of industrial affairs, remained ignorant of this inflexibility, and

[1] W. A. Brown, Jnr., *The International Gold Standard Re-interpreted, 1914–34,* 2 vols. (New York, 1940).

[2] Hawtrey, *Century of Bank Rate,* pp. 136, 257.

[3] *Committee on Finance and Industry, Report* (1931. Cmd. 3897), paras. 22, 29, 72–87, Appx. I, Table 3, pp. 296–7; also see Keynes, *Treatise on Money,* chapters 2, 25, 32; T. Balogh, *Studies in Financial Organisation* (Cambridge, 1947), pp. 39–40, 56 ff.; Nevin, *Cheap Money,* pp. 118–20; *Radcliffe Report,* paras. 506–11.

[4] Cmd. 3897, *Memorandum of Dissent* by Lord Bradbury, paras. 19–22.

[5] *Report of the Committee on the Working of the Monetary System* (1959. Cmnd. 827).

[6] W. Manning Dicey, 'Treasury Bills and the Money Supply', *Lloyd's Bank Review,* N.S., 55, 1960, p. 1, and *Money under Review* (1960), p. 11, also pp. 52–63; cf. also R. S. Sayers, *Central Banking after Bagehot* (1957), p. 21.

thus 'fundamentally economic policy and structural conditions were out of phase with each other'.[1]

The gold standard, re-established with great *éclat* by Britain, would have been difficult to work at the best of times, in view of the permanent structural changes; as it happened, it set out on its course in the most unfavourable circumstances. Some countries returned to gold on a 'gold exchange' basis, basing their convertibility on reserves held in the form of balances in London or New York which could be turned into gold, thus putting a dangerous burden on London, especially since the 'gold exchange' countries got their London balances, not by foreign trade surplus, but by short-term loans.[2] In the pre-war days the Bank of England had held sufficient short-term claims by London on foreign centres to balance roughly the foreign short-term claims on London, and to make the effects of a change in bank rate felt quickly in all parts of the globe; but in the 1920's, foreign short-term holdings in London greatly exceeded the sterling bills on foreign account and other similar assests by a margin estimated by the Macmillan Committee at £250–300 million.[3]

Moreover, several countries, including Japan, Poland, and France, returned to gold at rates which under-valued their currencies, thus giving their exporters an additional advantage over those of Britain, while others, including Italy, Belgium and France, stabilized their currency at high home price levels, allowing their industrialists to preserve their inflation gains of lower real wages and other fixed charges.[4] The slow fall of world prices after 1925 made the task of the export industries more difficult still.[5]

High rates to prevent gold drains became endemic[6] and dampened down incipient economic expansion in the late 1920's. The burden of high interest rates and restrictive bank policies could not be eased as long as internal costs stayed up,[7] and it proved impossible to lower these: wages in 1929 stood at 99·5 (1924 = 100). By the end of the decade the harmful effect of British monetary policy on industry and exports was widely understood, but short of allowing home prices to rise, which would mean jettisoning the gold parity, there seemed to be no practicable policy to solve the dilemma of the British economy.

6. THE YEARS OF CRISIS: 1929–1931

Up to 1929, Britain had been labouring under the special difficulties of over-large export industries and an over-valued currency, but the rest of

[1] David Williams, 'Montagu Norman and Banking Policy in the Nineteen-Twenties', *Yorkshire Bull.*, 11/1, 1959, p. 55. For a full-scale study see Sir Henry Clay, *Lord Norman* (1957).

[2] W. A. Lewis, *op. cit.*, p. 47.   [3] Cmd. 3897, paras, 92–3, 260, 347–9.

[4] Henry Clay, *The Post-War Unemployment Problem* (1929), p. 76.

[5] J. H. Jones, in *Britain in Depression* (1935), pp. 8–13; p. 220 above.

[6] Hawtrey, *Century of Bank Rate*, pp. 138–43.

[7] E.g. L. Robbins, *The Great Depression* (1934), chapter 5.

the world had witnessed something akin to the orthodox cyclical sequence: a speculative and inflationary boom in 1919-20, followed by collapse and depression in 1921-2, and succeeded, in turn, by a rise to general conditions of prosperity in the later 1920's, including a rapid increase in output, profits and incomes, and a boom in share prices which ended, after an orgy of stock exchange speculation, in a financial crash, signalizing the onset of yet another depression.

In conformity with the new distribution of economic power, the crash actually occurred in New York, in October 1929.[1] It was, to begin with, a purely financial phenomenon, the collapse of share prices from their unwarrantably high level to which they had been bid up, not by expectation of incomes, but by bull speculators trading on margins. The destruction of credit, the bankruptcies and financial losses soon transmitted themselves to the productive sectors, however, and as production and incomes contracted in the U.S.A., the supply of dollars to the rest of the world fell drastically, as described in section 2 above, and depression spread quickly to the rest of the world.

It proved to be far more severe and protracted than any previous slump, whether measured in decline of output or in the numbers unemployed. In the worst-affected countries, industrial output fell by one-half in three years. Prices and overseas trade also showed falls of unprecedented dimensions, and the unique severity of the depression was underlined by the inability of the world to pull out of it in the manner of the pre-1914 trade cycles. The onset of the depression in 1929 was further distinguished by a series of severe financial and foreign exchange crises. The background to these crises, the war debt and reparations obligations, the calamitous fall of primary product prices, and the maladjustment of the currencies of the leading countries, have been noted in earlier sections of this chapter. We may now turn to observe how they affected the United Kingdom in the crisis years.

The difficulties began, in fact, as early as 1928, with the abrupt cessation of American lending, when dollar funds were diverted to New York to participate in the stock exchange speculation. A number of continental countries, which had largely relied on American loans to keep their foreign exchange position in balance, were forced to look elsewhere, mainly to London and Paris. Paris, having under-valued its currency, went on serenely accumulating gold throughout this period, and the main strain fell on London, ill-equipped to bear it. When, at the end of 1929, the cessation of American lending was followed by the abrupt fall in American purchases, triggering off a general decline in world trade, each country tried to reduce its imports and increase its exports[2] by means of tariffs, restrictions and

---

[1] The best account is in J. K. Galbraith, *The Great Crash* (1955).
[2] A. J. Youngson, *The British Economy, 1920-1957* (1960), pp. 79-80; Herbert Heaton, *The British Way to Recovery* (Minneapolis, 1934), p. 7.

currency barriers, and this hit the British capacity to earn foreign exchange particularly hard.

In London, bank rate was raised to $6\frac{1}{2}\%$ late in September 1929, though it was reduced again with the inflow of funds from New York after the collapse there. But by now the world depression, carrying unemployment to industrial countries and loss of incomes to primary producing countries, had begun its inexorable march. Prices, employment and production all turned down sharply. The British figures were as follows:

	Wholesale Prices (Board of Trade) 1929 = 100	Registered Unemployed (Ministry of Labour)		Index of Industrial Activity[1]
		%	Numbers (000)	
1929	100	10·4	1,249	118·7
1930	87·5	16·1	1,975	107·4
1931	76·8	21·3	2,698	86·8
1932	74·9	22·1	2,813	81·1
1933	75·0	19·9	2,221	89·3

Elsewhere, the reduction was far greater. While British industrial production (1929 = 100) fell to 84 in 1932, it fell to 72 in France, and 53 in Germany and the U.S.A.

In the course of 1930, a drain of gold to Berlin was added to the earlier drain to Paris. The Bank of England was further weakened by the fall of share prices on the London Stock Exchange at the end of 1929, particularly those associated with the Hatry enterprises, and by the need to shore up much of Britain's basic industry by the Securities Management Trust (November 1929) and the Bankers' Industrial Development Co. (April 1930); it also had to meet its contribution to the Bank for International Settlements in May 1930.[2] To make matters worse, Paris added £95 million and New York £64 million to their gold reserves in the course of the year.[3] In 1930 the Bank of England succeeded in withstanding the strain by drawing gold from South Africa and Australia, but in 1931 it had to raise its rate well above those of New York and Paris, attracting funds

---

[1] W. H. Beveridge, *Full Employment in a Free Society* (1944), p. 313.
[2] H. H. Schloss, *The Bank for International Settlements* (Amsterdam, 1958).
[3] *Committee on Finance and Industry* (Cmd. 3897), paras. 163–6, 311; Hawtrey, *Gold Standard*, pp. 115–18; H. F. Fraser, *Great Britain and the Gold Standard* (1933), pp. 72 ff.; A. D. Gayer, *Monetary Policy and Economic Stabilisation* (1935), pp. 99–116; G. Cassel, *The Crisis in the World's Monetary System* (1932).

which were to add to the embarrassment of London when the European financial crisis set in.[1]

It began with the threatened collapse of the Austrian Kredit-Anstalt in May 1931, an institution controlling the majority of the banking and much of the industry of the country. Disaster was staved off, but meanwhile the crisis had spread to Germany, and then also to Hungary and Rumania. Germany had been denuded of working capital by inflation, and it had operated on short-term loans from abroad, including Britain, drawn there by exceptionally high interest rates. These funds were frozen by international moratorium as the crisis worsened later in the year, adding materially to the problems of London,[2] while Germany, having exhausted her aid from the Bank for International Settlements, was not precluded from continuing to draw on London. 'British short-term borrowing came to an abrupt end while its lending became indefinitely prolonged.'[3]

To balance this withdrawal of foreign short-term funds without losing too much of its gold, the London Money Market would before 1914 have looked to its second line of reserve, its bill portfolios. But these consisted now largely of bills frozen by moratoria, or of Treasury Bills unacceptable abroad, rather than of first-class commercial bills giving London large financial claims on the rest of the world. Thus the Bank's gold reserve had to stand most of the strain and quickly dropped to £130 million. Instead of defending itself by a high bank rate, it raised a loan of £50 million in New York and Paris, and the rate was put up to 4½% only. It was, in part, the depth of the slump and the level of unemployment which inhibited the raising of the bank rate to panic heights; in part, it was the realization that a high rate would, at best, only bring back some 'hot' money which would leave again at the first opportunity; and in part, it was the fear that a high rate would defeat its own object, by advertising a crisis of the kind which had scared off so many fund holders already.[4]

The irony was that New York and Paris, bloated with gold, experienced no drain at all. Theirs was to come only in 1933 and 1936 respectively, when they in turn had been brought to a position of weakness. Such was the inevitable logic of a financial system which left the economic fate of the world to be decided by international bankers and exchange

[1] *Committee on Finance and Industry*, para. 295; J. G. Smith and G. J. Walker, 'Currency and Banking', in *Britain in Depression* (1935).

[2] Sir Arthur Salter, *Recovery* (1932), pp. 43 ff.; Royal Institute of International Affairs, *Monetary Policy and the Depression* (1933), pp. 10–12; A. E. Kahn, *Great Britain in the World Economy* (1946), p. 38; W. A. Morton, *British Finance, 1930–1940* (Madison, 1943), pp. 30–7; Edward W. Bennett, *Germany and the Diplomacy of the Financial Crisis, 1931* (Cambridge, Mass., 1962), pp. 221 ff.

[3] U. K. Hicks, *Finance of the British Government, 1920–1936* (1938), p. 348.

[4] H. V. Hodson, *Slump and Recovery, 1929–1937* (1938), p. 67; Nevin, *Cheap Money*, p. 16; D. Williams, 'London and the 1931 Financial Crisis', *Ec. Hist. Rev.*, 2nd S., 15/3, 1963.

speculators swayed by fear and rumour. 'The classical remedy of an increase of the discount rate proved inoperative in checking the withdrawal of foreign funds, for the reason that mobile capital was seeking security, with little or no return, rather than high interest rates coupled with currency and credit risks.' [1] As soon as any centre showed signs of weakness, withdrawals began which turned the dreaded weakness into reality. In the summer of 1931, the holders of these mobile funds, mentioned several times already, the undesirable, but essential buttresses of sterling under an over-valued gold standard, began to attack London. In three weeks, Continental holders withdrew £41 million, and over the whole period of crisis, some £200 million of this 'hot' money was withdrawn.

The belief of the financiers in the weakness of London, which originated in the increasingly unfavourable trade balance of the United Kingdom and the threat to the gold reserve of the Bank of England, was further strengthened by the fact that it was a Labour Government which held office; by the emphasis of the Macmillan Report, which appeared on 14th July, on the unhealthy dependence of London on short-term funds; and by the threatened budget deficit, highlighted by the 'highly coloured account of the national finances' [2] of the May Committee Report presented on the last day of July.[3] To cap it all, a case of insubordination at Invergordon over cuts in naval pay was exaggerated in the world press as that final indignity, a mutiny in the Royal Navy. When the drain on London continued into August and the Treasury sought a further loan of £80 million in Paris and New York, the British Government was told bluntly that it must carry through at least some of the May Committee's recommendations, especially the severe cut in unemployment pay, before its application would be considered.

The crisis which hit London, it should be noted, was not one of unemployment or industrial depression, except in so far as these had caused a deficit in the Unemployment Fund. The bankers and the Governments concerned were not trying to increase employment or salvage industry, but merely to right the unbalances of the budget, trade and credit. Likewise, the solution to be imposed by the British Government was, yet again, as in 1914 and in 1925, the one demanded by the City.

Those who characterized the outcome as a 'bankers' ramp' [4] were, however, clearly misdirecting their criticism: bankers and speculators could not be blamed for seeking the best possible terms for themselves. The

---

[1] *Second Annual Report* of the Bank for International Settlements (Basle, 1932), quoted in Gayer, p. 27; cf. also N. F. Hall, *The Exchange Equalisation Account* (1935), p. 19.

[2] Smith and Walker, p. 36.   [3] pp. 212–13 above.

[4] Cf. the excellent discussion on this point in C. L. Mowat, *Britain Between the Wars* (1956 ed.), chapter 7, section 6. A detailed partisan account will be found in R. Bassett, *Nineteen Thirty One, Political Crisis* (1958).

fault, if any, lay with the still general belief that the limits of Government economic action lay in providing financial stability on the one hand, and assisting those who fell into pauperism because of the failure of the economy to employ them on the other. As long as it was believed that the sole function of Government in an economic crisis was to establish a favourable financial framework, the City could not be blamed for interpreting this as a framework favourable to itself. It was only in the 1930's that a change in attitude began to emerge, and by 1939 the Chancellor of the Exchequer went so far as to ask the banks to eliminate all foreign exchange and gold transactions of a speculative nature, and 'the authorities in America, France and Holland co-operated with the British in suppressing activities of the cosmopolitan speculator whose only concern is profit'.[1]

Faced by the ultimatum of the bankers over the £80 million loan in August 1931, the Labour Government split on the issue of how far to cut back unemployment relief at their behest, and several of its members, led by the Prime Minister, Ramsey MacDonald, joined by Conservative leaders and by some Liberals, formed a 'National' Government on August 24th to save the country from its financial perils.[2] The ousting of the Labour Government at once reduced the speculative pressure on sterling, even before the new Government had taken any action. Thus favoured, it obtained the foreign loan that had been refused its predecessor, and introduced a revised budget on 10th September which turned out to be only fractionally more severe than that which Labour had been prepared to accept. Indeed, the new Government, though confirmed in office by an overwhelming vote in the snap election of October 1931 by voters who fondly hoped it intended to cure depression when it merely wished to cause more effective deflation, stumbled into all the disasters which the Labour Government was ousted to prevent: the trade balance remained highly unfavourable, the payments to the sinking funds for debt redemption were partly suspended and, above all, the pound was driven off gold. Even in its decision to come off gold, the Bank of England's 'chief concern was not to gain advantages for British export trade by exploiting the new situation, but to conserve the international utility of the London money market'.[3]

This action, taken on 20th September 1931, followed a renewed drain of gold. It afforded instant relief, and was accompanied by the raising of the bank rate to 6%. Within ten days sterling had depreciated by 18% and at the end of the year it was down to $3.40.

[1] L. Waight, *The History and Mechanism of the Exchange Equalisation Account* (Cambridge, 1939), p. 143.

[2] Philip Viscount Snowden, *An Autobiography* (1934), chapters 76–80; Ramsay Muir, *The Record of the National Government* (1936), chapters 3–9; p. 213 above.

[3] W. A. Brown, Jnr., *The International Gold Standard Re-interpreted, 1914–1934*, 2 vols. (New York, 1940), Vol. 2, p. 1093. Robert Skidelsky, *Politicians and the Slump. The Labour Government of 1929–1931* (1967).

A large number of other countries inside and outside the sterling bloc, including the Dominions, Scandinavia and Japan, followed Britain off gold in the course of the next few months, but since the U.S.A., Germany, France, Belgium, Holland, Italy and Poland, among others, remained on gold for the time being, sterling goods enjoyed a sudden price advantage, reversing directly the unfavourable position of 1925–31.[1] Most of the countries adversely affected reacted by raising tariffs against British goods, but since Britain also introduced protection, the favourable impact on the trade balance remained for a time.

There was also relief in other ways. Foreign borrowers found repayment in sterling easier. Home prices kept very steady, the cost of living being virtually unchanged over 1931–6, and wholesale prices rising by 10% only, so that confidence in sterling was quickly restored and funds began to flow in again. The panic loans of £130 million from France and America were repaid with surprising ease.[2] The vast resources of the large joint-stock banks which had emerged from earlier amalgamations, ensured that Britain, unlike other countries, suffered no bank collapses or defaults.

By April 1932, with the pound stabilized, a balanced budget and effective protection, the financial crisis was over. Bank rate was steadily reduced, reaching 2% in June. The industrial depression was at its worst in the third quarter of 1932, but thenceforward all indices showed a strong upward trend, leading up to the boom of 1937.

7. FINANCIAL POLICY AND INSTITUTIONS IN THE NINETEEN-THIRTIES

The 'cheap money' policy of a 2% bank rate ushered in a period of stable prices, stable interest rates and stable exchange rates. Stability in the foreign exchanges was achieved by means of the Exchange Equalization Account, established in April 1932, and its supporting measures.[3] It was one of the major innovations introduced into the British financial scene in the age of 'managed' currencies. Originally launched with a sum of £175 million in Treasury Bills, it began operations at a period when sterling was very strong and it was thus able quickly to acquire a large quantity of foreign currency in exchange for its sterling bills. In November 1932, however, it had virtually lost its foreign currency holding again and was helpless to prevent the temporary fall of sterling to $3.15.[4] As a result, its financial basis was enlarged by £200 million in May 1933, and a further sum of £200 million was added in 1937.

---

[1] W. A. Lewis, *Economic Survey, 1919–1939* (1949), pp. 63–5; H. W. Arndt, *The Economic Lessons of the Nineteen-Thirties* (1944), pp. 96–9.
[2] J. H. Richardson, *British Economic Foreign Policy* (1936), pp. 36 ff.
[3] J. G. Smith and G. J. Walker, 'Currency and Banking', in *Britain in Depression* (1935), p. 45.
[4] J. H. Richardson, *British Economic Foreign Policy* (1936), pp. 45–50; H. F. Fraser, *Great Britain and the Gold Standard* (1933), pp. 131–2.

The duty of the fund was to counteract, by suitable purchases and sales, any temporary divergence from the stabilized exchange rates which otherwise in the then nervous state of foreign exchange markets, might easily degenerate into a cumulative exchange crisis. While it was not to originate any long-term changes in the exchange rates,[1] the Account appeared deliberately to depress the value of the pound below its natural level in order to favour the British balance of payments.[2] In the process it accumulated a large gold hoard, which stood it in good stead when a heavy drain to France set in in 1938;[3] but it must also take its share of the blame for forcing the U.S.A. to retaliate and to wreck the World Economic Conference in 1933 by insisting on a free hand to devalue the dollar.

The U.S.A., one of the worst sufferers in the depression, went off gold in April 1933, and the dollar was ultimately stabilized at 59% of the old gold parity, the pound being then closely linked with it at the old ratio. With the dollar and sterling blocs devalued, and Germany's foreign trade tightly controlled at several different artificial exchange rates, France and the other gold bloc members were left alone at a higher price level. The resulting unemployment and outflow of capital (partly, as in Britain in 1931, politically motivated), occurring in anticipation of devaluation, forced France to devalue also in 1936.[4] The three main currencies, the pound, dollar and franc, were thus all off gold, but were tied, in practice, to each other and to gold, and the three monetary authorities concluded a Tripartite Agreement, undertaking not to alter their exchange rates without prior consultation.

The currency areas covered by the Tripartite Agreement formed the only important region in which international trade in the old sense was still carried on, but even there it proved possible to isolate each country from changes occurring in the others. Thus the collapse of the American prosperity in 1937 had far less effect on the rest of the world than the crash of 1929.[5] The currency systems of Germany and the countries in its orbit, pursuing their different policies of rearmament and autarchy, were even more immune from the effects of alterations in world trade, gold movements or exchange rates.[6]

[1] W. Manning Dacey, 'The Technique of Insulation', *The Banker*, 48/153, Oct. 1938; L. Waight, *The History and Mechanism of the Exchange Equalisation Account* (Cambridge, 1939), p. 11; N. F. Hall, *The Exchange Equalisation Account* (1935).

[2] N. F. Hall, 'The Foreign Exchanges, 1932–1937', in *Britain in Recovery* (1938); A. E. Kahn, *Great Britain in the World Economy* (1946), pp. 202–3.

[3] A. E. Kahn, pp. 196–8; R. G. Hawtrey, *The Gold Standard in Theory and Practice* (5th ed., 1947), p. 221.

[4] H. V. Hodson, *Slump and Recovery, 1929–1937* (1938), chapters 6, 10, 11; R. G. Hawtrey, *Gold Standard*, pp. 161–73.

[5] W. A. Lewis, *Economic Survey, 1919–1939* (1949), pp. 67–72.

[6] Royal Institute of International Affairs, *Monetary Policy and the Depression* (1933), Appx. IV.

Financial Policy and Institutions in the Nineteen-Thirties

After the financial strains of 1931, Britain was thus able to sail into calmer waters of protection, a managed currency, a balanced budget and cheap money. Before following out the consequences of these policies, it will be advisable to trace the main changes of the financial institutions of the United Kingdom between 1913 and the 1930's.

At the centre, the Bank of England was less active than in earlier periods. As its bank rate was left unaltered for seven years at 2%, it could no longer be used as a weapon. Instead, rates were kept low by suitable supplies of cash, and the Central Bank exerted what influence it required by 'quality control'. The cash supply could safely be expanded as long as the American cash base was enlarged still faster under the 'New Deal' policies.[1] The responsibility over the foreign exchanges was transferred to the Exchange Equalization Account.

The joint-stock banks had, by the early 1930's, fully completed the process of amalgamation that was all but consummated by 1920.[2] Between 1922 and 1924, the number of banks was further reduced by eight, one of which went bankrupt, the others being absorbed by the larger systems. In 1927-8, the Liverpool-based Martin's Bank was established out of a merger of three firms, having a large regional, if not quite national, coverage, and in 1935 a similar merger created the District Bank, based on Manchester, as the eleventh member of the London Clearing House in 1936. Thus by mergers and associations, the last area of banking independence, South Lancashire, was being brought into the national system. At the end of 1938, there remained only four London clearing banks, four Scottish and three Irish banks, the other nominally independent banks all being associated with one or the other of these major institutions, besides the 'Big Five'. The dominance of the latter, the Midland, Barclay's, Lloyd's, the National Provincial and the Westminster Banks, is shown by the following comparison of deposits, capital and reserves on 31st December 1938:[3]

'Big Five' banks	£2,299 mn.
Other English banks	239
Scottish banks	248
Northern Irish banks	151

Fundamentally, the policy of British banks remained unchanged in this period. Their loans, as far as they were made to industry or agriculture, were intended to be self-liquidating or short-term, and for the rest the

[1] R. S. Sayers, *Central Banking After Bagehot* (1957), pp. 29–31; G. D. H. Cole, *Money, Trade and Investment* (1954), p. 84.

[2] Joseph Sykes, *The Amalgamation Movement in English Banking* (1926).

[3] T. Balogh, *Studies in Financial Organisation* (Cambridge, 1947), pp. 14–15, 114–18; H. Compton and E. H. Bott, *British Industry* (1940), p. 171; R. J. Truptil, *British Banks and the London Money Market* (1936), part I, chapters 2 and 6.

banks preferred to be liquid, investing in short-dated bills or in gilt-edged securities that were easily marketable. Direct investment in the share or loan capital of industry continued to be shunned.

Before 1914 there had indeed been little demand on bank funds for home investment. British industry generally succeeded in financing its own expansion by ploughing back profits or tapping local resources,[1] and few purely industrial issues were floated in London. The most highly specialized institutions were those arranging overseas investment.

After the war, the scope of overseas investment was much reduced, and at the same time the rate of saving had markedly decreased. There was a general tendency, nurtured by the heady post-war boom, to live at a higher rate of personal expenditure in relation to income than was the case before 1914, in defiance of the destruction of capital during the war. There was also, in addition to this general increase in the propensity to consume, the special effect of the relative decline in the incomes of the rich, by higher taxation and by the normal tendency of the share of profits to fall in all great depressions, and this also worked in the direction of reducing the national rate of saving. According to one estimate, gross investment fell from 25% to 16%, and net investment from 17% to 6–7% of national income between 1911 and 1938.[2] Of the diminished stream of savings, industry received little: investors steered clear of the depressed old staple trades, and the new industries, by their very nature untried or consisting originally of small firms, found access to the capital market equally difficult in any but the boom years, such as 1919–20 and perhaps 1928–9.[3] It even became possible to argue, as did Keynes, that large as was the fall in savings, the fall in home investment plans was larger still.

This problem was noted by the Balfour Committee, but it received its first important public recognition in the Report of the Macmillan Committee. Its terms of reference, provided by the Labour Government, to 'inquire into banking, finance and credit . . . and to make recommendations calculated to enable these agencies to promote the development of trade and commerce and the employment of labour', were a sign of the new preoccupation with the welfare of industry. In its Report, the Committee strongly recommended a closer, and more continuous, interest of the banks in industry. In particular, it approved of the German practice of associating a bank with several competing firms in one industry, which

[1] F. Lavington, *The English Capital Market* (1921), chapters 31–33.
[2] A. E. Kahn, pp. 137–8; T. Balogh, p. 277; Colin Clark, *National Income and Outlay* (1937), pp. 185, 250–3; W. H. Beveridge, *Full Employment in a Free Society* (1944), pp. 104–5; J. B. Jefferys and Dorothy Walters, 'National Income and Expenditure of the U.K. 1870–1952', *Income and Wealth*, Series V, 1955, p. 17.
[3] A. B. Levy, *Private Corporations and Their Control* (1950), Vol. 1, pp. 164–5; A. T. K. Grant, *A Study of the Capital Market in Post-War Britain* (1937), chapter 8.

led to 'rationalization' and the strengthening of the industry by the elimination of competition:

> British companies in the iron and steel, electrical and other industries [it reported] must meet in the gate their great American and German competitors who are generally financially powerful and closely supported by banking and financial groups, with whom they have continuous relationships. British Industry, without similar support, will undoubtedly be at a disadvantage. But such effective support cannot be obtained merely for a particular occasion. It can only be the result of intimate co-operation over years during which the financial interests get an insight into the problems and the requirements of the industry in question.[1]

This was a general plea. There was also particular reference to medium-term finance extended over 1–5 years; to long-dated industrial capital; and to small and medium-sized firms, needing capital in sums of up to £200,000, for which the City made very inadequate provision—the 'Macmillan gap'.[2] A greater concern for the long-term rate of interest, including presumably industrial investment, was also urged on the Bank of England.[3]

In this respect, the Committee was swimming with the tide. Several banks had become reluctant holders of shares or bonds in various enterprises in the collapse of 1920–1, and others had taken an interest in restrictive control schemes. The Bank of England itself had formed a separate agency, Securities Management Trust, in 1929 to administer with the help of a small, expert staff the large and varied industrial property which had fallen into its lap, and this was enlarged in 1930 into the Bankers Industrial Development Co.[4] That concern was launched with a capital of £6 million, of which the Bank of England provided one-quarter, other large banks providing the rest. It was instrumental in financing reconstruction schemes concerned with destroying surplus capacity, including National Shipbuilders Security Ltd. and the Lancashire Cotton Corporation, and with providing loans for the steel industry. The Bank of England also took part in the flotation of the United Dominions Trust with its various subsidiaries one of which, Credit for Industry Ltd. (1934), was specifically designed to help smaller firms with long-term loans.[5]

---

[1] *Report of the Committee on Finance and Industry* (1931. Cmd. 3897), para. 384, also paras. 378–383, 386; R. F. Harrod, *John Maynard Keynes* (1951), pp. 413–16.

[2] Cmd. 3897, paras. 392–404. Also see S. E. Thomas, *British Banks and the Finance of Industry* (1930), chapters 4–6; U. K. Hicks, *The Finance of the British Government, 1920–1936* (1938), p. 259.

[3] Cmd. 3897, para. 306 (iv).

[4] Sir Henry Clay, *Lord Norman* (1957), chapter 8; p. 118 above.

[5] T. Balogh, *op. cit.*, pp. 199–201; A. Beacham, *Economics of Industrial Organisation* (3rd ed., 1955), pp. 22–4; Grant, pp. 215–17.

These developments, however, could scarcely be said to have met the recommendations of the Macmillan Committee in full. The 'Macmillan gap' remained unbridged in the 1930's.[1] The banks, far from increasing their participation in industry, found in the 1930's that their industrial holdings of the slump years, which had largely arisen because of the inability of firms to repay their loans or reduce their overdrafts, were being wiped out as soon as the recovery began.[2] As a result, the banks, though willing to hold 55–60% of deposits in the form of 'advances' to industry, could seldom manage to place more than 40%, and were obliged to hold the rest in the form of 'investments', i.e. Government securities. Their holdings of these thereby rose from £264 million in February 1932 to £610 million in October 1936. As this was such an appreciable part of the total, precipitate sales would have forced down the price and caused capital losses, so that bank 'investments', formerly considered fairly liquid, in practice became far less so.[3]

The absence of a demand for bank loans on the part of industry did not mean that industry had no need of finance. It merely meant that bank accommodation was not found suitable. Compared with pre-war years, industry obtained more of its capital from outside, and as its needs grew with the investment programmes of the recovery years, especially of the new industries,[4] it was forced to tap new sources. The institutions formed or expanded to cater for its needs included Investment Trusts, in which the joint-stock banks largely participated, mainly concerned with taking up existing securities; Finance Companies, also generally linked with banks or merchant banks, growing especially in the recovery years of the 1930's, and concerned with new industrial issues, and Hire-Purchase Finance firms.[5]

It was a reflection of the general rise in incomes that an increasing share of the national savings came from 'small' and institutional savers, mainly the Building Societies and the Insurance Companies. Both were benefiting from the increase in freely disposable incomes and the rise in numbers of the lower middle classes, by showing remarkable increases in assets, including investments, and the insurance companies in particular began to place a larger share of their investments in debentures and even in equities of industry.[6] Few of the 'small' savers were working-class

---

[1] (Radcliffe) *Committee on the Working of the Monetary System* (1959. Cmnd. 827), paras. 229–34, 932.
[2] Sir Arthur Salter, *Recovery* (1932), pp. 90–1.
[3] Truptil, *op. cit.*, p. 306; also *Radcliffe Report*, paras. 139–40; T. Balogh, pp. 73–4.
[4] E. Nevin, *Cheap Money*, pp. 264–5; Compton and Bott, *British Industry*, p. 193.   [5] T. Balogh, pp. 158 ff., 256–9, 278–88.
[6] Nevin, *Cheap Money*, pp. 264–5; Sir Harold Bellman, *Bricks and Mortals* (1961), chapters 7–9.

households,[1] but the sources of the funds were drawn more widely than before.

These 'small' savings, which had amounted to only £32 million a year, or 13·2% of net accumulation, in 1901–13, had risen to £110·3 million a year, or over half the total net investment, in 1924–35. Of this latter sum, the Insurance Companies were responsible for £57½ million, Building Societies for £51½ million, and Post Office and Trustee Savings Banks for £1½ million. The total funds represented by deposits of these savings institutions, as well as by Building Societies' deposits and shares, and by the assets of Industrial and Provident Societies, rose from £607 million in 1919 to £972 million in 1929 and £1,760 million in 1937.[2]

In contrast with the rising opportunities of these new institutions, the older types of financial houses, notably the Acceptance Houses (merchant bankers) and the Discount Houses, found many of their pre-war markets closed or shrinking.[3] The former were adversely affected by the decline in international trade and lending, and after the moratoria of 1931, which froze most of their current assets, might easily have been destroyed, had not the Bank of England come to their rescue by rediscount facilities. In the course of the 1930's many of their overseas assets were gradually funded or liquidated,[4] and several houses went under.

The Discount Houses continued to occupy their very special position as the crucial link between the Bank of England and the clearing banks because of the rule that the clearing banks did not seek direct re-discounting business with the Bank of England. But the discount market, as its name implies, operated with bills, and bills were becoming increasingly scarce. Even before 1914 the cheque had replaced the inland bill as the main means of payment of large sums;[5] after the war the decline in foreign trade, and the foreign branches of the clearing banks, greatly reduced the need for foreign bills of exchange, and this was accelerated by the world-wide currency restrictions after 1931.

The yearly average of all commercial bills outstanding, both inland-drawn and foreign-drawn, was within the range of £400–650 million in the 1920's; it fell to well below £300 million in the 1930's,[6] and of the foreign acceptance business the clearing banks had captured a large share.[7] This might not have mattered so much, had not the supply of Treasury Bills

---

[1] John Hilton, *Rich Man, Poor Man* (1944, 3rd imp. 1947), chapter 2; Colin Clark, 'Determination of the Multiplier from National Income Statistics', *Econ. J.*, 48/191, 1938, p. 436.

[2] E. H. Phelps-Brown and Bernard Weber, 'Accumulation, Productivity and Distribution in the British Economy, 1870–1938', *Econ. J.*, 63/250, June 1953; T. Balogh, p. 96.

[3] *Macmillan Report*, paras. 88–95; Truptil, *op. cit.*, chapters 3 and 4, pp. 307–9.

[4] T. Balogh, pp. 263–5.   [5] p. 15 above.

[6] T. Balogh, pp. 167, 177–82.   [7] J. Sykes, *op. cit.*, p. 171.

also shown signs of drying up, because of successful funding operations at a time of cheap money on the one hand, and large increases in the holdings of Government departments and of foreigners on the other.[1] The result was a 'bill famine', which drove down the rate on Treasury Bills issued by tender from about 4–5% in the years 1925–32 to 0·6% from 1933 onward, i.e. nearly 1½% below bank rate. It was made tolerable only by the agreement of the joint-stock banks not to compete directly for these bills, and by the formation of a 'syndicate' of Discount Houses to end competition and make a single bid for them.[2] The decline in the quantity and the interest rate of both commercial and Treasury bills severely restricted the scope of the traditional business of the discount market.

With these changes in the institutional framework in mind, we may now turn to the course of the cheap money policy itself. In the beginning, in 1932, the policy was not the result of deliberate decision: rates were pulled down by a 'tangled mass of forces'.[3] The advantages of cheap money, which led to its retention for nineteen years, until 1951, became apparent and acceptable only gradually. Market rates had been falling, and the prices of Consols and other gilt-edged securities rising, from September 1931 onward, long before the official policy of low rates was inaugurated. The reasons for this are not clear, as a price rise was expected, and against this equities would be a better hedge than fixed-interest securities, nor was there any increase in the quantity of money at that stage. Perhaps basically the change was psychological, the increased confidence in a Conservative-minded Government. However it was brought about, the fall in market rates gave the Government an indication of direction. As soon as the foreign loans of £130 million, raised during the crisis, were paid off, the bank rate began to be reduced in March 1932[4] to reach 2% in June, where it remained. Around it, the structure of other rates also settled down to exceptionally low levels, bill rates, in particular, staying round ½% until 1939, as noted above, and even long-term rates being distinctly lower than in the 1920's.

There were at least four major reasons which launched, and kept, the Government on its cheap money course once it had been laid down. First, low rates in London would isolate the British economy from the short-term fluctuations induced by changes abroad, and keep away foreign 'hot' money. This consideration may have weighed heavily in the early period of this policy. Later on, the isolation was performed by the Exchange

[1] A. J. Youngson, *The British Economy, 1920–1957* (1960), pp. 194–5.
[2] T. Balogh, pp. 61 ff., 133, and Appx. I to Part II by F. W. Paish; Nevin, *Cheap Money*, pp. 134–43, 179.
[3] E. Nevin, *The Mechanism of Cheap Money, 1931–39* (Cardiff, 1955), pp. 107–8, also 57–8.
[4] E. Nevin, 'The Origins of Cheap Money', *Economica*, N.S., 20/77, 1953.

Equalization Account. Secondly, low rates were a simple device for reducing Government expenditure without causing social unrest. This, also, was an early motive, and was triumphantly vindicated by the great conversion of 1932, although low market rates were not the only pre-condition of success. The conversion and funding operations were also assisted by the growth of departmental funds, including the health and unemployment insurance funds, Post Office and Trustee Savings Bank funds, the Treasury Pension Fund, and part of the backing for the fiduciary issue as well as the funds of the Exchange Equalization Account, all of which gave the Treasury much greater freedom over the timing of its issues, compared with the constant stream of renewals which tied the Government's hands in the 1920's.[1] Thirdly, there may have been the desire, in the face of an apparent decline in entrepreneurship in the British economy, to favour by low interest rates the active as against the passive members of the community: a step in the direction of what Keynes came to call the 'euthanasia of the rentier'.

Lastly, the authorities also began to look on cheap money as a method of increasing the total level of activity in the economy. This motive became operative, at the earliest, in 1933, but was later responsible for the continuation of the policy in the face of many changing circumstances. Whether low rates actually stimulated the economy in the 1930's is in some doubt. They were certainly accompanied by a large increase in the quantity of credit,[2] even though much of the gold inflow was sterilized in the Exchange Equalization Account, but as noted above on p. 234 there were few industrial borrowers in the early 1930's in the face of willing lenders—a circumstance which helped to depress rates still further. In the later 1930's the net effect of the Government's policy was in the opposite direction. The shortage of bills made the banks, which had began to watch their 'liquidity ratio' as well as the pure cash ratio, too illiquid and unwilling to lend, and in the incipient boom of 1936–7 the authorities induced a distinct cash shortage, which went directly and deliberately, though only temporarily, against the overall expansionary effect of cheap money.

How far Government policy as a whole, including other measures, could be held responsible for the industrial recovery has been subject to much debate, but few would give it much weight today. Low rates might, according to Hawtrey, have had directly beneficial effects in 1931, but by 1932 it was too late, and the recovery had to wait for other, more general factors.[3] Home capital issues, which one would have expected to be

---

[1] U. K. Hicks, *Finance of the British Government*, pp. 364–9.
[2] Truptil, p. 298; H. W. Arndt, *The Economic Lessons of the Nineteen-Thirties* (1944), chapter 4.
[3] Hawtrey, *Gold Standard*, pp. 149–52.

among the first indices to show the benefits of cheap money, did not begin to rise until some eighteen months after the beginning of the upswing. Moreover, even the cheap money policy of 1932 was directly counteracted by deflationary budgets until 1934, and by the decision taken in 1931, at the depth of the depression, to work off the accumulated deficit of £115 million of the Unemployment Fund by collecting more in contributions than was paid out in benefits. The investments by the public utilities were all timed to begin much too late to affect the recovery, except for the electricity grid which by sheer accident rose to the peak of its constructional work in the depression. Thus public investment probably amplified, rather than evened out, cyclical fluctuations.[1] More positive was the contribution made by the tariff. It is possible to argue not only that protection brought certain immediate sectional benefits, e.g. to the iron and steel industry, but also, more generally, that by reducing imports it reduced the extent by which British incomes had to decline by virtue of the decline in exports, i.e. that the downward multiplier was cut off. Further, by taxing imports (as well as by banning foreign capital issues) the protectionist policy encouraged expenditure in such sectors as building and the service trades at home, which were undoubtedly connected with the onset of the recovery.[2]

Basically, the claim that the Government's cheap money policy assisted the economic recovery must rest on the claim that it helped to bring about the building boom of the 1930's. The building boom was at once the symbol and a main carrier of British industrial recovery from the Great Depression. It began largely as a boom in the building of private dwellings, as distinct from local authority building.[3] Starting from the relatively high level of building of the 1920's, when an average of 150,000 dwellings a year of all kinds was completed, output stayed around the 200,000 mark in 1930–3, and then rose rapidly to well over 350,000 dwellings a year. In those totals, the figure of dwellings completed by local authorities remained fairly constantly at about 75,000 a year. From 1934 on, the boom was further boosted by industrial and commercial building which showed the usual accelerator effects during the upswing of a trade cycle.[4]

Building employed only 6–7½% of all insured workers in the 1930's, but it accounted for 20% of the increase in employment in 1932–5, or 30% if the increase in the indigenous building materials industry is included. If

---

[1] U. K. Hicks, *Finance of the British Government*, pp. 280–95, 376–7; also E. Nevin, pp. 229 ff.; R. F. Bretherton, F. A. Burchardt, R. S. G. Rutherford, *Public Investment and the Trade Cycle in Great Britain* (1941), p. 407.

[2] A. E. Kahn, pp. 154–6, 262–4; W. A. Morton, *British Finance, 1930–1940* (Madison, 1943), p. 82, also chapters 14–17.

[3] G. D. H. Cole, *Building and Planning* (1945), pp. 96–7.

[4] Figures in E. Nevin, *Cheap Money*, p. 269; cf. B. Weber and J. Parry Lewis, 'Industrial Building in Great Britain, 1923–38', *Scot. J. Pol. Econ.*, 8/1, Feb. 1961.

to this are added the usual multiplier effects and the increased demand for furniture, as well as the fact that the building indices were leading the others in the upswing, it is clear that here was a critical mechanism for stimulating British recovery at work.[1] To find the causes of the building boom is to find, in large measure, the causes of the recovery.

To explain the building boom solely by the cheap money policy is to look largely to the supply side, and to ignore other factors affecting supply even then. Nor were the effects of low rates entirely clear-cut. Most of the building, and 75% of the dwelling houses, were financed by building societies, the phenomenal growth of which was one of the most striking aspects of the boom, their total balances out on mortage rising from £316 million at the end of 1930 to £706 million at the end of 1939. Yet building society rates fell only slowly, from an average of 5·87% in 1931 to 4·80% in 1939.[2] While a reduction of 1% in mortgage rates is a very substantial reduction in the total weekly cost of a house, it took eight years to achieve: the average reduction by 1933, when building was in full swing, was only 0·3%. Most of the remainder of the houses were built by local authorities, and were affected by Government policy rather than by the falling mortgage rates of the 1930's.[3] In sum, the direct effect of cheap money on the supply side could not have been large. On the other hand, the fact that building societies kept up their rates on shares and deposits while others dropped, diverted increasing funds to them, and allowed them to expand their lending and offer easier terms. Moreover, a large proportion of building was for investment, and it was clear that it was low interest rates at a time when rents showed no disposition to fall which made returns on housing investment so attractive.[4]

The other main factor at work on the supply side was the reduction in cost: a house costing £350 in 1931 fell to well below £300 in 1933–4,[5] and despite a rise in the general price level, its price did not increase again until 1937. For this fall in the cost curve both materials and labour were responsible: building materials showing a sharp reduction in price, and labour a marked increase in output per head after the low level of the early post-war years.[6]

---

[1] G. D. A. MacDougall, 'General Survey, 1929–1937', in *Britain in Recovery* (1938), pp. 46–8, also Sir Harold Bellman, 'The Building Trades', in *ibid.*; W. A. Lewis, *Economic Survey, 1919–39* (1949), p. 87; A. P. Becker, 'Housing in England and Wales during the Business Depression of the 1930's', *Ec. Hist. Rev.*, 2nd S., 3/3, 1951, p. 325.　　　　　　　[2] Becker, p. 335.
[3] U. K. Hicks, *Finance of the British Government*, p. 131.
[4] Nevin, *Cheap Money*, pp. 272 ff.
[5] L. R. Connor, 'Urban Housing in England and Wales', *J. R. Stat. S.*, 99/1, 1936, p. 39.
[6] I. Bowen, 'Building Output and the Trade Cycle (U.K., 1924–38)', *Oxf. Ec. P.*, 3, 1940, p. 116; R. L. Reiss, *Municipal and Private Enterprise Housing* (1945), pp. 24–6.

Commercial and Financial Developments

Of at least equal importance were the changes on the demand side. The well-known 'building cycle', which was held back from its expected upswing in the 1920's because of the generally depressed condition of the country and the effects of rent restriction,[1] began to operate with full force in the 1930's. A shortage of houses, estimated at 700,000–1,200,000 in 1920, increased to an estimated peak of 1·2 to 2 million in 1930: the backlog of suspension of building in war-time, the natural wear and tear of old buildings which needed replacement, the rapid increase in the number of families (as distinct from the number of people),[2] and rising standards of consumption and of housing by-laws which condemned many houses as unfit to live in, contributed to this pent-up demand in the 1930's.[3]

In addition to these factors common to most upswings of the 'building cycle', there were two special factors in this period. One was the migration of industry and population, calling for new houses, roads, and public buildings in new areas quite irrespective of the total demand-supply position, and the other was the rise in real incomes, largely achieved by the increasingly favourable terms of trade in the years before 1931.[4] This latter factor has wider implications also.

The housing boom may have been the most visible and the largest single component of the upswing in economic activity which signalized the end of the slump, but it was by no means the only one. There were also remarkable increases in many service trades, entertainments, and other 'sheltered' industries. They were the kind of goods and services which the bulk of the lower middle classes and skilled workers demanded with their increased real incomes, and the rise in their real wages or salaries, in turn, was achieved, not by rising money payments, but by falling prices, pulled down by falling prices of imports. In all this, Government action, even cheap money, played a relatively minor part. The impetus came from a rising demand, which was based in the final analysis on the greatly improved terms of trade and on lowered real costs of production, and the main positive action of the Government consisted in channelling the additional demand into home-produced goods and services rather than imports.

In the United States, the slow recovery received a sharp setback in 1937 and all indices pointed to a renewed depression, even though neither in America nor on this side of the Atlantic had a position of full employment been approached at the peak of the 'boom'. This time, how-

[1] W. A. Lewis, *Economic Survey*, p. 86.
[2] J. B. Cullingworth, *Housing Needs and Planning Policy* (1960), chapter 2.
[3] Herbert W. Robinson, *The Economics of Building* (1939), pp. 119–22; W. F. Stolper, 'British Monetary Policy and the Housing Boom', *Quarterly Journal of Economics*, 56/1, Part II, Nov. 1941; Reiss, *passim*; C. L. Mowat, *Britain Between the Wars*, pp. 458–61.
[4] F. Benham, *Great Britain Under Protection* (New York, 1941), chapter 9.

ever, the shock of the American recession on the rest of the world, insulated by 'managed' currencies and other protection, was small. In Britain, re-armament quickly took up the slack,[1] and with building still booming, the recession of 1938–9 was milder than that following 1929, and was short-lived. The needs of war soon led to the full employment of all available resources.

[1] H. V. Hodson, *Slump and Recovery, 1929–1937* (1938), chapter 12.

CHAPTER V

Social Conditions between the Wars

I. THE AGE OF MASS UNEMPLOYMENT

Industrially, the main development in Britain between the wars was the enforced shift of resources from the old to the new industries, from the export trades to the sheltered home industries. The last chapter traced the consequences of this shift on the trading and financial position of Britain in the world economy. This chapter will follow out its consequences on the well-being of different sections of the population, and in particular, the contrast between the high and rising incomes among those in full employment in the expanding sectors, and the poverty and long-period unemployment of many of those in the declining sectors. Unemployment of men and of resources occupies a central place in the history of the inter-war years.

At the end of the war, some transitional unemployment was expected as soldiers and war-workers were being demobilized and fitted into their normal peace-time occupations, but the actual transfer from the forces to civilian occupations was accomplished with remarkable smoothness, helped as it was by the high level of employment, and the 28 days' paid leave granted to demobilized soldiers. Between the armistice and April 1920, 2,900,000 men were added to civilian employment, while the number of females in civilian employment dropped by 500,000 and numbers in the Forces were reduced by 3,600,000. Throughout this period of gigantic changes, unemployment remained generally below the half million mark. A maximum of 1,093,000 were paid out-of-work donation in April 1919,[1] but it is doubtful how many of them were truly unemployed; a year later there was an acute labour shortage in most areas.[2]

No sooner was the apparatus of economic control dismantled in 1920, in the belief that the effects of war-time dislocation had been overcome, than employment began to shrink. By March 1921 unemployment in the insured trades reached 15%. The coal stoppage of April to June raised the figure to 22%, but even after the dispute was over, the proportion remained obstinately at 16–17%. In view of the fact that the pre-war

[1] A. C. Pigou, *Aspects of British Economic History, 1918–1925* (1947), pp. 36–40.
[2] E. V. Morgan, *Studies in British Financial Policy, 1914–25* (1952), pp. 70–2.

maximum rate over a period of 60 years or more had been 11%, and the average 4½% (and that the insurance scheme had been built on the actuarial assumption of such a rate), this high level of unemployment was confidently expected to be temporary only. The confidence was misplaced. Employment improved in 1924, and was at a high level again in 1927–9, but even in the best months, the official unemployment rate stood at 9–10%, or over a million unemployed. Fluctuations in unemployment similar to those of the pre-1914 era seemed to be superimposed on an irreducible 'hard core' of close on a million unemployed men.[1]

The summer of 1929, in which one out of eleven among the insured trades was out of work, proved to be the high point of prosperity. The 'Great Depression' of the early 1930's brought with it a level of unemployment that put even the 1920's in the shade. The official unemployment rate reached a peak of 23% or nearly one-quarter of the insured population in August 1932, and stayed above 20% for over two years. In terms of numbers, this meant a figure of nearly 3 million people without work, but there were in addition several important sections of the population outside the field of insurance, and therefore excluded from the official statistics. Among them were agricultural workers, domestic servants, self-employed persons, persons employed by members of their immediate family, and salaried employees normally earning over £250 a year, besides civil servants, police, armed forces and railwaymen who were not normally subject to unemployment. Further, in the bad years of the slump, many who were willing and able to work, especially among the elderly and the married women, had ceased to register with the Ministry of Labour, as they had exhausted their unemployment insurance benefits and considered it unlikely that they would ever be found work again. Including these groups, the total true number unemployed has been estimated at 3,289,000 in 1931 and 3,750,000 in the peak period of September 1932.[2] Some 6–7 million people were living on the dole.

Improvement set in in 1933, and while the numbers out of work fell to a minimum of 9% (1,400,000 on the official register) by September 1937, the numbers in employment rose faster still. Some 2 million persons were added to the employed population between 1933 and 1937, of whom fewer than 1½ million came from the ranks of the registered unemployed, most of the remainder being persons who had withdrawn from the live register of the Labour Exchanges in the depth of the slump.[3] The position worsened in 1938–9, when 1,800,000–1,900,000 persons (12%) were on the official unemployment registers, in spite of re-armament, and if it

[1] Henry Clay, *The Post-War Unemployment Problem* (1929), pp. 24, 28.
[2] Colin Clark, *National Income and Outlay* (1937), p. 31; H. W. Robinson, 'Employment and Unemployment', in *Britain in Recovery* (1938), p. 95.
[3] R. C. Davison, *British Unemployment Policy since 1930* (1938), p. 49.

had not been for the outbreak of war, in September 1939, all the signs are that the figures would have deteriorated further to usher in a renewed depression.

General unemployment percentages hide very great differences between industries, areas, workers of different skills, ages or sex. In the years before 1914 it was London and the south which had the highest unemployment percentages, while the old industrial north had the lowest, and as late as 1919 it was assumed that industries such as coal and cotton would have so little unemployment compared with other occupations, that they would want to establish their own 'special' insurance schemes at more favourable rates.[1] In the event, it was the old industrial areas and the old staple export trades which suffered most.

In the early 1920's, the heaviest unemployment rates were recorded n the industries which had been over-expanded during the war: ship-building, engineering and the metal industries generally. After 1925, coal and cotton came to the forefront, while some sections of engineering, at least, experienced better trade. On the whole, however, it was becoming clear by the end of the decade that it was the staple export trades, above all coal mining, but also cotton, wool, tinplate, iron and steel and pottery, which fared the worst in the general depression.[2] By contrast, industries which were rapidly expanding, like electrical engineering or motor engineering, or which catered largely for the home market, like distribution or motor transport, had a relatively low rate of unemployment.

In 1929–31 the effects of a general world economic depression were added to the special problems of the export industries, and there were further changes. The new industries and services continued to enjoy the lowest unemployment figures until 1931, but they failed to show the same rate of recovery as the rest of the country in the next few years. By contrast, the declining staples showed remarkable reductions in unemployment as also in the total labour force attached, when the recovery began. In the bad years, the workers in them stayed put and hung on to their old trade, where they were established and had acquired rights to draw benefits. As soon as better trade offered, they rushed into the expanding industries in such numbers as to overstrain their capacity of absorbing labour[3] (see facing page).

There was a further complicating factor. Industries producing durable capital goods, which are usually subject to much greater cyclical fluctuations than those producing consumer goods, had a much more than

---

[1] W. H. Beveridge, *Unemployment, a Problem of Industry* (1930), pp. 291, 405.

[2] Clay, *op. cit.*, pp. 27–8, 41–52, 81–4, 92–5, 108; Pigou, *op. cit.*, pp. 46–50.

[3] W. H. Beveridge, *Full Employment in a Free Society* (1944), pp. 49–59, 83, Table 33 (pp. 316–20), based on his series of three articles, 'An Analysis of Unemployment', *Economica*, N.S., 3 and 4, Nos. 12–14, 1936–7, esp. No. 12, Nov. 1936, p. 374.

The Age of Mass Unemployment

Unemployment Percentages in Selected Industries

	1932	1937
(A) Expanding Industries:		
Building	29·0	13·8
Motor vehicles, etc.	20·0	4·8
Electrical engineering	16·3	3·1
Food industries	16·6	12·4
Hotel, etc., service	17·3	14·2
Distributive trades	12·2	8·8
(B) Declining Industries:		
Coal mining	33·9	14·7
Woollen and worsted	20·7	10·2
Cotton	28·5	11·5
Shipbuilding	62·2	23·8
Jute	42·2	26·8
Pig-iron making	43·5	9·8

normally rapid expansion in the 1930's,[1] having been held back for almost twenty years, first by the war and then by the 'doldrums' of the 1920's.

Within industry it was, as ever, the unskilled workers who bore the brunt of the unemployment, and the salaried employees and 'employers' and managers who suffered least. According to the calculations of Colin Clark, based on the Census of 1931, there were in that year 30·5% of unskilled labourers unemployed and 14·4% of skilled and semi-skilled industrial workers, but only 5–8% of white-collar workers, and a bare ½–2% of working proprietors of businesses or shops, and farmers.[2] If persons temporarily stopped were included also, the differences between these groups would be greater still.

In view of the strong localization of most of the basic and staple industries, the high incidence of unemployment in them was reflected in high local rates of unemployment in certain areas. This topic has been treated in some detail above[3] and need only be alluded to here. In 1934 with recovery on its way for some time, most of the industrial towns in the Welsh valleys, and many towns on the Tyne and in Durham, had unemployment rates of over 50%, and some well over 70% of the total workers insured. In West Cumberland, where closed coal mines left whole populations stranded without any prospective means of support, there were towns like Frizington, where a bare 33 men were on unemployment insurance benefit, while 515 had been unemployed for so long that they

[1] E. H. Phelps-Brown and G. L. S. Shackle, 'British Economic Fluctuations', *Oxf. Econ. P.*, No. 2, 1939.
[2] Colin Clark, *National Income and Outlay*, p. 46, and *The Conditions of Economic Progress* (1951 ed), p. 470.
[3] Chapter 3, section 4.

had exhausted their insurance claims and were kept on 'Transitional Payments'.[1]

Unemployment of such extent and durations was a social, as well as an economic problem. The man who was on the dole for a long period, in a community in which there were many others like him, could not just be put into cold storage, to be taken out, unchanged, as soon as a new job offered itself.[2] He lost some of his skill and his self-respect, and often also the will to work, and some permanent damage to his personality was only too likely. Men became bitter, cynical and disillusioned, and less sure of their moral bearings when they were denied work and found themselves and their families in poverty in the midst of a rich society. For a time the unemployed even became a political force, but owing to the impermanent nature of the status of 'unemployed', they made no sustained impact on the country's political life.[3]

There were also special problem groups among them. There were boys and girls, shunted into dead-end jobs when leaving school and then thrown on the labour market when old enough to claim full wages, without skill and without a trade, and there were the youths who never secured a steady job at all, even for a time. There were the older men who found it impossible, once they were dismissed, ever to gain new employment, and whose only hope lay in by-employment, such as allotment keeping or poultry farming. There were labourers with large families who secured almost as much, if not more, on the dole, because of the family allowance element in it, as when they were working, and who had therefore no incentive to seek work; there were craftsmen, proud of their skill, who refused inferior jobs and failed to realize that their craft had become out-of-date; and there were workers, especially in the coal districts, who were known as active trade unionists or Communists and were, in effect, blacklisted with no hope of ever finding employment in their own industry again.

In the relatively prosperous districts unemployment was often felt as a stigma and kept secret, and men out of work preferred isolation. In the depressed areas, where unemployment was the common lot of many or most workers, there was often comradeship in distress, which was greatly to be preferred to isolation, but tended to sap the overriding desire to be at work again. There were, further, often local or perhaps even national differences in attitude: the proud families of Crook Town, keeping up an

---

[1] Ministry of Labour, *Reports of Investigations into the Industrial Conditions of Certain Depressed Areas* (1934. Cmd. 4728), pp. 27, 106, 136.

[2] H. W. Singer, *Unemployment and the Unemployed* (1940), chapter 12. Cf. also M. Bruce, *The Coming of the Welfare State* (1961), pp. 228–40.

[3] Wal Hannington, *Unemployed Struggles, 1919–1936* (1936); H. L. Beales and R. S. Lambert (ed.), *Memoirs of the Unemployed* (1934).

outward appearance of serenity and respectability, contrasted with the gregarious families of the Welsh valleys, only too eager to exaggerate their distress and dramatize their ill-luck.[1] Whatever the area, however, much social waste and personal suffering have to be added to the economic loss of output, of skill and of willingness to work, as the costs of prolonged periods of unemployment.

Among applicants for benefit of allowances in 1929, only 4·7% had been unemployed twelve months or more, and many of these were coal miners who had not been re-employed after the strike of 1926. But the proportion rose to 16·4% in August 1932, 25·0% in August 1936 and (after a change in the classification) 22·6% in August 1939.[2] Thus the numbers of the long-term unemployed, though relatively small, were rising in the depression, and could not be brought down again in the recovery. It was estimated that 300,000 workers were in this category of long-term unemployment in early 1932, over 480,000 in July 1933, and 265,000 still at the peak of the boom, in the autumn of 1937. In some of the badly hit areas, the proportions were very much higher. In September 1936, while only 0·4% of the insured fell into this category in prosperous Deptford, the proportion was 18·8% in Crook and 28·1% in the Rhondda, in both these places forming over one-half of the unemployed population.[3] Similarly, there were industries with half or more of the unemployed in the long-period unemployment group.[4]

By contrast, the proportion in continuous unemployment for three months or less was 78·5% of those registered in 1929, 59% in August 1932 and fluctuated around this proportion in the later 1930's. This high proportion gave rise to the phrase of the 'stage army' of the unemployed, the same figure representing an ever-changing set of individuals dropping out of employment, but not suffering unduly from prolonged spells of lack of work. In depression years, however, the spell of work consisted often of a few days' or a few weeks' employment only, perhaps as relief drivers or postmen, interrupting years of general unemployment, so that a high proportion of those nominally on the register for a short period only were in fact long-period cases.[5]

After years of such experiences, even sympathetic reformers began fatalistically to accept large-scale unemployment as inevitable. Sir William

---

[1] (Pilgrim Trust), *Men Without Work* (Cambridge, 1938) is a report of six typical urban areas in 1936, including Crook and the Rhondda. Cf. also C. L. Mowat, *Britain Between the Wars* (1956 ed.), pp. 480–90; A. J. Lush, *Disinherited Youth* (Edinburgh, 1943).

[2] Beveridge, *Full Employment*, Table 8, p. 64. Cf. also Clark, *National Income and Outlay*, p. 48.

[3] *Men Without Work*, *passim*. The Report deals largely with those unemployed for 12 months or more.   [4] Beveridge, *Full Employment*, p. 83.

[5] H. W. Singer, *op. cit.*, chapter 1.

(later Lord) Beveridge, the most prominent among them, recognized in 1937 three main groups: (*a*) short-period, fractional or seasonal unemployment, amounting to 6–8% of the insured population, or 800,000–1,000,000 people and accepted as inescapable; (*b*) long-period hard-core unemployed in contracting industries, living in regions of declining industry, or handicapped by old age, numbering 4%, or 500,000, who might be reduced in numbers in the long run; and (*c*) cyclical unemployment of workers temporarily thrown out of work by a recession of whom there were none at the time, but of whom there might be up to 6%, or 800,000, at the bottom of a slump. The numbers referred to insured persons only; there would be others outside the insurance scheme. The pre-war long-term average of $4\frac{1}{2}$% unemployment could never be attained again because of structural changes in industry.[1] It has since become clear that such pessimistic assumptions were merely elevating the experiences of one or two trade cycles into immutable laws: the post-1939 economy has managed well on unemployment figures under 3%, and for long periods even under 1%.

The pre-war insurance scheme in certain industries was extended in 1916 to cover some 4 million workers. In November 1918, when the Government was anxious to avoid the political and social dangers of throwing large numbers of returned soldiers or discharged munitions workers on the Poor Law Institutions, an Out-of-Work Donation scheme was started as a temporary measure. It covered both returning soldiers and, on slightly different terms, virtually all civilian workers. The benefits were entirely non-contributory, the cost being borne by the Exchequer, and were so much more generous than the insurance benefit rates that the latter were virtually suspended, all workers preferring to draw Donation instead. Widespread allegations of abuse were made but not confirmed by the Aberconway Committee of Inquiry,[2] and the scheme was successful inasmuch as it carried the burden of the transitional months and allowed the more permanent Act of 1920 to be introduced at leisure. The civilian scheme ended in November 1919 and the service scheme in 1921, and their total cost of £66 million[3] seemed a small price to pay for social peace at a critical time.

The Unemployment Insurance Act of 1920 contained all the main prin-

---

[1] Sir William Beveridge, 'An Analysis of Unemployment, III', *Economica*, N.S., 4/14, 1937, pp. 180–2. Cf. also R. C. Davison, *The Unemployed, Old Policies and New* (1929), chapter 6.

[2] *Reports* (1919. Cmd. 196 and 305).

[3] Karl de Schweinitz, *England's Road to Social Security*, p. 218; E. M. Burns, *British Unemployment Programs, 1920–1938* (Washington, 1941), p. 7. Miss Burns' work, together with the works by Davison and Lord Beveridge quoted earlier in this section, form the main sources for the study of unemployment insurance and assistance in this period.

ciples of the Act of 1911, but extended its scope to virtually all employments.[1] Eleven million workers were included, rising gradually over the period to 15·4 million in 1938,[2] and all official unemployment statistics were based on that category of insured persons. Contributions and benefit rights were much as they had been in the earlier, more limited scheme, and so was the assumed unemployment rate of about 4%.

The Act had hardly been put into effect when the slump set in, raising unemployment rates to well over 10% for the decade instead of 4%. Even at the existing rates and conditions of benefit, the finances of the fund were severely strained, and minor relaxations, such as the extension of the period of benefits, soon wiped out the accumulated surplus of £22 million from the earlier scheme and ran the Fund into deficits. Yet even this extravagant management would still have thrown hundreds of thousands of able-bodied workers into the arms of the Poor Law, and the Government, in 1921, was thus presented with the dilemma which was to dog all administrations for the next two decades: how to preserve the 'insurance' principle of the original scheme, while at the same time preventing the hundreds of thousands who had exhausted their benefit entitlement from being treated as paupers. It was to solve this that a third type of benefit was interposed, neither insurance nor charity, but with some of the characteristics of both, changing in detail several times in the inter-war years, but remaining in essentials the same.

This solution was all the easier since the 'insurance' part itself could hardly be said to be run on strict insurance principles. The accumulated contributions of one group were used in 1921 to subsidize a much larger group; trades with lower risks were added at similar rates to help trades with higher risks of unemployment; and the Exchequer contribution crept up in the course of the decade from under one-third to about one-half of the income. Nevertheless, the insurance scheme was based on compulsory statutory contributions, in return for which there was a contractual right to certain benefits, though the exact terms were changed from time to time. For the other types of benefit there was no such right; they were subject to some form of means or needs test.

These 'intermediate' schemes, being neither insurance nor Poor Law, were improvisations, and there were no fewer than 18 amending Acts to the Unemployment Insurance Act between 1920 and 1930 and more in the 1930's. At first the intermediate scheme, called 'uncovenanted benefit' in 1921–4, then 'extended benefit' in 1924–8 and 'transitional benefit' in 1928–31, was paid out of the Insurance Fund, but since this destroyed its solvency, its cost was transferred to the Treasury. Until 1928 the continued tendency for the rates of unemployment to exceed the estimates on

---

[1] The main groups exempted are listed on p. 243 above.
[2] Alan T. Peacock, *The Economics of National Insurance* (1952), p. 15.

which insurance and relief rates were based, subjected this system to a series of great strains. In order to prevent too many persons falling out of benefit, conditions of drawing and rates of benefit were eased several times, especially by the Labour Government in 1924, and this in turn caused rates of contribution to be raised, placing an unwarrantably heavy burden on the industries with little unemployment. Even so, the Fund ran nto debt to the tune of £25 million by 1928, while there were almost as many unemployed who had exhausted their benefit and were on the supplementary scheme as there were on the full insurance scheme. Another group, numbering 120,000–140,000 insured, and making with their dependants some half million persons, had slipped through the meshes of both and had to be looked after by the Poor Law Guardians.

In both the Poor Law and the supplementary schemes, relief was given according to needs, and local administration and interpretation differed widely. Already in 1921, some of the Labour Councillors and Guardian in Poplar, a poor London borough with a large unemployment problem, had forced some redistribution of the burden from local shoulders by going to prison rather than contribute their quota of rates for the London County Council, and by 1926 three Poor Law Unions had gone bankrupt, having exhausted their borrowing powers, and were replaced by Ministry nominees. In general, 'the level of assistance has varied with the political complexion, the social theories, and the financial status of the individual relief authorities'.[1]

The Blanesburgh Departmental Committee on Unemployment Insurance, which reported in 1927,[2] recommended the abolition of 'extended benefit' by relaxing the conditions of receiving insurance benefit to the extent of granting indefinite drawing rights to all those who had 30 weeks' contributions in the past two years to their credit. Even this easy rule, it was found, would exclude one-seventh of the insured, and when the recommendation was incorporated in the Unemployment Act of 1927, which became operative in 1928, the rule was postponed, and meanwhile 8 contributions in the past two years, or 30 weeks' contributions at any time, would qualify.[3] Contributions and benefits were lowered, in order to render the scheme financially sound.

But this scheme also went gravely astray in its actuarial estimate of financial burden and return. Being launched in what was probably the least depressed year of the 1920's, it assumed an average unemployment rate of 6%, or 1,160,000 persons out of work; in fact, the rate rose from 9% in 1927 to 13·6% in March 1930, 19·6% in December of that year,

---

[1] E. M. Burns, p. 28.
[2] *Report of the Departmental Committee on Unemployment Insurance* (1927).
[3] G. P. Jones and A. G. Pool, *A Hundred Years of Economic Development in Great Britain* (1959 ed.), pp. 392–5.

and then stayed above 20% for over two years, or nearly 3 million insured unemployed. The heavy outpayments which plunged the Fund deeper into nominal debt (the distinction between the growing Treasury 'contribution' to the Fund and the Treasury 'loans' were of no great immediate economic significance) helped to precipitate the economic and political crisis of 1931, as described in chapter 4 above. It also forced the Government to consider anew the principles of unemployment insurance.

Meanwhile, the burden of unemployment and the poverty it brought in its wake was also undermining the old Poor Law. Throughout the 1920's a minimum of 350,000–450,000 persons out of work received outdoor relief in Great Britain, and at certain times these numbers were very much higher: there were 1,244,000 persons in June 1922, for example, and over 1½ million during the prolonged coal strike of 1926. The local system of Poor Law Guardians was not designed to take such strains on top of its normal duties of looking after the non-able-bodied paupers,[1] and the Poor Law had to be entirely re-cast.

The new law, the Local Government Act of 1929 (and a similar Act for Scotland), confirmed by the Poor Law Act of 1930, followed the Royal Commission of 1909 and the Report of the Onslow Commission, which had sat since 1923.[2] A centuries-old tradition was ended and an era in public welfare provision opened when Poor Law Unions and their Guardians were abolished as from 1930, and their work transferred to Public Assistance Committees of County Councils and County Borough Councils. Perhaps the most significant change was the turning of the labour 'test' for the able-bodied from a deterrent into the 'primary objective . . . to maintain the employability of those able and willing to work, so that when opportunity offers, these men may have no difficulty in resuming their places in industry'.[3] The 'genuinely seeking work' clause, dating from 1924, was also abolished, since the notion of 'voluntary unemployment' had become patently unhelpful in existing conditions.

In 1930 a Royal Commission on Unemployment Insurance was set up to consider the thorough reconstruction of the original scheme, which by 1931 'was hardly recognizable through the tangled mass of opportunist legislation'.[4] Its report of 1932 was the basis of the more permanent legislation of 1934. Meanwhile, however, there was an immediate crisis in all out-of-work benefit and relief schemes with the deepening of the depression in 1931, as the deficits of the Unemployment Fund mounted to new heights, even though the Treasury had taken over the total current

[1] C. L. Mowat, *Britain Between the Wars* (1956 ed.), pp. 126–9.
[2] *Report of the Royal Commission on Local Government* (1928. Cmd. 3213); David C. Marsh, *National Insurance and Assistance in Great Britain* (1950), pp. 22–5.
[3] E. M. Burns, *op. cit.*, p. 26, quoting from a Ministry of Health circular of 1930.
[4] Marsh, p. 44, quoting P.E.P., *Report on British Social Services* (1937).

costs of the 'transitional' benefits. It led to drastic cuts in benefits and increases in contributions. The total weekly contribution per adult male worker was raised from 22½d. to 30d. per week, and the benefit rates were cut by about one-tenth. The terms on which benefit was granted were tightened up to the extent of reducing by some 700,000 the numbers receiving insurance benefits, matched by a rise of only about 250,000 in the numbers receiving transitional payments. Within a year about 180,000 persons were removed from the register altogether.[1]

Once a person had exhausted his insurance benefit, now reduced to a maximum of 26 weeks, he was forced to turn to the intermediate scheme, now called 'transitional', with a searching needs test, and the widespread bitterness resulting from reductions in the 'dole' because of earnings of other members of the family, or some small property, dates mainly from those years. The local standards of needs tests differed widely in practice, even after the Transitional Payments (Determination of Needs) Act of 1932 had been passed to make them uniform, while many deplored, with Sir Henry Betterton, the Minister of Labour, the 'complete divorce between the responsibility of the central authority, which is providing the money, and that of the local authority which disburses it'.[2] The total savings, compared with the costs of the earlier scheme which had brought down the Labour Government, was only £24 million in the first year, but with all its faults, this was the system which saw Britain through the worst of the depression from 1931 to 1934, until a more permanent solution could be devised.

The Holman Gregory Commission of 1930, noted above, reported in 1932, and on its Reports[3] was based the new Unemployment Act of 1934, which was to put the unemployment scheme at last on a sound and permanent footing. It was in two parts, dealing with insurance and assistance respectively. The insurance scheme was to remain actuarially sound, and watched over by an Unemployment Insurance Statutory Committee which was not subject to direct political pressures. In the event, with better trade leading up to the boom of 1937, and rates of unemployment much below the calculated break-even rate of 16¾% (the rate of 1934), the Fund succeeded not only in staying solvent, but could also afford to raise benefits and lower contributions, while paying off much of the accumulated debt. In 1936 agricultural workers were catered for by a new parallel scheme, and in 1937 several other groups formerly excluded were brought in.

For those whose spell out of work exceeded the limit of 26 weeks, and

---

[1] G. D. H. and Margaret Cole, *The Condition of Britain* (1937), chapter 4.
[2] H.o.C., 30.11.1933.
[3] *Interim Report of the Royal Commission on Unemployment Insurance* (1931. Cmd. 3872), *Final Report* (1932. Cmd. 4185).

for many of those outside the insurable classes altogether, the transitional benefits were to be replaced by a new scheme, administered by a central Unemployment Assistance Board, with its own staff of full-time officers, in place of the local Committees. This Board, like the Statutory Committee, was also to be taken out of politics, it was to guarantee national uniformity, all its funds save small token payments by local authorities were to come out of the national exchequer, and it was given fairly wide latitude in granting claims as long as 'capacity to work', 'availability for work' and 'need', less narrowly defined, were proved. It was to take over most able-bodied but uninsured persons from the Poor Law, and it was to pitch its benefits high enough to avoid any need for supplementation by it. In this way it was hoped to reduce the burden on the Poor Law, now administered by the Public Assistance Committees of the local authorities.

When the details were announced, however, it was found that the rates payable were in many cases below those paid earlier under the transitional scheme. There was a public outcry, especially by the organized unemployed themselves, popular indignation against the system of the 'dole' became greater than ever, and the Board was at once pitched back into the political arena. A Standstill Act of February 1935 left the old rates wherever they were more favourable, and kept the old Poor Law cases with the local authorities instead of transferring them to the Board. Two years were to elapse before the 'second appointed day', 1st April 1937, when the Board took over about 100,000 Poor Law cases, mostly able-bodied persons, and began everywhere to pay its own rates, which were generally scaled up so as not to lead to any actual reductions.

The growth in the number of those who had been unemployed so long that they had exhausted their insurance benefits was shown by the fact that those aided by the 'transitional' and 'assistance' schemes were throughout only slightly fewer than those who drew insurance benefits, while the aggregate sums paid out to the former were actually higher in most years. In spite of the existence of the Unemployment Assistance Board, there were still some 150,000 unemployed, plus 250,000 dependants, thrown on the Poor Law until March 1937. From April 1937 on (the second appointed day), their numbers shrunk to 30,000 and 40,000 respectively. In September 1939 those distressed by war and some other classes were added to the responsibility of the Board, and in March 1940, in view of its additional responsibilities, its name was changed to that of Assistance Board.

Public authorities also originated other measures of relief, besides direct benefit payments. Local schemes to help the depressed areas have been noted in chapter 3, section 4, above,[1] and the aid to land settlement

[1] A brief list will be found in the *Report of the Royal Commission on the Distribution of the Industrial Population* (Barlow Report) (1940. Cmd. 6153), pp. 146 ff.

was noted in the same chapter, section 5. Industrial Transfer Boards, established in 1928, helped individuals and whole families in their removal in search of work, though in practice voluntary migration achieved much more than assisted transfer. Until 1929 there were also substantial sums expended in assisting migration overseas.[1] The establishment of Government Training Centres, of residential Instructional Centres, and other means of training[2] had been of some help to young persons and to those returning from the armed services after the war; but in face of the general mass unemployment of the 1930's there seemed little purpose in learning a trade when fully skilled men were themselves still out of work.

Abroad, one of the main methods of dealing with unemployment was the provision of public works. In this country, as noted on p. 209 above, such policies enjoyed little official support, and were suspended in 1931 just at the time when the depression had reached really serious proportions. In the 1920's, however, they were of some importance. From 1921 on, local authorities undertook construction schemes, and there were some Government grants for the maintenance of public buildings and for afforestation, partly with the unemployed in mind. But the Central Government's contribution to road building in the 1920's came largely out of the Road Fund, and the important trunk road programme and five years' programme of 1929 were cut in 1931, for reasons of economy, when they might have been of the greatest use. The Unemployment Grants Committee itself spent £69·5 million between December 1920 and January 1932 assisting local authorities with public works, but this compared with the £600 million paid out in the same period in benefit and relief. A maximum of 60,000 men worked on these schemes in 1931, when total unemployment was over 2½ million. Even this grudging aid was suspended in 1931, and though public opinion became more favourable towards public works from 1935 on,[3] little was done before the war.

2. HOUSING, HEALTH AND OTHER WELFARE PROVISIONS

The social conscience of the Edwardians had been remarkably fertile of ideas and expedients, quite apart from the unemployment insurance scheme, and many of these came to be widely, even generally adopted by the subjects of George V. Among the most significant was the introduction of public subsidies for housing.

The nineteenth century believed that the housing of ordinary families

---

[1] pp. 282–3 below.
[2] R. C. Davison, *Unemployment Policy*, chapter 6, and *The Unemployed*, chapter 7.
[3] J. H. Richardson, *British Economic Foreign, Policy* (1936), p. 44.

could safely be left to the forces of unfettered demand and supply. The sorry results of this policy of *laissez-faire* in house building are with us still. Even the nineteenth century was forced to deal with the worst consequences of this unchecked town building for profit, from the 1840's onwards, on grounds of health, and from the 1890's on, also on grounds of the loss of amenities for the urban population as a whole.[1] The Housing and Town Planning Act of 1909 was the latest attempt to take account of the amenity value to the community lost or gained by private building, but still left all the initiative to local authorities, and the public provision of housing for the poorer classes before 1914, in spite of the enabling legislation of 1875 and 1890, was still little more than experimental, and was limited to some slum-clearance schemes of a few progressive town councils.

The war completely revolutionized the market for houses for letting. Rent control, imposed as a result of protests by Glasgow munition workers in 1915 to keep down the cost of living, reduced the real level of rents in a period of rising prices, though ultimately an increase of 40–50% on pre-war rents was permitted. After the war, the housing shortage caused by the interruption of building, and aggravated by the expectations aroused by the slogan of 'homes for heroes', would have raised rents so much beyond the pre-war figures as to cause widespread hardship and unrest. Hence rent control was kept on after 1918 and was, in fact, extended to more expensive property in 1919 and 1920.

Thus the returns on house owning were kept low, and new houses, even if built to pre-war standards, would have, to be economic, to let at rents so much higher than 'controlled' dwellings as to make their occupation unlikely. But building could not be kept down to pre-war standards; generally rising expectations of civilized minima for working-class houses, well expressed by the recommendations of the Tudor Walters Committee of the Ministry of Reconstruction in 1917–18, made it necessary to plan post-war houses on a more generous scale, further widening the gap between the economic rents required for new buildings and the old controlled rents. As a result of these developments, three interrelated conditions came to determine the housing market from 1919 onward. First, there remained an intractable shortage of working-class dwellings to let at current (controlled) rents; secondly, the level of rents of a large proportion of dwellings was artificial, being either controlled below its market level or subsidized; and thirdly, a gap had opened between the weekly rent which wage-earners were prepared to pay, and the costs of the sort of accommodation which they (and society) as a whole were coming to expect as a minimum.

The shortage of houses in 1919 has been variously computed at between

[1] W. Ashworth, *The Genesis of Modern British Town Planning* (1954).

600,000 and 1 million,[1] mostly in the cheaper range of houses. Since private investment in houses built for letting had been made unprofitable, it was certain that none would take place, yet a building programme had become an urgent social and political necessity. The obvious solution was a Government subsidy, and in the current generous mood regarding public expenditure this met with no serious opposition. It was made all the easier since the need was believed to be temporary only. The diagnosis of at least one official commission that the shortage was likely to be endemic[2] was held to apply, at most, to North Britain only, especially Tyneside and Scotland, where overcrowding was well known to be far worse than further south. In the event, housing needs grew faster than new dwellings and subsidized housing became one of the corner-stones of public welfare provision.

The first measure, the Housing and Town Planning Act of 1919 (the 'Addison Act'), bore all the signs of a hurried emergency measure. It introduced three major new principles: the building of houses was made obligatory on the local authorities rather than permissive, it was to fill general needs, not merely to apply to slum clearance, and it was to attract a Government subsidy. Houses built by local authorities were to receive a subsidy to the extent of the entire loss beyond the proceeds of a penny rate, and subsidies were available also for Housing Associations and non-profit-making Housing Trusts. Private enterprise was excluded, but could claim a capital subsidy of £260 a house under certain easy conditions.

The Ministry of Health had certain powers over the building and the rents charged, and this ensured that subsidized houses were indeed built for those in most urgent need, irrespective of the rent they could afford. But the overriding need to produce the maximum number of houses at any cost, and the fact that the Act gave no incentive to local authorities, who were in immediate charge of the building, to practise economy at a time of shortages and rising prices in the boom of 1919–20, caused the building under the Addison Act to be completed on the most extravagant terms. A large part of the subsidies flowed directly into the pockets of profiteering builders, to the tune of £1 a week per house. In March 1921, tenders for a non-parlour type of house reached £838 a house, compared with £371 in January 1923 and about £300 ten years later. Building under the Addison Act was suspended in 1922 as part of the economy campaign of that year. By March 1923, the houses built in England and Wales under the legislation of 1919 totalled 155,000 by local authorities, 44,000

---

[1] p. 240 above; W. F. Stolper,'British Monetary Policy and the Housing Boom', *Q.J.E.*, 56/1, part II, Nov. 1941, p. 90; Seymour J. Price, *Building Societies, Their Origin and History* (1958), pp. 292–3.

[2] *Royal Commission on Housing of the Industrial Population in Scotland* (1917. Cd. 8731).

by private enterprise with subsidy, and 54,000 without. The additional need since 1919, because of the net increase in the number of families, was estimated at 460,000 in the same period, so that the shortage had increased by some 200,000 dwellings, in spite of the extravagant spending.[1]

New principles of subsidizing building became necessary, and were introduced by the ('Chamberlain') Housing Act of 1923. Local economies were encouraged by limiting the subsidy for each house to £6 a year for 20 years, all the remainder of the loss to be borne by the local authority. This method proved effective in ensuring local economy in housing management, and was retained in later legislation; but the Act failed to encourage the building of working-class housing (if that, indeed, was its object), for under the high rate of interest then ruling, the subsidy was too low to permit rents which working-class families could afford. On the other hand, the Act was used by private enterprise builders, and nearly 400,000 of their houses ultimately claimed and received subsidies under it, mostly built for sale to the middle classes. The Act also provided for subsidies for slum clearance, but the housing shortage was too great to demolish any existing accommodation, no matter how unsatisfactory.

The tendency of the Chamberlain Act to use the taxpayers' money to subsidize the housing of those who needed it least, while leaving the large working-class demand unfulfilled, was redressed to some extent by the Labour Government in the following year. Its ('Wheatley') Housing (Financial Provisions) Act of 1924 raised the subsidy per house to £9 a year for forty years in the towns, and higher still in agricultural parishes, provided that the house was built for letting, that it was built at 'fair wages', and that the rent did not exceed the 'appropriate normal rent' of the district, unless the loss falling thereby on the rates were to become £4 10s. a year or over.[2] Local authorities were stimulated by its provisions to provide large numbers of houses for the better-off artisan classes, but since the rates were calculated so as to leave little or no profit to the house owner, private enterprise was not attracted by them, and preferred the Chamberlain scheme, the two schemes continuing side by side, one used by local authorities, the other by private builders. In 1927 the rates of subsidies on both were drastically reduced, and in 1929 the Chamberlain Act subsidies were ended, the Wheatley subsidies being abolished by the Housing Act of 1933.

The total number of houses built under the two schemes in England and Wales was nearly 960,000, of which 580,000 were provided by local authorities (358,000 of them by 1930) and 378,000 by private enterprise,

[1] R. L. Reiss, *Municipal and Private Enterprise Housing* (1945), pp. 32 ff.; Marian Bowley, *Housing and the State* (1945), chapter 2; C. L. Mowat, *Britain Between the Wars* (1956 ed.), p. 44.
[2] Richard W. Lyman, *The First Labour Government, 1924* (1957), chapter 8.

nearly all of them by 1930. Including some 536,000 houses built since the end of the war without subsidy, the total of new houses built in England and Wales by the end of 1930 was almost 1½ million, and from 1926 onwards the rate of construction had been 200,000 dwellings a year. Official opinion began to believe that the basic housing needs were now being met, and the general subsidy schemes began to be wound up, the subsidies of the 1930's being designed for special purposes only, such as slum clearance and the abolition of overcrowding.

At the same time, rent control was also eased. The Act of 1923 had permitted the decontrol of rents on changes of tenancy, but the effects of this measure were necessarily limited. It was the Housing Act of 1933 which freed all large houses (of £45 rateable value or over in London, £45 or over in Scotland and £35 or over elsewhere) from rent control, continued decontrol on change of tenancy only in medium-sized houses (below these limits and above £20, £26 5s. and £13 respectively) and maintained full rent control in houses below these sizes, of which there were about 4 million, or 40% of the total. The Housing Act of 1938, after six years of building boom, maintained rent control for the smaller buildings (below the limits of £35, £35 and £20 respectively).

These rent control provisions reflected the fact that, in spite of the repeal of the general housing subsidies, the housing shortage was by no means over for the poorer classes of the community.[1] The number of separate families, a rough guide to the housing needs of the community, was still growing more rapidly than the number of dwellings until 1930. In 1931 the number of unoccupied houses was still round the remarkably low figure of 200,000 for the United Kingdom as a whole. But in this total housing market, the demand for the more expensive accommodation was now being met, and successive Governments were increasingly unwilling to subsidize those who could afford the lowest rents only. Instead, a private-enterprise housing boom developed in the 1930's[2] which provided almost 3 million new houses, virtually all for better-off owners and tenants. Those who occupied the cheaper houses could, in theory, find accommodation by 'filtering up' into dwellings thus vacated,[3] but mobility was low, partly as a result of rent control, and by the end of the 1930's there developed strong signs of an over-supply of expensive houses, while the shortage of cheap accommodation was as acute as ever.

The general subsidies had thus been cut off too soon while the legislation of the 1930's dealt with special cases only. The first of the new Acts, the ('Greenwood') Housing Act of 1930, offered Government subsidies to

[1] G. D. H. and M. I. Cole, *The Condition of Britain* (1937), chapter 3.
[2] pp. 239–40 above.
[3] A. P. Becker, 'Housing in England and Wales during the Business Depression of the 1930's', *Ec. Hist. Rev.*, 2nd S.. 3/3, 1951, p. 323.

local authorities for slum clearance schemes.[1] Up to then, it was estimated that only 11,000 slum houses in England and Wales had been pulled down and replaced, largely because of the absolute shortage of dwellings, but the new Act started from the assumption that the shortage was beginning to wane, and that replacement of slum property could begin. With the repeal of the existing general subsidies in 1933, it became the main effective subsidy scheme.

The Greenwood Act had the novel feature that subsidies varied, not with the number of houses, but with the number of people displaced and rehoused. The local authorities were given £2 5s. a year for forty years per person re-housed, with certain additions in special cases, and thus had a strong incentive to tackle the most populous areas first, and to provide new houses as fast as the old slums were pulled down. Further, all authorities with populations of over 20,000 were required to prepare five-year schemes for slum clearance, and continue them until all slums had been removed. The response to this was poor at first, but the Housing (Financial Provisions) Act of 1933, which ended the other subsidies, led local authorities to concentrate on slum clearance. Even then, the plans envisaged the scrapping of only 250,000 houses (out of at least 750,000 unfit), the building of 285,000 and the re-housing of $1\frac{1}{4}$ million people.

In 1935 a further Act extended subsidies to building designed to abate overcrowding, especially if high-cost flats were required. By then, according to the Report on Overcrowding in England and Wales, published by the Ministry of Health in 1936,[2] only 3·8% of dwellings were judged to be 'overcrowded', but this figure hid large regional concentrations, especially on Tyneside, where working-class flats were still typical, and in Scotland (not covered by this Report) where 22·6% of working class dwellings were overcrowded in 1935. In any case, 'overcrowding' depends on the standards adopted, and a slightly more rigorous standard produced an average of 9·5%.[3] The Act of 1935 also allowed local authorities to spread their housing costs so that council tenants in houses built under different schemes might pay comparable rents.

The consolidating Housing Act of 1936 added, in Part II, provisions which forced private owners of small property to undertake adequate repairs and gave local authorities power to clear slum property without compensation, in default. Part III dealt with slum clearance, including complete clearances of 'redevelopment areas', Part IV with abatement of overcrowding, and Part V with powers of local authorities to provide additional dwellings. The subsidy rates were reduced for general cases, and raised for special cases, like urban flats and agricultural areas, by the

---

[1] E. D. (Lord) Simon, *The Anti-Slum Campaign* (1933), esp. chapter 13.
[2] Ministry of Health, *Report of Overcrowding Survey of England and Wales* (1936).
[3] Mowat, p. 507; G. D. H. Cole, *Building and Planning* (1945), pp. 102–3.

Housing Act of 1938. The total number of houses built in England and Wales under the legislation of the 1930's was 289,000 by local authorities and 8,000 by private enterprise.

With this selective building by local authorities and the private housing boom in full swing, much of the overcrowding of 1936 had been abolished by 1939. Of the 1¼ million persons to be rehoused, only 239,000 were left in their old quarters, nearly half of them in five cities—London, Leeds, Liverpool, Manchester and Sheffield. In many areas the five-year plans had been completed, and in others they were all but complete on the outbreak of war. But elsewhere slums were newly developing: in 1939, some 550,000 dwellings were still left which were fit for destruction under the slum clearance Acts, and 350,000 'marginal' dwellings, likely to become slums in a few years' time.

In Scotland, where housing needs were far greater and conditions far worse, more houses were built by local authorities and fewer by private enterprise than in England and Wales. The total number of dwellings completed between the wars in Great Britain compared as follows (in 000):[1]

Built in:	England and Wales	Scotland	Great Britain
By local authorities	1,163	230	1,393
By private enterprise with subsidy	433	43	476
By private enterprise without subsidy	2,596	63	2,659
	4,192	336	4,528

New building thus amounted to 4½ million *dwellings*, of which over two-thirds were built by private enterprise. Virtually all of these, except for 48,000 built by Housing Associations, were for letting to middle-class tenants or for sale to owner-occupiers, again for the middle classes and the top group of artisans. Many of the remainder, built by local authorities, were also let at rents which could be afforded by the better-off workers only.

Bearing in mind that about 700,000 dwellings were pulled down or converted, the net addition was of the order of 3·8 million. The total stock of *houses* in the United Kingdom increased from 9¼ million in 1920 to over 12½ million, or a net addition of 3¼ million.[2] Since the number of families was estimated to have risen by 3·3 million, the gap was closed, mainly in the late 1930's, to the extent of half a million dwellings since 1919, or not quite enough to meet the estimated shortage of 1919. There

[1] Reiss, p. 15; Miss Bowley's figures vary slightly from these, *op. cit.*, Table 2, p. 271, and Appx. I.
[2] Richard Stone, *The Measurement of Consumers' Expenditure and Behaviour in the United Kingdom, 1920–1938*, Vol. 1 (Cambridge, 1954), Table 92 and chapter 15.

was still a considerable shortage of cheap accommodation in 1938, besides the slum property condemned and waiting to be cleared and replaced.[1]

Nevertheless, there had been substantial improvements. Over one-third of the stock of houses in existence had been built in the past twenty years, to much higher standards than pre-war working-class dwellings. The Town and Country Planning Act of 1932, which gave local authorities powers to determine the uses of areas, was beginning to be applied,[2] and together with the general acceptance of the housing estate as the main form of large-scale building[3] led to the consideration not only of individual houses, but of the total amenities of urban living. Compared with pre-war years, 'the majority of those who benefited by the increase in the national income and by the more equal distribution of this income, tended to enjoy the bulk of their gains in terms of better housing conditions'.[4] Virtually all those with weekly incomes of under £3, and most of those with incomes £3–5, had to rely on old controlled accommodation or on new housing provided by the public authorities. Housing, like public health and education, was increasingly recognized to be an important public service.

Health insurance had covered from its beginnings in 1911 many more persons than the selective trade groups embraced by unemployment insurance. By 1921, over 15 million persons were included, and by 1938 the numbers insured had increased to nearly 20 million. Only the numbers of those insured under the Widows', Orphans' and Old-Age Pensions scheme exceeded those insured by the health scheme (by about 1 million) in 1938.[5] In this period the basic principles of health insurance, including the central position of the 'approved societies', remained unchanged, in spite of much criticism of the wasteful and uneven administration of the latter.

There was little attempt made to integrate the insurance scheme with the public health legislation with its very different origins and administrative structure, in spite of the establishment of the Ministry of Health in 1919, responsible for both, but there were other changes.[6] As early as January 1918, the Maclean Committee, one of the Committees of the Ministry

---

[1] M. J. Elsas, *Housing Before the War and After* (1942).

[2] *Report of the Royal Commission on the Distribution of the Industrial Population* (Barlow Report) (1940. Cmd. 6153), chapter 8; *Report of the Committee on Land Utilization in Rural Areas* (Scott Report) (1942. Cmd. 6378), chapter 6.

[3] H. and M. Wickwar, *The Social Services, an Historical Survey* (2nd ed., 1949), pp. 144–52.

[4] Mark Abrams, *The Condition of the British People, 1911–1945* (1945), p. 44.

[5] Alan T. Peacock, *The Economics of National Insurance* (1952), p. 15; D. C. Marsh, *National Insurance and Assistance in Great Britain* (1950), chapter 3; P.E.P., *Report on the British Social Services* (1937), p. 123.

[6] Sir George Newman, *The Building of a Nation's Health* (1939), chapter 4.

of Reconstruction, suggested the abolition of the Poor Law Unions, and the transfer of their duties and property (including the hospitals) to County and County Borough Councils. This reform was accomplished by Chamberlain's Local Government Act of 1929. Others had to wait longer. The Lawrence Commission, appointed in 1924 and reporting in 1926,[1] deplored the separation of the health insurance scheme from the public health authorities, with their duties in the field of preventive medicine, and the great variety in the additional benefits provided by the various approved societies. It proposed to make generally available to all insured persons, first, complete dental services, secondly, an 'out-patient service' to supplement the work of the general practitioners, thirdly, allowances for dependants of the insured sick, and fourthly, an extension of maternity benefits, in collaboration with the local authorities. A minority report went much further, asking for treatment for dependants among the urgent next steps within the scheme. The majority report, however, was more impressed with the immediate needs for economy, and in practice no action followed its report.[2]

Meanwhile, the variety of standards and the lack of co-ordination among the voluntary hospitals had been criticized by an Interim Report of the Dawson Committee in 1920, and by the Report of the Cave Committee in 1921, and as a result, a Voluntary Hospitals Commission was set up, under Lord Onslow, with a Government grant which was to be used to induce them to collaborate more closely. The Boards of the voluntary hospitals proved difficult to rouse to action, however, until the Council (ex-Poor Law) hospitals in 1930 provided some direct competitive spur. Only in the 1930's were standards gradually raised, and some collaboration between the local authority hospitals and the voluntary hospitals in their regions established. Hospital contributory schemes increased greatly, and by 1937 there were at least 5 million voluntary contributors, paying for at least 10 million persons, including dependants, yet the voluntary hospitals found it hard to make ends meet, and could not enlarge the number of beds; instead more contributing patients were treated in Council hospitals, while the total number of beds available remained distinctly low.[3]

Infectious diseases had been the responsibility of the local health authorities since the nineteenth century, and many of them maintained extensive isolation hospitals, tuberculosis sanatoria and similar institutions. In 1918, the Maternity and Child Welfare Act gave local authorities greater power to extend their facilities in this field, including the provision

[1] *Royal Commission on National Health Insurance* (1926. Cmd. 2596); Hermann Levy, *National Health Insurance* (Cambridge, 1944), chapters 3, 5.

[2] J. S. Ross, *The National Health Service in Great Britain* (1952), pp. 41–56.

[3] Levy, pp. 167–71; W. M. Frazer, *A History of English Public Health, 1834–1939* (1950), pp. 390–3; P.E.P., *The British Health Services* (1937), p. 16; Harry Eckstein, *The English Health Service* (Cambridge. Mass., 1959), chapter 5.

of clinics, and the Midwives Act of 1936 required them to provide trained midwives. In a little over twenty years, the number of Infant Welfare Centres had risen from a handful to 3,580 in 1938, and the number of ante-natal clinics to 1,795 in England and Wales.[1] The Venereal Diseases Act of 1917 and the Mental Treatment Act of 1930 opened up new fields in the public health services. The Blind Persons Act of 1920 made Counties and County Boroughs responsible for the welfare of the blind, and granted them non-contributory pensions at the age of 50, lowered to 40 in 1938. Meanwhile, the Nurses Registration Act of 1919 gave an enhanced status to the nursing profession, followed later by similar statutory qualifications for other medical auxiliaries.

Thus at the end of the 1930's, there had been substantial progress made in many separate fields, without bringing the different aspects of public health administrations any closer together, except, perhaps, in the hands of the Local Medical Officer of Health. The insurance scheme covered only about half the adult population; it excluded some 15 million wives of insured persons except when they were child-bearing, and it failed to provide most types of specialist and hospital treatment even for those it covered. Youths of 14–16 years of age were brought in only in 1938, and children between one and five not at all.

The local authorities were entirely separate from those administering the insurance scheme, yet they gave medical and dental inspection, but not always treatment, to schoolchildren[2] and provided school milk to 3·2 million children in 1937, free to ½ million of them and to the rest at reduced prices. They were also responsible for medical services in which the protection of the public was as important as the cure of the individual, such as the treatment of infectious diseases, venereal diseases and insanity, as well as for more general legislation as to building, sewage, slaughter houses, food adulteration, and so forth. The Acts relating to most of these functions were consolidated by the Public Health Act of 1936, extended by the Food and Drugs Act of 1938 which adopted clauses found useful in local Acts. Since taking over the functions of the Poor Law Guardians in 1930, the Public Assistance Committees of the larger local authorities also controlled many hospitals, and were responsible for all medical assistance required by paupers. The other public hospitals, including the teaching hospitals, continued to be managed by yet a third set of authorities, the voluntary committees. Of the 3,029 hospitals in existence in Great Britain, 1,013 were voluntary, 116 were general public hospitals, 523 were Poor Law hospitals, and the rest was made up of special hospitals and sanatoria managed by the local authorities.[3]

[1] R. M. Titmuss, *Birth, Poverty and Health* (1943), p. 33.
[2] H. and M. Wickwar, *The Social Services, an Historical Survey* (2nd ed., 1949), p. 120. [3] C. L. Mowat, *Britain Between the Wars* (1956 ed.), p. 497.

Efforts to unify these various services were, however, becoming more numerous. In 1930 the B.M.A. issued its *Proposals for a General Medical Service for the Nation*, brought up to date and re-issued in 1938, which urged the extension of health insurance to all of like economic status as those in the scheme, and to all the members of their families. It further proposed to extend benefits to include specialist and consultant services, as well as ophthalmic, dental and maternity services. Finally, it suggested that all public health administration should be concentrated on single, all-embracing local authorities of fair size, except for hospitals, which should be treated on a regional basis.

In 1937, the authors of a most comprehensive report on the British Health Services, published by P.E.P., were also in favour of a major reorganization.[1] More significant was the report of the Cathcart Committee on Scottish Health Services, which sat from 1933 to 1936.[2] The Committee was greatly impressed by the inferior state of the national health of Scotland compared with that of England and Wales (not to mention other countries), though legislation had followed closely parallel paths after the foundation of the Scottish Board of Health in 1919. It demanded an extension of insurance benefits and a comprehensive national health policy, to aim at 'the fitness of the people', including preventive as well as curative measures. Thus public opinion before the war was being prepared for the changes that were to occur after it.

The third pre-1914 benefit scheme, the non-contributory old-age pension, was not changed in principle in this period, but payments were raised to 10s. a week and the income limits (above which no payments were made) were raised periodically also. The Old Age and Widows' Pension Act of 1940 provided for pensioners to draw supplementary pensions from the Assistance Board, after a means test. This Act also reduced, for no very convincing reason, the retirement age for women to 60 in place of 65.

Superimposed on this scheme were the new contributory pensions which would, in due course, be paid out as a right and without a needs test, and begin at the age of 65 instead of 70. They were linked with several other benefits in the comprehensive Widows', Orphans' and Old Age Contributory Pensions Act of 1925. Apart from old-age pensions for insured men (at 10s. a week), there were to be pensions for widows, children's allowances for widows, and payments for orphans of insured persons. An Act of 1937 opened this scheme, on a voluntary basis, to independent workers of small means.[3]

[1] P.E.P., *op. cit.*, p. 25.
[2] *Report of the Committee on the Scottish Health Services* (1936. Cmd. 5204).
[3] Marsh, *op. cit.*, chapter 6; Charles E. Clarke, *Social Insurance in Britain* (Cambridge, 1950), pp. 7-9.

The war and the brave hopes for the post-war world brought major changes in the field of public education also. The Fisher Education Act of 1918 gave the Board of Education, and the Counties and County Boroughs, as local education authorities, strong encouragement and greater power to develop a comprehensive system of education from the nursery school to the evening class. The Board's financial aid to the local authorities was increased to at least 50% of expenditure, and was awarded on a different basis which implied a new partnership between them. Full-time education to the age of 14 was made compulsory by revoking all concessions to part-timers and early leavers. Local authorities were permitted to raise the school-leaving age to 15, or, in default, to provide day continuation schools for youths aged 14 to 16 for one day a week. Finally, the noble aspiration was written into the Act, that 'adequate provision shall be made in order to secure that children and young persons shall not be debarred from receiving the benefits of any form of education by which they are capable of profiting through inability to pay fees'.

The hopes which had inspired the Act were largely disappointed. The Geddes axe and the general spirit of economy after 1921 killed all continuation schools except the one at Rugby. The school-leaving age remained at 14, and measures to tackle the overcrowding, the poor equipment, the lack of staff in so many of the ordinary Council schools were deferred for yet another decade. Yet some impetus remained from the Fisher Act, particularly in the field of secondary education. The Hadow Report,[1] the work of a committee appointed by the Labour Government of 1924, was one of its consequences, and in dealing with the problem of finding a more valuable content for the education of those who now stayed on to the age of 14 and would soon stay on until 15, it made some proposals that were to be of far-reaching significance.

Assuming that the school-leaving age would be raised to 15 within five years, i.e. by 1932, it would be necessary to end 'elementary' education at 11, and devise more useful curricula beyond that age after separating out children of differing abilities. In addition to the existing grammar schools and the junior technical and trade schools with their strong vocational bias, there should also be so-called 'modern' schools, selective and non-selective, which should combine practical teaching with a liberal approach, and should thus fill a gap between the other two types, while claiming staff and equipment comparable with those of grammar schools. 'Senior' classes should be provided preferably away from the 'primary' school for children under 11, and transfer between the different types of school should be made possible.

The Report was adopted, and reorganization proceeded throughout

[1] Board of Education Consultative Committee, *Report on the Education of the Adolescent* (1927).

the rest of the inter-war period, though progress was slow in rural areas and among the 'voluntary schools' in which one-third of the children of elementary schools were partly provided for and controlled by the churches.[1] By 1938, 63·5% of all children over 11 were in reorganized ('modern') schools, and the innovations introduced by the Hadow Report had become common property.[2] The influential Spens Committee, appointed in 1933 and reporting in 1938,[3] further elaborated the idea of a type of school having parity of esteem with the grammar school, but giving a more practical education in place of the stress on classics and the preparation for a University. It suggested the foundation of 'Technical High Schools', giving a general education from 11 to 13, and a more scientific, if liberal, education from 13+ to 16+, with a leaving certificate after a minimum leaving age of 16.[4]

The extension of schooling to 15, planned by the Labour Government for 1931, was thwarted largely by the opposition of the churches, but was re-enacted in 1936, when the churches were appeased by large grants. Timed to come into effect in September 1939, it was again held up, by the war. Throughout the period, children from poorer homes continued in practice to be denied the opportunity of higher education in all but the most exceptional circumstances.[5] Higher education was still mainly for the rich, rather than for those best able to profit by it.

Taken all in all, the more generous impulses and the more ambitious social demands of the war years had not been entirely rendered nugatory by the reaction of the early 1920's. There was a considerable expansion of the public services into new fields, formerly cultivated by the voluntary social services or by private enterprise. There was, at the same time, a gradual abandonment of comprehensive poor relief based on destitution, and its replacement by contractual insurance benefits, or specialist services provided on a basis of common citizenship. Administratively, also, there was a distinct movement away from *ad hoc* bodies, and the transfer of functions to the many-sided, elective, normal local authority, supported by Exchequer grants.[6] These tendencies appeared to meet with general approval; and the last years before the war saw numerous proposals, made by official and unofficial bodies of influence, to proceed farther in the same direction.

[1] H. and M. Wickwar, *The Social Services*, pp. 73–82; G. A. N. Lowndes, *The Silent Social Revolution* (1937), p. 101.
[2] A. M. Carr-Saunders and D. Caradog Jones, *A Survey of the Social Structure of England and Wales* (Oxford, 2nd ed., 1937), chapter 11.
[3] Board of Education Consultative Committee, *Report on Secondary Education* (1938).
[4] John Graves, *Policy and Progress in Secondary Education, 1902–1942* (1943), chapters 16–22.
[5] K. Lindsay, *Social Progress and Educational Waste* (1926); R. M. Titmuss, *op. cit.*, pp. 63–4.   [6] P.E.P., *Social Services*, pp. 11–12.

3. THE TRADE UNIONS AND THE POLITICS OF POVERTY

The war had brought about a remarkable increase in the power, status and size of trade unions. The peak of their membership was reached in 1920, when it stood at 8·3 million; after that it declined to 4·4 million in 1933, to recover again to 6·3 million in 1939. The membership of the unions affiliated to the Trades Union Congress in these years was 6·5 million, 3·5 million and 4·7 million respectively.[1] Several factors accounted for the war-time growth. There was the unions' success in raising wages and improving conditions, especially for unskilled workers and women workers, even though it was based on a price inflation and a labour shortage. The automatic application of war-time arbitration awards to all workers, including non-unionists, provided a potent demonstration of the unions' powers and functions to the latter. The growth of the community spirit, fostered during the war, and the knowledge of common hardships, helped to claim adherence and loyalty. Full employment removed the former fear of the blacklisting of union members. The momentous leftward impetus given to political thought by the heightened political awareness of soldiers and war workers, further focussed attention on the unions and on the role they might play. Conversely, the inability of the unions to hold their high money wage level after 1920 (though adequately explained by the general deflation), the mass unemployment, the disillusionment with the political impotence of Labour, and the return of the spirit of individualistic self-seeking were not without influence on the decline of trade-union membership after 1920.

In their appearances before manpower boards, arbitration tribunals and various public authorities in the war, the trade unions within each industry had been forced to collaborate closely, and this encouraged a movement towards the amalgamation of the numerous small societies to be found in most industries, into larger bodies. The Trade Union (Amalgamation) Act of 1917 made amalgamation easier, and the widespread support for industrial unionism given by many of the shop stewards' committees during the war[2] worked in the same direction. The outcome was a series of major amalgamations establishing the small number of very large unions which have dominated the union world to the present day. Among them was the amalgamation of the A.S.E. with nine smaller societies in 1920 to form the Amalgamated Engineering Union, the National Union of Foundry Workers formed in the same year, the N.U. of General and Municipal Workers in 1924, the Transport and General Workers' Union in 1922, the Amalgamated Union of Building Trade

[1] N. Barou, *British Trade Unions* (1947), Appx. XIV.
[2] Branko Pribićević, *The Shop Stewards' Movement and Workers' Control, 1910–1922* (Oxford, 1959).

Workers in 1921, the Amalgamated Society of Woodworkers in 1921, and the Iron and Steel Trades Confederation in 1917.[1] Other amalgamations formed in the years 1920-2 led to the formation of the N.U. of Textile Workers, the N.U. of Distributive and Allied Workers, the N.U. of Printing, Bookbinding and Paper Workers, the Union of Post Office Workers, the Tailors' and Garment Workers' Union, the Civil Service Clerical Association, the N.U. of Sheet Metal Workers and the N.U. of Blastfurnacemen.

These amalgamations and others like them gave an appearance of greater strength to the unions concerned. But the resultant large societies, having several hundred thousand members each, were not only burdened in the first instance by an over-large staff, too many conflicting rules, varying contribution systems and other teething troubles; even in the longer run, size, while likely to affect the character of trade unionism in various ways, was not necessarily bound to strengthen it. There inevitably developed a large full-time bureaucracy, not in immediate contact with members' problems; the voice and power of the local branch was necessarily diminished in national councils, and this contributed both to the growth of apathy among members, and to the outbreaks of unofficial strikes, signs that communication with the union leadership had broken down. The leaders themselves, instead of having spent their younger years battling for their society, came increasingly to be men who had worked their way up inside a safe, strong, hierarchical and generally recognized organization, more concerned to preserve peace with employers and to safeguard their benefit funds than to sanction more positive or adventurous drives to recruit new members or raise wages.

This tendency to settle down to respectable and responsible trade union policies became more evident after 1926, the year of the General Strike. By contrast, before about 1906 a policy of caution had been obligatory on many unions because of their weakness. The years in between, forming an interlude of stationary real wages in the secular upward movement of working-class living standards,[2] and interrupted by the war which gave its own strong impetus to trade union militancy, formed a unique period in which trade unions were both strong enough, and militant enough, to challenge their employers repeatedly and per-

---

[1] J. B. Jefferys, *The Story of the Engineers, 1800-1945* (1945), pp. 191-4; H. J. Fyrth and Henry Collins, *The Foundry Workers, a Trade Union History* (1959), pp. 151-8; H. A. Clegg, *General Union* (Oxford, 1954), Part I; V. L. Allen, *Trade Union Leadership* (1957), chapter 3 and Appendices; Alan Bullock, *The Life and Times of Ernest Bevin*, Vol. I (1960), pp. 153 ff.; (Arthur Pugh) *Men of Steel* (1951), chapter 13; R. W. Postgate, *The Builders' History* (1923), chapter 18; S. Higgenbottam, *Our Society's History* (1939); G. D. H. Cole, *Organised Labour* (1924), Part 4; P.E.P., *British Trade Unionism* (1948), pp. 97, 103-4.
[2] E. H. Phelps-Brown, *The Growth of British Industrial Relations* (1959), p. 354.

sistently, both in narrow skirmishes and on a broad front. There were four main issues in the strikes of this watershed of trade union history: first, the recognition of trade unions by employers; secondly, increases in wages in the era of rising prices up to 1920, and resistance to the attempts to cut wage costs ahead of prices in the slump years afterwards; thirdly, the integration of new types of skill or semi-skilled work, from machine minding to bus driving, into the old-established categories of skilled, apprenticed crafts; and fourthly, the permanent retention of some of the gains in working conditions achieved in the period of labour shortage, 1915–20, above all, the shorter working week without loss of pay, introduced in most industries in 1919–20.[1] In addition, there were the political demands: 'Labour is challenging the whole structure of capitalist industry as it now exists,' wrote one group of moderate leaders in 1919; 'it demands a system of industrial control which shall be truly democratic in character.'[2]

The earliest of the important post-war strikes took place on the Clyde, the storm centre of the war years, and in Belfast, where the engineers, led by their shop stewards, came out for a forty and forty-four hour week respectively in January and February 1919. They were defeated, but not without violent street battles and many arrests. Perhaps more significant for the unsettled conditions of the times was the police strike, in July 1919, following a successful action a year earlier, but ending in the defeat of the strikers and legislation outlawing the union.[3] The miners' threat to strike for the nationalization of coal in February 1919 had been staved off by the appointment of the Sankey Commission, and by its report in favour of nationalization, which it was believed the Government would accept, but in June there was a strike of cotton workers, and in July of Yorkshire miners. The national railway strike of September–October 1919, to enforce a wage settlement, was important for being, in effect, conducted against the Government which was then still administering the railways, and for the widespread publicity, achieved by skilful propaganda, as well as the large amount of sympathy it aroused among many other transport workers and the public at large.[4]

There were other disputes, concerned mainly with purely industrial questions. The foundry workers struck for four months for a wage increase, but had to go back, defeated, in January 1920. In the same year a Special Court of Inquiry was set up under the Industrial Courts Act to hear the

---

[1] See p. 90 above.

[2] D. F. MacDonald, *The State and the Trade Unions* (1960), p. 98.

[3] V. L. Allen, 'The National Union of Police and Prison Officers', *Ec. Hist. Rev.*, 2nd S., 11/1, 1958.

[4] G. D. H. Cole, *A Short History of the British Working-Class Movement, 1789–1947* (1952 ed.), pp. 392–3; G. W. Alcock, *Fifty Years of Railway Trade Unionism* (1922).

case of the Transport Workers' Federation for higher wages and de-casualization in the docks. The union's case was brilliantly presented by Ernest Bevin, who earned the title the 'Dockers' K.C.' by his advocacy, and the court awarded a national minimum wage as well as proposing a scheme for regulating the labour market at the docks, though this latter was ignored by the employers. The largest of the post-war disputes outside the coal mining industry began in March 1922, when the engineering employers locked out all members of the A.E.U. and of 47 other unions in their industry over the refusal of the men to permit unlimited overtime working at the discretion of the employers—the issue of 'managerial functions'. The struggle went on until June when the men, having exhausted their funds, returned to work on the employers' terms.

The high incidence of strikes in the post-war years is brought out in the following tabulation:[1]

Average of Years	No. of Strikes Beginning in Year	Workers Involved in Strikes Beginning in Year (million)	Working Days Lost by Strikes During the Year (million)
1911–14	1,034	0·88	17·9
1915–18	775	0·68	4·2
1919–21	1,241	2·11	49·1
1922–26[2]	568	0·63	38·8[3]
1927–39	570	0·31	3·1

The industrial unrest illustrated by these strike statistics was combined with much political activity on the part of labour. The electoral defeat in the 'coupon election' of 1918 was, to some extent, neutralized by sweeping victories of Labour candidates in the municipal elections in November 1919. In the General Election of November 1923, Labour polled 4,350,000 votes, only 1 million fewer than the Conservatives. With 258 seats going to the latter, 192 to Labour, and 157 to Asquith's Liberals, the result was the formation of the first Labour Government early in 1924, governing with Liberal support.[4] Though the Government did not last out the year, Labour was henceforth the official opposition in the years in which it did not form the Government.

A bare four years earlier, in 1919 or 1920, the temper of the working classes had been such that Liberal support for a Labour Government would

[1] K. G. J. C. Knowles, *Strikes—A Study in Industrial Conflict* (Oxford, 1952), Appx. Table 1. [2] Excluding the General Strike.
[3] Average 1922–5; 11·7 million.
[4] C. L. Mowat, *Britain Between the Wars* (1956 ed.), pp. 145, 168 ff.; B. C. Roberts, *The Trades Union Congress, 1868–1921* (1958), pp. 315 ff.

have been very doubtful indeed. The war had left a relic of class hatred, and with the example of the Bolshevik Revolution and other Continental revolutions before them, the working classes took to more revolutionary politics. 'Nationalization of the mines, the railways, and the land; workers' control of industry; a capital levy; work or maintenance; an end to class distinction; the abolition of poverty and riches—these were the slogans which captured a considerable section of the working classes.' [1] The high point of activity, perhaps, occurred in August 1920, when a 'Council of Action' was set up by the Labour Party Executive and the Parliamentary Committee of the T.U.C., and hundreds of local 'Councils of Action' sprang up in all parts of the country, to stop the sending of military aid by the British Government to the armies with which the young Soviet Union was still at war. This campaign was successful, and in the same year a Communist Party was formed, but was refused affiliation to the Labour Party.

In 1920–1 the organization of the T.U.C. was overhauled, as that of the Labour Party had been in 1917–18. The Parliamentary Committee was replaced by a 'General Council', more fully representative of all important sections of workers and with far wider industrial powers and duties. In 1924, further steps in the same direction were taken when Congress voted in favour of the 'Industrial Workers Charter', proposing to form one single union for each industry, with the object of maximizing its power. Congress also demanded the nationalization of the key industries, and the General Council was strengthened.[2] At the same time federations and industrial alliances of several unions were established or discussed, and an approach made, in 1924–5, to the Soviet trade unions for closer collaboration.

The militancy of both the political and the industrial wings of the Labour Movement was met by the Government by some temporary expedients, like the Wages (Temporary Regulations) Act of November 1918, which prohibited any reduction of wages in the course of the next six months, the 'out-of-work donation', described in the last section, and the Industrial Conference. Some gains were of permanent benefit, including legislation to promote arbitration, conciliation and the fixing of wages.[3]

The scheme of joint industrial councils based on the reports of the Whitley Committee of the Ministry of Reconstruction[4] was, after its initial widespread acceptance, not as successful as had been hoped. The high point of the movement was reached at the end of 1920, when there

---

[1] Alan Bullock, *The Life and Times of Ernest Bevin*, Vol. I (1960), p. 99.
[2] W. Milne-Bailey, *Trade Union Documents* (1929), No. 83.
[3] See pp. 88, 90–1 above.
[4] Cd. 8606 (1917), Cd. 9001, 9002, 9099, 9153 (1918).

were 75 J.I.C.s, covering 3½ million workers, and 33 'Interim Industrial Reconstruction Committees' which the Government hoped to develop into fully fledged councils. In the 1920's, many were dissolved and others never came to life properly, and the most durable machinery was that established in the Civil Service and by statutory authority elsewhere, as on the railways under the Railway Act of 1921 and in agriculture under the Agricultural Wages (Regulation) Act of 1924.[1]

The scope of Trade Boards was extended by an Amending Act in 1918 to cover not only sweated trades, but all those in which no other formal negotiating machinery existed. Between 1919 and 1921, 33 new boards were set up, but in 1922, when the immediate need to pacify Labour had passed, the Cave Committee reported against the further extension of this compulsory method of wage-fixing, and only about ten new industries were added between 1922 and 1939, apart from 18 in Northern Ireland. The total number of workers covered was about 1½ million.[2]

The third organization to emerge from the recommendations of the Whitley Committee was the Industrial Court, set up under the Industrial Courts Act of 1919. Composed of members drawn from three sections, employers, employed and 'independents', the Courts could be appointed only on the request of both parties. Its decisions were not binding, but out of 1,700 awards in the nineteen years to 1939, only four were questioned by one or the other party to the dispute.[3] In 1936 the Civil Service Arbitration Tribunal, working to much the same rules, was set up to deal with all Civil Service cases. The Industrial Court was also given additional jurisdiction from time to time, such as powers to arbitrate on hours and conditions under the Road Traffic Act, 1930 (amended 1933), under the Sugar Industry (Reorganization) Act of 1936, the Air Navigation Act of 1936, and the Road Haulage Wages Act of 1938. This latter Act also included the unusual principle, first introduced by the Cotton Manufacturing Industry (Temporary Provisions) Act of 1934, of giving statutory sanction to wages arrived at by collective bargaining, and making them applicable to all firms.

In the period of the post-war unrest, the cockpit of the industrial struggles was the coal industry. While forming only 6·2% of the industrial population, the miners furnished 41·8% of all strikers between 1911 and 1945, and if the General Strike of 1926 is excluded, in which the other

[1] J. B. Seymour, *The Whitley Councils Scheme* (1932); J. H. Richardson, *Industrial Relations in Great Britain* (Geneva, 1933), chapter 4.

[2] J. J. Mallon, 'Trade Boards', in G. D. H. Cole, *British Trade Unions To-day* (1939); Dorothy Sells, *The British Trade Boards System* (1923); Milne-Bailey, Nos. 116–18.

[3] F. E. Gannett and B. F. Catherwood, *Industrial and Labour Relations in Great Britain* (1939), p. 18; G. P. Jones and A. G. Pool, *A Hundred Years of Economic Development in Great Britain* (1959 ed.), pp. 386–9.

trades were striking in support of the miners' demands, the miner was eight times as likely to strike as the average worker; the only other major industries above the average were textiles (2·2 times), metal working, etc. (1·4) and transport (1·5).[1] The history of the Miners' Federation of Great Britain in this period thus deserves special attention.

Among all the groups of workers demanding the nationalization of their industry after the war, the miners were the most insistent, and enjoyed the most widespread support. In view of the great coal shortage in Europe, and the ugly temper in many mining districts, the Government felt constrained to appoint the Sankey Commission early in 1919 to stave off a threatened miners' strike on this question, though it could not avoid a month's strike in the Yorkshire coalfield in July–August 1919 about the application of the Coal Controller's wage award on the introduction of the seven-hour shift. The Government's disregard of the recommendation of Lord Sankey for nationalization persuaded the miners that they had been tricked into calling off their strike when it stood the greatest chance of success, in February 1919, in order to enter into a period of procrastination in which their industrial power would steadily diminish. To the distrust of the coal owners, dating from pre-war years, there was added distrust of the Government.[2] All the miners could do was to move the T.U.C. to vote overwhelmingly for nationalization in September 1919, and confirm this decision in two special Congresses in December 1919 and March 1920.

Meanwhile, in 1920, the industry was still riding the high wave of prosperity and selling its exports at unprecedented prices. In July 1920 the miners asked for an increase in wages together with a reduction in coal prices. The Government, which was still administering the mines, turned down both demands, and the miners determined on a strike to begin on 25th September, calling the other two partners in the much-feared 'Triple Alliance', the transport workers and railwaymen, to their aid. The Triple Alliance, which had shown its weakness once already, a year earlier, in the course of the railway strike when J. H. Thomas of the N.U.R. had refused to call in his allies, was again found wanting, and did little more than delay, by further negotiations, the strike notices by a few weeks. The national coal strike began on 16th October and lasted three weeks, ending in a partial victory for the miners. A wage increase was granted, but made conditional upon increased output, the so-called 'datum line', and permanent terms were to be worked out by the end of March 1921. Meanwhile, despite its failure on this occasion, the threat of the Triple Alliance had led the Government to introduce the Emergency

---

[1] Knowles, *Strikes*, p. 203.
[2] A. Hutt, *The Post-War History of the British Working Class* (1937), chapter 1, and *British Trade Unionism* (1952 ed.), chapter 7; also pp. 111–12 above.

Powers Act of 1920, which empowered the Government to declare a 'state of emergency' and govern by decree, on threat of any action 'of such a nature and on so extensive a scale as to be calculated, by interfering with the supply and distribution of food, water, fuel, or light, or with the means of locomotion, to deprive the community, or any substantial portion of the community, of the essentials of life'.[1] It was put into force and used with some effect in the mining disputes of 1921 and 1926.

Before the new permanent rate of mining wages could be worked out, a sharp slump of coal export prices reduced the surplus available (home coal price having been kept down throughout this period) and the Government announced its intention of handing the industry back to the owners on 31st March 1921 instead of 31st August. The owners, faced with large losses at existing wages and prices, at once determined on drastic wage reductions and locked out the miners on 31st March. This time the other members of the Triple Alliance appeared to be willing to strike in support of the miners from April 12th, while the Government declared a State of Emergency and made even more extensive military preparations than in the strikes of 1919 and 1920. There followed a series of manœuvres and negotiations behind the scenes, which ended in the withdrawal of the other allies from the strike threat on 15th April, 'Black Friday'. Their decision has often been termed a betrayal, and in view of the later career of some of the leaders involved, such a view may not be entirely without foundation, but basically the structure of the Alliance itself was at fault, for it did not define whether in the case of a dispute of one section, aided by the others, the section alone or the whole Alliance should be empowered to make terms. On this issue the Alliance broke up, in effect, in 1921.[2]

Left in the lurch by their allies, the miners suffered a crushing defeat and had to return to work on the owners' terms in June 1921, when their funds were exhausted. They had to submit not only to a wage cut, but also to a return from the national wage agreements of war-time to the earlier district agreements, bitterly opposed by the Miners' Federation which remembered the pre-war methods of depressing wages by playing off one district against another.[3] The defeat was felt by the trade union world as a whole, as it was followed by large-scale wage reductions and by a mass defection of membership in many industries. The bargaining positions in the labour market had radically changed with the change in the economic climate, from boom to slump.

Mass unemployment might have contributed to bring in the Labour

---

[1] Emergency Powers Act, 1920, 10 & 11 Geo. V, ch. 55, sec. 1.
[2] Francis Williams, *Magnificent Journey* (1954), chapter 21.
[3] J. W. F. Rowe, *Wages in the Coal Industry* (1923); J. R. Raynes, *Coal and its Conflicts* (1928).

Administration of 1924, but it did little to strengthen the hands of the trade unions, which continued to be powerless to stop wage reductions large enough to cause loss of membership, but too small to allow export prices to fall and exports to expand. The first Labour Government did not, in its short span of office, come up to the fears of its enemies, nor did it fulfil the hopes of its more revolutionary supporters, who had assumed that Socialist measures might be introduced.[1] When it was defeated, by the combined action of a press stunt and its own pathological fear of being labelled 'revolutionary', it became clear that the post-war settlement of the labour question, the more permanent equilibrium of forces after the disorientation of the war years, would be decided in the industrial field, not the political. Again it was the coal mining industry which became the scene of battle.

In 1924, owing to improved coal prices, and the threat of a new Miners' Minimum Wages Act to be passed by the Labour Government then in power, the owners granted a substantial wage increase for one year. Before it expired in the summer of 1925, coal prices and sales had begun their rapid and permanent decline, and the owners demanded, not only a return to the wages of 1921-4, but also the repeal of the Seven Hours Act of 1919 and its replacement by eight-hour shifts. In view of the unfavourable market situation and their own depleted finances after the stoppage of 1921, the miners felt unable to resist these demands unaided, and turned for help to the General Council of the T.U.C., recently provided with authority which seemed to fit the new situation. Trade union rates were under attack all along the line, especially in the export industries, which were desperately anxious to reduce costs, and there was little doubt that the outcome of the miners' dispute would largely determine other wage levels. Moreover, many leaders were attempting to make good the 'betrayal' of 1921, especially since the miner with his dangerous, strenuous and ill-paid job could always count on the maximum sympathy of other trade unionists. In July 1925, the Trades Union Congress pledged its full support to the miners, to the extent of being prepared to call a general sympathetic strike.

Faced with this threat, the Government (which collaborated with the mine owners throughout this dispute) climbed down on 'Red Friday'. It decided to offer a temporary subsidy to enable the mine owners to con: tinue to pay existing wage rates, and to appoint a Royal Commission. The Commission, presided over by Sir Herbert Samuel, the fourth official body to inquire into the industry since 1918, made various useful minor proposals, and repeated the Sankey Commission's recommendation to nationalize coal royalties, but it could offer no solution to the immediate

[1] G. D. H. Cole, *History of the Labour Party Since 1914* (1948); Richard W. Lyman, *The First Labour Government, 1924* (1957).

275

wage problem. Its proposal to keep to existing working hours and enforce rather smaller wage cuts than those demanded by the owners satisfied neither party, and the whole Report was subsequently ignored.

The subsidy had, however, given a breathing space of nine months which the Government used to prepare for an all-out struggle with the miners' union and the T.U.C. Large coal stocks were built up, the country was divided into ten areas under Civil Commissioners provided with wide powers, an Emergency Committee for Supply and Transport was appointed, and an Organization for the Maintenance of Supplies was set up on private initiative, to marshal volunteer strike breakers. By contrast, the General Council of the T.U.C. made no preparations whatever; it did not even consider the issue which had broken the Triple Alliance five years earlier, namely whether, in the case of a sympathetic strike, all the unions involved, or the miners alone, should have the right to decide on the terms of settlement.[1]

The subsidy expired at the end of April, the miners were locked out, and the General Council called a 'general strike' in support of the miners' case for midnight, Monday, 3rd May. The 'first line' of trades, including transport, iron and steel, printing, building and electricity and gas workers, was called out at once, and the 'second line' of engineers and shipbuilders was called out on 11th May.

Despite the lack of preparation, the response of the rank and file exceeded all expectations. The strike, in the trades called out, was virtually complete. As most of the fuel supplies and transport were affected, local trades or other *ad hoc* bodies took over some of the functions of local government to provide necessary services to hospitals, etc., and others attempted, in the absence of newspapers, to counter the information and propaganda of the B.B.C., which was wholly under the influence of the Government, by information sheets of their own.

The strike brought forth much capacity for organization, enthusiasm and solidarity of the ordinary membership, but these were wholly nullified by the attitude of its leaders. 'For the rank and file the strike was a triumph: for most of its national leaders a humiliation.' [2] The General Council itself virtually disintegrated as a directing organ. Whatever positive directive was given from the centre, was due to individuals, above all Ernest Bevin, though most of the initiative seemed to come from below.

---

[1] Cole and Postgate, *The Common People*, pp. 564–5.

[2] C. L. Mowat, *Britain Between the Wars*, p. 313. Other good accounts of the General Strike will be found in: Julian Symons, *The General Strike* (1957); W. H. Crook, *The General Strike* (1931); A. J. Cook, *The Nine Days* (1927); Hamilton Fyfe, *Behind the Scenes of the Great Strike* (1926); Alan Bullock, *op. cit.*, pp. 299–344; Milne-Bailey, Nos. 141–52.

The members of the General Council, having committed their organization to strike action without preparation and without thinking out its consequences, were from the first intent to call it off at the earliest opportunity. What was to have been a gesture of sympathy and solidarity with the miners had become, by the deliberate decision of the Government, a challenge to the Government and to the constitution, which neither the trade union leadership nor even the miners' leaders were willing to support. Unwilling to win, they could not compromise either, since the Cabinet, temporarily under the sway of its more ebullient members led by Winston Churchill, was determined to achieve complete victory. In the end, using the pretext that a compromise formula suggested by Sir Herbert Samuel might be adopted, the General Council called off the strike on 12th May, after nine days, without any conditions or promises on the part of Government or owners. The strikers, who had only begun to get into their stride, were unable to understand this submission, but discipline again prevailed and most of them returned to work. There was relatively little victimization, apart from the railway companies, which used the strike to institute wholesale dismissals: 45,000 men had not gone back by October.

The miners' leaders had scarcely been consulted. While the rest of the country went back to work, the miners stayed out. Their funds had been low, and the subscriptions to their aid, totalling £1·8 million, a large part of which had come from the Russian miners, were insufficient for a prolonged struggle. As starvation began to enter the mining villages after weary months of attrition, the owners became more confident, irritating even the Government by their unwillingness to make the slightest concession. At length, after nearly eight months, the men were broken, and agreements were made district by district, in each case involving major reductions in wages and increases in hours to 7½ or 8 per shift. Apart from G. A. Spencer's breakaway union in Nottinghamshire, however, the loyalty of the miners to their trade union was unshaken even after that disaster.[1]

The immediate cost of the coal strike was the loss of 28 million tons of coal for export; the total losses, including losses of wages, have been put at £175–270 million. Among trade union leaders, the main consequence was the determination to avoid at all costs a repetition of the head-on clash with the Government. Not only sympathetic strikes, but even ordinary strikes began to be frowned on, and there were very few full-scale national strikes after 1927: disputes remained local and short and were often unofficial.[2] The years beginning in 1927 were among the

[1] R. Page Arnot, *The Miners: Years of Struggle* (1953), chapters 12–14; D. H. Robertson, 'A Narrative of the Coal Strike', *Econ. J.*, 36/143, 1926.
[2] Knowles, pp. 155–7; H. A. Clegg and R. Adams, *The Employers' Challenge*

most peaceful in recorded history, as trade union leaders showed signs of 'exhaustion, disillusionment and recognition of the futility of industrial stoppages following the disastrous experiences of 1926'.[1] Only the cotton industry showed an upsurge of industrial disputes in 1929, 1931 and 1932, losing in those three years 15½ million working days, or over 70% of the number lost in all industries.

The leading trade unionists turned to collaboration with the owners and managers of their own industries. They were met more than half-way by those employers who were coming to look for a solution to the grave industrial problems of the age in rationalization, association or a corporate form of industrial organization in which the workers' representatives would play a part.[2] 'We realise', wrote Sir Alfred Mond (later Lord Melchett) and twenty other large employers to the General Council of the T.U.C. in November 1927, 'that industrial reconstruction can be undertaken only in conjunction with and with the co-operation of those entitled and empowered to speak for organised Labour.' They initiated the so-called 'Mond-Turner' conversations, with the full official support of the General Council of the T.U.C. which told the 1928 Congress that it was

> for the trade union movement to say boldly that not only is it concerned with the prosperity of industry, but that it is going to have a voice in the way industry is carried on . . . the unions can use their power to promote and guide the scientific reorganization of industry.[3]

Although the conversations were never officially supported by any employers' organization, they helped to give trade unions a breathing space after their defeat of 1926, and to allow industry to reap the benefit of the boom of 1927–9 without being subject to claims for increased wages.

The General Strike also closed an epoch which began in 1907, in which unions relied on putting pressure on the public at large in order to induce the Government to mediate and enforce some concessions on the employers.[4] Henceforward for many years to come no trade union leader would dare to challenge the intervention of the Government. Henceforward also those in the trade union world who were in favour of State Socialism or Guild Socialism, and who appeared to sweep all before them in 1919–24, were to be overwhelmed by those favouring slow

---

(Oxford, 1957), chapter 1; G. D. H. Cole, *An Introduction to Trade Unionism* (1953), chapter X/1.
[1] J. H. Richardson, 'Industrial Relations', in *Britain in Depression* (1935), pp. 59–60; also his 'Industrial Relations' in *Britain in Recovery* (1938), pp. 115–17.
[2] E.g. Sir Alfred Mond, *Industry and Politics* (1927); Bullock, *op. cit.*, chapter 15.
[3] Quoted in A. Hutt, *Post-War History of the British Working Class*, p. 178. Also Ben Turner, *About Myself* (1930).
[4] Phelps-Brown, *op. cit.*, pp. 348–9; p. 30 above.

reform as the programme for the Labour Party. Finally, the fiasco of the General Strike destroyed the 'myth' of the efficacy of this ultimate weapon in the armoury of the working classes, which had haunted them since the days of Syndicalism before 1914.

The strike also left its mark on the Statute Book. Apart from the Eight Hours Act, passed in 1926, which permitted the lengthening of the miners' working day as part of the settlement, the employers' victory was embodied in the Trade Disputes and Trade Unions Act of 1927. This made general strikes illegal, mainly by outlawing all sympathy strikes which were held by the Courts to be designed to coerce the Government either directly or by inflicting hardship on the public. It forbade State employees to belong to societies or federations not consisting wholly of State employees. Further, it altered the law of picketing almost to the restrictive position it had occupied in the nineteenth century, and gave the Government the power, by injunction, to attack trade union funds, the worst aspect of these sections of the Act being their vagueness and consequent uncertainty. Finally, it substituted 'contracting in' for 'contracting out' of the political levy, and thus at once reduced sharply the trade union contributions to Labour Party funds.

This measure, which in some respects put the trade unions back fifty years, was widely deplored as a needless act of vengeance, and contributed to the General Election result of 1929, which returned Labour as the largest party in the House. It gained 289 seats, the Conservatives having 260 and the Liberals, now on their precipitate downward movement as the third party in the British electoral system, a mere 58. Labour took office again under James Ramsay MacDonald, with Liberal support.

The second Labour Government did little to further the cause of the trade unions or of its own Socialist supporters. It was quite unable to deal on orthodox lines with the effects of the great depression and worsening unemployment and was unwilling to strike out on its own. The result was a fatal split in the Cabinet, followed by an ignominious defeat at the polls at the end of 1931, decimating the party in the House and wiping out its chances of office for the next decade.

The new National Government carried out the kind of cuts in the dole and in other social welfare provisions which Labour had feared most. Yet when the immediate pressure of the slump had lifted by 1934, it was found that public opinion in general and the Government in particular had come round to supporting more generous social welfare provisions, as described in the last two sections above, and that the political and industrial struggles of the 1920's had thus by no means been in vain.

The trade unions, at the same time, began to register large increases in membership. The conservatism of their leaders did not go unchallenged. The Minority Movement, founded in 1923-4, survived as a goad towards more radical policies and more militant action. The National Unemployed Workers' Movement remained active, and was largely instrumental in forcing the Government to postpone and finally abandon the cuts in the dole which were to operate under Part II of the Unemployment Act of 1934, even though the official trade union leadership opposed its policies and hampered its actions. There were numerous unofficial strikes, directed against the union leadership as much as against the employers. In a few cases, as among the London busmen, breakaway unions were formed out of the despair of making the leadership responsive to a more active rank and file. By and large, however, the trade unions maintained their character of solidity, hoping to gain better terms for their members by collaboration with the employers rather than by opposing them, and forming a steadying, conservative influence on the Labour Party itself.

4. CHANGES IN POPULATION AND SOCIAL STRUCTURE

The population increase which had accompanied the industrialization of this country continued between the wars, the United Kingdom figures rising from 43·74 million in the middle of 1920 to 47·49 million in the middle of 1938,[1] but the rate of increase had begun to decline sharply in the second decade of the twentieth century. It contracted further in the 1920's and 1930's at such a headlong rate that fears began to be expressed about the ultimate absolute decline of the population of the United Kingdom,[2] some demographers estimating that it would be halved before the end of the century.

In absolute terms, the natural increase of population in Great Britain was at its highest in 1901–11, when births exceeded deaths by nearly 4·6 million, but because of the heavy rate of emigration in that decade, the net increase in the home population had been higher in the 1890's, at almost 4 million, compared with only 3·8 million in 1901–11.[3] In the following decade, 1911–21, the natural increase fell to 2·8 million (net, 1·9 million) and there were further drops after the war, the increase for 1921–31 being only 2·6 million (2·0 million) and in 1931–41 1·2 million, though there was a net increase of 1·8 million then, because of some net immigration. As the total population was rising throughout this period, the proportionate decline in the rate of increase was faster than these figures suggest; and since the death rate was falling it follows that the fall in the birth rate was precipitate.

The population increase between the wars was associated with a

---

[1] Richard Stone, *Measurement of Consumers' Expenditure and Behaviour in the United Kingdom, 1920–1938* (Cambridge, 1954), Table 116, p. 414.

[2] E.g. D. V. Glass, *The Struggle for Population* (1936).

[3] *Report of the Royal Commission on Population* (1948. Cmd. 7695), Table IV, p. 9; most of this section is based on this report.

geographical shift, but it was in a direction different from that of the nineteenth century:[1]

Regional Distribution (R = largely rural)	Population in 1938 (million)	% Change 1921-38	Multiplication of Population 1801-1921
South-east	14·49	+18·1	5
Midlands	7·21	+11·6	4
West Riding	3·46	+6·0	5½
Eastern Counties (R)	1·85	+3·7	2
Lancashire and Cheshire	6·16	+3·5	7
South-west (R)	2·08	+3·3	2
Northern Rural Belt (R)	1·29	+3·1	3
Scotland	4·99	+2·1	3
Northumberland and Durham	2·20	−1·0	7
North and Central Wales (R)	0·68	−4·8	2
South Wales	1·78	−8·1	9
Great Britain	46·20	+8·0	4

The fastest growing areas between 1800 and 1921, Lancashire and Cheshire, South Wales and Northumberland and Durham, were well down the list, the latter two even declining absolutely in the inter-war period; by contrast, the only two regions exceeding the national average increase in 1921–38 were the South-east (including London) and the Midlands. The South-east, in fact, absorbed 2¼ million people in this period, and the Midlands ¾ million out of a total national population increase of 3½ million. The growth of the inter-war period was also accompanied by further urbanization, and it was still largely the rural areas that acted as population reservoirs for the growing towns. The main growth, however, occurred no longer in the large cities of north Britain, but rather in the smaller towns with growing industries (e.g. Oxford, York, Leicester and Norwich) and in the expanding coal and iron ore fields of the east Midlands.[2] The conurbations remained stationary or declined in population, with the exception of London and Birmingham,[3] whose unrestricted sprawl created some of the main social and transport problems of the age.

There was some emigration in the first post-war decade, mainly to Empire countries, but it was at an average rate of about 130,000 a year, or a mere 40% of the immediate pre-war rate,[4] and even then it had to be

[1] Mark Abrams, *The Condition of the British People, 1911–1945* (1945), p. 22. Cf. also A. Beacham, *Structure of British Industry* (1955 ed.), p. 150; G. D. H. Cole and R. Postgate, *The Common People, 1746–1938* (1938), pp. 612–13.

[2] P.E.P., *Report on the Location of Industry in Great Britain* (1939), p. 197, map on p. 171 and Appx. III, pp. 294–9.

[3] David C. Marsh, *The Changing Social Structure of England and Wales, 1871–1951* (1958), chapter 4; Mark Abrams, *op. cit.*, p. 35.

[4] W. A. Carrothers, *Emigration from the British Isles* (1929), Appx. I and IV.

officially supported to a much larger extent than before 1914. Emigration to areas outside the Empire, like the U.S.A. and South America, which had taken many migrants both from the British Isles and from other parts of Europe before the war, was very sharply reduced. It was not only that there were fewer potential emigrants: most receiving countries had reversed their attitude, and instead of welcoming the additional hands to open up their empty territories, had begun to be conscious of having reached their frontiers. Among the other causes of the new restrictiveness were unemployment in the towns and the weakness of primary product prices.

The United States, for example, changed within a few years from virtually unlimited immigration for persons of European stock at a rate exceeding 1 million before 1914, to the most severe restrictions. The first to be imposed was the literacy test of 1917, but in 1921, 805,000 immigrants entered in spite of it. Restriction was therefore made more severe by the Quota Act of 1921, admitting annually from each country no more than 3% of the numbers born there and resident in the U.S.A. in 1910, or a maximum of 358,000 a year. This was further reduced in 1924 to a maximum of 165,000 in 1925-9, and 154,000 from 1930 on, for those born outside the American continent.[1] Many other countries also became highly restrictive, though exact methods varied. Even Britain became less liberal: the Aliens Act of 1914 and 1919 led to the Aliens Order of 1920, under which immigrants were admitted only if they could prove their ability to maintain themselves and their families.

The Dominions at first formed an exception, for they were eager to have British immigrants, even though in part at least this was due to their anxiety to avoid having to admit others. During the war, two studies on Empire migration appeared, one by the Empire Settlement Committee, appointed in 1917 to report on the settlement of ex-members of the forces, and the other by the Dominions Royal Commission, appointed in 1912 following the Imperial Conference. Both reports were issued in 1917 and led to official aid for migration within the Empire. In 1919 the Government's free passage scheme for ex-service men and their families assisted 86,000 persons to emigrate within three years. When it had become clear that there would be very little unaided migration on the pre-war scale, the Imperial Conference of 1921 proposed further assistance, and the Empire Settlement Act of 1922 authorized an expenditure of up to £3 million a year, provided the receiving Governments matched it by at least equal sums. 400,000 migrants in the next nine years benefited from aid under this Act, but most of them only by small sums, and it is doubtful how far these actually contributed to their decision to emigrate. Special schemes of settlement, as for example one

[1] Julius Isaac, *Economics of Migration* (1947), p. 56.

designed to open up new land in Western Australia, failed dismally. In 1925, an agreement was made with Australia to settle 450,000 immigrants from Britain in ten years, Australia to raise a total of £34 million for land, development and farm buildings, and the United Kingdom to add one-fifth of the expenditure to that of Australia, provided that for every £150,000 so contributed, 10,000 people were settled within this period. This scheme, also, was a failure and was terminated in 1932 after £4·3 million had been spent.[1] Other assisted schemes elsewhere failed also, and an official report in May 1938 pronounced against any further programmes of this kind.[2]

Long before this, however, the conditions relating to migration had changed. As the Great Depression began to affect overseas countries as well as the European centres, the doors of most receiving countries, already half-shut, were closed almost completely. Even Canada began to restrict immigration from Britain by using the clause in her Immigration Act which excluded those who might become a public charge, and reception elsewhere also became more frigid, while the official subsidies for migration were being withdrawn. Meanwhile the wish to emigrate had evaporated even faster than the official encouragements. There was, in fact, in the 1930's for the first time since figures were recorded a heavy net immigration into Britain, mostly on the part of disillusioned former emigrants, many of whom found even living on the dole in Britain better than their experience overseas. The *net* annual immigration was at a rate of 35,000 a year in 1931–4, and 13,000 a year in 1935–8,[3] though it should be noted that the net increase was confined to England. Scotland and Wales continued to lose population.

Not only migration, but the other two factors affecting the change in the population, the birth rate and the death rate, were greatly influenced by economic and social conditions. The death rate had been falling steadily for over a century, and the fall had been particularly marked since the 1890's.[4] The 'standardized' death rate for England and Wales had fallen from 13·5 per thousand in 1911–14 to 9·3 in 1937, though it was still 13·3 in Scotland in that year.[5] 'The expectation of life for men increased from 43·7 years in 1881 to 61·8 years in 1938, and for women from 47·2 to 65·8 for the corresponding years. It serves as an admirable indication of changes in social conditions.'[6]

More important still as a measure of social conditions was the fall in

[1] N. H. Carrier and J. R. Jeffery, *External Migration, a Study of the Available Statistics, 1815–1950* (1953).
[2] *Report of the British Overseas Settlement Board* (1938. Cmd. 5766).
[3] Isaac, Table 6, p. 64.
[4] *Report of the Royal Commission on Population*, pp. 18–20.
[5] C. L. Mowat, *Britain Between the Wars* (1956 ed.), pp. 513–14.
[6] Eva M. Hubback, *The Population of Britain* (1947), p. 23.

the maternity and the infantile death rate. 'Infantile mortality is the most sensitive index we possess of social welfare and of sanitary administration, especially under urban conditions.' [1] While the infantile death rate (deaths in the first year of life per 1,000 live births) fell from 110 in 1911–15 to 58 in 1937 in England and Wales (but standing at 80 in Scotland in the latter year), the differences between classes and between regions were not being reduced, and in some cases tended even to widen. The following tabulation relates to the social class of the father:[2]

Infant Mortality per 1,000 Legitimate Live Births

		1911	1930–2
Social Class I	(Upper and Middle)	76	33
,, ,, II	(Between I and III)	106	45
,, ,, III	(Skilled Labour)	113	58
,, ,, IV	(Between III and V)	122	67
,, ,, V	(Unskilled Labour)	153	77

The labourer's infant mortality rate was double the best rate in 1911, but more than double in 1930–2; in the latter year, in spite of all the intervening medical and social progress, it was only at the middle-class level of 1911. Where they could be isolated more exactly than in this crude general tabulation, the class differences were greater still.

The differences between regions were equally startling. Thus in 1935, the infant mortality rate was 57 for England and Wales and 77 for Scotland, but it was 32 in Coulsdon and Purley and 41 in Surrey as a whole, compared with 76 in Durham and 114 in Jarrow. There were similar differences in child mortality and maternal mortality:[3]

	Deaths at Ages		Maternal Mortality per 1,000 Births, 1936
	1–2	2–5	
	(per 1,000 living, 1931–4)		
North I (Durham and Northumberland)	22·05	6·57	5·29
Wales I (4 Southern Counties)	15·44	5·34	4·78
South-east England	10·94	3·80	2·57
Greater London	12·55	4·25	2·16

[1] Sir Arthur Newsholme, quoted in R. M. Titmuss, *Birth, Poverty and Wealth, a Study of Infant Mortality* (1943), p. 12. Cf. also Fred Grundy, *The New Public Health* (1957), pp. 136–45.   [2] Titmuss, *op. cit.*, p. 26.
[3] Richard M. Titmuss, *Poverty and Population* (1938), pp. 80, 102–3, 144.

Comparisons between smaller areas, such as towns or urban districts, showed still greater differences,[1] and more detailed analysis pointed to the conclusion that the largest part of them was due to distress and debilities that could be prevented by better sanitary conditions, by better nutrition and better care. Thus even in the 1930's, in spite of the welcome fall in ,death rates, it was still true that a large number of unnecessary deaths were permitted to occur because of poverty.

If the death rate was falling, the birth rate was falling faster still. The crude birth rate declined from 23·6 per thousand in England and Wales in 1911–15 (25·4 in Scotland) to 15·1 (17·7) in 1938. The annual number of births fell from about 1 million before 1914 to a minimum of 580,000 in 1932 and hovered around 700,000 for most of the 1930's, in spite of a larger total population. The excess of births over deaths fell to about 2½ per thousand, or a mere 110,000 a year,[2] but even this positive figure hid an underlying tendency towards an absolute decline, since the age pyramid was unduly distorted by the exceptionally large 'years' born in 1900–14 who were of child-bearing age in the 1930's and thus produced a temporarily large annual number of births. On the basis of the 'net reproduction rate' of the number of girls born and likely to survive to child-bearing age to replace the existing female population of the same age group,[3] England and Wales failed to reach a rate of 1 (i.e a long-run stationary population) from 1922 onward; in 1933 the rate fell to 0·75.

The causes for the fall in the birth rate were complex.[4] In part they lay in improved technical means and wider knowledge of methods of birth control, and in the relaxation of obedience to religious prohibition of their use; in part they were to be found in the improved status of women; in part they were the effects of the 'social example' of the upper classes which throughout this period had, on average, smaller families than the lower, and were thus ahead of them in the downward march. To a large extent, however, the causes were economic: on the one hand, the Education Acts ensured that children had ceased to be a source of income to their families until they were near marriageable age; on the other, rising incomes made the alternatives that were available if the family size was kept down relatively more attractive. Higher economic hopes and social ambition increased further the sacrifices imposed by additional children on those already born.

[1] E.g. A. Hutt, *The Condition of the Working Class in Britain* (1933), pp. 41–2, 164.
[2] A. M. Carr-Saunders, D. Caradog Jones and C. A. Moser, *A Survey of Social Conditions in England and Wales* (Oxford, 1958), chapter 2.
[3] Hubback, pp. 18–25.
[4] The best brief discussion will be found in *Royal Commission on Population. Report* (1949), chapters 4 and 5. Cf. also Hubback, *op. cit.*, Part II.

The economic effects of these population changes worked mainly through the declining size of families, and the changed age structure of the population. The average number of live births per married woman born in 1841–5 was 5·71, and in 1861–5 it was 4·66; women married in 1900–9 had only an average of 3·37 live births, and those married in 1925–9 only 2·19. In other words, the typical Victorian family had 5 children, while the typical modern family had 2 only.[1] As the span of life lengthened at the same time, the proportion of the lifetime spent with the children living at home was falling also, and the average family household size was falling even faster than the birth figures would indicate. Thus between 1911 and 1939, the number of families consisting of 1 or 2 persons almost doubled, from 1·9 million to 3·7 million; the families of 3 or 4 persons increased by ⅔, from 3·3 million to 5·45 million; while the number of large families, of 5 persons or more, actually fell from 3·7 million to 3·1 million.[2] Throughout this period, the size of family still increased however, as one descended the social scale.[3]

Thus for any given size of population there was an increasing number of families, demanding their separate households and contributing to the housing shortage and the building boom. For every adult wage-earner there was a smaller number of dependants—a potent cause of the improvement in living standards. With smaller families, married women found it easier to go out to work and could do so for a larger proportion of their married lives, and they found it easier to manage without domestic servants. The working housewife and the relative decline in the number of domestic servants for households of equivalent standing were, in turn, contributing factors to the great increase in the production of tinned foods, household gadgets, ready-made clothes, and other mass-produced consumption goods, as well as of services like laundries and restaurants. At the same time, the decline of the large household forced many elderly people, who had formerly found room within it, into the care of public authorities.

There was a growing proportion of older people in the population, but there were fewer children also, and for the time being, those two movements more than held each other in balance: the percentage of children under 14 dropped faster between 1911 and 1939, from 30·8% to 21·4%, than the proportion of people over 65 increased (from 5·3% to 8·9%), so that the population of working age could increase from 63·9% to 69·7% of the total population, or in absolute numbers, from 26·1 to 32·3 million. The proportion of people of working age had been increasing for some time, but this had been neutralized by the raising of the school-

---

[1] *Royal Commission on Population*, Tables 15, 16 and 17.
[2] Mark Abrams, *op. cit.*, p. 41; Marsh, chapter 3.
[3] E. H. Phelps-Brown, *The Growth of British Industrial Relations* (1959), pp. 4–8.

leaving age; in this period it contributed materially to the rising standard of income per head.[1] Meanwhile, among the consequences of the changing age structure were the growing burden of old-age pensions and, because of rising standards and expectation of life, the growth of private and company pension schemes, as well as the increasing rigidity which this ageing process of a whole society imposed on the economy. In districts losing heavily by emigration, such as South Wales or the north-east coast, the ageing of the remaining population was particularly noteworthy.

These changes in population were inextricably interwoven with changes in the social structure of Britain. The decline in the birth rate, in particular, was closely connected with the social and economic ambitions that became possible for all classes of society, and with the relative growth in numbers of the professional and lower middle classes who tended to have smaller families than the manual working classes. The outstanding social change in this period was, in fact, the growth of the 'white-collar' workers. This change, in turn, was a compound of two closely connected factors, the growth of the 'salariat' in industry and elsewhere, and the growth of the kind of occupations, like retail distribution, local government and entertainments, which employed a very high proportion of salaried persons.

The growth of the salaried personnel in industry is difficult to measure. One estimate, based on the Censuses of production, put the proportion of administrative staff at 11·8 in 1924, 15·1 in 1935 and 20·0 in 1948 (operatives = 100).[2] Another estimate puts the increase of salaried personnel in private industry between the Census years 1911 and 1931 at 1,170,000 (from 1·04 million to 2·21 million), and in public administration (including teaching) at 200,000 (from 489,000 to 687,000), or a total increase of nearly 1·4 million persons, of whom 650,000 were women.[3]

There are more reliable estimates available for the growth in the service industries and in tertiary industries generally. The following statement reproduces some of the best estimates (see table on next page).

In their totals (excluding defence) Chapman and Knight register an increase of 1,246,000 salaried persons, or 35%, as against an increase in the number of wage-earners of 1,686,000, or 14%, between 1920-2 and 1937-8. Insurance statistics suggest a rise in the proportion of salaried workers from 22·0% in 1924 to 25·5% in 1938, and a corresponding fall

---

[1] p. 291 below.
[2] P. S. Florence, *The Logic of British and American Industry* (1953), Table IVA, p. 139; L. Rostas, 'Industrial Production, Productivity and Distribution in Britain, Germany and the United States', *Econ. J.*, 53/20, 1943, p. 51.
[3] J. G. Marley and H. Campion, 'Changes in Salaries in Great Britain, 1924-1939', in A. L. Bowley, *Studies in the National Income, 1924-1938* (Cambridge, 1942), p. 86.

Social Conditions Between the Wars

	Changes in Numbers Employed (000)			(Chapman & Knight)[4]		
	1921–31 (Marsh)[1]	1931–9 (Frankel)[2]	Total Change 1921–39[3]	Average Employment		Change 1920–2 to 1937–8
				1920–2	1937–8	
Primary Industries	−466	−419	−885	2,135	1,586	−549
Secondary Industries	−491	+1,050	+559	8,099	9,448	+1,349
Tertiary Industries	+873	+1,210	+2,083	5,301	7,336	+2,035
All Employment	−74	+1,841	+1,767	15,535	18,370	+2,835

in the proportion of wage-earners from 75·8% to 72·2%, the rest being armed forces.[5]

This tendency of the growth of the service industries, and of the growth of the 'salariat' within each industry, was common to all advanced countries.[6] It was well in evidence even before the war. Looking back to a period as recent as the 1870's, 'we wonder to-day that the world ever went on with so few to administer its services and apply and advance its techniques'.[7] This growing class contributed a certain factor of stability to incomes, since its rate of unemployment was much lower than that of manual workers and its salaries also kept up better in the depressions (though they rose slower in the recovery, also),[8] and without it the depression would have been even worse.

There were social effects also. The service trades offered particularly attractive careers to women, whose numbers in many branches went up even faster than those of men. The professions themselves were transformed, lowered, perhaps, in status since their early exclusiveness, but

[1] Marsh, op. cit., p. 105; excludes defence and 'Miscellaneous'.

[2] H. Frankel, 'The Industrial Distribution of the Population of Great Britain in July 1939', J. R. Stat. S., 108/3–4, 1945, pp. 420–1.

[3] A combination of the previous two columns; as they are not drawn up strictly on the same basis, this total should be taken as approximate only.

[4] Agatha L. Chapman and Rose Knight, Wages and Salaries in the United Kingdom, 1920–1938 (Cambridge, 1953), p. 18. Excludes armed forces.

[5] Cf. also Colin Clark, National Income and Outlay (1937), p. 38, Table 13, and The Conditions of Economic Progress (2nd ed., 1951), pp. 316–25; G. D. H. and M. I. Cole, The Condition of Britain (1937), pp. 45–9; C. W. McMahon and G. D. N. Worswick, 'The Growth of Services in the Economy I', District Bank Review, No. 136, Dec. 1960.

[6] For the American experience, see G. J. Stigler, Trends in Employment in the Service Industries (Princeton, 1956).

[7] E. H. Phelps-Brown, Growth of British Industrial Relations, p. 61; also David Lockwood, The Blackcoated Worker (1958), p. 36; D. Caradog Jones, 'Some Notes on the Census of Occupations for England and Wales', J. R. Stat. S., 1915, 78/1; Elie Halevy, A History of the English People (1926), Vol. 6/I, pp. 262–5.

[8] Marley and Campion, loc. cit., pp. 92–4.

imparting a higher standing and sense of responsibility to many activities newly crystallized out as separate professions with their recognized training and codes of conduct.[1] The growing salaried and professional groups at the same time added greatly to the social stability of the country also, for with a birth rate below the average, it was invariably largely recruited from below, offering opportunities for advancement to many ambitious and capable working-class children who would have otherwise joined the most rebellious ranks of Labour.[2]

5. THE RISE IN THE STANDARD OF LIVING

It is time to draw together the many strands of information available and weave out of them a picture of general economic progress. The statistics of national income have been widely used as the most general measuring rod of economic welfare since the pioneer work by Bowley, Stamp and Colin Clark. A. R. Prest's more recent figures are summarized below:[3]

Average of Years	Net National Income of the U.K. at Factor Cost, £mn.	Index of National Income at Constant (1900) Prices, 1900 = 100	
		National Income	Income per Head
1912–14	2,301	118·4	106·6
1919–20	5,562	124·7	113·8
1921–4	4,020	110·6	102·4
1925–6	3,947	117·9	107·5
1927–9	4,159	130·1	117·5
1930–2	3,730	129·7	115·8
1933–5	4,006	143·1	126·1
1936–8	4,558	155·1	134·9

In spite of some apparent increases in the post-war boom, real national income (as well as income per head) had barely reached the pre-war level by 1924. Total output probably exceeded the best of the years before 1914,

[1] Two opposing views will be found in A. M. Carr-Saunders and P. A. Wilson, *The Professions* (1933), and R. Lewis and Angus Maude, *Professional People* (1952).
[2] Lockwood, *passim*, esp. chapter 4; F. D. Klingender, *Clerical Labour in Britain* (1935).
[3] A. R. Prest, 'National Income of the United Kingdom 1870–1946', *Econ. J.*, 58/229, 1948; A. L. Bowley, *Studies in the National Income, 1924–1938* (Cambridge, 1942), esp. Table IX, p. 81; Colin Clark, *The Conditions of Economic Progress* (1951 ed.), esp. p. 63; A. L. Bowley and J. C. Stamp, *The National Income, 1924* (1927); Colin Clark, *National Income and Outlay* (1937), Table 37, p. 88, also pp. 267–9; J. B. Jefferys and D. Walters, 'National Income and Expenditure of the U.K., 1870–1952', *Income and Wealth*, Series V, p. 19, Table VIII.

Social Conditions Between the Wars

but it was neutralized by the loss of income from abroad owing to the sale of assets during the war. From 1925 onward a remarkable and sustained rise set in, barely held back by the depression. From the beginning of the recovery onward the rate of increase was speeded up, the late 1930's showing as much increase as the whole of the period between 1913 and the mid-1930's. This was true both of total national income, and of income per head, in real terms.

Within these totals of all incomes, real wages also rose substantially, though their rise was more evenly spread between the 1920's and the 1930's. The main changes may be summarized as follows (1930 = 100):[1]

	Cost-of-Living Index	Average Annual Real Earnings (Salaries and Wages)	Index of Intra-Industry Real Earnings of Wage-earners	Net Real Wages per Full-time Week (Kuczynski)	Real Wage Rates
1920	157·6	84·1	90·9	97·1	94·7
1924	110·8	90·7	91·3	88·3	91·9
1929	103·8	96·5	97·2	93·2	96·7
1932	91·1	106·5	105·9	102·9	106·1
1937	97·5	105·2	105·9	101·0	105·2
1938	98·7	107·1	108·7	103·9	107·0

It should be noted that these figures of real earnings depend heavily on the cost-of-living index, which was itself the subject of much debate. The second column refers to wages plus salaries, and the last three to wages only, but in the main the movements are not dissimilar. After stagnation in the early 1920's,[2] real wages rose by about 10% to 1930 and continued to rise in the depression years, remaining almost stationary for the rest of the 1930's.

This picture would be strongly modified by the incidence of unemployment. It is, in particular, to a large extent the improved employment position which caused the national income to rise in the late 1930's while real wages per head of employed worker remained constant. Further, if the earnings of the men in work were spread over the whole of the working class, including those out of work, the post-war position would compare

[1] A. L. Chapman and Rose Knight, *Wages and Salaries in the United Kingdom, 1920–1938* (Cambridge, 1953), Tables 11, 14, pp. 30–3; J. Kuczynski, *A Short History of Labour Conditions in Great Britain, 1750 to the Present Day* (1946 ed.), p. 120; last column based on E. C. Ramsbottom, 'The Course of Wage Rates in the United Kingdom, 1921–1934', *J. R. Stat. S.*, 98/4, 1935, 'Wage Rates in the United Kingdom, 1934–1937', *ibid.*, 101/1, 1938, and 'Wage Rates in the United Kingdom in 1938', *ibid.*, 102/2, 1939.

[2] E. V. Morgan, *Studies in British Financial Policy, 1914–25* (1952), pp. 284–6.

far less favourably with that of pre-war. The inclusion of unemployment (and unemployment benefit) would postpone the date at which the high wages of 1913 were being earned again from 1927 to 1930, and would put the post-war peak of 1937 at a bare 5%, instead of 13%, above the 1913 real wage rate.[1] Some observers, however, expressed the more optimistic view that 'the British (working class) consumer, in fact, has for several years been getting the best of both worlds. From 1929 to 1932 the fall in prices outweighed to his advantage the fall in employment. And from 1933 to 1937 the rise in employment outweighed to his advantage the rise in prices.'[2] Most estimates put the increase in real weekly wages between the pre-war years and 1937-8 at between 20% and 33%, while the working day was shorter by about one hour.[3]

The rise in living standards, and especially in real incomes of the working classes, was the outcome of several factors, some of which have been discussed already. Among them was the increase in output per man-hour,[4] the improvement in the terms of trade,[5] and an increase in the proportion of the national product consumed.[6] Other relevant factors were a change in the age structure, an increase in the proportion of salaried, i.e. higher-paid, employees, and a slight tendency towards greater equality in incomes. The main factor working in the opposite direction, and cancelling a large part of these advantages, was the heavy increase in unemployment.[7]

The change in the age structure was of considerable importance:

> Between 1891 and 1947 the number of people aged 15–64 per con-
> sumer has risen from ·60 to ·68. Thus if we still had the 19th century
> age distribution the national income per head would be—other things
> being equal—about one-eighth lower than it actually is . . . this change
> in age balance has been an appreciable factor in the rise in our standard
> of life over the last seventy years.[8]

---

[1] J. Kuczynski, *A Short History of Labour Conditions in Great Britain, 1750 to the Present Day* (1946 ed.), p. 120; cf. also G. D. H. Cole and R. Postgate, *The Common People, 1746–1938* (1938), chapter 49.

[2] *Economist*, 1.1.1938, p. 14; also in G. D. A. MacDougall, 'General Survey, 1929–1937', in *Britain in Recovery* (1938), pp. 26–7.

[3] E. H. Phelps-Brown, *The Growth of British Industrial Relations* (1959), p. 345; W. A. Lewis, *Economic Survey, 1919–1939* (1949), p. 139.

[4] pp. 96–7 above. Also K. S. Lomax, 'Production and Productivity Movements in the U.K. since 1900', *J. R. Stat. S.*, 122/2, 1959; T. M. Ridley, 'Industrial Production in the U.K., 1900–1953', *Economica*, N.S., 22/85, 1955; Colin Clark, *The Conditions of Economic Progress* (1951 ed.), pp. 63, 269.

[5] p. 189 above.

[6] p. 232 above.

[7] Section 1 of this chapter. Cf. also A. E. Kahn, *Great Britain in the World Economy* (New York, 1946), p. 265.

[8] *Report of the Royal Commission on Population* (1949. Cmd. 7695), p. 112.

Social Conditions Between the Wars

A more refined calculation, taking into account not only the changes among producers, but also the changing composition of the consuming public (e.g. children counting as a fraction of adults), reached the following conclusion:[1]

	'Producer Units'	'Consumer Units'
1911	31·85 million	30·9 million
1938	40·46 ,,	36·515 ,,
Increase	+27%	+18%

Before the war, a large part, perhaps one-half, of the long-term increase in real wages had been due simply to a shift of wage-earners into better jobs, but in the inter-war years this effect was negligible.[2] Instead, there was a marked shift into salaried occupations, and in spite of their low remuneration in some cases,[3] this shift normally meant both an increase in weekly pay, and a reduction in the incidence of unemployment.

Lastly, real wages rose because of a redistribution of income in favour of wage-earners. The constancy of the wage bill as a proportion of total national income around the 40% mark has often been noted; but in view of the fact that wage-earners formed a steadily falling proportion of the total occupied population, from 78·0% in 1900 to 74·1% in 1913, 73·0% in 1924 and 71·4% in 1938, according to Phelps-Brown and Hart,[4] their constant share of the total national income clearly represents a relative rise in their income.

The parallel long-run egalitarian tendency in the distribution of property, however, was so slight as to be hardly perceptible. In spite of heavy progressive death duties and direct taxation, the economic system evidently worked so much in favour of those owning capital that total distribution was left virtually unchanged. According to estate duty returns, in 1911–13, 96·9% of persons owning property owned under £1,000 each, and in 1936–8 the figure was still 93·0%. At the other end of the scale, 0·4% of property owners owned 55·6% of the total capital in 1911–13, and in 1936–8, 0·95% of owners owned 55·68% of the capital,[5] and even then

---

[1] Mark Abrams, *The Condition of the British People, 1911–1945* (1945), p. 29, also p. 56; Colin Clark, *National Income and Outlay*, pp. 15–16.

[2] A. L. Bowley, *Wages and Incomes in the U.K. since 1860* (Cambridge, 1937), Appx. C; Chapman and Knight, *op. cit.*, pp. 33–4.

[3] A. Hutt, *The Condition of the Working Class in Britain* (1933), chapter 8.

[4] E. H. Phelps-Brown and P. E. Hart, 'The Share of Wages in the National Income', *Econ. J.*, 62/246, 1952, pp. 276–7; Clark, *National Income*, pp. 94, 100–1, 125; Bowley, *Studies in the National Income*, pp. 56–8; Chapman and Knight, pp. 18–23.

[5] H. Campion, *Public and Private Property in Great Britain* (1939); Kathleen M. Langley, 'The Distribution of Capital in Private Hands, 1936–1938 and 1946–1947', *Bull. Oxf. Inst. Stat.*, 12/12, 1950, Table on p. 355 and 13/2, 1951, pp. 45–7; G. W. Daniels and H. Campion, *The Distribution of the National Capital* (Manchester,

much of the apparent redistribution was clearly caused by precautions taken against the incidence of death duties.

In sum, there was in this period an appreciable rise in the standards of comfort and welfare of working-class families, particularly those in which the wage-earners were in regular employment. This conclusion is supported by the remarkable increase in small savings, including working-class savings, showing some margin of income above bare subsistence.[1] It is also supported by the significant change in the pattern of working-class expenditure, as shown in the budgets used by the Ministry of Labour, after large-scale sample inquiries, for its cost-of-living index.[2]

These budgets show that in 1937–8, as compared with before 1914, the 'average' working-class family had fewer people between whom the larger income was divided, and that there were consequent reductions in the shares of income expended in food, clothing and rent, leaving quite large increases in expenditure for non-necessities and semi-luxuries. These were often the very items which could be cheapened by mass-production, so that the improvement of the material conditions of life for the large majority of the population was very much greater than the monetary measure might imply. Statistics fail to take full account of the difference made by electricity instead of candles, and gas cookers instead of coal or coke ranges, as standard equipment in working-class homes; of improved housing, including indoor water and sanitation; or of radio, the cinema and newspapers within almost everybody's reach. A most significant pointer was the adoption, in 1938, of one week's paid holiday as standard practice, after the report of Lord Amulree's Committee on Holidays with Pay,[3] in all the industries in which conditions were governed by Trade Boards or Agricultural Wage Boards. It might have been enforced elsewhere but for the war. Up to 1937, only $1\frac{1}{2}$–$1\frac{3}{4}$ million wage-earners received paid holidays by collective agreement, though the total receiving paid holidays was nearer 4 millions out of the $18\frac{1}{2}$ millions earning £250 a year or less; in 1939 it was 11 millions, or the large majority, though few of these had the resources of experience as yet to spend their holidays away from home.[4]

1936); G. D. H. and M. I. Cole, *The Condition of Britain* (1937), p. 75; C. L. Mowat, *Britain Between the Wars* (1956 ed.), p. 494.

[1] pp. 234–5 above, also G. D. H. Cole, *Money, Trade and Investment* (1954), pp. 220–1; Esme Preston, 'Personal Savings Through Institutional Channels (1937–1949)', *Bull. Oxf. Inst. Stat.*, 12/9, 1950, Table 7, p. 252; Henry Durant and J. Goldmann, 'The Distribution of Working-Class Savings', *ibid.*, 7/1, 1945.

[2] pp. 177–8 above, Mark Abrams, *op. cit.*, pp. 84–5; *Min. Labour Gazette*, Dec. 1940.

[3] Cmd. 5724 (1938).

[4] C. L. Mowat, *Britain Between the Wars* (1956 ed.), pp. 500–1; Phelps-Brown, *op. cit.*, pp. 347–8; Elizabeth Brunner, *Holiday Making and Holiday Trades* (1945), pp. 9, 13–15; J. A. R. Pimlott, *The Englishman's Holiday* (1947), pp. 214–15.

Within the basic food bill itself, there was a decline in the consumption of the cheap filler and substitute foods, while the consumption of foodstuffs of which the demand was highly elastic with respect to incomes, or which were considered semi-luxuries, increased rapidly. The consumption of wheat, for example, fell from 4·28 lb. per head per week in 1910–14 to 4·05 lb. in 1924 and 3·77 lb. in 1938. Other foods are shown below:[1]

	Annual Consumption	
	1920–2	1937–8
Potatoes (tons per head)	0·083	0·074
Fresh milk (mn. gall.)	848	1,000
Cream (mn. gall.)	3·22	9·19
Eggs (mn.)	3,915	9,385
Soft drinks (mn. gall.)	1·72	5·79
Sugar, chocolate, confectionery (mn. tons)	1·06	1·53

The improvement in the general standard of nutrition is shown in the increase in the consumption of calories per head from 3,057 a day in 1901–13 to 3,139 in 1924–8 and 3,398 in 1937–8. Other indices compared as follows:[2]

Nutrients available per Head per Day in the U.K.

	Average 1920–2	Average 1937–8
Protein (g.)	87·2	90·55
Fat (g.)	127·1	152·9
Carbohydrates (g.)	413·0	414·95
Calcium (mg.)	754	815
Vitamin A (i.u.)	3,616	4,749
„ B_1 (mg.)	1·31	1·375
„ C (mg.)	118·0	135·5
Riboflavin (mg.)	1·71	1·90

Yet, in the face of all this indubitable progress, there were still enormous areas of poverty left, much preventible misery and illness and many premature deaths. To some extent, it was precisely the great progress already achieved which drew attention to the tasks which still awaited the social reformer. In part, it was the greatly enlarged and more detailed knowledge of the poor and their problems which brought these tasks more urgently before the public eye. This derived from various official statistics resulting from the new welfare and insurance schemes,

[1] Stone, *Consumers' Expenditure*, Tables 10, 21, 35, 45, 53, 109, 116; H. V. Edwards, 'Flour Milling', in *Further Studies in Industrial Organisation* (1948), ed. M. P. Fogarty, p. 77.
[2] Stone, *op. cit.*, Table 61; John Boyd Orr, *Food, Health and Income* (2nd ed., 1937), pp. 24–5.

and from social surveys, which followed the brilliant pioneer work of Booth and Rowntree at the turn of the century. The best-known social surveys in this period were those for London, Merseyside, Southampton, York, Tyneside, Becontree and Dagenham, Brynmawr, Bristol and Sheffield.[1] The inquiries in York and London could be directly compared with the pre-war surveys, and this was also the case in the less ambitious survey made by A. L. Bowley in five Midland towns.[2]

'Primary poverty', poverty so great that the lack of the necessary food and shelter actually impaired health and efficiency, occurred in York, in 1899, among 15·46% of the working classes, and in 1936 among 6·8%. But the definition of 'primary poverty' on which these figures were based set an impossible standard of housekeeping: it assumed that the whole income was spent in the best possible way on the most nutritious food and on other bare necessities bought in the cheapest market. It assumed that nothing was spent on more interesting food, on travelling or postage, on entertainment or smoking. In practice, human psychological needs would demand more than this bare physical minimum,[3] and a realistic standard would require a rather higher income level to meet some non-necessities as well as the minimum physical needs—the 'poverty line'. In York in 1936, 31·1% of working-class families (or 17·7% of the total population) fell below this line, and in Bristol in 1937 (a boom year), 10·7% of working-class families fell below it. In the other surveys, the 'poverty standard' differed. The London Survey used a lower figure, according to which 9·8% of the London working-class families lived in poverty in 1928, another good year. On the same standard, the proportion on Merseyside (1929) was 17·3%, in Liverpool (1929) 16·1% and in Southampton (1931) 20·0%. On the Rowntree standard, the Merseyside proportion would have been about 30%. On a different, even more rigorous physical needs standard, the Pilgrim Trust found 30% of the long-term unemployed to be in poverty, and another 14% just above it.[4]

A different study in this field was made by John (now Lord) Boyd Orr

---

[1] H. A. Mess, *Industrial Tyneside: a Social Survey* (1928); Sir. H. Llewellyn Smith (Director), *The New Survey of London Life and Labour* (9 vols., 1930–5); P. Ford, *Work and Wealth in a Modern Port: an Economic Survey of Southampton* (1934); B. Seebohm Rowntree, *Poverty and Progress* (1941); D. Caradog Jones, *Social Survey of Merseyside* (3 vols., Liverpool, 1934); Terence Young, *Becontree and Dagenham* (1934); Hilda Jennings, *Brynmawr: A Study of a Distressed Area* (1934); Herbert Tout, *Standard of Living in Bristol* (Bristol, 1938); A. D. K. Owen, *Housing Problem in Sheffield* (Sheffield, 1931), *Unemployment in Sheffield* (Sheffield, 1932), *Juvenile Employment and Welfare in Sheffield* and *Standard of Living in Sheffield* (Sheffield, 1933); and, in general, A. F. Wells, *The Local Social Survey in Great Britain* (1935).
[2] A. L. Bowley and A. R. Burnett-Hurst, *Livelihood and Poverty* (1915), and A. L. Bowley and M. H. Hogg, *Has Poverty Diminished?* (1925).
[3] G. D. H. and M. I. Cole, *Condition of Britain*, pp. 134–8.
[4] Pilgrim Trust, *Men Without Work* (Cambridge, 1938), p. 109.

in 1936,[1] who showed that about one-tenth of the total population was unable, on its income, to buy food that would be sufficient either in vitamins or in calories, and that as much as half the population was bound to have diets deficient in some respects even in the most prosperous years of the 1930's: the food consumption of the lower-income groups would have to rise by 12–25% before it became sufficient for maintaining perfect health. At the same time, at least two-thirds of the population, or the large majority of working-class homes, had no savings to fall back on to eke out longer periods of inadequate wages.[2]

With the general reduction in the size of families, the economic effects of children took on a new importance. 'The incidence of poverty', stated the Report to the Pilgrim Trust,[3] 'is progressively greater according to the number of children under working age in the family concerned.' Looked at from another angle, this meant that a far larger proportion of children than of adults lived in poverty such as to affect their health and growth. In York, Rowntree found that while only 31·1% of the working-class population lived below the poverty line, 52·5% of the children under one and 49·7% of the children from one to five did so. Similarly, in Birmingham, in a sample survey in 1939, it was found that 14% of the families, but 30% of the children, had insufficient food.[4] The social conscience of many who were not perturbed by the poverty of adults was roused by the thought of poverty among children, and a strong movement developed, led by Eleanor Rathbone,[5] for family allowances for all, including those in work, in order to reduce the economic burdens of children in working-class households.

The causes of poverty were essentially the same as before 1914: the interruption of the earning power of the main breadwinner owing to illness, to casual type of work, or, above all, to unemployment; an inadequate wage; and a large family of dependants. Several of these causes could be present at the same time. There had been progress, but there was still much poverty, and much reluctance to extend further the social welfare provisions already in existence. It was not the least of the consequences of the second World War that the hopes and dreams of the small minority with the most sensitive social conscience in the 1930's became acceptable as social legislation to the large majority after 1945.

---

[1] J. Boyd Orr, *Food, Health and Income* (1936, 2nd ed. 1937); also Sir George Newman, *The Building of a Nation's Health* (1939), pp. 352–9.
[2] John Hilton, *Rich Man, Poor Man* (1944, 3rd impr. 1947), pp. 23–6.
[3] *Op. cit.*, p. 11.
[4] Mark Abrams, *op. cit.*, pp. 99 ff.
[5] See esp. E. F. Rathbone, *The Disinherited Family* (1924, new ed. 1949), and Mary Stocks, *Eleanor Rathbone* (1949), chapter 8.

CHAPTER VI

The British Economy in Total War, 1939–1945

1. THE WAR ECONOMY AND ECONOMIC PLANNING

The outbreak of the second World War in September 1939 found the British Government prepared to a much greater extent for the policies of economic control than it had been in 1914. The experience of 1914–18 had not been entirely forgotten. From the early 1930's on, several Government departments had been engaged in preparing elaborate war plans, and some of the necessary legislation was passed within a few days of the declaration of war. Some of the very officials chosen to implement economic war policy in 1939–40 were the same persons who had administered the controls of 1917–18. As a result, the war economy shifted into gear more quickly in the second World War than the first, and many of the earlier errors were avoided.

In 1914 the strain on the economy caused by maintaining a large army in the field had been ludicrously underestimated. Instead of requiring merely an enlargement of the munitions industry, to be called forth by the usual method of placing orders, it was found that the effects of war production were such that the necessary controls had to be pushed further and further back, until finally virtually all civilian activities were brought under the purview of Government departments. In 1939 it was, therefore, understood that the apparatus of control would have to reach back far beyond the munitions industry, though at first few concrete steps were taken.[1] The second main lesson digested, perhaps too well, was the need to enlist the voluntary support of labour, particularly in the munitions and other essential industries, and the Ministry of Labour in particular, mindful of the costly strikes of 1914–18, fell over backwards to retain the goodwill of workers and their leaders.

There were also other lessons of value carried over from the first war to the second, such as the methods of civilian food rationing, and the Schedule of Reserved Occupations evolved in the 1930's, on the basis of

[1] E.g. I. Bowen and G. D. N. Worswick, 'The Controls and War Finance' (1940), in Oxford Institute of Statistics, *Studies in War Economics* (Oxford, 1947).

the Schedule of Protected Occupations of the earlier war, to prevent the call-up of key workers.[1] Nevertheless, it seems in retrospect that many lessons that ought to have been learnt had been forgotten, or were applied too late after great and unnecessary cost. The control of civilian trade and consumption, the control over the foreign exchanges and capital movements, the control over labour demand and supply, rationing of food and the expansion of munition-making and machine tool capacity all appeared as belated measures forced on the Government by the march of events rather than as orderly stages of the creation of a war economy. Even some specific errors of the first World War were repeated, including a rash over-recruitment from the mines, resulting in a fuel shortage later, an agricultural expansion programme neglecting the importance of saving the bulkiest imports, and an over-optimistic assessment of shipping needs and resources which seriously endangered military operations and civilian supplies at several critical points during the war.

There was a certain basic similarity between the two World Wars, as far as British economic strategy was concerned. Both wars were fought against the same main enemy, Germany, occupying with her Allies the centre of the European continent, and relying largely on vast initial superiority and on U-boat power at sea, while Britain and her Allies, entering the war far less prepared, depended on their command of the world's resources outside Europe to build up gradually a power superior to Germany's with which to crush her after weakening her by means of an economic blockade. But here the similarity ends, for quite apart from the obvious consequences of technical changes, such as the vulnerability of Britain to serious air attacks, the second World War saw Britain, after less than one year's hostilities, facing without a major continental ally a powerful enemy who controlled most of Europe, and above all the coastline opposite these islands. Whereas in the first World War the position of the chief belligerents in the west was never seriously threatened, the second World War, besides the much greater part played in it by non-European battlefields, witnessed several startling reverses of fortune, including the fall of France and the successive entry of Soviet Russia, the U.S.A. and Japan, besides minor powers, into the war. Each of these imposed major changes of economic policy, so that the economic history of this period is best treated in the light of the needs of these successive phases of the war, rather than as a gradually emergent controlled economy, as in 1914–18.

[1] W. K. Hancock and M. M. Gowing, *British War Economy* (1949), pp. 48 ff. The present section is based largely on that work, which forms the central volume in the Official History of the Second World War, United Kingdom Civil Series (H.S.W.W.), as well as on the other volumes in that series. An excellent summary of Hancock and Gowing will be found in the form of chapter 5 of A. J. Youngson, *The British Economy, 1920–1957* (1960).

The War Economy and Economic Planning

Four main phases of the war may be distinguished. The first period, the 'phoney war', was essentially a period of waiting, in which the Allies, apparently secure behind the Channel and the Maginot line, expected to be allowed to build up their military strength while Germany, with vastly superior forces on land and in the air, stood idly by. This pipe dream was shattered by the German invasion and occupation of Norway, Denmark, Holland, Belgium and part of France, and the period ended with the evacuation of the British Expeditionary Force from Dunkirk. The second period ran from the summer of 1940 to the Japanese attack on Pearl Harbour in December 1941. It began with the air 'Battle of Britain' designed to paralyse British defences and permit a German invasion of these shores, and continued as a war of attrition by air attacks and attacks on British merchant shipping. Germany also consolidated her power in the Mediterranean and seriously threatened the British positions in the Middle East. This was the period when Britain virtually stood alone and prospects seemed bleakest, as even in the distant future there seemed to be no way of overcoming the superior economic and manpower resources of the enemy. Even the German attack in the east in the summer of 1941, which was ultimately to prove so disastrous to the Axis powers, gave no immediate relief to Britain who, on the contrary, made some of her scarce resources available to her new Russian ally.

With the entry of the U.S.A. into the war in December 1941 ultimate victory for the Allies seemed again a reasonable hope, but meanwhile the third phase of the war, which lasted until the invasion of Normandy in June 1944, had opened disastrously with the sinkings at Pearl Harbour, withdrawals in the Middle East, the loss of much of South-Eastern Asia to the Japanese and severe shipping losses in the Atlantic. Further, in the first year the entry of America increased rather than relieved the pressure on the British economy, for American Lend-Lease shipments were reduced in favour of American mobilization, and much valuable British tonnage was diverted to the use of the American services. It took some time for the vast productive potential of the U.S.A. to be converted into actual munitions, but when these began to come off the production lines, North Africa was invaded and cleared of the enemy, and Allied landings in Italy were paralleled by the Russian counter-offensives in the east and victorious American actions in the Pacific.

The fourth phase was ushered in by the invasion of Normandy by British and American forces after the Allies had established complete superiority at sea and in the air (apart from the unmanned V-weapons launched against Britain). Despite the successful establishment of a bridgehead in the west, and the advance of the Red Army in the east, the war against Germany, contrary to expectations, dragged on until May 1945, causing great strain, particularly on the Allied transport system. By contrast, the fighting against Japan, estimated to take 12–18 months after 'V.E.-day', was over in a few weeks, thanks largely to the grim destruction wrought by the atom bombs on Hiroshima and Nagasaki.

The term 'phoney war' referred to military operations, but it could with equal justice have been applied to British economic warfare. Actual preparations for the war, as distinct from paper planning, had been negligible with a single exception. This was the remarkably effective, and perhaps decisive, creation of aircraft building capacity under the programmes of 1936 and after, both by the expansion of aircraft firms and by calling into being 'shadow' aircraft factories set up by motor and electrical equipment manufacturers and others.[1] Even the eleventh-hour suggestion by Sir Arthur Salter of stockpiling certain strategic raw materials, and the bulk-purchasing agreements for Australian and New Zealand wool, were made too late to bring tangible results before the actual declaration of war on 3rd September 1939.[2]

This declaration, it is true, was accompanied by a formidable array of legislation, prepared beforehand. The Emergency Powers (Defence) Act, 1939, had been passed on 24th August and gave the most far-reaching powers to the Government, acting by Statutory Rules and Orders: these were confirmed, though scarcely extended, by two further Emergency Powers Acts in 1940. In addition, some sixty other statutes were passed in the early weeks of the war. By 1st September several new Ministries had been created, including the Ministries of Supply, of Economic Warfare, of Home Security, of Information, of Food and of Shipping, united in May 1941 with Transport to become the Ministry of War Transport. Recruitment was added to the duties of the Ministry of Labour, which thus became the Ministry of Labour and National Service and as such played one of the central parts in the combined economic and military strategy of the war. There were also innumerable co-ordinating, planning and emergency committees and boards established at an early date.

The crucial role of translating the needs of the Services into orders for industry, and converting industry to a war footing to supply them, was intended for the Ministry of Supply. In the event, the Admiralty successfully stood out for independent control over the shipbuilding programme, both naval and mercantile,[3] and the R.A.F. was allowed to control its own supply of aircraft, so that the Ministry of Supply was restricted to supplying the Army, and a limited range of arms and stores to the other two

[1] P. W. S. Andrews and E. Brunner, *Life of Lord Nuffield* (Oxford, 1955), Part IV, chapter 6; P.E.P., *Engineering Reports II: Motor Vehicles* (1950), pp. 39–40.

[2] J. Hurstfield, *The Control of Raw Materials* (H.S.W.W., 1953), p. 79, Appx. I, pp. 427–30, also his 'Control of Raw Material Supplies, 1919–1939', *Ec. Hist. Rev.*, 14/1–2, 1944, pp. 25–6.

[3] J. D. Scott and Richard Hughes, *The Administration of War Production* (H.S.W.W., 1955), pp. 140–7, 213–16.

The War Economy and Economic Planning

Services. In 1940 the Ministry of Aircraft Production was set up, occupying the centre of the stage in the critical summer months of 1940, and continuing as the third supply department thereafter.[1]

There was thus a great deal of administrative activity, but there was as yet little positive action to show for it. Deeming the country secure from direct attack, the Government went ahead with its leisurely plan of gearing British production to a target of eventual superiority over Germany three years hence. Government expenditure ran at £20 million a week at the outbreak of war and was still only £33½ million weekly in the sixth month, and much of that increase was due to price rises. The production of munitions was nowhere near the limits of physical capacity. Even though the shortage of foreign exchange had been one of the most serious problems in the 1914–18 war, control was still lax. While British holdings of foreign securities had to be registered, and Treasury permission for payments abroad had become obligatory, foreign holders of sterling balances could still engage in exchange dealings, and there was still freedom of payments within the Sterling Area until May 1940.[2]

The numbers in the Services had risen from 480,000 in June 1939 to 1,850,000 at the end of March 1940, but there were still 1 million unemployed in April 1940, and little consideration was as yet given to a planned allocation of manpower. Similarly, because of the surplus tonnage of the 1930's, and the expectation that the shipping of many neutral countries could be hired, if necessary, there was no serious rationing of shipping space, so that in the first eight months of war, when conditions were so much easier than they were to become later, there was actually a fall in some of the most vital stocks, including fats, sugar, timber, oil and iron ore. At the same time the production of many inessentials continued unhindered.[3]

Since so many resources were still not fully employed, there appeared to be as yet no need of general economic planning, and departments pursued their own policies, even competing for the same scarce resources without co-ordination with their neighbours. The authorities were aware of the need for preserving the right pace of mobilization: there was no point, for example, in conscripting soldiers who could not be provided with equipment, and since there was assumed to be no great urgency in expanding the armed forces, the programme of building munition-making capacity was allowed to gather momentum at its own pace, dictating the

[1] Scott and Hughes, Part IV.
[2] T. Balogh, 'The Drift Towards a Rational Foreign Exchange Policy', *Economica*, N.S., 7/27, 1940, and 'Foreign Exchange and Export Trade Policy', *Econ. J.*, 50/197, 1940; R. F. Harrod, *The Life of John Maynard Keynes* (1951), pp. 494 ff.
[3] E. L. Hargreaves and M. M. Gowing, *Civil Industry and Trade* (H.S.W.W., 1952), pp. 16–18.

speed of mobilization.[1] 'Reflecting upon this first period of the war, the historian finds himself oppressed by a feeling of lost opportunity.' [2]

The Government was at this stage still concerned with providing specific items demanded by the Services, such as aircraft and guns, rather than with the total planning of resources. It was sensitive to only one general index of the growing strain on resources, the rise in the cost of living, which actually proceeded faster in the early months of the second World War than it had done in the first, and conjured up dangers of similar labour troubles. In the official index, certain foods were heavily overweighted, so that it was possible, while negotiating with the unions for wage restraint in November 1939, to extend, secretly, the first food subsidy to some of these items as a cheap way of keeping down the cost-of-living *index*.[3] From this beginning was gradually built up a consistent policy of large-scale subsidy for items within the working-class cost-of-living index, and of heavy taxation of goods outside it. In the early months, however, subsidies, combined with the limitation of profit margins, operating from the 1st January 1940, merely served to create an irrational price structure.

By April–May 1940 the growing impact of mobilization was beginning to affect the economy at several points at once. The engineering industry, as the basis of the munitions industry, began to feel a shortage of skilled workers as well as of machine tools, a large proportion of which had to be imported; there was a drain on the foreign exchange reserves and a consequent need to divert resources to exports; there was need to build up stocks, in the face of a growing shipping shortage. These and other pressures were on the point of enforcing their own logic of a more thorough-going system of economic control, when the German offensive, ending in the collapse of France, completely shattered the long-term time-table to which the British war economy had been geared.

The debacle in the west was not, as it turned out, an unmitigated disaster. It led to the replacement of Chamberlain's Conservative Ministry by a Coalition Government led by Winston Churchill, which infused great vigour at once into all Government operations, and, enjoying the confidence of the whole nation, including labour, could pursue and enforce policies of a harshness which its predecessor would not have dared to contemplate. The British people as a whole had been shocked into a willingness to work and to bear privations both of material standards and of traditional liberties inconceivable before May 1940. The very isolation of Britain in Europe brought the realities of the war home to the American

[1] M. M. Postan, *British War Production* (H.S.W.W., 1952), p. 102.
[2] Hancock and Gowing, p. 149.
[3] H. M. D. Parker, *Manpower, a Study of War-Time Policy and Administration* (H.S.W.W., 1957), p. 82; R. S. Sayers, *Financial Policy, 1939–1945* (H.S.W.W., 1956), pp. 63–4.

people to a sufficient extent to permit President Roosevelt to authorize aid culminating in Lend-Lease in March 1941.[1] Lastly, there were more immediate and tangible benefits, such as the end of the need to supply France with scarce coal, and the addition to shipping tonnage under British control as Norwegian, Dutch and other masters sought refuge in ports in Allied hands.

All these, however, were minor advantages compared with the strategic and economic problems posed by the devastating military reverse. Britain lay open to German bombing by air, especially of communications and war industries, and the production drive was thus severely hampered by delays, precautions, dispersals, as well as by direct damage. The dangers to shipping were immeasurably increased, and the east coast ports had to be closed to the larger vessels, blocking up still further the bottle-necks at the west coast ports. The supply of several important raw materials, including high-grade iron ore, was cut off at once. The hope of strangling Germany by blockade was converted into an immediate danger of a blockade of this country, carried out by U-boats, mines and aircraft.[2] Meanwhile, contrary to Britain's tradition of providing ships and material to aid an allied Continental army, she had for the first time to build up a large army herself, while strengthening the equipment of the other two Services also. The sudden increases of demand on home industry, resources and manpower drove Britain to a hasty improvisation of innumerable economic controls. They were only slowly built up into an integrated system in the following years.

The controls had to be set up in the midst of the air Battle of Britain, when by the orders of the new Minister of Aircraft Production, Lord Beaverbrook, the building of aircraft became number one priority, and in view of the threatening invasion, the projects that could be completed quickly had overriding priority claims to all resources. The air battle was won by such means, but only at the expense of disrupting long-term mobilization plans. From the autumn of 1940 onward, however, great strides were made in techniques of planning as well as in methods of financial control.

The year 1941 was certainly a watershed in the conduct of the war, producing firm policies of taxation, of free and forced saving, of price control, of rationing and control of civilian supplies, together with exhaustive discussions of wages policy. In 1941, too, these problems were considered as parts of one another. The whole economic situation was illuminated in that year by the new statistical analysis contained in the first white paper on national income and expenditure.[3]

---

[1] R. D. Hall, *North American Supply* (H.S.W.W., 1955), p. 127.
[2] W. N. Medlicott, *The Economic Blockade*, Vol. 1 (H.S.W.W., 1952), chapter 12.
[3] Hancock and Gowing, p. 152. See pp. 324–6 below.

Economists and statisticians, basically in favour of the national income approach, were employed in increasing numbers in key departmental posts. Those in the War Cabinet Secretariat were split into the 'Central Statistical Office' and the 'Economic Section' in January 1941, and Keynes himself had become economic adviser to the Treasury some months earlier.[1] One of the earliest lessons they taught was the interchangeable nature of scarce resources. Thus, for example, food could be brought in from North America, a short trip using little tonnage, but costly in hard currency, or it could be brought in from Australia, using only sterling currency, but much more costly in tonnage. Scarce shipping and scarce foreign exchange were thus substitutes for one another up to a point, and since both could be saved by employing more labour in home agriculture to raise British home output, scarce labour could be used as a substitute for either.

A second principle was also established as a result of the experience of the aircraft programme of the summer of 1940. 'Priorities' as a method of control had proved utterly unsuitable, except for the occasional crash programme, for often the higher-priority product was produced only at great cost in terms of another product, only slightly less essential, and a system of relative priorities ultimately left the decision to the individual manufacturer and his ability to secure his own supplies of components, raw materials and labour. Instead, a system of allocation was evolved, which ensured to each department, and each manufacturer, a designated quantum of supplies, the total allocation being equivalent to the total quantity available.[2]

Such a system could work only if there was a basis of knowledge of the resources available, and if there was some supreme authority, capable of deciding between different claims on scarce resources, in the light of strategic needs and, in particular, between the claims of the Services as a whole and the need to provide sufficient civilian goods to maintain morale and efficiency at home.[3] It was in this period that many new statistical services and methods were evolved, and that the Production Executive, a Committee of the War Cabinet under the Lord President of the Council, emerged as the main arbiter on planning, with the Joint War Production Staff below it.[4] From it radiated the lines of command and communication

[1] U. K. Hicks, *Public Finance* (1947), p. 41; Harrod, *Life of Keynes*, pp. 501-3; D. N. Chester, 'The Central Machinery for Economic Policy', in *Lessons of the British War Economy* (Cambridge, 1951).

[2] Hurstfield, *op. cit.*, pp. 89 ff.; Postan, pp. 159-61.

[3] Hargreaves and Gowing, chapter 13.

[4] Postan, pp. 142 ff., 248 ff; Scott and Hughes, Part 5; also Gilbert Walker, *Economic Planning by Programme and Control in Great Britain* (1957), chapter 3; E. A. G. Robinson, 'The Overall Allocation of Resources', E. Devons, 'The Problem of Co-ordination in Aircraft Production', R. Pares, 'The Work of a Departmental Priority Office', in *Lessons of the British War Economy*.

which ultimately made up the economic planning machine. In February 1942, the Ministry of Production was created as a further co-ordinating agency.

There was, in all this, little direct control of industry, though powers existed for it. Apart from the State-owned Royal Ordnance factories, which at their peak employed 300,000 workers,[1] the dockyards and the 170 'agency' factories, the Government did not own any enterprises itself. It had immediate direction of some basic industries and services, such as the railways or the ports, and it gave some detailed directives elsewhere, as in the 'concentration' schemes, organized by the Board of Trade in 1941 in the hosiery, cotton and other less essential industries, with the object of minimizing their use of resources without destroying their peace-time markets.[2] But by and large private managements were left in control of their firms, being made to conform to central plans indirectly, by allocations of raw materials[3] and labour, by licensing of capital equipment and maintenance, by controlled prices, especially by the Goods and Services (Price Control) Act of 1941, by taxes and by other incentives.

Similarly, in spite of the unrestricted powers of conscription of workers, given to the Minister by S.R. & O. (1940), No. 781, and in spite of the fact that the manpower budget and allocation became the central planning tool, labour, while directed in some isolated cases (the selective coal-mining scheme of August 1943, yielding 22,000 as 'Bevin boys' to the mines, being perhaps the most spectacular), was not normally individually conscripted. Under the Essential Works Order and the Registration for Employment Order, S.R. & O. (1941), Nos. 302 and 368, workers could be sent to, or kept in, essential industries or occupations, according to their age, sex and skill, but their actual employers and their right to move was left to their own choice as far as possible.

Finally, there were no full and self-consistent economic plans made for each period *ab initio*, as was attempted in the U.S.A.: the most that could be done with existing knowledge and powers and machinery was to 'allocate upon the user basis for preceding periods, modified where necessary by changes in the requirements or supply situations'.[4] Some sectors, retail distribution being perhaps the most important, could not be controlled at all for the purpose of yielding up resources (other than

---

[1] William Hornby, *Factories and Plant* (H.S.W.W., 1958), p. 89; P. Inman, *Labour in the Munitions Industries* (H.S.W.W., 1957), p. 180.

[2] Board of Trade, *Concentration of Production* (1941. Cmd. 6258); Hargreaves and Gowing, chapter 10; G. D. N. Worswick, 'Concentration in the Leicester Hosiery Industry', *Bull. Oxf. Inst. Stat.*, 3/6, 1941, and 'Concentration, Success or Failure?' *ibid.*, 3/16, 1941; G. C. Allen, 'The Concentration of Production Policy', in D. N. Chester (ed.), *Lessons of the British War Economy*.

[3] W. Ashworth, *Contracts and Finance* (H.S.W.W., 1953), pp. 41 ff.

[4] Hurstfield, *op. cit.*, p. 95.

labour) for the war effort, in spite of several determined attempts to do so.[1]

Nevertheless, the mechanism evolved was capable of mobilizing the British economy to an extent unmatched by any other belligerent,[2] permitting it at the same time to withstand several major shocks. As far as manpower was concerned, for example, Britain mobilized between mid-1939 and the peak period of September 1943, no fewer than 8½ million insured persons (18% of the total population) for the Forces, the auxiliary Forces, and the munitions industries, beside some 400,000 workers past insurable age, 160,000 from Ireland (North and South), many thousands of other immigrants and refugees, and ultimately 224,000 prisoners of war. 4¾ million were drawn from civilian industries, 1¼ million from among the unemployed, and 2½ million from formerly non-industrial classes, mainly housewives and domestic workers.[3] These shifts, in turn, caused other complex shifts and replacements, from jobs of lesser war importance to jobs of greater importance. There were also the special schemes of allocating scarce craftsmen, the geographical transfer of factories from scarce labour areas to areas of surplus labour, the dilution of skills and re-designing of jobs, and many other adjustments.[4] The conscription of women, authorized in December 1941, was an unprecedented move, a symbol of the extent to which the country was prepared to accept control over labour.

Similarly, with a shipping tonnage scarcely above the pre-war level,[5] and far less effective because of the convoy system and congestion at the ports, Britain succeeded in supplying the booming munitions and other industries with raw materials, in transporting and supplying troops to distant theatres of war, in sending convoys to Russia, in transporting American troops and their supplies to this country, and in launching the sea-borne invasions of North Africa, Italy, Southern France and, finally, Normandy, while not neglecting to supply her dependent territories in

[1] Henry Smith, *Retail Distribution* (2nd ed., 1948), p. 145, chapter 6; J. B. Jefferys, *Retail Trading in Britain, 1850–1950* (Cambridge, 1954), chapter 3; H. Levy, *Retail Trade Associations* (1942), chapter 19; Board of Trade, *Reports of the Retail Trade Committee* (1941–42).

[2] C. T. Saunders, 'Manpower Distribution 1939–1945: Some International Comparisons', *Manchester School*, 14/2, 1946, p. 19; A. J. Brown, *Applied Economics* (1947), p. 23.

[3] Ministry of Labour and National Service, *Report for the Years 1939–1946* (1947. Cmd. 7225), pp. 4, 54–7; Sir Godfrey Ince, 'The Mobilisation of Manpower in Great Britain for the Second World War', *Manchester School*, 14/1, 1946; M. Kalecki, 'Labour in the War Industries of Britain and the U.S.A.' (1943), in Oxford Inst. of Statistics, *Studies in War Economics*; Alan Bullock, *The Life and Times of Ernest Bevin II: Minister of Labour 1940–1945* (1967).

[4] P. Inman, *Labour in the Munitions Industries; Statistics Relating to the War Effort of the United Kingdom* (1944. Cmd. 6564), section 1.

[5] E.g. Central Statistical Office, *Statistical Digest of the War* (H.S.W.W., 1951), Table 70.

Africa or India by 'cross traffic' and to feed the home population better in many respects than it had been fed before the war.[1]

Again, rationing required a major planning effort in itself, and extended to food and clothing, as well as furniture and furnishing, the points and coupons being like a second system of prices and cash, except that the initial distribution was different,[2] and the total calculated not to exceed available supplies. It was supported by agricultural planning on the one hand, and by the unique British 'utility' scheme for clothing and furniture on the other, the latter begun under S.R. & O. (1941), No. 1281, and quickly spreading, to permit control of standards, of prices and of supplies of materials to the producers.[3]

The entry of America into the war in its third phase did not permit any relaxation of the tight control over the British economy. Ultimately, from the middle of 1943 onward, it proved possible to co-ordinate to some extent the production and use of resources of the two countries. Thus the U.S.A. increasingly produced materials of war, including merchant ships, for both, while Britain's productive potential could be used to most effect in building, e.g., warships or airfields and hutments for American troops stationed in Britain and in freeing men for the Armed Forces.[4] American ingenuity also began to take increasing account of Allied needs, devising, for example, methods of dehydrating or otherwise concentrating the foodstuffs supplied to Britain in order to save shipping space. By 1943-4, the U.S.A. supplied about one-quarter of the munitions need of the Empire, the United Kingdom still supplying well over 60%.[5]

This co-ordination was not without its own dangers and difficulties for Britain. The method of Lend-Lease put Britain in a position where she could not order, merely request, and her requests were subject to disconcerting amendment as a result of simultaneous demands by the American Services. As far as shipping was concerned, while in 1942 the losses were sustained by the British mercantile marine, the additions were made to the American, and the summer months of 1942 saw the most

[1] C. B. A. Behrens, *Merchant Shipping and the Demands of War* (H.S.W.W., 1955), chapters 12-17.

[2] L. Robbins, *The Economic Problem in Peace and War* (1947), pp. 7-8; W. B. Reddaway, 'Rationing', in *Lessons of the British War Economy*, p. 191.

[3] H. E. Wadsworth, 'Utility Cloth and Clothing Scheme', *Rev. Econ. Studies*, 16(2)/40, 1949-50; E. L. Hargreaves, 'Price Control of (Non-food) Consumer Goods', *Oxf. Econ. P.*, No. 8, 1947; M. Kalecki, 'Rationing and Price Control', *Bull. Oxf. Inst. Stat.*, 6/2, 1944 (also in *Studies in War Economics*); P. Ady, 'Utility Goods', *ibid.*, 4/15, 1942; H. A. Silverman, 'The Boot and Shoe Industry', in *Studies in Industrial Organisation* (1946), p. 230.

[4] H. D. Hall and C. C. Wrigley, *Studies of Overseas Supply* (H.S.W.W., 1956), chapters 4-6.

[5] R. G. D. Allen, 'Mutual Aid Between the U.S. and the British Empire, 1941-5', *J. R. Stat. S.*, 109/3, 1946, p. 268.

serious shipping crisis of the war. In spite of its vast absolute amount, American war production formed a much smaller share of the total national output than the British and was, unlike the British, achieved by addition to civilian output, and not at its expense.[1] American agencies, therefore, found it difficult to appreciate on what narrow margins British economic planning had to operate.

From the autumn of 1943 onward, in the last phase of the war, the Allied output of aircraft, ships, tanks, vehicles and guns had become so vastly greater than that of the Axis powers, that production had ceased to be a problem, and the main problem was to come to grips with the enemy to make the superiority effective. In Britain there could still be no relaxation, however. Manpower began to be transferred from industry to the Forces, and production and strategic allocations were afoot to deal with Japan, as well as with the reconstruction and export needs of the first years of peace, particularly their expected critical foreign exchange position. The manpower budget for the first year after Victory in Europe, but before the defeat of Japan, estimated that 2·6 million persons of those released from the Forces and war industries would be available for employment. Against this, the necessary increase in the production of civilian consumption goods, capital goods and exports were estimated to require 3·4 million workers, so that there was still an estimated shortfall of 800,000 workers.

2. INDUSTRY IN THE WAR YEARS

Britain being within easy reach of German aircraft and missiles, there was much direct damage to industry caused by bombing, and indirect damage caused by the necessary air raid precautions and salvaging operations. But beyond these, and in the long run more decisive, was the enforced consumption of capital. Total war demanded all the resources that could be spared, and among those spared most easily in the short run were those normally used for the replacement and upkeep of capital.

According to official estimates, annual net non-war capital formation in the United Kingdom fell from £214 million in 1938 to about £−1,000 million (capital consumption) in 1940-5, or from 5% of net national income to −12%.[2] These figures are net, i.e. after the expansion in such sectors as agriculture and engineering have been taken into account, and they represent a staggering cumulative total of neglect, decline and loss of efficiency in many vital industries and services. In addition, there was the incalculable damage done by such war-time makeshifts as working by

---

[1] Morris A. Copeland and others, *The Impact of the War on Civilian Consumption in the U.K., the U.S.A. and Canada* (1945).

[2] *National Income and Expenditure of the U.K., 1938-1945* (1946. Cmd. 6784), Table 4.

green labour, the irregular or inferior supply of raw materials, spare parts and fuel, the over-felling of timber or the selective working of the easiest coal seams. Finally, the lack of opportunity of industrial training among the men and women drafted into the Forces must be reckoned an additional capital loss.

War gave a violent twist to the allocation of resources, affecting different industries very differently. Those which catered mainly for civilian demands were cut down drastically. Among the major occupations, retail distribution, pottery, textiles, clothing and building and construction each lost about one-half of their manpower, despite the substantial military orders for the latter two and despite the decision, after some years of war, to consider a certain minimum output of such goods as furniture, saucepans and crockery, as a necessity for the maintenance of civilian morale. Other civilian supply industries, with scarcely even that justification, like furs or carpets,[1] lost an even larger percentage of their labour force. As supplies were restricted, capital was run down, and much of the labour consisted of unskilled or female replacements, output fell often even more than employment figures.

Further, shortages of materials or skilled labour led necessarily to simpler styles, plainer finishes and, often, lower quality, and, in some cases, as in clothing and furniture, these became the 'utility' grade, supervised by the Board of Trade. Official 'utility' schemes introduced methods of mass-production and quality control, but elsewhere standards often lapsed haphazardly, without any corresponding benefits. Craftsmen and others came to forget the practices of high-class work, and others grew up who had never learnt them. Both consumers and producers came to accept the second best and the general attitude of the sellers' market, and this attitude was difficult to combat when the export drive after the war brought British industry again into competition with foreign manufacturers.

Other problems, as they affected the post-war position of many non-munitions industries, are aptly summed up in the following references to building. It should be noted, however, that they were coloured by the need to explain the poor performance of the building industry, in terms of output per man-hour, even several years after the end of the war:[2]

> During the war, the industry lost a large part of its experienced labour force, and for six years the normal process of recruitment and training was interrupted. Many young craftsmen and apprentices were

---

[1] Board of Trade, *Working Party Reports; Carpets* (1947), p. 4.

[2] Working Party Report, *Building* (1950), pp. 12–13; also Ministry of Labour and National Service, *Report for the Years 1939–1946* (1947. Cmd. 7225), pp. 87–91; I. Bowen, 'The Control of Building', in D. N. Chester, *Lessons of the British War Economy* (Cambridge, 1951).

conscripted for national service before they had gained experience in industry. Other men who left the industry during the war had lost much of their skill by the time they returned while those who remained in the industry throughout the war were employed on work which usually differed markedly from that of peace time. . . . Similar causes affected the efficiency of management. . . . Principals and members of their staff who had been on war service had to pick up the threads of their work, and new staff had to be engaged from among persons who had lost, or lacked, experience. . . . Directing and supervising staff had then to adapt themselves to a situation in which emphasis was no longer laid on speed of construction rather than on costs . . . the Essential Work (Building and Civil Engineering) Order which was in force between 1941 and 1947 left its mark on the industry in the form of relaxed discipline.

The poor performance of industries such as building was, however, counterbalanced by the advances made in others. In the war years the influx of unskilled and female workers, among other factors, was bound to affect productivity adversely: one estimate put the decline in output per man-hour in industry in the war years as high as 8% (1939–46).[1] This would be reversed when male labour returned, and manufacturing in particular appeared to have suffered no irreparable permanent damage in efficiency. Between the Census of Production years 1935 and 1948, output *per employee hour* changed as follows (1907 = 100):[2]

	1935	1948
Iron and steel	154	175
Engineering, shipbuilding, vehicles	196	224
Non-ferrous metals	131	190
Chemicals	174	206
Clay and building materials	180	247
Paper, printing and publishing	208	221
Food, drink and tobacco	108	142
Textiles	155	198
Clothing	146	136
Leather	136	141
Miscellaneous	228	278
All manufacturing	171	203

In fact, against the direct damage, the lack of investment, and the loss of skill must be set certain distinctly favourable effects of the war. Among the most important were the scientific and technological advances in-

[1] A. Maddison, 'Output, Employment and Productivity in British Manufacturing in the Last Half-century', *Bull. Oxf. Inst. Stat.*, 17/4, 1955, p. 380.
[2] Colin Clark, *The Conditions of Economic Progress* (2nd ed., 1951), p. 270.

duced by military and industrial demands, and the direct stimulus to a few industries of great strategic importance, in particular engineering in the widest sense, including vehicles and aircraft, iron and steel and other metals, chemicals and agriculture.

The scientific discoveries of the war years, and those applied on a large scale for the first time during the war, are legion. Among the best known are magnetron valves, centimetric radar and other devices built on them, jet engines and other revolutionary aircraft developments, nuclear fission, electronic computing and control systems, antibiotics, D.D.T. and other insecticides, and, on the other side, ballistic missiles;[1] several of these being developments of a whole series of interdependent discoveries. Many were called forth by military demands, but others were developed to fill new industrial needs or to replace scarce raw materials, such as artificial rubber and nylon and other plastics.

The war also fostered a new attitude to science, and the practice of a massive deployment of scientists and technologists of many specialisms on a broad front, to solve given problems. To the scientists were given not only traditional, 'laboratory' tasks such as the development of a new apparatus or chemical, but also the solution of such logistic problems as the right order and balance of the loading of ships for D-day, an exercise in computation which has since, in principle, been followed in the internal organization of some large firms.

The scientists in Government service in particular developed from isolated and subordinate specialists into members of co-ordinated teams, who in the end had to be allowed to question even the policy and strategy behind the tasks they were set. 'When one compares the freedom and authority enjoyed by the civilian scientists and technicians,' noted two historians of the war,[2] 'both at headquarters and in the establishments, in the period 1943-5 with the isolation and subjection of pre-war days, the change is among the most striking features of the organization of British war production.' Even at the very top, Winston Churchill leaned heavily on Lord Cherwell and a brilliant and unorthodox team of scientists who accounted for the peculiar shape of 'Britain's Government in the war . . . which was largely personal and yet free from the intellectual limitations of an autocracy'.[3] This enhanced role of the scientist, and his employment in large teams and with elaborate equipment, has since been adopted by

---

[1] E.g. W. H. G. Armytage, *A Social History of Engineering* (1961), pp. 310 ff.

[2] J. D. Scott and Richard Hughes, *The Administration of War Production* (1955), p. 288, also pp. 327-8.

[3] M. M. Postan, *British War Production* (1952), p. 144; J. D. Scott, 'Scientific Collaboration between the United Kingdom and North America', in H. D. Hall and C. C. Wrigley, *Studies of Overseas Supply* (H.S.W.W., 1956), chapter 8; G. D. A. MacDougall, 'The Prime Minister's Statistical Section,' in Chester (ed.), *Lessons of the War Economy*; but see C. P. Snow, *Science and Government* (1961).

many of the major firms. Its roots in the war economy were still evident in the 1950's and 1960's by the large proportion of scientific research, even in non-Government establishments, devoted to 'defence', as well as by the continued concentration of research in a few industries with strong strategic importance, notably aircraft, electrical engineering and chemicals.[1]

It was also these industries, together with engineering and agriculture, which received the main benefits of expansion and modernization during the war. Engineering, though one of the most rapidly growing industries in the inter-war period, was in the late 1930's, technically and organizationally, still inferior in many respects to the best examples abroad. In one oɩ its most backward sectors, the machine tool industry, tooling-up for re-armament led to an expansion of production by British makers from 20,000 machine tools in 1935 to 35,000 in 1939 and 100,000 in 1942, and employment in the industry rose from 21,000 in 1935 to a maximum of 68,600 in March 1943; at the same time, imports of American machine tools were expanded from 8,000 in 1939 to a maximum of 33,000 in 1940, many of them being responsible for introducing new methods here. The output of small tools, fine measuring tools and measuring instruments and industrial electrical equipment increased likewise.[2]

Much of the expanded munitions industry had a direct peace-time value, especially the works producing motor vehicles and aircraft. Of the 3·3 million people employed in armaments, excluding chemicals, explosives and iron and steel, at the peak of 1943, 2·2 million were in industries with a civilian base.[3]

The output of aircraft increased from 2,800 in 1938 to nearly 8,000 in 1939, 20,000 in 1941 and over 26,000 in 1943 and 1944. Because of their growing complexity and the growing proportion of heavier aircraft, the structural weight increased even faster, from 9·8 million lb. to 28·9, 87·2 and about 200 million lb. in the same years. The aircraft repaired and engines delivered and repaired rose in the same proportion, and required an industrial effort almost as large as the new building. The capacity of the motor trade was also expanded, though much of the productive capacity turned over to army vehicles, tracked carriers and tanks, as well as aircraft, had been converted from plant designed for civilian motor vehicles rather than newly built. Shipbuilding, limited by shortages of labour, of steel and even of berths, after the deliberate destruction of the 1930's, did not expand as much; the output of mercantile tonnage rose to an average of well over 1·1 million g.t. annually in 1941–4, while the launchings of naval and landing craft increased from 94,000 dw. tons in 1939 to 260,000

---

[1] John Jewkes, David Sawers, Richard Stillerman, *The Sources of Invention* (1958), pp. 148–52; p. 94 above.
[2] Postan, pp. 206–7; Wm. Hornby, *Factories and Plant* (1958), chapters 10–13.
[3] Hornby, pp. 28–30.

dw.t. in 1940 and 600,000 dw.t. in 1943.[1] Each of these trades, in turn, depended on large numbers of outside suppliers for materials and components, so that their expansion fertilized a whole range of other modern industries. In the radio, electrical and electronics industry, for example, the output of radio valves rose from under 12 million a year in 1940 to over 35 million in 1944, and special facilities for the mass-production of electrical components were created in the process.

The permanent enlargement of the vital engineering group of industries during the war is illustrated in the following tabulation:[2]

	June 1939	November 1946	% Increase
Non-ferrous metal manufacture	55·9	87·8	57·1
Shipbuilding and repair	144·7	219·8	51·9
Constructional engineering	49·0	66·5	35·7
Electric cable, apparatus	195·9	265·5	35·5
Explosives, chemicals	174·3	235·5	35·1
Scientific instruments	48·3	65·0	34·6
Marine engineering	52·2	70·2	34·5
General engineering	704·7	944·3	34·0

Table heading: Insured Persons (000)

The change was not merely one of size. The necessities of war taught new methods of mass-production, of industrial control and management, of design and quality control, and spread this knowledge among a host of sub-contractors. War-time training schemes increased the numbers of key workers, such as draughtsmen and tool-room operators. The capital equipment was greatly enlarged, the Government alone, according to one calculation, investing in 1936–45 over £1,000 million in fixed capital, made up of £89 million in works for the Admiralty, £384 million for aircraft production, and £556 million for the War Office and the Ministry of Supply, spread over both Government-owned and agency factories, and capital subsidies to contractors.[3] At the end of the war, machine tools alone worth £100 million from Government factories were sold to private industry, the normal pre-war intake being about £5 million a year, and 75 million square feet of factory space made available to peace-time industry.[4] To this have to be added private contractors' investments, which were particularly high in some public utilities, such as electricity generation.

[1] Central Statistical Office, *Statistical Digest of the War* (1951), Tables 111, 130–1; H. F. Heath and A. L. Hetherington, *Industrial Research and Development in the United Kingdom* (1946), pp. 200 ff.

[2] Postan, p. 385; also C. E. V. Leser, 'Changes in Level and Diversity of Employment in Regions of Great Britain, 1939–47', *Econ. J.*, 59/235, 1949, Table 4.

[3] Postan, p. 448. Hornby, *op. cit.*, chapter 14, puts the Government expenditure in the same years at £425·6 million for aircraft production, and £460·4 million for War Office and Supply.

[4] W. K. Hancock and M. M. Gowing, *British War Economy* (1949), pp. 551–2.

The British Economy in Total War, 1939–1945

The iron and steel industry was another important sector to be enlarged and modernized. To fill the gap caused by the loss of the high-grade ores after the summer of 1940, the output of home ores had to be expanded from 14 million tons to nearly 20 m.t., and blast furnace capacity enlarged and altered to produce the same quantity of 8 m.t. out of the poorer home ores. The required increase in the output of steel had to be based on greater utilization of steel scrap. The bulk steel capacity raised to 13 m.t. a year by the schemes of the 1930's proved sufficient for the needs of war, provided it was used fully and continuously, but the sudden increase in the demand for alloy steel could not be met from existing furnaces, and capacity was raised from 500,000 tons (200,000 tons of which was in electric furnaces) before the war to $1\frac{3}{4}$ m.t. (half of it in electric furnaces) by 1942. Government subventions to the extension of alloy steel capacity amounted to £7 million, to foundry capacity £8 million, to drop forgings, one of the most serious early bottlenecks, £7 million, and gun forgings £4 million. At the same time, the ingot capacity for aluminium, a vital structural material for aircraft, was raised to 31,000 tons in 1939 and increased further to 54,000 tons by 1943; the demand, by that time, had risen to 300,000 tons, of which 100,000 tons were provided from scrap by new plant set up during the war, and the remainder from imports.[1] The capacity for other raw materials and semi-manufactures had similarly to be enlarged, *pari passu* with the expansion of the engineering industry.

The other industry to emerge very much strengthened by the war was agriculture. The subsidies, Government-sponsored marketing schemes and protection of the 1930's laid a broad basis of State influence over agriculture in the 1930's. In June 1939, under the terms of the Agricultural Development Act, a subsidy of £2 an acre was paid for the ploughing up of land which had lain unploughed for the past seven years, and this indicated the main direction of Government war-time policy: the enlargement of arable production.

In the late 1930's about 70% of the country's consumption of calories was supplied from abroad, but the proportion was 84% in the case of sugar, oils and fats, 88% of wheat and flour and 91% of butter.[2] As in 1914–18, shipping space for such bulky commodities as grain, and foreign exchange to pay for it, were among the most critical shortages, and agricultural policy was accordingly designed to reduce the dependence on imported food, despite a declining labour force and in the face of short-

---

[1] J. Hurstfield, *The Control of Raw Materials* (1953), pp. 335–48; J. Roepke, *Movements of the British Iron and Steel Industry, 1720–1951* (Urbana, Ill., 1956), chapter 7; P. Inman, *Labour in the Munitions Industries* (1957), p. 158; Duncan Burn, *The Steel Industry 1939–1959* (Cambridge, 1961), chapters 1 and 2.
[2] R. J. Hammond, *Food.*, Vol. 1 (H.S.W.W., 1951), Table V, p. 394.

ages of equipment, imported fertilizer and imported feeding stuffs. It succeeded to the extent of raising home production by 70%, measured in calories and protein, and in saving thereby about half the food imports, without depriving the home population of its necessary food intake. Measured net of imported feeding stuffs, which were drastically reduced to save shipping space, home output increased from 14·7 milliard calories in 1938–9 to 20·0 milliard in 1941–2 and 28·1 milliard in 1943–4, or by 36% and 91% respectively. Total home food production, by value, rose from 42% to 52% of consumption between 1938 and 1946.[1]

The basic feature of the Government's agricultural policy was the ploughing-up campaign, which raised the area under arable cultivation from just under 12 million to just under 18 million acres.[2] Allowing for land under temporary grass, the actual increase of the land in tillage was over 5 million acres by the end of the war. This increase, which was achieved by gradual expansion year by year, was fairly evenly spread among wheat, barley and oats, and potatoes and root crops. It was obtained at the cost of a corresponding decline in the acreage under permanent grass (the rough grazing remaining constant) and thereby involved a marked shift from animal husbandry to arable: between 1939 and 1945, the number of sheep and lambs, for example, in Great Britain fell from 26 million to 19½ million, pigs from 3·8 million to 1·9 million, and poultry from 64 million head to 45 million. Only cattle were encouraged, and their numbers grew from about 8 million to 8·7 million head, in order to increase the home supply of milk. Imports could thus be converted from bulky cattle feeding stuffs to the more concentrated food values contained in meat, eggs, etc., while British soil was converted to maintain the largest number of people per acre. Up to 1941, the prices of imports were a major consideration. Lend-lease arrangements removed this limitation, and imports were determined thereafter largely on the basis of their use of scarce shipping space.

The increase in the arable acreage was accompanied by remarkable increases in yields per acre, at least of grain crops. Thus the yield of wheat rose from 17·7 cwt. in 1936–8 to 19·7 cwt. in 1942–5, of barley from 16·4 to 18·5 cwt. and of oats from 15·7 to 16·7 cwt., despite the likelihood that much of the newly ploughed land was marginal. Additional labour could scarcely be credited with this increase, for much of it was female or casual: if a conversion factor is applied, to allow for the changing composition of the labour force, the index of agricultural employment in terms of

[1] E. F. Nash, 'War-Time Control of Food and Agricultural Prices', in D. N. Chester (ed.), *Lessons of the War Economy.*
[2] *Statistical Digest of the War,* Table 55, p. 57; H. T. Williams, *Principles for British Agricultural Policy* (1960), chapter 5.

man years stood at 99 in 1939–40 (1937 = 100) and crept up only to 108 in 1943–4 and 109 in 1944–5, working an acreage increased by 50%.[1] The increase in home food production, made up of enlarged yields on a greatly increased acreage, was, in fact, achieved by large-scale mechanization and increased use of fertilizers.

Between 1938–9 and 1945–6 the quantity of fertilizers used on United Kingdom farms (in terms of 1,000 tons) increased as follows: nitrogen, from 60 to 165; phosphate, from 170 to 359; potash, from 75 to 101; and lime, from 1,300 to 2,000. Similarly, between 1939 and 1946 total mechanical horse power on British farms rose from just under 2 million to just under 5 million. The change in these seven years had been greater than in the preceding fourteen years of peace.[2] Tractors increased from 56,000 to 203,000 in this period, and the increase of other equipment was as follows (in 000):[3]

	May 1942	April 1944	June 1946
Disc harrows	33·8	58·9	65·2
Cultivators (grubbers)	161·7	191·4	247·8
Binders	131·6	144·0	149·5
Combine harvesters	1·0	2·5	3·8
Milking machines	29·5	37·8	48·3

This transformation was brought about almost entirely by deliberate Government planning and direction. Official agricultural policy was administered locally, as in the first World War, by County War Agricultural Committees which were given wide powers, including those of determining land use, and allocating labour, machinery and other scarce resources to make their decisions effective.[4] To this direct control was added a whole battery of financial inducements. The Government encouraged capital investment by subsidies for ditching, draining and water supplies, and by grants of between 25% and 75% for approved land reclamation schemes. For current costs, the 50% lime subsidy was continued and subsidies for hill sheep and cattle were added, while there were acreage payments for wheat and potatoes, the production of which was considered particularly desirable, and loans for 'agricultural requisites'.

All these were additional to the main pre-war incentive, the guaranteed

[1] K. A. H. Murray, *Agriculture* (H.S.W.W., 1955), pp. 85, 273.

[2] D. K. Britton and I. F. Keith, 'A Note on the Statistics of Farm Power Supplies in Great Britain', *The Farm Economist*, 6/6, 1950; Hancock and Gowing, p. 550.

[3] Murray, p. 276; *Statistical Digest of the War*, Table 64; cf. also P.E.P., *Agricultural Machinery* (1949), p. 95.

[4] A. W. Menzies Kitchin, 'Local Administration of Agricultural Policy', in *Lessons of the British War Economy*.

price, which was now greatly extended in scope. Wages were raised substantially ιο prevent the wholesale emigration of adult male workers to the booming munitions industries, though they still remained well below the absolute level of industrial wages; but agricultural prices under the guaranteed price scheme rose much faster than costs, and there was some justification in the widespread criticism that farmers had been given too great a voice in the annual price review. Prices rose as follows (index, 1936–8 = 100):

	Official Cost of Living	Retail Food Prices	Agricultural Prices
1939	104	103	103
1941	130	123	172
1943	130	121	186
1945	133	125	196

The widening gap between farm prices and the prices paid by consumers involved the State in ever-increasing food subsidies, quite apart from the direct subsidies and grants rising to £37 million a year in 1943–5, and their results were mainly to raise *net* farm receipts much faster than any other type of incomes.[1] The price guarantees were extended to at least one year after the termination of hostilities, and farmers were encouraged also by other methods, such as increased security of tenancy, granted in 1941.[2] Thus fostered, encouraged, cajoled and directed by the Government, agriculture emerged from the war in a healthier and more prosperous state than it had enjoyed for seventy years.

Not all primary production at home was equally fortunate. Elsewhere, the pressure to obtain the largest possible immediate return at the least outlay in real resources could lead to a long-run weakening of the industry by the running down of its capital, and the exhaustion of the easiest sources of supply. This may be illustrated by the timber and coal industries.

The shortage of timber was felt only after the Continent became closed to British shipping; then timber became one of the scarcest of materials. The country went to inordinate lengths to reduce its consumption and to find substitutes, often of other scarce materials, such as steel, but at least part of the gap had to be filled by increased home fellings. They rose from an average of 150,000 tons in 1935–8 to a maximum of 1,251,000 tons in 1943 in the case of hardwood, from 180,000 tons to 861,000 tons (1942) in the case of softwood, and from 120,000 tons to

[1] Murray, *op. cit.*, chapter 11; E. F. Nash, 'War-Time Control of Food and Agricultural Prices', in *Lessons of the British War Economy*.
[2] S. G. Sturmey, 'Owner-Farming in England and Wales, 1900–1950', *Manchester School*, 23/3, 1955, p. 264.

1,765,000 tons (1943) in the case of pitwood.[1] The cost of these fellings to the long-term forestry supply of the country was prodigious:

By the end of 1945 some 60 per cent of Great Britain's softwoods had been taken, and some 40 per cent of the hardwoods. The residue of mature softwoods is miserably small, and though the quantity of mature hardwood is considerably larger, the best had gone. Moreover, the heavy cuttings in the 30–60 year classes has further jeopardised the future prospect. The distribution of age classes . . . is completely out of joint.[2]

The problems of coal mining during the war were more complex. After fifteen years of overproduction and unemployment, it was difficult to believe that the coal supply would fall short of needs. It was estimated that output some 10% above the peace-time level would be required to supplant German coal, especially in France, and a Coal Production Council was established to organize a long-term expansion of output, but it had hardly begun to function when the fall of France and the closure of virtually all other export markets in the summer of 1940 reduced prospective consumption to about 10% *below* prospective output. There was unemployment in the export districts, and the recruitment of miners into the Forces was encouraged. The coal shortage in the winter of 1940–1 was due to transport difficulties, not shortage of supply.[3]

Output, however, was falling. The quantity of total saleable coal had been 231 million tons in 1939, and 224 m.t. in 1940. It fell to 206 m.t. in 1941, and to 204 m.t., 194 m.t., 184 m.t. and 175 m.t. in the following years. Up to 1941, the fall was simply due to the fall in the number of wage-earners on the colliery books, from 766,000 in 1939 to 698,000 in 1941. From then onwards, the numbers remained constant while output per manshift fell, largely because of the ageing of the work force, the deterioration of the fixed equipment, the general long-term downward curve of British coal mining as the best seams were being worked out, faulty planning and administration and, not least, because of smouldering discontent over wages, the Essential Works Order and the much-publicized campaigns to end absenteeism in the pits. When, in 1942, booming heavy industries and others began to push up the demand for coal there developed a major fuel crisis.

In the mines, as ever, the bad industrial relations of the past had their influence on current problems. The Government, having contributed to the defeat of the miners in 1926, considered itself duty bound not to permit nationalization by the back door, and its war-time coal control was

---

[1] Postan, *op. cit.*, pp. 156, 216; P. Ford, 'The Allocation of Timber', in *Lessons of British War Economy*.

[2] Russell Meiggs, *Home Timber Production* (1949), p. 43.

[3] Hancock and Gowing, chapter XVI (ii).

therefore completely decentralized, not only geographically, by regions, but even functionally within the regions, between Coal Supply Officers, Coal Export Officers and the Divisional Coal Officers, with the owners' District Executive Boards still determining output and pit-head prices under the cartel scheme. As the coal crisis developed in 1942, this chaotic structure could not stand the strain, while efforts to reduce the demand for coal by consumer rationing also failed, largely owing to transport difficulties. A new policy for the mines became urgent, and in June 1942 a new department, the Ministry of Fuel and Power, was created to administer it.[1]

One of its first acts was to take over the Coal Charges Account with its compensating levies scheme from the owners, designed to even out the effects of rising costs and varying prices between districts. Coal control became centralized by Group Production Directors, responsible to Area Controllers, though there was still no question of nationalization, and the new minister set about raising the output of coal.

The most urgent problems related to labour. Though miners' wage and earnings had risen faster than most since the start of the war, they were still, in absolute terms, below the earnings of workers in the munitions industries and in other heavy, unpleasant trades. Voluntary recruitment, either of miners or of others, was therefore a failure, and even the conscripted 'Bevin boys' were recruited only in numbers to make good the wastage, and not to increase the work force. On the advice of a Board of investigation under Lord Greene (the 'Greene Committee'), whose first Report appeared in June 1942[2] (three others appearing later in 1942–3), a substantial wage advance of 2s. 6d. per shift and a national minimum wage were applied at once in 1942. The industry also adopted the National Conciliation Scheme drafted by the Greene Committee, and granted further wage awards to the miners during the war. Yet unrest in the mines was not abated, and in 1943–4 the bad industrial relations in the industry were the nearest approach to the rebellious spirit which was manifest in a wide range of industries in the later years of the 1914–18 war.

The capital position of the industry gave equal grounds for concern. Mechanization had been interrupted by the fall of France and the consequent fear of overproduction, but as the coal crisis developed, some of the country's scarce engineering capacity was turned over to mining engineering, and with the aid of Government finance, the provision of equipment was greatly increased. The proportion of coal cut by machinery rose from 61% in 1939 to 72% in 1945, and of coal conveyed mechanically from 58% to 71%,[3] but output, both absolute and per man-shift, continued to

---

[1] W. H. B. Court, *Coal* (H.S.W.W., 1951), chapters 9 and 10.
[2] *Report of the Board of Investigation into the Immediate Wage Issue in the Coal-Mining Industry* (1942).   [3] Court, p. 279.

fall year by year. If it had not been for opencast coal, rising from 1·3 million tons in 1942 to 8½ m.t. in 1944, it would have fallen more rapidly still. As it was, stocks were down to dangerous levels in the winter of 1944–5. With its equipment run down, and its manpower depleted and in an unco-operative mood, that unhappy industry, after nearly twenty years of sagging demand and excess capacity, emerged from the war with an almost limitless demand, but an utter inability to meet it.

If coal had its own special problems, the running down of capital was nowhere more marked than in inland transport, where maintenance and replacement could fairly safely be neglected for several years, only to leave an increased burden to the post-war generation. Further, ports and railway centres became special targets for enemy bomb attacks. The capital equipment suffered all the more since the public transport system had to carry a load in 1939–45 well above its normal peace-time weight, because of the virtual suspension of private motoring, the enforced residence of millions of people away from home, the military movements, and the disruption or lengthening of the normal supply routes of goods traffic. The increased load on the railways is evident from the following figures:[1]

Railways		1938	1942	1944
Freight tonnage (mn. tons)	coal	173	163	151
	other	93	132	142
Net ton-miles (mn. tons)	coal	8,104	9,951	9,267
	other	8,162	13,871	15,177
Wagon miles (mn.)	loaded	3,003	3,983	4,064
	empty	1,492	1,412	1,427
Passenger miles, main line companies, milliard		19[2]	—	32

Apart from the greatly increased traffic, this tabulation shows that while the quantity of coal transported was steadily reduced, its ton mileage increased; in other words, the diversion of supplies from the export fields to home use caused longer runs, despite the zoning. It further points to an increasingly effective control over wagon loads, as full wagon mileage was raised by one-third without any increase in the empty wagon mileage.

In the later years of the war, the Central Transport Committee, set up in 1941, reduced the burdens on the railways to some extent by allocating an increasing quantity of goods to canals and coastal shipping. The traffic on the roads, by contrast, began to be curtailed from 1941 onward, owing to severe shortages of rubber and petrol.[3] Private cars lost their petrol ration completely in March 1942, *C* licence vehicles were severely restricted by zoning and other schemes, and *A* and *B* licence vehicles were gradually

---

[1] Hancock and Gowing, p. 481.   [2] September 1938–August 1939 inclusive.
[3] C. I. Savage, *Inland Transport* (H.S.W.W., 1957).

diverted from long-distance traffic, which was to be the responsibility of the railways, to short-distance goods traffic especially after bombings and from the congested western ports. Vehicles could be directed to some extent from the beginning by the judicious allocation of the motor fuel ration, but gradually the Government took over complete control of road haulage, first by commandeering certain special vehicles, e.g. the meat pool of the Ministry of Food in 1940, and later by controlling all journeys over 60 miles. By 1943 a special Road Haulage organization was set up under the Ministry of War Transport which came to control 388 large organizations, and all long-distance vehicles, a total of 34,000 goods vehicles.[1] Road passenger vehicles were left under the control of the Regional Transport Commissioners.

As in the first World War, the railways had been placed at once under Government control, the proprietors receiving a guaranteed income, settled at the end of 1940 at £43 million, Government and railways to share war damage costs equally. In view of the greatly increased traffic and the virtual suspension of maintenance, actual net receipts soon exceeded this figure and in 1943, the peak year, reached the total of £105½ million.

At the end of the hostilities, however, it was found that

the railways had been overloaded during the war almost to the point of breakdown. . . . The immediate post-war years found the railways with heavy arrears of replacement and repair of permanent way, locomotives and rolling stock to be made good. Indeed the ultimate consequences of overstraining the inland transport system during the war were only felt in 1946, 1947 and afterwards. . . . Other branches of inland transport were also suffering from the strain of the war years and the difficulty of renewing their equipment—many buses and goods vehicles for example were in need of replacement. But the railways had sustained the heaviest impact during the war and it was to take five years or more to restore them to good working order.[2]

The war, it may be concluded, had profoundly affected British productive capacity, but its consequences, and the post-war position of the different branches of manufacturing industry, agriculture, transport and the public utilities, were very different. Some important sectors were forced to contract, losing skill, connections and capital equipment; others were forced to expand on a shrinking capital base; but the effects of war were not wholly unfavourable to all. Some industries, notably engineering, metals and chemicals as well as agriculture, expanded and profited greatly. It was fortunate that these included many of the industries that were destined to play a leading part in the post-war reconstruction of Britain.

[1] Gilbert Walker, *Road and Rail* (2nd ed., 1947), p. 230.
[2] Savage, *Inland Transport*, pp. 634, 638–9.

3. FISCAL AND FINANCIAL POLICY DURING THE WAR

The mobilization of the British industrial potential for the war was not to be carried through solely by physical controls. Since most enterprises were still managed immediately by their former managers, even if working under Government direction, and the efforts of employees were also mainly motivated by the hope of gain, fiscal and financial weapons were still needed to ensure that resources yielded their maximum return and were at their highest possible level of productivity. Further, Britain's dependence on imports made it necessary to maintain the foreign value of the pound sterling as well as to husband the limited foreign exchange reserves for the needs of war and the peace to follow. Finally, as Government taxation and borrowing were the immediate sources which fed the stream of military expenditure, it was one of the objectives of the fiscal system to distribute the necessary burden fairly between classes and between individuals.[1]

Finance, then, though it had ceased to be the arbiter of military policy, was still one of its major instruments. Provided the physical resources were there, it was a criterion of the efficiency of the financial instruments that it should not stand in the way of their use. 'In the sense that financial obstacles were never allowed to obstruct the war effort, British policy in the second World War was undoubtedly successful.'[2]

The subordination of finance to strategy was achieved virtually from the start. 'On the whole', it was judged, 'at the outbreak of war the financial limits to rearmament became so wide as no longer to limit.'[3] For this, the experience of the first World War, in which finance had too long and disastrously claimed prime consideration, was as much responsible as the fact that the country's re-armament effort was still small and therefore not too hard to bear. In those early months of 'phoney war', fiscal and financial policy still operated in the framework of the former war, and as such, had two main closely interrelated objectives: the prevention of inflationary price rises, which might lead to labour unrest and have other undesirable social repercussions, and the meeting of the costs of the war as far as possible out of increased taxation rather than by borrowing.

The early preoccupation with the level of retail prices may have been somewhat premature. In the first weeks of the war there occurred an inevitable rise in the costs of certain materials in short supply, and of some wages, notably those of miners, accompanied by a corresponding rise in the price of coal. These increases pushed up the cost of living figure by some 10%, but there was clearly as yet no general inflationary pressure in

---

[1] W. K. Hancock and M. M. Gowing, *British War Economy* (1949), pp. 48 ff.
[2] R. S. Sayers, *Financial Policy, 1939–45* (H.S.W.W., 1956), p. 21.
[3] M. M. Postan, *British War Production* (1952), p. 82.

the economy[1] when the Government, as noted above,[2] was stampeded into subsidizing certain foods to keep down the official index. At first intended to be temporary only, until the trade unions had agreed to a wage standstill, the subsidies grew with a momentum of their own. By January 1940 the Chancellor announced their continuation on a broad front, though still hedged round with many qualifications,[3] and within six months they had become an integral component of war policy. The budget of April 1941 laid it down that the cost-of-living index would be stabilized in the range of 25–30% above the immediate pre-war level. Later in the war, even some necessities outside the official index were held down in price, though others were deliberately allowed to rise to great heights.

The early food subsidies had been easy to apply, since the Government, as bulk importer, could simply absorb the rising costs abroad and pass on the foodstuffs to home distributors at any desired price level. There was some early Treasury opposition to the rising 'trading' losses which resulted from these operations by the Ministry of Food, while farmers had to be subsidized in various other ways[4] to bridge the gap between home food production costs and the artificially low prices, but since food accounted for 60% of the weight in the index, the results were considered to warrant the expense. Another item, rent, was held down equally easily by rent control, and the Government also had powers to keep down the price to the consumer of several other goods and services, such as coal and railway fares. In the case of clothing, and what little furniture and other household durables came on the market after 1941, the 'utility' scheme was combined with price control. There were also some general provisions, such as the Goods and Services (Price Control) Act of July 1941, though price control was never quite complete.[5] By contrast, the Government could afford to levy a large part of its revenue by steeply increasing duties on tobacco and alcohol, since their weight in the official index was minute, and even the purchase tax, by careful discrimination, was gradually developed so as to raise the maximum of revenue with the minimum disturbance to the cost-of-living index.

The success of the retail price policy in its objective of limiting the war-time inflation and insulating the home consumer from world price changes may be judged by the following stattisics:[6]

---

[1] Hancock and Gowing, pp. 153–7.
[2] p. 302 above.
[3] *H.o.C. Debates*, Vol. 356, cols. 1154–9, 31 January, 1940.
[4] p. 317 above.
[5] E. L. Hargreaves and M. M. Gowing, *Civil Industry and Trade* (1952), p. 122; Hancock and Gowing, pp. 501–4.
[6] G. D. H. Cole, *Money, Trade and Investment* (1954), p. 95; subsidy figures from white paper on *National Income and Expenditure of the United Kingdom 1938 to 1946* (1947. Cmd. 7099), Table 19: these *exclude* housing subsidies.

Price Index (First Half 1939 = 100)				Subsidies (£ million)
Wholesale Prices			Cost of Living	
Board of Trade	Economist	Statist		
1940	140	139	144	121	72
1941	157	151	159	129	138
1942	164	160	169	130	164
1943	167	164	172	129	177
1944	171	168	177	131	215
1945	174	172	182	132	250

Subsidies for retail commodity prices could only deal with the symptoms of the inflationary problem. Its essence was the fact that the Government was attempting to absorb a much larger share of the national resources than individuals and firms were willing to forgo; and since physical controls could never be made quite tight enough to achieve this transfer unaided there developed inevitable shortages leading to price rises, which became particularly acute whenever there occurred a change in Government policy involving a major switch in resources. This underlying cause of inflation could ultimately be combated only by a conscious withdrawal of purchasing power from the public by a high level of taxation.

To begin with, however, revenue by taxation was increased for the traditional reason of keeping borrowing to a mimimum. There was an autumn war budget in September 1939, which estimated the total expenditure for the financial year 1939-40 at £1,933 million, some £116 million more than the Government were actually to spend. Defence expenditure amounted to only £1,000 million, compared with £382 million in 1938-9. The budget proposals in April 1940 were equally timid, and of the limited sums required, about one-half was raised by taxation, and half by borrowing.

By this time budgetary policy had come under sharp criticism. The critics were led, once again, by J. M. Keynes. In correspondence to The Times in November 1939, published as a pamphlet early in 1940,[1] he condemned the traditional assessment of revenue according to the principle of what the taxpayer would bear, which turned out to be about half the required expenditure. By starting at the other end, and calculating the national income and its main components first, it would be possible at once to determine the capacity for war-making available, and the level of

[1] J. M. Keynes, How to Pay for the War (1940); cf. also R. F. Harrod, The Life of John Maynard Keynes (1951), pp. 489 ff.

324

taxation necessary to transfer that part of the national income to the Government without creating an inflation. At existing levels of incomes and taxation, for example, he calculated that there was an inflationary 'gap', which could most usefully be viewed as the difference between the proposed Government expenditure and the total of taxes plus savings plus any income or dissaving available from abroad. He therefore proposed increased taxes, sweetened by promises to repay part of them after the war as 'deferred pay' (the later 'post-war credits'), and in particular, regressive taxes on the poorer two-thirds of the population who had hitherto been but lightly taxed.

'There can be no doubt at all that his hold upon the professional economist was from the first a major factor in leading public opinion to acceptance of a relatively strong financial policy.' [1] In his proposals of November 1939, however, he faced initially opposition both from Conservative opinion within the Treasury, which distrusted his figures, and from Labour opinion outside, which objected to the heavy taxation of the working classes. But he was swimming with the tide. In April 1940 the *Economist* pointed out that even after its great increase, the British war budget was still well below that of Germany, though it had several years' start to make up.[2] The Chancellor of the Exchequer himself was becoming impatient with the inability of his Treasury officials to suggest means of stopping the inflation, and in March a war loan of a mere £300 million had been a failure. Above all, it was the shock of the defeats of the summer of 1940 and the change of Government which precipitated the changeover to Keynesian policies, with some support even from within the Treasury.

The new, more vigorous, tax policies allowed war expenditure in the current year to be raised from a prospective £2,000 to £2,800 million. The Chancellor, Sir Kingsley Wood, at once raised the standard rate of income tax by 1s. to 8s. 6d., while reducing exemption limits and raising other rates and surtax rates. Purchase tax was imposed on a broad front, and the Excess Profits Tax was raised from 60% to 100% (i.e. taxing the total increase in profits over a standard pre-war period) for all industries, though it was later softened by various concessions, including a 20% post-war credit on the tax paid.[3] With Keynes and other leading economists installed at the Treasury by the end of 1940, and others in the Cabinet Office, the transformation was complete.

Kingsley Wood's budget of April 1941 marked the turning point.[4] It

[1] Sayers, *op. cit.*, p. 3.
[2] 'A Budget of Delusions', *Economist*, 27th April 1940, pp. 759–60.
[3] J. R. Hicks, U. K. Hicks and L. Rostas, *The Taxation of War Wealth* (Oxford, 2nd ed., 1942), chapters 11 and 12; A. J. Youngson, *The British Economy 1920–1957* (1960), pp. 150–1; Hancock and Gowing, pp. 327–30.
[4] S. H. Beer, *Treasury Control* (Oxford, 1956), p. 66.

was conceived in national income terms, and to symbolize the new approach, was accompanied by a white paper setting out the official estimates of the national income and expenditure,[1] the first of the series which has become, together with the Government Social Survey and other tools developed in war-time, the indispensable guide to economic policy since. According to the official estimates, the 'gap' at existing rates of income and taxation would be of the order of £500 million, of which £200–300 million would be found by increased personal savings, and £250 million by additional taxation, over and above the estimated revenue of £1,636 million. This was to take the form of raising the standard rate of income tax by 1s. 6d. to 10s. in the pound, and other rates in proportion.

The actual figures underlying the budget of 1941 might have been unreliable, as some critics alleged;[2] certainly, the queues at the shops continued, and widespread rationing and price control had to be introduced, after all. But the principle was sound, and the remaining war budgets, 1942–5, showed little change in their mode of calculation or their method of presentation. The only major innovations were 'Pay As You Earn', introduced in September 1943 and applying to about 16 million earners, of whom 12 million were taxable, and the development of the purchase tax as a finer, discriminating weapon, not only for the raising of revenue, but also to restrict and generally influence consumption.[3] Up to 1942, direct and indirect taxation had roughly increased in step, the former by 177% over 1939, and the latter by 145%. In the later years of the war, the gap widened considerably, contributing to the welfare policies which were also evident in the highly discriminatory incidence of subsidies. By 1945 the revenue from direct taxes had increased by 300%, while that from indirect taxes had risen by only 160%.

The success of fiscal policy during the war has to be judged against the size of the problem: at the height of the war, about half the current consumption was diverted to the Government, while civilian consumption, in real terms, had to be reduced to something like 80% of the pre-war level[4] (see table opposite).

In this table, the totals of columns A and B are equal to the totals of

[1] *The Sources of War Finance. An Analysis and an Estimate of the National Income and Expenditure in 1938 and 1940* (1941. Cmd. 6261). Cf. also J. E. Meade and R. Stone, *National Income and Expenditure* (1944 ed.); R. Stone, 'The Use and Development of National Income and Expenditure Estimates', in *Lessons of the British War Economy*; E. F. Jackson, 'The Recent Use of Social Accounting in the United Kingdom', *Income and Weatlh*, Series I (1950).
[2] M. Kalecki, 'The Budget and Inflation', *Bull. Oxf. Inst. Stat.*, 3/6, 1941.
[3] Sayers, *op. cit.*, chapter 4.
[4] Statistics based on *National Income and Expenditure of the United Kingdom, 1938–1945* (1946. Cmd. 6784), Tables 4 and 5. Some of the figures have been slightly revised since. Cf. also *Statistics Relating to the War Effort of the United Kingdom* (1944. Cmd. 6564).

	Comparison of Net National Product: % Distribution					
	Personal and Government Consumption A	War B	Personal Consumption C	Total Government Consumption, Civil and War D	Net Non-War Capital Formation E	Real Personal Consumption[1] F
1938	88	7	78	17	5	100
1939	83	15	73½	24½	2	100
1940	72	44	64	52	−16	90
1941	63	54	56	61	−17	83
1942	60	52	52	60	−12	82
1943	56	56	49	63	−12	79
1944	58	54	51	61	−12	83
1945	61	49	54	56	−10	86

C and D, but the two pairs of columns are differently grouped. Either pair, together with column E, totals 100, i.e. the Net National Product. According to the first division of the product, it will be seen that at the peak of the war effort, in 1943, armament alone equalled the rest of national consumption. The other division (columns C and D) which isolates the total share taken by the Government, and therefore forms a more realistic indicator of budgetary policy, shows that the Government share exceeded private consumption for the whole of the period 1941–45 inclusive. The table also illustrates the gradual increase of mobilization to its high point in 1943, and the important contribution made by capital consumption to the total war effort.[2]

Government expenditure at such a rate could not conceivably be met entirely out of current revenue. Government borrowing covered, for the whole period 1939–45, about half the expenditure, but significantly its proportion fell progressively in the course of the war[3] (see table on next page).

Omitting lend-lease and other gifts from abroad, virtually the whole deficit was met by borrowing at home. The skill of the Government's borrowing policy is indicated by the fact that of £14,800 million so raised in the course of the war, only £770 million were raised by the printing press, i.e. by increasing the fiduciary bank note issue.[4] To achieve it, the whole of the savings in the private sector had to be made available to the Government.

Savings were channelled into the hands of the Government partly by what might be called direct controls, and partly by the more normal methods of making attractive offers for them. Among the direct controls were the suspension of opportunities for investments in new capital goods,

[1] Index, 1938 prices.
[2] Cf. also U. K. Hicks, *Public Finance* (1947), pp. 110–11; J. Hurstfield, *The Control of Raw Materials* (1953), pp. 106, 126.
[3] Sayers, Appx. I, Tables 4 and 5.   [4] Sayers, p. 223.

	Total Tax Revenue (£mn.)	Total Income, incl. Income from Property after Paying National Debt Interest (£mn.)	Total Deficit on Current Account (£mn.)	Of which Raised by Public Borrowing at Home (£mn.)	Ratio A : D
	A	B	C	D	E
1939	980	771	490	352	—
1940	1,382	1,158	2,115	1,550	0·89
1941	2,143	1,905	2,828	2,553	0·84
1942	2,563	2,314	2,909	2,576	1·00
1943	3,052	2,759	2,826	2,972[1]	1·03
1944	3,262	2,897	2,672	2,792[1]	1·17
1945	3,265	2,806	2,131	2,442[1]	1·34

the licensing and allocation of materials, etc., as well as the control over new capital issues of over £10,000 by the Capital Issues Committee, set up under the Defence (Finance) Regulation, S.R. & O. (1939), No. 1620. Annual capital issues of companies, as a result, fell from £160 million in 1938 and £73½ million in 1939, to an average of £14 million in 1940–4.[2] Pressure was also brought to bear on the clearing banks to turn all their available resources over to the Government and to restrict bank advances intended to be used for capital construction.

The methods of raising Government loans showed a degree of subtlety far superior to that of the first World War.[3] Their essence was the exploitation of a discriminating monopoly, i.e. the offer of separate terms to each sector of the market, in each case at the lowest rate necessary to bring forth the loans. The 'cheap money' of the 1930's had lowered general expectations of interest levels, and since there was little hope of attracting foreign lenders to London by high rates, and there were other means available to the Government for inhibiting competing claims for savings, there seemed to be no very good reason for raising the rate structure and thus increasing the interest burden on the Government. The bank rate, after seven years at the 2% level, was raised to 4% on 24th August 1939 for reasons which are still obscure, but in view of the pointlessness of this gesture, it was lowered again to 3%, and the authorities were able to conduct a '3% war' by mopping up all the available savings at low and steady rates.

[1] There was some net lending abroad in these years.
[2] W. Ashworth, *Contracts and Finance* (1953), p. 222.
[3] The following paragraphs are largely based on Sayers, *op. cit.*, chapter 7.

For the small saver, the 'National Savings' movement, which had survived from the first World War, was again made the vehicle of strong patriotic appeals, and savers were offered, besides the Post Office and the Trustee Savings Banks and similar holdings, a series of National Savings Certificates and Defence Bonds. For the larger savers, National War Bonds at $2\frac{1}{2}\%$ were provided on tap, i.e. as a continuous supply on application, and 3% Savings Bonds were also on offer, at slightly different terms, their maturity being well spaced out over the post-war period so as to avoid a repetition of the vast conversion operation of 1932. At the end of 1941 yet another type of security began to be issued, the Tax Reserve Certificate, to take advantage of the idle funds held by prudent firms in readiness for their tax liability.

Any funds not invested in any of these alternative loans would normally find their way into the banks, and the Government accordingly developed a whole battery of methods to absorb all 'idle' bank balances, including Ways and Means Advances, Treasury Bills and Treasury Deposit Receipts. The first, being considered inflationary, were used as little as possible, and the main weight fell on Treasury Bills. At first the demand for them greatly exceeded the supply. Of £1,100 million outstanding at the outbreak of war, over £707 million were issued on 'tap' to departments, only £411 million being outstanding on 'tender' to the market. Further, in the early months of the war, the flight from the pound drove a windfall of sterling balances into the Exchange Equalization Account, absorbing bills for six months. Later, however, Treasury Bills gradually increased in importance as a method of transferring funds from the Money Market to the Government.

Yet even the Treasury Bill still left some funds untapped, and in the perilous days of July 1940 a new security was issued to the banks, the Treasury Deposit Receipt. It was rather less liquid than the Treasury Bill, having a currency of six months, and being non-negotiable, though it could be repaid in full for bonds for either the banks or their customers, but its rate, delicately fixed at $1\frac{1}{8}\%$, was just above the Bill rate which then stood at a shade over 1%. This meticulous mopping-up of bank liquid reserves was driven to such lengths that occasionally the cash reserves of the clearing banks were actually reduced below the safety level.

At the same time, concrete restrictions placed on individual spending and on business investment, forced businesses and individuals to accumulate their funds in the banks, unless, indeed, they invested them directly in Government paper. For this reason, as well as because of the general inflation, total bank deposits rose from £2,730 million in 1939 to £5,551 million in 1945 (or by 103%), while total bank clearings, indicating the velocity of circulation, only rose from £36·6 milliard to £66·9 milliard, or by 83%. The London clearing banks alone held average net deposits of £1,257 million in 1939, and £4,035 million at the end of 1945. But of this

329

latter sum, only £1,339 million were private deposits, the rest being business deposits, which had thus risen during the war by over £1,500 million,[1] representing one aspect of the 'forced saving' which consisted of denying firms the real resources for investment in the private sector.

The assets of the London clearing banks were, however, much further distorted by war finance than the liabilities. Commercial advances, as a proportion of deposits, declined dramatically from 44·1% in 1939 to a bare 16·1% in 1945, being smaller even in absolute terms than before the war, and bills discounted fell from 11·3% to 4·0%. Against this, T.D.R.s rose from nil to 38·6%, while 'investments' kept a constant share of the total. In August 1945, Government paper and cash amounted to 83·3% of the deposits of the London clearing banks. They had thus become principally agents for the absorption of funds from the public for the use of the Government, and other financial institutions, for much the same reasons, had their investment portfolios similarly filled with Government paper.

4. THE PROBLEM OF THE FOREIGN BALANCE OF PAYMENTS

The foreign exchanges, it was well understood even before 1939, would require special care during the war. In the course of 1914–18 there had been tight control, particularly over the dollar exchange, but in the second World War this had to be greatly strengthened. For while the last years of peace before 1914 had seen large annual surpluses on current account, the balance of payments in the late 1930's had left no margin, despite protection, controls and artificial support through the Exchange Equalization Account. Moreover, while the immediate panic in August 1914 led to a world shortage of sterling, the crisis of the spring of 1938 had led to a *withdrawal* of foreign funds to the extent of £150 million, and an actual declaration of war could be expected to lead to a large-scale flight from sterling.[2]

The threat to the value of sterling lay largely in the probable adverse balance of payments during the war, though few would have imagined its eventual size. While imports were unlikely to be below their peace-time levels, home industry, increasingly diverted to war production, could scarcely be expected to maintain the same level of exports, and Britain's 'invisible exports' were also likely to shrink. Compared with 1914–18, the large buffer of foreign investments which might be sold off to pay for current imports and meanwhile provided invisible earnings had also been severely diminished.[3] Against this, the possible fall in some raw material prices, as Axis purchases were cut off, would afford but little relief.

---

[1] Ashworth, *op. cit.*, pp. 234–5, Appx. I, Table L, p. 260.
[2] R. S. Sayers, *Central Banking After Bagehot* (1957), p. 65.
[3] Cf. J. M. Keynes, *How to Pay for the War* (1940), Appx., p. 86. Though not very accurate, the figures represent the beliefs current at the outbreak of war.

The Problem of the Foreign Balance of Payments

The critical factor was thus the adverse trade balance, especially with dollar countries. The gold and dollar reserve, estimated at £450 million at the outbreak of war, and planned to be rationed out to last for three years at £150 million a year, was soon being depleted at a much greater rate.[1] Hence a major export drive, particularly to 'hard currency' countries, was undertaken in February 1940, and by April–May it contributed in no small measure to the growing shortage of resources. It had hardly got into its stride, however, before the military collapse in the west, the danger of a German invasion and the consequent need for war production at all costs, forced the country to sacrifice its exports and its gold and dollar reserve. As a result, at the end of the supreme effort of the summer and autumn of 1940, the hope of meeting all foreign payments necessary to maintain the much enlarged armament programme at home had become plainly illusory. The dollar import problem was solved by 'Lend-Lease', and it became possible to switch exports from areas with the 'hardest' currencies to areas with the most vital strategic materials to sell in return. In the process, Britain lost many of her traditional markets, which were forced to turn to the U.S.A. instead,[2] and the volume of her exports fell to less than one-third of the pre-war figure. At the end of the war, less than 2% of the labour force was engaged on exports, compared with 9·5% before the war.

To the huge adverse balance on visible trade account, shown below, have to be added the expenditure by British troops overseas, and the free deliveries from the dollar area:[3]

	Exports (£mn.)	Imports (£mn.)	Visible Adverse Balance (£mn.)	Volume Index	
				Exports	Imports
1938	471	858	387	100	100
1939	440	840	400	94	97
1941	365	1,132	767	56	82
1943	234	1,228	994	29	77
1945	399	1,053	654	46	62

Taking those additional items into account, over the war period as a whole (September 1939 to December 1945 inclusive), total British current

[1] W. K. Hancock and M. M. Gowing, *British War Economy* (1949), pp. 112–17; J. Hurstfield, *The Control of Raw Materials* (1953), pp. 108–13; M. M. Postan, *British War Production* (1952), pp. 82–3.

[2] E. L. Hargreaves and M. M. Gowing, *Civil Industry and Trade* (1952), pp. 44 ff., chapters 7–9.

[3] Re-exports and corresponding imports omitted. Central Statistical Office, *Statistical Digest of the War* (1951), Table 142.

debits amounted to £16,900 million, of which visible imports accounted for £12,200 million. Of this sum, only £6,900 million, or about 40%, was requited by goods and services by the United Kingdom; the rest was financed by sales of capital (£1,200 million), running up debts with other countries (£3,500 million) and *net* grants, mainly from the U.S.A. and Canada (£5,400 million).[1]

To keep the pound at a fixed value, settled at $4.03 (some 20% below the old gold parity), under conditions of such strain, two major weapons were used: import controls and financial controls. The import drain was controlled only by degrees. Imports of luxuries were restricted at once by a licensing system operated by the Board of Trade, and before long most necessities were imported by the Ministry of Food and Ministry of Supply. But this still left many private importers as well as departments to compete, costing Britain £50 million in foreign exchange in needlessly increased prices.[2] It was not until all imports of food were transferred to the Ministry in March 1940, that private importers were virtually squeezed out. Formal general import control was not imposed until June 1940.

Direct financial controls also took time to evolve. Dealings in gold and foreign exchange were put under Treasury control at once; payments abroad and purchases of foreign assets required Treasury sanction and holdings of foreign securities had to be registered with the Treasury for possible sale by the Government in return for sterling payments to the former holders. But these early controls, like those of imports, left several major loopholes. For one thing, payments within the 'Sterling Area' were left free, and in some of it leakages occurred more easily than in the United Kingdom. The 'Sterling Area' in its modern sense with its single pool of gold and dollar resources evolved under the lead of the United Kingdom only in 1939–41.[3] Above all, foreign holders of sterling balances could still engage in exchange dealings,[4] and many exchanged their sterling for dollars or other 'hard' currency, which then escaped control. The loss of these precious balances in the early months was estimated at $737 million,[5] but was considered necessary in order not to alienate American holders of sterling. Only in May were foreign-held securities blocked, the balances having by then become negligible, and all further leaks were then stopped by bilateral trade treaties.

The history of the methods of raising external loans in the two main

[1] R. S. Sayers, *Financial Policy, 1939–45* (1956), Appx. I, Table 10, p. 499.
[2] T. Balogh, 'The Drift Towards a Rational Foreign Exchange Policy' (1940), in Oxford Institute of Statistics, *Studies in War Economics* (1947), p. 66.
[3] *Report of the Committee on the Working of the Monetary System* (Radcliffe Report) (1959. Cmnd. 827), paras. 647, 723 ff.; A. R. Conan, *The Sterling Area* (1952), p. 52; D. F. McCurrach, 'Britain's U.S. Dollar Problem, 1939–45', *Econ. J.*, 58/231, 1948, p. 356.   [4] See p. 301 above.
[5] H. Duncan Hall, *North American Supply* (H.S.W.W., 1955), p. 270.

currencies, the dollar and the pound sterling, differed greatly, but between them they permitted the United Kingdom to emerge from the war in the summer of 1945 without being crippled by foreign loans of the 1914–1918 type. The only loans outstanding of that type were secured, in the case of Canada and the U.S.A., by assets held in those countries, and in the case of Portugal, by gold earmarked for that purpose.[1]

The 'Sterling Balances', i.e. the credits of other countries held in London in blocked accounts, were owed largely, though not wholly, within the 'Sterling Area'. The largest holder was India, whose credit in London rose to well over £1 milliard at the end of the war even after more than £300 million of capital assets had been sold off by Britain. 'The main origin [of these credits] was when India was used as the operational basis and arsenal of democracy in the East against Japan.'[2] Other large sums were held by Egypt, Palestine and the Sudan, again on account of the supply and expenditure of Empire troops in their area, but these countries were less eager to supply 'forced loans' to Britain, and they were more sensitive to later suggestions to freeze them. Substantial balance also accrued to other Colonial areas, and to South Africa, Australia and New Zealand. Outside the Empire, the Argentine held about £100 million at the end of the war, and Brazil about £40 million, the total of the Western Hemisphere being over £300 million; and several of the Western European Governments-in-Exile had also accumulated substantial sterling claims, either by transferring their gold to the United Kingdom, or by the active trade balance of their colonies.

The total indebtedness grew at a steady rate of £600 million a year throughout the later war years, and by mid-1945 had reached the following amounts (in £mn.):[3]

Australia, N.Z., S. Africa, Eire	384
India, Burma, Middle East	1,732
Colonies and other Sterling Area	607
Total Sterling Area	**2,723**
South and North America	303
European States and Dependencies	267
Rest of the World	62
Grand Total	**3,355**

[1] R. S. Sayers, *Financial Policy*, p. 438.

[2] H. A. Shannon, 'The Sterling Balances of the Sterling Area 1939–1949', *Econ. J.*, 60/239, 1950, p. 540; H. D. Hall and C. C. Wrigley, *Studies of Overseas Supply* (H.S.W.W., 1956), chapter 9; Sir Dennis H. Robertson, *Britain in the World Economy* (1954), p. 40.

[3] Sayers, *Financial Policy*, p. 439; cf. also chapters, 9, 10, 14; T. Balogh, 'The International Aspect', in G. D. N. Worswick and P. H. Ady, *The British Economy, 1945–1950* (Oxford, 1952), pp. 480–3.

The British Economy in Total War, 1939–1945

It might be held that it would be a poor recompense for the United Kingdom to have borne the brunt of the fighting and of war production, only to find herself at the end of the war crippled by debt, much of it due to inflation created by British expenditure itself,[1] to the very countries which she saved by her efforts. The issue was not so simple, however. Some of the countries concerned were not necessarily friendly to the British side, and their supplies would not have been forthcoming without payment; as it was, their willingness to let their sterling credits accumulate represented a considerable concession on the part of populations which had a vastly lower standard of living than Great Britain, even in the worst months of the war. Again, the independent countries of South America were prepared to trust Britain with their sterling credits for their deliveries to Britain, even though Britain cut off her traditional exports to them, because there were British capital assets within their borders at least equal in value;[2] attempts to default on the sterling balances would have simply led to the confiscation of these assets. Lastly, the European Governments-in-Exile could claim that their countries, at the end of the war, were in far greater need of rehabilitation than was Britain, and were therefore in no position to provide loans for the latter.

The sterling balances thus had many origins and many types of owners. While they accumulated, they allowed Britain to fight the war with resources greater than her own, without bankruptcy and without damage to the international value of the pound sterling. At the end of the war, however, they represented a large financial burden, even when not subject to demands of withdrawal. The annual interest and service charge payable abroad, a striking reversal of the old role of Britain as international lender, was hard to bear in the early post-war years; while the need to hold credit balances against them, in order to keep them active and maintain the pound as an international currency, was to lead to serious misunderstandings with the Americans.

By means of external borrowing, and by the sale of capital assets, the United Kingdom obtained from the non-dollar world a total of some £4 milliard in 1939–45,[3] a sum of the same order of magnitude as the total British foreign investment at the outbreak of war. Yet it was put in the shade by the contribution of the dollar world (the U.S.A. and Canada), which provided £7·5 milliard (£6·2 milliard net) by gifts and over £1 milliard by sales of investments, gold and by accumulating liabilities.

The Canadian contribution, large as it was in relation to the resources of the Dominion, was made with the minimum of friction. Having used

---

[1] E. M. H. Lloyd, *Food and Inflation in the Middle East, 1940–45* (Stanford, 1956).
[2] J. Fred Rippy, *British Investments in South America, 1822–1949* (Minneapolis, 1959), 186.
[3] R. F. Harrod, *Life of John Maynard Keynes* (1951), p. 606.

up its liquid Canadian resources, the United Kingdom was granted an interest-free loan of $700 million in 1942, and when that was exhausted, the Canadians voted their magnificent 'billion-dollar gift' in 1943. It was followed by two 'mutual aid' appropriations, without strings, totalling $1,800 million in 1943-4, and further credits lasted until 1946. Total gifts and free aids came to $3,468 million, and total supplies and services to the United Kingdom (including those paid for) to $7,441 million, or nearly £2 milliard.[1]

Very different were the relations with the United States, bedevilled as they were by the strong neutralist and isolationist sector of American public opinion, and by widespread suspicions of Britain's motives. At the outbreak of war, there were two legal limits to British purchases in the United States: the Neutrality Act prohibited sales of war materials to belligerents, and the Johnson Act of 1934 prohibited loans to foreign Governments which had defaulted on their first World War loans, including the United Kingdom Government. Purchases were therefore limited to non-war goods, in quantities which the country could afford to pay for in cash. In November 1939 the Neutrality Act was amended to permit purchases of munitions in foreign ships, and the remaining limits were thus purely financial, but very real none the less. It was in this period of 'cash and carry', of careful husbanding of gold and dollar reserves, that the British Purchasing Commission under Arthur B. Purvis (as well as its French counterpart) established itself, to play henceforth a crucial part in economic warfare and in the delicate but vital relationship of the two Anglo-Saxon powers.[2]

Apart from machine tools, the principal British need was for aircraft, and in this first period they formed the most important military item ordered in the U.S.A. (as well as in Canada). Aircraft factories, however, are not built overnight, and long before Britain could receive substantial supplies of American aircraft, the calamity of the fall of France had overtaken the Allies. With her back suddenly against the wall, the United Kingdom was forced to readjust her economic sights and to plan for a far larger contribution from North American production in the long run, if she were ever to match the Axis powers; at the same time, she had to increase her immediate orders from America, especially her aeroplane demands, and she took over the French orders placed there, which alone committed her to an ultimate expenditure of $612 million.

British orders both for immediate use and for long-term supply were, therefore, stepped up enormously in the second half of 1940, but neither

[1] Sayers, *Financial Policy*, chapter 11; Hall, *op. cit.*, chapters 1, 2, pp. 483-7; Hall and Wrigley, pp. 46-65.
[2] M. Jean Monnet of the French Commission was taken on the British staff after the fall of France.

led to any tangible results. The immediate orders failed to materialize because of the sheer inability of American industry, increasingly drawn upon by the American forces also, to meet them quickly enough. It was estimated that at least $200 million of precious British reserves had gone by March 1941, not into buying arms, but into building factories in the U.S.A. and in Canada. For all her vast outlay and large future commitments, the United Kingdom had as yet, in the critical months to the end of 1940, received only the minimal actual supplies of munitions. Aircraft, for example, from the U.S.A., perhaps the most critical item, only numbered 700 in 1939 and 2,000 for the whole of 1940 (compared with a British home production of 8,000 and 15,000 respectively).[1] Supplies of food, raw materials and other peace-time goods were, however, much more satisfactory: for the whole of 1939–41, their imports from the U.S.A. amounted to £667 million, as against £133 million for munitions; only in 1943 did munitions supply begin to exceed the imports of non-war goods.[2]

Far more disturbing than the short-term delay was the long-term prospect. Even though the gold and dollar reserves had been enlarged by current earnings of $2,000 million between September 1939 and December 1940 ($345 by United Kingdom earnings, $670 by Empire commodities and $965 by Dominion gold),[3] the position had been reached by that latter date where the total liquid reserves, including saleable capital assets in the dollar area, were only just sufficient to pay for orders already placed. There was nothing left even to begin to pay the very much enlarged programme for 1941, necessary for the ultimate defeat of the Axis.

This position had been foreseen some months earlier, and as the date of the absolute impoverishment of Britain and her Allies loomed nearer, it was becoming clear that in the last resort the United States would not deny her help. There had been some piece-meal expansion of American aid, as far as her position as a neutral and her Congress and public opinion allowed. The 50 destroyers, for example, handed over in September 1940 in return for British bases, were a welcome immediate contribution,[4] while the United States co-operated in denying some crucial war materials, such as molybdenum, to Germany and to neutrals within her control.[5] By December 1940 more comprehensive action had become necessary, and President Roosevelt met it by announcing the provision of 'Lend-Lease'.

[1] Hall and Wrigley, p. 30.
[2] J. Hurstfield, *Control of Raw Materials*, p. 98.
[3] McCurrach, *loc. cit.*, pp. 358 ff.; Hall, *North American Supplies*, pp. 269–70,
[4] W. S. Churchill, *The Second World War. Vol. II. Their Finest Hour* (1949). chapter 20.   [5] Hall, *North American Supplies*, chapter 3–6.

The Problem of the Foreign Balance of Payments

Lend-lease meant the supply, free of charge, for the duration of the war, of all goods and services needed by Britain and available in the U.S.A.; it was granted on the same terms to the other Allies, including Soviet Russia and China. Though lend-lease supplies were, until 1943-4 at least, only marginal to the United Kingdom's war effort, they solved the problem set by the running out of reserves. Further, by allowing Britain to concentrate on a more limited field of production, to dovetail with American supply, lend-lease removed one of the most harmful effects of the dollar shortage. Its vast bulk, some $27 milliard being made available to the United Kingdom, and $6 milliard by the United Kingdom to the U.S.A. in 'reciprocal aid' or 'reverse lend-lease', dominated British economic warfare, and its conditions dominated British economic relations with the U.S.A. and the rest of the world.[1]

The lend-lease Act, though called the 'most unsordid act' in history, had to pass through Congress while America was still neutral and it had to run an annual gauntlet of renewal; and in this process several onerous conditions were exacted. To begin with, Britain had to strip herself bare of dollars and all capital assets in the U.S.A., and great pressure was brought to bear on her to sell even those which could be sold only at a large loss. This reserve gone, the accumulation of a new one, even if desperately required as backing for the 'sterling balances', was viewed with the greatest hostility and suspicion.

Secondly, many months were to elapse before the first substantial lend-lease deliveries actually arrived in Britain, and over two years were to elapse before they exceeded the deliveries paid for in cash. In the interim Britain would, in fact, have been bankrupt if it had not been for a loan of $425 million extended by the Reconstruction Finance Corporation, an American Government agency, against the collateral of British-held American assets valued at $700 million.

Thirdly, lend-lease supplies were, in form, deliveries by the American Government to Allied Governments 'for the defence of the U.S.A.', so that, in the last resort, they depended not on the wishes of the receiving country, but on those of the American Government. Thus, in spite of growing collaboration between the Supply Boards of the Allied Governments, British and other Allied deliveries were still liable to sudden cancellation in favour of the American Services, whose shopping lists were usually grossly inflated by British austerity standards.

Fourthly, there were the 'strings' deliberately put in. Some were

---

[1] For the history of 'lend-lease', see Edward R. Stettinius, Jnr., *Lend-Lease* (New York, 1944); Sayers, *Financial Policy*, chapters 13, 15; Hall, *North American Supplies*, chapters 8-11; Hancock and Gowing, chapter 9; Hall and Wrigley, chapter 3; Hurstfield, chapter 19; A. J. Youngson, *British Economy, 1920–1957* (1960), pp. 152-6.

reasonable in principle, such as the proviso that no private profit should be made out of lend-lease deliveries. Others were less so, above all the demand for a prohibition of all British exports containing any raw materials which were also supplied through lend-lease, so that American exporters should not have to compete with the British who were subsidized by the American taxpayer. This extreme demand was somewhat toned down later, but it was still highly restrictive, when the British Government decided to accept it voluntarily in the Export White Paper of 19th September 1941,[1] before the American entry into the war. The other main condition related to the post-war world. By the famous Article VII of the Mutual Aid Agreement of 1942,[2] Britain had to subscribe to the pronouncement against 'discrimination' in international trade after the war, generally understood to be an attack on Imperial preference.

There might have been some justification for this treatment while America was still neutral, but even after Pearl Harbour, when America became a belligerent ally, 'Britain's position remained what it had been through 1941, that of the dependent partner receiving aid'.[3] Neither did it change when Britain and the Empire granted 'reverse lend-lease' without any strings, representing, though it was much smaller in amount, as high a proportion of the donor's national income, and a greater sacrifice.[4] Besides, the U.S.A. derived much advantage from British scientific knowledge supplied free for such projects as radar, jet engines and nuclear fission.[5] Lastly, the American insistence on unilateral treatment made it impossible for Britain to propose pooling arrangements among her other Allies, so that lend-lease was, in a sense, responsible for the extent of the burdensome Sterling Balances at the end of the war.

If conditions of lend-lease were restrictive in 1941–2, when sympathy with the dangerously exposed position of Britain was at its height, they became even more so later as the immediate danger receded and American troops began to take part themselves in the fighting. Further, as their expenditure in Britain and elsewhere in the Sterling Area began to raise the dollar reserve, which the American president, unknown to the British, had determined should not exceed $1,000 million, there began a further series of restrictions to reduce them to that level. Tobacco for civilian consumption was removed from the lend-lease list and in November 1943 capital goods were taken out, at a cost to the sterling area of $200 million.

[1] Cmd. 6311.
[2] *Treaty Series No. 7* (1942). Cmd. 6391 and Cmd. 6341.
[3] Sayers, *Financial Policy*, p. 375.
[4] R. G. D. Allen, 'Mutual Aid between the U.S.A. and the British Empire 1941–5', *J. R. Stat. S.*, 109/3, 1946; Hancock and Gowing, p. 353, Table 3(c).
[5] Hall and Wrigley, chapter 8.

Moreover, Congress was reducing the overall appropriations for lend-lease just as the American troops were leaving Allied soil and the dollar reserves began to fall again, and it was made clear that after the defeat of Germany, lend-lease supplies would be sent only for troops actually fighting the Japanese, and no longer for civilians.

Basing himself on the agreement between the President and the Prime Minister at Quebec, Keynes secured some concessions at the Washington Conference in October 1944 from this intransigent position. The importance of exports to the survival of Britain was recognized and she was allowed to convert some of her export industries even before V.E. day; as from the beginning of 1945, she was also given greater freedom to export by paying for her raw materials. But the relief was short-lived. In March 1945 lend-lease was renewed, but for war purposes only; in April President Roosevelt died; and V.E. day, in June, was followed quickly by the surrender of Japan on August 14th. A week later, lend-lease was abruptly stopped, and Britain was faced with the immediate necessity of paying in dollars for goods already in the country or 'in the pipeline' to the tune of $650 million, as well as for continuation orders, if she was not to be starved of necessary food and raw materials.

During the war, the British economy had become utterly dependent on a large import surplus from America, not only of war materials, but also of peace-time commodities. With her capital equipment run down, more resources devoted to war and needing reconversion to a larger extent than any other Ally, her overseas earnings cut by the loss of one-quarter of her shipping and almost half her investments, she was quite unable to earn the necessary dollars, even if the standard of consumption were cut further. The rest of the world, much of it devastated and disorganized, was in no position to supply the needs hitherto filled from dollar sources, and was itself in need of dollar aid. The only possible course for Britain was to obtain an American loan of the type which she had succeeded in avoiding throughout the war, and at the end of the war Keynes was sent to Washington once again to negotiate it.

5. WORK AND WELFARE IN THE WAR YEARS

It was suggested above[1] that the Government, in its anxiety not to repeat the mistakes of the first World War, was perhaps over-sensitive to the views of organized workers. There were several reasons why the costly strikes and the class hatred of the first World War were not repeated in the second. For one thing, the unions and their leaders enjoyed from the outset much greater official recognition, and when, in May 1940, Labour entered the Coalition Government, the outstanding trade unionist of the day, Ernest Bevin, was in charge of policy relating to manpower as

[1] p. 297.

Minister of Labour and National Service. Secondly, Labour was politically much more in sympathy with this war and its declared war aims than with the first, and exerted more positive influence on the schemes for post-war reconstruction. Thirdly, the Government's efforts to ensure a fair distribution of food and other necessities, and to enlarge social welfare schemes, by themselves contributed to the social peace of the war years. Finally, unlike the years before 1914, the 1930's had seen very few large strikes, so that, perhaps, it was not surprising that apart from the coal mines, some engineers' strikes in 1940 and a boilermakers' strike in 1944, the war-time strikes were short, small and unofficial.[1]

As prices rose in the early weeks of war, and a shortage of some types of labour made itself felt, the trade unions, distrusting the Chamberlain Government, refused to submit either to compulsory settlement of wages or to legal prohibition of strikes, nor was the Ministry of Labour eager to see such measures enacted. As a result, it was not possible to hold down wages, and the Government itself, by allowing the very first major wage claim, that of the miners in October 1939, at the cost of raising the price of coal, set a poor example to employers who wished to be intransigent.[2]

The formation of the Coalition Government and the arrival of Mr. Bevin at the Ministry of Labour created confidence between the Government and the unions. Manpower policy became more positive, though the Government continued to keep its drastic legal powers in the background, and relied as far as possible on the voluntary co-operation of the unions and the use of voluntary, peace-time machinery.

As far as collective bargaining was concerned, the basic provision, the Conditions of Employment and National Arbitration Order S.R. & O. (1940), No. 1305, preserved all the existing negotiating machinery, including arbitration and the powers of the Industrial Court. It was only for issues in which agreement could not be reached by existing methods that it established a new National Arbitration Tribunal. Strikes and lock-outs were prohibited, unless the Ministry of Labour failed to act for three weeks after receiving notice of a dispute. Normally the Ministry would refer a dispute either to the National Arbitration Tribunal or to any of the other existing arbitration bodies, and in that case their awards were to have legal force.[3] Altogether, in 1939-45, 816 decisions were handed down by the N.A.T., 692 by other arbitrators, and there were about 2,150 conciliation settlements. Strikes could not entirely be prevented and

---

[1] Allan Flanders, *Trade Unions* (1952), p. 100; K. G. J. C. Knowles, *Strikes, A Study in Industrial Conflict* (Oxford, 1952), pp. 162–3; Central Statistical Office, *Statistical Digest of the War* (1951), Table 36; A. L. Bowley, 'Labour Disputes in Wartime', *London & Cambridge Economic Service*, No. 103 (1945), p. 8.

[2] W. K. Hancock and M. M. Gowing, *British War Economy* (1949), pp. 164–5.

[3] N. Barou, *British Trade Unions* (1947), pp. 153–4; H. M. D. Parker, *Manpower, a Study in War-Time Policy and Administration* (H.S.W.W., 1957), chapter 25.

against large-scale strikes the Government was as helpless as in 1914–18, but there were only 109 prosecutions during the war. In April 1944, the Minister, perhaps remembering with bitterness his struggle with 'unofficial' leaders in his own union, pushed through amendments to the Defence Regulations 1A and Regulation 1AA giving powers to deal severely with incitement to strike, but they were repealed again in the following year.

The direction of labour was based on the drastic Essential Works Order, S.R. & O. No. 302, of March 1941,[1] but its powers were used sparingly for fear of industrial troubles such as accompanied the combouts after 1915. Dilution also relied heavily on the experience of 1915–18, and in the engineering industry was negotiated as early as August 1939. It led to some difficulty in Coventry and Glasgow in February 1940, but gave little trouble once the Coalition Government was in power. It was combined with a system of training, and between mid-1939 and mid-1943 the proportion of women workers in engineering was raised from 10·5% to 31·2%.[2]

Where labour was virtually conscripted into 'controlled' establishments, 'the Minister of Labour was convinced that he could not expect men to give up the right to free choice of employment without guaranteeing them certain conditions of work, including a guaranteed week and the restriction of the employers' right to dismiss them'.[3] This conviction moved him to provide for the expansion of welfare facilities,[4] the improvements in working conditions even in the midst of the war-time difficulties, the strengthening of the 'fair wages' clause in Government contracts, and the extension of statutory wage determination to trades hitherto poorly organized.

These last received much attention during the war years. Road Haulage had been covered just before the outbreak of war, though it was several years before the new wage rates were actually enforced. A Joint Council for the Distributive Trades was set up in 1940, and separate Whitley Councils for different sections of the trade later. In 1943, the Catering Wages Act established the Catering Wages Commission, and Wages Boards to fix pay and conditions of work in the different sections of the trade. The Central Agricultural Wages Board was given powers in 1940 to fix national minimum wage rates for adult male workers, and in 1942 wage-fixing powers in general were transferred to it from the counties. Lastly, in coal mining, owners and miners agreed to a national conciliation scheme, including a National Reference Tribunal of three neutral members. These developments culminated in the Wages Council

---

[1] p. 305 above; Parker, pp. 134, 448–54.
[2] P. Inman, *Labour in the Munition Industries* (H.S.W.W., 1957), p. 80.
[3] Inman, p. 103.   [4] pp. 346–7 below.

Act of 1945 which converted the existing Trade Boards and the Road Haulage Wages Board into Wages Councils, gave them additional powers over earnings and conditions, and fostered their extension into other industries with poor facilities for collective bargaining. Elsewhere, 56 joint industrial councils were established or re-established in the war years, partly with a view to laying down 'recognized' conditions of employment as stipulated by the Essential Works Order.[1] Mr. Bevin's greatest personal triumph was perhaps the decasualization of dock labour, which began in 1941.[2]

As in 1914–18, the trade unions grew greatly in stature and power during the war years. Membership rose from $6\frac{1}{4}$ million in 1939 to nearly 8 million in 1945. Quite apart from their representation on the National Joint Advisory Council to the Minister of Labour, trade union leaders were increasingly drawn into the machinery of Government. The Regional Boards for Industry, set up in 1941, and the National Production Advisory Council of 1942, among others, gave them considerable influence over industrial planning. Joint consultation, originated in engineering in 1942, spread to many other industries, and Joint Production Committees, beginning spontaneously in Woolwich in 1940, covered $3\frac{1}{2}$ million workers by the end of 1944.[3] Again, the T.U.C. Interim Report of 1944[4] carried great weight with the Labour Party, which was destined to govern the country after the war. The leaders of the large trade unions, in fact, became so eager to show a sense of responsibility for the economy as a whole, that they laid themselves open to legitimate attacks by their own members for neglecting their interests.

If they had exerted their power to the full, like, for example, the farmers,[5] the trade unions could not indeed have been prevented from enforcing wage increases that would have destroyed any hopes of containing the war-time inflation. As it was, it was only real *earnings* which showed any substantial increase, real wage *rates* rising more slowly than the cost of living, though faster than the official cost-of-living index, which working people were well aware was grossly unrepresentative and had its components selectively held down in price[6] (compare columns B and C below). At the same time, regular hours of work if not overtime, night

---

[1] D. F. MacDonald, *The State and the Trade Unions* (1960), chapter 9; P.E.P., *British Trade Unionism* (1948), pp. 39–54; Min. of Labour and Nat. Service, *Report for 1939–46*, pp. 269–294; Allan Flanders, 'Industrial Relations', in G. D. N. Worswick and P. H. Ady, *The British Economy 1945–1950* (Oxford, 1952), pp. 112–115.

[2] Hancock and Gowing, p. 240.

[3] Industrial Welfare Society, *Works Councils and Committees* (1943); N. Barou, p. 170.

[4] T.U.C., *Interim Report on Post-War Reconstruction* (1944). Cf. p. 348 below.

[5] p. 317 above.   [6] Hancock and Gowing, pp. 164–9, 333–5.

shifts and week-end work, together with much piecework and up-grading of workers, raised actual earnings a good deal more than wage rates:[1]

	Wage Rates[2]	Official Cost-of-Living Index	Wage-earners' True Cost-of-Living Index	Weekly Earnings Oct.
				1938 = 100[3]
	Sept. 1939 = 100		1938 = 100	
	A	B	C	D
1939	104	104	$102\frac{1}{2}$	—
1940	113–14	121	120	130
1941	122	128	135	142
1942	131–2	129	143	160
1943	136–7	129	148	176
1944	143–4	130	150	$181\frac{1}{2}$
1945	150–1	$133\frac{1}{2}$	—	$180\frac{1}{2}$

Of the total increase in money earnings of 81%, it was estimated that 32% was due to a rise in wage rates, 9% to changes as between industries, 6% to increases in the hours of work, −1% to changes in the proportion of men, women, boys and girls employed, and 20% to all remaining factors, including overtime and piecework.[4] It was thus largely the longer hours and the harder or more skilled work which raised the real earnings of the working classes above those of peace-time.

Average wages, as always, hide many divergent movements in different industries. As soon as full employment conditions permitted, there began an irresistible pressure to raise the wages of many unskilled and agricultural workers, whose incomes were held to be below a reasonable subsistence level, and of those who received less than others in comparable work, such as miners and railwaymen. Wage rates also had to be boosted in industries which had to attract much new labour quickly, such as engineering and aircraft, and the Government itself, in its white paper on *Price Stabilization and Industrial Policy* of July 1941,[5] admitted the justice of raising wages where productivity had risen, where earnings had been

[1] Ministry of Labour, *Report 1939–46*, pp. 304–5; Parker, *Manpower*, p. 433. J. L. Nicholson, 'Employment and National Income during the War', *Bull. Oxf. Inst. Stat.*, 7/14, 1945, Table 6, and 'Earnings and Hours of Labour', *ibid.*, 8/5, 1946, Table 2; Hancock and Gowing, p. 152; J. Kuczynski, *A Short History of Labour Conditions in Great Britain, 1750 to the Present Day* (3rd ed., 1947), chapter 4.
[2] July figures.   [3] Current weights.
[4] Nicholson, 'Earnings and Hours'; N. Barou, pp. 159–60.
[5] Cmd. 6294. Cf. also B. C. Roberts, *National Wages Policy in War and Peace* (1958), chapter 2.

below a reasonable minimum or where there were changes in the form or volume of production. Thus there were many forces pushing up wage rates, while women's rates rose more than men's, and unskilled rates crept up from about 70% to about 80% of skilled rates in the course of the war.

The maintenance or increase of real wages at a time when measures of profit limitation were in force, when house rents were frozen by the Rent and Mortgage Interest Restriction Act of 1939, and when heavy burdens of taxation reduced the real incomes of the rich, implied for the second World War, as it did in the first, a substantial redistribution of incomes in favour of wage-earners. The tax burden of the war on wage-earners was estimated at only 13–17% in the later years of the war, compared with 35–44% on non-wage-earners.[1]

As a result, while wage incomes (at constant, 1947 prices and after taxation) rose by 18% between 1938 and 1947, and 'social incomes' by 57%, incomes from property fell by 15% and salaries by 21%.[2] In the following comparison between 1938 and 1949, a year for which better statistics are available, the extent of the redistribution is somewhat exaggerated, since, like the official national income statistics and others based on them, it omits the very large share of income from property represented by undistributed profits and capital appreciation[3] (see table opposite).

The war also saw a redistribution of property, though it was less marked than that in incomes. For example, the capital owned by owners of £100,000 and over fell from 22% in 1936–8 to 16·1% of the total in 1946–7, and that held by owners of £1,000–£10,000 rose from 29·3% to 32·8%,[4] but allowance has to be made for the changing value of the pound.

The more equitable distribution of war-time was achieved not only by the money flow of incomes, taxation and subsidies, but also by direct control over goods. The luxuries and non-necessities consumed by the rich were reduced most drastically, while many of the non-necessities of the poor, including tobacco, alcohol and cinemas, were maintained deliberately (and heavily taxed) for the combined purposes of maintaining morale, mopping up spending power and providing a broad tax base.

[1] J. L. Nicholson, 'Employment and National Income', *loc. cit.*, Table 8; *National Income and Expenditure of the United Kingdom, 1938–1945* (1946. Cmd. 6784), Table 9.

[2] Dudley Seers, *Changes in the Cost-of-Living and the Distribution of Income since 1938* (Oxford, 1949), p. 64.

[3] Dudley Seers, 'The Levelling of Incomes', *Bull. Oxf. Inst. Stat.*, 12/10 (1950), pp. 278–9.

[4] Kathleen M. Langley, 'The Distribution of Capital in Private Hands in 1936–8 and 1946–7, Part II', *Bull. Oxf. Inst. Stat.*, 13/2, 1951.

	Post-tax Real Average Incomes in 1949. Index 1938 = 100	Percentage Share in Post tax Personal Incomes at Constant (1938) Prices	
		1938	1949
Wages	122	37	47
Salaries	83	23	22
Forces' pay	82	2	3
Total work income	—	62	71
Farming income	191 ⎫		
Professional earnings	89 ⎬	12	10
Sole traders' profit	82 ⎭		
Distributed property income	—	20	10
Social income	—	6	9
		100	100

While food consumption as a whole was cut by one-sixth in money terms at constant prices,[1] the supplies of many basic foods were maintained at their peace-time levels, and others were even increased. These included liquid milk, flour and other cereals (partly by a higher extraction rate), potatoes, and fats other than butter. The basic foods were rationed in 1940 and consumption per head of meat (including bacon and ham), of sugar and of tea was cut substantially in the following years.[2] At the end of 1941 there followed the 'points system' rationing for canned goods, biscuits, syrup, breakfast cereals, etc., as well as clothes rationing, and in 1942 'personal points' for sweets. Bread was not rationed at all during the war.[3] Among other goods, the consumption of tobacco and beer, as well as travel, increased most; consumption of fuel and light remained fairly constant; but consumption of clothing was down to less than one-half, and of household goods to less than 40% of pre-war. Private motoring was suspended, restaurant meals limited to 5s. and service reduced accordingly. In general, it would be broadly true to state that personal

[1] *National Income and Expenditure of the United Kingdom, 1938–1945* (1946. Cmd. 6784), Table 9.

[2] *Statistical Digest of the War*, Tables, 67, 70; *Food Consumption Levels in the United Kingdom* (1947. Cmd. 7203).

[3] A. S. MacNalty, *The Civilian Health and Medical Services*, Vol. 1 (H.S.W.W., 1953), chapter 5; Hargreaves and Gowing, *Civil Industry*, chapter 14; W. B. Reddaway, 'Rationing', in *Lessons of the British War Economy*; R. J. Hammond, *Food*, Vol. 1 (1951), esp. chapters 8, 14, 15, 22, 23; Vol. 2 (1956), Part C.

consumption was stabilized at the pre-war skilled artisan level, and that of other classes cut down to approach it.[1]

There was also positive intervention, usually on grounds of national efficiency, in the direction of extending the State welfare provisions. For example, school meals were instituted, partly with a view to permitting housewives to take up outside work, but in part designed to help out the families which could not afford to buy even their basic rations, and they were served to all children, rich and poor alike. In the same way, nurseries were established for working mothers and for others. The cheap milk scheme for young children and expectant mothers began in 1940 and there followed the provision for orange juice, cod liver oil, the special egg allocation and vitamin tablets.[2] The initial impulse, again, may have been with the Health Authorities anxious to protect children from the ill-effects of rationing, but the ultimate effect was a welfare policy providing certain minimum needs for all classes alike, as a right of citizenship. By these means there was achieved, after a slight deterioration in 1940 and 1941, a substantial improvement in the health of the country, especially in that of children, in spite of air raids, food shortages, overcrowding, the strain on medical services and other adverse factors. While the general death rate, continued its slow secular fall, the infant mortality rate, perhaps the most sensitive index, declined substantially from 56 per 1,000 live births in England (77 in Scotland) in 1936–8 to 45 (58) in 1944–6.[3]

Munition workers and those employed in essential industries received special attention. Sometimes the interests of efficiency demanded it, as when the long hours worked in the summer of 1940 had to be reduced because of the obvious signs of fatigue, and sometimes it was necessary in order to attract and keep workers in factories inconveniently sited; but in part it was, again, called forth by the new spirit fostered by the common experience of the war. There was much new-found humanity as well as an intelligent search for efficiency behind the increase from 35 whole-time and 70 part-time factory doctors in the whole country at the outbreak of war to 181 and 890 by 1944, and the increase from 1,500 industrial nurses to 8,000 in 1943. From November 1940 on, factory inspectors had power to make canteens compulsory in the large works, and in these they increased threefold, to 5,000, while in the smaller firms, not subject to the Order of 1940, they grew from 1,400 to 6,800, beside docks' canteens and seamen's welfare centres. The factory inspectorate was also given

---

[1] J. Hurstfield, *The Control of Raw Materials* (1953), Appx. 15, Tables 1–3, Appx. 16; Hancock and Gowing, pp. 324, 492–5.
[2] Sheila Ferguson and Hilde Fitzgerald, *Studies in the Social Services* (H.S.W.W., 1954), chapters 5, 6 and 7; MacNalty, *op. cit.*, chapter 4.
[3] R. M. Titmuss, *Problems of Social Policy* (H.S.W.W., 1950), p. 521, also pp. 509 ff.

powers, by an earlier Order of July 1940, to insist on the appointment of welfare officers in large factories of 250 workers and over; and their number rose from 1,500 to 5,378 in January 1944. Special training schemes were organized for them by the Ministry, and their employment symbolized the new enlightened attitude to personnel management.[1]

In the spirit of the times, welfare provisions could not be limited to the special classes of expectant mothers, children and war workers. 'It would, in any relative sense, be true to say that by the end of the Second World War the Government had, through the agency of newly established or existing services, assumed and developed a measure of direct concern for the health and well-being of the population which, by contrast with the role of the Government in the nineteen-thirties, was little short of remarkable.' [2] Factory canteens were matched for the general public by the local authorities' 'British Restaurants'.[3] The evacuation of schoolchildren from the large cities involved the organization of innumerable public services of a kind normally provided privately only. In the face of the danger from bombing, class distinction tended to pall also: provision in shelters, emergency hospitals and evacuation centres was alike for all.

As a result, the association of public welfare with charity and degradation was beginning to fade. Unemployment had been virtually abolished from the middle of 1941 on, but there were still many persons in need, and for them public aid was made more humane. The Determination of Needs Act of 1941 abolished the needs test inquiry into the whole family, limiting it to the person seeking relief. The transfer, in 1940, of pensions, relief of war distress and allowances to families of men in the Forces to the re-named 'Assistance Board' did much also to change the attitude of that institution. The more sympathetic handling of these cases also improved the treatment of old-age pensioners who drew supplementary relief under the Act of 1940,[4] and of other paupers.

It was therefore not surprising that the committee of officials, set up in June 1941 under the chairmanship of Sir William Beveridge to report on social insurance and allied services after the war, should have been irresistibly drawn towards one single comprehensive scheme, with similar benefit rates for all kinds of need, available to all as of right. Its report, issued (since its proposals were controversial) under Beveridge's name alone in November 1942, had an immediate and startling popular appeal

---

[1] Inman, chapter 9; Parker, chapter 23; Ministry of Labour, *Report 1939–46*, p. 113.
[2] R. M. Titmuss, p. 506. Cf. also Alan T. Peacock and Jack Wiseman, *The Growth of Public Expenditure in the United Kingdom* (1961).
[3] R. J. Hammond, *Food*, Vol. 2, chapters 23–25.
[4] W. H. Beveridge, *Full Employment in a Free Society* (1945 ed.), Part III; D. C. Marsh, *National Insurance and Assistance in Great Britain* (1950), pp. 51–2.

as the 'Beveridge Report' [1] and became one of the pillars of the country's post-war plans.

6. PLANS FOR POST-WAR RECONSTRUCTION

The common national disaster and triumph of Dunkirk, and the sharing of the hardships and dangers afterwards, had created a new spirit of national consciousness, demanding a new approach to the country's future. In response to 'the strong impulse to fuse the will to victory with aspirations for a better world after victory',[2] Churchill's Coalition Government set up a War Aims Committee of the War Cabinet in August 1940, although it was only in 1943 that a Minister of Reconstruction was appointed. A Minister without Portfolio had been assigned the duty of post-war planning since 1940, and it was as such that Mr. Arthur Greenwood invited Sir William Beveridge to report on the insurance services. Beveridge's own belief was 'that the purpose of victory is to live into a better world than the old world; that each individual is more likely to concentrate upon his war effort if he feels that his Government will be ready with plans for that better world; that, if these plans are to be ready in time, they must be made now'.[3]

The immediate occasion of the appointment of the Beveridge Committee was the protest by the trade unions at the suspension of the work of the Royal Commission on Workmen's Compensation in 1940, because of the alleged inability of the employers to submit evidence. This protest, it may be noted in passing, was not the only contribution of the unions to post-war planning. The hopes of the T.U.C. were embodied in its Interim Report of 1944,[4] which proposed joint Industrial Boards for industrial development—the later Development Boards—as well as demanding policies for full employment. Most of the larger unions also made their own post-war plans, the miners, for example, drawing up the twelve-point 'Miners' Charter'.[5]

The Beveridge Report appeared in November 1942. Its main points were embodied in its six 'principles'.[6] The first was its comprehensiveness. It covered all the known causes of the 'giant', Want, by providing for unemployment benefit, sickness benefit, disability benefit, workmen's compensation, old age, widows' and orphans' pensions and benefits, funeral grants and maternity benefit. In addition to these financial provisions,

---

[1] Sir William Beveridge, *Social Insurance and Allied Services* (1942. Cmd. 6404).
[2] W. K. Hancock and M. M. Gowing, *British War Economy* (1949), p. 534.
[3] Sir William Beveridge, *Social Insurance and Allied Services* (1942. Cmd. 6404), para. 458; also R. M. Titmuss, *Problems of Social Policy* (1950), p. 508.
[4] See p. 342 above.
[5] N. Barou, *British Trade Unions* (1947), pp. 184–5, chapter 16; P.E.P., *British Trade Unionism* (1948), p. 147; D. F. MacDonald, *The State and the Trade Unions* (1960), p. 134.   [6] Paras. 303–9.

the Report was also based on the assumptions that a comprehensive health and rehabilitation service was to be established, its full resources available to all, in place of the uneven and haphazard hospital and medical services before the war, and it made the further proposal that children's allowances should be paid to all. These two suggestions, translated into the National Health Service and Family Allowances, became as vital to the fabric of the Welfare State as social insurance itself. Lastly, a system of 'National Assistance' was to be maintained to cover those who despite all forethought did not fit into any of the categories of beneficiaries and those for whom the benefits paid were insufficient. The scheme was to be comprehensive also in the sense of covering the whole population, whether employed, occupied or unoccupied.

The second principle was that of unification of administrative responsibility. Instead of the nine different Government departments, three different sets of local authorities and the multitude of 'approved societies' administering the existing ten separate schemes,[1] there was to be a single scheme, a single Ministry, and a single weekly stamp to be paid by the insured person and his employer to cover all the insurance provisions.

Thirdly, there was classification. In place of the varying coverage and obligation under existing schemes which had grown up separately, the whole population was grouped from the outset in six main classes, and their contribution rates and benefit rights laid down from the beginning, though in some cases, as for housewives out at work, some choice was possible. The classes were: wage and salary earners, others gainfully occupied, housewives, others of working age, those below working age and retired persons above working age.

The fourth principle was that of adequate benefits. After careful study, the minimum needs were established and (subject to variations of the cost of living) laid down as the standard benefits to be paid, the 'national minimum income for subsistence' below which no one was allowed to fall.[2] This minimum rate was to be the same for all types of benefit, in place of the illogical differences of the rates under existing schemes. Only two exceptions were to be made, a lower rate for old-age pensioners in the early years of the scheme, because of their lower contributions in the course of their working life, and a higher rate in some cases of prolonged incapacity and industrial injury, the former 'workmen's compensation'.

The fifth principle, closely allied to the fourth, was that of flat-rate benefits, according to the size of the family, and irrespective of normal earnings or length of benefit. Corresponding to it was the sixth principle, flat-rate contribution. Though higher than before, the insured persons' contribution was still to be within the reach of every person employed.

[1] W. A. Robson (ed.), *Social Security* (3rd ed., 1948), Introduction, p. 35.
[2] Cf. pp. 37, 89 above.

Of the tripartite income of the Insurance Fund, the Exchequer and local authorities were to contribute about 50%, insured persons (including the self-employed) about 30%, and employers about 20%. The scheme as a whole implied a considerable increase in social security payments. For 1945, for example, these would rise to 10·7% of net national income, compared with 6·4% under the old rates and 7·1% before the war. In future years, this proportion would drop slightly with rising national income, in spite of the heavier burden of the old-age pensions.[1]

Though radical in the changes it proposed, the Beveridge Plan was not revolutionary. It resembled the British educational system in providing a national minimum by the State while allowing those who could afford it to buy better provisions, in the field of superannuation, for example, and, as it turned out, in the medical service also. Moreover, it was the natural culmination of the development of the 1930's and this perhaps explains the remarkable support it received from so many temporary and permanent civil servants on the Committee and outside it, despite the large number of changes it proposed. Its popular appeal was immense, 250,000 copies of the full report and 350,000 of an official abridgement being sold within a few months, besides 42,000 in the United States, and innumerable translations. Only the Government appeared hostile, though it did not oppose the plan openly.[2]

The hostility of the Government was the less understandable since its most likely ground for misgivings, finance, was taken care of by Beveridge's 'deal' with Keynes representing the Treasury, whereby the additional burdens on the Treasury in the early years were limited to £100 million per annum, largely by postponing the full benefits for old-age pensioners. The Government's own proposals, set forth in two white papers in September 1944,[3] dealing with social insurance including family allowances, and with the industrial injuries respectively, fell short of Beveridge's proposals, especially in respect of the principle of 'adequacy', but in many other respects followed them closely. The two parallel proposals for a complete and comprehensive health service after the war, which owed a great deal to the *Draft Interim Report* of the Medical Planning Commission of the B.M.A. and the Royal Colleges in 1942,[4] and for family allowances

---

[1] R. W. B. Clarke, 'The Beveridge Report and After', and 'Social Security Housekeeping', in *Social Security*; D. C. Marsh, *National Insurance and Assistance in Great Britain* (1950), pp. 65–9; Karl de Schweinitz, *England's Road to Social Security* (1943), pp. 228–44; Sir W. H. Beveridge, *Pillars of Security* (1942).

[2] Lord Beveridge, *Power and Influence* (1953), chapters 14, 15. For a critical view, see J. W. Nisbet and others, *The Beveridge Plan* (1943).

[3] *Social Insurance*, Part I (1944. Cmd. 6550) and Part II (1944. Cmd. 6551). W. H. Beveridge, 'Epilogue', in *Social Security*, pp. 412–17.

[4] *A National Health Service* (Feb. 1944. Cmd. 6502); *British Medical Journal*, 20th June 1942, pp. 743–53.

respectively, were, however, adopted by the Coalition Government during the war, the latter being enacted in June 1945.

Though social security bulked largest in the public eye, the central place in the Government's social reconstruction plan was reserved to the policy for full employment. The Beveridge Report also had made its maintenance one of its basic requirements. It had to assume unemployment at no less than the disastrously high average rate of $8\frac{1}{2}\%$, but as soon as it had been completed, Beveridge, with the help of a brilliant team of economists, prepared a second, unofficial report, proposing means of reducing the post-war unemployment rate to 3%.[1] Even before its appearance in November 1944, the Government had brought out its own white paper on Employment Policy[2] in May. Though still hedged with qualifications and, in particular, fighting shy of committing itself to deficit financing in the slump and to State action to increase productivity,[3] the white paper marks a decisive turning point in the Government's acceptance 'as one of their primary aims and responsibilities . . . the maintenance of a high and stable level of employment after the war', and of Keynesian methods of achieving it.

The Government also prepared other social reconstruction plans. The policy for education was outlined in a white paper[4] and incorporated in the Education Act of 1944. This raised the school age to 15 (postponed, in the event, to 1947), foreshadowed its extension to 16, and enacted free secondary education for all. The uses of land and town planning were discussed in three official reports and in a Government white paper in 1944,[5] and in 1943 an independent Ministry of Town and Country Planning was set up, though no legislation was passed before the end of the war. There were also specific plans made for housing after the war, and the target programme of March 1945 was for 300,000 permanent houses built or building by the end of the second year after V.E.-day, plus an expenditure of £150 million on prefabricated houses.[6] In 1944 agriculture had its fixed prices and assured markets extended to at least the 1947 harvest. In 1944 there was also a white paper on 'Scientific Research and Development'.[7]

These were long-term plans of reconstruction, but there were the immediate problems of demobilization also. 'The "run-down" of war

---

[1] W. H. Beveridge, *Full Employment in a Free Society* (1944), pp. 21, 126–8.
[2] Cmd. 6527.
[3] U. K. Hicks, *Public Finance* (1947), pp. 325–9, chapter 18.
[4] *Educational Reconstruction* (1944. Cmd. 6548).
[5] *Royal Commission on the Distribution of the Industrial Population* (Barlow Report) (1939. Cmd. 6153); *Committee on Land Utilisation in Rural Areas* (Scott Report) (1942. Cmd. 6378); *Expert Committee on Compensation and Betterment* (Uthwatt Report) (1942. Cmd. 6386); *The Control of Land Use* (1944. Cmd. 6537).
[6] *Housing* (1945. Cmd. 6609).   [7] Cmd. 6514.

industry had begun a long time before victory in Europe was in sight and continued long after it had been achieved.'[1] The labour force in the munitions industry had begun to be reduced in 1943, permitting some increased recruitment to the Forces, as well as conversion to peacetime and export needs. From the autumn of 1944 on, war contracts were broken on a large scale.[2] When hostilities were actually at an end, a vast controlled demobilization programme from the Forces and the war industries, as well as tremendous shifts between industries, had to be carried out. Between the middle of 1945 and the end of 1946, for example, engineering lost half a million workers, mostly women, and building gained over half a million, nearly all men. Much of this transition had been planned well before the end of the war.[3]

Besides planning for the immediate and long-term post-war social and economic development, post-war planning also had to consider international economic relationships and policies. During the war, the negotiations relating to them were in part mere diplomatic jockeying for position,[4] and in part they were propagandist. But governments and peoples alike felt that international economic relations had been among the least satisfactory aspects of the pre-war world, they had undoubtedly contributed to poverty, unemployment, international hatred and war, and there was much room for reform in the post-war world. While the world lay at their feet, the two principal western Allies, Britain and the U.S.A., discussed these reforms and ultimately Canada and the other Allies, including the Soviet Union and China, were drawn in, and the economic plans then took their place, beside the political framework of the United Nations, as the operative conditions of post-war economic life.

One of the basic weaknesses in the 1930's, inhibiting international trade by a vicious circle of tariffs and restrictions, had been international illiquidity, the shortage in the hands of potential buyers of currencies of the potential sellers. An international bank, holding a generally acceptable currency, could provide the initial liquidity on which could be built a superstructure of mutual obligations that could carry a much higher level of international trade on the basis of similar national resources. Plans to create such a world authority were first drafted in 1941 by Keynes in Britain and by Harry D. White in the U.S.A., and as both tended to reflect the particular needs of their countries, they found their respective schemes championed by the two Governments. The economic strength of

---

[1] M. M. Postan, *British War Production* (1952), p. 371.
[2] W. Ashworth, *Contracts and Finance* (1953), p. 64.
[3] E. L. Hargreaves and M. M. Gowing, *Civil Industry and Trade* (1952), pp. 618–27; H. M. D. Parker, *Manpower* (1957), chapter 16; Ministry of Labour and National Service, *Report, 1939–1946*, pp. 73 ff., 194 ff.
[4] Cf. p. 338 above.

the United States ensured that her proposal was the one which was ultimately accepted, but not before many amendments representing British views had been inserted.[1]

The final scheme, as agreed to at the historic Bretton Woods Conference in July 1944,[2] was in two parts, one dealing with the problem of international liquidity by means of the 'International Monetary Fund, and the other establishing a 'Bank for Reconstruction and Development' for long-term loans, expressly excluded from the I.M.F. The Bank was limited in its loans to $10 milliard, or £2,500 million;[3] in any case for Britain the Fund was of far greater importance.

By the rules adopted by the I.M.F., each country paid a contribution to the Fund roughly according to its economic strength, and this was to be made partly in gold and largely in the member's own currency. These quota contributions were held by the Fund, to be available to any member state finding itself short of the currency of another, in return for its own, at fixed parity rates. It was clear to all the delegates that the I.M.F. (as indeed the Bank) would in the first instance be used largely to make United States dollars available to the rest of the world, and their attitudes to the provisions of the Fund were largely coloured by that fact. Thus the United States insisted successfully on 'limited liability', i.e. a fixed quota, so that there was a clear limit to the total dollars to be contributed. Further, members were limited in this easy way of acquiring foreign exchange to 25% of their own quota in any one year and 100% of their quota in all, and there was also a graduated charge. There was thus a penalty on being a persistent international borrower on short-term account, but it was a measure of British influence on American thinking that there was also a penalty on the country running a persistent surplus—the 'scarce currency' clause, which permitted other members to take protective measures against the country whose currency was in such demand that the Fund's holding of it was running down; in the circumstances, this was most likely to be the American dollar.

The Fund could not, and was not intended to, correct a fundamental and persistent disequilibrium; it was merely to act as a substantial buffer

[1] R. F. Harrod, *Life of John Maynard Keynes* (1951), chapter 13; Richard N. Gardner, *Sterling-Dollar Diplomacy* (Oxford, 1956), chapter 5; J. H. Williams, *Post-War Monetary Plans* (N.Y., 1947), essays 8–11; Joan Robinson, 'The International Currency Proposals', in *The New Economics* (ed. Seymour E. Harris) (1949); R. Triffin, *Europe and the Money Muddle* (New Haven, 1957), chapter 3; Jacob Viner, 'Two Plans for International Monetary Stabilization', in *International Economics* (Glencoe, Ill., 1951); Brian Tew, *International Monetary Co-operation 1945–1952* (1952), chapters 6, 7; Alvin H. Hansen, *America's Role in the World Economy* (1945), chapters 4–7; A. J. Youngson, *The British Economy 1920–1957* (1960), pp. 155–6.

[2] *United Nations Monetary and Financial Conference, Final Act* (1944. Cmd. 6546).

[3] P.E.P., *Britain and World Trade* (1947), pp. 34–7.

between a temporary unbalance and the need to take the kind of major corrective action, such as currency depreciation or trade restrictions, which had disrupted trade in the 1930's. Member states bound themselves not to devalue their currencies, except under certain conditions to 'correct a fundamental disequilibrium', not to discriminate against other member states and, after a transitional period, not to place restrictions on current international payments. There were, at the time, further negotiations in progress to lower tariffs and other trade restrictions and discriminations, and these ultimately led to the General Agreement on Tariffs and Trade (G.A.T.T.) in 1947.

Other international obligations undertaken by Britain included the agreement to share in the costs of the United Nations Relief and Rehabilitation Administration (U.N.R.R.A.),[1] the agency which prevented starvation and diseases from ravaging much of Europe, Asia and other parts of the world after the fighting; the Hot Springs Agreement, establishing the Food and Agriculture Organization (F.A.O.),[2] to prevent shortages in the early post-war years, and the glut of the inter-war years after; and the International Labour Organization (I.L.O.) surviving from the days of the League of Nations.[3]

Throughout all the discussions that were to shape the post-war world, however, Britain seemed to demand undue protection and discrimination in her favour, as against the liberalism which appeared to motivate the Americans. There were good reasons for this. Having lost so many sources of her invisible earnings, and, at least temporarily, her power to produce for export, Britain foresaw the most dire threat to the pound sterling and to her balance of payments if freedom of trade and exchange were to be allowed too quickly. From the viewpoint of mid-1945, before the war had yet ended, the British current balance for 1946, after the end of lend-lease, appeared as follows (£ million):[4]

	1938	1946 estimate
Deficit on visible trade	−300	−650
Government expenditure abroad	−16	−300
Net invisible income	+248	+120
Total unfavourable balance (including some other items)	—	−750

[1] U.N.R.R.A., *Resolutions and Reports Adopted by the Council* (1943. Cmd. 6497).
[2] *Final Act of the United Nations Conference on Food and Agriculture* (1943. Cmd. 6451); *Documents relating to the Food and Agriculture Oragnisation of the United Nations* (1945. Cmd. 6590).
[3] Hansen, chapters 10–13; Sir Frederick Leggett, 'The Contribution of the I.L.O.', in Ministry of Labour and National Service, *The Worker in Industry* (1952).
[4] Hancock and Gowing, p. 549.

Plans for Post-War Reconstruction

Even with the most vigorous export drive and import controls, the adverse balance was unlikely to disappear before 1951, by which time it might have accumulated to a total of £1,250 million. The Treasury experts making these forecasts could not then know that the war against Japan would barely outlast that in Europe, that lend-lease would be abolished at once at its end, and that several other unfavourable factors would combine to make Britain's post-war position far worse than they had dared to imagine in their most pessimistic moments.

CHAPTER VII

Reconversion to Peace, 1945–1950

1. THE DOLLAR PROBLEM AND THE STERLING CRISES

The gloomy forecasts about the British balance of payments, with which the last chapter ended, rested on two basic facts. The first was that Britain had for years lived beyond her means by consuming her capital, by borrowing and by gifts from abroad, and that these had to cease in the summer of 1945, leaving a large gap. The second was that the disruption and diversion of British productive capacity during the war had been so violent that several years would be needed before it could be restored to its full peace-time efficiency, to fill that gap. The years of that restoration form the framework of this chapter.

The year chosen as the end of that period, 1950, is a somewhat arbitrary mark. In some respects 1949 would be a better date, seeing the end, for example, of the period of basic foreign exchange disequilibrium; if the Korean War is taken as an aftermath of the last war instead of a prelude to the next, its economic repercussions did not give way to 'normalcy' until 1952 or 1953; if the political view is taken, 1951 was the year in which the Labour Government handed over to the Conservatives. In this chapter the artificial limit of the date chosen will be broken whenever events require it. But, broadly, 1950 may be taken as indicating the watershed when the worst of the effects of the war were over, when Britain had returned to a position comparable with that at the outbreak of war, and when progress beyond it could begin.

The war had left several fundamental economic problems, and some of these will be discussed in the next section; but the foreign balance was the most obvious, and appeared the most urgent. Unless large unrequited imports could be brought in to replace lend-lease supplies, the economy was likely to grind to a standstill for lack of fuel, raw materials and food. The only possible sources of supply in a war-ravaged world were in North America, and in order to tap them, Britain had to ask for an American loan.

In the negotiations over this loan, the causes of Britain's foreign trade weakness were put most succinctly.[1] While imports for a larger, more

[1] *Statistical Material Presented During the Washington Negotiations* (December

356

active population could not be cut much below those of pre-war, commodity exports had been reduced to little more than a third, in the interest of war production, and the sources of invisible exports had also greatly diminished: total merchant shipping, for example, was down from 22·1 to 15·9 million dw. tons (ocean-going vessels of 1,600 tons and over); one-quarter of overseas investments, worth £1,118 million, had been sold off, while the overseas debt was increased by a rise in 'sterling balances' from £476 million to £3,355 million by June 1945 and £3,567 million by the end of the year. To meet this gap, exports would have to be raised by at least 50% in volume above pre-war; to meet at the same time the need of repaying the sterling debt, of building up a shrunken gold and dollar reserve, and of investments in the more backward parts of the Empire, the volume of exports would have to be raised by 75%, at least, and this figure became one of the main 'targets' of economic planning. Even that level was unduly optimistic, for it neglected the import content of increased export goods production (perhaps +15% of exports) and the likely deterioration in the terms of trade.[1] It would take 3–5 years to reach that level of 175% of pre-war exports, and meanwhile an adverse balance of at least £1,250 million would have accumulated. This was the sum which the Americans were asked to cover by a loan.

Keynes and the other British delegates found the atmosphere in Washington very much more frigid than during the war. It was not only that the dangers of war were over, and the American public was looking forward to enjoying the fruits of victory in unexampled wealth and prosperity; from the American point of view, Britain was only one of many countries seeking aid, and among them she was the least to claim pity on grounds of poverty, and the most to be feared as a potential trade rival.

In the end a 'line of credit' of $3,750 million was granted to Britain, plus $650 million to pay the outstanding lend-lease debts, and to this the Canadians added a loan, on the same terms, of $1,250 million. The terms themselves were not ungenerous, interest being at 2%, to become payable, together with the capital repayments over fifty years, only in 1951. But there were 'strings'. One was the undertaking by Britain to deal with her sterling creditors, either by immediate repayment, by gradual release beginning in 1951, or by 'adjustment' in consideration of other services. Much more serious was the obligation to apply the Bretton Woods terms, not within five years after ratification, as originally agreed, but within a year of the actual granting of the loan, i.e. by July 1947.

1945. Cmd. 6707); cf. also H. S. Booker, *The Problem of Britain's Overseas Trade* (1948), chapters, 5, 9.

[1] P.E.P., *Britain and World Trade* (1947), pp. 61 ff.

This latter condition would inevitably endanger the Sterling Area's 'dollar pool', the Sterling Area itself, and the pound sterling. In a world in which Britain was still in desperate need of export and import controls, and in which her strong importer position allowed her to use bilateral trade treaties to the greatest effect, she was to be prohibited from protecting herself in this way, while the Americans did not even undertake to *reduce* their tariff. With the 1930's in mind, Britain was particularly alarmed at being left defenceless against an American slump, which would, it was generally believed, again lead to a more than proportionate fall in U.S. imports and, hence, aggravate the dollar payments problem.[1] There was widespread opposition to the acceptance of these onerous terms,[2] but the United Kingdom was not in a position to refuse.

Meanwhile, the high hopes placed on the international institutions designed to ensure a freer flow of trade were being generally disappointed. The International Trade Organization, proposed in December 1945,[3] was stillborn, and the more modest General Agreement on Tariffs and Trade[4] (the Havana Charter), designed to *eliminate* discrimination but only *reduce* tariffs, was being ratified very slowly and came into operation only in 1948. Of the two Bretton Woods institutions, the Bank made a very slow start, lending only $800 million in its first six years, and then mostly for political, not economic purposes, and the performance of the International Monetary Fund was, perhaps, even less satisfactory. Its funds proved too small to carry the strain of the vast unbalance in world trade that was rapidly developing; its total transactions amounted to $600 million while American aid outside it (excluding U.N.R.R.A. and lend-lease) amounted to $20 milliard.[5] It had, in fact, been designed to deal with deflationary policies and fears of depression spreading from one country to another, not with persistent dollar shortages: with the problems, in other words, of the 1930's and not of the late 1940's. It could, therefore, do little to cure the world's main economic ailment, which appeared in every country in turn as a dollar shortage or a dollar 'gap'.

[1] P.E.P., *op. cit.*, chapters 7, 9; O. Hoeffding, 'The U.S., and World Trade', in Mark Abrams (ed.), *Britain and Her Export Trade* (1946).
[2] *Financial Agreement Between the Governments of the United States and the United Kingdom* (1945. Cmd. 6708); Richard N. Gardner, *Sterling-Dollar Diplomacy* (Oxford, 1956), chapters 10, 11; R. D. Hall, *North American Supply* (1955), pp. 477–9; but see R. F. Harrod, *A Page of British Folly* (1946).
[3] *Proposals for Consideration by an International Conference on Trade and Employment* (1945. Cmd. 6709). [4] 1947. Cmd. 7258.
[5] T. Balogh, 'The International Aspect', in G. D. N. Worswick and P. H. Ady, *The British Economy, 1945–1950* (Oxford, 1952), pp. 504–5; Gardner, chapters 14–17; J. H. Williams, *Post-War Monetary Plans* (Oxford, 1949), essays 5–7; Brian Tew, *International Monetary Co-operation 1945–1952* (1952), chapters 7, 8; Sir Hubert D. Henderson, 'A Criticism of the Havana Charter', *Amer. Econ. Rev.*, 39/3, 1949; Donald B. Marsh, *World Trade and Investment* (New York, 1951), pp. 423–4, chapters 26–29, 32.

The Dollar Problem and the Sterling Crises

In concrete terms, the dollar shortage in the rest of the world, as in Britain, was caused by the desperate need for goods and services which could be obtained only in the dollar area—for dollars. In a sense, therefore, it was a transient phenomenon, a consequence of the shattering of productive capacity in the war without a parallel reduction either in people's expected real income or in their monetary resources. Its very universality and duration, however, induced the widespread belief that it was permanent and part of the structure of the world's economy, and that it had begun in the inter-war years:[1]

I began to form the view before the war [declared Sir Geoffrey Crowther roundly] that there was an obstruction in the world's exchange markets of a kind and size wholly different from anything that has been previously known. This new factor was a chronic tendency towards a shortage of dollars.[2]

Europe's population was rising and its food production falling behind:[3]

Average of Years	Index of Population	Index of Output, 5 Grains	Average of Years	Index of Output, 7 Crops, Weighted by Value
1912–14	100	100	1909–13	100
1937–9	115	110	1934–8	113
1947–9	113	84	1949–50	103

In addition, many of the European raw materials were nearing exhaustion and had to be replaced by imported materials and fuels. The terms of trade were bound to turn against the industrialized countries,[4] and Western Europe was bound to lose her trade surplus even with the non-dollar primary producers. Since, further, American productivity was rising faster than that of the rest of the world, and the U.S.A., unlike Britain in the days of her hegemony, neither allowed imports freely into the country, nor invested her surpluses freely abroad, but, on the contrary, went in for deflationary policies, the dollar gap was growing ever wider.[5]

[1] p. 187 above; also J. R. Sargent, 'Britain and Europe', in *The British Economy 1945–1950*; Elliott Zupnick, *Britain's Postwar Dollar Problem* (New York, 1957) chapters 5 and 6.

[2] G. Crowther, *Balances and Imbalances of Payments* (Boston, Mass., 1957), p. 34.

[3] Ingvar Svennilsen, *Growth and Stagnation in the European Economy* (U.N., Geneva, 1954), pp. 236–7, 247, *passim*.

[4] C. P. Kindleberger, 'Industrial Europe's Terms of Trade on Current Account, 1870–1953', *Econ. J.*, 65/257, 1955.

[5] E.g. T. Balogh, *The Dollar Crisis, Cause and Cure* (Oxford, 1950), chapter 1, and 'The Dollar Crisis Revisited', *Oxf. Econ. P.*, N.S., 6/2, 1954; J. H. Williams,

Keynes was almost alone in maintaining, in a posthumous article,[1] that the dollar shortage would be short-lived, and he clearly underestimated its power.[2]

Whether temporary or permanent, Britain had to adjust herself to the dollar shortage for the time being. Considerable successes were achieved by controls, financial incentives and persuasion, to expand British exports, especially to dollar and other 'hard currency' areas, but the drain on the gold and dollar reserves continued. In July 1946, the dollars of the 'line of credit' became available, and it was intended that they should last until 1951, by which time equilibrium was to be restored. Even though it was understood that the deficits were likely to be much greater in the early years than in the later, it soon became clear that the loan was drawn on much more rapidly than was safe: in the year to 30th June 1947, purchases from hard currency areas totalled $1,540 million, sales to them only $340 million. A harsh winter was followed by a fuel crisis which held up production and transport and was estimated to have cost £200 million in exports; invisible earnings were disappointing; and the terms of trade turned sharply against the United Kingdom, adding £329 million to the import bill in 1947.[3]

It was in these unpropitious circumstances that the convertibility of sterling had to be permitted on July 15th, under the terms of the dollar loan. The convertibility applied only to sterling currently earned and not to accumulated balances, but even so, the run on the dollar pool was immediate, as almost every country with sterling earnings hurried to convert them into dollars, with which so many more useful purchases could be made.[4] The drain on the dollar reserve was so alarming that the restrictions had to be put on again after barely one month. The gold and dollar reserves fell in the course of 1947 by over $600 million, or one-quarter. On current balance of payments, there was a deficit of £545 million in the course of the year; with the dollar area alone, of £571 million.[5]

Economic Stability in the Modern World (Oxford, 1952); A. J. Brown, 'Dollars and Crises', *Ec. Hist. Rev.*, 2nd S., 12/2, 1959, pp. 287–90; Seymour E. Harris, *The European Recovery Program* (Cambridge, Mass., 1948), pp. 96 ff.; R. G. Hawtrey, *The Balance of Payments and the Standard of Living* (1950), chapters 4 and 5; Donald MacDougall, *The World Dollar Problem* (1957), esp. chapter 15, Appx. IA and XVc.

[1] J. M. Keynes, 'The Balance of Payments of the United States', *Econ. J.*, 56/222, 1946; cf. also R. F. Harrod, *Life of John Maynard Keynes* (1951), p. 621.

[2] R. Triffin, *Gold and the Dollar Crisis* (New Haven, 1960), p. 5.

[3] A. J. Youngson, *The British Economy 1920–1957* (1960), pp. 164–8.

[4] Cf. Paul Bareau, 'The Position of Sterling in International Trade', in Institute of Bankers, *Banking and Foreign Trade* (1953).

[5] *U.K. Balance of Payments 1946–1950* (No. 2) (1951. Cmd. 8201).

A similar dollar crisis hit the whole of Western Europe in 1947, threatening European recovery and standards of living. In April 1947 the Moscow Conference confirmed the post-war split between East and West, and in the emergent 'cold war' the economic prosperity of the West suddenly acquired strategic significance for the U.S.A. In June 1947, General Marshall offered massive American aid to Europe, provided Europe adopted a measure of economic co-operation. This was eagerly accepted by the governments of Western Europe, who met in September 1947 as the Committee of European Economic Co-operation (C.E.E.C.) of sixteen nations and prepared a four-year 'plan'. Before the end of the year President Truman was authorizing 'interim aid' while putting before Congress a total demand of $17 milliard for European recovery. Congress approved 'Marshall Aid' in April 1948, and in September 1948 Western Europe agreed on its distribution. The European Recovery Programme (E.R.P.) provided over $6 milliard in its first year (1948–9) and $3·8 milliard in the next year, plus $700 million for military aid ('Mutual Defence Assistance'). Thereafter recovery aid tapered off, Britain declining Marshall Aid after the end of 1950, and it was replaced by military assistance, but the Marshall plan had fulfilled its main function of carrying Europe over its critical deficit years.[1] It had also induced closer co-operation among European nations, beginning with the first inter-European payments scheme in October 1948 and ending in the fully-fledged European Payments Union (E.P.U.) of 1950, which encouraged European trade by creating liquidity and mutual credit.[2]

The United Kingdom drew its share of Marshall Aid, while her trade balance also improved impressively in 1948. Little was done, however, to strengthen the reserves, and when the relaxation of controls at the end of 1948 and the booming home demand again made inroads into the precarious balance of payments,[3] while a slight recession in the U.S.A. made dollar sales more difficult, a sustained attack on sterling began in international markets[4] and forced the Chancellor to devalue the pound sterling in September 1949, from $4.03 to $2.80.

The extent of the devaluation, 30·5%, was far larger than seemed

[1] J. H. Williams, 'The Task of Economic Recovery', in *Post War Monetary Plans* (Oxford, 1949); H. B. Price, *The Marshall Plan and Its Meaning* (Ithaca, N.Y.), 1955; Robert E. Summers (ed.), *Economic Aid to Europe: The Marshall Plan* (New York, 1948); O.E.E.C., *9th Report. A Decade of Co-operation. Achievements and Perspectives* (Paris, 1958); Triffin, *Europe and the Money Muddle* (New Haven, 1957), chapters 3 and 4; T. Balogh, *Dollar Crisis*, chapter 2.

[2] R. Triffin, *Europe and the Money Muddle*, chapter 5; but see Per Jacobsson, 'Trade and Financial Relations between Countries—the Progress Towards Multilateralism', in Institute of Bankers, *Banking and Foreign Trade* (1953).

[3] Gilbert Walker, *Economic Planning* (1957), pp. 109–29; p. 371 below.

[4] A. A. Rogow, *The Labour Government and British Industry 1945–1951* (Oxford, 1955), pp. 35–6, 121–2.

warranted by internal purchasing power or by international markets. Apart from the Sterling Area itself, few of the other countries followed Britain's devaluation to that extreme, Italy, for example, devaluing by 8%, Belgium by 13% and Germany by 20%.[1]

Further, the decision to devalue at all was questionable, for in the existing conditions of import control little could be hoped for from reduced imports, while exports had still been held back, not so much by high costs as by sheer inability to produce. After the devaluation, more resources would have to be devoted to exports to buy the identical quantum of imports, and the under-valuation of the pound would inevitably lead to price rises at home, and was bound to breach the frail barriers against inflation built up over the years.[2] The reason for the extent of the drop was probably 'psychological', to show the world the Government's determination to rectify the British balance of payments; but both the cause of the speculators' attack on sterling and its cure bore a disheartening resemblance to those of 1931.

In many ways, the devaluation was a turning point. It marked the failure of the Government's economic policy, and no alternative was evolved before its defeat at the polls in 1951. It was a flagrant violation of the Bretton Woods Agreement, in spirit if not in letter (the Fund being forced to sanction it as a virtual *fait accompli*), and contributed no little to its weakness and to the general disillusionment with the post-war international institutions. With the ending of the speculative attack, the gold and dollar reserves rose again quickly, from $1,425 million at the end of September 1949 to $2,422 million in mid-1950, and by that time the rapidly rising volume of output and exports was beginning to restore the long-term trade balance. Though the Korean War and the stockpiling crisis associated with it in 1951 caused the third of what threatened to be regular economic crises in alternate years, British economic recovery was by then too firmly set to be imperilled by it.

The main movements are illustrated by the following statistics (£mn. except the last two columns)[3] (see table opposite).

The success of the export drive was quite outstanding, exports increasing even in real terms by 77% between 1946 and 1950, though some of its benefits were lost by the worsening terms of trade. By 1948, the successes in the dollar market improved the current balance, though there was still a heavy deficit year by year in absolute terms, met largely by

[1] Tew, *op. cit.*, chapter 9.

[2] Hawtrey, *op. cit.*, pp. 99–111; Triffin, *Money Muddle*, p. 75; R. F. Harrod, *Policy Against Inflation* (1958), pp. 132–51.

[3] *United Kingdom Balance of Payments, 1946–1954* (1954. Cmd. 9291); also *Committee on the Working of the Monetary System* (Radcliffe Report) (1959. Cmnd. 827), p. 234; G. D. H. Cole, *The Post-War Condition of Britain* (1956), chapters 13, 14; *Annual Abstract of Statistics*.

Exports	Balance of Visible Trade	Total Current Balance of Payments	Change in Sterling Liabilities	Inter-Government Transactions, + =Receipts by U.K. − =Payments by U.K.	Other Capital Movements	Changes in Gold and Dollar Reserves	Terms of Trade Board of Trade, 1947=100	Terms of Trade E.C.A. Mission,[1] 1938=100
A	B	C	D	E	F	G	H	
946 917	−165	−295	+ 43	+240	+ 99	+ 87	87[2]	108
947 1,145	−415	−442	−112	+639	−301	−216	100	117
948 1,602	−192	+7	−346	+437	−167	− 69	102	121
949 1,841	−137	+38	− 9	+160	−207	− 18	101	122
950 2,250	−133	+297	+340	+127	− 81	+683	108	133
951 2,748	−733	−419	+ 94	− 36	−266	−627	123	159[3]

the net dollar earnings of the raw materials producers of the rest of the Sterling Area.[4] After devaluation in 1949, the Sterling Area trade deficit with the dollar area was virtually eliminated. At the same time, British trade with the rest of the Sterling Area also became increasingly favourable.[5]

What was at least as heartening as the 'phenomenal growth of British exports' which 'would have staggered the reconstruction planners of 1943–5 and even the Marshall Aid planners of 1947'[6] was their changed composition. Unlike her balance of the inter-war years, Britain was largely concentrating on the growth sectors of world trade:[7]

Proportion of Exports in 1952–3	United Kingdom	World
Among expanding commodities	65·0%	53·6%
Among stable commodities	4·7	17·5
Among declining commodities	30·3	28·9

The improvement in the current balance of payments (tabulation above, column C), except for the disastrous Korean War year of 1951, plus the proceeds from loans and aid (column E) were dissipated, not in strengthening the precarious reserves (column G), but in making foreign investments, probably under-estimated in the table,[8] in undetected exports of capital,[9] and in paying off some of the sterling balances (columns F and

[1] M.S.A. Mission to the United Kingdom, *Economic Development in the United Kingdom, 1850–1950*, pp. 104–5.   [2] 1938.   [3] June 1951.
[4] *Radcliffe Report*, paras. 649–56; D. H. Robertson, *Britain in the World Economy* (1954), p. 49; *United Kingdom Balance of Payments 1946–1953* (1953. Cmd. 8976).
[5] J. R. Sargent, 'Britain and the Sterling Area', in *The British Economy, 1945–1950*.   [6] *Radcliffe Report*, para. 402.
[7] P. D. Henderson, 'Britain's International Position', in *The British Economy, 1945–1950*, p. 70; F. H. Awad, 'The Structure of the World Export Trade, 1926–1952', *Yorkshire Bulletin*, 11/1, 1959, p. 35; P.E.P., *Britain and World Trade* (1947), p. 117, also chapter 8.
[8] A. R. Conan, *Capital Imports into Sterling Countries* (1960), pp. 82–6.
[9] E.C.E., *Economic Survey of Europe in 1949* (Geneva, 1950), pp. 124–6.

D), without, however, 'funding' the latter in any way.[1] Thus the weakness of sterling at the beginning of the period was not yet cured at the end. With a reserve of barely £1,000 million, a swing of £200–300 million in any one year, relatively minute in comparison with the total trade of the Sterling Area, of £10,000, would cause a major crisis, and this vulnerability remained after 1951.

Critics were not wanting who attacked the order of priorities. Foreign investments at the rate of £1,650 million in six years 1945–51, of which £350 million was public investment,[2] were considered to be too high. Expenditure on maintaining troops abroad could also have been cut, and a strong case could be made for cutting imports rather than increasing exports, with the incidental merit of not turning the terms of trade so sharply against Britain.[3]

The dollar 'gap' and the foreign balance as a whole could not, in fact, be divorced from general economic policy. External unbalance after the war had the same roots as the domestic inflation, namely a rate of incomes and welfare schemes incommensurate with real output and thus a level of *ex-ante* plans of real consumption spending and investment which production did not warrant,[4] but which all classes considered to be their right as victors in a long and weary struggle: 'It is expected', British officials informed the Americans while negotiating the 1945 loan, 'that the standard of output and efficiency which will have been reached should bring some improvement in the standard of life.'[5] Formally, it was the same excess of incomes over output which created the foreign unbalance and the domestic inflationary pressure, and to understand the former fully, it is therefore necessary to turn to a consideration of domestic economic policy.

2. FULL EMPLOYMENT POLICIES IN PRACTICE

Economic policy making by the post-war Government was dominated by its inheritance of a large measure of suppressed inflation, i.e. an excess of purchasing power over goods available at current prices, prevented from resulting in open inflation only by price control and physical restrictions. In that sense the war-time Keynesian 'National Income' budgeting had been a failure, for even with the immense aid of free lend-lease supplies, it had been unable to prevent the accumulation of potentially inflationary funds, ready to burst forth as soon as the control barriers

---

[1] R. F. Harrod, *Policy Against Inflation* (1958), pp. 111 ff.
[2] *Radcliffe Report*, Table 33.
[3] R. F. Harrod, *Are These Hardships Necessary?* (1947), and *Life of Keynes*, pp. 615–16; H. S. Booker, *op. cit.*, pp. 168–71; S. E. Harris, *European Recovery Program*, pp. 37–41.
[4] Triffin, *Money Muddle*, chapter 2.   [5] Cmd. 6707, para. 11.

were removed. Personal 'forced savings', in the absence of any goods to spend incomes on, and firms' accumulated balances, were waiting to be spent after years of austerity, and the banks had been forced into a state of over-liquidity which was potentially even more dangerous.[1]

The liquid assets of the personal sector had changed as follows:[2]

	£ million			% Change
	1938	1946	1951	1938-46
Net personal deposits in London Clearing Banks	*c.* 560	1,423	1,675	*c.* +154
Building Society deposits and shares	682	785	1,216	+ 15
Post Office savings bank deposits	495	1,910	1,902	+286
Trustee savings bank deposits	233	643	917	+176
Total liquid assets	*c.* 1,970	4,762	5,710	*c.* +142
Personal disposable income	4,675	7,569	10,389	+62
Liquid assets as % of incomes	42%	63%	55%	

Similarly, 'tender' Treasury Bills had risen from £650 million before the war to £1,800 million, the banks held £1,800 million of T.D.R.s, and total 'money supply' as a proportion of national income was 52·4% in 1939, 69·6% in 1945, and after rising to a peak of 79·2% in 1947, dropped steadily to 62·1% in 1951.[3] The total excess liquidity in the economy was of the order of magnitude of £3 milliard, or a year's tax revenue.[4]

This state of suppressed inflation was highly unstable, but opinion differed widely on the best methods of dealing with it. One method was to follow the model of 1918-19 by removing the controls as quickly as possible; but this would most likely have led to a rapid inflation, with high speculative profits for some and hardships for many, followed by a slump. It would also have played havoc with the foreign balance, and in the post-war mood, which had brought the Labour Party into power with a large majority on a programme of economic and social reform, this course was hardly practical politics.

[1] Cf., in general, G. D. N. Worswick, 'The British Economy 1945-50', in G. D. N. Worswick and P. H. Ady, *The British Economy 1945-1950* (Oxford, 1952); also R. F. Harrod, *Policy Against Inflation* (1958), pp. 93-106.
[2] *Committee on the Working of the Monetary System (Radcliffe Report)* (1959. Cmnd. 827), Table 22.
[3] W. Manning Dacey, *The British Banking Mechanism* (2nd rev. ed., 1958), p. 176; *Radcliffe Report*, para. 46.
[4] R. G. Hawtrey, *The Balance of Payments and the Standard of Living* (1950), pp. 34-45.

A more realistic proposal was a tax on capital or savings, disguised, perhaps, as a currency 'reform'. 'There were good grounds for supposing that nothing short of a thoroughgoing monetary reform, on the continental model, would have wrung from the system the excess liquidity that had been brought into existence by the war', when consumers, merchants, producers, 'all were oozing surplus liquidity'.[1] The methods used in several continental countries were ably canvassed here,[2] but the Labour Government at no time seriously considered any measure of confiscating capital, apart from the small 'special contribution' of the budget of April 1948. A third group of proposals, favoured by many economists, was for a deflationary policy, including high interest rates, in order to let 'the market', rather than the Government, decide where the necessary cuts were to be made.[3] Apart from the fact, however, that to be effective, rates would have to be fantastically high, for 'however great the shortage of capital in the sense of current savings, there was no corresponding shortage of liquid funds', this policy greatly overestimated the flexibility of factors of production, and was basically only a more sophisticated version of the first, involving unemployment.

In the policy which it eventually adopted, the Government had the advantage of possessing vastly greater economic powers than any peace-time Government had ever possessed before, and it disposed of a larger share of the national income, public revenue (including that of local authorities and the Insurance Funds) amounting to $37 \cdot 7\%$ of gross national product in 1946 and $34 \cdot 9\%$ in 1951, compared with $19 \cdot 0\%$ in 1938.[4] But it had also more objectives to be pursued simultaneously. These included full employment, high and rising productivity, the retention of the more equable income distribution and the welfare scheme of the war years, a healthy foreign trade balance, the maintenance of the value of the pound, and a speedy dismantling of the more irksome of the war restrictions and controls, among others.[5]

The Labour Government placed the greatest weight on the first two and considered the last two rather less important than some of the critics and this largely accounts for the differences in views.[6] But in pursuing so many

---

[1] *Radcliffe Report*, para. 45.

[2] E.g. F. W. Paish, 'Planning and the Price System', in *The Post-War Financial Problem and Other Essays* (1950). Cf. also Thomas Wilson, *Inflation* (Oxford, 1961), pp. 153 ff. Keynes, in his essay *How to Pay for the War*, had also suggested a capital levy after the war.

[3] J. E. Meade, *Planning and the Price Mechanism* (1948); John Jewkes, *Ordeal by Planning* (1948).

[4] J. C. R. Dow, 'Fiscal Policy and Monetary Policy as Instruments of Economic Control', *Westminster Bank Review*, Aug. 1960, p. 12.

[5] E.g. *Radcliffe Report*, paras. 53–71.

[6] Hugh Dalton, *High Tide and After, Memoirs 1945–1960* (1962).

objectives at once, it could not help, in common with all other post-war Governments, promoting measures which pulled in different directions.

Its main concern was undoubtedly to raise output as fast as possible, particularly of the basic and the export industries, but this brought it up against the shortage of capital. According to one estimate, the loss of capital during the war amounted to £9 milliard at 1948 prices, or one-fifth of the stock of 1939 (£2 milliard direct damage, £3 milliard running down of capital and stocks, and £4 milliard of overseas capital losses);[1] in addition there were the needs of rapid technological progress, the need to substitute capital for imports in order to save foreign currency, and the optimism of businessmen induced by the sellers' market.[2] Yet savings had already been low in the 1930's and would be reduced still further by the redistribution of incomes and the high rate of taxation, and it was clear that much of the investment would have to be made by the Government itself. Further, a regular budget surplus seemed an absolute necessity if the threat of the suppressed inflation were ever to be removed. The Government was therefore obliged to maintain a high rate of taxation, diminishing thereby the source of private savings still further, reducing incentives and encouraging waste, and making it necessary to preserve the regressive high indirect taxes.[3] Accordingly, the Government was torn between opposite taxation policies. In its first budget, it reduced the standard rate of income tax by 1s. and made other concessions, but later the need for a budget surplus, disinflation and high revenue to carry through the welfare and investment programme required periodic upward revision of tax rates.

The results of these (and other) conflicting aims behind the budget may be summarized as follows (£ mn.):

	Revenue	Expenditure Excl. Transfer to Capital Account	Surplus	Transfer to Capital Account	Direct Taxes on Capital	Taxes on Outlay	Subsidies	Taxes on Outlay, less Subsidies
1938	1,017	1,099	−82	9	78	410	32	378
1946	3,364	3,742	−378	552	143	1,282	350	932
1947	3,440	3,271	169	393	164	1,478	444	1,034
1948	3,985	3,323	662	219	215	1,703	542	1,161
1949	4,270	3,519	751	248	254	1,655	496	1,159
1950	4,323	3,513	810	160	190	1,722	455	1,267

[1] F. W. Paish, 'Savings and Investment', *op. cit.*; cf. also C. A. R. Crosland, *Britain's Economic Problem* (1953), pp. 20–3.

[2] *Radcliffe Report*, paras. 31–41; F. W. Paish, 'The Post-War Financial Problem', *loc. cit.*; I. Bowen, *Britain's Industrial Survival* (1947), pp. 110 ff.

[3] Findlay Weaver, 'Taxation and Redistribution in the United Kingdom', *Rev. of Econ. and Statistics*, 32/3, 1950.

The most serious conflict, however, appeared to exist between the anti-inflationary budget and what became the most controversial of Dr. Dalton's financial policies, the policy of 'cheap money'. Low and steady interest rates had been in operation since 1932 and were one of the accepted weapons to counteract a threatened depression. The post-war Chancellor, however, maintained them in a period of full employment and inflation, when the opposite policy was prescribed by Keynesian doctrine. Whatever the exact weight of influence of interest rates on the economy (and few were, after the '3% war', disposed to rate them very highly),[1] it was exerted in the wrong direction and meant, in effect, that the monetary weapon could not be used until 'cheap money' was ended in 1951.[2] The policy was not, however, entirely without justification.

To begin with, full employment could by no means be taken for granted at the end of the war. The white paper had assumed an average of $1\frac{1}{2}$ million persons out of work, the insurance contributions were calculated on a basis of $8\frac{1}{2}\%$ unemployment, and there was substantial unemployment in several continental countries at the time, notably among those curing inflation by 'orthodox' policies. A cheap money policy at least removed that danger. It was only after the fuel crisis in 1947 that scarcity, rather than surplus, was generally taken to be the main problem,[3] and only in 1951 that the Insurance Scheme officially used lower unemployment figures as the basis for its actuarial calculations.[4]

Secondly, low interest rates kept down the cost of borrowing, not only of the Government, but also of the local authorities, mainly for house building, and of some of the basic industries after their nationalization. They also kept down the sums payable abroad, as Britain was a net short-term borrower. These reductions, apart from being desirable in themselves, helped the first reconstruction schemes to be concentrated, not in the industries promising the highest quick return, but in the basic industries and in the biggest export earners. Thirdly, the policy permitted the Government to preserve, for some years, the redistributive gains of the war years in favour of the lower incomes.[5]

Against this policy it was urged that it weakened and distorted economic incentives, that it was inflationary and that, therefore, thirdly, it made necessary the retention of many irksome and inhibiting controls.[6] As for

[1] C. M. Kennedy, 'Monetary Policy', in *The British Economy, 1945–1950*.
[2] For the state of opinion on using monetary policy again at that time, see the discussion in *Bull. Oxf. Inst. Stat.*, Vol. 14, Nos. 4, 5, 8, 1952.
[3] Especially *Economic Survey* (1947. Cmd. 7046).
[4] A. T. Peacock, *The Economics of National Insurance* (1952), pp. 27, 119–20; *Report on Social Insurance and Allied Services (Beveridge Report)* (1942. Cmd. 6404), Appx. A., para. 14.
[5] F. W. Paish, 'Cheap Money Policy', *loc. cit.*; W. Manning Dacey, pp. 116 ff.
[6] A. J. Youngson, *The British Economy, 1920–1957* (1960), pp. 159–61.

the first of these, the weakened incentive was the concomitant of full employment, and while some of the critics were consistent enough to state that 'a moderate degree of unemployment would do a great deal of good— on the two conditions . . . that it does not exceed 5 to 7 per cent . . . and that the total does not contain many pockets of heavy or long-continued unemployment',[1] this was a policy which all the political parties were specifically pledged to avoid. The 'misdirection' of resources was a matter of opinion: many of the controls were specifically imposed to correct the undesirable allocations by market forces: 'had borrowing been more difficult, the volume of investment might have been somewhat reduced, but the projects held up would have frequently been the wrong ones'.[2]

The other two arguments, which were closely linked, had more substance. The lowering of the rate on Consols by $\frac{3}{8}\%$ to $2\frac{1}{2}\%$ in January 1947 involved a large-scale creation of new short-term debt and of additional liquidity: deposits of the eleven clearing banks rose by £900 million in this period, of which perhaps one-half was due to this operation. Rates were not lowered further after that, and from 1947 long-term rates were allowed to rise slowly, but the serried ranks of Government paper, added to the balances and the outstanding short- and medium-term loans of the war years, which had to be renewed at a rate of £600–£1,000 a year, made financial control of the Money Market by the Government (other than keeping the rates down) quite impossible.

Basically, the institutions of the Money Market had not changed during or after the war. The Bank of England was nationalized in 1946, the holdings of Government paper by the 'Departments' had increased, and the clearing banks had been persuaded in 1946 to end 'window-dressing', which reduced the cash reserve shown from about 10% to about 8%,[3] but any modicum of increased Government control that might have derived from these changes was more than counter-balanced by the dead weight of liquidity created. Investments of the clearing banks had fallen from the pre-war figure of 70% of deposits to 46·8% in 1948, the rest of the mounting deposits being covered largely by Government short-term paper. The total bill holdings of the London clearing banks increased from £369 million at the end of 1945 to £1,408 million at the end of 1950, or nearly four-fold, while the total of investments plus advances was allowed to rise only from £2,049 million to £3,175 million, or by 50%.[4] In these conditions, the withdrawal of cash from the banks by the authorities was not

---

[1] *Economist*, 4th June 1949, p. 1026. In terms of numbers, 5–7% meant 1–1½ million unemployed.

[2] P.E.P., *Government and Industry* (1952), p. 41.

[3] R. S. Sayers, *Central Banking After Bagehot* (1957), p. 23.

[4] W. Manning Dacey, chapter 8; C. N. Ward-Perkins, 'Banking Developments', in *The British Economy, 1945–1950*.

pyramided into a substantial restriction of credit: it merely led to the reduction (or a refusal to take up more) of the banks' holdings of Treasury Bills and, up to 1952, T.D.R.s. Nor was any other 'credit squeeze' likely to be effective when so much surplus liquidity was left in the system.[1]

The rest of the Money Market, including the Discount Houses, was also so gorged with Government paper as to be insensitive to its change of policy, while the Acceptance Houses could be moved, at best, only by exhortation. Other institutions, like Insurance Companies or pension funds, had dutifully absorbed much Government paper during the war and after; but the risk of capital losses (i.e. the risk that low rates could not be indefinitely maintained) was beginning to make them also unwilling to absorb more and to increase their equity holdings instead, with prospects of capital gains in a period of inflation.[2]

Recognizing, in practice, that Government paper, rather than the availability of cash as such, was the source of liquidity, 'there has been no attempt in the post-war period to operate on the banking position by limiting the supply of cash: the banks have always been automatically provided with whatever was necessary to make their cash ratios fit the 8 per cent. rule imposed since 1946'.[3] The limit of the fiduciary issue was after 1939 raised without question according to the needs for cash,[4] and the inflationary pressures generated after 1945 ran up against no money barriers. 'In these conditions, there was no escape from continued restraint by direct controls and austere budgets.'[5]

Here, indeed, lay the root cause for complaint, for in the prevailing boom conditions it seemed to each entrepreneur that only 'the controls' stood between him and the opportunities for making much greater profits, even though he might, in reality, have been far worse off in the chaos of their removal. The pressure for their abolition may have come from a very small section of society only, but it was a powerful section, and, exactly as after the 1914–18 war, it forced the Government steadily and relentlessly to dismantle the apparatus of control inherited from the war.[6] The real accusation against the cheap money policy was that it slowed down this process of dismantling.

[1] Sir Oliver Franks, 'Bank Advances as an Object of Policy', *Lloyds Bank Review*, N.S., No. 59, 1961, pp. 5–6.

[2] *Radcliffe Report*, paras. 145–8, 162 ff., 185 ff., 252 ff., also chapters 5, 9; G. Clayton, 'The Role of the British Life Assurance Companies in the Capital Market, *Econ. J.*, 61/241, 1951, pp. 91/2; G. Clayton and W. T. Osborn, 'Insurance Companies and the Finance of Industry', *Oxf. Econ. P.*, N.S., 10/1, 1958.

[3] *Radcliffe Report*, para. 430.

[4] W. Manning Dacey, chapter 11.

[5] *Radcliffe Report*, para. 402.

[6] A. A. Rogow, *The Labour Government and British Industry 1945–1951* (Oxford, 1955), chapter 3, pp. 138–72; J. D. Stewart, *British Pressure Groups* (Oxford, 1958); S. E. Finer, *Anonymous Empire* (1958), pp. 8–10.

The controls surviving after 1945 were many and various. Consumer rationing of clothing, furniture, petrol, soap and many foodstuffs was abolished by 1950, but the main foodstuffs were still rationed and coal still 'allocated', and there were still restrictions on tourists' expenditure and on hire purchase agreements. These provided cause for popular grumbling, but were not the main reason for the gathering campaign for economic 'freedom'. Rationed foods (and others) were, however, subsidized, and subsidies could be attacked as contributing to the high taxation which reduced incentives for the higher income earners. Sir Stafford Cripps drastically reduced food subsidies in 1949 from an estimated £568 million to a maximum limit of £465 million, and to £410 million in 1950.

In other sectors, 'recovery and rising production removed many of the more serious shortages during 1948, 1949 and 1950, and the controls were steadily relaxed as supplies increased and as their disadvantages appeared all too clearly to outweigh their advantages'.[1] Price control of non-food goods, raw material allocation, including that of steel, control over labour (re-imposed briefly and ineffectually in 1947) had all been repealed by 1950, timber only remaining to 1951; in October 1948, a veritable 'bonfire of controls' had been lit by the Board of Trade, and by 1951 most of the 'utility specifications' had lost their bite.[2] Apart from exchange restrictions under the Exchange Control Act of 1947, and import restrictions, therefore, there was very little to restrain private enterprise in its current spending.

Controls were much more persistent in the capital investment field.[3] Building licences were still tightly controlled and normally required a sponsoring Government department, and attempts were still made to put into practice the war-time blueprints for the planned use of land;[4] the vast profits realized by 'developers' since, explain in part the bitter opposition to these controls. Other powers survived after 1951, including the Town and Country Planning Act which gave Counties and County Boroughs a veto over the siting of industries conflicting with their long-term plans. The six 'Development Areas', extensions of the former 'Special Areas', were aided under the Distribution of Industry Acts of 1945 and 1950, by Government funds for the construction of factories to be let to light industry at pre-war rents, and by other inducements, including services, facilities and loans. It was the difficulty of obtaining labour, licences and facilities

---

[1] Gilbert Walker, *Economic Planning by Programme and Control in Great Britain* (1957), p. 147.
[2] G. D. N. Worswick, 'Direct Controls', in *The British Economy, 1945–1950*.
[3] P.E.P., *Government and Industry*, chapter 2; Rogow, pp. 27 ff.
[4] See p. 351 above; also N. Rosenberg, *Economic Planning in the British Building Industry, 1945–1949* (1960).

elsewhere that made the efforts to deal with the deep-set problems of these districts temporarily successful.[1]

Apart from the physical controls over building and siting, the Capital Issues Committee survived from the war years and its powers were extended by the Borrowing (Control and Guarantees) Act of 1946, which made Treasury sanction necessary for any new borrowing or raising capital by share issue of sums over £50,000, the C.I.C. acting as adviser to the Treasury.[2] At the same time, banks were issued with memoranda on the lending policy they were to adopt, though there was not statutory sanction behind these. Capital exports came under particularly severe scrutiny. To these negative measures was added positive aid. In 1946, the Industrial and Commercial Finance Corporation was set up by the Bank of England, the London clearing banks and the Scottish banks, in order to provide loans in the range of £5,000–£200,000, the 'Macmillan gap', while the Finance Corporation for Industry was established to finance larger schemes, particularly in rapidly expanding industries, which might for other reasons find a direct approach to the market difficult.[3] The Export Credits Guarantee Department provided insurance cover for exports, while 'in the early post-war years the discount market played an important part in absorbing offerings of short-dated bonds sold by industrial companies to finance reconversion, and a series of increases in the capital of the market was approved by the Capital Issues Committee to enable it to perform this special function'.[4]

It was generally assumed that these various controls were the tools of an integrated Labour Party policy of economic 'planning'. The significance of such a policy was, however, very much in doubt. At one extreme, it could be taken to mean little more than that the Government would determine the level of the total national expenditure, enforcing it with the various weapons at its command, but would leave the detailed distribution to the decision of the market; this was the minimum programme of the war-time white paper on employment, to which all the coalition parties agreed. At the other extreme, it could imply complete control over all actual industries and services, an extension of the nationalization policy to the whole economy. In practice, the Government's policy of 'democratic

[1] Michael P. Fogarty, 'The Location of Industry', in *The British Economy, 1945–1950*, pp. 266, 275; *Distribution of Industry* (1948. Cmd. 7540), Parts II and III; *Town and Country Planning, 1943–1951* (1951. Cmd. 8204); Board of Trade, *The Development Areas Today* (1947); R. S. Edwards and H. Townsend, *Business Enterprise, its Growth and Organisation* (1959), chapter 16; also see p. 403 below.

[2] *Radcliffe Report*, paras. 272, 966, *passim*; *Memorandum of Guidance* (1945. Cmd. 6645).

[3] C. N. Ward-Perkins, 'Banking Developments', in *The British Economy 1945–1950*, pp. 218, 223; Raymond Frost, 'The Macmillan Gap 1931–53', *Oxf. Econ. P.*, N.S., 6/2, 1954.

[4] Dacey, p. 65.

planning' was to be somewhere in between, eclectic, varied, and changing rapidly in its brief years of office.[1]

The actual controls taken over from the Caretaker Government at the end of the war and continued by the Supplies and Services (Transitional Powers) Act of 1945 contained fiscal, financial and physical planning powers: 'the use of quantitative production programmes' has been called 'the outstanding feature of our war-time economic organization'.[2] They might have survived into the peace economy.

> The essence of planning and control by the State in relation to productive industry and commercial activity must be the same in war and peace [it was said in 1947],[3] . . . the essential elements are plans consisting of decisions of policy quantitatively expressed in the form of programmes and such measures as . . . may be necessary to ensure the performance of these programmes.

Such a policy appealed strongly to the Socialists among the Labour Government's supporters, but in fact it was not developed further.

Instead, with Germany and Japan out of the way as competitors, the dollar loans secured, and industrial output rising, Labour Ministers and officials were remarkably self-satisfied about their economic policy,[4] and many quantitative controls were allowed to lapse before the crises of early 1947 shocked the Government out of its complacency. One of the gravest weaknesses had been shown to be the lack of co-ordination between departments, in spite of the survival of the Lord President's Ministerial Committee until 1947, and as a result, an inter-departmental planning staff under a Chief Planning Officer, Sir Edwin Plowden, was appointed. The change was made leisurely, and it was only in July 1947 that the names and functions of the Economic Planning Board were announced. In August, the exchange crisis occurred, but it was not until the end of September that economic policy was taken seriously enough to cause the appointment of Sir Stafford Cripps, hitherto President of the Board of Trade, to the newly created post of Minister of Economic Affairs, with the Economic Planning Staff, the Economic Information Unit and the surviving Economic Section of the Cabinet Secretariat to assist him. The relationship of this new Department to the Treasury was, however, never clarified, for almost at once Dr. Dalton resigned from his post as Chancellor of the Exchequer following the autumn budget indiscretion, and Sir Stafford became Chancellor, taking most of his department with him.

---

[1] The best account will be found in A. A. Rogow, *op. cit.*, esp. chapters 1 and 2.
[2] Sir Hubert Henderson, *The Uses and Abuses of Economic Planning* (Cambridge, 1947), p. 10.
[3] Sir Oliver Franks, *Central Planning and Control in War and Peace* (1947), p. 17.
[4] D. N. Chester, 'Machinery of Government and Planning', in *The British Economy, 1945–1950*, p. 341.

With this chance event in its favour, and the general opposition of the business world and even of some Labour opinion[1] against physical controls, the Treasury found it easy to reassert its former authority by concentrating all power in the financial and fiscal weapons of control. The cheap money policy was maintained with less force, and doubt about its future was by itself likely to send up long-term rates. The budget became increasingly the main instrument of control and 'the *Economic Surveys* became annually less ambitious. The "targets" of 1947 and 1948 became the "estimates" of 1949; in 1950 and 1951 the estimates became less detailed and more cautious; by 1952 they had almost disappeared.' [2]

With weak co-ordination, divided counsel and uncertain aim, the Government's post-war economic policy could not be said to have been a successful demonstration of the benefits of economic planning. But the picture drawn by some critics of a bureaucracy-ridden, atrophied planned economy, waiting with bated breath for a dash to economic freedom, bore little semblance to reality. In fact, the period 1945–50 was essentially one in which, despite the colour of the Government, war-time controls were dismantled as fast as the highly vulnerable external position of the country and the need to preserve full employment would permit.

The evidence makes it equally difficult to sustain the charge that a misguided cheap money policy was responsible for continuing inflation. The inflation was world-wide and its progress in Britain not exceptional. In an economy in which prices and wages moved rigidly together,[3] rising import prices alone could cause it quite as much as home monetary policy. The change of policy after 1951 did not end the inflation, despite the fact that the most adverse factor before 1951 was turning into the Government's favour: import prices were falling. Inflation even after 1951 could only be temporarily halted at the cost of creating unemployment. Further, it should be noted that while none of the paper schemes for reducing the liquidity in the system was politically feasible after 1945, the actual policy followed was not entirely unsuccessful in reducing the weight of the suppressed inflation.[4]

Both these were objectives which had a relatively low priority in the Government programme. Its economic policy should mainly be judged by its chief objectives of maintaining full employment, a rising output, and a high and socially desirable allocation of investment. The employment policy was successful beyond all hope: apart from the fuel crisis in

---

[1] E.g. W. A. Lewis, *The Principles of Economic Planning* (1949).

[2] A. J. Youngson, *op. cit.*, p. 264; Samuel H. Beer, *Treasury Control* (Oxford, 1956), pp. 79 ff.; Gilbert Walker, *op. cit.*, chapters 4, 5.

[3] J. C. R. Dow, 'Analysis of the Generation of Price Inflation. A Study of Cost and Price Changes in the United Kingdom 1946–1954', *Oxf. Econ. P.*, N.S., 8/3, 1956, pp. 252–301.   [4] Cf. the figures on p. 367 above.

February–March 1947, unemployment was generally below 400,000 of insured workers (i.e. under 2%), many of whom were either unemployable or waiting between jobs. Capital investment was also at a rate higher than many had believed possible: by 1948–52, net domestic capital formation (including stocks) was running at 10·6% of net national product, compared with only 7·7% in 1934–8, while an additional 0·2% was made available for foreign investment (compared with —0·5%).[1] Much of it was investment by public authorities in the basic industries, in housing, and in other fields disastrously neglected in the past or vital for the future.[2] There might be disagreement as to detail at the time,[3] but its general aptness and right proportions are in retrospect hardly open to doubt.[4]

Partly with the aid of this improved equipment, production as well as productivity showed the most encouraging rise, despite the reduction in the average (actual) working week.[5] The annual increase in manufacturing output was 8% and the *per capita* increase in all industry was 3%, which compared well with any previous period in British history and with other countries, including those of Western Europe and North America.[6] It was also bound to make the most effective contribution to the solution of the other major problems, including the foreign trade gap and the inflation. It is therefore not a little surprising that the period appears in much of the contemporary literature as a period of chaos and failure.

Much of this was no more than the normal bias of economic literature which regularly tends to portray periods of low profits as 'depressions' even though output and wage incomes are booming.[7] But something was also due to genuine causes. One was that higher production was not fairly matched by higher incomes. On a rough calculation, of the £2,050 million increase in national output between 1938 and 1950 (£2,000 million at constant 1948 prices), £700 million was 'lost' by changes in world prices, £400 million by the need to increase exports to cover loss of foreign income,

---

[1] J. B. Jefferys and Dorothy Walters, 'National Income and Expenditure of the U.K. 1870–1952', *Income and Wealth*, Series 5 (1955), p. 19, Table VIII.

[2] Gilbert Walker, *Economic Planning*, p. 156; U. K. Hicks, *British Public Finances, their Structure and Development, 1880–1952* (1954), p. 65.

[3] E. Devons, 'The Progress of Reconversion', *Manchester School*, 15/1, 1947, pp. 12–17.

[4] Sir Dennis H. Robertson, *Britain in the World Economy* (1954), pp. 11–20; E. Nevin, 'Social Priorities and the Flow of Capital', *Three Banks' Review*, No. 19, 1953; Elliott Zupnick, *Britain's Postwar Dollar Problem* (New York, 1961), pp. 61–5.

[5] Dudley Seers, 'National Income, Production and Consumption', in *The British Economy, 1945–1950*, p. 38; figures on p. 378 below.

[6] K. S. Lomax, 'Production and Productivity Movements in the U.K. since 1900', *J. R. Stat. S.*, 122/2, 1959, pp. 201–3.

[7] E.g. H. L. Beales, 'The "Great Depression" in Industry and Trade', *Ec. Hist. Rev.*, 5/1, 1934.

£100 million by a higher rate of capital investment, and £350 million by higher Government spending. The consumers were left with only a quarter of the increase, £500 million,[1] to share between an additional 6% of the population. Another calculation shows the real output per head in the United Kingdom to have risen, between 1937 and 1950, by about 25%, while the real income per head only rose by 7%.[2]

Secondly, there were the periodic crises and uncertainties. It might be true that the twentieth century was never without them, and that the extreme economic vulnerability of the United Kingdom in the post-war years, and the erratic nature of American aid, were largely responsible for the fluctuations and crises after 1945, but each critic believed that his own solution would have prevented any particular crisis, and rated Government policy accordingly. Moreover, the only reasonable alternatives offered included deflation or unemployment as a calculated risk, and for this the country was not ready. 'If there is a lesson of the years 1945–50,' an observer summed up, 'it is that the recurrence of alternate periods of apparent austerity and apparent ease of supply is the price of stability of employment.'[3]

Lastly, there was the dissatisfaction with restrictions, with lack of choice, with continued shortages and high taxes. There was some substance in the complaints that there were too many resources devoted to manning the controls and to avoiding them, instead of to productive purposes. The gross unbalance of the late 1940's inevitably called for controls and austerity, but the solid foundations of reconstruction laid then, could make an expansion possible which might well need greater freedom for enterprise, both public and private. In an economy in which at least 80% of industry was run by the profit motive (and none of the major parties seemed willing to change this ratio much in 1951), greater freedom had to mean greater freedom to make profits, and it was, perhaps, fortunate that in post-war Britain the Governments were politically biassed in favour of central control in the 1940's, and private enterprise in the 1950's. Yet a doubt remains: for after decades of association, rationalization and control, British industry appeared to have lost the zest for enterprise,[4] and this lack, especially by comparison with businessmen of other advanced countries, constituted one of the major weaknesses of the 1950's.

3. INDUSTRIAL RECONSTRUCTION

The most encouraging aspects of the post-war economy were undoubtedly the maintenance of a high level of employment, and of a high and

[1] Seers, *loc. cit.*, p. 46.
[2] C. F. Carter, 'The Real Product of the United Kingdom 1946–1950', *London and Cambridge Economic Service*, 29/3, 1951.
[3] G. D. N. Worswick, 'Direct Controls', p. 311.
[4] Economist Intelligence Unit, *Britain and Europe* (1957), p. 62.

rising level of output. These were achieved even though the capital equipment of the country was seriously run down, there were raw material and fuel shortages, the hours of labour had been reduced, and the system of control and the high level of taxation were said to stifle enterprise, while full employment was said to be detrimental to industrial discipline. The high rate of production increase was, in fact, maintained well past the demobilization years into the 1950's, and was then slowed down only by deliberate Government policies of deflation and restriction.

For this progress, science and technology, firmly based on their achievement in war,[1] claimed a growing share of the credit. Never before had the resources devoted to science been greater, yet never had there been so much criticism of their inadequacy.[2] There was some truth in the complaint that the traditions of British industry were against the use of academic knowledge and in favour of skill and experience learnt on the job, even on the part of senior management,[3] but they were the last relics of the days when the old staple industries dominated the economic scene, and they were now being eradicated.

Several different estimates have been made, but they all agree in the main on the order of magnitude of the increase in production achieved (recalculated to 1946 = 100)[4] (see table on next page).

With a population increase of barely 3% between 1938 and 1946 and another 3% in 1946–50, the rise in output per head was substantial.[5] While in the war years the (nominal) 'production' of services, including

[1] See pp. 310–11 above.

[2] Sir F. H. Heath and A. L. Hetherington, *Industrial Research and Development in the United Kingdom* (1946), chapter 39; R. S. Edwards, *Co-operative Industrial Research* (1950); C. F. Carter and B. R. Williams, *Investment in Innovation* (1958), pp. 138–40, and *Industry and Technical Progress* (1957), chapters 1–3; R. L. Meier, 'The Role of Science in the British Economy', *Manchester School*, 18/2, 1950, pp. 101–2, 114–18; Duncan Burn, in *Structure of the British Economy*, Vol. 2, pp. 436–40; Lord Hankey, 'Technical and Scientific Manpower', in Ministry of Labour and National Service, *The Worker in Industry* (1952).

[3] Stephen F. Cotgrove, *Technical Education and Social Change* (1958), chapter 7; *First Annual Report of the Advisory Council on Scientific Policy* (1948. Cmd. 7465), p. 15.

[4] *National Income and Expenditure, passim*, linked to pre-war figures according to A. R. Prest, 'National Income of the United Kingdom 1870–1946', *Econ. J.*, 58/229, 1948; *London and Cambridge Economic Service, passim*; C. F. Carter, 'The Real Product of the United Kingdom', *ibid.*, 29/3, 1951; Dudley Seers, 'National Income, Production and Consumption', in G. D. N. Worswick and P. H. Ady, *The British Economy, 1945–1950* (Oxford, 1952), pp. 38 ff.; G. D. N. Worswick, *ibid.*, pp. 6–8, 18–19; K. S. Lomax, 'Production and Productivity Movements in the U.K. since 1900', *J. R. Stat. S.*, 122/2, 1959, p. 192; T. M. Ridley, 'Industrial Production in the U.K., 1900–1953', *Economica*, N.S., 22/85, 1955, p. 12; W. G. Hoffmann, *British Industry, 1700–1950* (Oxford, 1955), Table 54; G. D. H. Cole, *The Post-War Condition of Britain* (1956), chapter 5.

[5] E.g. N. H. Leyland, Productivity', in *The British Economy, 1945–1950*, p. 393; L. Rostas, 'Changes in the Productivity of British Industry, 1945–50', *Econ. J.*, 62/245, 1952.

Total Production		All Industries					Manufacturing Industry Only		
Gross National Product at 1948 Factor Cost	Total Real Product (Carter)	Board of Trade	Ridley	Lomax	L. & C. Econ. Service 'B' Index	Hoff- mann	Board of Trade	Carter	Lomax
Average									
1936–8	97·2	—	104[1]	103·1	97·9	106	108·1	—	—	96·2
1946	100	100	100	100	100	100	100	100	100	100
1947	101·0	101	108	106·2	106·2	108	109·1	109	104	107·0
1948	105·7	106	121	114·9	114·9	118	121·2	123	115	116·1
1949	110·3	112	129	122·3	122·2	126	128·8	132	123	124·0
1950	114·8	115	140	130·6	130·6	135	137·8	145	133	134·0

administration and entertainments, fell less than that of manufacturing,[2] after the war it was manufacturing industry which expanded the fastest, leaving mining, building and utilities far behind; transport and the services as a whole rose even more slowly, being pulled down by actual declines in railway transport and domestic service.

Within manufacturing, again, the progress was very uneven. It was greatest in metals, engineering, chemicals and related industries. Unlike the post-war period twenty-five years earlier, the heavy industries, including shipbuilding and coal, as well as agriculture, were driven to increase their output even beyond the artificially high levels attained in war-time, instead of suffering a painful contraction.[3] Others, like paper, printing, textiles, distribution and building, which had had to contract in the war years, were also urged to expand.[4] In general, however, reconstruction was dominated by the capital goods and the export industries,[5] largely because of deliberate policies designed to save imports, especially from the dollar area, to increase exports, and re-equip British ndustry.

There was also a marked shift from some of the older industries to some of the newer, accompanied by improved capital equipment and better techniques, including management techniques, in the latter. The industries which showed the most consistent expansion throughout, showed also the largest increase in labour productivity: 'large increases in output

[1] 1938.
[2] A. Beacham, *Economics of Industrial Organisation* (3rd ed., 1955), p. 175.
[3] *Committee on the Working of the Monetary System* (Radcliffe Report) (1959. Cmnd. 827), para. 20.
[4] For employment statistics, see Beacham, pp. 155 *passim*, and D. C. Marsh, *The Changing Social Structure of England and Wales, 1871–1951* (1958), chapter 6.
[5] E. Devons, 'The Progress of Reconversion', *Manchester School*, 15/1, 1947.

per head are associated with large increases in output, substantial declines in relative costs, and falling prices'.[1]

The course of industrial change may be summarized in the following statistics of selected main industries:[2]

	Index of Industrial Production (1924 = 100)			Average Rate of Productivity Increase (%)[3]	
	Average 1936–8	1946	1950	1935–49	1949–55
Metal manufacture	139	157½	201½	1·2	3·3
Engineering, shipbuilding, electrical engineering	141	179	256	1·0	3·3
Vehicles	215	245	339	4·0	3·9
Chemicals	143	210	289	2·7	6·2
Textiles	118½	86½	128	2·0	1·4
Clothing	130	85	110	0·3	2·0
Food, drink, tobacco	141	163	181	1·6	0·5
All manufacturing	148	154	207	2·0	3·1
Building, contracting	174	132	157	−3·6	3·6
Gas, water, electricity	206	290	372	3·7	4·5
Mining and quarrying	92	71	80	−0·4	−0·1
All industry	146	149	195	1·3	3·2

Among the main industries, the progress of coal was the most disappointing. Output crept up from the nadir of 175 million tons in 1945 to 204 m.t. in 1950, but this increase was largely due to an opencast output of 12 m.t. and an increased labour force, output per man-shift reaching the pre-war figure only in 1950, in spite of heavy investment in new equipment. As a result, a shortage of fuel remained one of the most serious brakes on recovery, and it culminated in the crisis of February–March 1947 when several million workers were kept idle for lack of power and export markets were disappointed also.

Coal mining was the first industry to be nationalized, but it was not until 1950 that the N.C.B. published its long-term plan.[4] The tasks of the

[1] W. E. G. Salter, *Productivity and Technical Change* (Cambridge, 1960), pp. 109, 144, 177–83. This is based on a study of 28 selected industries in the period 1924–50; cf. also Rostas, 'Changes in Productivity', pp. 23–4.
[2] Lomax, *loc. cit.*, pp. 192–3, 203.
[3] Output per operative hour.
[4] N.C.B., *Plan for Coal* (1950); also A. Beacham, 'Planned Investment in the Coal Industry', *Oxf. Econ. P.*, N.S., 3/2, 1951.

Board were indeed formidable, for the industry had much leeway in capital equipment to make up,[1] at a time when geological conditions required heavy investment merely to keep output from falling, and when the absolute coal shortage made the continuance of uneconomic pits essential.[2] It had also to deal with a militant work force expecting rapid improvements in wages and conditions under national ownership, while much of the old managerial class left, depriving the Coal Board of one complete level of management.[3] The obligation on the N.C.B. to charge less than market prices (except for exports) gave the rest of industry cheap coal, but stimulated demand artificially, and made it impossible to accumulate reserve funds, for investment or as buffer to offset future losses. The coal problem survived to the end of the 1950's, when it was solved by the gradual fall in demand.[4]

The iron and steel industry also had much leeway to make up, but it found it easier to recruit additional labour, and it benefited more quickly from its capital investment. Its supervisory Board, appointed after the war, left the initiative to the firms, but on the request by the Government the Federation had to prepare a five-year plan of expansion which was published in 1946.[5] The plan bore all the signs of being a combination of the budgets of the several firms prepared for their own purposes, as distinct from a single national programme. It was criticized in particular for 'patching' existing plants everywhere rather than proposing bold new construction in the low cost areas, and for reflecting the companies' fear of overproduction, by not being sufficiently ambitious. After some scrapping of obsolete plant, it proposed to increase the total steel capacity only to 15–16 million tons and pig iron capacity to $8\frac{1}{2}$–9 m.t. In the event the targets were raised again in 1948, but capacity continued to lag behind demand, though the average performance was easily raised by new works, in view of the inefficiency of the plant which they replaced.[6]

---

[1] *Coal Mining. Report of the Technical Advisory Committee (Reid Report)* (1945. Cmd. 6610); A. Beacham, 'Efficiency and Organisation of the British Coal Industry', *Econ. J.*, 55/218–19, 1945.

[2] Sir Hubert Houldsworth, 'The National Coal Board', in Institute of Public Administration, *Efficiency in the Nationalised Industries* (1952).

[3] *Report of the Advisory Committee on Organisation (Fleck Report)* (1955).

[4] G. C. Allen, *British Industries and Their Organisation* (3rd ed., 1951), pp. 56–9, 77–83; cf. also 4th ed. (1959). These volumes will also be found useful for the other staple industries. Cf. also Cole, *op. cit.*, pp. 130–7; A. J. Youngson, *The British Economy, 1920–1957* (1960), pp. 193 ff.

[5] *Report of the British Iron and Steel Federation and the Joint Iron Council on the Iron and Steel Industry* (1946. Cmd. 6811).

[6] B.I.S.F., *Monthly Statistical Bulletin, passim*; Duncan Burn, *The Steel Industry 1939–1959* (Cambridge, 1961), chapters 3–5, and 'Steel', in *Structure of British Industry*, Vol. 1; Anglo-American Council on Productivity, *Iron and Steel* (1952); H. G. Roepke, *Movements in the British Iron and Steel Industry, 1720–1951* (Urbana Ill., 1956), chapters 7 and 8; Cole, pp. 155–161.

Industrial Reconstruction

	United Kingdom Output (m.t.)		Index of Output per Man-year (1938 = 100)
	Steel	Pig Iron	
Average			
1937–8	11·7	7·6	108
1946	12·7	7·8	115 (1947)
1950	16·3	9·6	139

Within these totals, there was a large expansion of the output of basic open-hearth furnaces and of electric furnaces, and a beginning was at last made in the building of a large integrated plate mill at Margam, as well as in the replacement of the old pack mills by modern continuous tinplate mills.[1]

The increasing supplies of steel, as of other metals, permitted the manifold branches of engineering and metal goods industries to extend beyond their enlarged war-time capacity. Among them, the centre of the picture came to be held by the motor-car industry. Reconversion from war-time production was relatively easy, the pre-war peak output of 526,000 units (cars, commercial vehicles and tractors) in 1937 being almost reached in 1947 and exceeded in 1948, when 626,000 units were produced, and further large expansion schemes brought the output in 1950 up to 903,000 units, excluding motor cycles. In view of the much slower recovery of Western European production, the United Kingdom accounted for 66% of the European output of cars in 1946–8 and for 52% still in 1949–50, and since American cars were not generally available because of the dollar shortage, export markets were wide open and limited only by productive capacity. Since then, British makes have been steadily pushed out by more competitive foreign products, in spite of their initial advantage, and of powerful Government incentives to export cars even at the cost of long waiting lists at home. In particular, British makers could be accused of making too many models, of building for the needs of British rather than of foreign roads, and of neglecting the vital aspects of service and spare parts, especially overseas.[2] There was some concentration in the industry, the 'big six' (reduced to five by the formation of the B.M.C.) producing 85% of the cars and commercial vehicles by number, and 60% by value, in 1948.[3]

The aircraft industry, heavily subsidized by the taxpayer, showed few of the faults of traditional British industrial organization, most of its firms being large and up-to-date. It also succeeded in maintaining its technical

[1] W. E. Minchinton, *The British Tinplate Industry* (Oxford, 1957), chapter 8.
[2] P.E.P., *Engineering Reports II: Motor Vehicles* (1950), p. 25.
[3] Aubrey Silberston, 'The Motor Industry', in *The Structure of British Industry*, Vol. 2.

lead and international competitive power. The shipbuilders and marine engineers, by contrast, failed to make use of the sellers' market in 1945–50 to modernize the yards and works and were soon to be driven out of neutral markets by builders in Germany, Japan, Sweden, Holland and elsewhere. Their output rose only from 1,133,000 gross tons in 1946 to 1,315,000 in 1950, compared with an average of 1,342,000 in 1920–4 and 1,660,000 in 1910–14.[1]

There was expansion also in many other sections of the engineering trade. The machine tool industry, though still much inferior to the American in efficiency, maintained its high output of the war years: total production in the United Kingdom, by value, rose from £6½ million in 1935 to £47 million in 1951. Some of the most spectacular developments occurred in the electronics industry with the introduction of radar devices and of computers. The pre-war output of radio receivers was reached in 1947, when over ½ million television sets were produced also. Employment in the whole electronics industry fell from 98,000 in 1943–4 to about 80,000 in 1946–7, to reach 93,000 again in 1950, though it doubled afterwards in only five years. Like electrical engineering as a whole, it was dominated from the beginning by a few giant firms and agreements and associations between them.[2]

The chemicals and allied industries also continued to expand, even after the artificial military stimulus was removed. The temporary eclipse of the main competitor, Germany, turned Britain from an importer into a large-scale exporter and permitted the industry to build up substantial markets abroad. At the same time, there occurred a phenomenal growth of demand for some of the industry's diverse products, notably plastics and pharmaceutical goods. Production of synthetic resin, for example, rose from 16,000 tons in 1941 to 25,000 in 1945 and 52,500 in 1950. The volume of output of the whole complex of chemical industries rose from an index number of 100 in 1946 to 120 in 1948 and 142 in 1950,[3] and exports rose from £77 million in 1947 to £117 million in 1950, at constant (1950) prices. The industry remained dominated by a handful of very large firms and riddled by restrictive practices, but this did not impair either its rate of expansion or its technical efficiency.[4]

[1] Ely Devons, 'The Aircraft Industry', and A. K. Cairncross and J. R. Parkinson, 'The Shipbuilding Industry', in *The Structure of British Industry*, Vol. 2; L. Jones, *Shipbuilding in Britain* (Cardiff, 1957), chapter 9.

[2] M. E. Beesley and G. W. Troup, 'The Machine Tool Industry', in *The Structure of British Industry*, Vol. 1; T. Wilson, 'The Electronics Industry', *ibid.*, Vol. 2; S. G. Sturmey, *The Economic Development of Radio* (1958), pp. 181–5, 209–11.

[3] *Annual Abstract of Statistics*.

[4] W. B. Reddaway, 'The Chemical Industry', in *The Structure of British Industry*, Vol. 1; C. J. Thomas, 'The Pharmaceutical Industry', *ibid.*, Vol. 2; T. I. Williams, *The Chemical Industry* (1953), Part II; Association of British Chemical Manufacturers, *Report on the Chemical Industry, 1949* (1950) and *Supplement, 1953* (1954).

Particular mention must be made of oil refining, which Britain was driven to undertake after the war in order to save dollars by substituting imports of crude Middle Eastern oil for refined American motor spirit. By large-scale projects, some of them built on virgin sites after the war, rated capacity was increased seven-fold between 1938 and 1953, and the range of finished products and of by-products was greatly widened. Oil refining formed one of the prime examples of the substitution of capital for imports after the war.[1] The rising demand of the industry was made up of many components, of which the growing number of motor cars, the conversion of oil by-products into other chemicals, and wide-spread change-over to oil firing in industry were the most important.

Among investment industries only building lagged behind, having by 1950 scarcely recovered its pre-war position. The typical building firm was still small: by 1949, 6·5% of the skilled operatives and 20·6% of the others worked for very large firms employing over one thousand employees each, but these were clearly firms of very different structure from the small craftsmen firms which built and repaired most dwelling houses. Repair and maintenance accounted for about half the output of the industry, new building being shared between domestic and industrial or commercial building in the ratio of 3 : 2. By the end of 1949, one million houses had been built or reconstructed, and the ratio of houses to population was beginning to exceed the pre-war ratio, but unfulfilled demand remained as high as ever, because of smaller families and rising expectations of living standards, and the shortages of both domestic and industrial and commercial buildings were among the most severe shortages felt by the public.[2]

In contrast with the industries noted so far, most consumption goods industries showed relatively modest increases in output. Domestic demand for their products was often held down by rationing, and exports generally played a relatively minor part. Nevertheless, there were some major changes in structure or materials.

Textiles were, perhaps, the outstanding example. War conditions had greatly reduced the output and the labour force of the traditional textile industries, and even in the post-war period they enjoyed a low priority and little hope of permanent expansion. Employment in the cotton industry dropped by 42% between 1937 and 1945, and in the woollen and

---

[1] Duncan Burn, 'The Oil Industry', in *The Structure of British Industry*, Vol. 1; Richard Evely and I. M. D. Little, *Concentration in British Industry. An Empirical Study of the Structure of British Production 1935-51* (Cambridge, 1960), pp. 203-8; Institute of Petroleum, *The Post-War Expansion of the U.K. Petroleum Industry* (1954).

[2] Working Party Report, *Building* (1950); C. F. Carter, 'The Building Industry', and B. R. Williams, 'The Building Materials Industry', in *The Structure of British Industry*, Vol. 1; Anglo-American Council on Productivity, Report on *Building* (1950).

worsted industries it dropped by 37% between 1939 and 1945; much of the equipment was out of date and most firms were small.[1] After a brief post-war boom, exports of cotton goods were to slump again in 1952, and even the home market of the industry was no longer safe. The woollen and worsted industries fared rather better, reaching by 1950 an output just below the pre-war level.[2] Man-made fibres on the other hand were being developed very rapidly. In 1952–3 nylon and rayon accounted for 80% of production of ladies' seamless hose, and for 90% of fully-fashioned ladies' hose. New fibres, such as 'Terylene', for which a pilot plant was set up in 1950, 'Orlon' and 'Ardil' which went into production in 1951, were also being developed for other uses. The proportion of employment accounted for by nylon and rayon spinning was still quite small, being 2·8% of all textile employment in July 1946 and 4·9% in 1950,[3] but its growth rate was significant.

Among other consumer goods industries, the food industries were continuing to be transformed by canning and other methods of preservation and preparation; a section of the furniture industry came for the first time under the control of large firms using new methods of production, selling and branding; and the paper and printing industries experienced a remarkable post-war expansion in spite of the severe restriction in the supply of wood pulp.

Agriculture, hard-pressed though it had been in the war to produce the maximum that the soil would yield, was urged to produce still more after the war, in view of the shortage of foreign currency and the world shortage of grain. In 1946 bread had to be temporarily rationed—a measure which had not been necessary in either the first or the second World War. The Agriculture Act of 1947 provided the framework for the official policy of 'stability and efficiency'. The former was to be achieved by annual price reviews and guaranteed markets for the most important farm products, which raised average farm incomes to six times their pre-war peak in 1949–50, and the latter by continued mechanization and the intelligent use of mixed farming techniques, encouraged by the 'National Agricultural Advisory Service' established in 1946, by tax concessions and by the initiative of the County Agricultural Executive Committees.

In 1947 the Government's 'plan' called for a 20% increase in output

---

[1] Working Party Reports: *Cotton* (1946), pp. 52 *passim*, *Wool* (1947), pp. 51 *passim*.

[2] G. W. Furness, 'The Cotton and Rayon Textile Industry', and G. F. Rainnie, 'The Woollen and Worsted Industry', in *The Structure of British Industry*, Vol. 2; J. F. Brothwell, 'The 1951 Depression in the British Wool Textile Industry', *Yorkshire Bull.*, 4/2, 1952, and 5/2, 1953.

[3] D. C. Hague, *The Economics of Man-made Fibres* (1957), p. 171, and 'The Man-made Fibres Industry', in *The Structure of British Industry*, Vol. 2; G. C. Allen, *op. cit.*, 1951 ed., pp. 184–5; 1959 ed., pp. 208–10.

(to 150% of pre-war) in five years, especially of dollar-saving crops. By 1950-1 the quantum of output reached, in fact, 146% of the pre-war level, a result achieved by holding the employment figure and the arable acreage (except in the uplands more suited to cattle) to their high war-time levels.[1] Most food crops and farm animals shared in this increase, as illustrated in the following comparative figures:

	1938	1946	1950
Crops harvested in G.B. (mn. tons):			
Grains	4·95	7·22	7·78
Potatoes	5·11	10·17	9·51
Fruit and vegetables	2·33	3·67	3·85
Animals on agricultural holdings in June (mn.):			
Cattle	8·76	9·63	10·62
Sheep and lambs	26·77	20·36	20·43
Pigs	4·38	1·95	2·99
Poultry	74·25	67·12	96·11

In sum, British industry proved to be more adaptable than many observers had believed possible.[2] Its flexibility, indispensable to a progressive economy, contrasted strongly with the tendency towards restriction and rigidity between the wars, and nowhere was the contrast more marked than in the attitude to monopoly before and after the war.[3]

In this period it was no longer certain whether the average size of plant was still growing. Between 1935 and 1948, it is true, average employment in all manufacturing plants rose from 107 to 124.[4] But a detailed study, comparing a sample of 41 industries between 1935 and 1951, concluded that 'there was a tendency for a concentration of production in larger

---

[1] A. J. Youngson, *op. cit.*, pp. 199-200; H. T. Williams, *Principles for British Agricultural Policy* (1960), pp. 44-58, 72 ff.; K. E. Hunt, *Changes in British Agriculture* (Oxford, dupl. 1952); P.E.P., *Agricultural Machinery* (1949), pp. 18-26, 95; H. C. Chew, 'Changes in Land Use and Stock over England and Wales, 1939 to 1951', *Geog. J.*, 122/4, 1956; John R. Raeburn, 'Agricultural Products and Marketing', in *The Structure of British Industry*, Vol. 1; D. K. Britton, 'Agriculture', in *The British Economy, 1945-1950*; *Agriculture Bill: Explanatory Memorandum* (1946. Cmd. 6996); C. H. Blagburn, 'Import Replacement by British Agriculture', *Econ. J.*, 60/237, 1950.

[2] E.g. E. A. G. Robinson, 'The Changing Structure of the British Economy', *Econ. J.*, 64/255, 1954.

[3] S. R. Dennison, 'New Industrial Development and Exports', in University of London and Institute of Bankers, *The Industrial Future of Great Britain* (1948).

[4] P. Sargant Florence, *The Logic of British and American Industry* (1953), p. 31; J. B. Jefferys, *Retail Trading in Britain, 1850-1950* (Cambridge, 1954), chapter 3.

plants by the older and larger units of a trade, some of which would themselves amalgamate, together with an entry of comparatively small newcomers'. There was also further evidence 'consistent with the operation of a process of amalgamation and the concentration of some production in larger and more efficient plants'.[1] Such comparisons, however, by their very nature excluded the new industries which arose after 1935, and which would reduce the overall degree of concentration; they also exclude the fact that the opportunities of making and keeping high profits were often greater for small firms than for large during the war, so that in the 1940's the long-term tendency towards industrial concentration was, on balance, slowed up or perhaps even halted altogether.[2]

Irrespective of these trends, however, it was the full employment policies which demanded the release from artificial restrictions. In the later war years, such bodies as the Federation of British Industries and the Association of British Chambers of Commerce might still favour trade associations in their reconstruction programmes, but the white paper on Employment Policy in 1944 already contained the first hint of the growing anti-restrictionist trend of public opinion.[3] It found expression in the Monopolies Act of 1948, which set up a Monopolies and Restrictive Practices Commission, with powers to inquire and to recommend action, but not to authorize action itself. By 1951 only two small industries had been reported on, but ultimately, it produced several valuable reports on individual industries and one general report,[4] and in 1956 an Act was passed giving power to curb restrictions which were deemed to be against the public interest. A separate Committee reported on resale price maintenance in 1949,[5] but the Labour Government's intention to restrict it in 1951 was thwarted by its electoral defeat.

By contrast, associations which were in the public interest were encouraged by the Government. In particular, since the economic problem was no longer the absorptive capacity of the market, but the productive capacity of the economy, the attention of economic policy makers turned to productivity, and to the enormous margin by which American pro-

[1] Richard Evely and I. M. D. Little, *Concentration in British Industry* (Cambridge, 1960), pp. 173–4, also chapter 12.

[2] P. E. Hart and S. J. Prais, 'The Analysis of Business Concentration: A Statistical Approach', *J. R. Stat. S.*, 119/2, 1956; P.E.P., *Government and Industry* (1952), p. 186.

[3] Cmd. 6527 (1944); I. Bowen, *Britain's Industrial Survival* (1947), pp. 63–4; S. R. Dennison, 'Restrictive Practices and the Act of 1956', *Lloyds Bank Review*, N.S., No. 59, 1961, pp. 36–7; Margaret Hall, 'Monopoly Policy', in *The British Economy, 1945–1950*; Cole, *op. cit.*, chapter 19.

[4] Monopolies and Restrictive Practices Commission, *Report on Collective Discrimination* (1955. Cmd. 9504).

[5] *Report of the Committee on Resale Price Maintenance* (Lloyd Jacobs Report) (1949. Cmd. 7696).

ductivity exceeded the British.[1] An Anglo-American Council on Productivity was set up in August 1948. It sent many teams selected from trade associations, trade unions and employers' federations to study American practices and publish their findings.

In the iron and steel industry a Board was set up in 1946 to steer the industry in the public interest. Elsewhere, it was decided in September 1945 to set up 'Working Parties' to inquire into individual industries and make recommendations. Seventeen were eventually appointed, and they reported in 1946–8, making many specific recommendations for improving industrial performances. One general result was the Industrial Organization and Development Act of 1947, which allowed the Government to set up Development Councils in any industry in which a substantial number of producers asked for them, with powers of compulsory levy from *all* firms in the industry. Among their functions were to be research, standardization, and sales promotion, but terms of remuneration and employment were specifically excluded. In spite of the specific recommendation of most Working Parties for Councils of this kind, the results of the Act were disappointing: apart from the transformation of the existing Cotton Board into a Development Council, there were only three Councils formed and three other Orders made, for compulsory levies for research and exports.[2]

Much more significant than these schemes was the programme of nationalization, which formed one of the main platforms of the Labour Government. Apart from the minor measures which were little more than formalities, including the Bank of England Act, 1946, the Cable and Wireless Act, 1946, and the Civil Aviation Act, 1946, which set up British European Airways (B.E.A.) and British South American Airways (the latter merged with B.O.A.C. in 1949), there were five major measures of nationalization: the Coal Industry Nationalization Act (1946), the Electricity Act (1947), the Transport Act (1947), the Gas Act (1948) and the Iron and Steel Act (1949). The Act nationalizing the steel industry was first held up by the House of Lords and its vesting date was further delayed until after the second post-war election, to 1951; by its provisions the firms were largely left intact and it was thus easy for the Conservative Governments to reverse the process of nationalization in the years after 1951 by selling the iron and steel firms back to private ownership. In the case of the other four major industries, the actual transfer took place in each case in the year following the passing of the Act.

[1] E.g. L. Rostas, *Comparative Productivity of British and American Industry* (Cambridge, 1948); E. Rothbarth, 'Causes of Superior Efficiency of American Industry', *Econ. J.*, 56/223, 1946.
[2] N. H. Leyland, 'Productivity', in *The British Economy, 1945–1950*; P. D. Henderson, 'Development Councils: an Industrial Experiment', *ibid.*

This programme of nationalization was probably the most controversial part of the post-war Government's policy,[1] largely because of its political, rather than its narrowly economic implications. On it were centred the hopes of Socialists, whether they were believers in 'State' socialism, in which the political authority would control industry by central planning, or whether they believed in Syndicalist or Guild Socialism, based on 'workers' control' and allowing a good deal of autonomy to each industry.[2] They hoped that the transfer of industry to public hands would alter the *rationale* of economic life by introducing production for use, in place of production for profit incidentally arising out of the process of production, and would remove the power of the capital-owning classes, and thus overturn the existing social and political structure and bring about a peaceful social revolution.

In retrospect it is clear that there was never any danger of such a revolution, much as many Labour supporters might have wished to see it,[3] and the heat and passion aroused by the controversy were largely misdirected. Industry was nationalized, the 'commanding heights' of the economy were occupied to the extent of 20%, not to dominate or transform the mainly profit-making industries composing the remaining 80% of the economy, but to serve society, including private industry, the more efficiently, and to give the Government additional powers, besides those it already possessed in the fiscal, monetary and other spheres, to pursue its economic objectives. The measures of nationalization actually carried out are therefore best seen not as representing a revolutionary economic doctrine, but as lying well within a long tradition of the growth of Government responsibility, represented by the Employment white paper of 1944, on the one hand, and by the pre-war public corporations[4] on the other: 'British experience of nationalization shows once more how one control leads to another.' [5] Some of the nationalized undertakings had, in fact, been public corporations (e.g. London Transport) or largely in the hands of local authorities (e.g. gas and electricity), though it should be noted that

the post-war public corporations differed from their predecessors not only in the wider scope of their monopolies and in the vastly greater

---

[1] E.g. R. Kelf-Cohen, *Nationalisation in Britain. The End of a Dogma* (1959).

[2] Cole, *op. cit.*, chapter 9, also his *The Case for Industrial Partnership* (1957); H. A. Clegg, *A New Approach to Industrial Democracy* (1960), esp. chapters 1, 2, 4, 16; Austen Albu, 'The Organization of Nationalized Industries and Services', in W. A. Robson (ed.), *Problems of Nationalized Industry* (1952).

[3] Cf. H. A. Clegg and T. E. Chester, *The Future of Nationalization* (Oxford, 1955), chapter 1; G. D. H. Cole, *Socialist Economics* (1950).

[4] See pp. 172–3 above.

[5] H. A. Clegg, 'Nationalized Industry', in *The British Economy, 1945–1950*, p. 246.

number of their employees, but also in their relationship with Parliament. The Acts gave the appropriate Minister specific authority over certain aspects of their work and over-all power to give directions of a general character.[1]

In line with tradition also was the fact that there was no 'pattern' of nationalization, but that the organization chosen for each industry differed fundamentally from all the others. Thus the National Coal Board began as a single unit controlling its numerous properties by a classic line-and-staff form of organization. In the electricity industry, by contrast, generation and bulk supply came under the (national) British Electicity Authority, while distribution was the preserve of the fairly autonomous Area Boards. The Gas Industry was split up entirely among 12 Area Gas Boards with very little co-ordination between them, and transport had the most complex organization of all, a Transport Commission controlling six main 'Executives'. Of these, the Railway, Docks and Inland Waterways, and Hotels Executives managed the property largely of the former four main line railways, the London Transport Executive that of the former L.P.T.B., the Road Haulage Executive managed some 40,000 long-distance vehicles nationalized or bought, and the Road Passenger Executive took over the road passenger interests of the railways, many of which consisted in partial shareholdings in privately or municipally controlled firms.[2]

This diversity was dictated by the diversity of the industries concerned, their differences in needs, structure and size. Their size compared as follows in 1950:

	Employees (000)	Fixed Assets (less Depreciation) (£mn.)	Gross Revenue (£mn.)
Coal	765	288	481
Electricity	170	548	214
Gas	141	211	192
Inland transport	888	1,341	560
Air transport	23	35	33
Grand Total	1,988	2,443	1,480

Even where some uniformity was desired, as in the principles of

[1] Clegg and Chester, p. 45; cf. also D. N. Chester, 'Organisation of the Nationalised Industries' and Ernest Davies, 'Ministerial Control and Parliamentary Responsibility of Nationalised Industries', in *Political Quarterly*, 21/2, 1950.
[2] Acton Society Trust, *Nationalised Industry. 9. Patterns of Organisation* (1951); D. N. Chester, *The Nationalised Industries* (2nd ed., 1951).

pricing,[1] different circumstances led to different results. In particular, the reluctance to allow the selling prices of nationalized industries to rise made it very much more difficult to break even in coal mining, where costs were rising exceedingly rapidly because of the great relative improvement in the miners' position and the high proportion of wage costs to total costs, as compared, for example, with electricity generation, where rapid technical advance and advantages of scale allowed the industry to absorb many of the cost increases. Similarly, the disconcerting short-term changes in Government policy regarding the heavy investment programme of the nationalized industries had varying effects on the industries concerned.

In the absence of any real intention of changing the structure of society, each separate act of nationalization has to stand on its own merits. On such a basis, the nationalization of coal mining and the railways was justifiable not only by such evident savings as the avoidance of over-lapping or of illogical boundaries, but also by the necessity of raising the morale of the labour force and providing a source of finance for the very large capital schemes required after decades of neglect. The nationalization of gas and electricity supply, while partly justifiable as permitting econo-mies of scale, and opportunity to bring the average up to the best practice,[2] as well as providing much necessary finance, would stand or fall much more with the possibility of general planning of the extensions and supply of all the means of fuel and power, excepting oil, but including atomic power which was from the beginning under Government control because of its obvious military significance.[3]

Under the Governments of the 1950's there was no hope of making nationalized industry a tool of economic planning in the national interest. With the sale of part of the road transport fleet to private ownership, and the independent control over passenger road transport, the attempt to plan and co-ordinate inland transport has been given up, with the result of chaos on the roads and continuous losses on the railways.[4] Elsewhere, as physical planning gave way, in the 1950's, to steering by fiscal and mone-tary methods and by exhortation, the nationalized industries, far from

---

[1] A vast literature grew up on the theoretical principles of pricing (as well as other managerial decisions by nationalized industry), but it cannot be said to have had any effect on actual policy. Much of the literature is reviewed in J. Wiseman, 'The Theory of Public Utility Price—An Empty Box', *Oxf. Econ. P.*, N.S., 9/1, 1957. More realistic accounts will be found in D. N. Chester, 'Note on the Price Policy indicated by the Nationalization Acts', *ibid.*, N.S. 2/1, 1950, and J. F. Sleeman, *British Public Utilities* (1953).

[2] E.g. *Report on the Gas Industry* (Heyworth Report) (1945. Cmd. 6699); H. F. H. Jones, 'The Gas Industry', and Lord Citrine, 'Electricity Supply', in Institute of Public Administration, *Efficiency in the Nationalised Industries* (1952).

[3] Youngson, pp. 187–97; E. Stanley Tucker, 'Fuel and Power', in *The Industrial Future of Great Britain*.

[4] Gilbert Walker, *Road and Rail* (2nd ed., 1947), chapter 12.

acting as instruments of controlling the rest of industry, were directed increasingly to become its servants, and to suffer the worst buffetings in their long-term investment plans with every change of wind of Government policy, with unfortunate results on their morale and their economic returns alike. Forced increasingly to deny the principle which they were established to promote, the principle of public service, and to justify themselves on the same commercial grounds as privately owned firms, the Boards of the nationalized industries have been neither able to maintain consistent financial policies nor give adequate attention to consumers' interests, despite the safeguards of consumers' councils written into the Acts,[1] nor can they defend their industries from the kind of attacks which would be unthinkable in the case of the owners or managers of private industry.

4. INCOMES AND WORK

The transition to peace involved a reduction in the numbers in the forces by $4\frac{1}{2}$ million persons and in the war industries by $3\frac{1}{4}$ million by the end of 1946, and their absorption into civilian industry or back into domestic duties.[2] The remarkable smoothness and absence of transitional unemployment with which this huge transfer of labour was carried through was due in the first place to careful planning by the Government, but was largely the result of the pressure of unfilled demands pervading all sectors of the economy. In spite of widespread misgivings, the high level of demand for labour preserved the flexibility of the British economy and permitted the rapid growth of some sectors at the expense of others.[3] By and large, labour was attracted to the expanding sectors by the offer of better wages and conditions, and this process, in a period of general labour shortage, contributed powerfully to the upward drive of wages.

Even without this additional element of propulsion given by 'bottleneck' wages, full employment was bound to contribute greatly to the bargaining strength of the trade unions. They could count on a friendly Government which passed, as one of its first measures, the Trade Disputes and Trade Unions Act of 1946, reversing the 1927 Act with its many

---

[1] J. A. G. Griffith, 'The Voice of the Consumer', *Political Quarterly*, 21/2 1950; A. M. de Neumann, *Consumers' Representation in the Public Sector of Industry* (Cambridge, 1950); Frank Milligan, 'The Consumer's Interest', in Robson (ed.), *Nationalized Industry*; W. A. Robson, *Nationalized Industry and Public Ownership* (1960), chapter 10.

[2] Ministry of Labour and National Service, *Report for the Years 1939–1946*, pp. 131–2, 151, 199–202, 225; T. Wilson, 'Manpower', in G. D. N. Worswick and P. H. Ady, *The British Economy, 1945–1950* (Oxford, 1952).

[3] G. D. N. Worswick, 'Personal Income Policy', in *The British Economy, 1945–1950*, pp. 320–4.

cramping provisions. Their membership continued its upsurge of the war years, rising from 7,875,000 in 1945 to 9,243,000 in 1950, to embrace 43% of all employees (53% of the men, 23% of the women), including an increasing number of non-manual workers.[1] The proposals of the T.U.C. General Council contained in the 'Interim Report on Trade Union Structure and Closer Unity' in 1944[2] remained as ineffective as earlier efforts to overhaul trade union organization, though there was a steady trickle of amalgamations, and in 1945 the National Union of Mineworkers replaced the earlier loose Federation. Trade union power was, however, increased by the extension of the Wages Council system under the Act of 1945,[3] which ensured that by 1950, 80% of employees were governed by statutory or voluntary forms of wage regulation; by the appointment of at least one former trade union officer to each of the Boards controlling the nationalized industries; by improved negotiating machinery in those industries; and by the continued Government consultation with trade union leaders on matters of economic policy, informally or formally through the National Joint Advisory Council, the Economic Planning Board, the Development Councils and elsewhere.[4]

On the whole, the trade unions used their increased political and economic power with a due sense of responsibility. The number of working days lost by disputes remained minute, averaging 2 million a year in 1945–50, nearly all in short strikes involving small numbers. 30% of working days lost were accounted for by transport workers, mainly dockers, and 25% by miners; there were also several flare-ups in shipbuilding and engineering, but the rest of industry experienced virtually no disputes at all. Nearly all strikes were unofficial: the war-time Order No. 1305 which made arbitration compulsory, in the last resort by the National Arbitration Tribunal, and made strikes without resort to arbitration illegal,[5] was operative throughout this period, and since the wage awards under it allowed wages to rise parallel with prices, it satisfied the leaders of most unions, particularly the weaker ones. The order did not, however, prevent unofficial strikes, in spite of some prosecutions, and when in 1951 the Government failed to secure the conviction of some dockers, a new Industrial Disputes Order was brought in.[6]

The 'responsible' attitude towards the problems of the whole economy and the support for the Labour Government at all costs were less evident in the lower trade union hierarchy than among the top leadership. It

[1] G. D. H. Cole, *The Post-War Condition of Britain* (1956), chapter 30.
[2] Trades Union Congress, *Annual Report*, 1944, pp. 341–76.
[3] See pp. 341–2 above.
[4] Allan Flanders, *Trade Unions* (1952), p. 100; P.E.P., *British Trade Unions* (1948), pp. 50, 114.
[5] pp. 340–1 above.
[6] D. F. MacDonald, *The State and the Trade Unions* (1960), pp. 177–8.

would be erroneous to assume that the organic link of the Trade Union Movement with the Labour Party ensured that there was no friction between them. On the question of the control over the nationalized industries, it is true, the trade union leadership (with few exceptions, of which the Union of Post Office Workers was the most conspicuous) agreed with the Government view that the trade unions should have no direct representation on the Boards, but should be free to criticize and represent their members' views as independent bodies. But there were many grounds for disagreements over wages policy.

Those who advocated a genuine 'wages policy' as an aspect of planning, generally had in mind the determination of the total wage increases feasible in any given future period, derived from the national income estimates, and their division among the different groups of workers according to agreed principles. Such proposals generally hoped to curb wage increases and thereby reduce the rate of inflation, as well as using the wage structure as an instrument of direct economic control and transfer of resources.[1] Quite apart from the theoretical objections to such a course, however, trade union leaders were too suspicious of the intention of Governments, and too jealous of their own powers, to sanction it, while experience in other countries showed that, whatever else might be said for it, a 'wages policy' would not cure an inflation.[2] A resolution proposing it was heavily defeated at the T.U.C. in 1951.

Instead, wages were determined by free collective bargaining between unions and employers' organizations, and by statutory bodies such as Wages Councils, which tended, in so far as they had a consistent policy, to keep their awards in line with the wages of comparable trades arrived at by union bargaining.[3] As soon as the war-time policy of keeping the cost of living stable was relaxed, rising prices, the labour shortage and union power began an upward push on wages which employers (including the nationalized industries) were unwilling to oppose, since they could easily recoup their higher costs by higher prices. This process would have made any Government policy of holding down prices impossible, had it not been for the deliberate restraint practised by the unions.

1946 was the only year in which increases in wage rates (and earnings)

[1] E.g. Allan Flanders, 'Wages Policy and Full Employment in Britain', *Bull. Oxf. Inst. Stat.*, 12/7–8, 1950, pp. 235–42, and 'Can Britain have a Wage Policy?', *Scot. J. Pol. Econ.*, 5/2, 1958 (Symposium on Wages Policy); C. W. Guillebaud, 'Problems of Wages Policy', in Min. of Labour and National Service, *The Worker in Industry* (1952).

[2] H. W. Singer, 'Wage Policy in Full Employment', *Econ. J.*, 57/228, 1947; E. H. Phelps-Brown and B. C. Roberts, 'Wages Policy in Great Britain', *Lloyds Bank Review*, N.S., No. 23, 1952; B. C. Roberts, *National Wages Policy in War and Peace* (1958); T. L. Johnstone, 'Wages Policies Abroad', *Scot. J. Pol. Econ.*, 5/2, 1958.

[3] Barbara Wootton, *The Social Foundations of Wage Policy* (1955).

exceeded the rise in the cost-of-living index; the restraint in personal income claims from 1947 onward is reflected in the following index figures:

	Average Weekly Earnings (M.o.Labour)	Wage Rates (Bowley)	Cost of Living (London and Cambridge Econ. S.)
1945 (1938 = 100)	180 (July)	154	148
1946 „ „	190 (Oct.)	167	150
1946 (1946 = 100)	100 „	100	100
1947 „ „	107 „	105	107
1948 „ „	116 „	$112\frac{1}{2}$	115
1949 „ „	$120\frac{1}{2}$ „	116	119
1950 „ „	126 „	118	123
1950 (1938 = 100)	240 „	197	184

Wage *rates*, in fact, rose less than prices after 1946, and real incomes were kept up only by the inflation of earnings by overtime and piece-rate payments, or by the upgrading of workers. The evidence that wages in this period followed, not led, prices has been noted above;[1] it could even be argued that the trade unions, whether by the inevitable delays of national wage bargaining, or by deliberate policy, kept wages lower than they would otherwise have been: 'the fact that the employers are willing to pay more than the negotiated wage rates in order to obtain the labour they require points to a situation where wages are lagging behind the levels that they would spontaneously reach as a result of market pressures'. Therefore, it could be said, 'it is in no small measure the employers who have undermined the standard rates and made further wage claims from the unions almost inevitable'.[2]

The official wage restraint policy into which the Government and the unions stumbled by accident rather than design between 1947 and 1951 had several distinct phases. In January 1947 the Government in its *Statement on the Economic Considerations affecting Relations between Employers and Workers*,[3] a white paper issued with the endorsement of the National Joint Advisory Council, drew attention to the need to keep incomes and prices down in order to remain competitive in world markets. The convertibility crisis of the summer further emphasized the foreign trade aspects of inflation. As its earlier exhortation had elicited only a limited

---

[1] p. 374 above.
[2] B. C. Roberts, *National Wages Policy*, p. 16; C. W. Guillebaud, *loc. cit.*, p. 46; also A. T. Peacock and W. J. L. Ryan, 'Wage Claims and the Pace of Inflation', *Econ. J.*, 63/250, 1953.   [3] Cmd. 7018.

response, the Government felt compelled to issue the much sharper *Statement on Personal Incomes, Costs and Prices* in February 1948.[1] This white paper, after referring to the anti-inflationary effects of the Government's policy of high taxation, demanded a total standstill of profits and rents at their present levels, and a qualified limitation of wage increases. Apart from industries in which wage increases were justified by increased productivity or by the national interest, e.g. in order to attract labour to undermanned occupations, there were to be no demands for higher wages, and no unofficial 'wage drift', ignoring national agreements. While disclaiming any intention of interfering in collective bargaining, the Government took care to bring its views to the attention of Wages Councils and other negotiating bodies.

Not unlike the white paper of 1941 in tone and effect,[2] this document marked a turning point in wages policy. The General Council of the T.U.C. fully endorsed the demand for wage restraint for the time being. A conference of trade union executives held in March 1948 also supported this, by a large majority, but it insisted on adding two further exceptions to the general wage standstill, beside the two permitted by the Government itself. One was the proviso to raise wages if they were found to be below a reasonable absolute minimum, and the other, to maintain differentials—a justification which the white paper had specifically rejected. These four grounds for exception would, between them, exempt from wage restraint virtually all the trade unions which voted for it, the others, a sizeable minority, voting against, so that the Government might be said to have won but a hollow victory. Yet it had committed the unions, at least on paper, to a policy in direct conflict with their reason for existence, and in practice their restraint in a period of full employment was greater than might have been expected.

After devaluation in September 1949, the General Council of the T.U.C. again urged a wage standstill, until the end of 1950, provided the interim retail price index did not rise by more than 5%, and asked the trades whose wages were tied to sliding scales to forgo increases due to them. Put before another meeting of trade union executives in January 1950, these propositions could, however, muster such a narrow majority only (4,263,000 against 3,606,000) as to lose all their moral force. 'The unions with sliding scales refused to sacrifice their advantages; the engineers and railwaymen continued to press their demands for wage increases, and the [miners and distributive workers voted to reject the policy which had been supported by their leaders.'[3] The General Council itself

---

[1] Cmd. 7321.   [2] p. 343 above.
[3] B. C. Roberts, *National Wages Policy*, p. 60; cf. also D. F. MacDonald, *The State and the Trade Unions* (1960), pp. 151 ff.; Allan Flanders, *Trade Unions* (1952), pp. 110–12.

abandoned its policy in June 1950 when it urged more 'flexibility' in wage negotiations. The impending crisis of 1951 led to a renewed attempt to peg wages with the help of enlarged subsidies, and Mr. Gaitskell proposed a statutory dividend limitation, but the Labour Government fell before these measures could be given a trial.

The labour shortage ensured that wages did not fall in the post-war years, as a proportion of the national income, but as usual, in a period of industrial boom, the share of profits went up, and it was rents and salaries which therefore had to bear the brunt of the necessary reductions. The available statistics fail to reflect fully the gains of dividend earners, since in view of the penal rates of taxation and the powerful pressures to dividend restraint, a much smaller proportion of dividends was distributed in the 1940's than in the pre-war years, and a larger proportion accumulated until more favourable times, or taken out as capital gains which remained untaxed and unrecorded.

Moreover, the proportion of wage-earners was falling: according to one calculation, wage-earners received 39·2% of the national income in 1938, when they formed 71·4% of the occupied population: in 1946 they received 40·5% and in 1950 41·9%, but by then they only formed 66·2% of the occupied population.[1] Conversely, the rising share of salaries has to be set against a rising number of salary earners: the growth of the 'salariat' interrupted or reversed during the war, was resumed with undiminished vigour after it.[2] The numbers employed in the trades with a large proportion of salary earners, insurance, banking and finance, public administration, professional services and the distributive trades, rose from 6·15 million in 1946 to 6·73 million in 1948 and (on a different statistical base) from 7·89 million in 1948 to 8·07 million in 1950; in industry, the proportion of administrative, clerical and technical employees to operatives rose from 13·5% in 1935 to 18·6% in 1948. The 'middle classes' of managerial, professional and white-collar workers, as well as proprietors, numbered 10·4 million, or over 20% of the population, in 1951; of these, 'proprietors and managerial' numbered 4·3 million.[3]

Statistics of pre-tax incomes like the following should be read with all these provisos in mind:[4]

[1] The figures are not quite on the same base. E. H. Phelps-Brown and P. E. Hart, 'The Share of Wages in National Incomes', *Econ. J.*, 62/246, 1952, p. 277.

[2] pp. 287–9 above. D. C. Marsh, *The Changing Social Structure of England and Wales, 1871–1951* (1958), pp. 105, 145, 194, *passim*.

[3] P.E.P., *Government and Industry* (1952), p. 171; Ministry of Labour and National Service, *Annual Reports*; C. W. McMahon and G. D. N. Worswick, 'The Growth of Services in the Economy', *District Bank Review*, No. 136, 1960; Cole, *op. cit.*, chapter 3.

[4] H. F. Lydall, 'The Long-Term Trend in the Size Distribution of Income', *J. R. Stat. S.*, 122/2, 1959, p. 17, Table 9. Cf. also pp. 344–5 above.

Proportion of Personal Incomes	1938	1949
Wages	37·8	41·9
Salaries	17·9	20·5
Other employment incomes	3·8	6·0
Self-employed	12·8	13·1
Rent, dividends, interest	22·3	11·4
Government transfers	5·4	7·1
	100	100

Whatever redistribution of incomes there had been, however, had largely occurred in the war period, not in the post-war years. No great accuracy is possible in estimating post-war shares of incomes, especially profits. Apart from undistributed profits (shown or hidden in the balance sheets) which yet were as much incomes of shareholders as those paid out, the period was also rich in tax evasion schemes, both for owners of shares and for top salaried persons in private industry and commerce. Various estimates exist for the understatement of these incomes in official statistics, but though it is known that it ran into hundreds of millions of pounds, in the nature of the case no reliable statements can be made. The inclusion of undistributed profits alone (including gains from stock appreciation) does, however, confirm the general impression of the constancy of the main shares of personal incomes in the gross national product in the post-war years:[1]

	1946	1950
Incomes of: Employees and Forces	57·2%	57·3%
Grants from public authorities	6·8	5·8
Self-employment	12·0	10·9
Property, including undistributed profits, additions to reserves	24·0	26·0

The tendency of the redistribution of private capital also largely ceased and the statistics of savings showed again the concentration of 'small' savings in the hands of a small minority of the working classes and in those of the middle classes; the building societies, attracting mainly middle-class savers, showed by far the largest increases.[2]

If Government policy failed to carry through a further redistribution of incomes, it still continued to restrict severely the spending of the higher income groups. In any case, a large part of their income was in the form of undistributed dividends, and was as yet only potential spending power; but

[1] Based on *National Income and Expenditure, 1946–1952* (1953), Table 9, excluding incomes of public authorities and public corporations, and remittances abroad. Cf. also Worswick, 'Personal Income Policy', pp. 315–17.

[2] Kathleen M. Langley, 'The Distribution of Private Capital, 1950–1', *Bull. Oxf. Inst. Stat.*, 16/1, 1954; Esme Preston, 'Personal Savings through Institutional Channels (1937–1949)', *ibid.*, 1950.

in addition, many consumption goods were still rationed, or their import restricted. The two largest reductions of personal expenditure (at constant, 1948, prices) occurred in the categories limited to the wealthier classes: expenditure on domestic service fell from £265 million in 1938 to £80 million in 1946 and £85 million in 1950, and private motoring from £250 million to £140 million and £160 million.[1]

The relative fall in salaries, as compared with wages, tended to level out earned incomes as a whole,[2] but there also took place a certain measure of levelling of wages during the war which was maintained in the post-war years. The differential of skill remained at about 20% of the unskilled wage, and women's and youths' wages were rising relatively to those of men. Above all, a large part of the bottom slice of the income pyramid, the population living in absolute poverty, was removed.

The virtual abolition of primary poverty in post-war Britain was only to a slight extent due to the rise in real wages. Much more important were two other developments: full employment on the one hand, and the State welfare provisions on the other. B. S. Rowntree, visiting York in 1950 to conduct his third social survey there,[3] found the proportion of the working-class population living in poverty to have dropped from 31·1% in 1936 to 2·8% in 1950; of those living below the poverty line, nearly one-third gave unemployment as the reason in 1936, while not one was found in 1950; in that year 68% attributed their poverty to old age. At the same time, Rowntree and Lavers calculated that if the welfare provisions (including subsidies) in 1950 had been only those of 1936, the proportion of working-class families living in poverty would have been, not 2·8%, but 22·2%. It seems reasonable to conclude that for the majority of the population, for those who before 1939 were never quite beyond the danger of want, either by unemployment, sickness or old age, the most important single development after 1945 was the creation of the 'Welfare State'.

5. THE WELFARE STATE

The measures passed by the post-war Government which established the 'Welfare State', and which helped to consolidate the abolition of poverty, have since become so universally accepted as to be unlikely to be modified in more than detail. Even the few who clamour for revision of principles[4] do not, openly at least, demand the reduction of welfare provisions for the poor, but only for the better-off.

[1] Dudley Seers, 'National Income, Production and Consumption', in *The British Economy, 1945–1950*, p. 47.
[2] David Lockwood, *The Black-Coated Workers* (1958), pp. 67–8.
[3] B. S. Rowntree and G. R. Lavers, *Poverty and the Welfare State* (1951), pp. 30–5.
[4] E.g. D. S. Lees, 'The Economics of Health Services', *Lloyds Bank Review*, N.S., 56, 1960.

The Welfare State

The limits of the 'Welfare State' are not easy to draw. At the centre, without a doubt, stood the Social Insurance scheme as proposed in the Beveridge Report,[1] and the National Health Service and the family allowances associated with it. The family allowances were enacted in 1945, providing 5s. a week for all children except the eldest; in November of that year, the new Ministery of National Insurance began to operate under an Act of 1944, and in 1946 the National Insurance Act, the National Insurance (Industrial Injuries) Act and the National Health Service Act were passed, coming into operation together on the 'appointed day', the 5th July 1948. In that year the National Assistance Act and the Children Act completed this group of reforms.

In spite of its many novel and detailed provisions, the Beveridge Report was followed remarkably faithfully. There were only two major departures from its principles. The first was caused by the rise in prices unmatched by increases in benefit rates, so that the principle of sufficiency was violated, the benefit rates, by themselves, were insufficient to sustain life, and the National Assistance scheme, intended only as a 'safety net' for a small minority, became a necessary standby for large numbers of insured persons. Thus by the end of 1950, 1,350,000 persons were receiving weekly allowances from the Assistance Board, of whom no fewer than 873,000 were persons who were in need because the benefits under the insurance scheme were too low; 650,000 of them were old-age pensioners.[2] This large-scale dependence on a National Assistance Board which was financed separately, was fairly independent of the Minister and had to apply a needs test, threatened to bring back the old Poor Law under a new guise.

The other important departure from the war-time recommendations was the decision to apply increased retirement pensions at once, instead of after an interval in which the beneficiaries might have accumulated sufficient credits by their in-payments; indeed, higher pensions were paid (except for dependants' allowances, which had to wait for the general scheme) as from October 1946, instead of waiting for July 1948, and the full rates were to come in after only 10 years instead of 20.[3] The numbers involved were 3·3 million persons in 1946 and 3·5 million in 1948.

This decision, made largely for political reasons, was doubly unfortunate from the point of view of the financial structure of the insurance scheme, since even at the less generous rates the growing number of retirement pensioners was certain to swallow a rapidly mounting share of its

[1] pp. 348–51 above. Also, M. Bruce, *The Coming of the Welfare State* (1961), chapter 7.
[2] G. D. H. Cole, *The Post-War Condition of Britain* (1956), chapter 23; D. C. Marsh, *National Insurance and Assistance in Great Britain* (1950), chapter 12.
[3] *Report of the Ministry of National Insurance for the Period 17th November 1944 to 4th July 1949* (1950. Cmd. 7955), chapters 4, 12; Lord Beveridge, 'Epilogue', in W. A. Robson (ed.), *Social Security* (3rd ed., 1948).

income. The number of people over 65 was expected to grow from 5·0 million in 1947 and 5·3 million in 1951 to 7·3 million in 1977, and, if mortality continued to decline, to as much as 8·2 million. As a proportion of the total population, they would increase from 10% in 1931 and 14% in 1951 to 18% in 1979. At the rates of the 1946 Act, the cost of the retirement pensions would then rise from £238 million in 1948 to £301 million in 1958 and £501 million in 1978, and the resulting deficit would fall entirely on the Exchequer, the contribution of which would grow quite disproportionately from £36 million to £107 million and £338 million respectively.[1]

Both the rates of subscription and the rates of benefits of the Insurance Fund were raised in the event, but the disproportion between the retirement pensions and the contribution rates remained, with the obligation on the Treasury to cover the widening gap. In strict logic, this took from the Insurance Fund the last vestiges of pretence of 'insurance'. Since the Treasury contributed a share of the normal income, adding sums at will or altering rates according to the short-term 'balance' of the Fund, as well as controlling the investment of the 'surplus' and finding most of the interest on it, the scheme was not run on insurance lines at all, but was a system of redistribution of incomes financed by three sets of taxes: a direct 'poll tax' on insured persons, an indirect tax in the form of the employer's contribution (which in the prevailing sellers' market he could be expected to pass on to consumers in higher prices) and the total tax base in the form of the Exchequer contributions.[2] But economic logic could take no account of the importance of at least the *nominal* maintenance of an insurance scheme for the sake of the abolition of the means test, the feeling of security it would bring to the members, the spirit in which they would claim its benefits, and the spirit with which it would be administered.

In other respects, the national insurance scheme, as enacted, followed the earlier proposals. It was compulsory and universal, the population being 'classified' into several separate classes of contributors and beneficiaries. The single insurance stamp provided unemployment, sickness and disablement benefits, and payments for retired persons, widows and orphans; there were also maternity benefits, death benefits (from July 1949) and associated schemes of family allowances (paid out of the Exchequer) and industrial injuries benefits (paid out of a separate fund), while the Insurance Fund also made an annual contribution to the Health

---

[1] *Report of the Royal Commission on Population* (1949. Cmd. 7695), pp. 112–17; *Report of the Committee on the Economic and Financial Provisions for Old Age* (Phillips Report) (1954. Cmd. 9333), esp. Table IV, paras. 117–22, and Section IV.

[2] Alan T. Peacock, *The Economics of National Insurance* (1952); cf. Douglas Jay in *Hansard*, H.o.C., 26th April 1951, Vol. 487, cols. 641–4; Walter Hagenbuch, *Social Economics* (Cambridge, 1958), pp. 265–7.

Service. The total numbers insured rose from about $15\frac{3}{4}$ million to $21\frac{1}{2}$ million for unemployment insurance and from $24\frac{1}{3}$ million to 25 million for other benefits.

By 1948, the rise in prices since 1939 had seriously reduced the real values of both contributions and benefits under the existing schemes, and the new monetary rates enacted were naturally higher; but a comparison of the *real* values of the new scheme in 1948 with those of the earlier schemes before the war[1] shows that both contributions and benefits of single men remained below the pre-war level, but the family allowances raised the real value of the benefits for family men considerably above it, while old-age pensioners enjoyed the largest rate of increase. For the fund as a whole, the absence of the drain of mass unemployment was of the utmost significance, and the social insurance budget, in spite of its rise in absolute terms, still fell short of its pre-war proportion of the total Government budget:[2]

	1938	1946	1950
Social Insurance contributions as % of total Government revenue	15·4	6·7	13·6
Social Insurance expenditure as % of total Government expenditure	13·6	3·9	11·3

The National Health Service, inaugurated on the same day, was also intended to be comprehensive, but the use of its facilities was not made compulsory and a small proportion of the population elected to pay for private service.[3] It was to provide, free of charge, all medical services and needs, in so far as they could be met from existing resources, and it was to bring into a single organization the many different insitutions that had grown up to form the existing variegated service. In practice, the scheme was greatly modified by the pressure of the B.M.A. and other interests,[4] and its regional and local administration remained split among three sets of authorities: the general practitioners' service was controlled by local Executive Councils; the hospitals by Regional Hospital Boards, the teaching hospitals retaining independent control; and the environmental services by the administrative Counties and County Boroughs. At the inauguration, the service had to overcome the handicap of much hostility, especially on the part of the medical profession; it inherited a severe shortage of hospitals, of equipment and of staff, and a geographical maldistribution of doctors, none of which could be remedied in the short run. Further, there was an unexpectedly large backlog of hidden demand, especially for

[1] E.g. D. C. Marsh, *op. cit.*, p. 116.
[2] Peacock, pp. 17–20.
[3] D. H. Hene, *The British Health Service* (1953), pp. 7–10.
[4] Harry Eckstein, *Pressure Group Politics* (1960), chapter 4.

dentures and glasses, which created long waiting lists and other early problems. The service also became quickly the victim of many ill-judged economy drives. In 1949 a measure permitting charges for medicines and appliances was passed (held in reserve and imposed by the Conservative Government after 1951), in 1950 a ceiling on total expenditure of £400 million gross was imposed, leading to charges for spectacles and dentures, and capital expenditure on hospitals was cut to the derisory figure of one-third of the pre-war level.[1]

Nevertheless, the National Health Service became one of the most popular and successful measures of the post-war years.[2] Thanks to its wide sweep, and to the great strides in medical science, many formerly fatal diseases, such as tuberculosis, typhoid and diphtheria, were beginning to be mastered, and the most sensitive index, the infant mortality rate, showed a welcome drop from 47·4 per thousand births in 1939 to 29·3 in 1949–50. The class differences still remained, however: in 1949–50, mortality ranged from 18·4 in the top (professional) class to 39·8 in the lowest (unskilled workers), while the differences in post-neo-natal deaths (at ages 4 weeks to 1 year), where environment counted for most, were greater still, ranging from 4·9 to 17·9.[3]

Housing standards had suffered perhaps more than any others from the war. By 1939, the backlog of cheaper houses had been reduced to perhaps ½ million, but in addition there was a net loss by enemy action of another ½ million houses plus the usual replacement needs and the cumulating demand caused by the larger numbers of households. The total shortage, estimated officially at 1¼ million houses in 1945, would by the time of the completion of that number, be of the order of magnitude of 3 million dwellings. According to the standards used, from 7·7% to 22·5% of dwellings were judged to be overcrowded in mid-1945 in England and Wales,[4] the Scottish figure being much higher. Thus the annual needs of building, for the next ten years, were set at a minimum of 300,000 houses,[5] compared with a maximum pre-war building rate of 350,000 dwellings. Since then, however, the building labour force had shrunk to half its size and its pre-war productivity per head had declined.

In the event, some 55,000 permanent buildings were completed in

---

[1] Brian Abel-Smith and R. M. Titmuss, *The Cost of the National Health Service in England and Wales* (Cambridge, 1956), pp. 137–8.

[2] Harry Eckstein, *The English Health Service* (Cambridge, Mass., 1959); J. S. Ross, *The National Health Service in Great Britain* (1952), Parts IV–VI.

[3] Cole. *op. cit.*, pp. 380–1.

[4] *Housing* (1945. Cmd. 6609); Geoffrey Thomas, *Population and Housing in England and Wales, Mid-45* (Social Survey, No. 60, 1946), p. 11.

[5] E.g. R. L. Reiss, *Municipal and Private Enterprise Housing* (1945), pp. 18–19; G. D. H. Cole, *Building and Planning* (1945), p. 150; Herbert Ashworth, *Housing in Great Britain* (1957), p. 43.

Great Britain in 1946, rising to 140,000 in 1947 and well over 200,000 a year for the next three years. In 1946–8, there were also 148,000 'temporary' prefabricated houses erected, financed by the Exchequer under the Act of 1944, so that at the time of the Census of 1951, the number of occupied dwellings, 13·3 million, exceeded the 1931 figure by over 3 million. Yet the number of households had been growing even faster, and in the Census year there were nearly 14½ million married households. The number of houses per 1,000 of the population was higher than pre-war, but the shortage was worse than ever.

New houses and re-buildings for private owners amounted to only 158,000 in 1945–50 and most of the post-war houses were built by local authorities, subsidized by the Government under Bevan's 1946 Act, in order to ensure that the new houses went to those in greatest need. Rent restriction kept the rents of older houses at their 1939 levels, and was extended to about 1 million furnished houses by an Act of 1946 which set up Rent Tribunals. The Landlord and Tenant (Rent Control) Act of 1949 gave the Tribunals the additional powers to fix rents for unfurnished houses for the first time, but at no time did the price of houses come under control.[1] This legislation kept down rents for a large proportion of the population in the face of an acute housing shortage, at the price of making families immobile, but it could not cure the shortage, estimated, after the building of well over 1¼ million post-war houses by 1951,[2] to be still between 1 and 2 million houses, nor could it prevent it falling, as ever, mainly on the poorer families.

The planning powers of the Town and Country Planning authorities, the Counties and County Boroughs, were greatly extended by the Act of 1947 which ensured that, on paper at least, the whole country was covered by long-term development plans. Special facilities, including trading estates, were provided for the 'Development Areas' and a more ambitious approach to town planning was symbolized by the creation of fourteen 'New Towns', eight of them in the London region. These were to end the unco-ordinated urban sprawl of the inter-war years by creating complete self-contained and balanced communities, offering local employment as well as housing. The capital was provided by specially formed public corporations which were to act also as local authorities in the initial stages. Though highly successful financially, it was doubtful how far the 'New Towns' have fulfilled all the hopes of their creators. Another significant attempt to realize the dreams of generations of reformers was the nationalization of the 'development value' of land, following the

---

[1] F. W. Paish, 'The Economics of Rent Restriction', in *The Post-War Financial Problem and Other Essays* (1950).

[2] Hagenbuch, *Social Economics*, p. 83; J. B. Cullingworth, *Housing Needs and Planning Policy* (1960), chapter 3.

Uthwatt Report,[1] with the object of transferring to the community the additional values created by the community rather than the individual. The scheme, however, was badly designed, it proved unpopular and troublesome to administer and was quickly modified out of existence by the Conservative Government.[2]

In education, also, the brave post-war plans were held up by the shortage of buildings and teachers, in spite of the imaginative post-war Emergency Teacher Training Scheme. The raising of the school-leaving age to 15 under the Butler Act of 1944 had to be postponed to April 1947, and its planned extension to 16 was postponed further, if not indefinitely.[3] Total expenditure on education, at constant prices, rose from an index of 76 in 1937–9 to 83 in 1946 and 122 in 1950 (1948 = 100), but as the birth rate 'bulge' loomed ahead, most of this was devoted to increasing quantity rather than quality.[4]

The 1944 Act made the education authorities explicitly responsible for three types of education, primary, secondary and further education, but the most important innovation of the post-war period was the creation of a universal and free secondary education system for children aged 11–15 and upwards. In practice, most authorities divided the children into three streams, grammar, technical and modern (not necessarily in separate schools), selected in most areas by an aptitude test taken at about the age of 11, the 'eleven-plus'. Though open in practice to many objections,[5] this reorganization of secondary education did more than any other previous measure to approach the ideals of educational democracy by making higher education available to capable children of all classes. It left untouched the privileged 'public school' system to those whose parents were able and willing to pay for it.

Besides social insurance, health, housing and education, there was also an expansion of many minor social services, for aged persons, for the blind, the mentally deficient, the problem families and others. In addition, there was still much scope for voluntary social work,[6] to fill the inevitable gaps left by national and local authorities. Finally, there were the provisions which involved no public expenditure, like Factory Acts, Food and Drug Acts, and rent control. Indeed, in its widest definition, the concept of the

[1] p. 351 above.
[2] G. D. H. Cole, *The Post-War Condition of Britain*, chapters 25, 26; Herbert Ashworth, chapters 17–19; Cullingworth, chapter 7; A. C. Duff, *Britain's New Towns* (1961).
[3] H. C. Dent, *Growth in English Education, 1946–1952* (1954), and *Secondary Education for All* (1949), chapter 4; Cole, *loc. cit.*, chapter 24.
[4] John Vaizey, *The Costs of Education* (1958), p. 70.
[5] E.g. Robin Pedley, *Comprehensive Education, a New Approach* (1956), also P. E. Vernon (ed.), *Secondary School Selection* (1957).
[6] G. Williams (ed.), *Voluntary Social Services since 1918* (1948); Lord Beveridge, *Voluntary Action* (1948); Hagenbuch, *op. cit.*, chapters 4, 7.

modern Welfare State was to focus much attention on intangible social improvements, such as the protection of personal rights including the prevention of neglect or cruelty to children, the fostering of the arts and recreational facilities, moral guidance and the abolition of ignorance and illiteracy, as well as of the grosser forms of inequality and privilege.[1] These ideals were not, however, as yet as widely approved as the more tangible material benefits of the Welfare State.

Not all the welfare schemes necessarily favoured the poor at the expense of the rich, or the working classes at the expense of the middle classes. The public education system, for example, benefited the average child of middle-income families much more than it benefited the lower-income child, even if the heavier taxation of the wealthier families is taken into account.[2] The Health Service, likewise, was to benefit the middle classes more than the working classes, who were generally insured before 1948, though there was some justification for describing it as mainly satisfying the quest for efficiency, always an important ingredient in Fabian and Labour Party doctrine, rather than the quest for social justice.[3] Whether the working classes as a whole gained from the social services, or whether the redistribution was merely 'horizontal', within classes, turned on definitions and assumptions. Working-class families certainly paid more in taxes and contributions than they received in social service benefits, but the question remains how much of the remainder of public expenditure should be assumed to be in their benefit and credited to them also, to set against their in-payments.[4] The major redistribution achieved by the social services was horizontal, e.g. from single and healthy men to large families, the sick, and the aged,[5] and this aspect of it met with widespread approval, for, after all, the net contributor, and the net beneficiary, was commonly the same person at different stages of his career.

It is also worth emphasizing that few of the post-war schemes were entirely novel: most of them developed naturally out of the older existing schemes. In spite of a widespread belief to the contrary, Britain did not spend significantly more on the social services after 1948 than she did

[1] W. A. Robson, The Welfare State (1957).
[2] Vaizey, The Costs of Education, p. 84.
[3] Eckstein, The English Health Service, esp. Introduction, and pp. 3 ff.
[4] Cf. pp. 367-8 above. Findlay Weaver, 'Taxation and Redistribution in the United Kingdom', Rev. of Econ. and Statistics, 32/3, 1950; A. T. Peacock and P. R. Browning, 'The Social Services in Great Britain and the Redistribution of Income', in Peacock (ed.), Income Redistribution and Social Policy (1954), esp. pp. 157-66; Asa Briggs, 'The Social Services', in G. D. N. Worswick and P. H. Ady, The British Economy 1945-1950 (Oxford, 1952), p. 373.
[5] R. M. Titmuss, 'Social Administration in a Changing Society', British Journal of Sociology, 2/3, 1951.

before 1939, apart from the retirement pensions. The Health Service, formerly administered largely by 'Approved Societies' and voluntary bodies, also came to swell the national figures, but did not represent a larger share of national outlay. The outlay on many services, in real terms or as a proportion of national income, had actually fallen. Comparisons are difficult and estimates differ widely. In terms of calendar years, the post-war growth, excluding capital expenditure, was of the following order of magnitude (in £mn.):[1]

	1946	1950
Subsidies (incl. local authorities)	387	475
Current grants to persons (incl. L.A.s)[2]	453	730
Net current Central Government expenditure on the Health Service	n.a.	401
Net current expenditure on social services by local authorities[3]	285	319
Totals	1,125	1,935

A different classification, omitting subsidies and some other transfers, and couched in terms of financial years, yields the following figures (£mn.):[4]

	1938–9	1947–8	1949–50
Social security services	310·5	559·8	714·8
Education	111·8	222·8	228·5
Health	74·4	174·7	408·6
Housing	23·7	55·8	54·5
	520·4	1013·1	1406·4

Most of this increase was accounted for by rises in prices and by the Health Service.[5] In comparison with the pre-war years, the increases in the old-age pensions, the family allowances and the subsidies were counter-balanced in part by a reduction in unemployment benefits, so that expenditure on transfers showed a much slower rise, and so did expenditure on capital (chiefly housing), both before and after July 1948:[6]

[1] *National Income and Expenditure 1946–52* (1953), Tables 27, 30, 34, 35.
[2] Excluding Forces' allowances and pensions, grants for research and post-war credit payments.
[3] Incl. Northern Ireland.
[4] Based on the *Monthly Digest of Statistics*; also John Vaizey, *The Cost of the Social Services* (Fabian Research Series, No. 166) (1954).
[5] Cf. other figures in A. J. Youngson, *The British Economy 1920–1957* (1960), p. 216; A. T. Peacock, *The Economics of National Insurance*, p. 24; Peacock and Browning, pp. 144–5; Hagenbuch, p. 213.
[6] Peacock and Browning, p. 151.

	1937–8	1947–8	1950–1
Total expenditure on the social services as % of gross national income at market prices, plus transfers	9·8	14·8	16·9
Transfer payments, as % of personal incomes before tax, including transfers	5·4	5·4	5·7
Gross capital expenditure on the social services, as % of gross domestic capital formation	10·4	15·3	14·8

Of equal importance with the growth in quantity and extent of the welfare services, was the new spirit behind the provisions of the 'Welfare State', a spirit of communal responsibility and humanity. This also had existed before 1939, though it was much fostered by the war and encouraged by the widespread benefits of full employment. The war hastened its application by removing, temporarily, the usual barriers of administrative conservatism and the power of vested interests. The changes planned in the last years of war were forced through in the early years of peace by the Labour Government, which could rightly claim to have been an administration of social reform, even if not, as its programme implied, of Socialism.

CHAPTER VIII

Britain in the Post-War World,
1950–1967

I. INDUSTRIAL GROWTH AND ORGANIZATION

By 1950 the immediate after-effects of the war had been overcome, both in the United Kingdom and abroad, and the world could settle down to the peaceful creation of wealth which most of its citizens expected after the holocaust. The Korean War, it is true, was soon to shatter the precarious peace and to distort prices and production once again; but in retrospect it appears as the first violent clash within the uneasy world balance of forces which marked the peace, rather than as the last battle of the war. The economic disturbances it caused were not strong enough to interrupt the upward movement of output and productivity, particularly among the advanced Western nations, which has become perhaps the most striking of all aspects of post-war economic history.

In the United Kingdom, as elsewhere in the West, the rate of saving, the level of investment in scientific research and development, and the rate of application of technical progress were very high in comparison with any earlier period of history and in consequence there was a faster rate of economic growth than perhaps at any previous age. Industrial output, the key factor, rose, according to one calculation, by 3·7% a year in 1948–60, compared with 3·1% in the inter-war years, 1·6% in 1877–1913 and just over 3% earlier in the nineteenth century,[1] when the population increase was much faster.

Again, limiting ourselves to certain industries, the series of 'physical' output shows the following comparisons of the pre-1950 and the post-1950 experience:[2]

Average Annual Rates of Increase, %	1924–50	1954–63
Volume of output	2·17	2·30
Employment	0·44	0·17
Output per head	1·60	1·84

[1] K. S. Lomax, 'Growth and Productivity in the United Kingdom', *Productivity Measurement Review*, 38 (1964), p. 6.

[2] W. B. Reddaway, in W. E. G. Salter, *Productivity and Technical Change* (2nd ed., Cambridge, 1966), p. 198.

Industrial Growth and Organization

Including all other sectors of the domestic economy, gross domestic product *per head* rose by 40% in 1950–66 and by 29% in the similar pre-war period, 1920–36.[1] It will be observed that this increase in output, though better than in earlier periods, was only marginally so.

Despite sharp annual variations, the growth in the gross domestic product was continuous throughout the whole period:[2]

G.D.P. *per Head of the Labour Force, at Constant*
(1958) Prices

1950	100·0
Average of years 1951–5	106·0
Average of years 1956–60	116·8
Average of years 1961–5	132·0
1966	141·4
First quarter 1967 (seasonally adjusted)	146·0

This amounted to an annual compound growth rate of G.D.P. of 2·2% per head, or a growth of total product of 2·9%, and a growth in the employed labour force of 0·7% a year, between 1950 and 1966.

Such an increase of nearly one-half, superimposed on a complex industrial society, was necessarily accompanied by a substantial change in the industrial and geographical distribution of employment, by the introduction of new technology and new products, and by the replacement of some existing industries by others. Much was heard in this period about the conservatism and restrictionism of the British worker and manager, about their unwillingness to innovate or to accept change, and about their fondness for tradition, and it is true that, in comparison with otherwise similar Continental economies, a society which suffered neither invasion nor revolution, nor even a major currency change in the past generation, was less inclined to scrap the old and accept the new. Yet the changes in industrial structure were large by any standards.

On the whole, they followed, and in some cases completed, the structural transformation of the economy which had begun in the 1920's. Its main components were a relative and, in some cases, an absolute decline of the old 'staple' and export industries, including shipping; their replacement by others fulfilling the same functions; and the creation of altogether new industries, meeting new needs or using new materials and components. It was a significant feature of this transformation that improved

[1] (London and Cambridge Economic Service), *The British Economy, Key Statistics 1900–1966*, Table C. Also see Angus Maddison, *Economic Growth in the West* (1964), p. 37.

[2] Ministry of Labour, *National Statistics on Incomes, Prices, Employment and Production*. Also Phyllis Deane and W. A. Cole, *British Economic Growth, 1688–1959* (2nd ed., Cambridge, 1967), Appx. Table 90, and *National Income and Expenditure* (annual).

technology and rising productivity were to be found both in the declining and in the expanding industries and occupations.

Agriculture was a good case in point. Its output rose from an index number of 88 in 1950 to 129 in 1966 while its employment declined sharply by about one-third.[1] This increase in output was spread over all the main products—grain, meat, dairy and market gardening. Land use, in fact, changed little over the period:

Land Utilization, United Kingdom[2]
(million acres)

	1948	1965
Tillage	13·2	12·0
Rotational grass	5·5	6·6
	18·7	18·6
Arable	18·7	18·6
Permanent grass	12·4	12·1
Rough grazing	17·2	17·8
Total Agricultural Area	48·3	48·5

Since land remained constant and labour declined,[3] the output increase was achieved largely by better equipment and better techniques. The equipment included the further extension of mechanization: the number of agricultural tractors licensed between 1951 and 1966 increased from 313,000 to 446,000, or nearly 1½ tractors per holding of any size. The new techniques included intensive breeding and better pest control. The stock of plant and machinery in agriculture, valued in constant (1958) prices at replacement cost, increased from £0·5 milliard in 1951 to £0·8 milliard in 1965.[4]

This heavy programme of investment in an industry still made up of relatively small units[5] reflected the confidence of farmers in a continuing policy of agricultural support by the Government. This confidence was only to a small extent based on the Agricultural Act of 1947: it largely relied on the assurance that in a highly protectionist country like post-war Britain agriculture, also, would have its particular security.

Agricultural policy, in fact, went through several phases. At first,

[1] *Key Statistics.*

[2] *Agricultural Statistics* (annual).

[3] As a share of farm *expenses*, labour fell from 42% in 1948–9 to 20% in 1965–6, while wages rose sharply.

[4] *National Income and Expenditure.* Also see S. G. Hooper, *The Finance of Farming in Great Britain* (1955); M. T. Stewart, 'Capital in Scottish Agriculture', *Scottish Agricultural Economics*, 15 (1965); and literature quoted in K. E. Hunt and K. R. Clark, *The State of British Agriculture*, 6, 1965–6 (Oxford, 1966), pp. 20–1.

[5] In England and Wales, the average size of holdings increased from 66·4 acres in 1949 to 75·5 in 1964, and the land in holdings of 500 acres and over, from 2,663,000 to 3,917,000 acres. Hunt and Clark, p. 58.

under Labour, the object was to secure higher production at all costs. This was continued up to the price review of 1952, when the saving of dollars was still stressed in a further expansion programme designed to raise output from 50% above pre-war, at which it stood then, to 60%. After this, policy changed sharply: the Government was no longer willing to 'plan' for specific quantities for any or all commodities, but, in parallel with its dismantling of food rationing and other controls, would undertake only to attempt to let supply and demand meet at acceptable consumer price levels. The actual mechanism of support was highly complex. Cereal and fatstock producers, who were in substantial competition with importers, were compensated by a set of 'deficiency payments' calculated retrospectively to meet the gap between the prices they obtained and the higher prices guaranteed by the annual review. From 1954, milk and potatoes, and from 1957, eggs, were sold by monopolistic official marketing boards which recovered and distributed the subsidies on behalf of the Government.[1] The system was designed both to give the consumer the benefit of (lower) world food prices, and to keep up efficiency incentives for farmers, while leaving the 'planning' of production to the farmer himself in the light of expected costs and prices and the variable subsidy.

In the mid-1950's the post-war world food shortage gave way to an incipient surplus in Western markets and it was largely due to the striking improvement in productivity and reduction in real costs that the subsidies declined in this period from the £382 million paid over in 1950 to an annual figure of around £250–£300 in the mid-1960's. The Agriculture Act of 1957 attempted to allay the farmers' fears of drastic cuts in support by limiting price reductions to 4% a year or 9% in three years, and the total values of guarantees to $2\frac{1}{2}$%, excluding changes in costs. In the 1965 annual price review, in a special white paper,[2] and in the National Plan for economic development of that year, the emphasis was again put on the increase in total output and on import savings. Output was to rise by 3·6% a year to 1970, compared with 3·2% in 1960–4, and in view of a further expected loss of manpower from 947,000 to 805,000, productivity was expected to continue to rise at a rate of 6% a year. Various measures, including the Agriculture Act of 1966, were to help particularly the small farmer and the hill farmer, by advice, credit facilities and direct support.

The system has been criticized for giving greater support to the well-off farmer who needs it least, and less support to the farmer on poorer land or with less managerial ability; from the mid-1950's on, this was borne in mind when price subsidies were sharply reduced, but improvement grants

[1] E.g., *Report on Agricultural Marketing Schemes for the Years 1938–55* (1957); *Guarantees for Home-Grown Cereals*, Cmd. 8947 (1953).

[2] *Annual Review and Determination of Guarantees*, Cmnd. 2621 (1965), *The Development of Agriculture*, Cmnd. 2738 (1965).

extended for capital investment under the Farm Improvement Scheme of 1957, and other direct grants to the small farmer under the Small Farm Scheme of 1959, the Horticulture Act of 1960 and the Agriculture and Horticulture Act of 1964. The system has also been criticized for attempting to achieve several, and partly contradictory aims:[1] the saving of foreign exchange, the improvement of home standards of nutrition, particularly milk consumption, and the provision of stable incomes and employment in agriculture. Certainly, over two-thirds of farmers' net income after the end of rationing has been provided by subsidies, which still left the average farmer's income at only £1,200 a year gross, or £900 net (i.e. after deducting interest on his capital), in 1960. Yet the gains were substantial. The increase in net output by 1960 was worth £300 m. a year, and more in foreign exchange, as higher British demand would have driven up world food prices, so that, in a generally protectionist country troubled by balance of payments deficits, agriculture's claim for support on grounds of import-saving as well as on social grounds was very great. But the strongest justification for the support which agriculture has received lies in its high rate of increase in output and, above all, in productivity; although, in turn, the reason for this success was its relative immunity from the repeated cuts and 'stops' by which Government policy prevented similar increases in the other sectors.[2]

Coal mining was another old staple industry which showed increases in productivity despite heavy losses in manpower. Here, also, rising efficiency was the result of better organization and heavy investment, though organizationally the industry was at the opposite pole from agriculture, consisting of a single nationalized decision-making centre instead of hundreds of thousands of small units.

Because of the run-down state of the industry, and the efforts which had to be devoted simply to reorganization in the early years of the National Coal Board, coal mining was slow to show any improvements in output per manshift after the war. Long-term improvement began with the plan of 1950[3] which proposed major reconstructions, the closure of 350–400 pits then working, new sinkings and general re-equipment to

---

[1] John R. Raeburn, 'Agricultural Production and Marketing', in Duncan Burn (ed.), *The Structure of British Industry* (2 vols., Cambridge, 1958), I, pp. 42–4; E. F. Nash, *Agricultural Policy in Britain: Selected Papers* (Cardiff, 1965).
[2] Peter Self and H. J. Storing, *The State and the Farmer* (1962), pp. 220 ff.; *Agriculture*, Cmnd. 1249 (1960); H. T. Williams, *Principles for British Agricultural Policy* (1960), pp. 64 ff., 167; Gavin McCrone, *The Economics of Subsidizing Agriculture. A Study of British Policy* (1962); O.E.C.D., *Agricultural Policies in 1966*.
[3] National Coal Board, *Plan for Coal* (1950); the revised plans were published as *Investing in Coal* (1956) and *Revised Plan for Coal* (1959). Cf. also A. Beacham, 'Planned Investment in the Coal Industry', *Oxf. Econ. P.*, 3/2 (1951) and K. S. Lomax, 'The Demand for Coal in Great Britain', *ibid.*, 4/1 (1952).

meet the estimated demand for coal for the next fifteen years, until 1965. In the early years, however, all the efforts did little beyond counteracting the natural tendency of mining costs to rise with the age of the workings. Output per manshift refused obstinately to reach the magic figure of 25 cwt., though it was on the brink of doing so in every year from 1950 to 1957. Total saleable output similarly did not rise beyond the 210 m.t. level, while from 1953 onward the number of workers in the industry actually began to fall. Throughout this period, the supply of coal was well below the demand, the gap being variously estimated as being between 15 and 20 million tons a year.[1] It is true that this 'gap' only existed because coal was seriously under-priced,[2] both in terms of costs (as the Coal Board used the lower average costs, instead of the higher marginal costs, as base) and in terms of what the market would bear, and coal thus became a hidden means of subsidizing British industry, even to the extent of negative dumping, or selling at a higher price abroad than at home. Yet the general assumption remained that coal would continue for many years to come to be in short supply, and the main problem would be to find means of expanding total output.

When the post-war world shortage of goods was followed, in the mid-1950's, by a world economic boom, including a marked expansion in Britain, the increase of demand found the industry unprepared to meet it. Incredible as it might have seemed to another age, coal had to be imported, to the tune of 25 million tons all told, much of it from the dollar area. Thus the booming demand led not just to full order books, full working, incentives to invest, and readiness thereby to meet the next expansion in demand, as it did elsewhere, but because of the neglect of earlier investment in productive capacity, to imports of a commodity traditionally produced at home.

However, the recession induced in 1957 and lasting until 1959 suddenly revealed the false basis of the planning for coal: a major change-over to oil, fostered by the coal shortage itself, was superimposed on the long-term decline in demand due to increasingly successful techniques of fuel-saving, and the beginnings of the conversion to atomic energy. Coal consumption in the United Kingdom fell from 214 million tons in 1956 to 187 million tons in 1959, while oil consumption rose from 18 to 33 million tons (coal equivalent) and 0·5 m.t. equivalent was produced by nuclear energy. Coal stocks began to build up to 8·6 m.t. at the end of 1957, 19·7 m.t. in 1958, and 35·7 m.t. or about two months' output at the end of 1959. Ironically, it was precisely at this point that the investment and reorganization of earlier years began to bear fruit. Productivity increased,

1 P.E.P., *Growth in the British Economy* (1960), pp. 99–103; Beacham, 'The Coal Industry', in Burn, *op. cit.*
2 I. M. D. Little, *The Price of Fuel* (Oxford, 1953).

413

and over-production, as in the inter-war years, appeared on the horizon. From the 1956 Plan, based on the belief that 'The National Coal Board's task is to raise the output of coal as high as they can to meet the country's increasing need for energy', there is a great gulf to the 1959 statement that 'In Britain, it is no longer necessary to plan to meet a continuous increase in demand.'[1]

This change in circumstances, which could easily have led to calamity for the industry, was overcome, and even turned to good account, by a consistent and massive programme of investment and reorganization. The plan of 1950 had involved the spending of £635 million in 1950–65. By 1956, the new plan envisaged a total of £1,350 million (or £500 million more, at 1955 prices) for a lower output target. The plan was changed again in 1959, in the light of the apparent permanent fall in demand, from the 1965 target of 240 m.t. to a target of 206 m.t., which was about the level of the actual 1959 production. This scaling down allowed the closing of high-cost pits to proceed even faster than had been intended, and the number of N.C.B. mines in production in Great Britain fell from 901 at the beginning of 1951 to 438 in March, 1967. Output per man-shift rose rapidly and continuously from 24·9 cwt. in 1957 to 36·6 cwt. in 1966–7, or by nearly one-half, and similarly output per man year stood at 293 t. in 1950 and 390 t. in 1966–7.

This striking success was reflected also in the accounts. In spite of the low-price policy, which deprived the National Coal Board of its own finance and forced it to increase its interest burden very heavily by outside borrowing, the rise in costs was kept below that of proceeds and in the mid-1960's it appeared that the Board might be permanently out of the red. The Board was also fortunate in its vigorous chairman, Lord Robens, who succeeded in reducing employment from a maximum of 711,000 in 1952 to 419,000 in 1967,[2] without arousing major opposition from the men. The care with which local closures and transfers of labour were prepared compared very favourably with the methods of some other industries in similar circumstances.

The reduction of the coal industry, however, is still only in its early stages. In November, 1967, a new White Paper[3] announced a planned reduction of manpower to one-sixth, or a mere 65,000 by 1980 in the seven main regions, and an expected share of coal of only 120 m.t. out of a national total of 350 m.t. coal equivalent by 1975, compared with 174·7 m.t. out of 297·7 m.t. in 1966. Despite the promised Government compensation payments of £133 million, of which £35 million was to go in

---

[1] The juxtaposition of these two views is in E. S. Simpson, *Coal and the Power Industries in Post-war Britain* (1966), p. 16.
[2] National Coal Board, *Annual Report and Accounts*.
[3] *Fuel Policy*, Cmnd. 3438 (1967).

redundancy pay to miners, the announcement caused bitter opposition in the mining areas.

In manufacturing, there were wide differences in the experience of different industries, some of which will be evident from the summary table below,[1] but space does not permit a detailed treatment of each. We must content ourselves with cursory descriptions of some select industries, representing respectively those rapidly expanding (motors, oil refining, chemicals), those growing at about the average rate (steel) and those actually declining (cotton, shipbuilding).

The motor car was, in many respects, the symbol of the post-war prosperity: a product of advanced technology and mass production, a luxury which had become a necessity, international in its influence and markets, a 'consumer durable' which permitted a distinct widening of the personal experiences, as well as an increase in the comforts of those possessing it, and, not least, typical in often being bought before it could be afforded, by means of credit. It was a colourful proof that the austerities and privations of the war years were over; it was also a yardstick of the producing country's industrial power.

The products of the British motor industry were destined both for the home market and for export, and the change from the post-war shortages, when markets were almost unlimited and the problem was merely one of capacity, came, as in most other industries, around the early 1950's. In the home market, supply did not catch up with the eager demand, and the sellers' market did not end, until 1955 or even later.[2] Abroad, the motor vehicle came to belong to the group of complex manufactured products for which there has been not only sharp and effective competition among exporters into the rapidly expanding markets which do not produce their own, but even expanding trade among the producing countries themselves.

On the face of it, Britain appeared to have done well, since her output rose 88% between 1955 and 1964 (or by 7·3% a year), compared with a world rise of only 63% (5·6). But world production outside the U.S.A. rose from 4,331,000 to 12,762,000 vehicles, or by no less than 195%,[3] and since then Japan has forged ahead much faster even than the Western European nations, to become the world's second largest producer, behind only the U.S.A. As for export performance, Britain kept her large share of the commercial vehicle market, but for private cars the story was typical of post-war development. At first, the United Kingdom occupied an unnaturally favourable position which she owed to the destruction wrought in the rest of Europe. By the late 1950's or early 1960's, however,

---

[1] pp. 426–7, below.
[2] G. Maxcy and A. Silberston, *The Motor Industry* (1959), pp. 18–19.
[3] A. Silberston, 'The Motor Industry 1955–1964', *Bull. Oxf. Inst. Stat.*, 27/4 (1965).

the leading competitors had not merely recaptured their share, but had overtaken the United Kingdom in the productivity of their plant and the skill of their salesmanship and presentation. Production of vehicles per employee year, 'adjusted' for certain incomparabilities, changed as follows:[1]

	1950	1959
France	3·2	5·7
W. Germany	2·2	5·6
U.K.	3·3	5·2
U.S.A.	10·0	10·3

Poor though this showing might be internationally, the annual increase of productivity of 4·5% compared well with only 2·4% per man year in industry as a whole. This rise was accompanied by a substantial increase in employment, so that the motor industry was undoubtedly one of the leading 'growth' industries in the post-war era:[2]

	Output, ooo vehicles		% exported	
	1951	1966	1951	1966
Passenger cars and taxis	476	1604	77	34
Commercial vehicles	258	439	53	36
Agricultural tractors	137	214	82	63

Total registrations of private cars increased in this period from under 2½ million to over 9½ million, and of commercial vehicles and tractors, from 1·4 million to 2·2 million. These figures do not tell the whole story, as motor vehicles did not remain the same. 'Quality' is a difficult concept, particularly in commodities as emotionally charged for some consumers as private motor cars, but there can be little doubt that the car of 1966 was technically a more efficient product than its equivalent of 1950, requiring less maintenance, standing up better to the rigours of long periods of fast motorway driving, and so on.

The motor industry thus repeated the experience of the main growth industries of the inter-war period. Rising demand owing to rising real incomes (demand for motor cars in this period increased three times as fast as incomes) met sharply falling cost curves at higher output. Important economies of scale began to occur at an annual output of 100,000 units, and the benefits of mass production continued to increase until at least the half-million output rate.[3] Mass production was achieved by a two-pronged approach. On the one hand, the number of models was reduced, though this movement was to some extent counter-acted by firms like

[1] *Ibid.*, p. 270.

[2] Min. of Transport. There was some re-classification, esp. of estate cars for export, between 1952 and 1953. The output of 1964 and 1965 had been substantially above that of 1966.

[3] A. Silberston, 'The Motor Industry', in D. L. Burn, *op. cit.*, II, p. 18.

Vauxhall which entered the small car market with the 'Victor', and most major firms tried to cash in on the success of the mini-car. The second and more effective method was a striking movement of amalgamation which, together with substantial American share purchases, turned the numerous firms of 1945 into little more than four large groups, of which one was British owned (Leyland–B.M.C.), and the other three were subsidiaries of the three major U.S. Companies, Ford, General Motors (Vauxhall) and Chrysler (Rootes). Between them, they controlled over 95% of car output and 90% of commercial vehicle output. Among the main landmarks were the mergers of Standard and Triumph (1945), Austin and Nuffield (1952), Rootes and Singer (1955), Jaguar and Daimler (1960), Leyland and Standard-Triumph (1961) and Leyland and B.M.C. (1968).[1] In the 1950's, at a time when the steel industry was unable to supply sufficient sheet steel to the British car industry, there was also a general scramble to link up with the body manufacturers, including Ford–Briggs Motor Bodies (1953), B.M.C.–Fisher & Ludlow (1953), B.S.A.–Car Bodies (1954), Standard–Mulliners (1958), and B.M.C.–Pressed Steel. The motor industry, as an assembly industry, pays over about half its costs to components manufacturers, other than body builders, and these also became dominated by a few large firms which might secure even longer runs by standardizing output between rival car makers: Joseph Lucas for electrical equipment, S. Smith and Sons, and Champion for sparking plugs and other equipment and Dunlop for tyres.

Like the motor car itself, the industry, with its high wages necessary to attract labour and its high expansion rate, became a major part of post-war industrial growth. Considerable pressure was applied to it by the Government to prevent its expansion in the prosperous Southern and Midland areas in which it was centred, like Dagenham, Luton, Birmingham and Coventry, and to move its new plants into the development areas. In the early 1960's, in consequence, Rootes opened a plant in Linwood, Scotland, for the production of the 'Imp' model, Vauxhall's developed a unit in Ellesmere Port, Standard-Triumph in Speke (Liverpool), Fords at Halewood (Merseyside) and B.M.C. in Llanelly. At the same time, the sharp decline in motor-car production after 1964, at a time when world demand was still expanding, illustrates perfectly the tragic consequences of an economic policy which seeks to ensure progress and prosperity by cutting production, creating idle capacity of plant and labour and severely damaging the incentive to invest.

Linked with the boom in motors was the expansion in oil refining.

---

[1] G. Maxcy, 'The Motor Industry', in P. Lesley Cook (ed.), *Effects of Mergers* (1958). In the B.M.C. (or more correctly, B. M. Holdings) merger with Leyland, official support was forthcoming with an investment of £25 million by the Industrial Re-organization Corporation.

Here the pre-war policy of siting the refineries abroad near the crude oil fields, and importing the refined products, has given way to the opposite policy of building up refining capacity in this country, sufficient to provide even for exports. The reasons were partly strategic and partly arose out of the need to save imports, but a home-based oil refining industry also provided some flexibility in varying the proportions of the product according to home needs and created a base for the petro-chemical industry. Again, there was a rapidly growing market, partly by replacing coal and partly by meeting new needs, as in transport;[1] and again, larger throughput led to lower costs, so that a refinery of a capacity of 10 million tons had little more than one-third of the unit costs of a refinery of a half-million ton capacity. Beginning with the Shell plant at Stanlow (1947) and the Esso refinery at Fawley (1951), capacity in Britain increased from 29 million tons in 1953 to 88 million tons at the end of 1966. At the latter date, all but 2% of the refining was carried out in plants of over 1 million tons capacity, and three plants were at, or near, the 10 million ton optimum: Fawley (Esso), Kent (B.P.) and Shell Haven (Shell).[2]

The industry is highly capital intensive, and the small labour force showed one of the fastest rises in productivity per man in British industry. It is dominated by a handful of giants, British, American and Dutch, all with large international interests, forming one of the world's most powerful oligopolies.[3] Nevertheless, competition was fierce in certain areas and one form which it took after 1945, the buying up and tying in of the retail outlets, the petrol stations, was in striking parallel to the action of the brewers over half a century earlier. Opinion was divided on the value of this system to the customers, but the Monopolies Commission refused to condemn it outright.[4]

Chemicals, the third among our examples of fast-growing industries, combines, like the other two, rapid technological progress with the opportunity of displacing older industries as well as creating new markets. The limits of the industry are ill-defined, and on some counts oil refining itself might be subsumed under it. A rough division into heavy chemicals and fine chemicals, such as pharmaceutical products, is often used, and there is also a dividing line between the production of intermediate raw materials and the production of finished or semi-finished goods such as

---

[1] E. S. Simpson, *op. cit.*, chapters 8 and 10; J. H. Dunning and C. J. Thomas, *British Industry, Change and Development in the Twentieth Century* (1961), pp. 89–92.

[2] C. Pratten and R. M. Dean, *The Economics of Large-Scale Production in British Industry* (Cambridge, 1965), pp. 93, 97; Duncan Burn, 'The Oil Industry', in *Structure of British Industry*, I.

[3] Peter Odell, *Oil: The New Commanding Height* (Fabian Society, 1965), pp. 5–7.

[4] Monopolies Commission, *Petrol: A Report on the Supply of Petrol to Retailers in the United Kingdom* (1965); Harry Townsend, 'Exclusive Dealing in Petrol: Some Comments', *Economica*, 32/128 (1965).

paints, plastics or man-made fibres. Yet the processes used, if not commercial considerations also, impose much vertical and horizontal integration and the chemical industry, in Britain and elsewhere, remained in this period one of the most highly concentrated of modern industries. I.C.I. alone employed about one-third of the labour force[1] and there have been several mergers among the other giants. The major take-over bid, by I.C.I., was, however, beaten off successfully by Courtauld's, the intended victim, in a dramatic battle in 1961, in which I.C.I. had obtained as much as 38% of the Courtauld shares.

Technical progress in this industry, also, though faster than in earlier periods, compared badly with the achievements of other countries. Britain, for example, delayed too long the switch from coal-based to gas- or oil-based technology, and fell behind in the production of plastics. In this, as in other faster-than-average growth industries heavily based on science and technology like electronics and man-made fibres, for which reasons of space forbid more detailed treatment,[2] we find the same story of inadequate investment in new capacity and tardy adoption of new technology, so that the windfall technical lead acquired during the war and still held in 1950 was lost and competitive power suffered.[3] In boom years, not even the home market could be supplied because of shortage of capacity and, instead of rising exports, there were merely sharp increases in imports. The similarity in the development of these varied industries leads to the conclusion that the 'fault', if any, did not lie with them, but derived from the circumstances in which they operated.

Among industries of near-average growth, the iron and steel industry occupied an important place. It was representative in providing the raw material both for capital goods, such as machines, ships, buildings, vehicles and bridges, as also for many of the durable consumer goods, on which so much of the newly increased income was expended.

The first iron and steel nationalization was only temporary: the Conservative Government announced at once its intention, achieved by the Iron and Steel Act of 1953, to sell the industry back to private owners, but leaving 'an adequate measure of public supervision'[4] to be exercised by the Iron and Steel Board. A separate Iron and Steel Holding and Realization Agency was to dispose of the shares and by 1957 had sold 86%; after 1963

---

[1] W. B. Reddaway, 'The Chemical Industry', in *Structure of British Industry*, I, and C. J. Thomas, 'The Pharmaceutical Industry', *ibid.*, II.

[2] E.g., Thomas Wilson, 'The Electronics Industry' and D. C. Hague, 'The Man-Made Fibres Industry', *ibid.*, II.

[3] The mid-1960's did, however, see some massive investments and the I.C.I. issue of £50 million in 1965 was the largest such private operation since the war. S. J. Wells, *Trade Policies for Britain* (1966), pp. 92–3.

[4] Quoted in A. J. Youngson, *Britain's Economic Growth, 1920–1966* (1967), p. 217.

those of only one firm, Richard Thomas & Baldwin, were left, and were held by the State until the second nationalization act.[1] The Board's function included the fixing of maximum prices at such a level 'as to make it very difficult indeed for the uneconomic unit to continue in existence',[2] investment policies, raw materials supplies and distribution, research and education, and welfare and labour relations. Within this fairly tight framework, each company was encouraged to maximize its profits competitively.

By 1950 capacity had been raised to 16 million tons of steel and was still very much below demand, particularly since artificially low coal and scrap prices kept steel prices down. A second 'plan' in 1952 envisaged investment at around £60 million a year, to raise capacity to over 20 million tons, later revised to 22½ million tons, by about 1957. This, however, was still well below national needs and forced Britain to spend foreign exchange on imports of sheet steel and other similar products in the 1950's. Indeed, so grave was the shortage that a system of home rationing, known as the 'distribution system', was not ended until 1953, and export restrictions or limitations persisted until 1959.

A third development plan was published in 1957, envisaging an increase in capacity to 29 million tons by 1962, and it was under its provision that some of the most important new plants were built and others extended, including the continuous strip mills at Ravenscraig and in South Wales and the R.T.B. Spencer Works at Newport, while the Dorman-Long Lockerby plant, a universal beam mill, was opened in 1958. Conversions to electricity and to oxygen processes, such as the L.D. or Kaldo furnaces, and extensions at Shotton, Appleby-Frodingham, Stocksbridge and elsewhere were also undertaken, though no complete new plant was put up. Fixed capital investment which had fluctuated around £60-80 million a year in 1947–55 (at constant, 1963 prices), rose to a peak of £207 million in 1961, only to drop back to c. £75 million by 1963-4.[3] A fourth plan, in April 1961, envisaged a further increase in capacity to 32 million tons in 1965, and a fifth plan, published under the shadow of nationalization in 1966, aimed at a capacity of 35·3 million tons in 1975, but the sellers' market had collapsed meanwhile and sales resistance was felt first in the recession of 1957–9, and more strongly after 1961. To some extent, steel was a victim of the failure of the economy as a whole to grow as fast as expected after 1957, having been an important cause of that failure before 1957; technological changes, steel 'economies' and displacement by

[1] Duncan Burn, 'Steel', in *Structure of British Industry*, I, pp. 298–300; G. W. Ross, *The Nationalization of Steel* (1965), pp. 153, *passim*.

[2] Aubrey Jones in a Commons debate, quoted in D. L. Burn, *The Steel Industry, 1939–1959* (Cambridge, 1961), p. 373.

[3] B. S. Keeling and A. E. G. Wright, *The Development of the Modern British Steel Industry* (1964), p. 129. See also J. C. Carr and W. Taplin, *History of the British Steel Industry* (Oxford, 1962).

other materials also played a part.[1] But British steel was also falling behind other countries in competitive power. The loss of technical leadership and the gap opening out between the lagging technology of the British industry as a whole, and its rapidly advancing chief foreign rivals, were among the most striking of any industry,[2] even before the massive production increases of the Japanese steel makers made themselves felt in traditional British markets. Thus, when the home market was depressed by Government policy, in the early 1960's, the industry found difficulty in disposing of its products abroad. Exports, which had had to be artificially kept down to $2\frac{1}{2}$–3 million tons in the 1950's, rose only to 4 million tons in the 1960's, while imports continued to be held down to around the 1 million ton mark by rising protective margins. Output in Britain doubled in 1950–66 and average furnace capacity, a fair measure of technical efficiency,[3] increased threefold; but in the same period world production almost quadrupled, the British average furnace was still much smaller than that of its main rivals in the E.E.C. and in Japan,[4] and the British share of world output fell from 10% in 1950 to 5% at the end of the period.

By the Iron and Steel Act of 1967, the fourteen major units of the industry were nationalized for the second time and the National Steel Corporation set up to administer them. It is too early to say how far the new ownership will speed up expansion and modernization, or how far the Corporation will become the victim, like other heavy capital spenders among the nationalized industries, of Treasury interference with their long-term capital plans for short-term reasons.

Among industries growing less than the average or in absolute decline, cotton was one of the most significant. In the early post-war years it experienced a striking expansion in demand, showing large increases in output and peaks in exports for piece goods in 1949 and yarn in 1951. In those years, every available worker was employed (though not all spindle and loom capacity) and more could have been exported, if it could have been produced.[5] From 1951, however, the decline was swift, and might

---

[1] Keeling and Wright, pp. 95–7; British Iron and Steel Federation, *The Steel Industry, Stage I Report of the Development Co-ordinating Committee* (1966).
[2] Burn, *Steel Industry*, pp. 558, *passim*.
[3] The notional index of costs was as follows:

Blast furnace:

capacity of			Open hearth furnace size:	
	100,000 t.p.a.	131	75 t.	131
	200,000 t.p.a.	100	150 t.	100
	1,000,000 t.p.a.	58	400 t.	85
	1,500,000 t.p.a.	52		

Pratten and Dean, pp. 67, 70.
[4] Wells, *op. cit.*, p. 99.
[5] G. W. Furness, 'The Cotton and Rayon Textile Industry', in *Structure of British Industry*, II.

have been swifter still but for quotas and high protection including voluntary ceilings of exports to Britain from Commonwealth countries since 1958, and regulations for imports from low wage countries, laid down by G.A.T.T. in 1962. When the decline set in, labour moved out fairly smoothly, since there was a general high level of employment in the area, but over-capacity in capital equipment was less easily dealt with. It was estimated in 1959 to have reached 30% in spinning, 60% in doubling, and 25–40% in finishing. The cotton industry thus appeared to be in an exceptionally unfavourable position in an otherwise booming Britain and the Government, in two minds whether to make grants for scrapping old plant or for installing new, was pressurized into doing both. The Cotton Industry Act, 1959, the first major post-war measure for aid towards the scrapping of obsolete plant, provided for the payment of two-thirds of the compensation by the Government, and one third by an industrial levy. Displaced labour was also to obtain compensation; and the Government, in addition, was to make grants covering a quarter of the cost of any new machinery installed before 1962. The effectiveness of the Act was greater and speedier than had been anticipated. Plans were completed for spinning, doubling and weaving in 1959, and for finishing in 1960. By the end of March, the number of spindles had been cut by nearly half (12·4 million out of 25·3 million), and the number of looms by two-fifths (105,000 out of 259,000); 300 mills were closed completely in 1959–60 and a total of over £30 million was ultimately paid out for scrapping and for new plant.[1]

The result was a remarkable rise in productivity as total employment fell. Even so, this rise was still much slower than the productivity rises abroad: between 1956 and 1961, the increase of 10% in the U.K. compared with 15% in Belgium, 28% in France and 52% in Italy.[2] Similar comparisons could be made in other declining or stagnant industries, as in wool and worsted spinning and weaving, in the clothing industry and in leather and furs.

Finally, among declining manufacturing industries, shipbuilding deserves a special mention. Again, following the short-term post-war competitive advantage because of the destruction of shipyard capacity among other belligerents, and the inability of the rest of the world to buy tonnage launched in the dollar areas, it is the relative British decline in competitiveness with the shipyards of other countries which is most striking. In the years 1949–51, the United Kingdom was still the leading producer for exports (i.e. foreign registration), selling 522,000 gross tons, or 38% of the

[1] P. D. Henderson, 'Government and Industry', in Worswick and Ady, *The British Economy in the Nineteen-Fifties* (1962), p. 351; *Reorganization of the Cotton Industry*, Cmnd. 744 (1959); *Economist*, 2nd April, 1960.

[2] Kenneth Keith, 'Finance and Structural Change in British Industry with Particular Reference to Cotton', *Moorgate and Wall Street* (Autumn, 1963), p. 26.

world total; by 1956, she had become a poor third behind Japan and Germany, selling 435,000 g.t., or less than 14%; by 1967, sales were an exceptional 612,000 g.t. but in 1964-6 they had averaged only 186,000 g.t. a year.[1] Similarly, total merchant tonnage launched in 1950 was 1,325,000 g.t., compared with a world total of 3,489,000 g.t., and in 1966 1,084,000 g.t. out of a world total of 14,307,000. In that year, Britain slipped to fourth place among the world's producing nations.

In the 1950's the chief competitors had been other European producers, such as Sweden and Germany, using mass production techniques on standardized vessels or standardized components, and a highly efficient technology. Since then, Japan has come to dominate the international market entirely, defeating opposition both on cost grounds and on technological ability of building super-tankers measuring hundreds of thousands of gross tons. Any growth of this magnitude attracts to itself the further advantages of mass production. Japan now produces twice the tonnage of her nearest three rivals together; and without hidden and other subsidies, her share would be larger still, and the British share much smaller. The Geddes report of 1966 found fault with out-of-date equipment, poor sites, divided trade union allegiance leading to costly demarcation disputes and relatively high costs of labour and raw materials in British yards. To become competitive, costs would have to be lowered by 15%, and the proposed remedies included rationalization, standardization and amalgamation. Government support, totalling some £68 million in credit and compensation for losses, was to be made available to bring about the amalgamation of the sixty-two yards into three or four large combines, of which two were to be in the North-East and one or two on the Clyde. The fifteen unions were similarly to amalgamate into five. In this way, the British share of the world market, which had fallen steadily to 10%, was to be raised to 12½%.[2] Meanwhile, the Fairfield yard on the Clyde, one of the best equipped in the country, had to be rescued from bankruptcy by the Government, which reconstructed the firm in February 1966, a month before the Geddes Committee Report, and provided £1½ million of the £2 million of new capital required. One of the objects of the new management under Iain Stewart was to improve labour relations and labour productivity, but its first productivity agreement went off to a bad start when it was caught by the insensitive axe of the total wage standstill of 1966.

Lastly, the post-war years have seen important changes also in the provision of services. In transport, the outstanding development has been

[1] A. K. Cairncross and J. R. Parkinson, 'The Shipbuilding Industry', in *Structure of British Industry*, II, p. 102; Lloyd's Register, *Annual Summary of Merchant Ships Launched*.

[2] *Shipbuilding Inquiry Committee 1965-6, Report*, Cmnd. 2937 (1966).

the progressive replacement of the railways and shipping by road and air transport, respectively. This had been a pre-war development, only interrupted by the war, and in the 1950's the trend was quickly resumed: every year saw a transfer of traffic to the roads. In consequence, the railways saw a yearly decline in the surplus out of which interest had to be paid; in 1956 they registered the first working deficit, i.e. before meeting central charges, and by 1958 the working deficit had rocketed to £48 million. As in the subsequent years the competitive position continued to deteriorate, all attempts to wipe out the deficit proved abortive, but meanwhile its existence led to a bewildering series of changes in policy, which could only have increased the difficulties of those who had actually to manage the railway system.

The avalanche of conflicting advice which descended upon British Railways had two broad targets: organization and technical equipment and control. On the first, the Transport Act of 1953 made provision for returning the road haulage services to private ownership. In the event, only a proportion of vehicles was sold before 1956, when the sales ended, and by the Transport (Disposal of Road Haulage Property) Act, 1956, British Road Services were to keep not only the parcels service of the railways, but also to retain a main trunk network. The Act of 1953 followed the white paper in laying down a policy of substantial autonomy for the Regions, and by abolishing the Railway Executive, it left the British Transport Commission to supervise, rather than manage, a series of disparate enterprises, including a substantial proportion of road vehicles.[1] More usefully, many of the restrictive powers of the Transport Tribunal were abolished, giving greater pricing freedom to the railways. A white paper of 1960[2] proposed to carry the policy of decentralization still further, by creating separate boards for railways, for London Transport, the docks, inland waterways and a holding company for the auxiliary services, such as British Road Services, buses, hotels and Thomas Cook and Son. Meanwhile, the Transport Tribunal, which had on several occasions considerably increased the losses of the railways by withholding or delaying rate increases, was to be shorn of its power, except for London.[3]

Further, the neglect and run-down of capital were at last to give way to some re-equipment from the mid-1950's onwards. A plan of 1955 envisaged the investment of £1,200 million (at 1954 prices) in fifteen years, divided about equally between maintenance and modernization of track, the introduction of diesel and electric drive, etc., and proposed the

---

[1] *Transport Policy*, Cmd. 8538 (1952); Gilbert Walker and C. I. Savage, 'Inland Carriage by Road and Rail', in *Structure of British Industry*, I.

[2] *Reorganization of the Nationalized Transport Undertakings*, Cmnd. 1248 (1960).

[3] D. L. Munby, 'The Nationalized Industries', in Worswick & Ady, *op. cit.*, p. 383; P.E.P., *Growth*, pp. 86 ff.

closing of unprofitable branch lines.[1] As in the case of the other major staple industries, such as coal and steel, there was an undue delay in the post-war years before plans for modernization were made and implemented; and, again as in other sectors, the rate of investment, which increased satisfactorily in the late 1950's, was soon cut down for reasons of short-term Treasury policy and because long-term prospects deteriorated. In the case of the railways, it was the mounting deficits and the loss of traffic which led to the reappraisal of reconstruction policies. Traffic volume and shares changed as follows:[2]

		Volume of Traffic		% Shares	
		1952	1962	1952	1962
Passengers	Railways	24·1	22·9	21	13
(billion passenger	Public Road	50·1	42·4	45	25
miles)	Private Road	37·9	103·7	34	61
Freight	Railways	22·4	16·1	54	32
(billion ton-miles)	Roads	18·8	33·6	46	68

Since then, motor traffic has increased from an index of 135 in 1962 (1958 = 100) to 186 in the first eleven months of 1967, and road ton miles from an index of 135 to 163, while rail ton miles fell from 89 to 80, and rail passenger journeys from 74 million to 64 million.[3]

In 1959 the earlier plan was optimistically extended to a total of £1,500 million (at 1958 prices), much of it to be spent in the next four years, when investment was to run at £200 million a year,[4] and it was still hoped to turn the annual deficit into a surplus by these means. But 1959-60 proved to be a turning-point. There was to be a new policy not only in organization, but also in equipment. Investment was cut down to about £100 million p.a. in 1963-4. Dr. Beeching, a leading industrialist, was called in in 1961 to advise, and while the 'Beeching Report',[5] which opened in 1963, did not disagree fundamentally with the diagnosis of 1955, the remedy was now put on closures rather than on re-equipment. The only mention of the latter in the report was an estimate of new rolling-stock, liner trains, etc., of £250 million over an unspecified period. The main

[1] British Transport Commission, *Modernization and Re-equipment of British Railways* (1955), and *Proposals for the Railways*, Cmd. 9880 (1956); M. Beesley and A. A. Walters, 'Investment in British Railways', *Westminster Bank Review* (May 1955).

[2] W. Beckerman and Associates, *The British Economy in 1975* (Cambridge, 1965), p. 326, Table 11.2.

[3] *Monthly Digest of Statistics.*

[4] British Transport Commission, *Reappraisal of the Plan for the Modernization and Re-equipment of British Railways*, Cmnd. 813 (1959).

[5] British Railways Board, *The Reshaping of British Railways* (1963); also D. L. Munby, 'The Reshaping of British Railways', *J. of Industrial Economics*, II/3 (1963).

proposal was the closure of 5,000 miles of track, together with 2,363 out of 4,293 passenger stations. Against this, freight handling was to be rationalized and the trunk lines were to provide a faster and more efficient competitive service. Thus the reduction in the deficit was to be achieved largely by cutting costs, rather than by attracting new traffic, and the reduction in the labour force by 1966 was put at 70,000. These proposals were accepted in principle, and many of the closures were carried out quickly, while the benefits of the better rolling-stock and some important track improvement like the electrification of the London–Manchester line, which derived from the earlier planned investment, also helped the management of the railways. Nevertheless, the deficit remained and no co-ordinated transport policy has yet emerged, though a battery of white papers issued in 1967[1] foreshadowed a major co-ordinating Transport Act in 1968.

On roads, curiously, new investment also lagged until the mid-1950's, but in their case, the momentum of the increase has been supported by powerful pressure groups and has been maintained. Even here, however, investment in major trunk road schemes and motorways has been too erratic to get the full economies of contractors' teamwork. Official figures of public expenditure on the roads show the slow start of new building (as against repair, etc.) and its sharp increase in the late 1950's (£mn current):[2]

	Expenditure on 'Roads and Public Lighting'			Road Expenditure (Min. Transport)	
Average of Years	Current	Capital Formation	Total	Fiscal Year	Total
1950–1	87	12	99	1949–50	71
1955–6	115	28	143	1955–56	111
1960–1	152	106	258	1960–61	196
1964–5	209	212	421	1965–66	369

In 1960, it was estimated that 10% of all urban roads and 4% of non-urban roads, or a total of nearly 11,000 miles, was 'overloaded'.[3] Since then, the number of motor vehicles licensed has increased faster than the road improvements, vehicles per mile having grown from 48·6 in 1960 to 65·8 in 1966, while a total of only 288 miles of motorway were opened since then, and 7,880 miles of other roads, or an increase of 8%, while traffic has increased by 44%. With current policies, the 'Buchanan Report' forecasts worsening urban congestion.[4]

This cursory review of certain sectors of the economy cannot give a complete picture of the development of the productive equipment of the

---

[1] *British Waterways*, Cmnd. 3401; *Railway Policy*, Cmnd. 3439; *The Transport of Freight*, Cmnd. 3470; *Public Transport and Traffic*, Cmnd. 3481.

[2] *National Income and Expenditure*; British Road Federation, *Basic Road Statistics* (1967).

[3] Beckerman, p. 358.

[4] *Traffic in Towns* (1963).

nation in 1950–67. It is intended merely as an illustration of some typical experiences of the primary, secondary and tertiary (service) industries in a period of solid, if chequered, expansion. An overall view reveals that few industries deviated very widely from the norm of slow annual rises in productivity and this is not, perhaps, surprising if we recall that it is essentially based on improved technology in its widest sense. This, by its nature, is likely to spread into most if not all fields. Where, however, new techniques were difficult to apply or were slow in appearance, e.g. in service trades like retail distribution, the rising real wages created by general productivity rises and transmitted by the pressures of the labour market and trade union power to the laggard sector, set up particularly strong incentives to save the now dearer labour by re-organization. The self-service revolution in retailing[1] typifies this reaction. Where, on the other hand, productivity rises were well above the average, then unless the industry was very small and in its early growth stages in this period, like oil refining, the general sluggishness of the growth of the economy as a whole held back the potential expansion of the favoured industry, and inhibited massive investment in new methods of the kind which could be absorbed by faster-growing economies like those of Germany or Japan.

Average Annual Percentage Rates of Growth by Industries, 1950–60[2]

		Net Output	Employment	Productivity
Primary Industries:	Agriculture, forestry, fishing	2·0	−2·5	4·5
	Coal mining	−1·1	−0·7	−0·4
	Other mining and quarrying	2·7	−1·1	3·8
Manufacturing Industries:	Mineral oil refining	11·3	3·2	8·1
	Motors and cycles	7·2	1·6	5·1
	Other chemicals	6·4	1·5	4·9
	Aircraft and railway rolling-stock	5·4	2·2	3·2
	Other manufacturing	4·6	1·8	2·8
	Paper, printing and publishing	4·5	1·9	2·6
	Engineering and electrical goods	3·8	1·5	2·3

[1] By 1966 it was estimated that 44% of grocery sales were in self-service stores or supermarkets, and the conversion rate was 150–200 stores per month.

[2] Beckerman, pp. 214, 216, 231, 233, Tables 7.6, 7.7, 7.11, 7.12. Cf. also K. S. Lomax, 'Growth and Productivity in the United Kingdom', *Productivity Measurement Review*, 38 (1964), p. 18, and 'Production and Productivity Movements in the United Kingdom since 1900', *J. R. Stat. S.*, 122/2, Series A (1959), for changes in annual average output per operative-hour in different industries; also C. H. Feinstein, 'Production and Productivity', *London and Cambridge Bulletin*, 48 (1963).

	Net Output	Employment	Productivity
Non-ferrous metals	3·1	1·8	1·5
Iron and steel	2·5	0·2	2·3
Food processing	2·5	1·7	0·8
Other metal goods	2·4	0·7	1·7
Drink and tobacco	2·2	0·4	1·8
Pottery and glass	2·0	−0·5	2·5
Timber, furniture	1·8	−0·2	2·0
Coke ovens	1·8	2·9	−1·1
Building materials	1·7	0·3	1·4
Leather, clothes, footwear	1·3	−0·8	2·1
Shipbuilding and marine engineering	0·6	−0·4	1·0
Textiles	−0·4	−1·8	1·4
Total manufacturing	*3·6*	*1·1*	*2·4*
Service and Other Industries: Construction	2·7	0·8	1·9
Gas	−0·8	−1·2	0·4
Electricity	8·4	1·5	6·9
Water	0·8	1·2	−0·4
Transport and communication	1·6	−0·6	2·2
Distributive trades	2·9	2·2	0·7
Other services	2·8	(1·3)	1·5
Total Gross Domestic Product	*2·5*	*0·7*	*1·8*

A cursory inspection will show the tendency for output and productivity in manufacturing to rise slightly faster than elsewhere and to pull the economy up with it, while productivity in the services tended to lag. Average output in the main sectors for 1964-6 compared as follows (1950–2 = 100):[1]

Agriculture, forestry, fishery	142
Industrial production	155
Transport and communications	139
Distributive trades	149
Other services (inc. Government)	136
Total output of goods and services	146·5

In productivity there was a similar differential. Output per person in the second quarter of 1967 for the economy as a whole was 39% above 1950 (35% in 1966), but in manufacturing it was 47% (45%), and output per man-hour in manufacturing, because of the shorter time worked, was as high as 56% (52%) above the 1950 level.[2]

On the other hand, the often expressed view that productivity gains were greatest in the fastest growing industries and vice versa, is not as

[1] Min. of Labour, *National Statistics on Incomes, Prices, Employment and Production* (re-calculated from base of 1958 = 100).

[2] *National Institute Economic Review*, 42 (November, 1967) and earlier issues, re-calculated from bases 1954 = 100 and 1958 = 100.

clearly borne out by the statistics as it once was. At the extremes, it is true, electricity, oil refining, motors and chemicals were leading on both counts, and coal mining and gas showed poor results in both production and productivity. On the other hand, agriculture, pottery and textiles had reasonable increases in productivity despite their overall stagnation or even decline, while the distributive trades and coke ovens had a poor productivity record, despite a fair growth. On a slightly different list of industries, the correlation coefficient of the rise in output with the rise in output per head was +0·81 for the years 1924–50, but only +0·69 for 1954–63. As the 'fit' was better among the faster growing industries than among the industries near the bottom of the table, some of which, like cotton, had a very good productivity record after the war (while before the war the correlation was good throughout), it has been suggested that full employment, creating labour shortages even in declining industries, has forced all industries, growing and declining alike, to substitute capital and organization for labour.[1] Insofar as it is true, it is a powerful argument

[1] W. E. G. Salter, with W. B. Reddaway, *Productivity and Technical Change* (2nd ed., Cambridge, 1966), pp. 82, 123, 206–7. The following figures for 1963 (index 1954 = 100) show the facts on which the judgment is based (p. 197):

	Gross Output	Total Employment	Output per Operative
Electricity	209·5	118·0	179·8
Chemicals (general)	186·9	117·2	171·9
Toilet preparations	155·3	146·2	109·1
Fertilizers, etc.	154·3	100·5	171·3
Misc. paper manufactures	147·1	109·3	139·0
Glass	146·8	111·0	140·6
Paper and board	139·4	120·5	121·1
Hosiery and knitted goods	136·0	98·6	142·0
Linoleum, leathercloth, etc.	135·9	120·5	123·3
Wire and wire manufactures	132·9	112·2	122·0
Rubber	126·5	108·7	124·6
Non-ferrous metals	125·9	102·6	125·8
Steel tubes	125·7	119·3	107·5
Brewing and malting	123·4	111·1	112·6
Paint and printing ink	122·8	94·4	140·2
Cement	117·2	111·9	108·7
Footwear	113·2	84·8	135·7
Iron and steel (general)	109·6	103·7	112·1
Bricks, fireclay, etc.	106·1	84·6	128·0
Dyestuffs	105·6	83·8	129·9
Cutlery	103·6	95·2	115·8
Jute	101·0	89·8	114·9
Cocoa and confectionery	97·5	93·7	108·6
Brushes and brooms	93·3	79·3	128·5
Coal mining	86·9	77·4	114·8
Coke ovens	86·4	90·5	98·9
Leather	85·9	71·8	118·3
Cotton spinning, etc.	69·2	55·0	129·1

against the notion, canvassed from time to time, that Britain should seek the salvation of a faster growth rate by maintaining a higher rate of unemployment since it suggests that it is the high demand, and high cost, of labour which induces technical innovation. It is noticeable, however, that the declining industries with best productivity records, namely agriculture, coal and cotton, have received direct Government support or incentives for massive investment and re-equipment.

It was also found that science-based industries (i.e. those with a high expenditure on research and development) grew faster than the average. Again, the correlation between such expenditure and the growth rate was better if the pre-war position is taken into account, the coefficient being $+0.93$ for 1935–58, but even for the post-war period it was still $+0.63$.[1]

The changes tabulated here hide a considerable switch in employment in a relatively short time. The flexibility of the labour market was at least as great as in any other period in recent history, in spite of full employment, the hoarding of labour by employers, rent control, pension schemes and other factors which were alleged to have inhibited it. Further, this switch occurred at a time when a large proportion of the most mobile population emigrated, and the actual increase in the male working population was very small, though the numbers, and proportions, of females seeking work outside the home continued to grow and made up (with the immigrants) most of the increase in the total.

The striking shift between 1948 and 1959 may be summarized as follows (in thousands):[2]

Gains: Increase in working		*Absorptions:* Manufacturing	973
population	1,188	Distribution	471
Released from:		Services	324
Defence	281	Local Govt.	81
Agriculture	178	Building and	
National Govt.	162	contracting	56
Mining	52		
	1,861		1,905

Since then, not only has the shift out of agriculture and mining accelerated, but within manufacturing itself, treated here as a single item, there have been substantial switches. Thus, between the end of 1950 and June 1967, there have been the following gains and losses in some individual industries (in thousands):[3]

[1] C. Freeman: 'Research and Development: A Comparison between British and American Industry', *National Institute Economic Review*, 20 (May 1962); B. Williams, 'Research Development and Economic Growth in the United Kingdom', *International Social Science Journal*, 18/3 (1966), pp. 413–14.
[2] Roy Harrod, *The British Economy* (New York, 1963), pp. 70–1.
[3] *Ministry of Labour Gazette*, 'Employees in Employment'.

Losses		Gains	
Vehicles	−149	Food, drink and tobacco	+29
Textiles	−332	Chemicals, etc.	+33
Leather, leather goods,		Metal manufacture	+48
fur	−23	Engineering, electrical and	
Clothing and footwear	−146	shipbuilding	+555
Timber, furniture	−8	Metal goods	+57
		Bricks, pottery, etc.	+14
		Paper, printing, publishing	+112

It will be seen that, in general, the pre-war trends have been maintained in this period.

Finally, the pre-war momentum towards greater concentration and a greater degree of monopolistic power was also sustained. Over the long term, there were signs of concentration both in terms of plant size and in terms of firm size,[1] pointing to the search for higher productivity by larger scale as at least part of the motivation behind the merger movement. From the early 1950's on, however, the commercial motive of reducing competition became more evident, and it was significant that stagnant or declining industries showed a greater tendency to concentration than expanding ones, in which technical advantages of scale were often high.[2]

One particular technique which attracted much attention at that time was the 'take-over bid', in which one company was able to acquire control of another by offering to buy out its shareholders at prices much above market quotations, and was able to do so profitably because balance sheet assets had been under-valued, or dividends had been kept unduly low in relation to earnings. Such a take-over represented a cashing in on hidden capital appreciation. Another method, particularly suitable in stores and offices, was to sell the premises or freehold, retaining a long lease, and use the capital thus freed to buy up similar property, to repeat the process in a snowballing series. Other entrepreneurs created holding companies in which their own limited holdings controlled large quantities of non-voting share capital. Some of the most spectacular post-war fortunes were made by these methods.[3] Indeed, speculation in urban land and city centre 'development' proved to be among the most profitable activities in the

[1] Alan Armstrong and Aubrey Silberston, 'Size of Plant, Size of Enterprise and Concentration in British Manufacturing Industry, 1935–1958', *J. R. Stat. S.*, 128/3, Series A (1965).
[2] K. D. George, 'Changes in British Industrial Concentration 1951–1958', *J. of Industrial Economics*, 15/3 (1967). This inverse correlation between growth and concentration was not, however, found by W. G. Shepherd, 'Changes in British Industrial Concentration, 1951–1958', *Oxf. Econ. P.*, 18/1 (1966).
[3] William Mennell, *Take-over: The Growth of Monopoly in Britain, 1951–1961* (1962); J. F. Wright, 'The Capital Market and the Finance of Industry', Worswick and Ady., *op. cit.*, pp. 464–73.

expansion years of the 1950's and diverted much scarce capital from more productive employment.

Take-overs, practised at first among smaller and poorly managed companies, quickly extended to the giants. Of the hundred largest companies (by assets) listed in 1954, eight had merged or been taken over by 1961 and so had 21% of all companies listed by the N.I.E.S.R. Of 1,882 companies with assets of £10,220 million listed in 1957, 274 (with 9% of assets) had been taken over five years later; the proportion, to be sure, was higher among the smaller ones, but even among the 180 largest companies, with assets of over £10 million each, twenty-one (6% of assets) had been merged or taken over within five years.[1] Altogether, larger firms tended to grow faster than smaller ones in these years, a difference which may be attributed in part to mergers, and in part to the greater conservatism among smaller companies.[2]

In the amalgamations of the giants the motives included both the hope for technical and cost advantages, and the desire to occupy monopolistic positions of strength. This was the case, for example, in the amalgamations and takeovers in the motor trade noted above, in the abortive bid by I.C.I. for Courtauld's in 1961, in the acquisition by Courtauld's of the Lancashire Cotton Corporation in 1964 and in the take-over of A.E.I. by G.E.C. in the electrical engineering field in 1967. In some cases the aim was near or total monopoly, as in the amalgamation of the aircraft industry into five units, of which two were to produce engines, two airframes, and one helicopters, all of which was engineered by the Government in 1959-60,[3] in the proposals of the Geddes Committee for the concentration of shipbuilding into three or four firms, or in the merger announced in March, 1968, of all British computer interests into a single combine, International Computer (Holdings) Limited, in which 10·5% was to be held by the Government.

In this period the merger movement extended also to the service industries. In retail distribution, for example, the 'multiples', or organizations having ten establishments or more, increased their share of the trade from 22% in 1950 to 35% in 1966.[4] Organizations with 100 establishments or over (excluding co-operatives), the real giants, increased their share of the trade from 12·9% in 1950 to 19·2% in 1961.[5] A high degree of con-

[1] Mennell, pp. 21, 35, 153; R. Evely and I. M. D. Little, *Concentration in British Industry* (1960).

[2] J. M. Samuels, 'Size and the Growth of Firms', *Rev. Econ. Studies* 32/90 (1965).

[3] For a good account, see P. D. Henderson, in 'Government and Industry', pp. 361–9.

[4] *Census of Distribution*, 1961, Part 14; and *Board of Trade Journal*, 23 February 1968. The figures refer to Great Britain.

[5] *Census of Distribution*, 1950 and 1961. Figures for 1966 were not yet available at the time of writing.

centration has developed in such other sectors as cinemas and newspapers and there have been important mergers among insurance companies. Perhaps most striking of all has been the scramble for mergers in banking as soon as it became known that the Treasury and the Bank of England had withdrawn their long-standing opposition to them. Within a matter of weeks, the two largest Scottish banks, the Royal Bank of Scotland and the National Commercial, had announced a merger and in England, the marriage of the National Provincial and the Westminster, and the proposed link-up of Barclays, Lloyds and Martins (which latter would become the second largest bank in the world)[1] promised to reduce the 'Big Five' to a mere 'Big Three'.

Meanwhile, control in the public interest over restrictive practices was slowly being built up by the authorities. The Commission set up under the Monopolies and Restrictive Practices (Inquiry and Control) Act of 1948 produced in the early 1950's reports on individual industries which showed the great variety in the methods. It was not, however, always clear whether the public suffered, or whether, as in the report on electric cables and on insulin, the monopoly merely provided countervailing power against another monopoly, or, perhaps, used its large size and control over supplies to achieve greater technical efficiency.

Little positive action arose out of these detailed reports, but the general report, commissioned in December 1952 and published in May 1955, *Collective Discrimination: A Report on Exclusive Dealing, Collective Boycotts, Aggregate Rebates and other Discriminatory Trade Practices*,[2] was followed by an important new measure. The Restrictive Trade Practices Act of 1956 set up a Restrictive Trade Practices Court, of the status of a High Court, and inaugurated the change from inquiry to control.[3] All restrictive agreements were to be registered and well over 2,000 were registered at once, the total, by 1963, being 2,430 proffered voluntarily and about 100 others brought to light in other ways. About 100 of these were laid before the Court by the Registrar as contrary to the public interest under the Act and, while most were abandoned before the hearings were completed, only a few of those heard to the end were not condemned as failing to satisfy the limited clauses which might make them acceptable.[4] As a result of the early

[1] *Economist*, 10th February 1968.
[2] Cmd. 9504 (1955).
[3] Catherine Brock, *The Control of Restrictive Practices from 1956* (1966); R. B. Stevens and B. S. Yamey, *The Restrictive Practices Court: The Judicial Process and Economic Policy* (1965); P. H. Guénault and J. M. Jackson, *The Control of Monopoly in the United Kingdom* (1960); Margaret Hall, 'The Consumer Sector', in Worswick and Ady, *op. cit.*, pp. 449–57; Alex Hunter, *Competitors and the Law* (1966); C. K. Rowley, *The British Monopoly Commission* (1966).
[4] In twenty-nine cases and forty-two issues decided in 1958–64, twenty-nine Agreements were declared contrary to the public interest and thirteen were

unfavourable judgments, over 1,500 agreements were abandoned or altered, and a further unknown number were abandoned in preference to registration.

In one respect, the Act allowed more restrictiveness than before: while prohibiting collective price fixing, it strengthened the power, hitherto very uncertain, of any individual firm to maintain the resale prices of its goods. When some firms actually used this power in a number of cases in order to force retailers to raise prices, it was shown up to be contrary to the spirit of the rest of the legislation, and in 1964 the Resale Prices Act aligned resale price maintenance with the other restrictive practices, by prohibiting it except in special cases where it could be shown to be necessary or in the public interest.

Thus, on paper, the anti-monopoly legislation had scored some formidable successes and, in some areas, particularly in retail trading, an unwonted freedom had by the mid-1960's replaced the earlier rigid price structure. Yet it was found to be easier to legislate against restrictive practices than to prevent them. For one thing, unofficial and unwritten agreements proved often as effectual as formal compacts. But secondly, the Government itself was not consistent, for while it hounded out and prohibited some monopolies, it created, encouraged or enforced others, as in the case of the aircraft industry, the Leyland–B.M.H. merger, shipbuilding, computer manufacture and agricultural marketing, described above. An attempt to discriminate more carefully between those restrictive actions that were in the public interest, and those which were not, was foreshadowed in a white paper prepared by the Conservative Government in 1964;[1] in the event, the proposals remained abortive, but the Monopolies and Mergers Act of 1965, passed by the new Government, gave the Board of Trade powers to impose conditions or to prohibit outright mergers which were referred to it. These powers were quickly brought into use.

2. FOREIGN TRADE AND TRADING RELATIONS

If the record of the British economy in 1950–67 compared well with the record of the past, it compared extremely badly with that of other contemporary advanced economies. The difference, the striking gap between the sluggish growth in output in Britain and the very much faster growth elsewhere, was so wide that the leading Continental countries, which for centuries had had much lower incomes and products *per capita*, began to catch up with and overtake Britain in absolute levels by the early

---

not. A. Sutherland, 'Economics in the Restrictive Practices Court', *Oxf. Econ. P.*, 17/3 (1965), pp. 427 ff.

[1] *Monopolies, Mergers and Restrictive Practices*, Cmnd. 2299 (1964).

Foreign Trade and Trading Relations

1960's. It was at that time that the poor growth performance of the United Kingdom became one of the main preoccupations of economists and policy makers and the main index of Britain's economic shortcomings. The basic facts are not in dispute:

Percentage Annual Average Compared Growth Rates[1]

	Output (G.D.P.) Beckerman, 1950–62	Postan, 1948–63	Productivity (G.N.P. per head of population) Beckerman, 1950–62	Postan, 1948–62	Maddison, 1955–64	G.D.P. at constant prices per head, Index for 1965 (1958=100)
Belgium	2·8	3·2	2·2	2·2	—	130
France	4·4	4·6	3·5	3·4	3·9	130
Germany	7·2	7·6	6·2	6·8	3·7	135
Italy	6·3	6·0	5·7	5·6	3·8	135
Netherlands	4·9	4·7	3·6	—	—	134
Sweden	3·7	3·4	3·1	2·6	—	134
United Kingdom	2·6	3·5	2·1	2·4	2·5	121
U.S.A.	3·0	—	1·3	—	1·6	123
Japan	—	—	—	—	7·6	188

This poor showing remains when the period is divided up in different ways, or when different base years are taken; fluctuations in the British economy were parallel to that of others, revolving merely around a much lower figure.[2]

The economic loss caused by this poorer performance in Britain is substantial. The British gross domestic product index in the first three quarters of 1967 stood at 159·6 (1950 = 100). At European growth rates of 4–5%, still a very low rate by European standards, it should have been somewhere between 194·8 and 229·2. The loss, in terms of 1967 values, was of the order of £7–14 milliard, or 22–44% of G.N.P.; and at current rates, such a European-type growth would have provided an additional personal disposable income per head, man, woman and child, of between £100 and £220 a year in 1967.[3] The discussion about the failure of the economy to grow is therefore a discussion about the loss of economic welfare of this

---

[1] W. Beckerman and Associates. *The British Economy in 1975* (Cambridge, 1965), p. 12; M. M. Postan, *An Economic History of Western Europe 1945–1964* (1967), pp. 12, 17; Angus Maddison, 'How Fast Can Britain Grow', *Lloyds Bank Review*, 79 (1966), p. 4; United Nations, *Annual Statistics*. For similar statistics, see Angus Maddison, *Economic Growth in the West* (1964), chapter 1, and 'Facts and Observations on Labour Productivity in Western Europe, North America and Japan', *Productivity Measurement Review*, 33 (1963); C. T. Saunders, 'International Comparison of Productivity Growth in the 1950's', *J. R. Stat. S.*, 126/2, Series A (1963); A. Lamfalussy, *The United Kingdom and the Six* (1963).

[2] C. A. Blyth, 'An International Comparison of Trend, Acceleration and Variation of the Rate of Growth of Productivity', *Productivity Measurement Review*, 39 (1964); T. Wilson, 'Instability and the Rate of Growth', *Lloyds Bank Review*, 81 (1966).

[3] See, e.g., Michael Stewart, *Keynes and After* (Penguin, 1967), p. 203.

order of magnitude. Even then, this calculation still excludes such other related losses as the breaches of international and internal contracts, the loss of goodwill and of confidence in labour relations, and the severe diminution of political independence, all of which were the result of the failure to expand real output at European rates.

From time to time, attempts have been made to account for the differences between the British and the other advanced economies by some particular handicaps. Among them was a permanent secular inability of the British economy to grow as fast as the others;[1] the technological gap of the 1940's, which Continental countries could bridge quickly or, in other words, the effects of a low starting-point; the crippling level of taxation for welfare purposes in Britain; the structural differences, allowing Continental countries to draw much labour from low productivity industries like agriculture into high productivity industries, but not open to Britain because the agricultural reservoir was so small; or the accession of labour from outside, particularly important for the West German economy, which was boosted by immigration from the east. Such explanations were, perhaps, permissible in the 1950's; by the 1960's, they could easily be shown to be trivial or irrelevant[2] as the absolute level of output, and the growth even in relation to, say, 1938, were higher on the Continent, which was yet growing faster. The Western economies were, in fact, sufficiently alike to allow a reasonably similar performance.[3] The technological gap between British practice and the best available at any one time and the rate of technological growth should have permitted comparable results in Britain after comparable effort. Taxation in Britain was lower than in many fast-growth countries.[4] As for the accession of labour,[5] the argument, indeed, should have gone the other way: for it is generally assumed in development economics that a rapid increase in the population, even if it is a working population, is a handicap, not an advantage, since it uses up

[1] J. Knapp and K. S. Lomax, 'Britain's Growth Performance: The Enigma of the 1950's', *Lloyds Bank Review*, 74 (1964).

[2] The best summaries of the argument will be found in Beckerman, chapter 1, and Postan, Part I. Also Beckerman, 'The Determinants of Economic Growth', in P. D. Henderson (ed.), *Economic Growth in Britain* (1966), pp. 61 ff.

[3] Some critics have pointed to unexplained differences *among* Continental nations, but even they usually agree that while in different periods the relative position of other countries may change, there is a striking similarity among European nations, shown on the table below, and a significant gap between their figures and the British. E.g. J. L. Stein, 'Economic Growth in the West', *Economica*, 32/125 (1965). Stein's forecast of a levelling off of the leading nations, it may be noticed, appears to have been falsified by events (pp. 83–7).

[4] First National City Bank of New York, *Monthly Economic Letter* (April 1968); Angus Maddison, 'Comparative Productivity Levels in the Developed Countries', *Banca Nazionale del Lavoro*, 83 (1967), p. 7.

[5] Stressed particularly in C. P. Kindleberger, *Europe's Post-war Growth. The Role of Labour Supply* (Cambridge, Mass., 1967).

resources for capital widening which would otherwise have led to a much more rapid *per capita* rise in productivity.[1]

The differences between Britain and the rest existed among all industries and sectors. The following table offers a sample of industries and of countries.

Changes in Productivity, Select Countries and Industries[2]

	Average Annual Growth Rates, % 1953–63			Productivity change, 1953–65. Index of Production as % of Index of Employment in 1965 (1953 = 100)[3]
	Production (a)	Employment (b)	Excess (a−b)	
Coal Mining				
France	−0·8	−2·8	2·0	138
W. Germany	0·7	−3·1	3·8	(154)
Italy	−1·0	−15·3	16·3	—
Japan	1·0	−7·8	8·8	300
United Kingdom	−1·1	−2·2	1·1	121
Textiles				
France	3·3	−1·5	4·8	149
W. Germany	5·5	−0·5	6·0	(191)
Italy	3·4	−1·1	4·5	(151)
Japan	9·1	2·5	6·6	223
United Kingdom	−1·0	−2·6	1·5	125
Chemicals				
W. Germany	10·7	4·6	6·1	(194)
Italy	14·1	3·4	10·7	(324)
Japan	15·1	6·0	9·1	292
United Kingdom	6·2	1·2	5·0	183
Electrical Machinery				
France	12·2	2·8	9·4	280
W. Germany	12·5	8·5	4·0	(155)
Italy	2·6	6·9	−4·3	(51)
Japan	28·1	13·5	14·6	353
United Kingdom	6·0	3·4	2·6	(130)
Iron and Steel				
W. Germany	5·4	2·9	2·6	(146)
Italy	11·7	2·6	9·1	(232)
Japan	14·2	6·9	7·3	—
United Kingdom	1·5	0·1	1·4	131
Electricity and Gas				
France	7·8	0·5	7·3	229
W. Germany	8·7	1·9	6·8	—
Italy	7·2	2·3	4·9	(171)
Japan	11·1	3·0	8·1	254
United Kingdom	5·5	0·6	4·9	172

[1] P.E.P., *Growth in the British Economy* (1960), p. 45, also quoting E.E.C.,

With the single and somewhat puzzling exception of electrical machinery manufacture in Italy, this table shows that in every field the British performance was in a class of its own. It will be noticed that the sharp rise in productivity abroad was not limited to growth industries, where it might perhaps be explained by the influx of labour, or a generally more optimistic economic framework: it was found equally in such industries as coal mining or textiles which were losing labour. Indeed, the gap between Britain and the rest tended to be wider in individual industries than in overall G.N.P., which is diluted by employment in such fields as administration, teaching or defence where rises in 'productivity' cannot be achieved or cannot be measured, or where it is easy to confuse costs and consumption.

Superficially, the explanation of this disparity is simple and is obvious to any visitor to, say, steelworks in Britain and abroad,[1] or to the Port of London and the Europort in Rotterdam. Whereas in 1950 Britain was level or ahead in technology, by 1968 the typical foreign worker operated with vastly superior equipment. The factor which has ensured that for the past two centuries or more it was the British workman who produced more, and enjoyed a higher real income than his Continental counterpart, now ensures the reverse and in precisely the same manner. In absolute terms, Britain has fallen from second place among Western nations, only the U.S.A. being ahead, to last but one, only Italy being still behind.[2]

---

cont. from p. 437
Economic Survey of Europe, 1958, pp. 37–8. See also the argument on immigration below, p. 500.
[2] Based on United Nations, Department of Economic and Social Affairs. *The Growth of World Industry, 1953–1965. National Tables* (New York, 1967). See also U.N., Economic Survey of Europe in 1961, Part 2, *Some Factors in Economic Growth in Europe during the 1950's* (Geneva, 1964), chapter 3; O.E.C.D., *Industrial Statistics, 1900–1962* (Paris, 1964), and figures on motor vehicles, above, p. 416.
[3] Figures in parentheses refer to 1964, with the same base of 1953.

---

[1] In 1959 the comparison of man-hours per unit of output in the steel industry was as follows:

	Overall	Taking into account differences in Processes
(Index, Germany = 100)		
Netherlands	62	59
Germany	100	100
Sweden	104	89
Italy	115	99
France	119	121
U.K.	157	146

Erik Ruist, 'Comparative Productivity in the Steel Industry', in J. T. Dunlop and V. P. Diatchenko (eds.), *Labour Productivity* (N.Y., 1964).
[2] Maddison, 'Comparative Productivity', p. 11, Table 12, and p. 15, Table 16.

Foreign Trade and Trading Relations

	Real Output at Factor Cost per Person Employed				Adjusted real output per man-hour (Index) 1965
	1938 $ U.S. prices	Rank	1965 $ U.S. prices	Rank	
U.S.A.	4432	1	8417	1	188·0
U.K.	2984	2	4598	9	100·0
Belgium	2895	3	5431	5	119·4
Netherlands	2831	4	5278	7	106·3
W. Germany	2826	5	6003	3	129·6
Canada	2763	6	6303	2	140·8
Norway	2659	7	5505	4	120·9
Denmark	2615	8	4679	8	104·2
France	2394	9	5335	6	110·7
Italy	1989	10	4041	10	88·5
U.S.S.R.	—	—	—	—	89·5
Japan	—	—	—	—	74·2

The only surprising aspect is the speed with which this change has come about, emphasizing the power of compound growth rates.

Inadequate equipment at home must be a reflection of inadequate investment. The relationship between investment and production increases, however, is by no means simple. There are no constant returns to scale on investment, no constant incremental capital-output ratios. Much ingenuity has been shown in recent economic literature, beginning with Solow's seminal essay,[1] in the exploration of the relationships between investment, technology and productivity changes in advanced economies. As far as concrete observation was concerned, two main phenomena have emerged in recent years in Britain and elsewhere.[2] The first is that the post-war increases in output were larger than the increases in the inputs of capital, labour and other factors. The second is that this 'extra' was the larger, the larger the addition to capital and the higher the growth rate, so that it grew more than proportionally with investment: 'there is . . . clear evidence that the residual is correlated with the growth rate':[3]

[1] R. Solow, 'Technical Change and the Aggregate Production Function', *Rev. of Econ. and Statistics*, 39/3 (1957). Also see Solow, 'Investment and Technological Progress', *Mathematical Methods in Social Science 1959* (Stanford, 1960), and literature quoted in J. C. R. Dow, *The Management of the British Economy 1945–1960* (Cambridge, 1965), p. 394; B. R. Williams, 'Investment and Technology in Growth', *Manchester School*, 32/1 (1964); P. A. David and Th. van der Klundert, 'Biased Efficiency, Growth and Capital-Labour Substitution in the U.S., 1899–1960', *Amer. Econ. Rev.*, 55/3 (1965); National Bureau of Economic Research, *Output, Input and Productivity Measurement* (Princeton, 1961).

[2] B. Williams, 'Research, Development and Economic Growth in the United Kingdom', *International Social Science Journal*, 18/3 (1966); United Nations, Economic Commission for Europe, *Some Factors in Economic Growth in Europe during the 1950's* (Geneva, 1964).

[3] Beckerman, p. 42, and Table 1.12 on p. 41. Also pp. 256–7. Cf. also T. P. Hill, 'Growth and Investment According to International Comparison', *Econ. J.*, 74/294 (1964).

Annual % growth of G.D.P. ascribed to:

	Increases in Labour and Capital		'Residual'	
	ECE (1949–59)	NIESR (1950–60)	ECE (1949–59)	NIESR (1950–60)
Germany	2·9	3·75	4·5	4·05
Belgium	1·0	1·45	2·0	1·35
Canada	3·6	2·25	0·6	0·55
France	1·1	1·45	3·4	2·95
Norway	1·6	2·05	1·8	1·15
Sweden	0·9	0·75	2·5	2·15
Netherlands	2·2	2·85	2·6	2·25
United Kingdom	1·3	1·15	1·1	1·2
U.S.A.	—	1·9	—	1·2

Neither of these observations should occasion much surprise. The first confirms that one kind of technological progress consists precisely in the creation of increased output per unit of capital-and-labour input. The second confirms that it is only by re-equipment and by investment in new methods, new organizations and new locations that this 'residual' can be created. Even with a similar technology, there are economies of scale in individual enterprises, which fast-growing economies, pressing against their capacity, reach more quickly.[1]

Physical investment in industry is a necessary concomitant of technical and even of social progress; new techniques of production, new commodities and changing tastes of consumers require new equipment.

[1] One recent study of the comparative growth of Britain and Germany attributes more of the difference to economies of scale than to technology—but the latter ('advance in knowledge') is an artificial and quite arbitrary figure, derived from the experience of the U.S.A., and is in this context quite indefensible.

Sources of Growth, annual growth rates, %

	U.K.	W. Germany
Input of Factors: Labour	0·35	0·94
Capital	0·80	1·57
Due to Factor Inputs	1·15	2·51
Other causes: Advance of Knowledge	0·76	0·76
Contraction of Agriculture and Self-Employment	0·09	0·66
Economies of Scale	0·43	1·25
Other	0·16	0·21
Due to other causes	1·12	2·88
Total observed growth in National Income	2·27	5·39

It is significant that Germany was assumed to operate at full capacity, while in Britain it was assumed that 0·54% p.a., or nearly one-fifth of total annual growth of capacity, had been wasted. Edward Dennison, *Why Growth Rates Differ* (1968).

Hence it is difficult to achieve a high rate of technical advance without a high level of investment. Conversely, a high level of investment tends to stimulate technical progress since it gives rise to increased opportunities to introducei mproved techniques and to experiment with new ideas. In short, a high level of investment and rapid technical progress go hand in hand and it is not practicable to answer the question what would happen to one in the absence of the other.

It is a more useful approach to regard technical progress and investment as different aspects of the same process, namely the application of new ideas to industry and the adaptation of industry to a changing environment.

All new methods require investment outlays before they can be utilized, irrespective of whether they are more mechanized or not . . . The relevant concept is gross investment; all investment expenditures increase productivity, either by bringing the capital stock up to date, or by increasing the degree of mechanization.[1]

Of course, there is no precise correlation between productivity increases and investment, for some investment may be misplaced; there are periods and industries in which a high incremental capital /output ratio must prevail, and some 'investment', like technical education, may not appear in any official statistics at all. Moreover, productivity increases come about partly by more intensive or more intelligent use of existing equipment, by smoother organization, by more rapid adaptations to market demands or the use of different raw material inputs. Yet, on the whole, it is only by investment that new methods of production can be introduced; it is only by a high level of investment that a high proportion of the total capital stock can be kept up to date; and given a similar structure of industry and a similar stage of technology, the country with a higher investment rate will cash in more on the 'residual' growth, while the country whose investment plans are brusquely cut by decisions originating outside industry, will find it particularly difficult to gain the full advantages of any new technology.[2]

[1] Tibor Barna, *Investment and Growth Policies in British Industrial Firms* (Cambridge, 1962), p. 1; Salter, *op. cit.*, p. 145. For obvious technical reasons, there was no correlation *as between industries* between investment and speed of productivity growth. R. J. Nicholson, 'Capital Stock, Employment and Output in British Industry 1948–1964', *Yorkshire Bulletin* 18/2 (1966), p. 83; also W. B. Reddaway and A. D. Smith, 'Progress in British Manufacturing Industries in the Period 1948–1954', *Econ. J.*, 70/277 (1960).

[2] This phenomenon is also well known in historical instances, e.g. P. Temin, 'The Relative Decline of the British Steel Industry, 1880–1913', in H. Rosovsky (ed.), *Industrialization in Two Systems: Essays in Honour of Alexander Gerschenkron* (N.Y., 1966). Also Kenneth Hilton, review of Beckerman, in *Bankers Magazine*, 203/1 (1967); T. P. Hill, 'Growth and Investment in International Comparison', *Econ. J.*, 74/294 (1964); and the general tenor of Richard E. Caves and Associates, *Britain's Economic Prospects* (Washington, D.C., 1968).

	Annual % Growth of G.N.P. 1950–60[1]	Average % of G.N.P.				
		Gross Domestic Investment, 1950–60	Net Investment 1949–59	Fixed Investment, less residential building, 1950–60	Gross Capital Formation, less residential building, 1955–63	Total Fixed Invest- ment, 1966
W. Germany	7·2	24·0	15·2	14·3	20·1	25·4
Italy	6·3	20·8	13·4	14·8	16·9	18·6
Austria	6·0	23·3*	16·7	—	—	—
Netherlands	4·9	24·2	14·9	16·3	—	—
France	4·4	19·1	10·2	13·6	15·7	21·8
Sweden	3·7	21·3	11·2	—	—	—
Belgium	2·8	16·5	7·4	11·5	—	—
U.K.	2·	15·4	8·0	9·9	13·7	17·8
Japan	—	—	—	—	30·2	31·5

*1949–59

The United Kingdom showed both a slow growth and a low investment rate. In productive industry, the British capital equipment became particularly dangerously antiquated. By the end of 1961, it was calculated, 60% of the buildings and 38% of plant and machinery in manufacturing and construction dated from before 1948. In some industries the proportion was much higher: 50% of the plant and machinery of the metal-using industries, 39% in textiles and 43% in paper and printing was built in 1947 or earlier. Similarly, 32% of all fixed capital in mining and quarrying, 78% of railway capital, 87% of docks and harbours and 71% of the capital sunk in roads, dated from before 1948.[2]

Why, then, was the rate of investment so low in Britain? In 1945–50, we have seen, investment had been held back by a variety of causes. One was the pressure for consumption, less restricted than in the rest of Europe where the widespread visible destruction made retrenchment generally acceptable. This pressure was hard to resist because of the high liquidity of the economy, which it took until 1950 to squeeze out. Another cause, however, was the deliberate decision of the Government, at each of the biennial exchange crises of 1947, 1949 and again 1951, to sacrifice investment to the vitally necessary export increases: 'whenever something went wrong with the balance of payments, domestic investment was hit on the

[1] Sources: *Some Factors in Economic Growth*, esp. Chapter 2; Maddison, *Economic Growth*, Tables III–1, III–6, 76, 81, and 'How Fast Can Britain Grow', p. 5; Beckerman, Tables 1.1, 1.8, pp. 12, 31. Also see Lamfalussy, *op. cit.*; *National Institute Economic Review*, 43 (1968), p. 23.

[2] G. A. Dean, 'The Stock of Fixed Capital in the United Kingdom in 1961', *J. R. Stat. S.*, 127/3, Series A (1964), pp. 338–9, 343.

head'.[1] As a result, the capital equipment per head was even by 1950 not yet fully restored to the pre-war level.[2]

Thus, in the crises of 1947–51, some future growth was sacrificed though the productive capacity was not wasted. It was merely diverted from investment to exports. Since then, however, this approach has become a permanent, and increasingly effective, feature of the British economy. Moreover, as it became increasingly difficult to market potential exports, the capacity abstracted from capital formation was no longer diverted to exports but was kept unemployed. Thus the main cause of the low investment, and hence the low growth rate, in Britain is easily stated: the whole of the considerable apparatus of Government economic power, especially as exercised by the Treasury, has been applied during the major part of the period under discussion to achieving it. In fact, it was usually an adverse balance of payments which in the post-war years caused the Government to decree a 'stop', exercised largely on home investment, though it also fell on home consumption, and at times even on Government expenditure. Government intervention was thus based wholly on short-term considerations, which changed from time to time in emphasis and will be discussed further below. Here it is our object to describe the consequences of the restrictions on investment.

Deflationary and restrictive policies affected investment in at least three ways, which varied in importance over this period. First, there was the direct Government instruction to the nationalized industries to cut or postpone their investment plans and, since they represented the public utilities and basic industries, investments there were large and critical[3] and cuts among them could be very effective. These were important in the early 1950's and come into prominence again in the 1960's. Secondly, deflationary measures were designed to affect all other investment directly, by high interest rates, by credit restrictions, by cuts in investment allowances and similar means. These were particularly prominent in the late 1950's. Thirdly, the repeated 'stops' and restrictions ultimately affected adversely the optimism and enterprise of private firms, which many observers have held to be the key factors in the world post-war boom. British enterprise remained surprisingly immune to this most dangerous consequence of official economic policy in the 1950's, but increasingly

[1] R. Nurkse, 'The Relation between Home Investment and External Balance in the Light of British Experience', *Rev. of Econ. and Statistics*, 38/2 (1956), p. 125. This is one of the most perceptive studies of the British economy published at the time.

[2] E. A. G. Robinson, 'British Economic Policy 1945–50', *London and Cambridge Economic Service Bulletin*, 28/2 (1950), p. 42; T. Balogh, 'Investment in Britain and the United States', *Bull. Oxf. Inst. Stat.*, 14/6 (1952).

[3] In 1955 the public sector was responsible for 57% of the total gross fixed capital formation, and in 1965, for 45%. *National Income and Expenditure.*

succumbed to it in the 1960's. By the mid-1960's, the damage had been done to the extent that it would take at least some years to convince the business community and the managers of nationalized industries again that it was safe to plan and invest for a high rate of growth.

If Government policy permitted the foreign balance of payments to affect investment and thus productivity, the latter in turn reacted on both via exports and imports. One of the outstanding characteristics of the period after 1950 was the failure of Britain to maintain the share of her exports in world markets. Her share of manufactured exports, which had been 21·3% in 1937, fell dramatically from 25·4% in 1950 to 16·2% in 1961 and 12·9% in 1966.[1] Had her exports kept up better, the balance of payments crises would have been avoided, and exports thus became a key issue.

Britain's poor export performance was not due, as it had been in the 1920's, to her concentration on stagnant, rather than on growth industries: on the contrary, her switch to new industries had been very successful, and in the post-war years Britain had a higher share of trade in the expanding industries than any of her leading competitors, except Germany.[2] Her area pattern, it is true, was slightly less favourable, since traditionally Britain was geared to supplying the underdeveloped areas of the world which grew more slowly in these years, than the European market which grew fastest,[3] but this was not of great significance and Japan, the most successful exporter, had an even less favourable area distribution from a growth point of view. What was significant was that Britain's exports did substantially less well than her competitors' in each main market separately. There may, perhaps, also have been a failure in salesmanship, though this is difficult to prove, and is in any case a part of economic efficiency.

The basic cause of the lag in exports is not in any doubt. Compared with the price level of all world imports, U.K. export prices rose, i.e. deteriorated competitively, by 14·5% in 1953–63; compared with total import prices into the Common Market, they rose 15·5% more; and compared with other imports into the U.S.A., their excess was 22·9%. Only U.S. export prices rose to the same extent as the British.[4]

Why, then, were British export prices so unfavourable? The prime cause has been described already. Exports were affected by the relative decline in British productivity, or the rise in real costs, relative to those of

[1] *Key Statistics*, Table N.

[2] Panic and Seward, p. 26; also H. Tyszynski, 'World Trade in Manufactured Commodities, 1899–1950', *Manchester School*, 19/3 (1951); S. Spiegelglass, 'World Export of Manufactures, 1956 vs. 1937', *ibid.*, 27/2 (1959); P.E.P., *Growth*, p. 166.

[3] S. J. Wells, *Trade Policies for Britain. A Study in Alternatives* (1966), p. 127.

[4] H. B. Junz and R. R. Rhomberg, 'Prices and Export Performance of Industrial Countries, 1953–1963', *I.M.F. Staff Papers*, 12/2 (1965), pp. 235, *passim*.

the chief competitors which tended to price British goods out of the competitive world markets. This tendency could, in theory, have been counteracted by a policy of deflating the British price-level parallel with Britain's inability to keep pace with the efficiency of her rivals, but neither of the two methods of doing this, lowering foreign prices by devaluation, or lowering home prices by a severe incomes policy, were open to the United Kingdom. An annual devaluation of 2–3% to reflect Britain's decline in relative productivity was unthinkable, since the whole programme of restrictions was kept in being precisely for the purpose of keeping up the sterling exchange rate. A severe incomes policy would, in the 1950's, not only have seemed a step backwards to the controls of war-time from which it was official policy to escape, but would also not seem to have been warranted, since as the table below shows strikingly, British wage rises were, if anything, well below those of most other countries. Moreover, it came to be increasingly clear that there was an 'institutional' element in a free society enjoying full employment and strong trade unions, which raised wages by around 5% a year as a matter of course.[1] The difference between British and foreign experience was not that money wages rose here; but that these increased costs were absorbed by rising productivity elsewhere, but not in the United Kingdom. (See Table below.)[2] In 1960, a direct attempt was first made to hold back the annual wage rise, mainly in Government employment and nationalized industry, and from 1966 the so-called 'incomes policy', based on a wage freeze and later very restricted increases, became the main prop of economic policy. The devaluation of 1967 was a belated application of the other type of measure to take account of Britain's failing competitiveness. Both of them were attempts to make prices reflect the relative impoverishment of Britain, rather than to remedy the causes of that impoverishment, and neither was successful even on its own misguided terms.

[1] A. G. Hines, 'Trade Unions and Wage Inflation in the United Kingdom, 1893–1961', *Rev. Econ. Studies*, 31/88 (1964); Colin Clark, 'An International Comparison of "Over-employment" Trends in Money Wages', *Oxf. Econ. P.*, 9/2 (1957); E. V. Morgan, 'Is Inflation Inevitable', *Econ. J.*, 76/301 (1966), p. 6; Dow, *Management*, pp. 355–6; L. A. Dicks-Mireau and J. C. R. Dow, 'The Determinants of Wage Inflation: United Kingdom, 1946–56', *J. R. Stat. S.*, 122/2, Ser. A. (1959); K. G. J. C. Knowles, 'Wages and Productivity', in Worswick and Ady, pp. 520 ff.

[2] Lamfalussy, *op. cit.*, p. 59, Table 13.

Wage Rates and Exports

Annual Percentage Growth Rates[1]

	Hourly Earnings[2]		Export Prices		Export Volume	
	Manufacturing 1948–63	All Labour 1963–7	1953–63	1963–7	1950–62	1963–7
Belgium	4·1	9·4	−0·6	+1·6	7·7	10·8[3]
France	9·7	6·2	0	+2·6	7·7	7·2
W. Germany	8·0	6·7	+0·7	+1·7[4]	14·8	10·1
Italy	6·3	8·0	−1·8	−0·2	17·9	14·7
Japan	7·7	11·1	−1·1	+0·2	15·5[5]	22·8[6]
Netherlands	6·9	10·7	+0·4	+0·7	9·5	9·4
Sweden	7·2	8·6	+0·8[1]	+1·2	7·0	7·0
U.K.	6·0	5·4	+1·7	+2·4	2·3	2·6
U.S.A.	4·2	3·6	+1·8	+1·6	3·2	—

It should be noted also that every restriction which made industry work at less than full capacity tended to raise costs. The exact effects are uncertain, but the following estimates are not untypical for capital-intensive industries:

Variation of Unit Costs with Capacity Working[7]

Unit Costs—Index

% Capacity working	Open Hearth Furnaces	Oil Refineries
100	100	100
90	104	109
80	110	118
70	—	129

These increased costs were not necessarily passed on to customers, particularly foreign ones; but if they were absorbed by the producers, they added to their unwillingness to expand their investment in the future.

[1] U.N., *Statistical Yearbook*; O.E.C.D., Dept. of Economics and Statistics, *Main Economic Indicators* (Paris, 1968); Beckerman, Table 2.2, p. 57, and 5.12, p. 176, also pp. 46–7, 58–9; Postan, p. 91; M. Panic and T. Seward, 'The Problem of U.K. Exports', *Bull. Oxf. Inst. Stat.*, 28/1 (1966), p. 22.

[2] Earnings Rates are daily for Belgium and Italy, and monthly for Japan.

[3] 1963–6.

[4] Manufactured export prices only.

[5] 1951–62.

[6] 1959–63.

[7] C. Pratten and R. M. Dean, *The Economics of Large-Scale Production in British Industry* (Cambridge, 1965), pp. 80, 89.

Thus, given common variations in input prices, like imports and wage rates, and given fixed exchange rates, Britain's failure to achieve the real cost reductions of other countries was bound to mean a relative rise in her export prices. Given the high demand elasticity, or in other words, the strongly competitive conditions in export markets, there is no alternative but to place the responsibility for the relative decline in British exports squarely on increasingly non-competitive price and quality, i.e. on a failure to keep up productive efficiency.[1] The circle is thus complete: failure in productivity led to losses in exports; these led to balance-of-payments difficulties, and these, in turn, led to Government short-term measures which were certain, in the long term, to make the productivity failures worse and start the circle up again, in less favourable conditions, as soon as the restrictions were taken off.

In the case of imports, the mechanism was even simpler. The fear had been often expressed in the late 1940's that expansion of incomes would lead to a proportionate increase in imports of raw materials, food and goods that could not be produced at home according to a calculable 'propensity to import'. In the event, it was true that every expansion between 1950 and 1967 led to an immediate sharp import rise; but just as the failure of exports to rise steeply was not simply due to the attractions of home demand, with which the negative correlation was weak,[2] but to a failure to produce, so this sharp rise in imports was not in commodities in which other countries enjoy national advantages in production, but on the contrary, the increase was greatest in machinery, steel and other capital goods, and in manufactures generally. In the motor industry, for example, the normal propensity to imports of 8%, rose to 15% near full capacity, because of the shortage of sheet steel.[3] For the economy in general in 1948–68 it was found that the elasticity of imports relative to home activity was higher for manufactures than for food.[4] Excess imports were thus largely due to non-necessities which could have been restricted, or to 'bottlenecks', i.e. failure to create sufficient capacity from home sources.

[1] See also Youngson, *Britain's Economic Growth 1920–1966* (1967), pp. 232–5; J. R. Parkinson, 'The Progress of United Kingdom Exports', *Scot. J. Pol. Econ.*, 13/1 (1966); M. FG. Scott, *A Study of United Kingdom Imports* (Cambridge, 1963); Lynden Moore, 'Factors Affecting Demand for British Exports', *Bull. Oxf. Inst. Stat.*, 26/4 (1964), p. 347.

[2] R. J. Ball, J. R. Eaton and M. D. Steuer, 'The Relationship between United Kingdom export performance in Manufactures and the Internal Pressure of Demand', *Econ. J.*, 76/301 (1966).

[3] Ian G. Stewart, 'Imports and the Terms of Trade', *Scot. J. Pol. Econ.*, 13/1 (1966), p. 30.

[4] Klein, Ball, Hazlewood and Vandome, *An Econometric Model of the United Kingdom* (Oxford, 1961), p. 97. Also Marc Nerlove, 'Two Models of the British Economy', *International Economic Review*, 6/1 (1965), p. 165.

To a varying extent, it was also due to a parallel sharp increase in inventories.[1] This may be put differently. Investment, the creation of productive capacity, was at no time undertaken in a quantity to sustain a higher growth rate, so that if income growth occurred at a rate approaching the average Continental experience, it expressed itself in an import surplus rather than a commensurate growth in output. This import surplus, as noted above, resulted in measures which injured the creation of productive capacity still further. For most of the time, in periods of restriction, output was at less than capacity, preventing the full use of home resources for such objectives as improving Britain's productive potential:[2] when the brakes were taken off, capacity was then found to be too inelastic and too low.

The N.E.D.C. Inquiry of 1965 investigated in detail the general rise of imports in 1954-64, and the sharp rise in 1962-4, of eight groups of manufactures. In three cases (chemicals, textiles, especially man-made fibres, and electrical household goods), shortage of capacity was given as the main reason; in three others, it was given as one of the main reasons (paper and board, iron and steel, building materials); and in the remaining two (engineering products, motor vehicles) performance and consumer preference were put to the fore.[3] Once again in the 1960's it was the shortage of machine-tool capacity which imperilled all hopes of faster growth, and its inadequacy was explained by the low and irregular demand it had met in the past.[4]

Moreover, the progressive deterioration of British technical competitiveness meant that at each crisis, the dependence on imports increased, and when the tide receded, left them at a higher level than before. This 'ratchet effect' was noted among all advanced countries, but in the United Kingdom it was particularly powerful in the case of machinery and other capital goods. Between 1948-57 and 1960-2, imports of food, drink and

---

[1] See, e.g., N.E.D.C., *Imported Manufactures: An Inquiry into Competitiveness* (1965); M. F. W. Hemming and G. F. Ray, 'Imports and Expansion', *National Institute Economic Review*, 2 (1959); A. Maizels, *Industrial Growth and World Trade* (Cambridge, 1963); Wells, *Trade*, p. 92; P.E.P., *Growth*, pp. 143 ff.; Lomax, 'Growth and Productivity', p. 14; Roy Harrod, *Towards a New Economic Policy* (Manchester, 1967), p. 25; P. M. Oppenheimer, 'Is Britain's Worsening Trade Gap due to bad management of the Business Cycle?', *Bull. Econ. and Stat.* (formerly *Bull. Oxf. Inst. Stat.*), 27/3 (1965). M. FG. Scott, 'The Volume of British Imports', in Worswick and Ady, *op. cit.*, though published in 1962, is still wholly couched in the terms of the immediate post-war problems, and is witness to the delay in recognizing the long-term post-war trend.

[2] W. A. H. Godley and J. R. Shepherd, 'Long-Term Growth and Short-Term Policy', *National Institute Economic Review*, 29 (1964).

[3] *Loc. cit.*, paras. 19, 26, 34, 48-50, 58, 61, 77-9, 82.

[4] E. W. Evans, 'Some Problems of Growth in the Machine Tool Industry', *Yorkshire Bulletin*, 18/1 (1966), pp. 43, 47-8.

tobacco rose by only 46%, and of basic materials (including mineral fuels), by only 28%; but imports of manufactures rose by 183%.[1]

Yet this is not the whole story. To understand the nature of this vicious spiral fully, it is important to look, not merely at commodity trade, but at all items in the balance of payments. The post-war foreign commodity trade balance was, in fact, exceptionally strong, compared with other recent periods. The immediate post-war task of raising exports by some three-quarters above the pre-war level without raising imports, had been astonishingly achieved by 1950.

Omitting the striking year-by-year fluctuations, which will be discussed below, it will be seen that the visible trade balance not only did not deteriorate, but actually improved over the period. To some extent, this was helped by the terms of trade, which turned into Britain's favour immediately after the price peak of 1951, to the extent of 30% by 1967. It made the export drive, in value if not in volume, correspondingly easier, compared with the difficult years of 1946–51 when the terms of trade were against Britain. The adverse excess of imports over exports actually fell from an average of £260 million in 1952–6 to £252 million in 1963–6, while the value of total trade, of which this was the balance, nearly doubled. As a proportion of G.N.P., exports were gaining on imports[2] and the exporting industries were achieving this success in the face of all the adverse conditions just discussed.

Among the 'invisibles', the returns from property, etc., abroad showed an increasing trend in monetary terms, though they declined in real terms. The other 'invisibles', however, showed a sad decline from their former importance in Britain's balance of payments. Civil aviation showed a small surplus year by year, but shipping, once a very large net earner of foreign currency, was a net loser in the 1960's: Britain paid more in shipping services to foreigners than she received in return. Travel and private transfers were growing negative items. Only financial and other services, the work of the City of London, was positive, and if it is borne in mind that the official statistics may slightly under-state the rise in these earnings,[3] these may have kept pace with prices and thus kept their real value.

Between them, these current items on private account created a strong

---

[1] Beckerman, Table 5.1, p. 149, Table 5.10, p. 170, and *passim*; Harrod, *British Economy*, pp. 149–50; F. Brechling and J. N. Wolfe, 'The End of Stop-go', *Lloyds Bank Review*, 75 (1965), pp. 27–8.

[2] P.E.P., *Growth*, p. 172; Harrod, *British Economy*, p. 31.

[3] A. E. Holmans, 'Invisible Earnings', *Scot. J. Pol. Econ.*, 13/1 (1966), pp. 56–7. Also, British National Export Council (William M. Clarke, Director of the Study), *Britain's Invisible Earnings* (1967); F. N. Burton and P. Galambos, 'The Role of Invisible Trade in the United Kingdom's Balance of Payments, 1952–1966', *National Provincial Bank Review*, 82 (1968).

U.K. Balance of Payments 1950–67[1] (£ million)

	Visible Trade Balance	Invisibles, Profits, Interest, etc. (net)	Other (net)	Total Private Current Balance	Government Current Transaction	Total Current Balance	Total Capital (net)[2]	Balance of Current and Capital Transactions
1950	(−51)	(+159)	(+334)	(+442)	(−136)	(+306)	—	—
1951	(−689)	(+147)	(+327)	(−215)	(−150)	(−365)	—	—
1952	−279	+252	+251	+224	−61	+163	−134	+29
1953	−244	+229	+226	+211	−66	+145	−194	−49
1954	−204	+250	+202	+248	−131	+117	−191	−74
1955	−313	+174	+122	−17	−138	−115	−122	−177
1956	+53	+229	+101	+383	−175	+208	−187	+21
1957	−29	+249	+157	+377	−144	+233	−106	+127
1958	+29	+294	+243	+566	−219	+347	−196	+151
1959	−118	+266	+228	+376	−227	+149	−255	−106
1960	−408	+240	+192	+24	−282	−258	−192	−450
1961	−153	+263	+227	+337	−332	+5	+68	+73
1962	−104	+346	+244	+486	−359	+127	−98	+29
1963	−83	+402	+178	+497	−381	+116	−55	−39
1964	−543	+409	+166	+32	−434	−402	−374	−776
1965	−269	+447	+170	+348	−458	−110	−232	−342
1966	−111	+371	+182	+442	−501	−59	−116	−175
1967 (3 qtrs)	−361	(+270)	(+202)	(+111)	(−342)	(−231)	(+29)	(−202)

[1] Central Statistical Office, *United Kingdom Balance of Payments*. (Annual) Figures for 1950 and 1951 are drawn from *United Kingdom Balance of Payments 1946–1957* (1959) and *Key Statistics*, and have not been corrected in the same way as the later figures. Figures for 1967 from C.S.O., *Financial Statistics*, 71 (March, 1968).

[2] Minus means net overseas investment; plus means net disinvestment.

positive balance year by year. By themselves, they would have placed Britain in a similarly favourable position as Germany and France in the 1960's, and would have made unnecessary the destructive restrictionist policies which the British economy had to endure. The items more than counter-balancing them, negatively, were Government expenditure and net foreign investment.

Among these, the Government account is much the more important. It was, in fact, larger than it appears from the table, since in addition to the current items shown here, a substantial and rapidly rising proportion of net capital investment, amounting to a net £386 million for the four years 1963–6, was also on Government account. Even omitting these large sums, the net expenditure[1] of Government abroad rose more than eight-fold in monetary terms in this period, and the purely military (net) expenditure within it rose even more sharply from £12 million in 1952 to £313 million in 1966. This item alone, therefore, was sufficient to wreck the delicate balance of payments of the United Kingdom since 1950, and to account for the worsening imbalances, in spite of the progressively improved trading accounts. Whether expenditure of this order of magnitude was wise or justifiable, or whether it contributed to the political strengthening of the United Kingdom, are political questions outside the purview of this book.[2] Given the unwillingness to impose overseas trading and payments restrictions which might have permitted Britain to incur this kind of expenditure without repeated deflation at home, the real cost-benefit analysis of British foreign policy would have to count the cost of Government activities abroad not merely in the hundreds of millions annually spent, but in the milliards annually lost in output and income because of the restrictions made necessary to maintain it.

The other negative item, which was of smaller absolute size and grew much more slowly, was net foreign investment. This expenditure has also come under attack from time to time as being greater than the economy could afford,[3] but its economic case is a much stronger one. Given a surplus on current account which obtained throughout, and which was maintained until 1959 even when Government expenditure was included, it was in the interest of world trade and prosperity, particularly of less developed countries hit by the adverse terms of trade which so helped Britain, to use Britain's trading surplus precisely in this traditional way.

---

[1] Gross expenditure rose less, it was the collapse of counterbalancing in-payments which caused the multiplication of the net figure.

[2] For other politically inspired burdens on the British economy, see R. N. Gardner, *Sterling-Dollar Diplomacy* (1956).

[3] E.g., A. R. Conan, 'The Unsolved Balance of Payments Problem', *Westminster Bank Review* (Nov. 1963), p. 11; F. W. Paish, 'Britain's Foreign Investment: the Post-War Record' (1956), in *Studies in an Inflationary Economy. The United Kingdom 1948–1961* (1962), chapter 9.

Moreover, this expenditure was productive and contributed to the growing 'invisible' surpluses on current account.

In concrete terms, many of these investments opened out and developed British markets and supply areas, mainly in the earlier years of the period. In the later years, they represented, in part, the necessary attempts of British firms to establish themselves behind tariff barriers. In the early 1950's, British private long-term investment rose rapidly from around £100 million to reach about £300 million by 1957, and it has stayed slightly above that figure, taking one year with another, ever since. As a result, private capital abroad, estimated at £3,300 million at the end of the war, rose to around £9,300 million in 1957 and to £11,800 million in 1961 according to one calculation.[1] Capital assets abroad are notoriously difficult to value, and official figures put private long-term investment abroad at £7,855 million at the end of 1962 and at £9,600 million at the end of 1966.[2]

In these totals, banking and portfolio investments showed some increases, but the largest growth was registered in direct investment of non-financial companies, and particularly in oil. According to Revell, these two items grew from £6,080 million in 1957 to £7,387 million in 1961, or by £325 million a year, and according to the official figures, direct investment rose from £3,755 million in 1962 to £4,900 million in 1966, and oil investment from £1,100 million to £1,500 million, or together by £385 million a year. Even more striking was the change in direction. Before 1960 most of British overseas investment went to areas like Canada and Australia, but since then it was made increasingly in Western Europe, both in the Common Market and the E.F.T.A. countries. As the return on investment was scarcely higher abroad than at home (7·8% as against 7·6% by 1960–2),[3] it was likely that many of these investments were made to enlarge markets rather than to find profitable outlets for capital.

This growth of real overseas long-term assets was in part matched by foreign investment in Britain. Inward investment grew from around 20% of outward capital flows in the early 1950's to 70–80% by the mid-1960's, and in 1961 and 1967 the balance was actually positive. The main components of capital imports, apart from the short-term funds that were to play an important part in the devaluation crisis of 1967, was direct invest-

---

[1] Jack Revell, *The Wealth of the Nation. The National Balance Sheet of the United Kingdom, 1957–1961* (Cambridge, 1967), Table 12.3, pp. 268–9, taking 'Private' and 'Direct Investments', less 'Cash and Short-Term Assets' and 'Bank Advances', which still overstates the long-term holdings.

[2] Central Statistical Office, *United Kingdom Balance of Payments*, 1967, Table 29. Also Alexander G. Kemp, 'Long-Term Capital Movements', *Scot. J. Pol. Econ.*, 13/1 (1966), pp. 143–9.

[3] J. H. Dunning, 'Does Foreign Investment Pay', *Moorgate and Wall Street* (Autumn, 1964); Wells, pp. 59–60; Beckerman, pp. 116–19.

ment, particularly by American firms, in subsidiaries to beat the British
tariff or to form bases for covering British and European markets. American investment in Britain was estimated at $847 million in 1950 and
$1,420 million in 1955, of which 80% was in oil and manufacturing; by
1967, it was estimated to have reached $7,000 mn. Total private foreign-
held capital was estimated at £3,150 million in 1957 and £5,750 million in
1961 by one calculation, and to have risen from £3,940 million in 1962 to
£4,900 million in 1966 by another.[1] In the context of the 1950's and 1960's,
American capital introduced into Britain the advantages of American
systems of management, as in the building of the Esso Fawley refinery,
or American technical know-how, as in the motor and other engineering
firms, and the American-owned plants were often much concerned with
exports or with import-saving.[2] In the long run, however, these investments were bound to burden the economy with their annual servicing
charges.

In addition to these private capital transfers, there were also official
investments, of which the 'sterling balances' were the most important.
Created first in war-time by the expenditure of British forces in such
countries as India and Egypt, they had become almost as large as British
investment overseas in the immediate post-war years. After 1950 the total
never moved far from the £3,500 million mark, of which 20–25% was held
by countries not in the sterling area; but within this total, India, Pakistan,
Ceylon and Egypt used up most of their holdings and those of Australia,
New Zealand and South Africa also declined, while, by contrast, the oil
countries of the Middle East, and some Far Eastern areas like Malaysia
and Hong-Kong, the surplus economies of the sterling area, greatly increased their holdings in London.[3]

The concept of the 'Sterling Area' itself underwent considerable
changes.[4] The level of the sterling balances proved that London was still
favoured by many countries, mainly those in the Commonwealth, as a
place to hold their reserves, and the high and rising interest rates payable
in London, a reflection of the increasing weakness of sterling, helped to
continue them in their resolve. On the other hand, the Commonwealth
received a small and falling share of British investments and a falling share

[1] *U.K. Balance of Payments*; Revell, *loc. cit.*; J. McMillan and Bernard Harris, *The American Take-Over of Britain* (1968).
[2] J. H. Dunning, *American Investment in British Manufacturing Industry* (1958), pp. 290–310, and 'U.S. Manufacturing Subsidiaries and Britain's Trade Balance', *District Bank Review*, 115 (1955).
[3] Beckerman, p. 113; Bank of England, *Quarterly Bulletin*; S. Strange, *The Sterling Problem and the Six* (P.E.P., European Series No. 4, 1967), Table 6, p. 68.
[4] C. W. McMahon, *Sterling in the Sixties*; Symposium in *Bull. Oxf. Inst. Stat.*, 21/4 (1959); J. M. Livingstone, *Britain and the World Economy* (Pelican 1966), chapter 2.

of British trade, as tariff preference margins were, on the whole, not increased, while the other attractions of other markets grew.[1] Sterling's role as an international currency also declined with British trade, British shipping and the importance of the London Money Market: by the mid-1960's, well under one-third of world transactions was left to be made in sterling.[2] The City of London itself, after the increasing liberalization of the 1950's culminating in the abolition of control over capital movements by non-residents and the effective convertibility of sterling, began to interest itself increasingly in credit transactions based on dollars rather than on sterling, the so-called 'Euro-Dollar' market.[3] British banks and other finance houses found it profitable in the 1960's to lend increasing sums on a short-term basis abroad and banks alone increased their lending from £800 million in 1962 to £1,200 million in 1967, some of these funds having, in turn, been obtained abroad.

It is now possible to summarize the main long-term trends in Britain's post-war overseas position. Omitting Government expenditure, the British economy produced sufficient surplus to have sustained both a rapid growth at home and net investment abroad. Burdened, however, as it was by the political fact of heavy and rapidly growing Government spending and lending abroad, the current balance was too small to sustain a heavy net foreign lending programme as well. Nevertheless, not only was this capital export programme permitted to continue but, in the late 1950's, when a few good years hid the underlying weakness of the economy, the pressure from the City ensured that the final reckless step was taken of making sterling wholly convertible,[4] so that the economy, which was already in imbalance because of a long-term lending programme it could not sustain, had to carry the further strain of short-term lending also.[5]

There was thus a gap in the balance of payments growing inexorably if irregularly throughout the period. It could not be financed by releasing the gold or convertible currency reserve, which had after the devaluation of 1949 quickly risen to just over £1,000 million,[6] since as it was it had to carry an increasing burden of trade and indebtedness with ever greater difficulty. Indeed, at this level it came to be accepted as barely adequate,

[1] G. D. A. MacDougall and R. Hutt, 'Imperial Preference: Quantitative Analysis', *Econ. J.*, 64/254 (1954); Wells, pp. 18 ff; G. Arnold, *Economic Co-operation in the Commonwealth* (1967), pp. 57–67.
[2] P. M. Oppenheimer, 'Monetary Movements and the International Position of Sterling', *Scot. J. Pol. Econ.*, 13/1 (1966).
[3] Paul Einzig, *The Euro-Dollar System* (1964).
[4] The main steps were taken in March 1954, February 1955 and at the end of December 1958. M. FG. Scott, 'The Balance of Payments Crisis', in Worswick and Ady, p. 210; Brian Tew, *International Monetary Co-operation 1945–1967* (1967), pp. 138–47.
[5] A. R. Conan, *The Problem of Sterling* (1966); Susan Strange, *op. cit.*
[6] E.g., Strange, Appx. Table 2, p. 65; Bank of England, *Quarterly Bulletin*.

and any diminution would have been the signal for a general run on sterling, so that it could scarcely be used for rectifying even minor fluctuations. If the use of the reserves were excluded, there were two other main methods open to Britain to fill that gap: attracting short-term capital from abroad and obtaining loans from Governmental organizations.

The short-term private loan, by speculative, 'volatile' capital, was particularly the method of the 1950's: it could be said with justice that Britain's lending long (and some of her lending short, also) was financed by borrowing short.[1] Foreign funds, like some of the official 'sterling balances', were attracted and held here very largely by the high interest rates, but they were volatile and reacted particularly sharply to any suggestion of devaluation; in consequence, the very thought of devaluation, which might at different times have afforded relief to the British economy, had to be firmly banished by successive Governments. As the gap widened, the foreign balances grew, and any alternative monetary policy of dealing with it became less and less workable, since the funds which would participate in a run on sterling, should it ever take place, grew increasingly beyond the power of the economy to withstand. The parallel, in many details, with the position of 1925–31, was striking. In both cases there was a weak balance of payments made weaker by maintaining sterling at an unrealistically high level; in both cases, the policy was maintained only by high interest rates and by restrictions and deflationary measures which hit industry and made long-term opportunities of breaking out of the circle increasingly difficult; in both cases, the priorities of the City were allowed to obscure totally the priorities of industry; and in both cases, the structure was held together only by large speculative funds which, though they had for years been fed by abnormally high interest earnings, would at the first sign of danger turn against sterling, leave London and turn a temporary embarrassment into a rout. In other respects, the setting was quite different: in 1966–7 the world economy was buoyant, not grinding to a halt as in 1929–31; Governments had new economic insights; and the British economy was far weaker, and far less important in relation to the world. Yet the speculative panic reactions of 1931 and 1966–7 were similar[2] and had the similar immediate consequence of forcing devaluation on sterling. The size of the monetary outflow in 1966 and 1967 showed up the extent to which in preceding years Britain had balanced her books with borrowed money.

The second line of defence was to use official resources, mainly of the International Monetary Fund and the European Payments Union and of

[1] T. M. Klein, 'The United Kingdom Balance-of-Payments Accounts', *Econ. J.*, 74/296 (1964).
[2] As early as March 1966 the private 'confidence drain' of sterling was estimated at £420 million. *Economist*, 2nd April 1966.

other Central Banks. Both the I.M.F. and the E.P.U. had been created to allow member countries to cover temporary deficits or surpluses without having to take the drastic steps more appropriate to a more fundamental disequilibrium.[1] In the 1950's the debts run up by the United Kingdom appeared to be of the temporary kind and were duly repaid. This included the negative balance of £340 million run up with E.P.U. in 1952, and the aid asked for after the post-Suez sterling crisis at the end of 1956, including the drawing of £201 million from the I.M.F., a loan of £179 million from the U.S. Export-Import Bank, a request to waive interest repayment on the U.S. and Canadian loans, and the granting of further drawing rights of £264 million from the I.M.F. Meanwhile, the E.P.U. obligations and the loans by Governments (mainly the post-war loans made by the U.S.A. and Canada) continued to be liquidated by yearly repayments, though at a depressingly slow rate.

Yet this apparent equilibrium of the 1950's hid a steady long-term deterioration. When the E.P.U. was wound up in 1958, Britain's balance with it was still negative to the tune of $379 million, and the European Monetary Agreement which replaced it was less elastic in its credit facilities.[2] At the same time, the I.M.F. and other Central Banks became loath to honour the original Bretton Woods formula of permitting devaluation in cases of fundamental disequilibrium; instead, they increasingly came to accept exchange rates as permanently fixed; and they failed to take into account the steady deterioration of the United Kingdom's balance-of-payments position.[3]

The balance-of-payments difficulties of the 1960's, ushered in by the crisis of 1960, were solved only by growing reliance on official foreign aid, which not only grew faster than it could be repaid, but after 1966 had to take the strain of the flight from the pound of speculative capital also. The run on the pound in 1960–61 was staved off only by the drawing of £536 million from the I.M.F. and further support from other central banks. Much of this was repaid quickly (£458 million in 1962), but confidence in the pound had been badly shaken. When the current balance showed the largest ever deficit of £750 million in 1964 the flood could no longer be held back, despite an unparalleled battery of restrictive measures at home, many of which had as their main object simply the restoration of confidence among foreign bankers and British and foreign speculators. £357 million were drawn from the I.M.F. in 1964, while the other central banks, with the Bank for International Settlements, ulti-

---

[1] See pp. 358, 361 above.

[2] Tew, pp. 111–23.

[3] R. S. Sayers, 'Co-operation Between Central Banks', *Three Banks Review* (September 1963); D. J. Coppock, 'The Alleged Case Against Devaluation', *Manchester School*, 33/3 (1965).

mately agreed to provide an equivalent of $3 milliard if necessary. In 1965 the I.M.F. was drawn on to the extent of £500 million and in 1966 a further £44 million, while there were credits also from the Federal Reserve Bank. In 1966 the Central Banks granted drawing facilities again of $1 milliard. After the devaluation of 1967, sterling was buttressed by an I.M.F. standby credit of $1,400 million, and credit facilities by other central banks exceeding $1,500 million. In so far as this was intended to hold up sterling, it made sterling into an internationally, rather than a British-backed currency.[1]

Increasingly in the period, the weakness of sterling was aggravated by the growing international weakness in reserves. World trade and indebtedness were rapidly increasing, but the world's gold reserve was not, so that each poundsworth of monetary gold had to bear an ever greater burden of transactions. Even if no country had been in basic deficit, world transactions would have become increasingly hampered thereby; but as the U.S.A. and Britain were both in fundamental disequilibrium, the former losing the gold which was being acquired by the surplus states, Germany and France, the deficit countries could not sustain the world boom indefinitely. The appreciation of the Mark and the Dutch Guilder in 1961 had shaken confidence; in 1964, the U.S.A. for the first time turned to the I.M.F. for $125 million in European currencies; the announcement in 1965 by the French Central Bank that it would convert some of its dollar reserves into gold further weakened the dollar; and when a renewed run on sterling began in 1967, its collapse could no longer be staved off even with the substantial loans and standby credits from other banks.

On 18 November 1967 sterling was devalued by one-seventh, from $2.80 to $2.40. Several other currencies followed, including those of Brazil, Ceylon, Denmark, Eire, Israel, New Zealand and Spain, but this time their importance was much less than in 1949 and they accounted for only about one-sixth of British trade. The international help, which alone allowed sterling to survive even at the lower rate and which refuted the claim of sterling to be considered a major independent, let alone a dominant currency, was emphasized by the humiliating terms of the 'Letter of Intent' which had to be pledged to the I.M.F. in return for its credits. Should the stringent restrictive policies imposed in 1967–8 turn out to be inadequate in the opinion of the I.M.F., the Fund would have to be consulted 'during the period of the standby arrangement and as long thereafter as the Fund holdings of sterling exceed 125 per cent of quota, to find appropriate solutions'.[2] Furthermore, this time, unlike 1931, or even

---

[1] *United Kingdom Balance of Payments*; Strange, pp. 15 ff.; Peter Oppenheimer, 'The Prospect for Sterling', *The Listener*, 15th February 1968.

[2] A useful brief account will be found in *Midland Bank Review* (February 1968), pp. 15–18.

457

1949, there was no immediate relief either in the trade balance, or on the speculative sterling markets. Instead of cheap money, the Bank Rate was put up to 8%, the highest since 1914. A battery of the most serious restrictive measures, including cuts in Government investment in public utilities, satisfied the Central and International Banks, but not apparently the speculators.

The reflux of foreign exchange fell a good way short of the very large outflow before devaluation. Nor was there much sign at this time (or indeed later in the period) that investment funds were returning, despite the 8% Bank Rate; or that forward sales of sterling were reversed before maturity.[1]

Indeed, the attack now shifted to the dollar—a development quite unthinkable twenty years earlier. The speculators went for gold and overwhelmed the 'gold pool', operated by eight leading central banks since 1961 with an estimated reserve of $270 million, though $3½ milliard of gold was sold to maintain the price. On 15th March 1968 dealings in the London gold market and American convertibility were suspended and a temporary moratorium declared. A meeting of world bankers agreed to take account of the free market situation by permitting transactions at a 'free price', while holding the official price, valid among Central Banks, at $35 an ounce. This was a half-way house; the dollar was not officially devalued, nor was gold demonetized. A second meeting on 29th and 30th March at Stockholm agreed, with only the French dissenting, to open mutual 'Special Drawing Rights' among Central Banks and the Bank for International Settlements. This may be looked upon as a belated victory for proposals, some of which go back to the 1940's, of breaking through the limitations of metallic reserves by creating expandable and internationally guaranteed paper reserves,[2] which obtained some recognition in the 'swap' system organized by the Federal Reserve System in 1962 and since extended, and would be put on a firmer basis when ratified in 1969.

International co-operation, deriving in part from the vision of the first peace years and unhampered by fears of massive unemployment, extended also to the field of trading agreements. G.A.T.T., after some initial successes in lowering tariffs on individual commodities which no country thought vital, soon found its success diminishing when it attempted to tackle those which member countries held to be important and it turned, instead, to across-the-board percentage cuts. However, the

---

[1] Bank of England, *Quarterly Bulletin*, 8/1 (1968), p. 4; also 7/4 (1967); *National Institute Economic Review*, 43 (1968), pp. 9–10.
[2] There is a large literature. See, e.g., H. G. Grubel (ed.), *World Monetary Reform* (1964).

'Kennedy round' came up against procedural and other difficulties, and few positive reductions were made.[1] Its main achievement was the prevention of indiscriminate tariff increases.

Much more significant were the regional agreements which sprang up in Europe. The European Economic Community, or Common Market, deriving from the earlier Coal, Iron and Steel Community among the 'Six' (Germany, France, Belgium, Holland, Italy and Luxemburg), was set up by the Treaty of Rome, signed in 1957. It came into operation in 1958 with a twelve-year programme of gradual removal of all barriers to trade among the members and the erection of a unitary tariff to the outside world. In the event, not only were the customs union provisions speeded up, but it proved possible to 'harmonize' many other economic activities, from social welfare provisions and agricultural protection to taxation, much faster than most observers had thought possible.[2]

The United Kingdom attempted to gain associate status at the foundation, offering an internal free-trade area without full economic integration, but this was turned down. In the event, the E.E.C. countries made immense economic progress in ;the years after the signing of the Treaty, although it is open to doubt how far this was as a result of it or how far they merely continued their earlier fast growth.[3] The large and expanding market among the 'Six' not only stimulated trade among the members, but even offered a market to British exporters which, in spite of the increasing tariff discrimination implicit in the Treaty, grew faster and became more important than any other.[4] The temptation to apply for full membership proved irresistible in the United Kingdom, despite many misgivings expressed in various quarters, and two attempts were made to join, in 1961–3 and in 1966–7, but both were turned down by French veto.

Meanwhile, after refusing to sign the Rome Treaty, the United Kingdom proceeded with her own proposal of a free-trade area, involving the abolition of tariffs and trading restrictions among the members, but not the harmonization of their tariffs against others, or of any other economic or social policies. In 1959 she was instrumental in setting up the European Free Trade Area, the 'Seven', by the Stockholm Convention. The other members were the three Western Scandinavian countries, Switzerland and Austria, both of whom were reluctant to imperil their status of neutrality

---

[1] Wells, pp. 28–32.

[2] M. Camps, *Britain and the European Community, 1955–1963* (1964) and *European Unification in the Sixties. From the Veto to the Crisis* (1967); U. Kitzinger, *The Politics and Economics of European Integration* (1962); J. F. Deniau, *The Common Market. Its Structure and Purpose* (1960); Sidney Dell, *Trade Blocs and Common Markets* (1963).

[3] A. Lamfalussy, 'Europe's Progress: Due to Common Market?', *Lloyds Bank Review*, 62 (1961).

[4] S. J. Wells, 'Trade with Europe', *Scot. J. Pol. Econ.*, 13/1 (1966).

by joining the E.E.C., and, somewhat incongruously, Portugal.[1] Finland became associated with them in 1961. The political and geographical viability of E.F.T.A. is much less obvious than that of the E.E.C. The 15% surcharge on imports imposed by the United Kingdom in 1964 without prior consultation caused grave offence, and it was clear that the United Kingdom and some other members were prepared to jettison E.F.T.A., had the British attempts to enter the E.E.C. succeeded. Nevertheless, the internal tariff reductions were kept in line with those of the E.E.C. to advance to full free trade by the end of 1966 instead of 1969, and, given the existence of one trading block, the members found clear advantages in belonging to another block with a population of nearly 100 million, a large proportion of whom enjoyed a very high standard of living.[2] There seemed at the time to be little likelihood of the acceptance by the E.E.C. of the repeated E.F.T.A. proposals to join both groups into a single Free Trade Area, though closer collaboration, including trading agreements, among them may be expected. For the time being, the United Kingdom tariff level against outside countries remained not only considerably higher than the common E.E.C. tariff, but even exceeded that of the protectionist United States.

3. FINANCE AND THE BANKING SYSTEM

Thanks to the heroic efforts of the later 1940's, the immediate danger posed by the high post-war financial liquidity in the British economy had been overcome by the end of the decade. Clearing bank deposits, which had risen nearly tenfold from pre-war days to 1950, were then held steady for three years, and rose by only 50% to 1967, much less than prices; the ratio of net bank deposits to G.D.P., which had been around 50% in the late 1930's and had risen to a maximum of 65% in 1947, fell steadily to a mere 30% in 1966. Currency circulation was also held at the same level over 1945–50, and afterwards rose less than incomes, and although deposits with acceptance houses and overseas banks rose much faster, these were not large enough to affect appreciably the general liquidity position.[3]

One of the main factors which helped to end the over-heating of the economy was the reduced pressure from the Government, whose borrowing had so much weakened the hands of the monetary policy makers in the

[1] F. V. Meyer, *The Seven* (1960); E.F.T.A., *Building E.F.T.A., A Free Trade Area in Europe* (Geneva, 1966).

[2] *E.F.T.A. Trade, 1959–1966* (Geneva, 1968); S. J. Wells, 'E.F.T.A.—The End of the Transition', *Lloyds Bank Review*, 82 (1966).

[3] *Financial Statistics*; London and Cambridge Economic Service, *Key Statistics 1900–1966*, Table M; G. L. Bell and L. S. Berman, 'Changes in the Money Supply in the United Kingdom, 1954 to 1964', *Economica*, 33/130 (1966), p. 149.

1920's and again in the 1940's. On current account, the Government achieved annual surpluses averaging £450 million a year, and while this was more than counterbalanced by heavy Government capital formation, so that on combined revenue and capital account there was still an annual deficit, it was so small that over much of the period it could be covered by the growth in the net National Savings. The decline of the latter in the mid-1960's, when they increased by only £175 million in the three years to the end of 1967, was not enough to weaken the Government's monetary control, which in any case depended on many other factors. As for short-term borrowing, 'the value of tender Treasury bills outstanding in 1965 was less than the sum of tender bills and Treasury deposit receipts outstanding in 1948', so that there was no floating debt increase either, to weaken monetary control.[1]

It was this more 'normal' money supply situation which allowed the Conservative Government to re-introduce monetary policy, including the bank rate, as the major innovation of the 1950's. After twenty years of a 2% Bank Rate, cheap money ended in 1951 and changes in the rate began to be used vigorously to support Government policies. However, as the long-term position of Britain worsened from 1956 on, the general tendency for the Bank Rate was upward. It never fell below 4% and the crisis rate of 7% was used with increasing frequency. When, following the Radcliffe Report of 1959, the lack of effectiveness of this kind of monetary policy became increasingly recognized, the rate (as in the 1920's) still had to stay up to avoid the collapse of sterling. Since 1966 it has always been above 6%, a near-crisis rate, and by the end of 1967 it stood at 8%; this medicine (like all the other dosages of restrictiveness) had also become ever less effective with increasing use. Its rise, meanwhile, was attracting the foreign short-term funds which had for years hidden the unhealthy balance-of-payments position from public recognition.

The Radcliffe Committee Report,[2] one of the most thorough and intelligent examinations of the British Monetary System, was in this respect very much a document of the 1950's. The Committee totally failed to see both the slow erosion of the United Kingdom's positive balance of payments, and her failure to keep up competitively with production and productivity increases abroad:

> The fact that there has been a substantial surplus on current account over the past ten years suggests . . . that there has been no fundamental lack of balance in the United Kingdom's trading position. Other countries have increased their exports more rapidly and, in a period when Germany and Japan were recovering their position, the

[1] W. B. Reddaway, 'Rising Prices for Ever?', *Lloyds Bank Review*, 81 (1966), p. 3; Bell and Berman, p. 163.
[2] *Committee on the Working of the Monetary System*, Cmnd. 827 (1959).

United Kingdom's share of the world market in manufactures has contracted. But exports and imports have roughly kept pace with one another; on the whole, the margin between the two has tended to widen and leave a rather more favourable balance. The repeated exchange crises have not been due, therefore, to any failure on the part of the United Kingdom to pay her way but to the volatility of various elements in the balance of payments and to the lack of reserves adequate to withstand the resulting pressure on them.[1]

The Committee was, no doubt, unfortunate in its timing: it could scarcely have been more mistaken in its diagnosis.

The attention of the Committee (like that of Montagu Norman in the 1920's) was of course largely concentrated on protecting the reserve and on suppressing inflation, still thought to be the main danger. Their particular concern was the monetary mechanism by which these aims could be accomplished, particularly in the crisis years of high pressure. In this field they made one of their most valuable contributions by showing that the traditional braking mechanism, the reduction of the 'liquidity' of the banks which forced them, in turn, to restrict their credit, was no longer working efficiently.

One of the main reasons for this was the transactions of the Government itself. We have seen that, in the long term, the Government finances were well in balance. In short-term management, however, the high absolute level of the floating debt, inherited from the 1940's, requiring the continuous attention and wooing of the market for renewals, was apt to clash, in any given year, with the needs of long-term borrowing, mostly for the capital programme of the nationalized industries. Neither could be switched off when the authorities wished, on general grounds, to reduce the creation of credit. The banking system therefore could compensate for any reduction of liquidity engineered by the authorities, by simply reducing its holdings of Government short-term debt, particularly Treasury Bills, and thus, in effect, force the authorities to restore its former liquid position. Particularly clear cases of this process in the restrictions of 1955 and 1957 were very much in the forefront of the Committee's mind to support their analysis.[2]

Put differently, the Committee were concerned to extend the concept of the 'supply of money', by which the authorities hoped to regulate demand, beyond the cash and bank deposits to which it used to be limited, to a much wider range of alternatives and to 'the state of liquidity of the whole economy'.[3] They were also concerned to evolve a mechanism

---

[1] Para. 633.
[2] Charles Kennedy, 'Monetary Policy', in Worswick and Ady, *op. cit.*, pp. 310–11; Harrod, *British Economy*, pp. 109–11.
[3] *Radcliffe Committee*, para. 981.

which would limit the effect on home activity of fluctuations caused by changes in the foreign balance.

For a time the Committee's ideas carried all before them,[1] but in recent years the debate has been reopened and there have been new defenders of the importance of the money base.[2] Others pointed out that the post-war mechanism tended to cushion, rather than transmit, the short-term effects of foreign imbalances, as the classic gold standard was said to have done: 'There was . . . little relationship between the changes in the payments position and changes in the money supply over the period considered.'[3]

As the revived traditional methods of monetary policy, consisting mainly of bank-rate changes and open market operations, showed themselves to be of failing efficiency in the 1950's, the Government had increasing resort to other means. Direct requests to the banks by Chancellors had been known before, but Macmillan's personal address to assembled bankers to exhort them to reduce their advances in 1956 represented a new step in that direction.[4] Since then, requests about both the volume and the type of bank advances to be permitted have become more and more specific. The proposal of the Bank of England to the Radcliffe Committee to provide legal sanction to the banks' traditional cash (8%) or liquid (30%) reserve, such as exist in other countries and would give the Central Bank much greater power to affect total credit by operating on those reserves, was turned down. Instead, the scheme actually adopted was to require the banks at times of restriction to open 'special deposits' with the Bank of England, which the latter could use to reduce liquidity, and which the banks would undertake by a gentlemen's agreement not to count among their cash reserve. Two such payments, of 1% each, were requested in 1960 and a third in 1961, each worth somewhat over £70 million.[5] The method was used again from 1965 on.

Other methods used were the control of new issues by the Capital Issues Committee, and the occasional restriction on building society lending, a rapidly growing mechanism of finance. Insurance funds, another important source of finance, could not be controlled. Curiously, one of the most effective means to be discovered in this period was the restriction of hire-purchase terms, partly because of the rapid growth of this method of finance, and partly since it took effect much more quickly and

---

[1] E.g., W. Manning Dicey, *Money Under Review*, and literature quoted in Worswick and Ady, p. 545.

[2] W. T. Newlyn, 'The Supply of Money and Its Control', *Econ. J.*, 74/294 (1964); R. L. Crouch, 'The Inadequacy of "New Orthodox Methods" of Monetary Control', *ibid.*, 74/296 (1964); A. B. Cramp, 'Control of the Money Supply', *ibid.*, 76/302 (1966).

[3] Bell and Berman, p. 163.　　　　　　　　[4] Dow, p. 240.

[5] Harrod, p. 111; *The Banker*, 108/391 (1958).

directly than any of the other methods:[1] 'If we look at the actual experience of the 1950's . . . we come to the conclusion that the really quick substantial effects were secured by hire purchase controls, just those which have the most concentrated directional effects.'[2] Further, while the other methods largely cut investment, hire-purchase control largely cut consumption, though it also affected the finance of smaller firms, and it was thus the one method which did no long-term damage to the economy. In the 1950's and 1960's, every major 'package' of restrictive or relaxing measures contained statutory changes in hire-purchase provisions. The advantages of such methods, which both worked at once and hit the right section of the economy, were evident, but on the whole the Treasury preferred to stick to controls which worked through the City rather than 'directly'.

As the long-term inflation of the post-war period proceeded, it led inevitably to·a re-examination of Keynesian theory on the subject and, in particular, to the elaboration of the distinction between 'demand-pull' and 'cost-push', or 'demand' and 'price' inflations,[3] the former caused by excessive demand throughout the economy and the latter by price rises of individual factors of production, particularly of labour. The issue became of vital importance for policy decisions.

If cost inflation was to blame, then the holding back of wage rises, as the main cost item under British control, became a major objective of policy. One extreme view, represented particularly by F. W. Paish, held that the only effective way of ensuring this was a substantial level of unemployment: 'The country must face the fact that, to check inflation permanently and to prevent the emergence of yet another balance-of-payments crisis, it must accept a permanent unemployment of some 500,000, or rather over 2 per cent.'[4] This view, apart from its obvious appeal to employers, has a certain superficial plausibility. A fast-growing economy which is constantly operating at less than full capacity is certainly conceivable in theory. Yet this view fails to take account of the obvious damage done to total welfare by not using available resources, and it is totally contradicted by the post-war experiences of other countries: some of the most successful growers, like Germany and the Netherlands, have done so with a high level of employment, while a high degree of un-

[1] J. K. S. Gandhi, 'Estimates of Hire Purchase and its Finance, 1948–1957' *Bull. Oxf. Inst. Stat.*, 28/4 (1966); Dow, pp. 246–8.

[2] *Radcliffe Committee*, para. 472.

[3] Dow, chapter 13: Thomas Wilson, *Inflation* (Oxford, 1961); Harrod, pp. 55 ff.; P. A. Samuelson and R. M. Solow, 'Analytical Aspects of Anti-Inflation Policy,' *Amer. Econ. Rev.*, 50 (1960).

[4] F. W. Paish, 'How the Economy Works', *Lloyds Bank Review*, 88 (1968), p. 21; also *Studies in an Inflationary Economy: The United Kingdom 1948–1961* (1962) esp. chapter 17.

employment did not prevent slow growth and balance of payments problems in the U.S.A., Canada and Belgium. Further, there is much evidence, including the experience of 1966–8, to show that unemployment rates, in order to be effective in holding back wage rises, would have to be very much higher than 2%. In fact, few economists have ever subscribed to the Paish doctrine in its extreme form, and the appearance of substantial 'wages drift', or payments of wages at rates beyond those officially negotiated, at least permit the conclusion that trade unions, far from pushing ahead of incomes in general, did not fully exploit their bargaining position.[1] Nevertheless, by force of circumstances and on the advice of the foreign banks whose loans have sustained sterling since 1964, something like the Paish doctrine has become official policy since 1966, and has been defended, by similar reasoning, both by members of the Government and by past and current Governors of the Bank of England. An alternative policy might have been a controlled system of wage rises, related to expected national income increases. The possibilities of a 'wages policy' have been much debated in academic circles,[2] but have never been accepted, even in principle, by the trade unions. Official attempts at an 'incomes policy', particularly those from 1966 onward, have in their unreasoning and untenable uniformity proved to be the very opposite of what a planned and rational wages policy was hoped to be.

Despite the clear theoretical distinction, it has not been easy to determine in practice which type of inflation prevailed in the United Kingdom.[3] Most observers would agree that both types have existed and there would have been periods when one or the other has been the predominant one. Since the early 1950's, when the after-effects of the drastic devaluation of 1949 were still making their inflationary path through the economy, there has been a tendency for the 'demand-pull' to decrease, and the 'cost-push' to increase, over the period, which also saw increasing unemployment in the later years. Clearly, from the point of view of economic welfare, inflation has not been a major problem and would have been a

---

[1] There is a large literature. See esp. E. H. Phelps Brown, 'Wage Drift', *Economica*, 29/116 (1962); T. Wilson, *Inflation* (Oxford, 1961), p. 252; *Statistics on Income, Prices, Employment and Production*, 24 (1968), Table B.14.

[2] J. C. R. Dow and L. A. Dicks-Mireau, 'Excess Demand for Labour in Britain: A Study in conditions in Great Britain, 1946–1956', *Oxf. Econ. P.*, 10/1, (1958); J. C. R. Dow, 'Analysis of the Generation of Price Inflation: A Study of Cost and Price changes in the United Kingdom, 1946–54', *ibid.*, 8/3 (1956); Symposium in *Bull. Oxf. Inst. Stat.*, 19/4 (1957); also in *Scot. J. Pol. Econ.*, Vol. 5 (1958); B. C. Roberts, *National Wages Policy in War and Peace* (1957); L. A. Dicks-Mireau and J. R. Shepherd, 'The Wages Structure and Some Implications for Incomes Policy', *National Institute Economic Review*, 22 (1962); Frank Blackaby and Michael Artis, 'On Incomes Policy', *District Bank Review*, 165 (1968).

[3] L. A. Dicks-Mireau, 'The Interrelationship between Cost and Price Changes, 1946–1959: A Study of Inflation in Post-War Britain', *Oxf. Econ. P.*, 13/3 (1961).

negligible one, had output grown at rates normal elsewhere, whereas 'in the past, attempts in the United Kingdom to halt inflation have often succeeded more conspicuously in halting growth'.[1] In practice, the restrictive measures adopted at each of the major crises did not distinguish very carefully between the possible sources of inflation, but sought to administer their cuts wherever they were thought most effective. As the restrictive dosage was increased from 1964 onwards, the weight of the measures which were directly inflationary increased more sharply. Among them were the 15% imports surcharge, the selective employment tax which companies were permitted to pass on to their customers, less than full capacity working and, most drastic of all, devaluation itself. In these measures, the stability of the internal price level has been sacrificed to what were considered the more urgent aims of the foreign payments balance and the external position of sterling.

In the normalization of the monetary system in the 1950's two further important developments have to be considered, one working in favour of the authorities, the other against them. In their favour was the startlingly rapid recovery of personal savings. Their virtual disappearance in the post-war years had been most perturbing and their re-emergence was not only a symbol, but also part cause, of more normal peaceful conditions: the post-war buying spree, the excessive velocity of circulation, had given way to a more balanced disposal of resources. In 1949–51, personal savings were still only 1–2% of G.N.P., but they jumped almost at once to 5%, and thenceforward remained at 6–7%.[2] The pressure was at once relieved on Government savings, which fell *pari passu*, while the savings of Companies and of Public Corporations remained at about the same level, the former showing a falling, and the latter a welcome rising tendency.

Percentage share in Total Savings[3]

	1950	Average 1954–6	Average 1959–61	Average 1965–6
Persons	−2·8	16·5	28·6	30·9
Companies	53·0	56·5	50·2	47·3
Public Corporations	5·1	6·3	6·5	10·0
Central and Local Government	42·2	18·3	16·0	16·5
Residual error	2·5	2·5	−1·3	−4·7
	100·0	100·0	100·0	100·0

[1] R. G. Opie, 'Inflation', in P. D. Henderson (ed.), *Economic Growth in Britain* (1966), p. 154.

[2] Richard Stone, 'Private Saving in Britain, Past, Present and Future' *Manchester School*, 32/2 (1964); *National Income and Expenditure*.

[3] Beckerman, p. 278; *National Income and Expenditure*; Elliot Zupnick, *Britain's Post-War Dollar Problem* (N.Y., 1957), pp. 54–5. See also *Bank for International Settlements. 38th Annual Report, 1967–1968* (Basle, 1968), p. 17.

Finance and the Banking System

At the same time, however, there occurred a marked revulsion against Government securities. This might have been no more than the wish to return to normal after the long years when the Government had absorbed most of the voluntary and involuntary savings made in the economy. But it aggravated the difficulties experienced by the authorities in the 1950's in placing their paper, and forced them at times to counteract their own restrictive policies to do so, while there seemed to be adequate savings generated for other purposes.

There was, in fact, a general movement away from fixed-interest securities into equities and the inflation itself was a major cause for this as it became more generally incorporated into expectations. Because of it, the rising trend of the bank rate was accompanied by a similar, apparently inexorable rise in the long-term interest rate, creating the 'reverse yield gap' from about 1960 onwards, i.e. a higher apparent yield for fixed-interest gilt-edged securities than for equity capital, which with its risks also carried the promise of capital appreciation.

The high and rising long-term interest rates were a creation of the Government in its defence of the balance of payments. It was alleged, at each crisis increase, that its object was to encourage saving and thus to bring savings and investment together to relieve the pressure on total demand. In fact, there was no real shortage of savings, which grew much faster than investment from a low point in 1954–5 onwards, and the high rate reflected the growing shortfall of quantity of money in relation to incomes. Thus, again in a manner evocative of the 1920's, the deflationary measure of dear money was superimposed on an economy which was already, basically and on a long-term basis, suffering from deflationary and contracting symptoms, particularly a decline in investment relative to savings.[1]

It will be seen from the table above that a high proportion of savings was generated and remained within the 'Companies' sector. Public issues remained at a relatively modest level. In 1966–7, an average of £121 million was issued in ordinary shares and £13 million in preference shares, for both home and foreign companies. Net loan issues were much higher, at £704 million, but of these £212 million were for local and public authorities. At the same time, saving became highly institutionalized. Among the most powerful agencies were insurance companies, building societies and investment and unit trusts. The insurance companies themselves reflected the switch into equities and away from gilt-edgeds. According to one calculation, while their total assets rose from £3,108 million in 1950 to £6,610 million in 1960, Government securities held by

[1] Harrod, *British Economy*, pp. 200–3 and *Economic Policy*, p. 10; Dow, *Management*, pp. 231–4.

467

them increased by only 30%, from £1,034 million to £1,332 million, but loan capital (much of it on mortgage secured on real estate) rose from £924 million to £2,285 million, and ordinary shares grew more than fourfold, from £338 million to £1,417 million. In 1964 their equity holdings were up to £2,253 million, and preference shares to £409 million, out of total assets of just over £10,000 million. Conversely, it was estimated in 1960, that insurance companies held 10% of all quoted equities and other financial institutions another 20%, and they invariably figured among the largest shareholders. Since then, their penetration of share ownership has certainly increased further.[1]

Among other institutional investors, Investment Trusts were still much the largest, holding assets worth over £3,000 million by the end of 1965, but the Unit Trusts, most of which had been formed only in the 1950's, were growing much more quickly, again with their main emphasis on a good spread among equities. From a mere £60 million in 1958, their funds reached £522 million by the end of 1965.[2] The change in the assets of the clearing banks was no less significant: in 1950, their investments were almost as large as their advances, £1,500 million as against £1,600 million. By 1966 the former had fallen to a little over £1,100 million, but the latter had increased threefold, to over £4,700 million.[3] Finally, the pre-war triumphal advance of the building societies was resumed, and proceeded at an annual rate of 10%. From assets of under £800 million in 1939 and £2,400 million in 1957, the societies had total assets of £6,300 million in 1966, of which 95% was used in lending on houses.[4]

The sources of new capital in recent years are illustrated by the table opposite:[5]

4. ECONOMIC POLICY: THE 'STOP–GO' CYCLE

In spite of the emergence of new weapons and techniques of monetary policy, and their partial rejection after 1959, the Budget still retained its central importance; the budget speech every year provided the keynote to the intentions of the Government planners and the Economic Survey preceding it provided their justification. The budget retained its tradi-

[1] Mennel, *op. cit.*, pp. 87–9, 128–36; Jack Revell, *The Wealth of the Nation* (Cambridge, 1967), pp. 218–19, *passim*; E. V. Morgan, *The Structure of Propert Ownership in Great Britain* (Oxford, 1960); *Annual Abstract of Statistics*.

[2] J. C. Gilbert, 'British Investment Trusts and Unit Trusts since 1960', *York-shire Bulletin*, 17/2 (1965), and 'British Investment and Unit Trusts and the Finance Act, 1965', *ibid.*, 18/2 (1966).

[3] *Key Statistics*. There were several changes in the bases of calculation between those years.

[4] Margaret Wray, 'Building Society Mortgages and the Housing Market', *Westminster Bank Review* (February 1968), pp. 31, 38.

[5] *Economist*, 23rd July 1966.

	£ million		
	1963	1964	1965
Net investment by:			
Personal sector	−567	−633	−687
Unit trusts	54	67	64
Investment Trusts (U.K. only)	72	14	11
Insurance companies	292	358	301
Superannuation funds	301	276	299
Untraced	92	160	140
Total	244	242	128
Raised by: Companies	438	513	442
less raised from other companies	209	337	333
Raised from investors	229	176	109
Overseas borrowers	15	66	19
Total	244	242	128

tional roles, such as providing finance for public expenditure, and contributing to such social aims as a fairer distribution of incomes and social security. But now its substantive role was to ensure that the call on resources was matched up with the resources available in any one year, both in the economy as a whole and in the separate sectors such as labour, investment or consumption, while at the same time supporting all the other goals of Government economic policy, including full and stable employment, stabilization of the value of the currency at home and of its foreign exchange rate, economic growth and the preservation of the framework and the incentives for private enterprise.[1]

Several technical innovations were introduced into the budget, generally reflecting either immediate needs or longer-term changes in policy. Income tax, among the most buoyant and prolific taxes during the two world wars, was largely left alone, the standard rate varying only marginally around the 8s. in the £ mark. The one major change was the massive reduction in surtax in Selwyn Lloyd's budget of 1961, achieved mainly by extending earned income and other allowances to much higher ranges. This single measure of redistribution in favour of the rich more than counteracted the slow rise in effective tax rates brought about when inflation pushed incomes of the same real value into ever higher tax brackets.[2]

By contrast, profits taxes were used more flexibly and changed more drastically. The 1950's opened with a sharp distinction between the

[1] I. M. D. Little, 'Fiscal Policy', in C. D. N. Worswick and P. Ady, *The British Economy in the Nineteen-Fifties* (Oxford, 1962), pp. 233–4.
[2] Little, chart on p. 280; *Economist*, 22nd April 1961.

taxation of distributed and undistributed profits, paying at rates of 25%
and 10% respectively, and the gap was widened to 50%: 10% in Gaitskell's budget of 1951, forming one of the main props of his deflationary
policy. In 1952 rates were reduced and henceforth they changed frequently, but the gap remained until 1958, when a single flat rate of 10%
was imposed. In April 1965 a new corporation tax was announced, to
come into operation after a year, which had the practical effect of higher
rates of taxation on both distributed and undistributed profits.

While the differential lasted, it penalized equities as against loans and
debentures, it penalized investment by shareholders in new ventures as
against capital accumulation in existing companies and it penalized risky
investments. The lowering of the tax in 1952 and the abolition of the
differential in 1958 were followed by quite significant upward jumps in the
proportions of profits distributed in 1953 and in 1959, and thus became
significant influences on the post-war patterns of distribution.[1]

A more direct impact on investment was achieved by investment
allowances and initial allowances. 'Initial allowances', permitting accelerated depreciation of capital installed and thus a delay in taxation and a
consequent gain in interest charges, had been introduced in 1945 as a
method of helping to finance investment. They were suspended in 1951, in
the budget which was perhaps the most damaging of all to long-term investment, but reintroduced in 1953.[2] They were subsequently varied frequently with changes in policy, but they were temporarily replaced in
1954 by 'investment allowances', which were true tax exemptions rather
than delays, and thus amounted to a direct subsidy. Both have since been
used at varying rates.

It may be noted that differential profits taxes and investment (initial)
allowances, which were designed to strengthen the incentive to invest,
were increasingly neutralized by high interest rates. The two policies were
contradictory but had this in common, that they constituted rising burdens
on the exchequer.[3] Because of inflation, however, the burden of annual
interest payments on the National Debt has remained constant as a share
of public expenditure and has been falling as a proportion of G.N.P., from
4·7% in 1950 to 4·4% in 1965.

Taxes on expenditure were used more flexibly than those on personal
incomes, and the detailed annual changes were too numerous to be summarized here. Two general trends do, however, stand out. One was that
the Exchequer continued to rely mainly on a small number of items of

---

[1] Little, p. 237 (footnote); *Royal Commission on the Taxation of Profits and Income,
Final Report*, Cmd. 9474 (1955), esp. chapter 20.
[2] Changes in the 1950's are summarized in J. C. R. Dow, *The Management of
the British Economy, 1945–1960* (Cambridge, 1965), p. 206.
[3] Dow, pp. 327–8.

mass consumption, such as tobacco, alcoholic drinks and fuel oils,[1] all very regressive in their incidence, and all (except for the special oil surcharge following the closing of the Suez Canal in 1956) showing a strong upward 'ratchet' effect, perhaps inevitable under rising prices when duties are specific. By contrast, purchase tax on a broad range of other items, calculated *ad valorem*, moved up and down much more freely. The second was the preservation, in principle, of the customs, excise and purchase tax system, rather than a conversion to turnover taxes, as favoured on the Continent, or expenditure taxes, as propagated with great skill by N. Kaldor.[2] The campaign for an expenditure tax has not remained entirely without effect, for the demonstration of the gaps left by the present system was one of the main factors behind the Capital Gains tax, one of the most interesting innovations of this period, introduced in 1965 at a rate of 30%. There was no change, however, in the basis of local taxation, which continued to be levied on capital rather than on labour, turnover or profit.

A further useful innovation was the right granted to the Chancellor in 1960 to vary during the year, and therefore free from the artificial timing of the budget proposals, purchase tax and excise duties by up to 10% either way. This was estimated to make, at its maximum, a difference of £200 million to revenue. A 10% surcharge was imposed almost at once, and since it was consolidated next year, it left the Chancellor free to use his powers again. A second similar grant of power to impose a payroll tax of 4s. per employee per week at about the same maximum yield of £200 million, which was granted at the same time, ran into much opposition and was withdrawn in 1962. The idea of a payroll tax was resuscitated by the Labour Government, but when Mr. Callaghan introduced it as the 'Selective Employment Tax' of 15% on payrolls in 1966, it was intended to perform a double function. In addition to the main objective which was to make labour more expensive and encourage labour-saving investment,[3] the tax had a distributional objective which largely cancelled out the first. Only the 'service industries' were to pay the tax effectively; some selected employments (e.g. hospitals) were to have the tax refunded after some delay; but manufacturing firms were in fact to gain more than they paid in. This discriminatory and arbitrary division into productive and unproductive employment ignored the fact that economic progress in general is accompanied by a decline in the primary and secondary industries and a growth of the tertiary occupations, both of which are penalized by the tax, and that in the British circumstances in particular, a penalty on high

---

[1] J. C. R. Dow, 'Fiscal Policy and Monetary Policy as Instruments of Economic Control', *Westminster Bank Review* (August 1960).

[2] N. Kaldor, *An Expenditure Tax* (1955); *Report of the Committee on Turnover Taxation*, Cmnd. 2300 (1964).

[3] J. R. Sargent, *Out of Stagnation* (Fabian Society, 1959).

(labour) costs would have been especially valuable in manufacturing industries working for exports.[1] To some extent, these distributive effects were met by the budget of 1968, which extended the effective range of the tax to all employees, but exempted the Development Areas.

Finally, the activities of the nationalized industries, including their capital programmes, were also made subject to overall economic policy as expressed in the budget. This was so particularly in the 1950's, and the wisdom and necessarily slow response of making long-term investment dependent on short-term considerations were much debated.[2] In the 1960's, the element of control lessened in the short-term sense, partly because the nationalized sector had more investment funds of its own, but its long-term expansion policies were even more severely affected by the toughening crisis measures.

As a share of national income, the Government sector fell sharply in the early 1950's, but by the mid-1960's had risen back slowly to its earlier proportion. Defence expenditure within the totals fell after the end of the Korean War, and social service expenditure increased. Other civil expenditure, including subsidies, fell slowly. Overall, however, there remained a basic stability in the public sector in spite of the sharp temporary fluctuations in policy.

Public Authorities Income and Expenditure (as % of G.N.P.)[3]

	Central Government Receipts			Public Authorities Current Expenditure of which:			
	Taxes on Income and Capital (inc. net Insurance Contributions)	Taxes on Expenditure	Total	Social Services	Defence	Debt Interest	Other
1950	20·8	14·7	33·2	13·6	7·1	4·7	7·8
1951	20·0	14·7	33·5	12·5	8·6	4·6	7·8
1964	18·1	11·5	33·0	16·1	6·8	4·4	5·7
1965	19·3	12·2	34·4	17·1	6·8	4·4	6·1

It is worth noting also that economic policy, including the 'stop-go' sequence, did in fact largely concern itself with marginal quantities and formed, in the long view, little more than ripples on the gently upward slope of production and incomes. Even the most drastic budget 'package' of all, the measures of 1968, were intended to cut consumption by less than £1 milliard in a full year, or 3% of national income. It is necessary to

[1] J. P. Hutton and K. Hartley, 'The Selective Employment Tax and the Labour Market', *British J. of Industrial Relations*, 4/3 (1966).

[2] *Public Investment in Great Britain*, Cmd. 1203 (1960); *The Financial and Economic Obligations of Nationalized Industries*, Cmd. 1337 (1961); *Committee on the Control of Public Expenditure* (Plowden Committee), Cmd. 1432 (1961); R. W. Bates, 'Stabilization Policy and Investment 1950–1960, with Special Reference to Electricity Supply', *Yorkshire Bulletin*, 18/1 (1966).

[3] *Key Statistics*, Table I.

compare this with the inter-war unemployment rates of up to 22%, in order to put the history of stop-go, and the problems of the economy, in their true perspective.

The year of 1951 saw a sudden deterioration of the balance of payments.[1] The largest part of this deficit was caused by a sharp decline of the terms of trade,[2] to their trough of the post-war years, precipitated by the Korean War and the stockpiling of imported raw materials in expectation of further price rises, which made inventories one of the most volatile of factors. Finally, the sudden re-armament programme, decided on in August 1950 at the request of the Americans, had already dangerously extended the home economy,[3] at a time when stocks had been already run down. Sharp restrictions were called for, but when Gaitskell's April budget was announced, the full extent of the deterioration in the balance of payments from the surplus of 1950 was not realized. Since the pressure was to come from re-armament, consumption cuts were not very relevant, and taxes on consumption were raised by £150 million only. The real cut was to fall on investment by such means as the suspension of 'initial allowances' and there was a hint of re-examining the merits of monetary policy shunned by Dr. Dalton.

As the crisis of 1951 turned out to be one of the foreign balance, a swing of £700 million from a surplus of £300 million in 1950 to a deficit of £400 million, the incoming Conservative Government proceeded almost at once to drastic import cuts and cuts in tourist allowances, in sharp reversal from a liberalizing trend before. A rise in the bank rate to $2\frac{1}{2}$% in November was to be followed by a further rise to 4% in March, 1952, accompanied by money market operations to make them effective, ushering in the new 'monetary' policy.[4] The budget of 1952 continued the policy of keeping consumption level and cutting investment in order to free resources for re-armament, but it also fulfilled some election pledges by a cut in subsidies and increases in indirect taxation, as well as cuts in incomes and profits taxes, all designed to redistribute income to the rich and to 'enterprise'. An excess profits levy was to prevent war profiteering.

The fall in import prices, some running down of stocks and the measures taken, together afforded gratifying relief to the balance of payments in 1952.[5] Home industrial output was cut by 3%, more sharply

---

[1] The year-by-year account of the following paragraphs is heavily indebted to Dow, *Management*, chapters 2 and 3, and I. M. D. Little, *loc. cit.*, pp. 257–73, for the 1950's, to the Annual Review in the *National Institute Economic Review*, February issues, for the 1960's, and to *Bank for International Settlements, Report, 1967–8*, pp. 3–16. The table on p. 450 above will also be found useful.

[2] Harrod, *British Economy*, pp. 133–5.

[3] Joan Mitchell, *Crisis in Britain* (1963), pp. 33–4, 106–7.

[4] A. J. Youngson, *Britain's Economic Growth, 1920–1966* (1967), p. 176.

[5] Joan Mitchell, chapter 9.

than had been intended, and tax revenue was also cut thereby, but the other indicators were more promising by the time of the 1953 budget. Butler, however, was still uncertain of the foreign balance, and the only concessions to expansion were the restoration of the initial allowances and some reduction in income and purchase taxes, calculated to add £100–£150 million to consumption. As a controlled boom got under way, some import and other restrictions were removed in 1953, and the bank rate was reduced by ½%. The most encouraging aspect was the buoyancy of exports, so that the boom was allowed to continue into 1954, when the economy again reached full employment. The budget of 1954 made no important changes apart from turning 'initial' into 'investment' allowances to encourage investment, but food rationing and building controls were abolished. Things seemed to be getting better every year and it was at this time that Mr. Butler announced his hope for a doubling of the standard of living in twenty-five years—the first important statement of concrete long-term growth as a major policy objective.

By the end of 1954 the boom was beginning to endanger the balance of payments, as consumption and imports exceeded the ability to produce and export. Measures early in 1955 including the raising of the bank rate in two steps from 3% to 4½%, and some hire-purchase restrictions. But in his budget, the Chancellor, misled perhaps by an improvement of sterling exchange rates rather than of the true balance, added to the expansion by an income tax cut of £150 million. By the summer, the economy was in crisis again, and the first cycle of the 1950's was completed. An autumn budget became necessary to rectify the balance of payments and to stop the speculation anticipating another devaluation. The *de facto* return to sterling convertibility about this time did not make the control of the economy any easier. There were sharp tax increases, and early in 1956 investment allowances were exchanged for the less valuable initial allowances, the bank rate was raised to 5½%, and there were hire-purchase restrictions. This crisis also saw some of the most savage cuts of the investment plans of nationalized industries.

On the whole, this credit squeeze was effective. The Budget was neutral, but contained Macmillan's best-known innovation, the premium bond to encourage saving. Output stagnated in 1956 and 1957, and so did investment, and imports actually fell, helped by a reduction in inventories. Exports showed an encouraging rise, and it is likely that in normal circumstances slow growth might have been resumed soon after, but instead the attack on Suez supervened at the end of 1956. The economic effects proved less destructive than might have been expected, though petrol was rationed once more, but it led, in September 1957, to a sharp speculative attack on sterling. The crisis of 1957 was thus not based on 'real' factors, nor did it reflect the performance of the economy which was reasonably healthy in that year. Nevertheless, it had to be met by the normal battery of squeeze measures, superimposed on a stagnant economy, and these prolonged the stagnation for another year. It was significant that the great price rise, which contributed to the sterling crisis, was based on a smaller than normal wage rise, but one which was not justified by a large enough increase in output. Further, the budget of 1957 had encouraged consumption by cuts in direct taxes, but failed to encourage investment, except in ships.

Thus the crisis of 1957 showed itself in a drain of the reserve, rather than a payments shortfall. It was precipitated by a number of circumstances: a *de facto* devaluation of the Franc, the refusal of Germany to revalue the Mark even though large quantities of gold had moved into that country, the decision to wind up the E.P.U., and by an attack launched from the City, led by the Governor and Deputy Governor of the Bank of England, recalling some aspects of the summer of 1931, on the alleged recklessness of the British Government in permitting credit expansion and wage increases. The Council on Prices, Productivity and Incomes, the 'Three Wise Men', had been set up in July 1957, and all seemed set for ever more drastic restrictions, but in fact Mr. Thorneycroft was not prepared to go much further than raise the bank rate to a sensational 7%, asking the banks to stop lending and arranging for cuts in Government spending and in the investment plans of the nationalized industries.

By early 1958 it was clear that the economy was in depression, and the budget laid the basis for only a slow expansion, since there were still fears of wage rises and another attack on the reserves. Heathcoat Amory raised 'initial' allowances, and made some moderate cuts in indirect taxes. Production stagnated but, owing to a substantial improvement in the terms of trade, Britain had the highest favourable trade balance of the post-war era, and the fall in import prices also kept home price level increases down to a low figure. Unemployment, at 2·8% in January 1959, was the highest since the war, and on this basis, Heathcoat Amory felt justified in introducing substantial boosts into the budget of 1959. Already during 1958, the ceiling on bank advances had been abolished, and hire-purchase restrictions taken off. Also, sterling was made fully convertible at what looked to be an auspicious time. Now the intention was to return to full employment. Among the considerable tax cuts, purchase tax was reduced by one sixth, the duty on beer cut, the standard income tax cut by 9*d.*, and the investment allowance reinstated. Altogether, £300 million was to be added to consumers' spendable incomes in a full year, plus £70 million in a once-for-all post-war credit repayment.

For a while output increased without exceeding the labour supply, though some bottlenecks, e.g., sheet steel, began to develop. During the year, industrial output rose 10%, national output 3-4%, and final expenditure, 6%. The external balance was less favourable, though still positive, and full capacity was being reached by the end of the year. In the budget of 1960 the changes were only minor, but the bank rate had been put up to 5% in January and went up to 6% in June, and the first 1% 'Special Deposits' was called for. In consequence, the consumption rise was held back, but the reduction was greater in production and exports, while imports and investment continued strongly. By now, policy-makers had become conscious of the very much faster rate of expansion sustained on the Continent, and for once, the attempt was made *not* to let the inevitable squeeze fall on investments. The total result of all these influences was a sharp deterioration in the balance of payments in 1960, making the end of the second cycle, in a form very similar to the crisis of 1955.

The budget of 1961 thus inaugurated another period of restriction and decline. There were tax increases, but these were of a kind to raise costs, and the balance of payments, while improving, was still weak. The large deficit of 1960 had been met, not by a drain of the reserves, but by more short-term loans, and now, in 1961, these turned against sterling, repeating the experience of a monetary, or speculative crisis of 1957, but this time much closer to the real deficit period, only some months earlier, which had caused it. The attack on sterling was beaten off with the help of large loans, including £323 million from the European Central Banks, and a £178 million standby credit, plus £535 million from the I.M.F., all of which weakened sterling still further in the long run. Meanwhile, the measures of July, 1961, the 'Little Budget', included a rise of the bank rate from 5% to 7%, another 10% surcharge on customs, excise and purchase tax, a further 1% special deposit, and promises of major Government cuts in expenditure, heralded by an immediate attempt to stop wage rises of employees in the public sector. These were sufficient to turn the modest expansion of the first half of 1961 into a sharp decline. The losses in economic growth now began to be considered more seriously, but the simultaneous (and partly contradictory) criticism was made that the collapse had come because expansion had been allowed to proceed too quickly.

The first type of criticism was perhaps best formulated by Harold Wilson, when moving the Amendment in the House of Commons.[1] The July measures, he alleged, were designed to keep the 'hot money' in London and, since a loan from the I.M.F. was necessary, to satisfy the international banking community by 'massive, masochistic and irrelevant cuts in our standard of living, harmful restrictions on our production, and needless increases in our cost and price structure (in the belief that speculators are impressed only by actions which in the long term harm the economy). The

---

[1] *H. of C. Debates*, vol. 645, cols. 441-2, 26th July 1961.

Government's policies are so bankrupt that sixteen years after the war we have to go for international aid. We will be a magnet again for hot money all over the world.'

The budget of 1962 showed only minor changes and the economy recovered only slowly, while more strenuous exhortations were uttered to hold down wages, and the N.E.D.C. began working on its long-term growth plan. A world economic boom allowed exports to increase slowly and to improve the balance so that a cautious reflationary policy could begin. By the end of the year indirect taxes had been reduced, the Special Deposits released, and investment allowances increased. However, the recovery was disappointing, industrial investment was still declining and unemployment was still substantial. For 1963 it was expected that the economy would move towards fuller capacity, and output would rise in line with the N.E.D.C. 4% target overall.[1] Maudling's Budget was openly expansionary, and tax remissions, including income tax concessions, together with the abolition of 'Schedule A' tax were estimated to amount to £269 million. There was also greater assistance to the Development Districts. Wage increases, however, were to be limited, mainly by exhortation, to the 'guiding light' of $3\frac{1}{2}$%. In the event, the recovery was substantial, output rose by 5–6%, but private investment was still depressed and there was still spare capacity, but at least the foreign balance had stood up well to the reflation and exports were rising.

1964 became the crisis year, marking the peak of the third cycle since 1951. The budget was still hopeful. It gambled on rising output, investment and productivity to break through the export price barrier to keep up a reasonable foreign balance; this, in turn, would permit expansion to continue at the existing rate, which was no more than the N.E.D.C. and others considered a minimum. The slight deflationary indirect tax increases were intended to hold expansion down to 4%, and if there had been any intention to impose tighter restrictions and cut short the boom, it was resisted in view of the coming General Election. In the event, the gamble failed. With the rise in consumption and investment, the foreign balance collapsed, and the balance-of-payments deficit was the largest ever, reaching nearly £700 million.

The new Labour Government announced a number of crisis measures in October almost immediately on taking office,[2] including a 15% surcharge on all imports of manufactures and semi-manufactures, which raised a storm of protest abroad, and some export rebates. In November a second budget increased petrol taxes at once, and announced an income tax increase and a new Corporation Tax, from April 1965, estimated to yield £215 million in a full year. Meanwhile, to stem the panic sterling

[1] N.E.D.C., *The National Plan*, Cmnd. 2764 (1965).
[2] Prime Minister's Office, *The Economic Situation* (1964).

477

outflow, the bank rate went up again to 7%, and an emergency credit of $3.000 million was raised abroad.

Callaghan's April budget of 1965 was only mildly deflationary, since he still hoped to increase exports by encouraging production rises at home. However, while incomes and imports rose in the United Kingdom, exports stayed down and by the end of the year the balance was still adverse. The budget in 1966 was delayed until May because of the General Election, but when it came, its most important deflationary provision, the S.E.T., which was calculated to bring in £315 million in the first year and to be equivalent to a £200 million purchase tax, could take effect only slowly. Meanwhile, the first half of the year had seen not only the drain on the reserves continuing, but some special features aggravating it, including the seamen's strike and a particularly heavy capital outflow matched by an unusually small inflow. There was thus a renewed run on sterling, which caused an even more severe application of the brake in the shape of the 'July measures'. They included severe hire-purchase restrictions; a 10% surcharge on purchase tax, petrol, and excise duties, except tobacco; savage cuts in Government spending, including investment by nationalized industries; tighter building controls; a 10% surcharge on surtax and various other measures, which together were calculated to reduce the pressure by £340 million in the current year and £516 million in a full year.

'The massive package thumped down . . .' commented the *Economist*, 'means that Mr. Wilson's Government is now following a right-wing policy of deflation more resolutely, more ruefully, more reactionarily . . . than any of its predecessors since the war . . .' 'And the measures will be operating', it added on another page, 'on an economy that was already showing signs of turning.'[1] The brief attempt to hold on to growth was abandoned; henceforth, the only reply to a sterling weakness would be further deflation and further squeezes.

The most controversial measure, perhaps, was the total wage freeze for six months, affecting even firms in which increases were to be paid for by increases in productivity, to be followed by a further six months of 'severe restraint'.[2] On its own premise, which was that incomes have to be cut to match productivity and not production raised to match incomes, it was a reasonable approach, though its effect was temporary, wage rises were postponed rather than abandoned and the damage done to industrial relations was incalculable. But the most significant result was that despite these most savage cuts, and five budgets in twenty months, the drain and the imbalance continued. Growth was duly slowed down, but exports did

[1] 23rd July 1966, pp. 329, 363.
[2] F. Blackaby and M. Artis, 'An Incomes Policy', *District Bank Review*, 165 (1968).

not thereby pick up. To some extent, again, there were special factors in 1967. World trade declined somewhat, while U.K. imports remained high and rising interest rates abroad weakened sterling; Mr. Wilson's application to join the E.E.C. renewed fears of a sterling devaluation; and the Middle East War in June again increased costs by closing the Suez Canal. This time the drain of funds out of London, particularly by speculative owners weary of three years' continuous crisis, could not be stopped by any amount of foreign lending, and in November the pound was devalued by one-seventh.[1]

As noted above, the flight from sterling was not stopped by devaluation but continued, and Britain required further large foreign loans. The measures taken at once in 1967, and the full budget of March 1968, exceeded all previous cuts in extent, and surprised even foreign bankers. No less than £923 million, or 3% of G.N.P., was to be diverted from consumption, one half to wipe off the foreign payments deficit and the other to build up an annual positive balance, to pay off the debts accumulated since 1964, and resume economic growth. Throughout these financial disasters, in which the confidence of overseas bankers and speculators had become at least as important as the real situation of the British economy,[2] it is important to note that some growth in output had continued, but the 4% target had long since been abandoned.

These violent fluctuations in the British economy fall into several well-marked phases.[3] The first, covering approximately the cycle of 1951–5, was still largely dominated by a seller's market at home and even abroad and by the Korean War, and its price rises were superimposed on the price rises following from the devaluation of 1949.[4] Capacity was still stretched to the full, and demand on resources was balanced with supply by deliberately cutting investment, in order to make the particularly scarce engineering products available first for export, and secondly for rearmament.[5] Policy was concerned mainly with liquidity, the price level

---

[1] *Bank of England Quarterly Bulletin*, 7/4 (1967), p. 335, and 8/1 (1968), pp. 4–8. *Midland Bank Review* (February 1968). See p. 457 above.

[2] 'The British Government had it brought home in no uncertain terms in late 1964, that it should not only steer the economy in what it thinks to be the right direction, but also in what foreign governments think to be the right direction.' A. R. Prest, 'The British Economy, 1945–1960', *Manchester School*, 33/2 (1965), p. 144.

[3] Dow, pp. 367 ff.

[4] Harrod, pp. 21–6; also 147–8, 165–9.

[5] 'In the long run our industries must have the equipment they need for expansion and efficiency. At the present time, however, some of them must needs be sacrificed because of the overriding importance of increasing exports of precisely those goods for which investment demand is heaviest. The Government has therefore taken steps to divert resources on a large scale from supplying engineering goods to the home market to production for exports.' *Economic Survey*,

at home and the payments balance abroad, and long-term growth was not a major issue, since British growth was satisfactory by historical standards. North American growth was slow, and Continental growth could be safely dismissed as a mere catching-up process after war damage.[1]

The second phase, 1955–60, which began with two years' stagnation ending in a purely financial crisis, saw substantial real income growth in its last three years. It saw the ending of controls, particularly over sterling convertibility and capital movement, which the economy could not possibly sustain without major structural alteration in view of the other burdens placed upon it, and it saw the peak and decline of the belief in 'monetary' means of economic control. In this period, Continental countries caught up with British absolute levels of output and income, and the first stirrings of disquiet about the slow British growth were heard.[2] Productive investment was less single-mindedly attacked by short-term policy-makers than in 1951–5,[3] investment in a real sense replaced exports,[4] and, taking the long view, the failure was less one of hitting investment thoughtlessly, but rather of allowing it too much freedom to turn into fields such as overseas companies or city centre properties which could not benefit British industrial competitiveness.

The third phase, 1960–4, was the most growth-conscious. It saw the setting up of the National Economic Development Council at the end of 1961 and its brave attempts to clear the path for a 4% growth rate.[5] The squeezes were designed to hit investment and production as little as possible, and various new encouragements to use resources productively were designed. Yet the massive backlog of investment, particularly in public utilities and capital-intensive basic industries, could not be made up in so

---

1952, Cmd. 8509 (1952), paras. 30–1; Joan Mitchell, *Crisis in Britain* (1963); P.E.P., *Growth*, pp. 139 ff.; R. Nurkse, 'The Relation between Home Investment and External Balance in the Light of British Experience, 1945–1955', *Review of Economics and Statistics*, 38/2 (1956).

[1] P.E.P., *Growth*, pp. 2–3.

[2] 'The Government is pledged to foster conditions', the white paper on the *Economic Implications of Full Employment* declared somewhat hesitantly, 'in which the nation can, if it so wills, realize its full potentialities for growth in terms of production and living standards.' Cmd. 9725 (1956), quoted in *Radcliffe Committee Report*, para. 58.

[3] 'A check to the expansion of investment was necessary, but it was also desirable to curb consumers' expenditure, so as to make room for a healthy growth of investment and a surplus in the balance of payments.' *Economic Survey 1956*, Cmd. 9278 (1956), para. 69. Nurkse, pp. 135 ff.

[4] Beckerman, Table 9.2, p. 271.

[5] E.g., 'The "Neddy" Experiment', *Midland Bank Review* (February 1968); Basil Taylor, 'The N.E.D.C. after Six Years', *Westminster Bank Review* (February 1968); Sir Robert Shone, 'Problems of Planning for Growth in a Mixed Economy', *Econ. J.*, 75/297 (1965); also M. F. G. Scott, 'The Balance of Payments' in P. D. Henderson, *Economic Growth in Britain* (1966), pp. 85, *passim*.

short a space of time. Indeed, capital formation was still lower than in any other comparable country and Great Britain's productivity fell behind more and more.

The balance-of-payments deficit of 1964 was the largest ever, and the years 1964–8 formed one long squeeze, punctuated by several financial crises. There was no period when the balance of policy was not deflationary, and over much of it new records in deflationary pressures were set up. Any plans for future growth gave way to current panic measures. N.E.D.C. and its 'Little Neddies', and the Department of Economic Affairs, both of which were dedicated to expansion and to a strengthening of the real industrial base, were effectively disarmed by the Treasury, an institution dedicated to the preservation of the financial base. Nevertheless, though all was sacrificed to it, the balance of payments remained obstinately negative, and year by year the burden of short-term debt and the annual interest payable on it had to be increased to finance it. When confidence fell away in the autumn of 1967, the second devaluation of sterling became inevitable, for although its immediate cause was speculative and financial, its underlying reality was that Britain's prices and costs had been left too high in relation to others by her failure to maintain similar increases in productivity. When most of the foreign private short-term capital had left, by early 1968, the total of official foreign lending (and the burden of its servicing and repayment) showed the extent to which Britain had been living beyond her means, by sustaining a quantity of foreign investment and Government expenditure abroad for which her economic strength had provided no justification.

Disclosed debt, repayable by 1975[1] *($ million)*

U.S. and Canadian Government, U.S. Eximbank (part of loans, repayable by 1975)	1,245
Bank for International Settlements	250
I.M.F. (loans of 1965 and 1966)	1,521
Swiss, German and Portuguese banks	193
	3,210

To this has to be added an estimated $2 milliard undisclosed debt, bringing the total to $5.3 milliard, matched by a reserve of $2.8 milliard, not all of which was owned by Britain, so that the crude deficit was some $2.5 milliard, or over £1 milliard.

Thus, on the face of it, British economic policy, the attempt to control the economy as a whole, proved to be astonishingly unsuccessful between 1950 and 1967, particularly by comparison with other countries similarly placed. It failed to maintain stability or the value of the currency. It led

---

[1] Well over half of this was repayable in 1970 or before. *Economist*, 23rd March 1968, p. 70, and 30th March 1968, p. 62.

to a lower rate of growth than technological improvements would have warranted. It demoralized employers and workers by periodic squeezes, discouragements to expansion and enforcements of breaches of collective agreements. It failed to preserve the Sterling Area as a credible entity, and yet failed to enter the European Economic Community as an alternative. And at the end of the period, it left Britain with a contrived level of unemployment and an accumulated debt, large enough to dismay even the most sanguine.

Not surprisingly, therefore, British policy came under repeated and varied attack in this period. How far has the criticism been justified? Much of the criticism was directed towards the technical handling of the short-term crises, and in particular, it has frequently been alleged that the Government permitted expansion to proceed too rapidly, thus exhausting spare capacity too quickly and creating bottlenecks by-passed by high imports. It may also be said with some justice that most of the measures taken operated too slowly, so that the squeezes came only when the economy was already depressed, and the expansion effects appeared only when resources were already over-extended.[1]

Much of this criticism seems misplaced. Not only did the successful, fast-growing economies fluctuate as widely as the British,[2] but the apparent alternative of slow stagnation in order to prevent the full stretch of the economy would make the cure as undesirable as the disease. In technical terms, the Treasury did as well as could be expected in dealing with *ad hoc* crises and usually had the financial and economic press on its side.

The principal fault lay in ignoring long-term benefits for the sake of solving short-term problems. To some extent, Britain was in a more difficult position here than other countries. Victory had induced expectations of an American standard of living[3] without the means to ensure it except by trenching into investments; and an inflation uncured by currency reform, as elsewhere, and continued by the Korean price rises which, by the time they had worked themselves out, had jointly set up an autonomous, institutionally inevitable annual round of leapfrogging incomes increases.[4] Moreover, in the early 1950's it was possible to believe that any restriction in productive capacity would be temporary only, and until the late 1950's it was still possible to believe that there were special temporary causes for the faster growth abroad. There was the additional burden of a political ambition greater than the economy could support, the usual fate

[1] E.g. F. Brechling and J. N. Wolfe, 'The End of Stop-Go', *Lloyds Bank Review*, 75 (1965); P. D. Henderson, *Economic Growth*, pp. 17–19; Youngson, pp. 259 ff.; Lomax, 'Growth and Productivity', pp. 14, *passim*.

[2] See p. 435 above.

[3] C. F. Carter, 'The International and Domestic Financial Policy of the United Kingdom', *Public Finance*, 8 (1953), p. 229.

[4] Dow, p. 391.

of an Empire in decline; and there were other historically determined burdens peculiar to Britain, such as the Sterling Area, and the long-term weakness in machine-tool production in particular and in investment in capital-goods industries in general.[1]

Above all, however, Britain was uniquely saddled with a complex of financial interests, the 'City', which were not directly dependent on the welfare of industry, as were financiers in other countries, and with an all-powerful Treasury with inadequate access either to economic science or to industry, so that it was totally subservient to the doctrines and the appraisals of the City, transmitted by the Bank of England. Indeed, as the balance of payments worsened in the 1960's, the Bank and its spokesmen came increasingly not only to influence policy behind the scenes, but also to press for their views in public if they contradicted Ministerial policy. Only this one-sided influence upon the Treasury can explain its failure to learn from British and other experience that growth need not mean inflation or an adverse trade balance; that a 'stop' need not mean stability; and that the policy of the past twenty years has led to a galloping deterioration, without even a theoretical model, let alone any practical example, that could lead one to hope for a break out of the vicious circle if more of the same medicine were continued.[2] After all, the information must have been available to the Treasury, as it has been to the public at large, that it was in 'stop' periods specifically designed to hold down prices, that prices rose fastest:[3]

	Expansion Periods (1953-5, 1958-60, 1962-4)	Stagnation Periods (1955-8, 1960-2, 1964-6)
Annual growth rate in U.K. Industrial Production	5·8%	0·9%
Annual rise in prices: retail	2·1	4·0
manufactures	1·4	2·9
Annual growth in volume: exports	4·9	2·7
imports	7·9	1·3

It is surely very irrational indeed to tolerate 'stop' measures, lasting two years or more, causing a loss of output of perhaps 3% of the national income in the first year and 6% in the second year, merely to correct a deficit amounting to 0·85% of national income . . . it is positively wrongful in relation to economic welfare.[4]

[1] P.E.P., *Growth*, pp. 173, 187; Youngson, p. 256.
[2] Harrod, pp. 189–206; Samuel Brittan, *The Treasury under the Tories 1951–1964* (Pelican, 1964).
[3] W. A. Eltis, 'Economic Growth and the British Balance of Payments', *District Bank Review*, 164 (1967), all figures based on *Key Statistics*. See also Harrod, *Towards a New Economic Policy*, p. 13; Michael Shanks, *The Stagnant Society* (Penguin, 1961), chapter 2; Norman MacRae, *Sunshades in October* (1963).
[4] Harrod, *op cit.*, p. 30.

We now had the new economies, it was alleged, and the

> philosophy of Keynes and Bretton Woods, which taught us that the right policy for a balance-of-payments deficit (unless it is caused by inflation which ours is not) was *not* internal deflation. It was to operate directly on the balance of payments, whether by import-restriction or export-promotion, thus giving time for long-term policies to increase efficiency to take effect.[1]

But no matter how firmly such views were held in other Ministries or by politicians out of office,[2] they could not prevail against the Treasury in office. 'If all the Labour Party speeches attacking stop-go were replayed one by one they would outlast the century. Yet on 20th July 1966 Mr. Wilson announced the most savage set of deflationary measures since the war.'[3] In May 1968 even the mere suggestion by the Institute of Economic and Social Research that preparations for possible import curbs might be advisable drew at once a sharp rebuke from Mr. Jenkins, the Chancellor of the Exchequer. The policy remains that of ever sharper and ever less effective credit squeezes. It could be only a financier's mind, unfamiliar with the workings of industry, that could have thought, after twenty years of consistent failure, of responding to the problem of inadequate productivity, not with 'produce more', but with 'consume and invest less'.

There was also a lack of drive from the productive sector. It may be, as has been suggested from time to time,[4] that it could have been called forth by leaving much more freedom to profit-making enterprise in the manner of the Germans; but for this, Britain was left at the end of the war with too strong an expectation of high incomes, too strong a trade union movement, to permit an investment drive at the German level. An alternative solution might have been to copy the French post-war plan of designating some areas of critical growth and allowing them to develop at all costs and in isolation from any cuts that might be imposed elsewhere; but there was never an emergency total enough to warrant such a drastic step, and the N.E.D.C. experiment, based consciously on the French model,[5] was easily defeated by the restrictionists. Perhaps it has been the tragedy of the British economy that at least until the late 1960's, it was never in severe enough danger to permit a thorough revision of the traditional policy, tried and found wanting since the 1920's.

---

[1] Anthony Crosland, *The British Economy in 1965* (Nottingham, 1965) pp. 13–14.
[2] For Harold Wilson's views, see pp. 476 above.
[3] Richard Pryke, *Though Cowards Flinch. An Alternative Economic Policy* (1967), p. 7.
[4] E.g., J. Jewkes, *New Ordeal by Planning* (1968).
[5] See the P.E.P. Publication, *Economic Planning in France* (1961); also Dow, pp. 298–9.

5. ECONOMIC POLICY: GOVERNMENT AND SOCIETY

There were few economic activities of the Government which were not related in some way to overall economic policy described in the last chapter, but some may conveniently be described separately, in the light of other social objectives. These activities were very numerous and together do not make a consistent whole, but a few important examples may make clear their general range and importance.

Since nationalization was carried through only in the late 1940's, the period covered by this chapter was the first to see it work in practice. Some of the questions concerning long-term investments within the nationalized industries have been noted above, but basically their problem was political, relating to the power exercised by the Treasury and the appropriate Ministry. Originally, the Boards of the nationalized industries had been given a great deal of autonomy, but political realities, including the power of the Minister to dismiss members of Boards of Public Corporations, led to a substantial degree of political control over the management, all the more effective for being unofficial. The extent of that development was well documented in the reports of the Select Committee on Nationalized Industries, under Sir Patrick Spens and later Sir Toby Low, who, according to one critic, between 1957 and 1961 'documented the extent to which Whitehall has exercised power without responsibility, by exerting pressure on the Boards of these "independent" corporations, but in such a way as not to be accountable to the public, and so as to enable blame to be thrown onto the Boards. They have also documented the amateurishness and incompetence of the civil servants responsible for the major economic decisions.'[1] After 1955 this control was further tightened by obliging the Boards to borrow from the Treasury, instead of the market, even though the public clearly and increasingly showed its dislike of gilt-edgeds; the Treasury had increasing difficulty in placing its paper; and Local Authorities were, at precisely the same time, given the directly opposite instructions to borrow outside.[2]

If, as it was widely thought, this development was inevitable,[3] many observers agreed with the Herbert Committee, that the Ministers' ultimate power should be exercised openly and in specific cases only.[4] A white paper criticized the interference with long-term investment plans in the

---

[1] D. L. Munby, 'The Nationalized Industries', in G. D. N. Worswick and P. H. Ady, *The British Economy in the Nineteen-Fifties* (1962), p. 384; also W. A. Robson, *Nationalized Industry and Public Ownership* (1962 ed.), pp. 144, 160.

[2] Harrod, *British Economy*, pp. 105-8.

[3] E.g., A. H. Hansen, *Parliament and Public Ownership* (1961), pp. 210 ff.

[4] *Report of the Committee of Inquiry into the Electricity Supply Industry*, Cmd. 9672 (1956).

interests of short-term policy.[1] Further, it was seen to be incongruous that these industries received, not the capital they needed, but the capital which the Treasury could spare from year to year, and that the Treasury's naïve aim of self-finance would lead to a wrong pricing policy.[2] By the end of the decade, a new relationship began to crystallize. A major white paper on the *Financial and Economic Obligations of the Nationalized Industries* laid down anew the divisions of power and the criteria of management. The Government, it stated, had the ultimate responsibility for seeing that the industries were administered economically and efficiently; further (in a passage begging all the main questions), 'although the industries have obligations of a national and non-economic kind, they are not, and ought not, to be regarded as social services absolved from economic and commercial justification'. More concretely, the industries were to accumulate adequate reserves, by depreciating at replacement, not historic cost; they were to plan to break even over five-year periods; and the rate of return expected from each of them was to be settled between the Minister and the Board and was to take account of any compulsory unprofitable activities. As a consequence, Electricity Boards agreed to aim at $12\frac{1}{2}\%$ on net assets, the Gas Board at $10\frac{1}{4}\%$, and the Coal Board, to break even, on certain assumptions.[3] A white paper of 1967[4] proposed that investments should be judged by discounted cash-flow techniques at a common discount rate of 8% which would make inter-industry comparisons among the nationalized industries possible. In the 1960's, the nationalized industries were able to find a larger share of their finance from their own resources.

Ultimately, the ambiguities over control reflected the ambiguities of purpose. The earlier Socialist hopes that the nationalized industries would usher in a regime of better industrial relations, a motivation of unselfishness and a social purpose in industry, were soon disappointed.[5] Instead, there was an amalgam of social and commercial objectives.

> The Coal Board is expected to keep down prices, and to make a profit, and to keep open a large number of uneconomic pits in Scotland, Wales and the North-East Coast. The Coal Board is, in fact, asked to act as a substitute for a proper national employment policy, and at the same time to meet commercial criteria.[6]

[1] *Public Investment,* Cmnd. 1203 (1960); also *Report of the (Plowden) Committee on the Control of Public Expenditure,* Cmnd. 1432 (1961), para. 23.
[2] Michael Shanks (ed.), *Lessons of Public Enterprise* (1963), p. 61.
[3] Cmnd. 1337 (1961); Pauline Gregg, *The Welfare State. The Economic and Social History of Great Britain from 1945 to the Present Day* (1967), p. 126.
[4] *Economic and Financial Obligations of Nationalized Industries,* Cmnd. 3477 (1967).
[5] Herbert Morrison, Foreword to Institute of Public Administration, *Efficiency in the Nationalized Industries* (1952); also Robson, *op. cit.,* pp. 460 ff.
[6] Roy Jenkins, in Shanks, *op. cit.,* p. 10.

The industries were put into impossible dilemmas. If they made large surpluses, they were accused of abusing their monopoly powers; if small profits or losses, of being inefficient. For years low coal prices and low railway freight rates were used as a deliberate subsidy to industry, and then the two industries were derided for failing to make ends meet and to supply their own capital needs. It needed an outside Court of Inquiry into a labour dispute on the railways to lay down the obvious, but at that time startling, principle that 'having willed the end (of a nationalized public utility), the Nation must will the means', implying that employees of such a nationalized service should receive a fair and adequate wage, and that, in broad terms, the railwayman should be in no worse case than his colleague in a comparable industry.[1] The industries were not only attacked for ideological reasons by partisans of free enterprise, but also freely by press and public at large[2] in terms which, had they been used against a private firm, would have resulted in large damages against the libeller. Shortcomings were put down freely to the fact of nationalization, while comparable shortcomings elsewhere were never blamed on private enterprise as such, but on weaknesses of individual firms. In fact, the main dilemma was that, far from becoming the spearhead of a Socialist economy, the nationalized industries remained anomalies in a private enterprise economy.

When the Labour Government had introduced its measures of nationalization, it had defended them more in terms of raised morale than in terms of the production record, but the practice has turned out to be the opposite: morale became the gravest weakness, while the production record was good, or at any rate better than it was likely to have been for these particular industries in private hands. Meanwhile, Labour's thinking on nationalization was much modified. On its return to office in 1964 and 1966 it was pledged only to re-nationalize steel, though it was difficult to argue that the iron and steel industry was outstanding among those which had 'failed the nation'. It is true that it had been slow to expand in the 1950's, and its lack of capacity, especially in sheet steel, caused some of the most costly import surpluses; but it was by no means the worst offender. The record of the machine-tools industry, for example, was almost certainly worse. The re-nationalization in 1967 of all major steel producers, i.e. those with an annual output of over 475,000 tons in 1963–4, under the National Steel Corporation was largely a political act.[3]

Beyond the nationalized industries, the Government also took a direct hand in influencing the development of production in many other sectors. Its activities in agriculture, aircraft production, cotton and ship-building

---

[1] *Interim Report*, Cmd. 9352 (1955), p. 6.
[2] Robson, pp. 409–10, 447–8.   [3] *Steel Nationalization*, Cmnd. 2651 (1965).

have been noted above. Other industries have seen methods too numerous to detail here, ranging from subsidies to export guarantees.[1] One method of particular interest was the promotion and support of scientific and technological research and training. These had been much boosted by the war and became again a method of improving the poor industrial performance of the 1960's. Government expenditure on civil research and development rose from £6·6 million in 1945–6 and £30 million in 1950–1 to an estimated £295 million in 1967–8, growing at a rate of 13% per annum.[2]

Official support for scientific research took mainly two forms: the work of the Scientific Civil Service and of Government-sponsored research institutions, and Government support for independent bodies.[3] The former were largely concerned with defence, but some, like the research activities of the Atomic Energy Authority, had important economic and industrial aspects and applications. The National Research Development Corporation, set up in 1948, had the task both of supervising the commercial exploitations of patents derived from public sponsored research and of supporting promising research which could not find industrial backers. Among the latter, the development of the hovercraft was perhaps the most spectacular.

In the support of outside civil research, the Department of Scientific and Industrial Research, strengthened by a new Act in 1956, was the main agency. It subsidized research associations formed by industries and also supported research in the Universities and similar institutions. Following the Trend Report[4] and following an electoral campaign in 1964 emphasizing the expansion of technological research and development, a Ministry of Technology was set up by the Science and Technology Act of 1965. The former D.S.I.R. was divided among two authorities, the Science Research Council and the National Environment Research Council, both under the Department of Education and Science. Apart from the continuing Medical and the Agricultural Research Councils and the Road Research Laboratory which went to the Ministry of Transport, most other Government research and development activity came under the new Ministry, which began by promising massive support to the British computer industry, the N.R.D.C. undertaking to invest £5 million in International Computers and Tabulators (I.C.T.). The Atomic Energy Authority was also permitted to engage in research outside the nuclear

[1] See esp. P. D. Henderson, 'Government and Industry', in Worswick and Ady; and J. W. Grove, *Government and Industry in Britain* (1962), Parts 3 and 5.

[2] Council for Scientific Policy, *Report on Science Policy*, Cmnd. 3007 (1966), para. 9 and p. 20, and *Second Report on Science Policy*, Cmnd. 3420 (1967), para. 10.

[3] Groves, chapter 11.

[4] *Report of the Committee of Enquiry into the Organization of the Civil Service*, Cmnd. 2171 (1963).

field, but there were no other immediate changes in policy and the post-war expansion has simply continued: the estimated vote for Technology and the Research Councils was £211 million in 1967–8 and £253 million for 1968–9.

Britain's expenditure on research was considerably higher than that o other European countries,[1] but this could not be said of her scientific and technological education, which became a major target of criticism when her poor productive performance had became evident in the late 1950's. The rising demand for more education of this type was superimposed on an existing upward curve of demand for all kinds of higher education, described most fully by the Robbins Report.[2] In 1956 the Government announced a five-year plan, estimated to cost £100 million, to expand the Technical Colleges both in their full-time and their part-time courses.[3] At a higher level, in addition to the foundation of seven new Universities, a number of Technical Colleges became Colleges of Advanced Technology and ultimately full Universities in the early 1960's, and others were elevated into a hierarchy of Polytechnics or Regional Colleges (which also offered degree courses), area colleges, and others.

At a lower level, the Industrial Training Act of 1964 broke new ground.[4] Under it the Minister of Labour was given statutory power to set up Industrial Training Boards in individual industries which would be authorized to make compulsory levies from all firms, and distribute them to those offering formal training facilities, thus providing a direct financial incentive to each firm to enlarge its own training activities in order to recoup its levy. By early 1968 some nineteen Boards had been formed.

In a strictly formal sense, there were few changes in this period in the Government's actions over wages and industrial relations. Some Wages Councils were abolished when the need for them had gone, including the one for chainmaking, one of the first four of 1909, and by the consolidating Wages Councils Act of 1959 the Minister of Labour was given power to order independent inquiries into industry and abolish Wages Councils on his own initiative. In the same year, the war-time method of compulsory arbitration, handled since 1951 by an Industrial Disputes Tribunal, was also abolished and any major breaches of agreement were to be put before the Industrial Court.

[1] % of G.N.P. spent on research and development:

U.S.A.	2·8	France	1·5
U.K.	2·3	W. Germany	1·3
Netherlands	1·8	Belgium	1·0

B. R. Williams, *Technology, Investment and Growth* (1967).
[2] *Report of the Committee on Higher Education,* Cmnd. 2154 (1963), and Appendices.
[3] *Better Opportunities in Technical Education,* Cmnd. 1254 (1961).
[4] *Industrial Training. General Proposals,* Cmnd. 1892 (1962).

Powers of conciliation and of originating Courts of Inquiry or Committees of Investigation, however, remained and were used frequently. The latter were particularly important in cases in which relatively limited disputes might have widespread repercussions elsewhere, so that the public would clamour for intervention. There were many such in the 1950's and 1960's.[1] Industrial relations in the nationalized industries, in which it was quite often the Government's policy that was responsible for the employer's intransigence, were particularly fit subjects for official or semi-official enquiries. In this regard, Selwyn Lloyd's 'July measures' of 1961 formed a landmark, for they actually included a total standstill for wage increases (except for those already sanctioned) among all Government employees and employers of nationalized industries and a similar directive to the Wages Boards, backed by the power of the Ministry of Labour to refer back proposed increases. Against this, there were only general exhortations to private industry. The discrimination caused an outcry, but had at last been brought into the open.

The real innovation of this period, however, was the growing interference with all collective bargaining by the Government in the interest of its own short-term policy. The justification, apart from the recurrent crises, was the inflationary framework in which, it was felt, employers were unable to provide a sufficient counter-weight to trade union pressure and were likely, instead, to raise prices against the public after conceding higher wages to their men. In some cases, e.g. in shipbuilding and the printing trades, it has been argued that this laxity at the ultimate expense of the consumer also exists in regard to manning, demarcation, 'overtime' and other matters.

Opinion may differ legitimately on how far the trade unions have abused their stronger position of the post-war years. The 'wages drift' and the large number of unofficial disputes won by employees point to the conclusion that they have not used their bargaining strength to the limit, but on the other side it is undeniable that they have raised costs in many industries by holding to antiquated manning and demarcation agreements. The charge, in other words, should not be that they were too militant, but that, like the employers they faced, they tended to cling too tenaciously to older ways. Total union membership has grown only very slowly, from about 9·3 million in 1950 to just over 10 million in 1967, or rather less than the rate of growth of the labour force. Trade unions have become more firmly entrenched in their positions and, while there have been some significant amalgamations following the Trade Union (Amalgamations) Act of 1964, including the Society of Graphical and

[1] Grove, *op. cit.*, chapters 8, 17; W. E. J. McCarthy and B. A. Clifford, 'The Work of Industrial Courts of Inquiry', *British Journal of Industrial Relations*, 4/1 (1966).

Allied Trades in printing in 1966 and the Amalgamated Engineering and
Foundry Workers' Union in engineering in 1967, and there has also been
an improvement in the competence of the bureaucracy, there seems little
hope of changing the structure or the methods of working of the trade
unions as a whole.[1]

We have noted in the last chapter the beginnings of voluntary wage
restraint and its mixed success in the late 1940's. Little was heard of it in
the early years of the Conservative Government, but in 1956 it was tried
again. Trade union opinion was hostile and, when the engineering
employers took the Government's exhortations seriously and determined
to fight against a wage claim early in 1957,

> the Government was forced to beat a hasty and humiliating retreat,
> conceding to the railwaymen a bigger wage increase than had been
> awarded to them by an independent arbitration tribunal and putting
> severe pressure on the engineering employers and their shipbuilding
> allies to come to terms with their own unions.[2]

The experience was repeated later in the year by the dock employers. This
retreat was, not unnaturally, resented by private employers, and under
their pressure the Government then went to the opposite extreme of
attempting to prevent at all costs pending wage rises in the public sector,
to the extent of overruling a Whitley Council award by the Ministry of
Health and a conciliation offer made in the London bus dispute, in 1957–
1958. The result was to discredit temporarily the official conciliation and
arbitration machinery, and in the next two years, Government intervention swung back again to the pole of leniency and tended to favour wage
increases for the sake of industrial peace.

Meanwhile, in August 1957, the Council on Productivity, Prices and
Incomes (the 'Three Wise Men') had been set up to advise the Government on the criteria by which wage claims should be judged, or, as the
trade unions alleged, to find respectable reasons for refusing wage increases. When the Council's first Report in 1958 seemed to confirm the
unions' suspicions, with the suggestion that 'wage advances have chiefly
been secured through the instrumentality of powerful trade unions',[3] that
a wage standstill was desirable, and an effective level of unemployment
might achieve it, 'the T.U.C. virtually boycotted the Council ever after'.[4]
In 1959 and 1960 official policy was again expansionist, and the Council's

[1] H. A. Turner, 'British Trade Union Structure: A New Approach?' *British
Journal of Industrial Relations*, 2/2 (1964). Also, T.U.C. *Annual Report*, 1966, pp. 114
ff.; John Hughes, *Change in the Trade Unions* (Fabian Society, 1964), pp. 14 ff.
[2] Michael Shanks, 'Public Policy and the Ministry of Labour', in B. C. Roberts
(ed.), *Industrial Relations: Contemporary Problems and Perspectives* (1962), pp. 263-4.
[3] *Council on Prices, Productivity and Incomes, First Report* (1958), p. 52.
[4] K. G. J. C. Knowles, 'Wages and Productivity', in Worswick and Ady, *op.
cit.*, p. 511.

pronouncements became less rigid, leaning increasingly towards the notion that total wage increases should not exceed total productivity increases. Its influence, however, had much waned by that time, and any development of its attempt at a more discriminating incomes policy was rudely cut short by the more severe freeze introduced in 1961. The Council was dissolved in 1962, together with the still-born Economic Planning Board proposed in 1961, on the formation of the N.E.D.C. In the same year the National Incomes Commission was set up to advise the Government on income claims.

Policy in the early 1960's, then, was to subject the total climate of collective bargaining to the temporary needs of the economy, and to exert the influence directly and precisely over wages in the public sector, but indirectly and generally only in the private sector. This remained so when the restrictionist policy of 1960-1 gave way to the easier conditions of 1962-3. Beginning with the severe crisis of late 1964, however, there was a further tightening up. Keeping wage incomes down to the low level of production increases achieved became a major aspect of policy.

The Declaration of Intent of December 1964 pledged the Government, the employers' organizations and the T.U.C., which was now once again amenable to steering by a Labour Government, to raise productivity, to keep income increases in line with output increases and hence to maintain a stable general price level. In February 1965 the agreement on the *Machinery for Prices and Incomes Policy* was published, which included the setting up of a National Board for Prices and Incomes, and an agreed white paper in April laid it down that all wage increases must be kept in line with the annual productivity rise, put somewhat optimistically at $3-3\frac{1}{2}\%$ p.a.[1]

The P.I.B., however, could look only at a few cases at a time, and neither the employers' organizations nor the unions were willing to operate a wider compulsory scheme themselves. There was also no effective scheme to hold price increases. In November 1965 the Government, therefore, instituted a voluntary notification scheme, whereby all wage claims were to be notified to the T.U.C. and the Ministry of Labour, and all price increases to the appropriate Ministry for the industry concerned, and neither was to be granted without the Ministry's or the P.I.B.'s consent.[2] In the sterling crisis of July 1966 a complete wage standstill for six months was decreed, followed by six months of severe restraint, and thereafter a return to something like the notification scheme, with the difference that the T.U.C. operated on a 'norm' of nil instead of $3-3\frac{1}{2}\%$, and the Government had power to delay any settlement for up to seven months.

[1] *Machinery for Prices and Incomes Policy*, Cmnd. 2577 (1965); *Prices and Incomes Policy*, Cmnd. 2639 (1965).
[2] *Prices and Incomes Policy: An Early Warning System*, Cmnd. 2809 (1965).

The result of this elaborate and demoralizing machinery was totally negative: in the twenty months before the 'freeze' (October 1964 to June 1966) earnings rose by $7\frac{1}{2}\%$, and in the fourteen months from June 1966 to October 1967, which included the freeze, by just over $5\frac{1}{2}\%$.[1] Bearing in mind the rising unemployment and consequent short-term working in the second period, this rate of increase was no less, and may well have been more, than the rates in the more normal years before the restrictions. Changes in prices (and profits) suggest that the policy has been no more successful in that respect, either.

Policy on industrial location was a little more effective, if not by much. The post-war legislation, based on assumptions of massive unemployment, was used less and less in the 1950's when that assumption proved wrong, though North-East Lancashire was added to the Scheduled Development Areas in 1953. Control was further reduced when building licensing was abolished in 1954, but then the recession of 1957–8 provided a new impetus. This was enhanced by the increasing traffic strangulation of London, the South-East and the Midlands, which made location policy necessary for the sake of the congested as well as the depressed areas. By the Distribution of Industry (Industrial Finances) Act, the powers of the Treasury to grant loans on grants for industrial buildings was extended to all forms of business, and to places outside the Development Areas with persistently high unemployment rates of over 4%. A major, consolidating measure in 1960, the Local Employment Act, provided for a new list of localities (Development Districts), based on actual and potential unemployment of $4\cdot5\%$ or above to qualify for the privileges, and made more effective the power of granting and withholding Industrial Development Certificates by lowering the limit to 3,000 square feet. Some 160 Districts were designated and the list varied from time to time. Grants and loans were to be more freely available also. Among the early successes was the setting up of branches of the main motor manufactures in those areas.[2]

In the Depression of 1962–3 a Secretary of State for Industry, Trade and Regional Development was appointed to deal with the disturbingly high unemployment figures of the traditional problem areas in Scotland, Wales and Northern England. Regional reports worked on the assumption that the solution lay in bringing work to these areas, rather than moving people out of them, and stressed the need for positive incentives and for amenities,[3] but in fact mobility was fairly high, and in ten years 18% of the population had moved outside their towns, and nearly 7% into another

[1] F. Blackaby and M. Artis, 'On Incomes Policy', *District Bank Review*, 165 (March 1968).
[2] P. D. Henderson, 'Government and Industry', pp. 337, *passim*.
[3] See also Colin Clark, 'Industrial Location and Economic Potential', *Lloyds Bank Review*, 82 (1966); Dunning and Thomas, *British Industry*, pp. 73–8.

region, mostly to London and the South-East.[1] The real watershed in post-war legislation came with the Local Employment Act of 1963, which provided for grants of 10% for machinery, 25% for buildings, an option of 'free' depreciation for industrialists, and a more stringent use of Industrial Development Certificates in congested areas.[2] Its effectiveness was also increased by a higher total incidence of unemployment.

In July 1965, Regional Planning Councils were set up to co-ordinate industrial and social policies with the needs of whole regions in mind. Their early experience does not, however, give much hope that they will be permitted much freedom of action outside the framework of national planning and short-term crisis policies. Moreover, local centres of heavy unemployment remained. In February 1968, for example, with the average unemployment rate for Great Britain at 2·7% (3·5% for men alone) and 7·5% for Northern Ireland, it was 4·6% in the North, 4·2% in Scotland and in Wales, but 6·0% in the Hartlepools, 7·1% in Greenock, 7·5% in the Rhondda and 5·8% in Workington, all still the black spots they had been in the 1930's.[3]

Finally, the post-war legislation had left the Government and Local Authorities with a much extended responsibility for education and welfare, and the growth of the importance of the social services is illustrated by the following comparison of expenditure:[4]

Public Expenditure on the Social Services

	1950 £mn.	1950 % of G.N.P.	1965 £mn.	1965 % of G.N.P.
Housing	340	2·9	934	3·0
Education			1,567	
Child care, school meals	442	3·8		5·8
Welfare services			230	
Health services	478	4·1	1,269	4·1
Nat. insurance, pensions, assistance	674	5·8	2,413	7·8
Total	1,934	16·5	6,413	20·7
G.N.P. at factor cost	11,687	100	30,904	100

Among the three most important items, education, the health service and other insurance and housing, the first has already been touched on

[1] A. J. Harris and R. Claussen (Government Social Survey), *Labour Mobility in Great Britain, 1953–1963*, S.S. 333 (1966), pp. 10–13.

[2] A. P. Thirlwall, 'The Local Employment Acts 1960–1963: A Progress Report', *Yorkshire Bulletin*, 18/1 (1966).

[3] *Ministry of Labour Gazette*; Michael Stewart, *Keynes and After* (Penguin, 1967), p. 157; Paul Burrows, 'Manpower Policy and the Structure of Unemployment in Britain', *Scot. J. Pol. Econ.*, 15/1 (1968), pp. 75–7.

[4] *National Income and Expenditure.*

briefly. Technical and higher education, it is true, greatly expanded and received a new impetus in the 1960's.[1] Other education, however, continued to be hamstrung by inadequate finance and services and, while the Robbins Report on Higher Education, with its ambitious plans for expansion was at once accepted in principle by the Government, the Newsom Report on the secondary modern schools which by chance appeared at almost the same time and a special Report by the National Union of Teachers,[2] both of which stressed the ill-effects of the neglect of the past, have so far failed to secure any marked improvement. As a proportion of national income, current net educational expenditure had not changed between the 1920's and the 1950's.[3] The economic crisis of 1967–8 has led once again to the postponement of the raising of the school leaving age to 16.

It was, perhaps, a significant pointer to the rise in affluence and in expectations and to the growing social mobility of the period, that one of the main provisions of the 1944 Education Act, the tripartite Secondary School system (hailed as a progressive step in its day), was in the process of being dismantled as too discriminatory and as too wasteful of the nation's talent,[4] little more than twenty years later. The idea of a 'comprehensive school' had gained ground in the 1950's[5] and the Labour election programme of 1964 included strong support for such a system. In July 1965 the Ministry of Education asked local authorities to prepare general plans for long-term changes in this direction, and by September 1967 it asked for detailed plans for the following three years, the request being made 'in accordance with the Government's declared objective of ending selection at the age of eleven-plus and of abolishing separatism in secondary education'.[6] The 'eleven-plus' examination, one of the most objectionable features,[7] was indeed likely to go among most authorities, but a different 'separatism', that between the local authority and the fee-paying schools, was likely to remain and even to be strengthened when local grammar schools, which had offered some privilege and some selectivity in the past, had been absorbed in a comprehensive system.

Even the new examinations designed at the beginning of the period

---

[1] See p. 489 above.
[2] Ministry of Education, *Half Our Future—A Report of the Central Advisory Council for Education* (England) (1963); N.U.T., *The State of Our Schools* (1963).
[3] John Vaizey, *The Costs of Education* (1958), p. 76.
[4] Ministry of Education, *15–18: A Report of the Central Advisory Council for Education* (Crowther Report) (1959–60); B. Jackson and D. Marsden, *Education and the Working Class* (1962).
[5] Robin Pedley, *The Comprehensive School* (Penguin, 1963).
[6] See Pauline Gregg, *Welfare State*, pp. 301, *passim*.
[7] W. Beckerman and Associates, *The British Economy in 1975* (Cambridge, 1965), p. 471.

or the General Certificate of Education at Ordinary ('O') and Advanced ('A') Level came under fire at the end. Neither has the Certificate of Secondary Education (C.S.E.), introduced in 1963 and operated first in 1965, designed specifically for the Secondary Modern Schools and controlled by the teachers, enjoyed universal support. Only the increase of the teacher training courses from two years to three introduced in 1960 in the training colleges (re-named Colleges of Education in 1965), and the introduction of B.Ed. degrees based on work in these Colleges and accepted by most Universities in 1966 or 1967, were advances which were likely to be permanent.

The Health Service which emerged from the post-war legislation saw very little change either in its organization or in its share of G.N.P.

Current Expenditure on Health and Welfare, U.K.[1]

| | Current Prices £mn. | | | At 1960 Prices | % of G.N.P. |
	Public	Private	Total	Public £mn.	Public and Personal
1951	487	93	580	665	4·49
1962	952	210	1,162	877	4·67

A committee set up in 1953 and reporting three years later[2] saw no justification for the widespread charges of extravagance and no grounds for changing the administrative structure. Government directives based on political or short-term economic considerations altered only minor aspects of the scheme, like prescription charges. Total expenditure, the numbers of doctors and nurses and the facilities offered increased slowly in this period, much more slowly than in the rest of Western Europe, most of which had overtaken Britain in the medical services offered by the 1960's. Hospital facilities, in particular, suffered like so much else, from lack of investment, and detailed plans prepared by Boards and Management Committees in England and Scotland to cover the years to 1971,[3] modest though they were by foreign standards, were most unlikely to be fulfilled. As a proportion of all fixed capital formation, capital expenditure on health and welfare rose from 0·8% in 1951–5 to 1·5% in 1963.[4] In this period the polarization between general practitioners and specialists was accentuated, and the country became increasingly dependent on coloured immigrants for manning the posts of junior hospital medical officers and for filling the ranks of the nurses.

---

[1] Beckerman, pp. 450–1.

[2] *Report of the (Guillebaud) Committee of Enquiry into the Cost of the National Health Service*, Cmd. 9663 (1956).

[3] *A Hospital Plan for England and Wales*, Cmnd. 1604 (1962), *A Hospital Plan for Scotland*, Cmnd. 1602 (1962), and see, in general, Pauline Gregg, *op. cit.*, chapter 14.

[4] Beckerman, pp. 437, 454.

The rest of the National Insurance Scheme saw only minor alterations, apart from the need to make contributions and benefits rise in line with general prices. In 1952 the Ministry of Pensions was amalgamated with the Ministry of National Insurance, and in 1966 that Ministry, in turn, was amalgamated with the National Assistance Board into the Ministry of Social Security. The basis of the Beveridge ideas stood firm, however, the only new principle being a graduated pension scheme in 1961 and unemployment and sickness benefits which by the National Insurance Act of 1966 were no longer geared to a national minimum, but related to wages.

Housing legislation, by contrast, saw considerable changes. The Conservative administration of the 1950's quickly redressed the balance of the 1940's, which had favoured the Local Authorities, and after the high point of 1954, when 249,000 local authority houses were built, the numbers fell rapidly to 125,000 in 1959, whereas houses built for private ownership increased sharply from 25,000 in 1951 to 153,000 in 1959 and just over 200,000 in the mid-sixties. 1954 was also the peak year for total numbers of houses completed at 354,000, but the numbers have generally kept above the 300,000 mark and Local Authority house building increased again after 1964. Total numbers rose to just over 400,000 in 1967. These numbers were large even by the standards of previous housing booms, and by 1956, when some 2½ million houses had been built since the war, it was considered that the worst of the housing shortage was over, and a specific action of slum clearance began. By 1963 over 480,000 slum houses had been replaced since early 1956, and a total of 4½ million dwellings had been built in Great Britain since the war, but both the total number of families in the country, and the number of houses turning into slums, were increasing also, and by 1965, 3 million families in Great Britain were still living in overcrowded or slum conditions. Of the housing stock of 1960, only 18% was under 10 years old and another 16%, 10–40 years. 15% was 70–100 years old, and 17% over 100 years. In terms of numbers of dwellings, 8·6 million, or nearly half, were built before 1919, and 2·8 million were over 100 years old. The Government's forecast for 1965–70 assumed the need of an annual output of 500,000 houses by 1970, of which 30,000 were to replace losses and demolitions, 150,000 to house additional households, and 320,000 for slum clearance and to create a 'vacancy rate' of 2%.[1]

The housing market remained throughout an artificial one. Subsidies which were paid by both central and local authorities ran at an annual level of just below £100 million in the early 1950's, rising to over £250

[1] *Annual Abstract of Statistics*; Beckerman, p. 381; Gregg, pp. 231 ff.; *Housing*, Cmnd. 2050 (1963), pp. 2–3; *The Housing Programme 1965–1970*, Cmnd. 2838 (1965); *The Scottish Housing Programme, 1965–1970*, Cmnd. 2839 (1965).

million by 1965.[1] Owner occupiers enjoyed substantial tax concessions in paying off their loans to building societies and insurance companies: in 1966 loans for house purchase amounted to £1,245 million by building societies, £147 million by insurance companies and £121 million by local authorities. The significance of the tax subsidy for this was recognized by legislation coming into effect in 1968 to compensate mortgage interest payers with incomes too low to get tax relief by an effective reduction of 2% in their rate.[2] There were also local authority improvement grants for private householders, used in 670,000 cases by 1963, and in 1959–61 the Government lent about £90 million to building societies to support tenants wishing to buy poorer-quality rented accommodation. The Housing Act 1961 (1962 for Scotland) also provided a sum of £25 million (plus £3 million for Scotland) as loans for non-profit-making housing associations.

In 1967 less than one-third of all houses were privately rented, but most of these (78% of the 1963 stock) were old and dated from before 1919. Only 6% of the post-1945 houses had been built privately for letting.[3] In the general dash for freedom in the 1950's, rent controls were loosened also. The Housing Repairs and Rents Act of 1954 permitted rent increases in the case of improvements, and the Rent Act of 1957 made even wider breaches by removing all larger property (estimated at ¾ million dwellings, but in practice only 317,000) from control after a brief period of transition, and permitting substantial increases in the remainder, about 4½ million dwellings.[4] In the event, the opportunities for eviction bore even harder on tenants than the rent increases, which became as incongruous themselves as the injustices they had been designed to redress.[5] Rack-renting and the eviction of rent-controlled tenants became a widespread evil particularly in London where it was known as 'Rachmanism', and in spite of the Housing Act of 1963, which gave Local Authorities new powers to deal with houses in multiple occupations, the Milner Holland Report of 1965[6] showed that substantial numbers of tenants lived in most sordid and inadequate conditions, with insecure tenancies and high rents, and that much even of the existing protective legislation was inadequate because of the ignorance of the ordinary tenant of an increasingly complex law. The

[1] *National Income and Expenditure.*

[2] Margaret Wray, 'Building Society Mortgages and the Housing Market', *Westminster Bank Review* (February 1968), pp. 32, 42.

[3] Beckerman, p. 383.

[4] Worswick and Ady, pp. 44–7; *Rent Act 1957. Report o, Enquiry*, Cmnd. 1246 (1960).

[5] M. F. W. Hemming, 'The Price of Accommodation', *National Institute Economic Review*, 29 (1964).

[6] *Report of the Committee on Housing in Greater London*, Cmnd. 2605 (1965); Ruth Glass and John Westergaard, *London's Housing Needs* (1965).

Rent Act of 1965 somewhat redressed the balance, giving security of tenure, controlled rents and some protection from harassment, and extended all this to furnished lettings as well.

Housing illustrated particularly well the post-war tendency away from the maximum Beveridge-type welfare scheme of the 1940's and towards the removal of one sector of welfare provision after another as soon as it could be shown that extreme grinding poverty no longer existed there. Against the total consensus of the two main political parties on issues of general economic policy, their contrasting views of welfare provisions, either as humane charity to the poor or as an aspect of a more egalitarian and mutually responsible and collaborative society, stand out as issues on which there is still major political debate.

6. WEALTH AND POVERTY

In the years from 1950 to 1967 the population of the United Kingdom increased from 50·2 million to 55·1 million (mid-year figures). This growth was based entirely on an excess of births over deaths. In the 1950's emigration was counter-balanced by an inward movement of equal size, and the net balance inward over the decade 1951–61 was less than 40,000, whilst since the legislation of 1962, outward migration has considerably exceeded immigration, by 113,000 for the two years 1964–5 alone. Up to 1962 the immigrants included, as always, the Irish, arriving at a rate of 60,000–70,000 a year; a somewhat smaller number from the White Commonwealth; and also a considerable number from Central and Western Europe. None of these, however, created as much political furore as the coloured immigrants, mainly from the West Indies, from East and West Africa, from India and from Pakistan, whose number was estimated at one million or more by 1964.[1] The highly controversial Commonwealth Immigrants Act of 1962 severely restricted further immigration[2] and, because of the loopholes it left, was followed by further restrictive measures; at the same time, the Race Relations Act of 1965, and the work of many private agencies, illustrates the potential threat which the issue of colour (as distinct from the issue of immigration) may pose to social cohesion. In the economic sphere, it would seem at first sight that immigrants would be of direct benefit, since they included a large proportion of working age, their claims on the social services were lower and, partly because of the bias of the Immigration Acts, they tended to flow into particularly

[1] R. B. Davison, *Commonwealth Immigrants* (1964) and *Black British* (1966); also, in general, Pauline Gregg, *The Welfare State* (1967), chapter 15; Annual *Abstract of Statistics*.

[2] Immigration from areas considered to be the origins of coloured immigrants averaged 37,000 a year in 1955–60, 154,000 from January 1961 to June 1962, in anticipation of restriction, and 54,000 in the three years following. *Immigration from the Commonwealth*, Cmnd. 2739 (1965), paras. 2, 9.

undermanned industries and occupations, such as local transport and the hospital service. The cost, however, lay in the capital provision, and it was over housing in overcrowded districts that much of the current racial prejudice was aroused,[1] just as it was mainly over the question of capital provision that some economists have found, on some questionable assumptions, that immigrants may have had a negative effect on the balance of payments.[2]

In a period of generally full employment the proportion of males at work remained consistently high, but there was a significant increase in the proportion of females at work. Of those of working age (15–64), employment rose from 40·5% in 1950 to 47·9% in 1965, reflecting the high demand for labour as well as continuing a long-term trend. Actual weekly working hours remained at over 46 in the early 1950's and were still 44·3 in 1966–8 despite the decline of the official working week from an average of 44·6 hours in 1951 to 40·5 hours in January 1968, but in the squeeze of 1962–3 and again in 1966–8, reduced pressure also showed itself in more short time, and less overtime worked.[3] Overtime work for men and female employment were the most sensitive to changes in demand for labour, though employment never fluctuated as much as total demand.[4] It was one of the (perhaps unintended) effects of S.E.T. to drive large numbers of females out of part-time employment in the service industries without providing any alternative openings for them.

A second secular trend of the inter-war period, the growth of the proportion of white-collar workers as against manual workers, also continued with undiminished force into the 1950's. This was associated both with technical changes within industry and the growth of the service trades at the expense of extractive and manufacturing industries. White-collar employees formed 30·9% of the occupied population in 1951 and 35·9% in 1961. Among them, scientists and engineers increased in number from 71,000 in 1931 to 187,000 in 1951 and 378,000 in 1961, more than doubling in one decade; and draughtsmen and laboratory technicians increased from 70,000 to 199,000 and 277,000 in the same years, or by 39% in one decade.[5]

---

[1] E.g. (Young Fabian Group), *Strangers Within* (Fabian Society, 1965).

[2] E. J. Mishan and L. Needleman, 'Immigration: Some Economic Effects', *Lloyds Bank Review*, 81 (1966).

[3] *Min. of Labour Gazette*; *Key Statistics*, Tables E and F; Beckerman, p. 83; *Statistics on Income, Prices, Employment and Production*, 24 (1968); E. G. Whybrew, *Overtime Working in Britain* (Research Paper No. 9 of the Royal Commission on Trade Unions and Employers' Associations) (1968).

[4] L. C. Hunter, 'Cyclical Variation in the Labour Supply: British Experience, 1951–60', *Oxf. Econ. P.*, 15/2 (1963); R. R. Neild, *Pricing and Employment in the Trade Cycle* (Cambridge, 1963), chapter 3; Harrod, *Economic Policy*, pp. 15–18.

[5] Paul Galambos, 'The Growth of the Employment of Non-Manual Workers in the British Manufacturing Industries, 1948–1962'; *Bull. Oxf. Inst. Stat.*, 26/3

Wealth and Poverty

This striking growth reflected the needs of a modern economy, but it also had powerful social consequences. Above all, it acted as a safety valve for the ambitious and gave millions of working-class children the opportunity to 'improve themselves' and live up to the expectations roused by their better education. It also strengthened social cohesion by filling the former gap between middle and working classes.

One proof of this could be found in the patterns of consumption. The motor car, once a middle-class status symbol, now became a leveller, as ownership extended yearly to lower income groups and it was closely paralleled by radio and television sets, by other domestic electric and gas appliances, by furniture and furnishings in the home and even by clothes and fashion goods, particularly among the young. The ambitions and the tastes among the classes came much closer together, though there were still differences detectable by the statisticians in the purchase of household goods, beside the main outstanding ambition by the middle classes to own, rather than rent, their home, and the desire to pay for private, privileged schooling and aim for a University education. Differences in expenditure patterns were now often larger between differently constituted families, e.g. those with many small children as compared with those with children who were earners themselves, than between social groups.[1]

The raising of the bulk of the population above a subsistence standard was reflected also in the national consumption statistics. In terms of quantity, the small increase in food and clothing contrasts with the sharp increase in 'luxuries', even though food rationing ended only in 1954 and coal rationing in 1958.[2] 'Expenditure elasticity' in the 1950's was found to be as high as 2·48 for transport and 1·57 for clothing, but only 1·05 for household expenses, 0·74 for drink and tobacco and 0·26 for food.[3] In terms of actual expenditure, however, because of the incidence of purchase tax and excise duties, and the increasing returns in the mass-production goods industries, the shares changed rather less, except for motor vehicles, which had still been held back by rationing in 1950, and among which increases in quantity greatly outweighed the relative reductions in costs.

Further, with rising standards, there were 'luxury' elements even

---

(1964); G. S. Bain, 'The Growth of White-Collar Unionism in Great Britain', *British J. of Industrial Relations*, 4/3 (1966); K. Prandy, *Professional Employees: A Study of Scientists and Engineers* (1965); *Scientific and Technological Manpower in Great Britain 1963*, Cmnd. 2146 (1963); R. M. Blackburn, *Union Character and Social Class: White-Collar Unionism* (1967).

[1] Ministry of Labour and National Service. *Report of an Enquiry into Household Expenditure in 1953–4* (1957); Ministry of Labour, *Family Expenditure Survey for 1963*.

[2] Margaret Hall, 'The Consumer Sector', in Worswick and Ady, p. 439.

[3] I.e., the percentage increase in expenditure corresponding to an increase in income of 1%. Beckerman, Table 6.1, p. 180.

Consumers' Expenditure, 1950–1965[1]

	Volume of consumption of 1965 (1950 = 100)	% of Consumers' Expenditure, current prices	
		1950	1965
Food	125·7	29·1	26·0
Drink, tobacco	129·8	16·5	12·8
Clothing	135·4	11·5	9·1
Housing and maintenance	137·3	8·6	11·1
Furniture, household goods	142·4	5·0	4·1
Radio, electrical	281·4	1·9	2·4
Motor vehicles and fuel	694·1	1·9	7·6
Population (1950 = 100)	(108·5)	—	—

among necessities. Thus, richer people still spent more on food per head than poorer people, and with the general rise in incomes, there was also a substantial replacement of 'inferior' foods by 'superior' ones:

Consumption per head in lb., U.K.[2]

		1944	1962
Increases:	Liquid milk	308	325
	Meat	114	157
	Eggs	27	34
	Butter	8	20
	Vegetables, fruit and nuts	192	235
Decreases:	Margarine	18	11
	Potatoes	275	214
	Wheat, flour and other cereals	253	177

The move towards uniformity, both of commodities available to the consumer and of the shops in which they were sold, which had been very evident between the wars, took further rapid strides forward, aided by the economies of mass-production and by advertising. Advertising, indeed, became one of Britain's most successful growth industries, particularly after the establishment of so-called Independent Television, and expenditure on it reached £590 million in 1965[3] and, after a temporary setback owing to the incidence of S.E.T., resumed its growth in 1967–8. It also called forth the consumers' countervailing power of self-protection by association and information. Consumer Co-operative Societies had performed this function in the nineteenth century, but in the mid-twentieth they were themselves producers, retailers and therefore competitors for the consumers' attention; besides, they were essentially working-class organizations. In 1957 the

[1] *National Income and Expenditure.*
[2] J. C. McKenzie, 'Past Dietary Trends as an Aid to Prediction', in T. C. Barker *et al.*, *Our Changing Fare* (1966), p. 136.
[3] Pauline Gregg, pp. 251–8.

Consumers' Association, a middle-class body, began to publish *Which?*, reporting objective tests on articles and services of widespread sale, and registered immediate and lasting success, with a membership of 400,000 at their tenth anniversary. *Shoppers' Guide*, also dating from 1957, a similar publication linked with the Consumer Advisory Council of the British Standards Institute, was less successful, but some of its work was transferred to a new magazine, *Focus*. Following the report of the Molony Committee,[1] official interest was also shown by the appointment of a national Consumer Council in 1963, and a tightening up of legislation protecting the consumers in the following years, culminating in the Trade Descriptions Act of 1968. Several cities, beginning with Sheffield, also appointed their own consumer protection officers. In one respect this movement simply made use of the possibilities provided by mass production and national chain stores to approach these problems nationally; in another, it represented a new way of dealing with monopolistic traders and producers, and with a full-employment economy in which loss of custom was not as powerful a threat to the inadequate seller as it once had been.

Incomes themselves did not show an even progression, and over the period as a whole, wages appeared to gain slightly at the expense of incomes from property.[2]

	Percentage Shares of Domestic Incomes		Index of Incomes (1950 = 100)	
	Av. 1950–2	Av. 1964–6	1966	3rd Quarter 1967
Wages and salaries	67·0	68·5	294·2	304·3
Trading profits of companies	15·6	14·5	218·5	229·7
Trading surplus of public corporations	2·0	3·5	339·1	345·1
Incomes from self-employment	15·5	13·6	117·8	284·0
Rent			361·6	
All incomes	100	100	284·0	296·5

However, these categories have only limited meanings, unless the changing numbers are borne in mind. In these years, in particular, the conversion of small businesses into companies, and the conversion of the incomes of their owners from profits to salaries, not to mention the tax avoidance among larger companies and richer individuals, all tended to favour property-owners more, and wage-earners less, than the official statistics would indicate.[3] Nevertheless, it is almost certain that wage earners kept

[1] *Final Report of the Consumer Protection Committee*, Cmnd. 1781 (1962).
[2] *Statistics on Incomes, Prices, Employment and Production.*
[3] S. Pollard and D. W. Crossley, *The Wealth of Britain, 1086–1966* (1968), p. 263.

all or nearly all of the gains they had made during the war years. Real wages of manual workers increased as follows:[1]

	Av. Hourly Real Wage Rates (1955 = 100)	Av. Real Weekly Earnings (1955 = 100)
1950	95·4	89·0
1955	100·0	100·0
1960	110·9	114·2
1965	120·1	128·9
1967	125·3	133·2

In relative terms, clerks' wages continued to fall, but otherwise the secular trend of wage differentials probably levelled off.[2] In a number of representative industries, the true ratios of unskilled wage rates were around 85% of those of the skilled. In earnings the gap was wider, the unskilled rates averaging between 71% and 87% of skilled earnings.

The levelling-up process was helped by the fiscal system, at least in the war years with their steep income taxes, their compulsory saving and their cutting down of luxury production, but in the following twenty years most, if not all the gains, were lost again. The most powerful influence of the public authorities in the direction of greater inequality included the decline of the food subsidies, the surtax concessions of 1961, the increase in indirect taxation, the greater use of the social services, particularly higher education and the health services, by the rich, and the greater skill in using tax concessions on mortgages and insurance and in devising ways of tax avoidance. One detailed study found that there has been 'little increase in the amount of vertical distribution between 1937 and 1959',[3] and since then the movement has certainly been the other way.[4]

Poverty has not entirely disappeared, though Seebohm Rowntree, returning to York in 1950 for a third time in half a century, found only 3% living in primary poverty.[5] Poverty is difficult to define. It is now the old, the large families among the the earners of low wages, the widows

---

[1] Calculated from *Statistics on Incomes*.

[2] G. Routh, *Occupation and Pay in Great Britain, 1906-60* (Cambridge, 1965), pp. 102–7; A. R. Thatcher, 'The Distribution of Earnings of Employees in Great Britain', *J. R. Stat. S.*, 131/1 (1968).

[3] R. J. Nicholson, 'Redistribution of Income in the U.K. in 1959, 1957 and 1953', repr. from *Income and Wealth Series*, X (1964), p. 61. Also R. M. Titmuss, *Income Distribution and Social Change* (1962); M. Postan, *An Economic History of Western Europe, 1945-1964* (1967), pp. 350–63; I.M.D. Little, 'Fiscal Policy', in Worswick and Ady, pp. 285–9. For an opposite view see H. F. Lydall, 'The Long-Term Trend in the Size Distribution of Income', *J. R. Stat. S.*, Series A, 122/1 (1959).

[4] R. J. Nicholson, 'The Distribution of Personal Income', *Lloyds Bank Review*, 83 (1967).

[5] B. S. Rowntree and G. R. Lavers, *Poverty and the Welfare State* (1951).

and chronically sick and the unemployed who have come to make up the ranks of the poor since the war. Estimates of their numbers have varied, but a recent study put it at 7½ million (15% of the population), of whom 2·6 million (5%) had incomes actually below national assistance rates.[1] Most of these were among the very young and the aged. For them there is still hunger, cold, preventable disease and there is still the demoralizing fear and the lowly social place that have ever been the lot of the poor. Moreover, they were made up not merely of the eccentrics or the unemployable, but of men and women passing through a phase in a normal life which might easily become a phase in the lives of many, perhaps of a majority of the population.

It is doubtless true that material goods are not the only things in life, and that the importance of economic problems can easily be exaggerated, yet it is particularly by reference to the bitter, painful and needless poverty still remaining that we can estimate the value of economic progress that has taken place since 1950. For many, it has opened up a fuller, more human life, others it has at least brought to the threshold of a higher experience, and many more were removed by it from suffering, from fear and from the other Giants whom Beveridge set out to slay in 1942. Moreover, men are very conscious of the value of economic progress, and economic failure brings inevitable tensions to the political, and ultimately the social, fabric of society. By all standards of the past, Britain's economic performance in 1950–67 was highly successful. Judged by the standards of our neighbours, by the standards of what was possible, posterity might well judge more harshly.

[1] Peter Townsend, *Poverty, Socialism and Labour in Power* (Fabian Society, 1966), pp. 10–11; also *idem.*, *The Family Life of Old People* (1954), chapter 12; Dorothy Wedderburn, 'Poverty in Britain Today. The Evidence', *Sociological Review*, 10 (1962); Gregg, pp. 265 ff.

FURTHER READING

This bibliography contains only a few titles of general works which the reader may find useful. For the rest of the recommended reading, students are referred to the Preface, pp. v–vi.

The only work covering most of the period considered here is A. J. Youngson, *Britain's Economic Growth 1920–1966* (1967). This is essentially a series of essays, mostly on economic policy, and requires some knowledge of the economic controversies of those years. A comprehensive volume of statistics is now available in B. R. Mitchell and Phyllis Deane, *Abstract of British Historical Statistics* (Cambridge, 1962).

For the years up to 1939, an elementary introduction will be found in M. W. Thomas (ed.), *A Survey of English Economic History* (1960 ed.), and more advanced treatment in G. P. Jones and A. G. Pool, *A Hundred Years of Economic Development* (1959 ed.), and W. Ashworth, *An Economic History of England 1870–1939* (1960). For the inter-war years specifically, W. A. Lewis, *Economic Survey 1919–1939* (1949), and two volumes published by the British Association, *Britain in Depression* (1935) and *Britain in Recovery* (1938), are strongly recommended.

The best account of the years of the second World War is in the main volume of the official series of war histories, W. K. Hancock and M. M. Gowing, *British War Economy* (1949). The most comprehensive study made to date of the immediate post-war years is the collective work, edited by G. D. N. Worswick and P. H. Ady, *The British Economy 1945–1950* (Oxford, 1952). This contains a valuable bibliography, as do most of the other works enumerated here.

For the years since 1950, see G. D. N. Worswick and P. H. Ady (ed.), *The British Economy in the Nineteen-Fifties* (1962); W. Beckerman and Associates, *The British Economy in 1975* (Cambridge, 1965); W. Beckerman (ed.), *The Labour Government's Economic Record, 1964–1970* (1972); and J. C. R. Dow, *The Management of the British Economy 1945–60* (Cambridge, 1965).

INDEX

Acceptance houses 235
Accounting practices 50, 55
Addison, Dr. Chr. 85, 88, 256
Advertising 159, 160, 176, 182
Age structure 286–7, 291–2, 400
Agricultural Credit Act (1928) 136, Holdings Act (1923) 136, Marketing Board 138–9, 141, 167, 172, Mortgage Corporation 136, Organization Society 137–8, Wages (Regulation) Act (1924) 142, 272
Agriculture (pre-1914) 8, (1914–18) 58–9, 77, (1919–39) 126, 134–45, (1939–45) 298, 307, 311, 312, 314–7, (1945–50) 321, 378, 384–5, (1950–67) 410–12, co-operation 137, derating 211, insurance 35, labour 40, 134, 142–3, 243, 252, 293, 315–16, 341, organization 162, 172, price support 217, 351, 411, protection 196, 199, research council 488
Agriculture Act (1920) 134, (1937) 139, (1947) 384, 410, (1957) 411, (1966) 411, other legislation (1950–67) 412
Aircraft (1914–18) 56, (1919–39) 94, (1939–45) 300, 311, 314, American supplies 335–6, industry (1914–18) 54, (1919–39) 103, 165, (1939–45) 303–4, 312, 343, (1945–50) 381–2, (1950–67), 432
Aircraft Production, Ministry of 301, 303
Air mail 156, 157
Air Navigation Act (1920) 156, (1936) 272
Air transport 156–7, 424, 449
Aliens Act (1914) 282
Allocation 304–5
Aluminium industry 106, 165, 314
Amalgamated Society of Engineers (A.E.U.) 81–2, 83, 87, 267, 270
Amalgamations, banking 14–15, 71–2, 168, 229, 231, coal mining 112, 169, cotton 122, industrial 10–12, 62, 170, 386, railway 146, road transport 152,

shipping 155, trade unions 33, 87, 267–8, 392
American loan 74, 224, 333, 335, 337, 339, 356–7, 360
Amory, H. 475
Approved Societies 37–8, 261–2, 349, 406
Arbitration 35, 45, 80, 82–3, 86, 91, 267, 271, 340, abolished 489
Army Contracts Department 46, 49–50
Artificial silk 97, 103, 164, 175
Ashfield, Lord 153
Askwith, Sir George 34
Asquith, H. H. 40, 71
Assistance Board 253, 264, 347, 399
Association, coal mining 112–13, 116, industrial 11–13, 101, 108, 166, 382, 386, retailing 179, trade 55, 62, 166–7, 170–2, 174, 182
Atomic Energy Authority 488
Atomic power 413
Austin Motors 102
Autarchy 125, 188, 230

Bacon Marketing Board 140–1, 142
Balance of payments (1950–67) 444, 449–51, 454–6, 461, 473, 476–7, 481
Balfour Committee 94, 169, 194, 232
Bank for International Settlements 456, 458
Bank of England 16–17, 67–9, 70, 73, 116, 136, 215–16, 218, 220, 222–3, 225, 228, 231–3, 235, 369, 387, 463, 483
Bankers' Industrial Development Corporation 118, 122, 225, 233
Bank rate 70, 215, 217, 220, 221, 223, 225–6, 228, 229 ff., 328, 458, 461, 467, 473–5, 476
Banks (pre-1914) 14–17, (1914–19) 68–72, (1920's) 216–17, 221–2, (1931) 227–8, (1930's) 231–5, (1939–45) 329–30, (1945–50) 369–70, (1950–1967) 433, and agriculture 136, amalgamation 11, 14–16, 55, 72, 231,

liquidity 222, 369–70, notes 68–9, 215–16, and rationalization 116, 233
Barlow Report 134
Battle of Britain 299, 303
Beaverbrook, Lord 303
Beeching Report 425
Beet sugar industry 136–7
Beveridge, Lord 248, 347 ff., 399, 497, 499, 505
Bevin, Ernest 220, 270, 276, 339, 340, 342, 403
Bevin boys 305, 319
'Big Five' banks 71, 231
Bilateral trade agreements 198, 332, 358
Birth rate 285, 286, 287, 289
Block grant 211
Borrowing (Controls and Guarantees) Act (1946) 372
Bradbury, Lord 222
Bread rationing 52, 384
Bretton Woods Conference 353, 357, 358, 362, 456, 484
Brewing industry 165
British Airways 157
British Broadcasting Company 159–61, Corporation 160–1, 172–3
British European Airways 387
British Iron and Steel Federation 116, 380
British Medical Association 401
British Overseas Airways Corporation 157, 172, 387
British Railways 424
British Road Services 424
British Shipping (Assistance) Act (1935) 118–19, 155
British Standard Institute 503
British Sugar Corporation 137
Broadcasting 159–61
Buchanan Report 426
Budgets 40–1, 63 ff., 200 ff., 215–16, 228–9, 230, 238, 323, 367–8, 407
Building boom 105, 108–9, 239–41, 258, 260, 286, contractors 167, 383, industry 108–9, 128, 167, 189, 256, 309–10, 352, 378, 383, 402–3, materials industry 11, societies 162, 234–5, 239, 397, 468
Butler, R. A. 474

Cable companies 158–9
Cables and Wireless Ltd., 159, 387
Callaghan, J. 471, 478

Canadian loan 74
Capital, accumulation 96, 163, 208, 215, 235, exports—*see* foreign investments, formation 308–9, 313, 328, 369, 374–5, levy 89, market 18, 161–3, 232–4, 468
Capital Issues Committee 192, 328, 372, 463
Cartels 113, 164, 167, 171, 172
Cash reserve 222, 370
Catering Wages Commission 341
Central banking—*see* Bank of England
Central Electricity Board 100, 172
Central Transport Committee 320
Chamberlain, Austen 77, Joseph 23, 35, Neville 84, 195, 211, 214, 257, 262, 302, 340
Charity Organization Society 37
Cheap money 229–30, 236–41, 328, 368–70, 374–5
Chemicals industry 6, 9, 11, 54, 94, 95, 103–5, 109, 164–6, 311, 312, 321, 378, 382, 418–19
Cherwell, Lord, 311
Children's allowances—*see* family allowances (also Act)
Churchill, Winston 31, 85, 150, 156, 209, 211, 212, 218, 277, 302, 311, 348
Clothing trade 8, 164, 309
Clynes, J. R. 51
Coal Act (1938) 113
Coal Controller 59, 273
Coal Mines Act (1930) 113, 116, 172
Coal Mines (Emergency) Act (1920) 112
Coal Mines Reorganization Commission 113
Coal mining (pre-1914) 4–5, (1914–18) 59–60, (1919–39) 110–14, 274–7, (1939–45), 318–20, (1945–50) 378–380, (1950–67) 487, amalgamation 111–14, 165, 167, 169, 172, control 59–60, 274, 319–20, depression 132, 148, 244, manpower 76–7, 298, 305, 318, 412, 414, nationalization 90, 111–12, 269, 273, 379–80, 387, strikes 272–3, (1919) 269, 273, (1920) 273–4, (1921) 274, (1926) 251, 276–277, technical progress 4–5, 94, 111, 319–20, 390, 412, unions (pre-1914) 31–3, (1914–21) 60, 79, 84, 90–1, (1919–39) 273–7, (1939–45) 340, (1945–50) 348, 392, wages 31–2, 341, 392

Coal Production Council 318
Coats, J. and P. 12, 168
Cohen Council 475, 491
Combinations 10–12, 55, 109, 123, 164, 168, 170–2
Committee on Production 80, 86, 87
Common Market 444, 452, 459
Communications 157–61
Computer industry 432, 485
Concentration, industrial 164–6, 381, schemes 305
Conciliation 30–1, 91, 146, 152, 271, 319, 340, 490
Conciliation Act 34
Conditions of Employment and National Arbitration Order (1940) 340
Conscription 47, 77, 305, 341
Conservative Government 92, (1905) 41, (1931) 236, (1951) 356, 402, 404, 473, 481, 487, Party 35, 40, 192, 279, 499
Consumers Advisory Centre 503
Consumers' Association 503
Consumers' expenditure 24, 51, 135, 177–8, 190, 232, 295–6, 326–7, 345, 398, 475, 478, 501–3
Control, government economic, employment level 209, 374–5, planning 368, 371–3, 375–6, 384, 388, 390, 393, post-war relaxation 168, 242, 361, 370, 374, 408, wartime 43 ff., 63, 89, 297 ff., 316, 322, 324
'Controlled' firms 45, 64, 341
Conversion (debt) 192, 202, 213, 222, 237
Co-operative societies 14, 107, 137–8, 162, 180–1, 183
Corn Production Act (1917) 59, 134
Cost-plus pricing 50
Cotton Control Board 61
Cotton industry 7, 61–2, 120–3, 167, 172, 244, 305, 383–4, 421–2
Cotton Industry Board 123
Cotton Industry (Reorganization) Act (1936) 123, (1939) 123, Act (1959), 422
Cotton Manufacturing (Temporary Provisions) Act (1934) 123, 272
Courtauld's 104, 168
Credit structure 222, 370–1
Cripps, Sir Stafford 373
Cunard Co. 155
Cunliffe Committee 67, 69, 215–16, 218–19, 221

Currency depreciation 188, 191, 193–4, 223, 228, 354, notes 68–9, 70

Dairy farming 140
Dalton, Dr. Hugh 368, 373
Death rate 39, 283–5, 346
Defence (Finance) Regulation (1939) 328
Defence of the Realm Act (1915) 45, Regulations 50, 53, 60
Deficits (budget) 66, 67, 200, 210–14, 227, 327, 351
Deflation 187, 208–9, 210, 214, 215–17, 221, 228, 238, 358–9, 376, 481, 484
Demobilization 88, 391
Department of Economic Affairs 481
Department of Education and Science 488
Department of Scientific and Industrial Research 54, 93, 488
Depressed areas 128 ff., 178–9, 247, 253, 371–2, 403, 472, 477, 493
Depression (1921) 92, 96, 168–9, 217, 223, 243–4, (1930's) agriculture 138, 144, American 186–7, 224, 230, 358, basic industries 92, 98, 101, 116, 122, 126, 131, 244, financial drain 186, 191, 200, 223 ff., incomes in 202, Keynesian policies 209, 220, profits in 375, railways 147, salaries in 228, shipping 154, social insurance in 279, unemployment 243–4, 252, wages in 290
De-rating—*see* local rating
Devaluation 361–2, 395, 445, 454–7, 479, 481
Development areas—*see* depressed areas
Development councils 348, 387, 392
Development (Loan Guarantee and Grants) Act (1929) 209
Dilke, Sir Charles 38
Dilution of Labour 45, 56, 77 ff., 82–3, 85–7, 341
Discount houses 235, 236, 370
Disputes (industrial) 30 ff., 60–2, 79–80, 82, 84–5, 87, 90, 110, 112, 242, 268–70, 273–8, 297, 339–41, 392, 478
Distress Committees 27–8
Distribution—*see* retail distribution
Distribution of Industry Acts (1945, 1950) 371, 493
Dock labour 31, 270, 342
Dollar exchange 73–4, 217–18, securities 74, 337, shortage 187, 190, 337, 339, 358 ff., 411, 459

Dunlop's 106
Dyestuffs (Import Regulation) Act (1920) 193

Economic Planning Board 392, 492
Economist 171, 325
Education 29, 34, 39, 203, 207, 211, 265–6, 350–1, 404–5, 489, 495–6, 501
Education Act (1902) 39, 285, (1918) 265, 285, (1944) 351, 404, 485
Electrical engineering (pre-1914) 6, 8, (1919–39) 97, 99, 101, 109, 119, 244, organization 164–5, science and 94–5, 312
Electricity grid 62, 99–100, 238, supply 99–101, 129, 143, 313, 387, 389, 390
Electronic computers 311
Electronics industry 313, 382
Emergency Powers Act (1920) 274–5, (1940) 300
Emergency Powers (Defence) Act (1939) 300
Emergency Teacher Training Scheme 404
Empire preference—*see* imperial preference
Empire Settlement Act (1922) 282
Employment exchanges—*see* labour exchanges
Engineering industry (pre-1914) 6–7, (1914–18) 55–6, (1919–39) 109, 119–20, (1939–45) 308, 311–14, (1945–50) 352, 378, 381, labour 76–8, 81–7, 244, 302, 341, 343, 392, organization 164, technical progress 94–5
Enterprise in industry 54, 237, 376
Essential Works Order (1941) 341–2
Euro-Dollars 454
European Central Banks 476
E.E.C. 459–60, 482
E.F.T.A. 452, 459–60
European Monetary Agreement 456
European Payments Union 361, 455–6, 475
European Recovery Programme 361
Excess Profits Duty 55, 64, 205, Tax 214, 325
Exchange Control Act (1947) 371
Exchange Equalization Account 229–231, 236–7, 329, 330
Exports (pre-1914) 4, 19, (1914–18) 46, 73–6, (1919–39) 184 ff., 197, 200,

coal 60, 111, 156, 169, credits guarantee 372, decline 173, 175, 228, 422–7, motor vehicles 103, restrictions 220–1, 223–4, staple industries 114, 119, 120–1, 123–5, 275, (1939–45) 331, (1945–50) drive 362, 364, expansion 308, 378, staple industries 379–84, (1950–67) 459, 474

Factory Acts 3, 39, 346–7, 404
Factory extensions 130, 313
Fair Trade 23
'Fair wages' 38, 152, 257, 341
Family Allowances 264, 296, 349, 350–351, 399, 406, size 181, 286, 293, 296, 383
Federal Reserve Bank 457–8
Federation of British Industries 166, 171, 386
Film industry 165, 194
Finance companies 234
Finance Corporation for Industry 372
Financial crisis 224–5, 227–9, 445, 454–7 461, 469, 476–8, 479–80, 495
Financial and economic obligations of nationalized industries 486
Flour milling 107–8, 167
Fluctuations of trade 62, 92, 116, 190–191, 200, 209–10, 216, 223 ff., 236, 244
Food Control Committees 52
Food, Ministry of 51, 53, 300, 323, 332
Food preservation 105, 108, 135, 286, 384
Food Production Department 59
Food rationing 51–3, 58, 297, 298, 307, 345, 371
Footwear industry 107
Ford Motors 102, 105, 168
Foreign balance of payments—*see* international balance of payments
Foreign exchanges (1914) 70, (1914–18) 73–5, (1919–25 restoration) 215, 217–18, 219, 221, (1929 crisis) 187, 224, (1931 crisis) 228–9, (1932 relief) 229–30, (1939–45 control) 298, 301, 322, 330 ff., (1945–50 crises and control) 308, 371
Foreign funds 220–1, 225–7, 236, 408
Foreign investments 19 ff., 72 ff., 185–187, 191–2, 196, 198, 216, 218, 226, 232, 235, 298, 330, 357, 363–4, 372, 375, 450–3, 454–5, 478

Foreign lending—*see* foreign investments
Forestry Commission 135, 172
Free trade 8, 98, 125, 138, 192–3, 199–200
Freight rates 48–9, 69, 118, 155–6
Friendly societies 36–7
Fuel shortage 298, 319, 360, 368, 379–380
Full employment 241–2, 267, 343, 348, 351, 366, 368, 374, 376, 386, 391, 398, 407, 445, 474, 500
Funding 202, 210, 222, 237, 364

Gaitskell, H. 396, 470, 473
Gas industry 389, 390
Geddes, Sir Eric 210, 217, 275, Sir Reay 423
General Agreement on Tariffs and Trade 354, 358, 422, 458
General strike 112, 268, 272, 275–9
George, David Lloyd 30, 40, 42, 45, 51, 90
Giffen, R. 1
Glass bottle making 11, 167
Glass making 105–6, 166
Gold and dollar reserves 331, 332, 336, 357, 360, 362–4, 454, 457, gold reserve 68–9, 70, 73–4, 188, 218, 221, 225, 226
Gold standard 17, 188, 195, 208, 215–223, 227–30, 463
Goods and Services (Price Control) Act (1941) 323
'Great Depression' 2
Greenwood Act (1930) 258–9
Gross domestic produce (1950–61) 409, 428, 435, 438, 440, 470
Guaranteed price 316–17
Guild Socialism 33, 278, 388

Hadow Report 265–6
Hard currencies 331, 332, 360
Health insurance 37–8, 261–4, 348 ff., 401–2
Henderson, Arthur 89
Herbert Committee 485
Herring Industry Board 172
Hire purchase finance firms 234
Holding Companies—*see* Monopoly
Holidays 293
Hop growers 137, 194
Hosiery industry 8, 107, 305
Hospitals 262–4, 401, 495
'Hot money'—*see* foreign funds

Hours of labour 54, 78, 82, 91, 112, 113, 152, 269, 273, 275, 277, 279, 342–3, 500
Household budgets 51, 177–8, 181, 293–5, 345
Housing 39, 154, 203, 240, 254–61, 286, 293, 351, 375, 402–4, 497, estates 177
Housing Act (1923) 257, (1924) 257, (1930) 258–9, (1933) 257, 258, 259, (1936) 259–60, (1938) 258, 260
Housing Repairs and Rents Act (1954) 498
Housing and Town Planning Act (1909) 39, 255, (1919) 91, 256

Immigration—*see* Population
Imperial Airways 156
Imperial Chemical Industries 104–5
Imperialism 21–2
Imperial preference 23, 196, 197, 199, 338
Imperial Tobacco Co. 13
Import Duties Act (1932) 138, 139, 195
Import Duties Advisory Committee 195
Imports (pre-1914) 4, (1914–18) 46, 73–6, (1919–39) 185 ff., cheaper 199–200, 220, 240, food 108, 135, 141, restrictions 194, 197, 224, (1939–45) 330, (1950–67) 447–8, 466, 473, food 298, 315, 332, 336, machine tools 312, (1945–50) 356, saving 364, 378
Income, inequalities 2, 30, 40, 65, 394–397, redistribution 65, 206–7, 208, 292, 344, 368, 397–8, 405, 407, 445, 503, tax 40, 63–5, 204–5, 214, 325–6, 367
Income, national—*see* national income
Independent T.V. 502
Industrial and Commercial Finance Corporation 372
Industrial Conference 90
Industrial Court 86, 91, 269, 272, 340
Industrial Development Certificates 494
Industrial Disputes Order (1951) 392
Industrial estates 133
Industrial organization 161 ff. 409, 414, 417, 431–2
Industrial Organization and Development Act (1947) 387
Industrial progress 3–5, 24, 53–4, 92–3, 96 ff., 129, 312–14, 315, 377 ff. 408–10, 427, 435, 441–7, 454, 483
Industrial relations 28 ff., 267 ff.
Industrial Training Act (1964), 489

Industrial Transfer Board 133, 254
Industrial unionism 33, 267, 271
Industrial unrest 45, 51, 52, 80–1, 87, 218, 270, 319, 322
Industrial welfare 77–8, 91, 346–7
Infantile mortality 39, 284–5, 346, 402
Inflation (1914–18) 46, 64, 67–9, 73, 80, 90, (1919–20) 134, 209, 210, 214–215, 223, (1920's German) 185, 208, (1939–45) 317, 322–5, 329, 334, (1945–50) 364–5, 367–9, 374–5, 393–401, (post-1950) 407, 464–7, 475
Institute of Economic and Social Research 485
Insurance companies 18, 37, 234–5, 467–8, Fund 350, 400, health—*see* health insurance, national 36–8, 203, 207, 294, 347–8, 368, 399–401, 404, unemployment—*see* unemployment insurance
Interest rates 67, 202, 209, 217, 220, 226, 230, 233, 236–40, 328, 366, 368–9; *see also* bank rate
Interlocking directorships 164–5
International balance of payments 73, 75, 185, 186, 195, 214, 217, 228, 330 ff., 354, 356 ff.
International Bank for Reconstruction and Development 353, 358
International cartels 104, 106, 109, 116, 167–8, 199
International Monetary Fund 353, 358, 362, 445–7, 476
Investment (1950–67)—*see* productivity
Investment trusts 234, 468
Invisible exports 19, 72, 73, 75, 191, 330, 354, 357, 360, 449
Iron and steel industry (pre-1914) 5, (1914–18) 57–8, (1919–39) 114–17, (1939–45) 311–12, 314, (1945–50) 380–1, Act (1953), 419, (1967) 421, combination 11, 55, 115, 164–6, 172, 196, 233, Holding and Realization Agency 419, nationalization 387, 408, 419–20, 487, protection 172, 194, 196, 199, 420, technical progress 57, 94, unemployment 244

Japan 416, 423, 444
Jenkins, R. 484
Joint Industrial Councils 88, 271–2, 342
Joint Production Committees 312
Joint-stock companies 10, 161–4, 173
Jute industry 7

Kaldor, N. 471
Key industries 62, 193, 196
Keynes, J. M. 3, 163, 195, 209, 219, 220, 221, 232, 304, 324–5, 339, 350, 351, 352, 357, 360, 364, 368, 484
Korean War 408, 472, 473, 479, 482
Kredit-Anstalt 226

Labour, Department (Board of Trade) 31, 34, exchanges 28, 37, 38, 129, 211, 234, Government (1924) 193, 211, 216–17, 250, 257, 265, 270, 275, (1929–31) 113, 209, 212–13, 227–8, 232, 252, 266, 279, (1945–51) 356, 366, 373, 386, 387, 392–3, 396, 407, (1950's) 452, 457, 477, 482, munitions 45, 305, occupational shifts 396, 500, Party 29, 32, 35, 89–90, 203, 267, 269–70, 271, 279, 325, 339, 342, 365, 372, 388, 393, 405, 484, 495, 499, Representation committee 28–9, shortage 46, 76 ff., 85, 129, 242, 301, 302, 305, 308, 340, 368, 391, 394, 395, 396, 427, 430, 475, 500, unrest—*see* industrial unrest
Laissez-faire 134, 141, 255
Lancashire Cotton Corporation 122, 233
Land Tax 40
Land use 410, 431–2
Larkin, James 31
Lend-lease 299, 303, 307, 315, 327, 331, 336–9, 354–7, 364
Lever Brothers 12, 104, 168
Liberal Government 29, 40, 71, 89, 92, Industrial Inquiry 162–3, 170–1, Party 89, 170, 211, 270, 279
Liberal–Labour Party 29
Liquidity (financial) 69, 72, 237, 329, 365, 366, 369–70, 440, 479, (international) 352, 353, 455–60
Live Stock Industry Act (1937) 141
Living standards 26–7, 125, 135, 154, 177, 179, 189, 268, 286, 289 ff., Index 394
Lloyd, S. 469, 490
Local Employment Act (1963) 484
Local Government Act (1929) 211, 251, 262
Local rating 136, 149, 203–4, 211, 213
Location of industry 93, 99, 102, 109–110, 115, 125 ff., 371–2, 493
London 126, 129, 131, 153, 250 money market 18, 69–71, 215, 22 ff., 236, 329, 369–70, 454, Passenger Transport Act (1933) 153–4

London—*cont.*
Passenger Transport Board 154, 172, 388, 389, Traffic Act (1924) 153
Low, Sir T. 485

MacDonald, J. R. 29, 228, 279
Machine tools industry 7, 56, 298, 302, 312, 382
Macmillan Committee 169, 213, 220, 222–3, 227, 232–4, 372
Macmillan, H. 463, 474
Managed currency 221, 229, 230, 241
Man-made fibres 103–4, 384
Mann, Tom 31, 33
Man-power Distribution Board 77, 84
Marconi Company 158–160, 161
Marine engineering 119
Market gardening 8, 135, 144
Marketing Acts—*see* Agricultural Marketing Act
Marshall Aid 361, 363
Mass production 101–2, 120, 125, 130, 165, 168, 175–6, 179, 286, 309, 313
Maternity and Child Welfare Act (1918) 262
Maudling, R. 477
May, Sir George 195, 212–13, 227
McKenna Duties 65, 102, 193, 194, 195–6, 211
Means test—*see* needs test
Meat control 50–1
Medical Research Council 488
Melchett, Lord 171, 278
Merchant bankers 18, firms 183–4
Metallurgy 95, 102, 311
Midwives Act (1936) 263
Migration 19–20, 128, 133, 254, 280–3
Milk Marketing Board 140
Milner Holland Report (1965) 498
Miners' Eight Hours Act (1908) 32, 39
Miners' unions—*see* coal mining unions
Minimum wage 32, 38–9, 83, 270
Mining Industry Act (1926) 112
Minority Movement 279–80
Molony Commission 503
Mond, Sir Alfred—*see* Melchett, Lord
Monetary policy 98, 125, 208, 215 ff., 368 ff., 408, 421, 425, 435, 458, 461–2, 464, 467, 469, 473, 478, 483, and Investment 443, 445
Monopolies 10–12, 104, 109, 116, 139, 146, 147–9, 157, 159, 163, 165–9, 173, 179, 385, Act (1948) 386, (1965) 434, Commission 418, Reports 433
Morris Motors 102

Morrison, Herbert 153
Most-favoured nation clause 198
Motor industry (1914–18) 56, (1919–1939) 95, 97, 101–3, 119, 129, exports 109, 415, organization 164–5, 417, protection 193, unemployment 244, (1939–45) 311–12, (1945–50) 381, (1950–67) 415–17, 447
Motor vehicles 102, 105, 106, 146, 147, 149–50, 176–7, 244, 383
Municipal enterprise 13
Munitions Act (1917) 85, of War Act (1915) 45, 79, 82, 84, of War (Amendment) Act (1916) 83
Munitions industry 44 ff., 76 ff., 297, 298, 301, 302, 306, 312, 346, levy 64, Ministry of 45, 46, 49, 50, 55, 56, 75, 76, 89, 166
Mutual Aid Agreement (1942) 338

National Arbitration Tribunal 340, 392
National Assistance Act (1948) 399, Board 497
National Board for Prices and Incomes 492
National Coal Board 379–80, 389, 412, 414
National debt 66–7, 201–3, 208, 210, 213, 220, 470, 481
National Economic Development Council (N.E.D.C.) 448, 477, 480–1 484, 492
National Environmental Research Council 488
National Government 92, 193, 199, 213, 228, 279
National Health Service 349, 350–1, 399, 400–2, 405, 406, Act (1946) 399, Expenditure 406, 496
National income 24 ff., 67, 209, 287, 289–90, 303–4, 324–5, 326, 350, 364, 392, 396, 472, Commission 492, Policy 492
National Insurance Act (1911) 36, 37, (1946) 399, (1966) 497, Ministry of 497
National Joint Advisory Council 392, 394
National Research Development Corporation 483
Nationalization, Bank of England 369, coal 59, 61, 62, 90–1, 111–13, 269, 273, 275, 319, 379, 387, and de-nationalization 408, Labour programme 89, 368, 372, 387–91, land

values 403, telephones 157, T.U.C.
programme 271, 392–3
'National minimum' 37, 89, 349
National Savings 461
National Shipbuilders' Security Limited 118, 119, 233
National Steel Corporation 421
National Union of Manufacturers 167
National Union of Teachers 495
Needs Test 252, 264, 347, 400
New Deal 231
Newsome Report 495
New Towns 403
Norman, Montagu 220, 462
Nuclear fission 311, 338
Nurses Registration Act (1919) 263
Nylon 93, 107, 311, 384

Oil refining 102, 105, 167, 383, 417–18, 452, 471
Old Age Pensions Act (1908) 36
Old age pensions—*see* Pensions
Oligopolies 174
Omnibus companies 149, 151, 177, *see also* road passenger transport
Open-cast coal 320, 379
Osborne judgement 29, 30
Ottawa Conference 195, 196–8
Overcrowding 258–60, 402
Overseas investment—*see* foreign investments
Owen's machine 11, 105

Paish, F. W. 464–5
Parliament Act (1911) 40
Parsons, Charles 6
Pay-as-you-earn 326
Pearl Harbour 299, 338
Pensions 35, 36, 203, 207, 211, 212, 261, 263, 264, 287, 348 ff., 399–401, 406, 407
'Phoney war' 299, 300, 322
Pig Marketing Board 140
Pilkington's 105–6
Planning 89, 90, 116, 169, 170, 197 ff., *see also* controls
Plastics 104, 106–7, 311
Ploughing-up campaign 58–9, 315
Political and Economic Planning (P.E.P.) 171, 264
Poor Law Act (1930) 251
Poor Laws 3, 27–8, 34, 36–7, 248, 250, 251, 253, 262, 263, 266, 399
Population increase 280–1, 283, 499
Port of London Authority 31, 173

Post-war credits 325
Potato Marketing Board 139–40, 141
Pottery industry 124, 194, 244, 309
Poverty 26–7, 34, 37, 251, 285, 294–6, 352, 398, 504–5
Prefabricated houses 403
Price control, Government 47, 60, 305, 323, 371, 390, 411, 492, fixing, private industry 62, 104, 116, 139–140, 167–8, 182, guarantee, Government 134, rises—*see* inflation
Primary products 185, 189, 190, 197, 224, 282, 359; *see also* raw materials
Printing industry 130, 131, 378, 384
Priorities 304
Production Executive 304, Ministry of 305
Productivity 24, 143, 310, 408, 418, 428–9, 437–8, 445, Council 387 and Investment 441–2, 448, 450
Professions 9, 288–9, 396
Profiteering 47, 48, 50, 51, 64, 80, 161, 256, Act (1919) 168
Property distribution 292–3, 344
Proprietary Articles Trade Association 182
Protection (pre-1914) 22–3, (1915–30) 65, 101, 102, 104, 106, 193, (1930's, general) 120, 190, 192–200, 206, 207, 229, 230, (abroad) 123–4, 125, (agricultural) 59, 138–44, 199, 205, (1945–50) 345 (1950–67) 410, 453, 459–60
Public assistance 207, 251, 253, 263
Public corporations 159–60, 162, 163, 170–3, 288–9, 403, 485, 486
Public health 34, 39, 261–4, 346, Act (1936) 263
Public works 209, 213, 254
Public Works Loan Board 208
Purchase Tax 323, 326

Race Relations Act (1965) 499
Radar 311, 338
Radcliffe Report 222, 461–3
Radio 94, 101, 158–61, 176, 313, 382
Railway Act (1921) 61, 145–6, 272
Railway and Canal Commission 112, 145
Railway Executive Committee 60, 424
Railway Rates Tribunal 145
Railways (1921–39) 145–9, (1939–45) 320–1, (1945–50) 378, (1950–67) 424, amalgamation 11, 55, 60–1, 145–6, 153, 172, de-rating 211, Government

Railways (1950–67)—*cont.*
war-time control 42, 90, 305, and location of industry 126, 130, nationalization 389–90, 426, trade unions 30–1, 33, 61, 146, 269, traffic 425
Railways (Agreement) Act (1935) 148
Rationalization 55, 107–8, 116, 167, 169, 171, 233, *see also* Beeching Report
Raw materials 167–8, 183, 185, 190, 195, 300, 303, 305, 306, 314, 339, 359, 363
Rayon 103–4, 107, 165, 384
Re-armament 117, 241, 243, 322
Reconstruction, post-war 87 ff., 255, 262, 271, 308, 348 ff., 368, 376, 407
Reform Acts (1867, 1884) 34
Regional Planning Council 494
Reith, J. C. W. 160
Rent restriction 84, 240, 255, 258, 323, 344, 403, 404, Act (1957) 498, Control Act (1949) 403
Reparations 186, 194, 224
Resale price maintenance 181–2, 386, Act (1964) 434
Research Associations 93
Research, scientific and industrial 54, 57, 93–5, 408, 430, 488–9
Restraint of trade 170, 182
Restrictive practices 55, 62, 101, 131, 382, 386, schemes 11, 92, 116, 118–119, 122, 125, 137, 166–8, 172, 174, 182, 233, 385
Retail distribution 128, 162, 167, 170, 175 ff., 244, 305–6, 309, 341, 378, 396, 432
Road Act (1920) 150
Road construction 426
Road Fund 150, 214, 254
Road Haulage Wages Act (1938) 153, 272, 341–2
Road and Rail Traffic Act (1933) 152
Road Research Laboratory 488
Road safety 150–1
Road Traffic Act (1930, 1934) 151, 272
Road transport 130, 148–54, 172, 320–1, 389–90, 424
Robbins Report 489, 495
Robens, Lord 414
Rowntree, B. S. 398, 504
Rubber industry 102, 106, 311

Safeguarding of Industries Act (1921) 124, 193–4, 195, 196, 212

Salaried persons 287–9, 291–2, 396, 398, 500
Salt Union 12
Samuel Commission 112, 275–6
Sankey Commission 60, 90, 111–12, 269, 273, 275
Savings 232, 234–5, 293, 296, 326, 327, 328–9, 365, 366, 367, 397, 408, 466–7, certificates 203
Science 1, 54, 92 ff., 109, 161, 310–12, 351, 377, 410, Research Council 488
Science and Technology Act 488
Scientific management 6, 82, 95–6
Scrap and build scheme 118, 155
Securities Management Trust 225, 233
Selective Employment Tax 466, 471, 478, 500, 502
Sellers' market 309, 367, 413, 415, 479
Service trades 9, 189, 240, 286, 287–8, 471
Shadow factories 103, 300
Shells supply 44–5, 47, 55
Sheltered industries 109, 144, 189, 240, 242
Shipbuilding industry (pre-1914) 6–7, 47, (1914–20) 48, 49, 56, labour 81, 83, 86, (1920–39) 117–19, organization 164, 165, 167, 172, tariff 199, technical progress 94–5, 422–3, unemployment 244, (1939–45) 300, (1945–50) 312–13, 378, 382
Shipping, industry 55, 56, 90, 117, 126, 154–6, 184, 191, 216, Ministry of 48–9, 'rings' 11, 155, 167, war-time 43, 47–9, 193, 298, 299, 301, 303, 306, 307–8, 314, 315
Shop Act (1904, 1911) 39
Shop stewards 80 ff., 87, 267, 269
Silk industry 7, 164, 194
Sinking Fund 212, 213, 228
Slum clearance 255, 258–61
Slump—*see* depression
Small holdings 136, 138, 144
Small Holdings and Allotments Act (1907) 40, (1926) 136
Smiles, Samuel 2
Snowden, Philip 211–12
Soap Trust 12, 105, 166
Social Security, Ministry of 497
Social surveys 295, 326, 398
Social welfare services 34 ff., 203–6, 211–12, 254 ff., 279, 294–6, 340, 346–7, 398, 399 ff., 404, 405, 497, expenditure 494, 496–7

Socialist policies 28-9, 33, 43, 53, 89, 170, 275, 373, 388, 407, 486-7
Special areas—*see* depressed areas
Special Areas (Amendment) Act (1937) 132
Special Areas Reconstruction (Agreement) Act (1936) 132
Special Areas Reconstruction Associations 132-3
Special Deposits 476
Spens Committee 266, 485
Standardization 56, 120
Staple industries 4 ff., 20-1, 110 ff., 124-5, 126 ff., 145, 189, 232, 244, 245, 377, 409, 414
Steel industry—*see* iron and steel industry
Sterling Area 301, 332, 333, 338, 358, 362, 363, 453, 482-3
Sterling balances 301, 332-4, 337-8, 357, 363-4, 453
"Stop-Go"—*see* monetary policy
Strikes—*see* disputes
Subsidies 396, 406, agricultural 135-4, 136-9, 141, 143-4, 205, 316, 317, 323, 410-12, 488, aircraft 156-7, 488, coal 112, food 53, 302, 317, 323, 371, foreign 194, 199, housing 207, 254-60, 497-8, shipping 119, 155
Suez 431, 474, 479
Sugar control 42-3, 52, 53, 181, convention 23
Sugar Industry (Reorganization) Act (1936) 137, 272
Sugar Subsidy Act (1925) 136
Supertax 40, 63-4
Supplies and Services (Transitional Powers) Act (1945) 372
Supply, Ministry of 300, 332
Sweated trades 3, 8, 38, 87, 272
Syndicalism 32, 83, 279, 388

Taff Vale case 28, 29, 30
"Take-Overs" 432, *see also* industrial organization
Tariffs (pre-1914) 22, (1919-39, abroad) 125, 142, 185, 186, 216, 224, (1932, general) 192 ff., 204, 229, (1932, iron and steel) 116, 196, (1945-50) 354, 358, (1950-67) 452, 460, *see also* protection
Taxation (pre-1914) 40-1, (1914-19) 63 ff., 89, (1919-39) 150, 204-6, 207, 208, 210, 213, 292, (1939-45) 302, 323 ff., 344, (1945-50) 366,

367, 395-6, 405, (post-1950) 407, 436, 469, 470-1, 473-5, 417
Tax evasion 397, 407
Tax Reserve Certificates 329
Technology 1, 92 ff., 310-11, 367, 377, 436, 438, 440, 441, 445, 453
Telegraph 158
Telephone 157-8
Television 101, 161, 382
Terms of trade 75, 189, 240, 291, 360, 364, 448, 451
Textile industry 7 ff., 129, 164, 309, 383-4, combinations 12-13, 166
Thorneycroft 475
Tillet, Ben 31
Timber 309, 317-18
Tin-plate industry 108, 244
Town and Country Planning Act (1932) 261, (1947) 403
Tractors 59, 143, 316
Trade boards 38, 87, 272, 293, *see also* wages boards
Trade Boards Act (1909) 38, (1918) 87, 272
Trade Descriptions Act (1968) 503
Trade Disputes Act (1906) 29
Trade Disputes and Trade Unions Act (1927) 279, 391-2, (1946) 391
Trade gap 190-1, 199, 355, 478
Trades Union Congress 33, 112, 267, 271, 273, 275-7, 278, 342, 348, 392, 393, 395-6, 491-2
Trade Union (Amalgamation) Act (1917) 267, (1964) 490
Trade Union (Amendment) Act (1913) 29
Trade unions (pre-1914) 28-34, 37, (1914-18) 45, 79-81, 83, 89, (1919-1939) 131, 267 ff., (1939-45) 339-40, 342, (1945-50) 391-4, (post-1950) 408, membership 490
Traffic Commissioners 151-2, 172
Transitional benefits 246, 249, 252, 253
Transport Acts (1953 and 1956) 424, (1968) 426
Transport Commission 389
Transport, Ministry of 488, Tribunal 424
Transport Workers' Federation 31, 33, 270
Treasury Agreement (1915) 45, 79, 82
Treasury bills 17, 67, 68, 72, 202, 203, 210, 222, 226, 229, 461-2, 485
Treasury Deposit Receipts 329-30, 365, 370

517

Index

'Treasury view' 209
Treaty of Rome 459
Trend Report 485
Tripartite Agreement (1936) 230
Triple Alliance 32, 33, 272–3, 276
Trunk Roads Act (1936) 150
Trusts 62, 166, 168, 170, 171

Under-employment 129
Unemployed Workmen Act (1905) 27
Unemployment (pre-1914) 27, 34,
(1914–18) 51, 76, (1919–39) 92, 96,
169, 173, 179, 211, 214–17, 224, 227,
242–54, 283, 288, 290–2, 295–6, 352,
398, (1939–45) 301, 347, (1945–50)
351, 366, 369, 375, 376, (post-1950)
475, 493, 494, Assistance Board 253,
depressed areas 128–9, 131, France
230, insurance 37, 91, 212–13, 243,
248–53, 254, 261, Insurance Fund
212–13, 227, 238, 249, 252, overseas
influence 186, 190, 199, policies 87–8,
108–9, 209, 220, 267, 274, 279, 430,
464–5, 482, relief 27, 204, 207, 212–
213, 227, 228, 246, 248–54, 291, 348
ff., 400, 406, staple industries 109–10,
114, 117, 124, 189, 318
Unemployment Act (1927) 250, (1934)
252, 280
Unemployment Insurance Act (1920)
248–9
Unilever—see Lever Brothers
Unofficial strikes 268, 392
U.N.R.R.A. 354, 358
Uthwatt Report 404
'Utility' scheme 307, 309, 323

Victimization 277
Votes of credit 63

Wages (pre-1914) 24–6, (1914–18) 30,
34, 51, 78–82, 85–7, 267, (1919–20)
60, 61, 91, 134, 215, 271, (1920–39)
112, 128, 142, 217, 218, 223, 268–9,
274–7, 290–1, 292, 296, control 113,
152–3, 272, (1939–45) 317, 319, 322,
340–4, (1945–50) 391–7, 398, (1950–
1967) 445–6, 490, 503, councils 341–
342, 392–3, 395, "drift" 465, 490,
policy 393, (post-1950) 445–6, 465,
477–8, 490–1
Wages Council Act (1945) 341–2, 392,
469
Wages (Temporary Regulation) Act
(1918) 86, 271
War Aims Committee 348
War Bonds 67
War economy 42 ff., 63, 297 ff., 391
War loans 186, 187, 202, 213, 224, 325,
328–9
Washington Conference (1944) 339
Webb, Sidney and Beatrice 3, 13, 36,
89
Welfare provisions—see social welfare
Welfare state 34, 41, 349, 398 ff., 407;
see also social welfare
Wheat 8, 43, 49, 52, 53, 58, 107, 134,
138–9, 195, 295, 315, 316
Wheat Act (1932) 138
Wheat Agreement 139
Wheatley Act (1924) 257
White collar workers—see salaries
Whitley Report 88, 91, 271–2, 341
Wholesale trade 182–3
Wilson, H. 436, 438, 479, 484
Wireless—see radio
Women in industry (1914–18) 55, 61,
77–9, 88, 119, 267, (1919–39) 107,
130, 286, 287, (1939–45) 306, 309–
310, 315, 341, (1945–50) 352, 398,
(1950–67) 430
Woollen and worsted industry 7, 44,
123–4, 167, 244, 383–4
Working Party Reports 387
Workmen's Compensation Act (1906)
36
Workmen's (Compensation for Acci-
dents) Act (1897) 35
World Economic Conference (1927)
216

York—see Social surveys